Contents

Constitutional Law:
THE MACHINERY OF GOVERNMENT

FOURTH EDITION

MICHAEL T MOLAN
BA, LLM (Lond), Barrister
Head of the Division of Law, South Bank University

OLD BAILEY PRESS

WITHDRAWN

OLD BAILEY PRESS
at Holborn College, Woolwich Road,
Charlton, London SE7 8LN

First published 1997
Fourth edition 2003

© The HLT Group Ltd 2003

ISBN 1 85836 489 2

British Library Cataloguing-in-Publication.
A CIP Catalogue record for this book is
available from the British Library.

Acknowledgement
The publishers and author would
like to thank the Incorporated
Council of Law Reporting for
England and Wales for kind
permission to reproduce extracts
from the Weekly Law Reports, and
Butterworths for their kind
permission to reproduce extracts
from the All England Law Reports.

Printed and bound in Great Britain

Preface

Old Bailey Press textbooks are written specifically for students. Whatever their course they will find our books clear and concise, providing comprehensive and up-to-date coverage. Written by specialists in their field, our textbooks are reviewed and updated on a regular basis. A companion 150 Leading Cases, Revision WorkBook and Statutes are also published.

Knowledge of recent cases is extremely important for those studying for their examinations. It demonstrates not only an active interest in the law as it develops, but also the dynamic nature of the law which is constantly adapting to changing social and economic trends.

This *Constitutional Law: The Machinery of Government* textbook is designed for use by any undergraduates who have constitutional law within their syllabus. It will be equally useful for all CPE/LLDip students who must study constitutional law as one of their 'core' subjects.

In addition, those studying for certain professional examinations, such as the Institute of Legal Executives, will find this textbook gives them sufficient information for their appropriate examinations in constitutional law.

The reorganisation of chapters in this fourth edition of this text reflects the changing emphasis in the study of constitutional law, with discrete chapters being devoted to the main rights protected under the European Convention on Human Rights. The constitutional impact of the Human Rights Act 1998 and its effect on the principles of judicial review are reflected in a number of cases considered in this new edition, including *R (On the Application of International Transport Roth GmbH)* v *Secretary of State for the Home Department*. A number of cases are considered that explore the developing area of confidentiality and privacy, including *A* v *B (A Company) and Another*, *Theakston* v *MGN Ltd* and *Campbell* v *MGN Ltd*. The developing nature of implied repeal where constitutionally significant legislation is in question is explored in *Thoburn* v *Sunderland City Council*. The latest developments in relation to House of Lords reform are examined, in particular the report of the Joint Committee on House of Lords Reform, as are the changes consequent upon the enactment of the Police Reform Act 2002.

The law is stated as of 1 January 2003.

Table of Cases

Table of Statutes and Other Materials

1

The Nature and Sources of Constitutional Law

1.1 Introduction

1.2 The classification of constitutions

1.3 The British constitution classified

1.4 The structure of the United Kingdom

1.5 Overview of the organs of government and the allocation of power

1.6 Legal rules of the constitution

1.7 Non-legal rules of the constitution

1.8 Constitutional reform

1.1 Introduction

What is a constitution? A simple answer would be that a constitution comprises a body of rules regulating the way in which an institution or organisation operates. Most clubs and associations have some sort of written constitution. Without a constitution there can at best be muddle and confusion as to how a body is to operate; at worst it can result in an organisation disintegrating, or being unable to perform the functions for which it was created. When the term constitution is used in the context of the government of a state, a more sophisticated analysis is required. One would expect a state's constitution to establish the organs of government; to detail the allocation of power between those organs of government; to provide for the resolution of disputes regarding the interpretation of the constitution; and to provide for amendment of the constitution where appropriate. A modern constitution would also be expected to detail the fundamental rights and duties of its citizens, to specify the protection afforded to those rights, and to provide due protection for minority groups.

For many, given the foregoing, to talk of the study of constitutional law, within the context of the British constitution, is something of a contradiction in terms. Use of the term 'law' suggests fixed rules that apply to all, that have to be consistently

1

observed, and can be readily ascertained. As will be seen, the British constitution is in fact based upon a strange amalgam of custom, precedent, convention and statute law that has evolved over many centuries, the product of historical accident and political expediency. It defies traditional analysis in terms of what lawyers traditionally think of as 'law'.

The scope of constitutional law as an academic discipline is, therefore, somewhat less clearly defined than might be the case with other areas of law such as the law of contract or the law of torts. Broadly, the subject is concerned with the functions discharged by the organs of government, the distribution of power between the organs of government, the law-making process, the relationship between individuals and the state in terms of the power of the state to interfere with the exercise of individual rights and freedoms, and the protection that the state can afford to its citizens.

Statehood and the organs of government

The study of constitutional law is based upon certain assumptions, not least of which is that there is an entity known as 'the State'. The reality is that this term has no legal significance whatsoever, in the sense that it is not formally defined, yet in political terms it is full of meaning, suggesting public governmental power and interests. The United Kingdom is a state, and its organs of government sometimes loosely referred to as 'the State'.

In terms of the recognition of states in the context of international law, the legal criteria of statehood are to be found in art 1 of the Montevideo Convention on Rights and Duties of States 1933 which provides:

'The state as a person of international law should possess the following qualifications: a permanent population; a defined territory; government; and capacity to enter into relations with other states.'

Organised government has traditionally been recognised as comprising three key functions:

1. legislative functions – the enactment of new law and the repeal or amendment of existing law;
2. executive functions – these include the making of policy and the conduct of government according to law;
3. judicial functions – these involve the determination of disputes between subjects, and between subjects and the state in accordance with the law.

Predictably, the organs of government are classified according to these functions, thus:

1. the *legislature* is the law-making body and consists in the United Kingdom of the Queen in Parliament, ie the House of Commons, the House of Lords and the Sovereign.

2. the *executive* is the body responsible for the execution or enforcement or carrying into effect of the laws laid down by the legislature. It also has responsibility for policy formulation. It consists of the government, ie the Prime Minister and other ministers, and a wide range of executive agencies such as tribunals, local authorities, chief constables, fire authorities, health authorities, public corporations, quangos etc.
3. the *judiciary*, responsible for settling legal disputes and interpreting and applying the law. It consists of the judges sitting in the courts of law, although other bodies sometimes discharge 'judicial' functions, such as tribunals and ministers.

1.2 The classification of constitutions

Constitutions can be classified in a number of different ways according to the form that they take, the distribution of power, and the ease with which they can be amended.

Written or unwritten

Constitutions can be classified as 'written' or 'unwritten' according to whether or not there is a single document containing the most fundamental constitutional rules, ie laying down the framework for the operation of the organs of government. This classification may be misleading, because an unwritten constitution may have many important constitutional rules in statutory form and, on the other hand, a written constitution may, in its operation, be modified and qualified by important unwritten rules. The term 'enacted constitution' is sometimes used instead of written constitution. The United Kingdom is now the only major country not to have a written constitution in the form of a constitution based on a document that represents some higher form of law. In many states there is a hierarchy of laws, with the law of the constitution being at the top of that hierarchy. This means that the rules of the constitution take precedence over any other law that is incompatible with the terms of the constitution. This law of the constitution is frequently found in a document referred to as the constitution. Suppose the 'higher' constitutional law decreed that all adults of sound mind should have the right to vote at parliamentary elections. If the legislature were then to pass an Act depriving women of the vote that Act could be challenged in the courts on the grounds that it was 'unconstitutional', ie it was incompatible with a specific rule of the constitution. In many states, therefore, a constitutional document imposes limits on what may be done by ordinary legislation. The United Kingdom, therefore, is one of the few countries where fundamental rights can be removed or diminished by 'ordinary' legislation. The lack of a constitution with any greater legal sanctity than the ordinary law of the land partly explains de Tocqueville's allegation that the English have no constitution. As Laws J observed in *R* v *Lord Chancellor, ex parte Witham* [1997] 2 All ER 779:

> 'The common law does not generally speak in the language of constitutional rights, for the good reason that in the absence of any sovereign text, a written constitution which is logically and legally prior to the power of legislature, executive and judiciary alike, there is on the face of it no hierarchy of rights such that any of them is more entrenched by the law than any other. And if the concept of a constitutional right is to have any meaning, it must surely sound in the protection which the law affords to it. Where a written constitution guarantees a right, there is no conceptual difficulty. The state authorities must give way to it, save to the extent that the constitution allows them to deny it. There may of course be other difficulties, such as whether on the constitution's true interpretation the right claimed exists at all. Even a superficial acquaintance with the jurisprudence of the Supreme Court of the United States shows that such problems may be acute. But they are not in the same category as the question: do we have constitutional rights at all?
>
> In the unwritten legal order of the British state, at a time when the common law continues to accord a legislative supremacy to Parliament, the notion of a constitutional right can in my judgment inhere only in this proposition, that the right in question cannot be abrogated by the state save by specific provision in an Act of Parliament, or by regulations whose vires in main legislation specifically confers the power to abrogate. General words will not suffice. And any such rights will be creatures of the common law, since their existence would not be the consequence of the democratic political process but would be logically prior to it.'

The absence of a higher constitutional law places the United Kingdom Parliament in a uniquely powerful position. This power to make or unmake any law is referred to as the doctrine of parliamentary sovereignty, considered at more length in Chapter 4. Somewhat ironically, as the colonies of the United Kingdom have had their independence returned to them it has been the invariable practice for the government at Westminster to be instrumental in ensuring that they have adopted written constitutions. A clear case of 'do as I say not as I do'.

Rigid or flexible

This classification was first proposed by Lord James Bryce in a series of Oxford lectures at the end of the nineteenth century. A flexible constitution, according to Lord Bryce's definition, is one where all the laws of the constitution can be amended by the ordinary law-making process. By contrast, in a rigid constitution, the laws of the constitution can only be amended by some special procedure. Thus, according to Lord Bryce, the United States has a rigid constitution, since constitutional amendments cannot be made by an ordinary Act of Congress (the normal law-making process), but require a special procedure involving a two-thirds majority in each House of Federal Congress, followed by ratification by at least three-quarters of the legislatures of the individual states of the Union. By contrast the United Kingdom constitution, any law of which can be changed by simple Act of Parliament, is flexible.

The terminology 'rigid' or 'flexible' was also adopted as one of six classifications of constitutions by Sir Kenneth Wheare in his book *Modern Constitutions* (1951). However, Wheare used the terminology in a different sense, namely, to distinguish constitutions according to whether they are, in practice, through the force of a variety of circumstances, easily and often altered, or not. On Wheare's classifications the United States constitution is 'rigid', because there have only been 26 amendments since its adoption in 1787. But the Swiss constitution, whose amendment requires a special procedure, usually a referendum of the people, is flexible because, in fact, it has often been amended. Proponents of the current constitutional framework, such as Lord Cranborne (former Conservative leader in the House of Lords) have argued:

> 'An unwritten constitution is by definition flexible. You need only pass a law to change it. It assumes that the status quo is not perfect because to change it is easy if there is a parliamentary majority for so doing. Evolution, rather than revolution, is built into the system. Evolution also ensures a sense of continuity and a sense of history, so important for a sense of nationhood. Continuity, evolutionary change, electoral authority – these add up to flexibility' (*The Times* 11 October 1996).

Unitary or federal

Under a federal constitution, government powers are divided between, on the one hand, the central (or federal) organs of state power and, on the other, the organs of the individual states or provinces that make up the federation. The United States of America, Canada, Australia, Malaysia and Nigeria are all examples of federal states. The essential point is that any alteration of the distribution of powers between the federal organs and the state organs can only be achieved by amendment of the constitution and not by simple act of the federal (central) Parliament. The individual states cannot have their powers reduced in that way. Any amendment to the constitution which involves a redistribution of powers between the federal and state organs will require some special procedure that, generally, allows the individual states some voice in the decision. Federal states have usually been formed by a group of states, each previously independent of one another or separately governed, coming together and transferring certain governmental powers to a set of central organs while retaining other powers themselves. Nigeria may be cited as an exception to this since the present 19 states of Nigeria were never separately governed.

Under a unitary constitution all state power is vested by the constitution in central organs. The United Kingdom has a unitary constitution since all state power is vested in central organs at Westminster and Whitehall. This is so despite the fact that the United Kingdom is regarded as having four component parts, England, Scotland, Wales and Northern Ireland, with Scotland, Wales and Northern Ireland enjoying varying degrees of devolved power. Ultimately Parliament at Westminster has power to make law for any of the regions and can repeal the legislation by which power was devolved. The United Kingdom also has a developed system of local government, local authorities having the power to make bye-laws and administer certain services in their particular locality. Again this does not detract from the nature of the United Kingdom as a unitary state, since at any time Parliament at Westminster could, by means of a simple Act of Parliament, reduce the powers of, or even abolish, these local authorities. For example, by means of the Local Government Act 1985 Parliament abolished the Greater London Council and the metropolitan county councils.

Other bases for classification

In addition to the above classifications, Wheare noted that constitutions are also distinguishable on the basis of other factors.

1. Whether the legislature is supreme or subordinate, ie can the legislature acting on its own amend the constitution? If so, the constitution is subordinate. If not, it is supreme.
2. Whether there is a discernible separation of powers, ie the extent to which the functions and the personnel of the three organs of state overlap.
3. Whether the state is monarchical or republican. This distinction is not as significant as it once was, since today many monarchies are, like the United Kingdom, constitutional monarchies where the monarch's power is not exercised personally but on her behalf by ministers of the democratically elected government.

The late S A de Smith in *Constitutional and Administrative Law* was influenced by Wheare's classifications. However, he abandoned the 'supreme or subordinate' distinction, and that based on 'fused or separated' powers, which he replaced by a distinction according to whether the state had a presidential or parliamentary executive. S A de Smith added two further classifications, the first being 'single-party and other constitutions'. The second classification he introduced was 'diarchical and other constitutions'. A diarchical constitution he describes as being one where there is a division of governmental competence between two or more authorities in the state otherwise than on a regional basis. He cites France, where the constitution gives both the legislature and the president separate law-making powers each within defined fields, and the Cyprus constitution of 1960, which gave certain law-making powers to separate Greek and Turkish communal chambers, the division being purely ethnic and not regional.

Leslie Wolf-Phillips introduces a classificatory scheme based on 13 elements according to which constitutions can be categorised. Some of these categories are the familiar ones of rigid or flexible, monarchical or republican, unitary or federal, but others include indigenous or adventitious (meaning home-produced or, alternatively, imposed from without for example by an imperial power); competitive or consolidatory (according to whether the constitution allows competition for power

between various elements in the state or, alternatively, consolidate
group, for example one party or one ethnic group); and
confirmatory (according to whether the constitution includes sta
to be fulfilled or whether it is, on the other hand, largely a
existing state of affairs). Wolf-Phillips also points out that most, if not ...,
have manifest constitutions and latent constitutions. The former refers to the formal
constitutional text and the latter refers to those areas of vital political activity, for
example the position and operations of political parties, which are unspecified in the
constitutional texts. This viewpoint, whilst an interesting one from which to analyse
other Commonwealth constitutions, may be less helpful in analysis of the United
Kingdom constitution because there is no formal constitutional text or written
constitution.

1.3 The British constitution classified

In the light of the above, the key aspect of the British constitution could be cited as
follows.

Unwritten: The United Kingdom does not have a written constitution. There is no
one document or group of documents providing a law of the constitution delimiting
the powers of the legislature, executive and judiciary.

Unitary: The United Kingdom is a unitary, as opposed to federal, state. Parliament,
sitting at Westminster, is the only body competent to legislate for the whole of the
United Kingdom.

Flexible: The British constitution is flexible in the sense that all law in the United
Kingdom, including laws relating to 'constitutional' issues may be enacted, repealed
or amended by the Queen in Parliament using the same procedure, ie changes can
be effected by ordinary legislation. Subject to the constraint imposed by membership
of the European Union (as to which see Chapters 2 and 4), Parliament may make or
unmake any law. There is no limit to its competence to legislate.

Headed by a constitutional monarchy: The Queen is the Head of State and
succession to the throne is hereditary. Although the monarch retains many of the
legal powers of government, by convention these powers are now exercised in her
name by her ministers.

Bicameralist: The United Kingdom legislature is composed of two Houses. The
House of Lords is the upper House of Parliament, and the House of Commons the
lower House of Parliament.

mocratic: The membership of the House of Commons is determined by the outcome of a general election based on universal adult suffrage conducted at least once every five years. The government is drawn from the political party that has the majority of seats in the House of Commons and ministers of the government are answerable to Parliament for the activities of their departments.

The position of the monarch

Historically the greater part of the machinery of central government emanates from the Crown. It is for that reason that from very early days the central government has been exercised in the name of the Sovereign. In the United Kingdom the legal Sovereign is the monarch (Queen Elizabeth II). But the monarch is not an absolute ruler. The United Kingdom has a constitutional monarchy, sovereignty being vested in the Queen in Parliament. In this respect a distinction must be made between the Sovereign and the Crown. When referring to the Queen's personal executive functions one speaks of 'the Sovereign'. When referring to the function of the central government generally, one speaks of the Crown.

The title to the Crown was originally elective and the notion of an hereditary monarchy grew gradually. At common law the title to the Crown of England was governed by the feudal rules of hereditary descent formerly applicable to land, except that in the case of a Sovereign dying and leaving no son but several daughters, the Crown descends to the eldest alone. She who holds the Crown in her own right as Queen of England has the same powers, prerogatives, rights and dignities as if she had been a King.

Ever since the Glorious Revolution of 1688 title to the Crown has been a matter which Parliament may regulate by statute. Today the Queen derives her title to the Crown from the Act of Settlement 1700, the Union with Scotland Act 1706, which constituted one Kingdom of Great Britain, and the Union with Ireland Act 1800 (as varied by the Government of Ireland Act 1920 and the Royal and Parliamentary Titles Act 1927), whereby the United Kingdom means Great Britain and Northern Ireland. By the Act of Settlement 1700 the Crown of England, France and Ireland was settled on Princess Sophia Electress of Hanover and granddaughter of James I, 'and the heirs of her body being Protestant'.

The Act of Settlement therefore disqualifies from the succession Roman Catholics and those who marry Roman Catholics. The Sovereign must also swear to maintain the Established Churches in England and Scotland, and must be in communion with the Church of England. His Majesty's Declaration of Abdication Act 1936 altered the hereditary succession to the Crown in that it provided that Edward VIII, his issue, if any, and the descendants of that issue, should not thereafter have any right to the succession.

By Royal Proclamation under the Great Seal issued under the Royal Titles Act 1953, the present royal title is: 'Elizabeth II by the Grace of God of the United Kingdom of Great Britain and Northern Ireland and of Her other Realms and

Territories Queen, Head of the Commonwealth, Defender of the Faith.' The forms of royal title adopted by other Member States of the Commonwealth for the Queen vary.

Under the Royal Marriages Act 1772, the marriage of a descendant of George II (other than the issue of princesses who have married into foreign families) shall be void unless the Sovereign has signified formal consent. Such a person may marry without the Sovereign's consent if he is over 25, provided 12 months' notice is given to the Privy Council and Parliament does not object.

Regency and Counsellors of State

The Regency Acts 1937–53 make provision for a regency in the event of the Sovereign being under the age of 18 years on his accession and in the event of the incapacity of the Sovereign through illness. They also make provision for the performance of certain of the royal functions in the Queen's name by Counsellors of State appointed by letters patent whenever she is absent or intends to be absent from the United Kingdom. In the case of regency, normally the regent will be the next person in the line of succession who is not disqualified by the Act of Settlement and is a British subject domiciled in the United Kingdom and of full age. The regent may exercise all royal functions except the granting of assent to a Bill to alter the succession to the throne, or to repeal the Scottish Act of 1706 securing the Scottish religion and Church. Counsellors of State may exercise those functions conferred upon them by letters patent. They may not, however, dissolve Parliament, except on the Sovereign's express instructions, nor grant any title or dignity of the peerage. The Counsellors of State must be the wife or husband of the Sovereign, the four persons next in line of succession to the Crown (unless disqualified from being regent or absent from the realm) and Queen Elizabeth, the Queen Mother.

Royal finance

Since the reign of George III it has been customary at the beginning of each reign for the Sovereign to surrender to Parliament for his life all the hereditary revenues of the Crown, including the Crown estates. In return Parliament grants the Civil List which is an annual sum to meet the salaries and other expenses of the royal household (Civil List Act 1952 as amended in 1972 and 1975), including sums for the use of those members of the Royal Family who undertake official duties on behalf of the Sovereign; other expenses are met by certain government departments. The royal yacht is maintained by the Ministry of Defence, for example, and the royal palaces by the Department of the Environment. The Prince of Wales receives the revenues of the Duchy of Cornwall. The Queen is personally exempt from taxation unless Parliament expressly or by necessary implication provides otherwise, or she consents to such taxation.

Duties of the Sovereign

Many activities of government require the participation of the Sovereign. Apart from her more public and ceremonial duties the Queen has a very full private work schedule. She receives Cabinet papers and minutes, Foreign Office dispatches and telegrams and other state papers, and receives the Prime Minister at a weekly audience at which she is kept informed of matters of state policy. The Queen presides over meetings of the Privy Council and receives visiting heads of state and foreign diplomatic representatives. She holds investitures to present honours and awards and gives her formal consent to major Crown appointments, including bishops and the senior judiciary. The Queen is head of the armed forces. Many state documents require her signature.

By convention, the Queen exercises her formal legal powers only upon and in accordance with the advice of her ministers. However, because of her long and wide experience of government, her guidance may prove invaluable. As Bagehot said, the Queen has the right to be consulted, the right to encourage, the right to warn.

The monarch is, technically, a party to the enactment of legislation, as the Royal Assent is required. By convention this is not withheld. In practice the monarch may even sign her assent before a Bill has completed all stages of its passage through Parliament if such action is expedient: see for example the rapid passage of the Terrorism and Conspiracy Act 1998.

The Queen as head of the Established Church

The Act of Supremacy 1534 declared Henry VIII supreme head of the Church in England and gave him control over its organisation. Queen Mary repealed that Act in the first year of her reign, but the Act of Supremacy 1558 passed in the first year of Elizabeth's reign reasserted the Church of England's independence from Rome and emphasised the monarch's ultimate authority over matters spiritual and ecclesiastical. It was originally entitled: 'An Act restoring to the Crown the ancient jurisdiction over the State ecclesiastical and spiritual and abolishing all foreign power repugnant to the same.' It enacted that:

> 'Such jurisdictions, privileges, superiorities and preeminences spiritual and ecclesiastical as by any spiritual or ecclesiastical power or authority had therefore been or might lawfully be exercised or used for the visitation of the ecclesiastical state and persons and for the reformation, order, and correction of the same and of all manners of errors, heresies, schisms, abuses and offences, contempts and enormities, should for ever by authority of Parliament be annexed to the Imperial Crown of this realm.'

An oath of allegiance was included, and failure to take it debarred a person from holding office in Church and State. It was not until the Roman Catholic Relief Act 1829 that members of the Catholic faith were rehabilitated to the extent of being entitled to sit and vote in Parliament. The Act of Supremacy 1558 is still the foundation of the Queen's ultimate authority over as head of the established Church.

What is 'the Crown'?

This matter was considered at some length by the House of Lords in *Town Investments Ltd* v *Department of the Environment* [1978] AC 359 where Lord Diplock, on behalf of the majority, expressed the view that:

'Where ... we are concerned with the legal nature of the exercise of executive powers of government, I believe that some of the more Athanasian like features of the debate in your Lordships' House could have been eliminated if instead of speaking of "the Crown" we were to speak of the "government" – a term appropriate to embrace both collectively and individually all of the ministers of the Crown and parliamentary secretaries under whose direction the administrative work of government is carried on by the civil servants employed in the various government departments. It is through them that the executive powers of Her Majesty's government in the United Kingdom are exercised, sometimes in the more important administrative matters in Her Majesty's name, but most often under their own official designation. Executive acts of government that are done by any of them are acts done by "the Crown" in the fictional sense in which that expression is now used in English public law.'

Demise of the Crown

'... the death of the Sovereign ... signifies merely a transfer of property; for when we say the demise of the Crown, we mean only that in consequence of the disunion of the Sovereign's natural body from his body politic, the Kingdom is transferred to his successor and so the royal dignity remains perpetual.' (Paraphrase of I Plowdens Reports 1550–80, page 177a.)

The paraphrase above explains as well as it is possible to do so the saying that 'the King never dies'. There may be a demise of the Crown on the death, abdication or deposition of the Sovereign. When any such event occurs the member of the Royal Family next in succession to the throne immediately accedes to the rights, privileges, and dignities of the monarch. The meeting of an Accession Council and the coronation are little more than public affirmations of the fact of the accession of the new monarch.

Formerly public business and tenure of public office were affected by a demise of the Crown, but this is no longer the case. Sections 4 and 5 of the Succession to the Crown Act 1707 and s51 of the Representation of the People Act 1867 provide that Parliament shall continue for its normal term despite the death of the reigning Sovereign, unless sooner prorogued or dissolved by his successor. The Demise of the Crown Act 1901, s1 provides that:

'The holding of any office under the Crown, whether within or without His Majesty's dominions, shall not be affected, nor shall any fresh appointment thereto be rendered necessary, by the demise of the Crown.'

1.4 The structure of the United Kingdom

The term 'United Kingdom' refers to the union of England, Wales, Scotland and Northern Ireland. Although the countries making up this union may enjoy distinct legal systems, and hence laws peculiar to themselves, they are not sovereign states as that term is used in constitutional law. The countries comprising the union are governed by Parliament at Westminster, and it is this body which, subject to the effect of EC law (see Chapter 4), enjoys sovereign power. It is in this sense, as considered above, that the United Kingdom constitution is described as being unitary in character.

The term 'Great Britain' should, strictly speaking, only be used when referring to the union of England, Scotland and Wales. 'British Isles' is a term of geographical, not constitutional significance, as it refers not only to the mainland, but also the Irish Republic and dependencies of the Crown such as the Isle of Man, Jersey and Guernsey.

Although the two centuries following the Norman conquest saw periodic assertions of independence by Welsh princes and others holding power over parts of the principality, the status of Wales as an English colony became increasingly apparent and was evidenced by the enactment of measures such as the Statute of Wales 1284. The political union was effectively complete by 1536 with the passing of the Act of Union, and in due course Welsh representation at Westminster, and the integration of the Welsh and English legal systems followed. In contrast to Wales, Scotland has a longer history of constitutional independence. Prior to the enactment of the Union with Scotland Act 1706, Scotland maintained its own monarchy, parliament and, as the history of military engagements between English and Scottish forces attests, defended its geographical integrity with varying degrees of success. The legislation of 1706, and the complimentary Union with England Act passed by the Scottish legislature in 1707, effectively secured a political and constitutional union of what by then had become England and Wales and Scotland.

The special needs of both Scotland and Wales were recognised at an executive level by the creation of government departments to take particular responsibility for aspects of regional policy. Thus, in 1884 the Scottish Office was created, and in 1892 the post of Minister for Scotland was accorded Cabinet rank. By 1926 the significance of the post was reflected in its being elevated to the rank of Secretary of State for Scotland. The post of Secretary of State for Wales was created in 1964, the holder being a member of the Cabinet. A Welsh Office, based in Cardiff, was created to provide an administrative base for its functions. The extent to which the creation of government departments based on regional lines has worked to the benefit of those regions remains open to question. The Welsh and Scottish Secretaries of State are, of course, bound by collective responsibility, and thus may have to be party to decisions that run counter to the interests of their regions as a whole. Given the secrecy attaching to Cabinet proceedings it is impossible to know the extent to which such ministers actually fight for their regions' interests. Perhaps effectiveness can only be measured in terms of economic prosperity.

The Welsh and Scottish Secretaries of State are answerable to the Westminster Parliament, but there is limited scope for scrutiny of their functions. Parliamentary questions for these ministers come around approximately once every three weeks. Since 1979 there have been select committees for Welsh and Scottish affairs, and there are standing committees which look at legislation exclusively concerned with Scotland.

Scottish and Welsh devolution

Some would argue that at the heart of the debate on devolution is the issue of legitimacy. Can a government based at Westminster claim to represent the whole country? During the 1980s some regarded it as iniquitous that a Conservative government exercised power over a region such as Scotland where at times it commanded less than 20 per cent of the popular vote. In the latter half of the twentieth century the significance of devolution as a political issue has ebbed and flowed, depending upon a whole host of factors. Disillusionment with central government, its apparent failure to take on board the needs of the regions, and grievances, both perceived and real, over the allocation of resources have provided fertile soil for the seeds of nationalism and calls for regional independence. This sense of alienation in regions such as Scotland and Wales was aggravated during the 1980s, with its prolonged period with a large Conservative majority in the House of Commons, by the perception in some quarters that what happened in the Scotland and Wales did not matter as there were few Conservative voters there anyway. Another factor relevant to the growth in nationalism and support for devolution may have been the decline in the power and influence of large (metropolitan) local authorities that had been gradually denuded of their functions and status. Municipal power bases for the Labour opposition in Wales and Scotland were effectively emasculated by successive reforms of local government in the period from 1979 to 1995. The resurgence of nationalism following the break-up of the former Soviet Union may also be a relevant underlying trend.

Opponents of devolution argued that it was unnecessary, would simply increase bureaucracy, would result in inconsistent standards in the delivery of public services, would place an unnecessary burden on the taxpayer, and could ultimately undermine the continued existence of the United Kingdom as a political entity and world power.

In order understand more fully these moral, political and economic arguments for and against devolution, some thought needs to be given to exactly what devolution involves. Should a regional government take functions and powers from central government or local government? Which would it more closely resemble? Would local government still be answerable to Parliament at Westminster or to the newly created regional assemblies? How would national standards in social services be maintained? Is there any real case for regional government in England?

Many of these issues were addressed by the by the Kilbrandon Commission (1973) which defined devolution (para 543) as 'the delegation of central government powers without the relinquishment of sovereignty'. This definition is necessarily imprecise, as the devolution of power can take a variety of forms, depending on the type of power being devolved and the degree of devolution involved. Broadly speaking it is possible to identify three variants.

1. Legislative devolution – the power to legislate for, and execute policy in relation to, certain defined matters delegated to a regional assembly. Central government retains an overriding power to legislate in respect of any matter (ie can repeal any measure introduced by the regional assembly).
2. Executive devolution – legislation is passed by Parliament at Westminster, with regional assemblies determining local policy and the manner in which it is to be put into effect.
3. Administrative devolution – does not involve the creation of a regional assembly. Central government arranges for the discharge of its policies on a regional basis.

The Kilbrandon Commission, which was set up in 1969 under the Labour government led by Harold Wilson, had its terms of reference related particularly to the question of the desirability or otherwise of devolving power to the regions. In its 1973 report the Commission claimed a lack of any significant 'grassroots' support for wholesale independence in Wales or Scotland, and emphasised the need for the United Kingdom to remain a coherent political and economic entity. A majority of its members favoured elected assemblies for Scotland and Wales with delegated legislative powers in relation to matters exclusive to those regions (ie largely co-terminus with the matters falling within the province of the respective Secretaries of State for Scotland and Wales). Dissenting voices amongst the Commission's members argued that the regions of England had an equally strong claim to the right to be well governed and could not agree to any scheme for devolution that overlooked the interests of the English regions. By the time the Commission's report was published in 1973, a Conservative government was in power and, perhaps unsurprisingly, the somewhat incoherent range of findings in the report led to its usefulness being doubted.

Although there had been a notable increase in the nationalist vote in parliamentary elections and by-elections in the late 1960s and early 1970s, it was not until the mid-to-late 1970s that a Labour government, heavily dependent upon the support of minority parties, took determined steps to put into effect policies designed to devolve power to regional assemblies for Wales and Scotland. Two measures were enacted, the Wales Act 1978 and the Scotland Act 1978, providing for legislative devolution in the case of the proposed Scottish assembly and executive devolution in the case of the Welsh assembly. The implementation of these proposals was made dependent upon the outcome of referendums to be held in

Scotland and Wales. As a result of back bench opposition to these Acts when they were before Parliament, a clause was inserted to the effect that both Acts would be repealed unless 40 per cent of those entitled to vote in the referendums voted in favour of the proposed assemblies. In the event only 11.9 per cent of registered voters in Wales supported the proposals and in Scotland the figure was 32.9 per cent. Thus the scheme came to nothing, and the Scottish National Party was to some extent responsible for the Labour government fall from power when it subsequently withdrew its support in the House of Commons in 1979.

The Labour Party has also, historically, embraced centralism as a means of effectively pursuing socialist policies. Much Labour support is, however, based in the more remote regions, and the Labour Party has shown greater readiness than the Conservative Party to recognise the moral argument for regional empowerment. A political difficulty for the Labour Party, however, is in espousing the nationalist cause, whilst retaining a political identity distinct from the nationalist parties. It is a difficult balancing act for any mainstream national political party to propose an effective and real devolution of power, without also advocating that the extent of its own writ as a party of government should not also be curtailed. In its 1987 election manifesto the Labour Party committed itself to legislating to establish an elected Scottish assembly with 'a wide range of powers over health, education and housing and over significant aspects of industrial and economic policy'. No mention was made of power to raise funds by way of taxation. Wales was promised a strengthened Welsh Development Agency and a separate Arts Council. The commitment to a Scottish assembly was reaffirmed in the 1992 manifesto, with an additional undertaking to introduce an elected Welsh assembly 'with powers and functions which reflect the existing administrative structure'.

In July 1997 the newly elected Labour government announced its plans for devolution in two White Papers, one dealing with Scotland (*Scotland's Parliament*), the other with Wales (*A Voice for Wales*). In due course, Scottish voters had the opportunity to express their views on the devolution question in a referendum held on 11 September 1997. The first question sought a 'Yes' or 'No' answer on the issue of the setting up of a Scottish Parliament in Edinburgh; the second related to whether or not that parliament should have tax-raising powers. On a turnout of 60.16 per cent, 74.29 per cent voted in favour of a Scottish Parliament being established, and 63.48 per cent voted in favour of that parliament being granted limited tax-varying powers. As indicated above, the main reason that the move towards devolution in 1978 became stalled was the failure to meet the requirement that the proposals would have to secure the support of at least 40 per cent of those eligible to vote. By contrast, in the 1997 referendum 44.7 per cent of all eligible Scottish voters voted in favour of a Scottish Parliament. However, only 38.2 per cent of those eligible to vote supported the granting of tax-varying powers.

The Scotland Act 1998 was duly passed providing for a Scottish Parliament. The first elections took place in 1999. The Parliament has 129 members, 73 members representing constituencies, the remaining 56 being drawn from party lists. Members serve four-year terms. Voters thus cast two votes. Section 44 of the 1998 Act provides for a Cabinet known as the Scottish Executive, led by a First Minister (Keeper of the Scottish Seal) who is responsible to the Crown. The First Minister has the power to appoint junior Scottish ministers and law officers. The Speaker of the Scottish Parliament is known as the Presiding Officer. The Scottish Parliament has power to deal with issues such as health, education, law and order, the environment, housing, economic development and consumer affairs. In relation to local government, it is able to authorise variations in local authority boundaries, functions and revenue raising powers.

The Scottish Parliament does not have power over foreign affairs, defence, constitutional matters, economic policy (beyond marginal revenue raising powers), and is not permitted to legislate in a manner that is inconsistent with Community law or the European Convention on Human Rights. In this sense the Scottish Parliament will be a subordinate body, required to act within the scope of its enabling legislation.

In the referendum held on 18 September 1997, Welsh voters voted in favour of a Welsh assembly, but by the narrowest of margins (a majority in favour of 7,000). Notwithstanding the narrow margin of victory for the pro-devolution campaigners, or the fact that voters in Cardiff, the site of the proposed Assembly, voted against devolution, the Government of Wales Act 1998 was enacted providing for a 60 member Assembly. The Assembly effectively takes over the powers currently exercised by the Welsh Office and a number of quangos, and a budget of over £7 billion (1997 figures), although the Secretary of State for Wales retains his seat in the Cabinet. The Assembly is empowered to make spending decisions in relation to health, education and related matters, and has the power to scrutinise European Union proposals and distribute funds allocated by Brussels. Members of the Assembly are elected to serve a four-year term. Forty members are elected on a constituency basis and 20 on a party list basis. The Assembly is structured on a local government model with powers conferred on the Assembly itself and exercised by multi-party subject committees and a single executive committee comprising the leaders of the subject committees. Parliament at Westminster retains control over issues such as foreign affairs, taxation, broadcasting, defence and social security.

Where a devolution issue arises in legal proceedings (meaning a question as to whether or not a devolved body has acted within the scope of its powers, has performed its duties, acted within the scope of Community law, or complied with the European Convention on Human Rights) the court seized of the issue should serve notice on the Attorney-General and the relevant devolved body (ie Scottish Parliament or Welsh Assembly) so that they can become parties to the action if they see fit. The issue in question can be further referred to the Judicial Committee of the Privy Council if necessary: see *Practice Direction (Supreme Court: Devolution)* [1999] 1 WLR 1592.

Ireland and Northern Ireland

Attempts by the Westminster Parliament to establish authority over Ireland, as evidenced by measures such as the Union with Ireland Act 1800, culminated, in the early part of the twentieth century, in events such as the 1916 Easter rising, a rebellion by Irish nationalists, and the emergence of revolutionary parties such as Sinn Fein. In due course the British government faced up to the reality of the continued armed Irish resistance to rule from Westminster, and by means of the Irish Free State (Agreement) Act 1922, Irish Free State (Constitution) Act 1922, and the Irish Free State (Consequential Provisions) Act 1922, created a situation whereby the new Irish Free State could become a dominion within the British Commonwealth, with the six counties, making up what is now referred to as Northern Ireland, having the right to opt out of the arrangement. By 1948 Ireland had left the British Commonwealth and achieved the status of an independent sovereign state. With the enactment of the Ireland Act 1949 the British government formally recognised this independence, but also enshrined in statute the 'loyalist veto' whereby the reunification of Ireland would only be permitted if a majority of the population of Northern Ireland agreed. Predictably the predominantly Protestant six counties of the North did exercise the right not to become part of a predominantly Catholic Irish state and, under the terms of the Government of Ireland Act 1920, came to be governed by a Northern Ireland parliament sitting at Stormont. This body had the power to enact legislation for the Province in most areas other than defence, foreign affairs and nationality, but financial control was effectively exercised from Westminster. Tension between the republican (Catholic) and loyalist (Protestant) communities in the North remained high, and following the outbreak of widespread civil disturbances in 1972 the Northern Ireland Parliament was disbanded and direct rule from Westminster imposed.

After two decades of unsuccessful attempts at sharing power between Westminster and Belfast, civil disobedience, public disorder, and terrorist atrocities committed by those on both sides of the sectarian divide, the prospects of a political settlement in Northern Ireland looked increasingly promising, and the Anglo–Irish agreement of 1985 was followed by the joint Anglo–Irish Downing Street declaration of 1993 and the 1994 cease fire declared by the paramilitary forces on both sides. In early 1995 the Dublin and Westminster governments agreed a joint framework document for the Province. Whilst reaffirming that a united Ireland could not be achieved without the consent of a majority of those in Northern Ireland (and noting that this recognition would require amendment of the Irish constitution), the joint framework document acknowledged the legitimacy of the aspirations of the Republican minority in Northern Ireland.

To promote cross-border co-operation, the document proposed the creation of a North–South body, comprising Heads of relevant executive departments, to 'discharge or oversee delegated executive, harmonising or consultative functions, as appropriate, over a range of matters that the two governments designate ... to discharge the functions ... designated for treatment on an all-Ireland basis ... to oversee the work of subsidiary bodies.' Moves towards a new settlement were delayed by the ending of the cease fire and the resumption of the IRA's mainland bombing campaign in February 1996, but work continued and, as a result of talks culminating in the 'Good Friday' agreement (also known as the 'Belfast Agreement') of April 1998, it was agreed that the Anglo–Irish agreement of 1985 should be replaced by a new British–Irish agreement. It was also agreed that the Irish constitution would be amended to provide that everyone born on the island of Ireland should be entitled to be part of the Irish nation.

A new art 3 inserted into the Irish constitution states:

'It is the firm will of the Irish nation ... to unite all the people who share the territory of the island of Ireland ... [but] recognising that a united Ireland shall be brought about only by peaceful means with the consent of a majority of the people ... in both jurisdictions.'

As part of the agreement the Government of Ireland Act 1920 has been repealed by the United Kingdom Parliament.

The agreement was supported by 71 per cent of the 81 per cent of the voters expressing a preference in a referendum in Northern Ireland in May 1998. In the Republic 94 per cent of those voting supported the agreement.

The Belfast Agreement also set out a new constitutional arrangement for Northern Ireland comprising three key bodies; a Northern Ireland Executive Committee; an Assembly; and a North-South Council of Ministers. The Northern Ireland Act 1998 was enacted to give effect to the main provisions of the agreement. The Assembly is, in effect, a parliament for the Province with power to legislate in areas previously dealt with by the six Northern Ireland government departments. Each of the 18 parliamentary constituencies returns six members elected by proportional representation. The Assembly has a chairman, a deputy chairman and committees to oversee government departments that currently run the Province. The Assembly liaises with a consultative Civic Forum, a body representing the business, trade union and voluntary sectors in Ulster. The Executive Committee is in effect a Cabinet, led by the First Minister and Deputy First Minister, with other ministerial posts being allocated in accordance with party representation in the Assembly. The First Minister and Deputy First Minister are elected by the Assembly. There are 12 ministers in all.

The agreement also provides for a North-South Council of Ministers, comprising ministers from both sides of the border meeting at least twice a year for plenary sessions. The general aim of the Council is to use its 'best endeavours to reach agreement on the adoption of common policies in areas where there is mutual cross-border and all-island benefit'. Specific areas of co-operation include: agriculture, education, transport and environment.

The operation of these new constitutional arrangements is overseen by a British-Irish Conference, although it does not have any executive powers as such. Its inaugural meeting was held in December 1999. In addition the 'Good Friday' agreement proposed the creation of a British-Irish Council (otherwise known as the 'Council of the Isles'), comprising representatives from British and Irish governments, the Northern Ireland Assembly, the Scottish Parliament, the Welsh Assembly and delegations from Jersey and Guernsey. The Council meets at summit level twice a year and at other times to deal with specific issues, such as transport links, agriculture, environmental, cultural and health issues. It also held its first meeting in December 1999.

Following the Review of the Implementation of the Belfast Agreement by Senator George Mitchell, legislative and executive authority over a number of issues was transferred to the Northern Ireland Assembly. Due to continuing political instability in the Province, however, the Northern Ireland Act 2000 was enacted (in two days) in February 2000 suspending the operation of the Northern Ireland Assembly. Pending the restoration of devolved government, legislation that would have been enacted by the Northern Ireland Assembly may be passed by Order in Council. The functions of the First and Deputy Ministers are exercised by the Secretary of State, and the functions of the Northern Ireland departments are discharged by the Northern Ireland Office.

Regionalism

Save the special arrangements that have existed in Northern Ireland from time to time during the twentieth century, the British constitution has not, prior to the Scotland Act 1998 and the Government of Wales Act 1998, featured any system of what might be termed 'regional government'. Powers and functions have been allocated between central government at Westminster and local government based on (largely) county boundaries. Given the devolution of power to Scotland and Wales that has now occurred, the question of devolving power to the regions of England has returned to the political agenda. In its 1997 election manifesto the Labour Party declared that:

> '... we will introduce legislation to allow the people, region by region, to decide in a referendum whether they want directly elected regional government. Only where clear popular consent is established will arrangements be made for elected regional assemblies. This would require a predominantly unitary system of local government, as presently exists in Scotland and Wales, and confirmation by independent auditors that no additional public expenditure overall would be involved. Our plans will not mean adding a new tier of government to the existing English system.'

To date this commitment to regionalism as regards England has been evidenced by the enactment of the Regional Development Agencies Act 1998, which created eight development agencies for areas outside London such as Leeds, Manchester, Bristol and Guildford. The primary tasks of the agencies is to develop regional economic plans, co-ordinate inward investment, market the regions as business centres and contribute to policies on transport, land use, health and education. The agencies will

over powers currently exercised by local governments in England. It
to be seen whether the work of these agencies can foster a sense of regional
sufficient to provide a basis for a more meaningful scheme of regional
government. The Select Committee on Environment, Transport and Regional
Affairs also has issues of regionalism within its remit.

1.5 Overview of the organs of government and the allocation of power

The modern British constitution is based on the revolution of the seventeenth
century that saw legislative supremacy slip from the grasp of the monarch to an
elected House of Commons. The Bill of Rights 1689, perhaps the closest thing the
British constitution has to a 'constitutional document' makes clear that, although the
monarch is a party to the legislative process, it is Parliament that is supreme. The
manifestation of Parliament's supremacy is legislation, to which the judges give
effect as evidence of their loyalty to Parliament. Within Parliament power resides
with the majority party in the House of Commons which, by convention, forms the
government. The leaders of the party forming the government, by convention, form
the Cabinet. Huge power is therefore concentrated in the hands of a few. The Prime
Minister selects his Cabinet, the Cabinet leads the government, and the government,
by definition, has overall power in the House of Commons. Power can be exercised
not only through the enactment of primary legalisation, but also by making
delegated legislation, and by ministers exercising prerogative power. Prerogative
powers are essentially those powers formerly exercised by the monarch that are now
exercised on her behalf by ministers. Examples include declaring war, deploying
troops, managing the Civil Service, issuing passports, and conducting foreign affairs.
Clearly not all executive functions are conducted by government ministers.
Functions are frequently allocated to other executive bodies such as local authorities
and other non-governmental organisations. The determination of disputes between
citizens, and between citizens and the state is the province of the judiciary. In this
respect the judiciary performs a vital role in ensuring that public authorities do not
exceed the scope of their powers. This control is achieved through the procedure
known as judicial review whereby a citizen with 'sufficient interest' can apply to the
courts for a determination of the legality of executive action. Without this safeguard
there would often be no effective control over the executive. Judicial functions are
also allocated to bodies such as tribunals where this is more appropriate than having
disputes determined by courts of law.

1.6 Legal rules of the constitution

As has been explained above the United Kingdom is unusual in not having a written constitution, ie a single document, or collection of documents, comprising the basic rules for the conduct of government. As a result, the study of constitutional law in the United Kingdom involves, on the one hand, an examination of those legal rules that can be classified as dealing with matters generally accepted as falling within the scope of constitutional law – such as the powers of the House of Lords; the right to vote; the regularity with which elections have to be held – and, on the other, those non-legal rules or conventions which provide evidence of how the organs of government actually operate in practice.

The term 'legal rules of the constitution' is used to refer to those principles that the courts will recognise as being enshrined in law, and thus enforceable in a court of law. In the United Kingdom there are two such sources of law, legislation and case law or common law.

Legislation

Of the two, legislation is the most important source of constitutional law, in the sense that the courts, in accordance with the doctrine of parliamentary sovereignty, will always give precedence to a statutory provision in favour of the common law. There are many major statutes of constitutional significance, examples include the Magna Carta 1215; Petition of Rights 1628; Bill of Rights 1689; Act of Settlement 1700; Union with Scotland Act 1706; Parliament Acts 1911 and 1949; Statute of Westminster 1931; Crown Proceedings Act 1947; the European Communities Act 1972 and the Human Rights Act 1998.

It should be noted that there is no exhaustive list of statutes that can be deemed 'constitutional' in their significance. It is not a term of art. In theory any piece of legislation that touches upon the rights and liberties of the subject could be classified as constitutional, but such an approach would encompass nearly every piece of legislation enacted. As a working definition it might be useful to proceed on the basis that aspects of the law relating to the constitution can be gleaned from legislation that deals with the key powers of the organs of state and the key rights and liberties of the individual.

What is significant is that although such legislation might deal with vital issues concerning the power of the state and the protection of the individual, it will enjoy no special status in terms of protection from repeal by any government with a sufficiently large majority.

In addition to domestic legislation, the law of the European Community also provides a source of constitutional law in the sense that, since the accession of the United Kingdom to membership of the European Communities on 1 January 1973, it impinges on the freedom of Parliament at Westminster to legislate as it sees fit, affects the approach of the judiciary to the interpretation of domestic legislation, and provides private individuals with enforceable rights against Member States. Community law is found in the Community treaties; regulations; directives and decisions of Community organs; and in rulings and decisions of the European Court of Justice. The nature of Community law is explored further in Chapter 2.

Common law

Some principles of constitutional law are enshrined in common law, ie the decisions of judges. Under the doctrine of precedent (or stare decisis) decisions of the superior courts are binding on all courts below, thus enabling a body of case law to be built up. Important rules of constitutional law may be found in many judicial decisions. For example, the case of *Entick* v *Carrington* (1765) 19 St Tr 1030 determined that general search warrants were illegal; in *M* v *Home Office* [1993] 3 WLR 433 the House of Lords considered the circumstances under which a minister could be held to have acted in contempt of court in his official capacity; and in *Council of Civil Service Unions* v *Minister for the Civil Service* [1985] AC 374 the House of Lords determined the circumstances in which an exercise of prerogative power would be reviewable by the courts.

These decisions illustrate the key role that the judiciary can play in the development of constitutional law, and their decisions remain in effect until such time as they are overturned by or consolidated in statute. The problem with the judicial contribution, however, is that it is necessarily sporadic and reactive, as opposed to concerted and dynamic. Judges can only adjudicate upon real cases that are litigated, hence the opportunity to develop the law on certain aspects of individual rights and freedoms, or ministerial or police powers may arise infrequently.

Rules of Parliament

As regards the operation of Parliament itself, there are rules relating to the functions, procedure, privileges and immunities of each House. Some are to be found in resolutions of each House, while others remain unwritten, being based solely on informal understandings or practice. Generally the ordinary courts have no jurisdiction over the law of Parliament.

1.7 Non-legal rules of the constitution

A great many rules of the constitution are not contained in Acts of Parliament or judicial decisions but are to be found in those rules of conduct called conventions. Conventions could be defined as rules of constitutional behaviour which are considered to be binding by and upon those who operate the constitution but which are not enforced by the law courts nor by the presiding officers in the Houses of Parliament.

The following examples will serve to indicate that constitutional conventions serve to regulate key aspects of the workings of government.

Of the conventions that regulate the powers of the executive perhaps the key examples are that: the Sovereign must not exercise (on her own initiative) her legal right to refuse to assent to Bills which have passed through both Houses of Parliament; the Sovereign must act in accordance with the advice of her ministers; the government shall be headed by a Prime Minister and the Prime Minister shall choose a Cabinet of ministers to lead the government; the Sovereign shall appoint as Prime Minister the leader of the party with the majority of seats in the House of Commons; the Prime Minister and the Chancellor of the Exchequer must be members of the House of Commons; ministers are collectively and individually responsible to Parliament; the government must resign or advise a dissolution of Parliament if it loses the confidence of the House of Commons; and ministers must be members of the House of Commons or the House of Lords.

The significant constitutional conventions relating to the operation of the legislature include the following: the majority in the House of Commons shall not expel the minority to gain political advantage; the House of Lords ought ultimately to defer to the will of the House of Commons; the representation of political parties in parliamentary committees ought to be proportionate to their strength in the House; money Bills shall only be introduced in the House of Commons and only by a government minister; and Parliament must be summoned to meet at least once a year.

In relation to the judiciary examples of key conventions are that judges should not be active in party politics, and that members of the House of Lords who have not been appointed Lords of Appeal in Ordinary must not participate in the judicial functions of the House.

Why conventions of the constitution are obeyed

According to Dicey:

> '... the sanction which constrains the boldest political adventurer to obey the fundamental principles of the constitution and the conventions in which these principles are expressed, is the fact that the breach of these principles and of these conventions will almost immediately bring the offender into conflict with the courts and the law of the land. ... For example, by convention Parliament must meet at least once each year. If that convention were disobeyed the government would soon find itself running out of money or having to raise illegal taxes, as the power to levy taxes is granted by Parliament for only a year at a time.'

However, there are many conventions the breach of which would not result in any illegality. For example, the conventions that lay peers do not take part in the judicial functions of the House, or that the majority in the Commons should not expel the opposition, or that Parliament should not legislate for a Dominion against its will. Therefore, obedience to conventions cannot be explained by reference to legal sanctions alone. As Professor Jennings has suggested, conventions are obeyed because of the political difficulties which follow if they are not. In a democracy this means the pressure exerted through public opinion and the opposition for government conforming to the principles on which the system is based.

The distinction between law and convention

According to Dicey the main distinction between law and convention is simply that laws are enforced by the courts, while conventions are not. He expressed the view that:

> '... the rules which make up constitutional laws, as the term is used in England, include two sets of principles or maxims of a totally distinct character. The one set of rules are in the strictest sense "laws" since they are rules which (whether written or unwritten, whether enacted by statute or derived from the mass of custom, tradition, or judge-made maxims known as the common law) are enforced by the courts; these rules constitute "constitutional law" in the proper sense of that term and may for the sake of distinction be called collectively "the law of the constitution". The other set of rules consists of conventions, understandings, habits or practice which, though they may regulate the conduct of the several members of the sovereign power, of the Ministry, and of other officials, are not in reality laws at all, since they are not enforced by the courts.'

However, Dicey's approach may be too simplistic. Not all rules of law are justiciable. Professor Jennings saw the real distinction between law and convention as resting upon the fact that when a rule is a rule of law, it is generally speaking the function of the courts to declare that it is broken. The legal rule is either formally expressed or formally illustrated by a decision of a court, whereas conventions arise out of practice. Formal enunciation through the proper constitutional authorities gives a rule of law a greater sanctity than a convention. The opposition feels that it has a more effective remedy if it can point out that the government has acted illegally, than it would have if it could say only that it has acted unconstitutionally.

Why not enact conventions as law?

Conventions have several advantages over legal rules in the context of constitutional law. They provide a means of bringing about constitutional change without the need for formal change in the law. For example, many conventions concern the powers of the Sovereign. They allow the legal powers of the Queen to remain intact while allowing the democratically elected government to exercise those powers and they allow flexibility. Law is rigid and may be difficult to change. Conventions allow the constitution to evolve and keep up to date with changing circumstances without the need for formal enactment or repeal of law. Law must be followed in every case. Conventions allow discretion and can be waived if the particular circumstances make this desirable. Most conventions concern matters of a political nature. Their non-legal nature thus helps to keep the judiciary and the courts out of politics and political controversy. As long as conventions are obeyed there is no need for legal codification. If a particular convention is disregarded then it can be formally enacted and given legal status.

The courts and conventions

Conventions, being non-legal rules, cannot be enforced through the courts. If a party to litigation seeks to rely on a constitutional convention that is incompatible with a statutory provision the courts have, to date, always given precedence to the statute, as illustrated in the Privy council's ruling in *Madzimbamuto* v *Lardner-Burke* [1969] 1 AC 645. In 1961 the United Kingdom government had recognised the existence of a convention to the effect that the Parliament at Westminster would not legislate for colonies such as Southern Rhodesia without their consent. In 1965 the government in Rhodesia declared unilateral independence. This declaration was not recognised by the United Kingdom government, and Parliament at Westminster enacted the Southern Rhodesia Act 1965 seeking to invalidate the acts of the Southern Rhodesian government. The Privy Council held (by a majority) that, regardless of the existence of a convention, the courts would enforce legislation duly enacted by Parliament. Lord Reid (referring to the convention in issue) observed:

> 'That was a very important convention but it had no legal effect in limiting the legal power of Parliament. It is often said that it would be unconstitutional for the United Kingdom Parliament to do certain things, meaning that the moral, political and other reasons against doing them are so strong that most people would regard it as highly improper if Parliament did these things. But that does mean that it is beyond the power of Parliament to do such things. If Parliament chose to do any of them the courts could not hold the Act of Parliament invalid. It may be that it would have been thought, before 1965, that it would be unconstitutional to disregard this convention. But it may also be that the unilateral Declaration of Independence released the United Kingdom from any obligation to observe the convention. Their Lordships in declaring the law are not concerned with these matters. They are only concerned with the legal powers of Parliament.'

The courts have been prepared, however, in appropriate cases, to recognise the existence of conventional rules when deciding points of law. For example, in *Liversidge* v *Anderson* [1942] AC 206, the court gave as one reason for refusing to exercise judicial review of a minister's discretionary power, the fact that through the convention of ministerial responsibility the minister was responsible to Parliament for the exercise of the power. Thus an alternative 'remedy' was available. Similarly, in *Attorney-General* v *Jonathan Cape Ltd* [1976] QB 752, where the court was considering whether to grant an order prohibiting the publication of a former Cabinet minister's diaries of his time in office, the Lord Chief Justice held that an injunction could, in suitable cases, be granted to protect Cabinet secrecy, and hence the convention of collective responsibility. What is significant is that he recognised the existence of the convention as providing a basis for granting a legal remedy. In *R v HM Treasury, ex parte Smedley* [1985] 1 QB 657 the Court of Appeal declined to review the legality of a draft order due to be laid before Parliament partly on the basis that the courts had no power to do so, and partly on the basis that, by convention, the courts did not rule on the legality of proceedings in Parliament. In explaining this ruling Sir John Donald MR observed:

'... it would clearly be a breach of the constitutional conventions for this court, or any court, to express a view, let alone take any action, concerning the decision to lay this draft Order in Council before Parliament or concerning the wisdom or otherwise of Parliament approving that draft. ... It is the function of Parliament to legislate and legislation is necessarily in written form. It is the function of the courts to construe and interpret that legislation. Putting it in popular language, it is for Parliament to make the laws and for the courts to tell the nation, including members of both Houses of Parliament, what those laws mean.'

Guidance as to how the courts might go about the task of determining the existence of a convention was provided by the decision in *Re Amendment of the Constitution of Canada* (1982) 125 DLR (3d) 1. The Canadian government had submitted to the United Kingdom proposals for a draft constitution that would effectively give Canada complete control over its own constitution. Provinces opposed to the changes sought, by way of a declaration, the view of the Supreme Court of Canada in relation to the following question:

'Is it a constitutional convention that the House of Commons and Senate of Canada will not request Her Majesty the Queen to lay before the Parliament of the United Kingdom of Great Britain and Northern Ireland a measure to amend the Constitution of Canada affecting federal-provincial relationships or the powers, rights or privileges granted or secured by the Constitution of Canada to the provinces, their legislatures or governments without first obtaining the agreement of the provinces?'

By a majority of six to three the court confirmed the existence of such a convention. In arriving at this conclusion the following observations were made in the majority judgment concerning the nature of conventions:

'The conventional rules of the Constitution present one striking peculiarity. In contradistinction to the laws of the Constitution, they are not enforced by the Courts. One reason for this situation is that, unlike common law rules, conventions are not judge-made rules. They are not based on judicial precedents but on precedents established by the institutions of government themselves. Nor are they in the nature of statutory commands which it is the function and duty of the Courts to obey and enforce. Furthermore, to enforce them would mean to administer some formal sanction when they are breached. But the legal system from which they are distinct does not contemplate formal sanctions for their breach. Perhaps the main reason why conventional rules cannot be enforced by the Courts is that they are generally in conflict with the legal rules which they postulate and the Courts are bound to enforce the legal rules. The conflict is not of a type which would entail the commission of any illegality. It results from the fact that legal rules create wide powers, discretions and rights which conventions prescribe should be exercised only in a certain limited manner, if at all.'

The court was also guided by the views of Sir Ivor Jennings expressed in *The Law and the Constitution* (5th ed, p136) where he stated:

'We have to ask ourselves three questions: first, what are the precedents; secondly, did the actors in the precedents believe that they were bound by a rule; and thirdly, is there a reason for the rule? A single precedent with a good reason may be enough to establish the rule. A whole string of precedents without such a reason will be of no avail, unless it is perfectly certain that the persons concerned regarded them[selves] as bound by it.'

The court's declaration was clearly not binding on the Canadian government as a matter of law, but it is significant that a revised proposal was drawn up to which all provinces agreed, with the exception of Quebec. The result was the enactment of the Canada Act 1982, which repatriated the Canadian constitution: see further *Manuel* v *Attorney-General* [1983] Ch 77.

1.8 Constitutional reform

As has been noted above, the British constitution is not the product of a thoughtful and reasoned design process. If one were to draft a constitution starting with a blank piece of paper it is unlikely that one would settle upon the British model as being the best that could be achieved. The debate about constitutional reform intensified in the run-up to the general election of May 1997 as a result of the great emphasis in the Labour Party's manifesto on the need to modernise key aspects of the constitution. Some changes have already taken place. The European Convention on Human Rights has been incorporated into domestic law with the enactment of the Human Rights Act 1998. Devolution in Scotland and Wales has been effected through the Scotland Act 1998 and the Government of Wales Act 1998. London has an elected assembly for the first time since 1985, headed by the mayor, Ken Livingston. Other changes are likely to take longer and be more difficult. Reform of the voting system for general elections has been considered by the Jenkins Commission, but there is no evidence to suggest that any changes will be introduced in the foreseeable future. Reform of the voting system for the elections for MEPs are ongoing, the debate at present being over what form of proportional representation should be used. Reform of the House of Lords is likely to prove the most controversial issue, the government having abolished the rights of hereditary peers to vote in the House of Lords. There is little agreement, however, on the longer term issue of what form a second chamber should take. The introduction of the Freedom of Information Act 2000 has disappointed many of the proponents of reform in this area.

2

The European Union

2.1 Introduction

2.2 The institutions of the European Union

2.3 The sources of European Community law

2.1 Introduction

The European Union, as it is has been called since 1992, can trace its origins back to the immediate post-war era of the late 1940s and early 1950s. Europe had been ravaged by two World Wars, and there was a political will to ensure that such a catastrophic breakdown in diplomatic relations, with consequent loss of life and systematic abuse of human rights, should not be allowed to recur. The belief was that the more the individual states of Europe became integrated and interdependent, the less likely it would be that any one state would resort to armed force against another. In May 1950 the French Foreign Minister, Robert Schuman (working closely with Jean Monnet) outlined the aims and methods of the so-called 'Schuman' plan, which sought to integrate the coal and steel industries of those Western European countries wishing participate in the scheme. It will be noted that the coal and steel industries were central to any country having militaristic ambitions, hence the impetus to achieve integration in these areas. The result was the European Coal and Steel Community (ECSC), formally established in 1951 when six countries – Belgium, France, the Federal Republic of Germany, Italy, Luxembourg and The Netherlands – signed the Treaty of Paris 1951. Common institutions were established to govern the operation and development of the coal and steel industries in the Member States. The establishment of the ECSC was seen by many as the first step towards greater unity in Europe, the intention being that, following the integration in areas of coal and steel production, economies as a whole of the member countries would be integrated. Once economic integration was completed it was thought that the way might be open to the formation of a United States of Europe. In 1957, the process of integration was taken a step further with the signing of the Treaty of Rome establishing what was, until 1992, known as the European Economic Community (EEC). This period also saw the formation of the European Atomic Energy Community (Euratom), to encourage co-operation in the peaceful use and development of nuclear energy.

Terminology

Following the signing of the Treaty on European Union (TEU) 1992 or 'Maastricht Treaty', the term 'European Economic Community' (EEC) was dropped in favour of 'European Community' (EC). The TEU 1992 also made it clear that the original Treaty of Rome, as amended by the Single European Act (SEA) 1986 and the TEU 1992, was henceforth to be known as the EC Treaty. Other terminological changes flowing from TEU 1992 are as follows: the Council of Ministers becomes the 'Council of the European Union'; the Commission becomes the 'European Commission'. The Treaty on European Union (TEU) 1997 or 'Amsterdam Treaty' provides that the EC is itself now part of a wider entity, the European Union (EU). The EU is based on three 'pillars': (i) the EC, including the European Coal and Steel Community and Euratom; (ii) the common foreign and security policy; and (iii) co-operation in the fields of justice and home affairs. EC institutions have no jurisdiction in relation to (ii) and (iii) unless the Council of the EC decides otherwise. Matters in (ii) and (iii) are governed by inter-governmental co-operation at a national level.

Although there is a tendency to use the terms 'EU law' and 'EC law' interchangeably, it is technically incorrect to use the former expression as the EU does not actually enact legislation. In the technical sense the expression 'Community law' should now only be used in respect of law arising under the EC Treaty.

The objectives of the European Union

The EC has as its aim the welding of Europe into a single prosperous area by abolishing restrictions affecting the movement of people, goods and capital; in effect an internal market without internal frontiers in which the free movement of goods, persons, services and capital can be achieved. Article 2 of the EC Treaty provides:

> 'The Community shall have as its task, by establishing a common market and progressively approximating the economic policies of Member States, to promote throughout the Community a harmonious development of economic activities, a continuous and balanced expansion, an increase in stability, an accelerated raising of the standard of living and closer relations between the states belonging to it.'

Article 3 of the Treaty details the means by which these aims are to be achieved. This includes, for example, the elimination of customs duties and quantitative restrictions on the import and export of goods between Member States. With the abolition of all customs duties between Member States there will be a single European market of approximately 270 million customers available to producers in Europe, and European manufacturers will be able to produce goods more cheaply on the scale that is practised for example in the United States. Article 3 also envisages the establishment of a common commercial policy, an internal market characterised by the abolition, as between Member States, of obstacles to free movement of goods, persons, services and capital. Under the common agricultural policy, designed to keep the price of foodstuffs at a sufficiently high level to ensure an adequate return for farmers without the need for subsidies, foodstuffs entering Member States from outside the European Union have levies placed upon them to make them as expensive as those offered for sale by producers in the EC. Prices are not allowed to fall to their natural level because producers can insist on designated national authorities intervening to buy foodstuffs at a certain price – the 'intervention' price fixed each year by the Council. Provision is also made in art 3 for the approximation of laws of Member States to the extent required for the proper functioning of internal market; development of a policy on environmental matters; and a common policy on transport. In all the above the EC aims to eliminate inequalities and to promote equality between men and women.

In 1973 the original six Member countries were joined by Denmark, Ireland and the United Kingdom. In January 1981 Greece joined the Community and Spain and Portugal also became Members on 1 January 1986. With effect from 1 January 1995 membership increased to 15, with the addition of Austria, Finland and Sweden. Following the Amsterdam Summit in 1997 negotiations are in train to admit Poland, Hungary, the Czech Republic, Slovenia, Estonia and Cyprus to an enlarged EU. The preconditions for membership are: stable democratic political institutions; observance of the rule of law; respect for human rights; and a viable market economy able to withstand competition from other Member States.

Towards a federal Europe: the Maastricht and Amsterdam Treaties

Following a meeting of heads of government of Members States in Maastricht in December 1991, the TEU 1992 (the 'Maastricht Treaty') was signed by all Member States, with certain exceptions being made by the United Kingdom, on 7 February 1992. The Treaty accelerated the move towards a federal, unified, Europe, providing, for example, that every national of each Member State was to be granted the status of citizen of the EU, in addition to national citizenship. The TEU 1992 laid down a timetable for monetary union, with the aim that a single currency (the ECU) should be in circulation by 1999.

As with previous EC treaties, and in accordance with constitutional requirements, the TEU 1992 had to be incorporated into United Kingdom law by means of domestic legislation, hence the enactment of the European Communities (Amendment) Act 1993. The Conservative government of the day sought an opt-out for the United Kingdom as regards certain aspects of the TEU 1992 'package' (eg limitation upon working hours etc), but the Labour government elected in May 1997 has agreed that the United Kingdom should be bound by them.

The ratification of the TEU 1992 prompted an application for judicial review in *R* v *Secretary of State for Foreign and Commonwealth Affairs, ex parte Rees Mogg* [1994] 2 WLR 115. The applicant sought a declaration that any such ratification would be unlawful on the ground (inter alia) that the establishment of a common foreign policy (under Title V of TEU 1992) would involve a loss of prerogative power, which could only be achieved by way of statutory enactment. Dismissing the application, the court held that, on the facts, the ratification of Title V of the Maastricht Treaty did not involve a diminution of prerogative power as it would be open to the United Kingdom to renege on its obligations under the Treaty, and re-assert the prerogative power to formulate and execute foreign policy in the areas affected.

The 'Amsterdam Treaty' (ie TEU 1997) seeks to consolidate each of the three 'pillars' of the EU put in place by TEU 1992. The Treaty was incorporated into domestic law by virtue of the European Communities (Amendment) Act 1998. In addition to addressing issues related to strengthening the operation of the EU institutions (as to which see below), specific matters addressed by TEU 1997 are as follows.

Rights of EU citizens

The EU will co-ordinate policies aimed at reducing unemployment, via the European Investment Bank. With the signing of the Treaty the United Kingdom has accepted the agreement on social policy providing for a maximum working week and a minimum wage. Under the Treaty the EU will monitor the extent to which Member States adhere to their obligations under the European Convention on Human Rights. The TEU 1997 contains a non-discrimination clause that allows the EU to take action against all forms of discrimination.

Removing remaining obstacles to freedom of movement and strengthening security

In accordance with the 1990 Schengen Agreement, identity checks will be abolished at internal frontiers with the exception of the borders of Ireland and the United Kingdom. Controls at external frontiers and ports will remain in place. The TEU 1997 also envisages a harmonisation of rules on the issuing of visas and the granting of asylum to those arriving from outside the EU. Minimum European norms will be established regarding facilities provided for asylum seekers. The role of Europol will be expanded and developed in respect of its data-gathering activities and investigative roles. There is no proposal that it should take over any of the policing functions of the forces of Member States. Note that the TEU 1997 moves some aspects of justice and home affairs, such as asylum and immigration, from the third pillar of the EU to the first, thus bringing them within the jurisdiction of the EC institutions, notable the European Court of Justice.

2.2 The institutions of the European Union

The Council of the European Union

The Council is the EC's principal decision-making body. The government of each of the 15 nations in the European Union has a seat on the Council. The foreign minister is usually a country's main representative, but a government is free to send any of its ministers to Council meetings. The Council's membership thus varies with the subject scheduled for discussion. Finance ministers will attend for discussion of economic issues, transport ministers for discussion of transport policy, agriculture ministers for discussion of the common agricultural policy, and so on. Unlike the European Commission, the Council's members represent their national interests first and foremost. The presidency of the Council rotates between the Member governments at six-monthly intervals.

Under art 202 EC Treaty (formerly art 145) the functions of the Council are stated as being to ensure that the objectives of the EC Treaty are attained, and to ensure the co-ordination of economic policies of Member States. The Council carries out these functions by making policy decisions, issuing regulations and directives, and acting upon proposals from the Commission.

The Council can determine issues by a simple majority vote, by qualified majority voting, or by means of a unanimous decision, depending on the procedure required by the EC Treaty, as amended. The provisions regulating the voting procedures of the Council attempt to fulfil two aims: first, to ensure that the Council cannot easily take a high-handed approach to Commission proposals; and, second, to ensure that important proposals aimed at promoting greater integration of Member States should not be held back by the veto of one Member State. Hence the Council may be able to accept Commission proposals by a qualified majority, but unanimity is required if it seeks to amend a Commission proposal against the wishes of the Commission. For some particularly important decisions, such as acceptance of a new Member State or changes in the number of commissioners, unanimity is required.

As art 205 EC Treaty (formerly art 148) explains, under the system of qualified majority voting the votes of Members are 'weighted' according to population. In effect a country will be allocated roughly one vote for every six million of population, although there are anomalies in respect of the smaller nations so as to ensure that their views are not totally marginalised. The entry into the European Union of Austria, Finland and Sweden has increased the total number of votes to 87, and the number of votes needed to form a 'blocking minority' has increased proportionately to 25. The use of qualified majority voting has gradually increased through measures introduced in the SEA 1986, and more recently in the TEU 1997, the latter extending its use to areas such as social exclusion, public health, equal opportunities and employment incentives.

Although in theory it should become more difficult for any one Member State to exercise a power of veto by opposing a measure in Council, in reality the Council has recognised that there may be a heavy political price to pay for enforcing on a Member State a measure that it bitterly opposes, and which is likely to cause widespread anti-EC sentiment within that Member State. Hence, under what is known as the Luxembourg Accord (the Luxembourg Agreement of 1966) the Council will not normally impose a decision on a Member State by way of qualified majority voting if a Member State can show that the decision would be detrimental to its vital national interests. The Luxembourg Accord has no legal status but has proved an important factor in negotiations between Member States. The Council is not bound to accept an assertion by a Member State that a matter ought not to be decided by qualified majority voting on the grounds that a vital national interest is affected. The ultimate decision rests with the Council.

Although the Council has a shifting membership, some stability and consistency is ensured by the work of the Committee of Permanent Representatives of Member States (COREPER), which not only undertakes the preparatory work for Council meetings but also co-ordinates meetings of senior civil servants from Member States. COREPER is organised on a committee basis, with work being split between the first committee dealing with social affairs and transport, and the second dealing with economic and foreign affairs. Agricultural issues fall under the responsibility of a separate agriculture committee.

The European Commission

The treaties assign the European Commission a wide range of duties. It is the guardian of the treaties setting up the EC and is responsible for seeing that they are implemented. It is the initiator of Community policy and oversees the execution of policy initiatives. The Commission can investigate instances of Member States failing to fulfil treaty obligations, and if necessary deliver a reasoned opinion. Non-compliance with such an opinion will result in the Commission referring the matter to the European Court of Justice: see art 226 EC Treaty.

The European Commission, an independent body with executive powers and responsibility, comprises 20 commissioners chosen for their all-round capability by agreement between the governments of the Member States. At present Germany, United Kingdom, France, Italy and Ireland have two commissioners each. A commissioner is obliged to act in the Community's interests as opposed to the interests of the country of which he or she is a national. Throughout their four-year term of office commissioners remain independent of their respective governments and of the Council.

The Council cannot remove any commissioner from office; only the European Parliament can compel the European Commission to resign as a body by passing a motion of censure. In January 1999 such a censure motion was only narrowly defeated following mounting concern regarding the failure of the Commission to deal properly with fraud, corruption and allegations of poor accountability. The Commission agreed to the appointment of a team of independent investigators who could look into the allegations. The resulting report, published in March 1999, was very critical of the way in which the Commission had conducted itself, and of the behaviour of certain individual commissioners. As a result all 20 serving commissioners resigned. Some were subsequently invited to take up different posts within the Commission; others, pointedly, were not.

The Commission as a whole is headed by a President, appointed by the Commission in consultation with Member States. Each commissioner heads a department with special responsibilities for one area of Community policy, such as economic affairs, agriculture, the environment and transport. Regular discussions are held between a commissioner's department and interested parties. As a result of these discussions the relevant commissioner formulates draft proposals which he believes will help to improve the quality of life of Community citizens. The draft proposals are discussed by all the commissioners who then decide on the nature of the final proposal. Decisions are taken on a collegiate basis.

The number of commissioners is likely to be reviewed prior to further enlargement of EU membership. The Treaty on European Union 1997 expands the scope of the European Commission's competence as regards policy initiatives in areas such as employment and health.

Economic and Social Committee

In addition, there is also a body known as the Economic and Social Committee that plays a consultative role in the decision-making processes of the Council and Commission. The Committee represents a wide spectrum of European Community interests, such as those of workers, consumers and farmers.

The European Parliament

The EC Parliament is not to be equated with the Westminster model. It cannot legislate in its own right and does not possess any form of parliamentary sovereignty. It does, however, exercise a limited, but growing, supervisory power in relation to legislative measures. In particular the Parliament:

1. advises the Council of the European Union on Commission proposals;
2. with the Council of the European Union, determines the budget for the EC;
3. exerts some political control over the Council and Commission; and
4. by debate can attract publicity to issues that then have to be considered by the Commission or the Council.

The European Parliament now has 626 members who represent the citizens of the European Union. Members are directly elected and serve for a period of five years. The composition of Parliament makes it a fully integrated Community institution, as the members do not sit in national groups but in political party groups. The six main political party groups at present are the Communists, Socialists, European People's Party, European Progressive Democrats, European Democrats and the Liberal and Democratic Group. The United Kingdom has 87 MEPs.

The European Parliament meets on average once a month, for sessions which last up to a week. It has 18 standing committees that discuss proposals put forward by the Commission under the consultation procedure. The committees present reports on these proposals for debate by the full Parliament. The Commission is not obliged to act upon the recommendations of these committees. Similarly, the Parliament can put forward its own policy initiatives, but the Commission is under no obligation to act upon them.

Despite worryingly low turnouts, particularly in the United Kingdom, direct elections have given the Parliament greater political authority and new prestige both inside and outside the European Union. The Parliament has the right to question members of the Commission and Council and is therefore able, to a limited extent, to monitor the work of these institutions. It has the power to dismiss the European Commission by a two-thirds majority vote, and can similarly reject the Council's proposals for the Community budget. As noted above, the inquiry into fraud and corruption within the Commission, instigated by the EC Parliament in January 1999, led to the resignation of all of the commissioners in March 1999.

The role of the Parliament has been strengthened by the provisions of the SEA 1986, TEU 1992 and TEU 1997. As a result the Parliament has a power of co-decision in relation to a wide range of matters such as freedom of movement, non-discrimination, transport policy, social security, rights of establishment of foreign nationals and rules governing professions. The Parliament considers the Council of Ministers' proposals, within a strict time limit, and can adopt, amend or reject them. Rejection or amendment requires an absolute majority of members. In the event of rejection or amendment, the conciliation procedures come into play whereby a Conciliation Committee, comprised equally of Parliament and Council members, seeks to achieve agreement. If agreement cannot be reached the measure in question is dropped.

The European Parliament now has an effective power of veto over applications for EU membership, can veto nominations for the appointment of commissioners, and the appointment of the EU President will require the endorsement of the Parliament.

The EC Ombudsman

In the wake of the 1994 European Parliament elections an Ombudsman for the EC was appointed by the European Parliament, pursuant to art 195 (formerly art 138e) of the EC Treaty, to investigate allegations of maladministration made by any EU citizen or resident against any EC institution other than the European Court of Justice. Complaints considered by the EC Ombudsman do not have to pass through an MEP filter (he can act on his own initiative), and are not subject to any specific time limit. Given that serious violations of EC law can be pursued by individuals taking cases to the European Court of Justice, it seems likely that the EC Ombudsman will be concerned with less serious cases, perhaps where there may be no obvious judicial remedy, and where political pressure to achieve a settlement or redress is more appropriate. The only sanction available to the EC Ombudsman in the event that he finds an institution guilty of maladministration is the making of an adverse report to the European Parliament. Jacob Soderman, the first European Ombudsman, presented his first report in October 1996, covering the last three months of 1995. During this period he received 298 complaints and carried out 16 investigations. Most of the complaints were found to be outside his jurisdiction.

The Court of Justice of the European Communities

The Court is the European Union's supreme judicial authority; there is no appeal against its rulings. Each of the treaties establishing the European Communities uses the same broad terms to define the specific responsibilities of the Court of Justice, which are to ensure that in the interpretation and application of these treaties the law is observed. The Court therefore interprets and applies the whole corpus of EC law from the basic treaties to the various implementing regulations, directives and decisions issued by the Council and the European Commission.

Although its jurisdiction is principally concerned with EC law, the Court is not cut off from national law, since it draws its inspiration from the legal traditions that are common to the Member States. This ensures respect both for the general principles of law and for fundamental human rights in so far as they have been incorporated into the European Community legal order.

The 15 judges of the Court are appointed by common accord of the governments of the Member States. The treaties require them to be chosen 'from persons whose independence is beyond doubt and who possess the qualifications required for appointment to the highest judicial offices in their respective countries or who are jurisconsults of recognised competence'. There is no specific nationality requirement, but at the present time the Court has one judge from each Member State. The judges select one of their number to be President for a renewable term of three years. Members of the Court hold office for a renewable term of six years. Every three years there is a partial replacement of the Court's membership: five or six judges and two or three advocates-general are replaced alternately. This ensures continuity of the Court's decisions, especially as most of the judges have had their term of office renewed at least once and sometimes twice. The independence of the judges is guaranteed by their status and is based on three fundamental rules of procedure: their deliberations are secret; judgments are reached by majority vote; and judgments are signed by all the judges who have taken part in the proceedings. Dissenting opinions are never published.

The Court is assisted in its work by the advocates-general who are appointed on the same terms as the judges, although nationality is immaterial. According to art 222 (formerly art 166) EC Treaty the functions of the advocates-general are to act with complete impartiality and independence, and to make, in open court, reasoned submissions on cases brought before the Court, in order to assist the Court in the performance of the tasks assigned to it. The advocates-general do not represent the Communities and cannot initiate proceedings themselves. At a separate hearing, some weeks after the lawyers have addressed the Court, the advocate-general comments on the various aspects of the case, weighs up the provisions of EC law involved, compares the case in point with previous rulings, and proposes a legal solution to the dispute. The advocate-general does not participate in the Court's deliberations. Once the advocate-general has delivered his opinion it is not open to the parties to submit any further written submissions unless requested to do so: see further *Emesa Sugar (Free Zone) NV* v *Aruba* (2000) The Times 29 February.

Since 1988 the European Court has been assisted in its work by the Court of First Instance, comprising 12 judges, created under the SEA 1986. Advocates-general may assist the Court of First Instance but there are none specifically assigned to it. The role of the Court of First Instance is to deal with cases that turn primarily on issues of fact, rather than law, brought by natural or legal persons, rather than Member States. Initially its caseload was limited to disputes related to production quotas, competition law and staff cases, but since 1993 its jurisdiction has been extended to all matters, other than cases involving anti-dumping proceedings. Appeal on a point of law lies to the European Court of Justice.

There are a variety of ways in which legal disputes can be brought before the European Court of Justice. A distinction is made between direct actions, which involve disputes between parties, and requests for preliminary rulings, which take the form of questions put by national judges. Direct actions may be divided into four categories:

1. proceedings against a Member State for failure to fulfil an obligation;
2. proceedings for annulment;
3. proceedings for failure to act; and
4. proceedings to establish liability.

As indicated above, if the Commission considers that any part of the administration of a Member State has not honoured an EC obligation, it asks that Member State to make its comments and then issues a reasoned opinion. If the Member State does not act on the opinion within the time allowed, the Commission may refer the matter to the Court on the basis that the Member State has failed to act as required: see art 226 (formerly art 169) EC Treaty. If the Court agrees that the case is well founded, it declares that an obligation has not been fulfilled: see for example *EC Commission* v *Italy* Case 39/72 [1973] ECR 101. All the authorities of the Member State concerned are required to take the necessary measures to comply with the Court's judgment in their respective areas of competence. If a state does not comply with the initial ruling, new proceedings may be brought for a declaration by the Court that the obligations arising from its first decision have not been complied with. *EC Commission* v *Italy* [1989] 3 CMLR 25 makes it clear that the Member State's duty in such cases is to make the necessary amendments to its domestic law. The TEU 1992 provided a framework for the introduction of a system of fines imposed upon Member States for non-compliance with EC obligations: see art 68 (formerly art 73p) EC Treaty. The European Commission has agreed that fines are to be imposed on a sliding scale, related to the 'wealth' of Member States.

Proceedings for annulment under art 230 (formerly art 173) EC Treaty are a way of reviewing the legality, under the treaties, of Community acts, Commission decisions and regulations, and of settling conflicts between the institutions over their respective powers under the treaties. The proceedings, which can be instigated by a Member State, the Council or the Commission, are directed against binding Community acts, be they general regulations and directives or decisions addressed to individuals, taken by the Council and the European Commission. The basis of such a challenge is that the impugned acts are unlawful because of lack of legal competence, infringement of an essential procedural requirement, infringement of the EC Treaty or any rule of law relating to its application, or misuse of powers. A notable recent example was the unsuccessful attempt by the United Kingdom to challenge the validity of the adoption of the 'working time directive' which sought to limit the average working week to 48 hours' duration: see further *United Kingdom* v *Council of Ministers of the European Communities* [1996] All ER (EC) 877. Because opinions and recommendations do not have binding force, proceedings may not be brought in respect of them.

Private citizens, companies and non-EC Member States may also initiate proceedings for annulment, but only against decisions which are specifically addressed to them or which, despite being in the form of regulations or decisions addressed to another person, concern them directly and individually. If the Court regards the action as well founded, it declares the act in question void and of no effect and the act then ceases to have any legal force as from the date when it originally took effect.

Proceedings for failure to act (under art 233 (formerly art 176) EC Treaty) provide a means of penalising inactivity on the part of the Council or the European Commission. Should the Council or the European Commission infringe the EC Treaty by failing to act, the Member States and the other institutions of the Community may bring an action before the Court of Justice to have the infringement established. Such actions are admissible only if the institution in question has previously been called upon to act. If it has not acted within two months of being invited to do so, an action may be brought within a further two months. Proceedings for failure to act can also be brought under identical conditions by private individuals or firms, who can accuse a Community institution of having failed to take a binding decision (ie one other than a recommendation or opinion) concerning them. Admissibility is subject to the same conditions as those that apply to actions for annulment – the act not taken must have been of direct and personal concern to the party initiating the proceedings.

Finally, the civil liability can be imposed by the Court for damage caused by EU institutions or servants in the performance of their duties in accordance with the general principles common to the laws of the Member States. The treaties confer on the Court of Justice the exclusive jurisdiction to order the EC to pay damages because of its actions or its legislative acts, on the principle of non-contractual liability. In exercising its unlimited jurisdiction, the Court decides the basis on which liability is to be determined, whether the damage is due to Community action, the amount of damage caused and the sum to be paid in compensation. By contrast, the EC's contractual liability is subject to the general law of the Member States and to the jurisdiction of their courts.

The European Court of Justice is, by its very nature, the supreme guardian of Community law. But it is not the only court that has the power to apply and interpret this body of law that is common to all the Member States. Unlike most classical forms of international treaty, there is a mass of provisions set out in the treaties themselves and in the secondary legislation of the Council and the European Commission, and in agreements entered into by the Community that are directly and immediately applicable in the legal systems of all the Member States. These acts have a direct effect in that they can confer individual rights on nationals of Member States (see below for an explanation of direct effect). Private individuals may invoke them in their national courts in relation to the national authorities and, in some circumstances, in relation to other private individuals and companies. The courts in each Member State have thus become, in a sense, 'Community courts'. To avoid differing and even conflicting interpretations, art 234 (formerly art 177) EC Treaty introduced a system of preliminary rulings that can be requested in order to test the validity of acts adopted by the institutions, and to provide clarification regarding the extent to which the domestic law of a Member State is at variance with the dictates of EC law.

Under the EC Treaty, where a national court from which appeals be made finds there is a problem regarding the interpretation of the treaties or of measures taken by the institutions, or some question arises as to the validity of these measures, it *may* apply, under art 234, to the European Court for a preliminary ruling if it considers that it needs to do so in order to come to its judgment. When a problem or question of this type arises in a national court against whose decisions there is no judicial remedy under national law (eg the House of Lords), that court *must* refer the matter to the Court of Justice. This system has resulted in valuable collaboration between the Court of Justice and national courts in ensuring the uniform application and interpretation of Community law.

In *Srl CILFIT* v *Ministry of Health* [1982] ECR 3415 the Court defined the extent and limits of the obligation on courts of final instance to request preliminary rulings. The Court stated that national courts did not need to refer questions if: the question raised was irrelevant, as, for instance, if it could have no possible influence on the outcome of the dispute; the Community rule in question had already been interpreted by the Court (whatever the circumstances and without the matters in dispute necessarily being absolutely identical); and there was no reasonable doubt about how the question should be answered.

Opinions vary on the authority enjoyed by preliminary rulings and particularly on whether they have general effect or are binding only on the parties concerned. However, three points seem to have been accepted regarding references for interpretation: the interpretation given by the Court is binding on the judge who requested it – he can refer the matter back to the Court if he considers that there is still a question to be answered; the interpretation serves as a basis for applying the relevant law in any subsequent case and other courts may invoke it without further reference to the Court of Justice; and a judge may always ask the Court of Justice for a new interpretation. A preliminary ruling may only be applied for by a national court or tribunal and not by the parties to the case. Once a ruling has been given the matter is taken back to the domestic court that made the reference for that court to give its ruling in the light of the European Court's decision.

As a consequence of the fact that any domestic court can, in theory, refer a case for consideration under art 234, concern is increasing at the extent to which the process is becoming overburdened by the number of cases so referred. At present the average length of time taken in dealing with a reference is 18 months. One possible reform that may be considered is to only permit the exercise of the right to make references once all domestic appeal procedures have been exhausted.

Given that the EC Treaty reflects its continental legal origins in the way in which it is drafted, as does the output of the Council in terms of other sources of EC law, it is not surprising to find that the approach of the European Court to the interpretation of the EC Treaty and other measures is markedly different from the approach adopted by UK courts when interpreting domestic legislation. As Lord Diplock observed in *Henn and Darby* v *DPP* [1981] AC 850 (at p852):

> 'The European Court, in contrast to English courts, applies teleological rather than historical methods to the interpretation of the treaties and other Community legislation. It seeks to give effect to what it conceives to be the spirit rather than the letter of the treaties; sometimes, indeed, to an English judge, it may seem to the exclusion of the letter. It views the Community as living and expanding organisms and the interpretation of the provisions of the treaties as changing to match their growth.'

The Council of Europe and the European Council

The Council of Europe exists quite independently of the EU, being the creation of the Treaty of Westminster in 1949. It has a much larger membership than the EU, comprising many states that, for political or economic reasons, find the concept of EU membership unacceptable or unattainable. The Council of Europe operates essentially as an inter-governmental organisation, that from time to time generates conventions on key aspects of international law. Its most notable achievement is the European Convention on Human Rights. A possible consequence of failing to comply with the Convention's requirements is expulsion from the Council of Europe. In 1967 Greece had its membership suspended following the military take-over and attendant human rights abuses. Similarly, in April 1995, the Council of Europe approved a resolution ordering Turkey's suspension unless it showed progress in withdrawing from Northern Iraq where it had intervened in relation to the Kurds.

The European Council has existed since the early 1970s and is comprised of the heads of EC Member States and the President of the European Commission. Although it originally existed as an ad hoc organisation, its existence has now been formerly recognised by the SEA 1986, and has had its status increased by virtue of the TEU 1997. The European Council provides a forum for discussion of strategic issues related to EU policy, such as economic and social matters, constitutional issues, and for reviewing the operation of the EU. Meetings, normally held three times a year, are chaired by the head of the member state currently holding the Presidency of EC.

Future developments – The Treaty of Nice

A number of factors underpinned the agreement reached by EU Member States at the Nice summit in December 2000. The first was the desire to enlarge membership from 15 to 27 Member States. The Treaty of Nice therefore paves the way for the admission of 12 new Member States: Bulgaria; Cyprus; the Czech Republic; Estonia; Hungary; Latvia; Lithuania; Malta; Poland; Romania; Slovakia; and Slovenia.

The second factor was the recognition that enlargement would necessitate a streamlining of decision making processes, especially with regard to qualified majority voting (QMV). Under the Treaty QMV is extended to 23 new areas including external border controls; freedom of movement for non-EU nationals; aspects of asylum and immigration rules; intra EU judicial co-operation on civil matters; social security provisions; state aid for industry; regional subsidies; and various procedural and administrative matters. Areas that remain outside the scope of QMV are taxation, core social security policy, trade issues concerning cultural and audio/visual sectors and core immigration policy.

The third factor was the desire on the part of the larger Member States to ensure that their influence was not diluted by an influx of many smaller Member States following enlargement. Although large Member States such as the United Kingdom, France, Germany and Italy will each lose one of their commissioners by 2005 (the total number of commissioners being capped at 27), between them Germany, France and the United Kingdom will form a dominant power block able to control the future direction of EU policy. The United Kingdom's influence within the EU will, arguably, be strengthened under the Treaty by virtue of the fact that it will have a larger share of votes in the Council of Ministers (29 out of 237 – ie 12.24 per cent, instead of 10 out of 87 – ie 11.49 per cent); there will be a higher threshold for a qualified majority vote (74 per cent of 239 votes, instead of 71.4 per cent). The Treaty will now have to be ratified by the United Kingdom Parliament.

2.3 The sources of European Community law

There are three main sources of EC law: the Community treaties; the Acts of the Community institutions; and the decisions of the Court of Justice of the European

Communities. Essential to the effective operation of the EC is the principle that its primary law, the treaties, applies to the same extent in the legal system of each Member State, and that it takes precedence over the domestic law of any Member State, to the extent that there is any conflict between the two.

Article 10 (formerly art 5) of the EC Treaty provides:

'Member States shall take all appropriate measures, whether general or particular, to ensure fulfilment of the obligations arising out of this Treaty or resulting from action taken by the institutions of the Community. They shall facilitate the achievement of the Community's tasks. They shall abstain from any measure which could jeopardise the attainment of the objectives of this Treaty.'

The 'appropriate measures' for the implementation of the Treaty depend upon the nature of the Member State's legal system. Where it is monist, the Treaty will automatically become part of domestic law that can be relied upon in the courts of that Member State (to the extent that it creates rights for individual litigants, as to which see below). Where the Member State has a dualist system, as is the case with the United Kingdom, the Treaty has to be incorporated into domestic law in order to be effective: see the European Communities Act 1972, the impact of which (as regards UK parliamentary sovereignty) is considered further in Chapter 4.

As regards the secondary legislation of the European Union, namely regulations, directives and decisions, art 249 (formerly art 189) of the EC Treaty provides:

'A regulation shall have general application. It shall be binding in its entirety and directly applicable in all Member States. A directive shall be binding, as to the result to be achieved, upon each Member State to whom it is addressed, but shall leave to the national authorities the choice of form and methods. A decision shall be binding in its entirety upon those to whom it is addressed. Recommendations and opinions shall have no binding force.'

Decisions of the Court of Justice may be treated as a secondary source of EC. The Court is not bound to follow its previous decisions and they may therefore be treated as persuasive rather than binding authority.

Any doubt as to the primacy of EC law over national law was resolved by the European Court of Justice in *Costa* v *ENEL* [1964] ECR 585 where the Court stated:

'By creating a Community of unlimited duration, having its own institutions, its own personality, its own legal capacity of representation on the international plane and, more particularly, real powers stemming from a limitation of sovereignty or a transfer of powers from the States to the Community, the Member States have limited their sovereign rights, albeit within limited fields, and have thus created a body of law which binds both their nationals and themselves. The integration into the laws of each Member State of provisions which derive from the Community, and more generally the terms and spirit of the Treaty, make it impossible for the States, as a corollary, to afford precedence to a unilateral and subsequent measure over a legal system accepted by them on a basis of reciprocity. ... The executive force of Community law cannot vary from one State to another in deference to subsequent domestic laws, without jeopardising the attainment of the objectives of the Treaty set out in art 5(2) [now art 10(2)] and giving rise to the discrimination prohibited by art 7 [now repealed]. The obligations undertaken under the Treaty establishing the Community would not be unconditional, but merely contingent, if they could be called in question by subsequent legislative acts of the signatories ...'

The primacy of EC law prevails even where the domestic law is penal in nature, thus creating a defence of reliance on European Community law: see *Pubblico Ministero* v *Ratti* Case 148/78 [1979] ECR 1629.

Direct applicability

It will be seen, therefore, that provisions contained in the treaties and regulations enacted by the Council are of 'direct applicability', by which is meant that they become part of the law of a Member State without further intervention by the Member State: see further *Van Duyn* v *Home Office* Case 41/74 [1974] ECR 1337 and *Re Export Tax on Art Treasures (No 2)* [1972] CMLR 699. As indicated above, proceedings can be brought in the European Court by any Member State against another Member State failing to fulfil its obligations under the treaties. Directives, by contrast, are not directly applicable in that they require further enactment by a Member State before they can take effect within its domestic law. Member States have no discretion as regards the object to be achieved by the implementation of the directive, but do have discretion as to how that objective is to be achieved. In the United Kingdom, for example, the implementation of a directive may take the form of primary or delegated legislation as appropriate. As to the consequences of an EC directive creating a conflict with existing UK primary legislation: see Chapter 4.

Direct effect

The extent to which the primacy of EC law is made effective depends largely upon the degree to which compliance is policed. Clearly, large-scale failure by a Member State to comply with the requirements of EC law would be raised by the European Commission, or other Member States. It is through the empowerment of individual EU citizens, however, that the monitoring process is made most effective, and this has been achieved by the European Court's development of the concept of 'direct effect'. In basic terms, if a given provision of EC law is held to have the characteristic of direct effect it can be invoked by a individual against a Member State in the courts of the relevant Member State.

This form of direct effect is sometime referred to as 'vertical' direct effect to distinguish it from 'horizontal' direct effect (considered below) where an individual seeks to invoke a provision of EC law against another private party.

Broadly, the criteria to be satisfied before a provision can be regarded as having direct effect are that it is sufficiently precise in its terms to be said to be creating individual rights, and does not require any further implementation in order to become effective in law.

That treaty provisions can have direct effect, where they are found to be sufficiently precise and unconditional in their effect, was established in *Van Gend en Loos* v *Nederlandse Administratie der Belastingen* [1963] ECR 1, where the Court observed that:

'The objective of the EEC Treaty, which is to establish a Common Market, the functioning of which is of direct concern to interested parties in the Community, implies that this Treaty is more than an agreement which merely creates mutual obligations between the contracting states. This view is confirmed by the preamble to the Treaty, which refers not only to governments but also to peoples. It is also confirmed more specifically by the establishment of institutions endowed with sovereign rights, the exercise of which affects Member States and also their citizens. Furthermore, it must be noted that the nationals of the states brought together in the Community are called upon to co-operate in the functioning of this Community through the intermediary of the European Parliament and the Economic and Social Committee ... the task assigned to the Court of Justice under art 177 [now art 234], the object of which is to secure uniform interpretation of the Treaty by national courts and tribunals, confirms that the states have acknowledged that Community law has an authority which can be invoked by their nationals before those courts and tribunals. The conclusion to be drawn from this is that the Community constitutes a new legal order of international law for the benefit of which the States have limited their sovereign rights, albeit within limited fields, and the subjects of which comprise not only Member States but also their nationals. Independently of the legislation of Member States, Community law therefore not only imposes obligations on individuals but is also intended to confer upon them rights which become part of their legal heritage. These rights arise not only where they are expressly granted by the Treaty, but also by reason of obligations which the Treaty imposes in a clearly defined way upon individuals as well as upon the Member States and upon the institutions of the Community ...'

See further *R* v *Secretary of State for the Home Department, ex parte Flynn* (1995) The Times 20 July (CA).

The same reasoning can be applied to regulations, provided the preconditions for direct effect are met: see *Politi* v *Ministry of Finance* [1971] ECR 1039.

Subject to certain conditions, directives can also have direct effect. The issue was considered by the European Court of Justice in *Van Duyn* v *Home Office* Case 41/74 [1974] ECR 1337. The United Kingdom government allowed the Church of Scientology to operate in England, but sought to limit its activities by not granting work permits to foreign nationals seeking to take up employment with the Church in England. Ms Van Duyn, a Dutch national offered employment by the Church in England, was refused a work permit by the Home Office. She sought a declaration that the minister's prohibition was in contravention of what was art 48 (now art 39) of the EC Treaty, and was not permitted under Council Directive 64/221/EEC. Amongst the question referred under what is now the art 234 procedure, the court asked whether the directive in issue was directly applicable so as to confer rights on individuals enforceable by them in the courts of a Member State. The European Court of Justice, holding that the directive could have direct effect, observed:

'If ... by virtue of the provisions of art 189 regulations are directly applicable and, consequently, may by their very nature have direct effect, it does not follow from this that other categories of acts mentioned in that article can never have similar effects. It would be incompatible with the binding effect attributed to a directive by art 189 to exclude, in principle, the possibility that the obligation which it imposes may be invoked by those concerned. In particular, where the Community authorities have, by directive, imposed on Member States the obligation to pursue a particular course of conduct, the useful effect of such an act would be weakened if individuals were prevented from relying on it before their national courts and if the latter were prevented from taking it into consideration as an element of Community law. Article 177, which empowers national courts to refer to the Court questions concerning the validity and interpretation of all acts of the Community institutions, without distinction, implies furthermore that these acts may be invoked by individuals in the national courts. It is necessary to examine, in every case, whether the nature, general scheme and wording of the provisions in question are capable of having direct effects on the relations between Member States and individuals.'

Becker v *Finanzamt Munster-Innenstadt* [1982] ECR 1-53 makes clear that the conditions for the direct effect of directives are that the Member State against whom the action is brought must have failed to transpose the directive into domestic law, or failed to do so correctly, and the directive must be sufficiently unconditional and precise in its terms. As was noted in *Marks & Spencer plc* v *Commissioner of Customs and Excise* [2000] STC 16, direct effect cannot be invoked where the directive has been correctly transposed but wrongly implemented. A further factor to be taken into account was highlighted by the Court in *Francovich (and Others)* v *Italian Republic* (see below), where the Court noted (at paras 11 and 26) that:

'Wherever the provisions of a directive appear, as far as their subject matter is concerned, to be unconditional and sufficiently precise, those provisions may ... be relied upon as against any national provision which is incompatible with the directive or in so far as the provisions of the directive define rights which individuals are able to assert against the State ... [but] ... even though the provisions ... [are] sufficiently precise and unconditional as regard[s] the determination of the persons entitled to the guarantee and as regards the content of that guarantee, those elements [may not be] sufficient to enable individuals to rely on those provisions before the national courts. [If] those provisions do not identify the person liable to provide the guarantee ... the State cannot be considered liable on the sole ground that it has failed to take transposition measures within the prescribed period.'

On this basis the Court of Appeal, in *Evans* v *Motor Insurers Bureau; Mighell* v *Reading and Another; White* v *White and Another* (1998) The Times 12 October held that the Second Council Directive 84/5/EEC (OJ 1984 L8/17), which dealt with the approximation of the laws of EU Member States regarding civil liability arising from the use of motor vehicles, was not of direct effect as it left it to the United Kingdom government to determine who should provide the scheme of compensation for those suffering losses caused by uninsured drivers.

What is a public body for the purposes of 'vertical' direct effect?

As has been noted above, the term vertical direct effect has been used to describe the position where a directive can be invoked by an individual against a Member State. The scope of vertical direct effect depends, therefore, on the extent to which defendant bodies are perceived to be emanations of the state, eg the armed forces, the police, regulatory bodies, colleges and universities etc. The extent to which an employer could be regarded as falling within the sphere of public law (and hence amenable to the doctrine) was considered in *Marshall* v *Southampton and South West Hampshire Area Health Authority* (below) and *Johnstone* v *Chief Constable of the Royal Ulster Constabulary* [1987] QB 129, where the European Court of Justice ruled respectively that employees of the National Health Service, and those of constitutionally independent authorities responsible for maintaining law and order, could invoke provisions contained in directives against their employers on the basis that they were agents of the national authority. In *Foster* v *British Gas* [1991] QB 405 the European Court of Justice suggested that:

> '... a body, whatever its legal form, which has been made responsible pursuant to a measure adopted by the State, for providing a public service under the control of the State and which has for that purpose special powers beyond those which result from the normal rules applicable in relations between individuals is included in any event among the bodies against which the provisions of a directive capable of having direct effect may be relied upon.'

Following this ruling the House of Lords proceeded on the basis that British Gas was a state body for the purposes of vertical effect. Similarly, in *National Union of Teachers and Others* v *Governing Body of St Mary's Church of England (Aided) Junior School and Others* [1997] ICR 334, the Court of Appeal held that the governing body of a voluntary aided school was an emanation of the state, for the purposes of the direct enforceability of a European Community directive. Citing *Foster*, Schiemann LJ noted that voluntary schools, once they chose to come within the state system, were subject to a considerable degree of control and influence by the Secretary of State, such that they could be regarded as coming within the 'control' of the state. In contrast see *Doughty* v *Rolls Royce* [1992] CMLR 1045 (ownership by the Crown not the sole determining factor).

Horizontal direct effect

Given the development of the doctrine of vertical direct effect, the question has arisen as to the extent to which treaty provisions, regulations and directives can have 'horizontal' direct effect, in the sense that they can be invoked by one individual against another natural or private legal person in the courts of Member States.

The horizontal direct effect of treaty provisions has been recognised by the European Court of Justice in decisions such as *Walrave and Koch* v *Union Cycliste Internationale* [1974] ECR 1405 and *Defrenne* v *Sabena* [1976] ECR 455, where it has been seen as a necessary step towards ensuring that the objectives of the Union are not thwarted by private law bodies exercising their rights to legal autonomy. A distinction has been drawn, however, between treaty provisions and regulations on the one hand, that are directly applicable and hence become part of domestic law without further enactment, and directives on the other, that require the State to which they are addressed to carry out the necessary procedures for implementation. Whilst it might be justifiable to permit proceedings against a private party for non-compliance with a treaty provision or regulation, should that private party be at risk of litigation because of the Member State's failure to implement a directive? In a number of cases, most notably *Marshall* v *Southampton and South West Hampshire Area Health Authority* [1986] QB 401 and *Faccini Dori* v *Recreb Srl* Case C–91/92 [1995] CMLR 833, the European Court of Justice has ruled that directives cannot have horizontal direct effect so as to impose liabilities and duties on individuals and private companies. As the Court observed, recognising the limits of the scope of Community law in *Faccini Dori* v *Recreb Srl*:

'The effect of extending ... to the sphere of relations between individuals [the case law on horizontal direct effect to directives] would be to recognise a power in the Community to enact obligations for individuals with immediate effect, whereas it has competence to do so only where it is empowered to adopt regulations.'

See also *R* v *Secretary of State for Employment, ex parte Seymour Smith* [1997] 2 All ER 273 and *El Cortes Ingles* v *Rivero* [1996] 2 CMLR 507.

The unwillingness of the European Court of Justice to recognise the horizontal direct effect of directives has, however, to be seen in the light of two other factors: the doctrine of indirect horizontal effect and the availability of damages against Member States for failure to implement directives.

Indirect effect

Although the European Court of Justice has balked at the prospect of openly recognising horizontal direct effect in respect of directives, not least because they are addressed to Member States and not individuals, it has developed a doctrine, sometimes referred to as indirect effect, whereby the responsibility of the Member State for the application by its courts of EC law is regarded as being the means by which they can be compelled to ensure that the objective of a given directive is achieved in the resolution of disputes in domestic courts.

In two cases, *Von Colson* v *Land Nordrhein-Westfalen* [1984] ECR 1891 and *Harz* v *Deutsche Tradex GmbH* [1984] ECR 1921, the plaintiffs sought compensation having had their job applications turned down on grounds of gender. Under German law the rejection of their applications was lawful, and their only entitlement was to reimbursement of their travelling expenses. The plaintiffs claimed that there had been a breach of art 6 of the Equal Treatment Directive. The European Court held that, notwithstanding whether the Directive gave rise to direct effect, the German

State was obliged, under art 10 (formerly art 5) of the EC Treaty, to ensure that its domestic courts interpreted domestic law in such a way as to secure compliance with the objectives of the Directive. Hence, even if the Directive was not one having direct effect, by this means it could be given indirect effect. Note that although Von Colson was pursuing her action against a public body (the German prison service), the claim in *Harz* was against a private company. This is significant because it means that the doctrine of indirect effect can operate vertically and horizontally.

Indirect effect places UK courts in a particular dilemma as the traditional approach is to give domestic legislation its ordinary and everyday meaning. How far should UK courts now go in attempting to interpret domestic law so as to ensure conformity with directives? In *Lister* v *Forth Dry Dock & Engineering Co Ltd* [1990] 1 AC 546 the House of Lords was willing to disregard the prima facie meaning of a statutory instrument in order to ensure compliance with a directive, notably because it was felt that the statutory instrument had been introduced specifically to ensure compliance with the directive (note also that this was litigation against a private party). Even where domestic legislation has not been enacted to secure compliance with a directive, the courts are still likely to strive for a meaning that ensures compatibility provided this can be done without doing undue violence to the terms of the domestic law: see *Webb* v *EMO Air Cargo Ltd (UK) (No 2)* [1995] 1 WLR 1454. Where no such accommodation is possible, the plaintiff would be advised to pursue a claim in damages against the Member State for non-compliance: see below.

In *Marleasing SA* v *La Comercial Internacional de Alimentacion SA* [1992] 1 CMLR 305 the doctrine of indirect effect was developed further to cover the situation where a directive had not been implemented. The plaintiff company had sought the nullification, in the Spanish courts, of the creation of the defendant company, on the basis that it had been formed with the sole purpose of defrauding creditors. The plaintiff's legal challenge was based on the provisions of Spanish law (sections 1261 and 1275 of the Civil Code) which rendered invalid contracts which were without legal purpose or caused unlawful consequences. The defendants called in aid art 11 of Council Directive 68/151 claiming that it listed exhaustively the circumstances in which the nullity of a company could be declared, and that the ground relied upon by the plaintiff was not listed therein. The Directive had not, at the time this issue came before the Spanish courts, been incorporated into the domestic law of Spain. The question referred to the European Court of Justice was as to whether the article in question was directly applicable so as to preclude a declaration of nullity of a public limited company on a ground other than those set out in the article. The European Court of Justice ruled that, whilst directives were not of themselves capable of having direct effect between individuals, the national courts of Member States were obliged to interpret domestic law so as to ensure conformity with EC directives, whether the domestic law originated before or after the incorporation of the directive. The effect of the decision was to prevent the Spanish court from declaring the defendant company to be a nullity on any ground other than one listed in the relevant directive: see further *Faccini Dori* v *Recreb Srl* (above). Note again that the decision gives rise to a measure having horizontal indirect effect. If it is simply impossible for the domestic court to interpret existing domestic law so as to achieve conformity with the objectives of the directive, the Member State may be liable in damages: see further *Wagner Miret* v *Fondo de Garantia Salaria* [1993] ECR 1–6911.

Remedies for non-compliance with Community law

The failure of a Member State to ensure compliance with the provisions of the EC Treaty or other Community legislation, or indeed to implement directives accurately and within given time limits, may give rise to a right in damages on the part of an individual adversely affected by the failure. The development of this form of State liability is of particular significance where there is no relevant domestic law upon which a plaintiff can base a legal claim. The possibility of such liability being imposed was recognised by the European Court of Justice in *Francovich (and Others)* v *Italian Republic* [1992] IRLR 84. A number of Italian workers who had been made redundant found that, following their employer's insolvency, there were insufficient funds to pay their salaries. The workers complained that the Italian government had failed to implement legislation, required by a directive, to guarantee that such salary arrears should be paid by the State. The European Court of Justice held that, even in situations such as presented by the case under consideration where (because of uncertainties relating to implementation) the directive in question could not be regarded as one having direct effect, Member States were obliged to provide protection for clearly defined individual rights granted by EC law to specific groups, and a failure to provide such protection, if resulting in economic loss to individuals within those groups, rendered the Member State in question liable in damages.

The Court based its reasoning on the ground that the full effectiveness of EC law might be called into question, and the protection of the rights which they conferred would be weakened, if individuals could not obtain compensation where their rights were infringed by a breach of EC law for which a Member State was responsible. In other words, a Member State should not be able to hide behind its own failure to implement a directive when defending such proceedings. The Court identified three precondition to liability: the directive had to be one conferring individual rights; the rights had to be identifiable on the basis of the provisions of the directive; and there had to be a causal link between the Member State's failure and the damage suffered. For these purposes a directive will generally be regarded as conferring individual rights if it is intended to provide protection for economic welfare (eg as regards consumer contracts), health (eg drinking water standards) or safety (eg product liability). In many ways this development is a logical extension of the doctrine that compliance with Community law will be most effectively policed by individuals within Member States. It simply provides them with a financial incentive to bring instances of non-implementation before the courts.

The European Court of Justice has since gone on to extend this right to damages to other instances of non-compliance by Member States, notably in *Brasserie du Pêcheur SA* v *Federal Republic of Germany* Case C–46/93; *R* v *Secretary of State for Transport, ex parte Factortame Ltd and Others (No 4)* Case C–48/93 [1996] 2 WLR 506. The first case concerned an action brought by a French beer producer in respect of losses caused through not being able to export its beer to Germany, following a ruling by the German authorities that its products did not comply with the German beer purity laws. The restriction imposed by the German authorities had, in previous proceedings, been found to be in contravention of EC Treaty articles seeking to eliminate quantitative restrictions on imports. The second case was brought by Spanish trawlermen seeking damages for losses caused by the enactment of Part II of the Merchant Shipping Act 1988 that had prevented them from operating fishing vessels that could be registered in the United Kingdom and thus permitted to fish against the British quota under the Common Fisheries policy. The 1988 Act had, in previous proceedings, been found to be in breach of Community law, in particular of the EC Treaty provisions ensuring freedom of establishment. The European Court ruled that the principle established in *Francovich* applied equally where the non-compliance was caused by any organ of government of the State, including the State's legislature, provided three conditions were met:

1. the rule of law infringed must be intended to confer rights on individuals;
2. the breach must be sufficiently serious; and
3. there must be a direct causal link between the breach of the obligation resting on the State and the damage sustained by the injured party.

On the facts the Court was satisfied that condition (1) was clearly satisfied in both cases. As regards condition (2), the test was whether or not a Member State had manifestly and gravely disregarded the limits on its discretion regarding the measures to be taken in ensuring compliance, due regard being had to factors such as whether the breach was intentional or voluntary, whether an excusable error of law had been made, whether the action of any Community institution might have contributed to the breach, and whether or not there were previous decisions of the European Court making clear the incompatibility of the domestic law in question. The issue of causation was to be determined by the domestic courts of Member States. See further *R* v *Secretary of State for Social Security, ex parte Sutton* [1997] 3 All ER (EC) 497.

Exemplary damages could be awarded in respect of such claims, provided they could be awarded on a similar basis under the domestic law of a Member State, subject always to the proviso that domestic law should not operate so as to make the obtaining of such reparation excessively difficult or impossible. In this regard, the requirement of English domestic law, to the effect that damages would only be recoverable in cases of misfeasance, was a measure that made the recovery of damages excessively difficult, if not impossible, given that the action that was the subject matter of the claim for damages was that of the legislature. Under EC law, the only permissible fault requirement for the award of damages was that there had been non-compliance with EC law. The measure of damages awarded had to be commensurate with the nature of the loss and damage suffered by the plaintiff, due regard being had to the extent to which the plaintiff had shown due diligence in mitigating the extent of any loss. In this respect, the proper protection of EC rights militated against the exclusion of a right to recover damages for loss of profit. Note that the Court rejected the contention that the right to damages should be limited to losses occurring only after the ruling by a competent court that there had been a violation of EC law.

The matter returned to the domestic courts of the UK in *R* v *Secretary of State for Transport, ex parte Factortame Ltd and Others (No 5)* [1999] 3 WLR 1062, where the House of Lords held that breaches of EC law by the United Kingdom in implementing the Merchant Shipping Act 1988 were sufficiently serious to give rise to liability in damages. The Secretary of State had contended that there should be no liability in damages as the legislation had been introduced to deal with a serious economic problem, the UK had enjoyed a wide margin of appreciation as regards the appropriate measure to introduce, and because there should be no liability in damages where the breach of EC law was 'excusable'. Rejecting these contentions Lord Slynn observed that the prohibition of discrimination on grounds of nationality was not to be found in an ambiguous directive but was clearly stated in (what had been) art 7. The action adopted by the UK government, albeit in good faith, had been deliberate, not accidental, and had (as its inevitable consequence) the harming of the interests of Spanish fishermen. The transitional period for compliance had been very short, as UK law stood at the time there was no effective means of securing interim relief, and the UK government had pressed ahead with the legislation despite the strong opposition expressed by the European Commission. His Lordship concluded that, taking all these factors into account, there had been the deliberate adoption of legislation that was clearly discriminatory amounting to a manifest breach of treaty obligations. The breach was grave both intrinsically and in terms of the consequences for those affected. The 'domicile' requirement fell to be regarded in the same way as the nationality requirement and was thus also a serious breach of EC law.

Lord Hoffmann expressed the view that what was fatal to the UK government's case was the divergence between the rhetoric and the solution adopted to deal with the problem of 'quota-hopping'. The rhetoric presented the problem as one of UK fishermen being robbed of the opportunity to fish in their own waters by Spanish fishermen effectively poaching the catch. The legislative solution adopted actually concerned itself with the residence of those who owned shares in the companies operating the fishing vessels. Lord Hope, concurring, added the view that if damages were not recoverable in a case such as this it would be hard to envisage when they would ever be available.

It is doubtful whether any one of these matters is, taken by itself, decisive as regards the availability of damages. Much will depend on the facts of a particular case. Where, for example, there is a lack of clarity as regards the relevant EC law, particularly where the meaning attributed to a provision of EC law by the UK legislature is one shared by other Member States acting in good faith, it seems that damages would not be forthcoming; see further *R* v *HM Treasury ex parte British Telecommunications plc* [1996] 3 WLR 203. The view of the European Commission as to how a provision of EC law should operate will be highly persuasive, but not decisive of the matter. In cases of doubt a Member State ought to be guided by the Commission; see further *R* v *Ministry of Agriculture ex parte Headley Lomas (Ireland) Ltd* [1996] 3 WLR 787, where the United Kingdom ban on the export of live sheep to Spain, on the basis that methods used in Spanish slaughterhouses were not consistent with those required by Council Directive 74/577/EEC, was held to give rise to a right to damages because art 34 (now art 29) (quantitative restriction on imports) created individual rights, and the breach of that article had been serious (there was no evidence that the slaughterhouses used by applicants were breaching the Directive).

As to the availability of punitive or exemplary damages see *Bourgoin SA and Others* v *Ministry of Agriculture, Fisheries and Food* [1986] QB 716. It is submitted that, unless a statute provides for punitive damages, only compensatory damages will be available. A breach of EC law by a Crown Servant is not necessarily to be equated with misfeasance. As to what would be required to establish an action based upon the tort of misfeasance (and hence open up the possibility of punitive damages) see further *Three Rivers District Council* v *Bank of England* [2000] 3 All ER 1.

Where a causal link cannot be established between the failure to implement Community law and financial loss on the part of the applicant, declaratory relief will be more appropriate: see *R* v *Secretary of State for Employment, ex parte Equal Opportunities Commission and Another* [1994] 2 WLR 409 and *R* v *Secretary of State for Employment, ex parte Seymour Smith* (above).

3

Constitutional Principles: The Separation of Powers, the Rule of Law and the Independence of the Judiciary

3.1 The rule of law

3.2 The separation of powers

3.3 Independence of the judiciary

3.1 The rule of law

Introduction

The United Kingdom is generally regarded as a country that has a tradition of respect for the rule of law. What does this mean? In general terms it means that there is a historical tradition of public bodies providing a specific legal justification for their actions, and of the courts adjudicating impartially on disputes between citizens and on disputes between citizens and the state. It also means that there is a tradition that those in power will abide by the rulings of the courts. Adherence to the rule of law does not mean that public authorities do not act illegally. There are thousands of examples in the area of administrative law of the courts ruling that a public body has exceeded its powers, or that a minister has acted unfairly. The central issue is that such unlawfulness is identified and remedied. Similarly adherence to the rule of law does not mean that citizens will never be assaulted or racially abused by police officers, that decisions of public bodies will be unbiased, or that citizens will not be wrongly deprived of their property. Again the point is that (although only effective to the extent that they are or can be invoked) procedures exist to investigate and rectify such transgressions. That such actions are seen as wrong is in itself evidence of the rule of law.

Many societies that, in their modern guises, expound the virtues of the doctrine of the rule of law will, in fact, have their origins in lawlessness, criminality, revolution and insurrection. The history of the United States is an example in point.

Where a revolution results in a transfer of power from one ruling group to another the actions of the insurrectionists will often be labelled as 'unlawful' by those purporting to be in power (such as a colonial government). Such labelling is justified by reference to the rule of law. Once the insurrectionists take power they establish their own legal order with their own concept of laws. They then rely on the doctrine of the rule of law to justify adherence to their laws. The crucial factor is that of judicial loyalty – do the judges give effect to the laws of the old rulers or the new one? In those cases where the judges are faced with a fait accompli the matter is simple – they either resign or give effect to the laws of the new regime. Whether or not they choose to remain in office would, one assumes, be related to the extent to which they regarded the new regime and its laws as having legitimacy. The events surrounding the unilateral declaration by the Rhodesian Prime Minister Ian Smith in 1965 are instructive in this regard. The British government regarded this act as unlawful and enacted the Southern Rhodesia Act 1965, by means of which it purported to reassert the power of Parliament at Westminster to legislate for the former colony. In *Madzimbamuto* v *Lardner-Burke* [1969] 1 AC 645 the question arose as to the validity of laws enacted by the Smith regime, under which Madzimbamuto was being detained. The Privy Council held that the United Kingdom legislation prevailed, notwithstanding the constitutional convention that Westminster would not legislate for a colony without its consent. Significantly, Lord Reid expressed the view that the 1965 Act would be applied by the courts even though regarded by some as morally or politically improper. Gradually the judges in Rhodesia began to give effect to the laws enacted by the Smith regime, albeit under the guise of a doctrine of 'necessity'. In due course the issue of laws having to be effective in order to be recognised as valid led to a change in the view of the Rhodesian judges as to what constituted a valid law.

The concept of the rule of law has been recognised since at least the fourth century BC when Aristotle expressed the view that the rule of the law was preferable to that of any individual. His view was that those in power should be subject to some sort of 'higher' law and should govern in accordance with that higher law. Underpinning this concept is the proposition that there exists what is sometimes called natural law, comprising certain basic and unalienable rights and concepts, in effect minimum standards of justice. This leads to the view that there may be situations where it would be right for an individual to ignore 'man-made' law because it is contrary to fundamental moral values. A number of writers have addressed this issue. In his book *Leviathan* (1651) Thomas Hobbes expressed the view that individuals, to some extent, gave up their autonomy for the greater good. This view presupposes a bargain or 'social contract' between the governed and the law-makers. At its most basic the terms of the contract are that there is no obligation to obey a state's laws if its commands are contrary to nature, and no obligation to obey a state's laws if it is no longer able to protect its citizens. Jean-Jacques Rousseau, writing in *The Social Contract and Discourses* (1762), also adhered to the social contract notion, but believed that sovereignty lay with the people.

Power was vested in government for the promotion of the common good. The government could only promulgate laws that were 'moral' and thus had the approval of the people. In *The Rights of Man* (1791), Thomas Paine expressed the view that individuals enjoyed both individualistic rights, such as the right to pursue happiness, and the civil right to 'fair government'. He argued that these rights should be protected by the law, in the form of a Bill of Rights, with the government holding power on trust to protect these rights. Whilst citizens were bound to observe the rule of law as regards a government that upheld these rights, citizens were also free to overthrow any government that purported to abrogate these rights. Contemporary writers, such as Raz (see Raz J 'The Rule of Law and Its Virtue' (1977) 93 LQR 195), have observed that the rule of law is a morally neutral concept – the moral content depends upon the nature of the law being enforced, eg it could be a law that most would regard as morally unacceptable, such as one providing for racial segregation. Hence whether or not one accepts the concept of the rule of law depends to some extent upon the law being applied. The 'formalist' view is that the rule of law must be obeyed provided the form of law is satisfactory (perhaps reflected in Margaret Thatcher's famous incantation that 'The law, is the law, is the law'). The 'substantivist' view would involve looking at the content of the law to see if it is a 'good' law. If the rule of law involves adherence to a statute providing that members of a minority group can be rounded up and exterminated, the notion of adherence becomes less absolute for the substantivist opposed to such a law on principle.

Writing in the Victorian era Professor A V Dicey, in his work *The Law of the Constitution* (1885) stated that the rule of law was one of the main features of the constitution of the United Kingdom and that, in this context, the phrase embraced at least three distinct though kindred concepts.

Dicey's (first) concept of the rule of law

Dicey expressed his first concept in these terms:

> 'That no man is punishable or can be lawfully made to suffer in body or goods except for a distinct breach of law established in the ordinary legal manner before the ordinary courts of the land. In this sense the rule of law is contrasted with every system of government based on the exercise by persons in authority of wide, arbitrary, or discretionary powers of constraint ... It means ... the absolute supremacy or predominance of regular law as opposed to the influence of arbitrary power, and excludes the existence of arbitrariness, of prerogative, or even of wide discretionary authority on the part of the government.'

Professor Jennings in his book *The Law and the Constitution* described Dicey's first concept as involving the notion that:

> '... all governmental powers, save those of the representative legislature, shall be distributed and determined by reasonably precise laws. Accordingly a King or other

person acting on behalf of the State cannot exercise a power unless he can point to some specific rule of law which authorises his act ...'

Hence what Dicey was asserting was that, in those societies where the rule of law obtains, the law does not give those in authority wide, discretionary powers to interfere with the personal freedom or property of subjects. Thus, according to Dicey, those in authority in the United Kingdom where, he claimed, the rule of law was most emphatically present, in contrast to continental countries such as Switzerland and France, could only interfere with the personal freedom or property of a subject if the subject had breached a specific law of the land and the breach had been established in the ordinary legal manner before the ordinary courts of the land.

For a contemporary example of the principle in application consider *Attorney-General* v *Blake* [2000] 3 WLR 625. The defendant had been employed as a member of the intelligence service prior to his conviction for spying. He published his autobiography *No Other Choice*, which divulged information acquired during the course of his employment. The Attorney-General sought to recover the profits made by the defendant on the basis that the defendant had breached his contract with the Crown, to whom he owed a fiduciary duty not to exploit his position as a Crown servant in order to publish the book. The Court of Appeal granted a 'freezing' order restraining Blake from receiving royalties until further notice. Although the House of Lords allowed the Attorney-General's claim based on breach of contract, it was not prepared to accept that there was a general common law right in the courts to grant orders to prevent wrongdoers benefiting from their actions. As Lord Nicholls explained:

'Although the [freezing] order is strictly only interlocutory in character "until further order", the basis on which the Court has made the order is that Blake will never receive any of the unpaid royalties. That is confiscation in substance, if not in form. In my view the Court has no power to make such an order. In respect of the proceeds of crime Parliament has conferred upon the Court power to make confiscation orders and ancillary restraint orders. In Part VI of the Criminal Justice Act 1988, since amended by the Proceeds of Crime Act 1995, Parliament has carefully marked out when these orders may be made. The common law has no power to remedy any perceived deficiencies in this statutory code. An attempt to do so would offend the established general principle, of high constitutional importance, that there is no common law power to take or confiscate property without compensation: see *Attorney-General* v *De Keyser's Royal Hotel Ltd* [1920] AC 508; *Burmah Oil Co Ltd* v *Lord Advocate* [1965] AC 75 ...'

Dicey's second concept of the rule of law

Dicey expressed his second concept in these terms:

'We mean in the second place, when we speak of the rule of law as a characteristic of our country, not only that with us no man is above the law, but (which is a different thing) that here every man, whatever be his rank or condition, is subject to the ordinary law of the realm and amenable to the jurisdiction of the ordinary tribunals. ... With us every official, from the Prime Minister down to a constable or a collector of taxes, is under the same responsibility for every act done without legal justification as any other citizen.'

Here Dicey was concerned to distinguish English law from the law of, for example, France, where there was, in contrast to England, a separate set of administrative courts for adjudicating in legal disputes between a subject and a government official. Such disputes would in England at that time be dealt with in the ordinary civil courts. In France they would be dealt with in the administrative courts, separate from the ordinary civil courts which dealt with disputes between subject and subject. The law applied in the administrative courts contained certain rules and principles different from those of the civil law applied in the ordinary civil courts. Dicey's contention was that in England every man, whether subject or government official, must justify his acts by reference to the same body of law, being the ordinary law applied in the ordinary courts of the land. Dicey wrote of this second concept:

> ' "The rule of law" in this sense excludes the idea of any exemption of officials or others from the duty of obedience to the law which governs other citizens or from the jurisdiction of the ordinary tribunals ... The notion which lies at the bottom of the administrative law known to foreign countries is, that affairs or disputes in which the government or its servants are concerned are beyond the sphere of the civil courts and must be dealt with by special and more or less official bodies ...'

By 'more or less official bodies' he meant tribunals or courts that were essentially a part of the executive machinery as opposed to part of the regular and independent court structure.

Dicey's third concept of the rule of law

Dicey expressed his third concept in these terms:

> '... the general principles of the constitution (as for example the right to personal liberty, or the right to public meeting) are with us as the result of judicial decisions determining the rights of private persons in particular cases brought before the courts; whereas under many foreign constitutions the security (such as it is) given to the rights of individuals results, or appears to result, from the general principles of the constitution ...'

The point being made by Dicey here is that in English law the rights of the individual were (at the time he was writing) determined by, and were dependent upon, the ordinary law of the land as developed by the ordinary courts adjudicating in particular cases. He would have had in mind that, in England, such rights would not have been based upon and special 'Bill of Rights' or other declaration in a written constitution. Dicey regarded the protection given to the rights of the individual in the United Kingdom as superior to that given in countries with a special declaration of rights or Bill of Rights, since he claimed the emphasis in English law was on giving a remedy when a right was infringed and not resting content with a mere statement or declaration of rights, which he would have regarded as a mere piece of paper.

Jennings' critique of Dicey

In his book, *The Law and the Constitution*, Sir Ivor Jennings carried out a sustained critique of Dicey's views, including his treatment of the rule of law. Jennings points out that the phrase could be used simply to denote a society where a state of law and order existed. For this usage, even an absolutist regime would qualify. Clearly, however, Dicey does not use the phrase to mean this and no more. Dicey is only prepared to give the label 'the rule of law' to societies where the legal rules on individual liberty and individual property rights conform to the standards he has set and which he considers desirable. To put it another way, Dicey makes a value judgment about what the content of law should be and then takes the next step of saying that that is what law is. The rule of law operates most strongly in those societies where the legal rules conform most perfectly to the standards he has set. It is Jennings who points out that Dicey's political views influence his judgment in setting those standards. Jennings states that those elements or features in the law of a society which Dicey relies on as constituting the rule of law are all consequences which follow naturally from the existence of a democracy with free elections and a recognition that criticism of the government is a positive merit. Jennings, by implication, denies that the prevalence of law is greater in a community that has these elements or features, than in a community where these features are absent. He is prepared to recognise that law may also rule in a society where the principles Dicey favours for the protection of individual liberty are quite absent. For Jennings states that the principles enunciated by Dicey depend essentially upon the existence of a democratic society and, by implication, Jennings is not prepared to deny that law prevails in a community where the political system is not one of the Western liberal democratic type favoured by Dicey. Jennings does not deny the desirability, in political terms, of the features Dicey stresses, but he does deny the specifically legal character of a community where they are present. He says of Dicey's three concepts:

> 'These are intangibles which nevertheless produce an impression on the mind of any observant person who crosses the boundary from a dictatorial state into a free country. They cannot easily be forced into a formal concept dignified by such a name as the rule of law ...'

Putting the matter more bluntly, he says of Dicey's use of the phrase 'the rule of law': 'If it is merely a phrase for distinguishing democratic ... government from dictatorship, it is wise to say so.'

Sir Ivor Jennings thus attempts to lay bare what he presumably believes to be the fallacy of supposing that societies adhering to political systems of the typical Western liberal-democratic type, with their stress on the rights of the individual, have any specially legal character which is missing in countries with political systems of the socialist, collectivist type. Two points may be made about this. First, political theorists and jurists in socialist countries of the Maoist type are well aware of the political connotations of the phrase the rule of law They write and speak of the desirability of their own societies conforming to socialist legality rather than to the rule of law. Second, there is a tendency on the part of jurists in many parts of the world to assume that law in the area of civil liberties has some logical and necessary connection with certain principles that those concerned hold dear. One might say more specifically, although also more tentatively, that there has been a tendency at times to stress respect for the individual as, in some sense, an essential of law.

The Declaration of Delhi 1959

The International Commission of Jurists, which is affiliated to UNESCO, convened a number of conferences for the purpose of agreeing upon an adaptation of Dicey's concept of the rule of law which could be made worldwide. At its 1959 conference in Delhi those attending completed a questionnaire regarding the nature of the rule of law. The resultant 'Declaration of Delhi' provided that respect for the supreme value of human personality should be taken as the basis of all law. It further provided that the rule of law involved: the right to representative and responsible government (ie the right to be governed by a representative body answerable to the people); provision to ensure that a citizen wronged by his government should have a remedy; observance of certain minimum standards regarding human rights; and the independence of the judiciary, including proper grounds and procedure for the removal of judges.

The influence of Dicey's first and second concepts can be seen in the declaration. His third concept was abandoned since most other countries in the world have a Bill of Rights of some description.

To what extent is Dicey's formulation of the rule of law relevant today?

Dicey's first concept

Notwithstanding Dicey's strongly expressed views there is nothing, in theory, to stop Parliament enacting legislation providing ministers, police officers, or other executive officers with wide powers to interfere with the rights and liberties of citizens. Some powers granted to the executive during wartime perhaps reflect this: see *Liversidge* v *Anderson* [1942] AC 206. Social and political developments in the twentieth century have also led to public authorities being given wide discretionary powers to interfere with the property and commercial interests of citizens, or to determine eligibility to publicly funded assistance. For example, a minister will often be given the power to determine an issue or grant a privilege, the power to be exercised 'if the minister sees fit'. Prima facie it is difficult to see how any challenge could be mounted to the exercise of such a power, raising the prospect of it being exercised in an arbitrary fashion without any legal redress for those affected.

In reality the courts have developed a complex and sophisticated body of law, generically referred to as administrative law, whereby they will review the exercise of executive discretion to ensure that it has been used lawfully (ie intra vires). If a minister, or any other public authority, is found to have abused a statutory discretion or other power affecting the public, the courts can, through the mechanism of judicial review, quash the decision on the grounds that it is outwith the discretion vested in the decision-maker (ie it is ultra vires). Hence, ostensibly wide powers are subject to judicial control on the basis that they have to be exercised reasonably, proportionately and fairly.

Dicey's first concept of the rule of law is also reflected in the way in which police powers have been codified in statutes such as the Police and Criminal Evidence Act 1984 (PACE). Some police officers might feel that their task would be much easier if they had an untrammelled power to stop search, arrest and detain anyone they felt like investigating. If such were the case the citizen would have very little protection from the arbitrary abuse of power. Instead PACE specifies the preconditions that have to be satisfied before police powers of arrest etc can be exercised. Typically an officer must have reasonable grounds for suspecting certain facts before exercising powers such as the power to arrest. PACE also contains strict rules on the length of time for which a suspect may be detained before being charged (see generally Chapter 10). A person who suspects that he is unlawfully detained may apply to the Divisional Court of the Queen's Bench Division of the High Court for a writ of habeas corpus ordering his release. The writ will be issued if the court is not satisfied that the detention is justified by law: see further the Petition of Rights 1628.

Dicey's second concept

It is not difficult to find examples that seem to contradict Dicey's notion that the United Kingdom constitution reflects the rule of law because the law applies equally to all. For example the monarch, in her personal capacity, is not subject to the jurisdiction of the ordinary courts of the land. Although the Crown Proceedings Act 1947 has reduced the legal immunities and privileges of the Crown in its public capacity, there are still many situations where the Crown, and to some extent other public bodies, enjoy a privileged position in litigation.

The public interest in the proper administration of justice has led to the rule that no civil legal action may be brought in respect of anything said or done by a judge in the exercise of his judicial functions (*Anderson* v *Gorrie* [1985] 1 QB 668); in respect of a jury verdict (*Bushell's Case* (1670) 6 St Tr 999); or in respect of words spoken by the parties, counsel or witnesses in the course of judicial proceedings: *Munster* v *Lamb* (1883) 11 QBD 588. Note also that the Crown cannot be sued in tort in respect of the actions of its servants discharging judicial functions. Under s1 of the State Immunity Act 1978 foreign states are immune from the jurisdiction of the English courts, save in a number of instances, most notably where commercial matters are in issue in respect of contracts to be performed in England, and as regards disputes relating to the possession and ownership of land in England. Section 20 of the 1978 Act (by reference to art 31 of the Vienna Convention on

Diplomatic Relations 1961) extends to serving heads of state the degree of immunity enjoyed by heads of diplomatic missions, including complete immunity from the criminal jurisdiction of the 'receiving' state. Even former heads of state continue to enjoy immunity (albeit of a more limited nature) in respect of criminal liability relating to acts performed in the exercise of the functions of the head of state: see *R v Bow Street Metropolitan Stipendiary Magistrate, ex parte Pinochet Ugarte* [1998] 4 All ER 897.

Government officials have a vast array of legal rights and powers not available to ordinary members of the public. For example, to take money as income tax, to exercise a power of compulsory purchase, to deport a person. In addition, the subject who wishes to contest whether the official has exercised these powers in accordance with law is often required by law to take the matter, not to the ordinary courts of the land, but to a special tribunal. In some cases there is an appeal on a point of law to the ordinary courts, but not in the case of every tribunal. The range of matters falling within the jurisdiction of bodies referred to generically as tribunals is vast. It encompasses the determination of tax due, eligibility for social security payments, regulation of civil aviation, awards of compensation to victims of crime, immigration, decisions to release prisoners on parole, rent assessment and regulation of broadcasting.

It is submitted, however, that none of the of above examples actually undermines Dicey's second concept. It is true that they all involve situations where the operation of the law is suspended in respect of certain individuals, or where individuals are prevented from securing redress before the ordinary courts, but the crucial point is that all these exceptions are regulated by law. They are not instances of an individual, or a public body, simply determining that a given law no longer applies to them. Arguably, even the immunity of the monarch subsists at common law only for as long as the courts are willing to permit it. As regards the suggestion that those who are required by statute to pursue their claims before tribunals are somehow denied their rights in law, it should be remembered that most important tribunals are listed in Sch 1 to the Tribunals and Inquiries Act 1992, thus ensuring that they are required to give reasons for their decisions if so requested, and that a right of appeal to the High Court on a point of law is available. As a last resort tribunal decisions will always be subject to judicial review if required.

Dicey's third concept

Prior to the enactment of the Human Rights Act 1998 the evidence to support Dicey's third concept was, at best, mixed. In cases such as *Malone* v *Metropolitan Police Commissioner* [1979] Ch 344 the court refused to recognise (in the absence of any statutory right) any right to privacy at common law that would render telephone-tapping unlawful. In declining to 'discover' any such protection at common law Sir Robert Megarry VC observed:

'One of the factors that must be relevant in such a case is the degree of particularity in the right that is claimed. The wider and more indefinite the right claimed, the greater the undesirability of holding that such a right exists. Wide and indefinite rights, while conferring an advantage on those who have them, may well gravely impair the position of those who are subject to the rights. To create a right for one person, you have to impose a corresponding duty on another ... It seems to me that where Parliament has abstained from legislating on a point that is plainly suitable for legislation, it is indeed difficult for the court to lay down new rules of common law or equity that will carry out the Crown's treaty obligations, or to discover for the first time that such rules have always existed.'

On the other hand judges from time to time asserted, in cases where a party sought to pray in aid an article of the European Convention on Human Rights, that reliance on the Convention was unnecessary, because it largely reflected the values expressed in the English common law. For example in *Derbyshire County Council* v *Times Newspapers Ltd and Others* [1993] 2 WLR 449, in determining that a local authority could not sue for defamation in respect of political criticism, Lord Keith rejected the notion that it was necessary to have regard to art 10 of the Convention as, in his view, 'the common law of England is consistent with obligations assumed by the Crown under the Treaty in this particular field.'

Dicey would doubtless have approved of such sentiments, but the incorporation of the Convention effected by the Human Rights Act 1998 means that, for the first time, statute law can now be cited as the basis for a number of fundamental human rights in English law, such as the right to life, liberty of the person, freedom of expression and privacy. Does this mean that Dicey's third concept becomes redundant? The answer must be a guarded 'no'. Under the Human Rights Act 1998 (considered further at Chapter 9) the courts will be required to interpret legislation so as to ensure conformity (so far as is possible) with the Convention rights protected by the 1998 Act. Thus the courts will still have to have regard to basic concepts of 'legality' in determining whether effect should be given to legislation that impinges on personal liberty.

De Smith has dismissed Dicey's concept of the rule of law as being 'rooted in Whiggish libertarianism ... very influential for two generations ... [but] today [it] no longer warrant detailed analysis.' It cannot, however, be denied that some general concept of the rule of law is frequently used today as a yardstick against which law on individual freedom is measured. It is not unusual to hear civil rights groups protest that certain legal provisions in the United Kingdom or other Commonwealth countries are 'contrary to the rule of law'. Often the speaker or writer might be strained to say exactly what he understands the rule of law to involve. The criticism is usually levelled at legal provisions which give to the executive branch of government power to deprive individuals of their personal liberty for a considerable time on the basis of some vague suspicion of wrongdoing, and without the courts having an opportunity to adjudicate on whether there is substantial ground for suspicion.

As Lord Steyn observed, in *R* v *Secretary of State for the Home Department, ex parte Pierson* [1997] 3 All ER 577, in the course of holding that the Home

Secretary's actions in retrospectively increasing sentencing tariffs would involve a violation of the principle of the rule of law (at p603):

'For at least a century it has been "thought to be in the highest degree improbable that Parliament would depart from the general system of law without expressing its intention with irresistible clearness". ... In his *Introduction to the Study of the Law of the Constitution* ... Dicey explained the context in which Parliament legislates as follows:

"By every path we come round to the same conclusion, that parliamentary sovereignty has favoured the rule of law, and that the supremacy of the law of the land both calls forth the exertion of parliamentary sovereignty, and leads to its being exercised in a spirit of legality."

But it is to Sir Rupert Cross that I turn for the best modern explanation of "the spirit of legality" or what has been called "the principle of legality". ... The passage appears in *Cross, Statutory Interpretation*, 3rd ed, at pp165–166 ... reads as follows:

"Statutes often go into considerable detail, but even so allowance must be made for the fact that they are not enacted in a vacuum. A great deal inevitably remains unsaid. Legislators and drafters assume that the courts will continue to act in accordance with well-recognised rules ... Longstanding principles of constitutional and administrative law are likewise taken for granted, or assumed by the courts to have been taken for granted, by Parliament. Examples are the principles that discretionary powers conferred in apparently absolute terms must be exercised reasonably, and that administrative tribunals and other such bodies must act in accordance with the principles of natural justice. One function of the word 'presumption' in the context of statutory interpretation is to state the result of this legislative reliance (real or assumed) on firmly established legal principles. There is a 'presumption' that mens rea is required in the case of statutory crimes, and a 'presumption' that statutory powers must be exercised reasonably. These presumptions apply although there is no question of linguistic ambiguity in the statutory wording under construction, and they may be described as 'presumptions of general application'. ... These presumptions of general application not only supplement the text, they also operate at a higher level as expressions of fundamental principles governing both civil liberties and the relations between Parliament, the executive and the courts. They operate here as constitutional principles which are not easily displaced by a statutory text ..."

And our public law is, of course, replete with other instances of the common law so supplementing statutes on the basis of the principle of legality ... the principle applies with equal force to protect substantive basic or fundamental rights.'

3.2 The separation of powers

Introduction

Although of great antiquity the modern basis for the doctrine of the separation of powers can be traced back to the writings of commentators such as John Locke who, in his *Second Treatise of Civil Government*, written in 1690, observed:

'The Three Organs of State must not get into one hand ... It may be too great a temptation to human frailty, apt to grasp at power, for the same persons who have the power of making laws, to have also in their hands the power to execute them, whereby they may exempt themselves from obedience to the laws they make, and suit the law, both in its making and execution, to their own private advantage.'

The doctrine was further examined by the French jurist Montesquieu (1689 – 1755) who based his exposition on the British constitution of the early eighteenth century.

In simple terms the doctrine recognises three functions of government, namely legislative, executive and judicial. In its purest form the doctrine holds that each of these three functions should be vested in separate organs of government – the legislature, the executive and the judiciary – with no overlap, as to concentrate more than one function in any one organ of government presents a threat to individual liberty.

If this doctrine is followed, the same persons should not form part of more than one of the three organs of government, for example ministers should not sit in Parliament; one organ of government should not control or interfere with the work of another, for example the judiciary should be independent of the executive, and ministers should not be responsible to Parliament; one organ of government should not exercise the functions of another, for example ministers should not have legislative powers.

Separation of powers in the constitution of the United States

In the United States Constitution of 1787, separation of powers was clearly expressed. Each of the three primary constitutional functions was vested in a distinct organ: legislative power was vested in Congress, consisting of a House of Representatives and a Senate; executive power was vested in the President; judicial power was vested in the Supreme Court and such other federal courts as might be established by Congress.

The President holds office for a fixed term of four years. If he resigns his deputy succeeds. He is not dependent on support in Congress to continue in office, and cannot use the threat of dissolution to make Congress, particularly those members who are of his party, co-operate. The President is separately elected from Congress, therefore he may be of a different party from that which has a majority in either or both Houses of Congress. The constitution states both the President's powers and the power of Congress. Heads of the chief departments of state are known as the Cabinet, but they are individually responsible to the President and not to Congress. That is, the President is directly answerable to the electorate because he is directly elected. In the United Kingdom, where ministers are not directly elected as such, they are answerable to Parliament, which is directly elected and therefore answerable to the electorate.

Neither the President nor members of his cabinet can sit or vote in Congress. They have no direct power to initiate Bills, but the President can recommend legislation in his message to Congress.

The President can veto legislation but can be overridden by a two-thirds vote in both Houses. Treaties are negotiated by the President, but must be approved by a two-thirds majority of the Senate. The President has the power to nominate certain key officers, including judges of the Supreme Court, but the Senate must confirm these appointments and may refuse to do so. Once appointed, the judges of the Supreme Court are independent of both Congress and the President. They may be removed by impeachment by the Senate, but only for treason, bribery or similar offences.

The Supreme Court has ruled that the separation of powers expressed in the constitution excludes any extensive delegation of legislative power by Congress to executive agencies: *Schechter Poultry Corporation v US* (1935). There is also the historic decision of Chief Justice Marshall in *Marbury v Madison* (1803) 1 Cranch 103, by which the Supreme Court assumed the power of declaring both Acts of Congress and Acts of the President to be unconstitutional.

In fact, the separation of powers in the United States constitution does not involve the isolation of each organ from the other two, but rather an elaborate system of checks and balances. The system rests upon an open recognition that particular functions belong primarily to a given organ, while at the same time superimposing a power of limited interference by another organ in order to ensure that the first does not exercise its acknowledged functions in an arbitrary and despotic manner.

It is generally agreed that the doctrine of the separation of powers is reflected in the British constitution, but not in any formalised way. As Lord Mustill observed in *R v Secretary of State for the Home Department, ex parte Fire Brigades Union and Others* [1995] 2 WLR 464:

> 'It is a feature of the peculiarly British conception of the separation of powers that Parliament, the executive and the courts have each their distinct and largely exclusive domain. Parliament has a legally unchallengeable right to make whatever laws it thinks right. The executive carries on the administration of the country in accordance with the powers conferred on it by law. The courts interpret the laws, and see that they are obeyed. Thus requires the courts on occasion to step into the territory which belongs to the executive, not only to verify that the powers asserted accord with the substantive law created by Parliament, but also that the manner in which they are exercised conforms with the standards of fairness which Parliament must have intended ... it is the task of Parliament and the executive in tandem, not of the courts, to govern the country ... [A]bsent a written constitution much sensitivity is required of the parliamentarian, administrator and judge if the delicate balance of the unwritten rules evolved ... in recent years is not to be disturbed, and all the recent advances undone.'

Similarly in *R v HM Treasury, ex parte Smedley* [1985] 1 QB 657, a case where the applicant sought judicial review of the Treasury's decision to lay before both Houses a draft Order in Council which, if approved, would authorise the payment of funds by the United Kingdom to the European Community, Sir John Donaldson MR observed:

'I think that I should say a word about the respective roles of Parliament and the courts. Although the United Kingdom has no written constitution, it is a constitutional convention of the highest importance that the legislature and the judicature are separate and independent of one another, subject to certain ultimate rights of Parliament over the judicature which are immaterial for present purposes. It therefore behoves the court to be ever sensitive to the paramount need to refrain from trespassing upon the province of Parliament or, so far as this can be avoided, even appearing to do so. Although it is not a matter for me, I would hope and expect that Parliament would be similarly sensitive to the need to refrain from trespassing upon the province of the courts ...'

The separation of powers under the British constitution – the legislature and executive

Fusion and separation

The Sovereign is head of the executive (ministers are 'the Queen's ministers') and also an integral part of the legislature, in the sense that she is party to the enactment of all primary domestic legislation. Given that the United Kingdom has a constitutional monarchy, the occasions when her role will be more than ceremonial will be few and far between. Perhaps more significantly, and in contrast to the United States, ministers are, by convention, members of the legislature, ie members of either the House of Commons or House of Lords. Whilst this is a breach of the doctrine of the separation of powers it can be rationalised on the basis that it promotes the responsibility of ministers to Parliament by ensuring that they can be questioned, take part in debates and make statements to the relevant House. The House of Commons is not capable of discharging all of the legislative functions necessary for a modern industrialised state, hence executive legislation is commonplace. Ministers have numerous powers under statute to enact subordinate legislation, usually in the form of statutory instruments. Ministers may also have powers under the prerogative to issue Orders in Council: see *R* v *Secretary of State for the Home Department, ex parte Fire Brigades Union and Others* (above). If these legislative powers were not discharged by ministers the legislative programme in the House of Commons would become unmanageable. Also the power to make subordinate legislation means that ministers can create new regulations to deal with unforeseen problems and threats rather than have to find time in the main legislative programme.

The doctrine is reflected in the fact that many office holders who make up the executive are disqualified from membership of the House of Commons. These include civil servants, members of the armed forces and police forces, and other holders of offices of profit under the Crown: see further the House of Commons Disqualification Act 1975.

Checks and balances

Ultimately the House of Commons controls the executive in that it can bring about the resignation of a government with a motion of no confidence. Less drastic control can be exercised in the form of question time, select committees, adjournment debates and opposition days. Delegated legislation is normally subject to some form of parliamentary scrutiny (typically being laid before the House) prior to its coming into effect, and will be subject to review in the courts if it goes beyond the powers delegated in the primary Act. The combined effects of the United Kingdom 'first past the post' electoral system together with strong party discipline means that, in practice, a government with an overall majority in the House of Commons has a large measure of control over Parliament. Government backbenchers will be unwilling to go too far in challenging the government for fear of causing a general election. The government also has available several devices for curtailing parliamentary debate. The House of Lords, even in its reformed state, can only delay the passage of legislation.

The separation of powers under the British constitution – the judiciary and executive

Fusion and separation

In theory it is for the executive, in the form of the Cabinet, to determine the policies underpinning proposals for changes in the law, and for the judges to apply the law. The constitutional significance of this is that the judiciary, being independent, can apply the law regardless of whether the result is at odds with what the government of the day may desire, or is otherwise politically unpopular. There is considerable evidence of judicial recognition of this separation of functions. In *Hinds* v *The Queen* [1977] AC 195, the Privy Council declared unconstitutional the 'gun court' set up in Jamaica because of the involvement of members of the executive in the sentencing of offenders. In *Browne* v *The Queen* (1999) The Times 11 May, the Privy Council declared that it was contrary to the constitution of St Christopher and Nevis for a defendant to be sentenced 'during the [Governor General's] pleasure', because it empowered a member of the executive to determine the severity of punishment. That was a judicial function to be exercised by the courts.

On the other hand, the most glaring breach of the doctrine of the separation of powers is provided by the functions performed by the Lord Chancellor. He is a member of the executive as head of the Lord Chancellor's department and therefore a member of the Cabinet. He is also the head of the judiciary, entitled to preside over the House of Lords when it sits as a court. As a member of the House of Lords, he is also a member of the legislature. Although this situation has been defended (by Lord Irvine amongst others) as being 'pragmatic', problems could arise if, for example, the Lord Chancellor were to give judgment in a House Lords ruling regarding the legality of action taken by a fellow Cabinet minister. The coming into effect of the Human Rights Act 1998 could well exacerbate matters as the judiciary could find themselves dealing with more highly politicised cases. It is possible that there could be a legal challenge to the statutory right of the Lord Chancellor to sit as a judge in the House of Lords (arising under the Judicial Committee Act 1833) on the grounds that his involvement is incompatible with art 6 of the European Convention on Human Rights (impartial tribunal for the determination of rights and obligations): see further *McGonnell* v *United Kingdom* (2000) The Times 22 February.

Difficulties have also arisen in respect of the role played by the Home Secretary in setting the tariff, ie the time to be spent in detention for the purposes of punishment and retribution where juveniles are sentenced to be detained at Her Majesty's pleasure. In *T* v *United Kingdom; V* v *United Kingdom* (1999) The Times 17 December, the European Court of Human Rights held that the setting of the tariff was a sentencing function that had to be conducted independently of the executive if it was to satisfy the requirements of art 6(1) of the European Convention on Human Rights. The judgment does not directly affect the power of the Home Secretary to determine the tariff in respect of adult prisoners convicted of murder, but it must call into question the continuing legality of such an arrangement, involving as it does a clear breach of the doctrine of the separation of powers.

At a less dramatic level there is a breach of the separation doctrine where judicial functions are performed by executive bodies, most notably tribunals. Again the justification for this breach of the doctrine is pragmatism. Tribunals may well have members appointed and dismissed by the executive and have rules of procedure laid down by the executive, but they are capable of dealing with specialised matters not suitable for resolution in the courts, such as welfare benefit claims, immigration matters, taxation and housing. They offer a speedier and cheaper alternative to going to court. Questions may well be asked as to the extent to which a tribunal is sufficiently 'independent' of the executive to satisfy the requirements of art 6 of the European Convention – provision of an independent and impartial tribunal: see *Smith* v *Secretary of State for Trade and Industry* [2000] ICR 69.

In addition, there may be disputes that a citizen has with a public body that will not be referred to a tribunal, but instead decided by a minister. These include disputes over refusal to grant planning permission by a local authority, or over the making of compulsory purchase orders. They fall for decision by the minister at the head of the relevant government department. This is a very clear example of the executive exercising a judicial function. The question can, of course, arise as to whether a particular function is more properly classified as 'administrative' or 'judicial'. The line between the two can be difficult to draw. For example, in an application for a licence or a dispute over the making of a clearance order, the deciding body has to apply the legal provisions of the relevant statute to the facts before it. But the legal provisions may allow for the exercise of considerable discretion on the part of the deciding body. Is the function then administrative or judicial?

Checks and balances

The executive exercises a degree of control over the judiciary in that it can determine who is appointed to a judicial role. Most members of the judiciary are appointed by the executive, or appointed by the Queen on the advice of the Prime Minister or Lord Chancellor, which is effectively the same thing (magistrates and circuit judges are appointed by the Lord Chancellor). Circuit judges are dismissable by the Lord Chancellor for incapacity or misbehaviour.

The most significant control mechanism in terms of the relationship between the judiciary and the executive is the common law power of the High Court to review the legality of administrative action taken by executive agencies, such as ministers, local authorities and other public bodies. A citizen with sufficient interest can apply for judicial review on the grounds that a public body has exceeded the limits of its powers, whether by acting unfairly or unreasonably. The same procedure could also be invoked by a person who alleges that he has been the victim of a breach of his Convention rights under the Human Rights Act 1998. The Divisional Court of the High Court can quash a decision of a public body on the basis that it has acted ultra vires (ie beyond its powers). By this means the citizen can seek some redress against the executive even in the absence of any express statutory right of appeal or other procedure for challenging its decisions. Key examples of the courts exercising this power of review include: *Council of Civil Service Unions* v *Minister for the Civil Service* [1985] AC 374 (prerogative power held to be reviewable by the courts); *Padfield* v *MAFF* [1968] AC 997 (minister's decision not to hold an inquiry unlawful due to the absence of any good reasons of not doing so); and *M* v *Home Office* [1993] 3 WLR 433 (remedies available against ministers of the Crown).

The separation of powers under the British constitution – the judiciary and legislature

Fusion and separation

The separation of the judiciary and legislature is expressly recognised in the House of Commons Disqualification Act 1975, which provides that holders of all full-time judicial appointments are disqualified from membership of the House of Commons. The House of Lords is, of course, both the second chamber of the legislature and the highest domestic court of appeal in the United Kingdom. Law Lords can sit and vote in the House of Lords whilst also sitting as Lords of Appeal in Ordinary in the Appellate Committee. By convention they sit as crossbenchers and do not become involved in overtly party political matters, although they do contribute to debates on the passage of law reform Bills. The Lord High Chancellor presides over the House of Lords when it is sitting in its legislative capacity, and is entitled to preside over the Appellate Committee when hearing appeals. Whether this particular intermingling of functions on the part of the Lord Chancellor will survive the coming into effect of the Human Rights Act 1998 remains to be seen. In *McGonnell* v *United Kingdom* (2000) The Times 22 February, the European Court of Human Rights ruled that the hearing of an appeal against a refusal of planning permission had violated art 6(1) of the European Convention on Human Rights, because the court had been presided over by the Bailiff of Guernsey who, in his legislative capacity, had presided over the States of Deliberation, Guernsey's legislative body, when it enacted the planning scheme being contested by the applicant.

Whilst the Court accepted that there was no evidence that the Bailiff had been personally prejudiced or biased, it concluded that any direct involvement in the passage of legislation was likely to be enough to call into question the judicial impartiality of a person who subsequently presided over a dispute as to the correct interpretation of the wording of the legislation or rules at issue. The ruling may have significant implications for constitutional arrangements in the United Kingdom. The Court stressed that it was not seeking to force signatory states to adopt any particular constitutional arrangements, but it is hard not to see the decision as an endorsement of the doctrine of the separation of powers. In theory, the Lord Chancellor would be in a doubtful position participating in any House of Lords' case dealing with a dispute as to the effect of legislation enacted since May 1997, or indeed legislation enacted prior to May 1997 where he was a vocal opposition spokesman. This could include litigation arising under the Human Rights Act 1998. Lord Irvine has indicated that he regards the ruling in *McGonnell* as being limited to its own facts and hence no bar on his right to sit in a judicial capacity, although he accepted that he was unlikely to be involved in any case where the government's interests were directly concerned.

Do judges make law? The creative or legislative function of the judiciary is perhaps greater in a common law system than in a civil law system based on a code. The 'declaratory' theory of precedent – the theory that judges do not make law but only declare the common law or common custom of the realm – persisted into the nineteenth century, but it is now generally recognised that the judges in the United Kingdom do exercise some law-making function, with the silent acquiescence of Parliament. A particularly striking example of this creative function was the House of Lords' decision in *Shaw* v *DPP* [1962] AC 220. Shaw proposed to publish a 'ladies directory' giving details of prostitutes. Prostitution is not, and was not at that time, a criminal offence in the United Kingdom. Shaw was convicted of conspiracy to corrupt public morals, and his conviction was upheld by the House of Lords, although this was not a statutory offence and there had never previously been a conviction for this offence. Indeed, when Shaw had consulted his lawyers and Scotland Yard to enquire whether, in the event of publication, he would be committing any criminal offence, the reply was that he would not. Viscount Simmonds, for the majority, observed:

> 'In the sphere of criminal law I entertain no doubt that there remains in the courts of law a residual power to enforce the supreme and fundamental purpose of the law, to conserve not only the safety and order but also the moral welfare of the state, and that it is their duty to guard it against attacks which may be the more insidious because they are novel and unprepared for.'

In 1972, in *Knuller* v *DPP* [1973] AC 435 the House of Lords upheld another conviction for conspiracy to corrupt public morals. It is indicative of the judiciary's power to create new law that Lord Reid, who had dissented in *Shaw*, taking the view that there could not be a conviction for such an offence, concurred in the decision in *Knuller*, feeling obliged to do so in view of the majority decision in *Shaw*.

Equally, however, the courts have been prepared to rely on the doctrine of the separation powers to justify a refusal to create new rights. Hence in *Malone* v *Metropolitan Police Commissioner* [1979] Ch 344 Sir Robert Megarry VC, declining to recognise any common law right to privacy, observed:

'... it is no function of the courts to legislate in a new field. The extension of the existing laws and principles is one thing, the creation of an altogether new right is another. At times judges must, and do, legislate; but as Holmes J once said, they do so only interstitially, and with molecular rather than molar motions: see *Southern Pacific Co* v *Jensen* (1917) 244 US 205, 221, in a dissenting judgment. Anything beyond that must be left for legislation. No new right in the law, fully-fledged with all the appropriate safeguards, can spring from the head of a judge deciding a particular case: only Parliament can create such a right. ... Where there is some major gap in the law, no doubt a judge would be capable of framing what he considered to be a proper code to fill it; and sometimes he may be tempted. But he has to remember that his function is judicial, not legislative, and that he ought not to use his office to legislate in the guise of exercising his judicial powers. ... The more complex and indefinite the subject matter, the greater the difficulty in the court doing what it is really appropriate, and only appropriate, for the legislature to do. Any regulation of so complex a matter as telephone tapping is essentially a matter for Parliament, not the courts.'

Checks and balances

Parliament can control the courts, in a sense, by legislation. But judges' salaries are charged on the consolidated fund, meaning that their payment is permanently authorised, and this authority does not need to be renewed, and hence reviewed, each year by Parliament. Thus Parliament is denied an annual opportunity to discuss and possibly criticise the activities of judges. Superior judges, under the Act of Settlement 1700, hold office during their good behaviour, rather than at Her Majesty's pleasure, but can be removed upon an address from both Houses of Parliament. The Supreme Court Act 1981 re-enacted the provision of 1700 in slightly different words, stating that judges of the High Court and Court of Appeal hold office during their good behaviour, subject to a power of removal by the Queen on an address by both Houses of Parliament. A similar provision applies to Lords of Appeal in Ordinary: s6 Appellate Jurisdiction Act 1876. This power of removal upon an address from Parliament has only been exercised once since 1700. In 1830 Jonah Barrington, an Irish judge, was removed, having misappropriated money belonging to litigants and having ceased to perform his judicial duties many years previously.

There is also a long-standing rule of the House of Commons that, except upon a substantive motion on the question of whether to request dismissal, Members of Parliament should not make comments or reflections upon the activities of particular judges, or judges generally. This convention is recorded in Erskine May. Members of Parliament may, with the exception of those holding office in the government, criticise a judgment rather than a judge. It is for the Speaker to ensure that MPs observe this nice distinction, which may be no easy task. When he was sitting as a judge several of Lord Denning's judgments caused an angry response among some MPs. On the occasion of his judgment in the Court of Appeal in *Duport Steels Ltd* v *Sirs* (reversed on appeal by the House of Lords ([1980] 1 WLR 142)), where adverse comment was made on the highly political flavour of parts of Lord Denning's judgment, the Speaker quoted a ruling given by the late Selwyn Lloyd when Speaker:

'It can be argued that the judge made a mistake and was wrong and the reason for this contention can be given within certain limits. What is wrong is to impute any motives to judges acting in their responsible office.'

Regarding judicial control of the legislature, the doctrine of parliamentary sovereignty applicable in the United Kingdom must be contrasted with those written constitutions which vest in a state's Supreme Court the power to declare legislation unconstitutional and invalid. No such power exists in the United Kingdom, in relation to primary legislation, although under the Human Rights Act 1998 a court can grant a declaration of incompatibility if it finds that domestic legislation cannot be interpreted in a manner that ensures compatibility with Convention rights. It will then be for the relevant minister to take remedial action to amend the legislation in question to ensure compliance (see further Chapter 9). Where a statute appears to be in breach of EC law a domestic court can grant an injunction to prevent the statute being put into effect, pending resolution of the issue of incompatibility by the European Court of Justice: see *R* v *Secretary of State for Transport, ex parte Factorame Ltd (No 2)* [1990] 3 WLR 818. Subject to this a judge is not at liberty to pick and choose between measures that he sees fit to give effect to and those that he does not. As Lord Diplock observed in *Duport Steels Ltd* v *Sirs*:

'... at a time when more and more cases involve the application of legislation which gives effect to policies that are the subject of bitter public and parliamentary controversy, it cannot be too strongly emphasised that the British constitution, though largely unwritten, is firmly based upon the separation of powers; Parliament makes the laws, the judiciary interpret them. ... In controversial matters such as are involved in industrial relations there is room for differences of opinion as to what is expedient, what is just and what is morally justifiable. Under our constitution it is Parliament's opinion on these matters that is paramount ... it is for Parliament, not for the judiciary, to decide whether any changes should be made to the law ...'

The same cannot be said of the judicial function in respect of delegated legislation. If, on an application for judicial review, a court finds that subordinate legislation has been made that goes beyond the powers of the enabling primary Act it may declare it to be invalid.

The approach of the courts to Parliament at Westminster is to be contrasted with the approach taken to the Scottish Parliament. *Whalley and Others* v *Watson* (2000) The Times 21 March confirms that the courts have the same powers over the Scottish Parliament as any other statutory body, save to the extent that s40 of the Scotland Act 1998 limited the range of remedies that could be granted. The Court of Session observed that, whilst the Westminster Parliament was respected as sovereign by the courts, the Scottish Parliament belonged to that wider family of parliaments, modelled in some respects on Westminster, that owed their powers to statute and were in various ways subject to the law and the courts.

3.3 Independence of the judiciary

It could be argued that the separation of powers means little more than that the judiciary should be independent of the executive. This minimal requirement can usually be met by ensuring that judges have security of tenure, are immune from civil and criminal liability as regards the discharge of judicial functions, and that their decisions are not subject to criticism in parliamentary debate.

Security of tenure

Magistrates may be dismissed by the Lord Chancellor without cause shown and judges of inferior courts may be dismissed by the Lord Chancellor for incapacity or misbehaviour. Judges of superior courts – High Court, Court of Appeal and House of Lords – hold office during good behaviour subject to a power of removal by the Queen on an address to the Queen by both Houses of Parliament: Act of Settlement 1700, re-enacted in the Appellate Jurisdiction Act 1981 and the Supreme Court Act 1981.

Freedom from criticism

By convention the judicial conduct of judges may not be the subject of criticism in parliamentary debate, except upon a motion for an address for their removal. Breach of this convention may amount to a contempt of Parliament. Criticism of a judge may also amount to contempt of court.

Judicial immunity

Judges are immune from suit in the law of defamation for anything said in court, as are parties, lawyers and witnesses. This applies to all the judges no matter what their rank in the judicial hierarchy. However, the liability of judges in tort for actions in the course of judicial proceedings depends upon the rank of the judge concerned. In the superior courts a judge is not liable even for an act in excess of his jurisdiction, provided he was acting bona fide.

In *Sirros* v *Moore* [1974] 3 All ER 776 the plaintiff, a citizen of Turkey, was brought before a magistrate for breach of the Aliens Order 1953. The magistrate fined him £50, recommended that he be deported, but directed that he should not be detained pending the Home Secretary's decision on deportation. The plaintiff appealed to the Crown Court against the recommendation for deportation. At the hearing the judge accepted the prosecution's submission that the court had no jurisdiction to hear an appeal against a recommendation for deportation, and announced the court's decision that the appeal be dismissed. Thereupon the plaintiff made his way out of the court, but when the judge realised that he was leaving court he called out 'stop him' and sent police officers after him. They found him in the street and brought him back to the cells where he was detained. On the following day the plaintiff successfully applied to the Divisional Court for habeas corpus. He later issued a writ claiming damages for assault and false imprisonment against, inter alia, the circuit judge in the Crown Court who had given the decision on appeal. The Court of Appeal held that the Crown Court had jurisdiction to hear the appeal, but as the Crown Court had dismissed the appeal there was, at the time the plaintiff's detention was ordered, no order under which the plaintiff could be detained. The instruction from the judge that he be detained was therefore unlawful. The plaintiff had, however, no cause of action against the judge in respect of this unlawful detention. The majority of the Court (Lord Denning MR and Ormerod LJ) stated that every judge of the superior and inferior courts, including a Justice of the Peace, was entitled to protection from liability and damages in respect of what he had done provided that he was acting judicially and under the honest belief that his act was within his jurisdiction. This was to be so even though, in consequence of a mistake of law or fact, what the judge had done might be outside his jurisdiction.

The dicta of the majority in *Sirros* v *Moore*, to the effect that all judges should enjoy the same immunity, were disapproved by the House of Lords in *Re McC* [1984] 3 All ER 908, where damages were awarded against magistrates who had failed to notify an accused of his right to legal representation before imposing a custodial sentence. The House of Lords considered that the historic distinction between judges of the superior and inferior courts should be preserved. They affirmed that judges of the inferior courts remain liable for acts in excess of their jurisdiction. Immunity applies to both civil and criminal liability and is based upon public policy requiring the judiciary to be free to pursue the administration of justice.

Common law rules against bias

In the sphere of public law there is a doctrine known as natural justice. One aspect of this doctrine is the notion that the decisions of public bodies must not only be free of actual bias on the part of the decision-maker, but must also be seen to free of bias.

If a judge has a financial interest related to an issue arising in the case before him he should not continue to preside. In *Dimes* v *Grand Junction Canal Proprietors* (1852) 3 HL Cas 759 Lord Cottenham LC had affirmed decrees made by the Vice-Chancellor in litigation between Dimes and the canal proprietors. Dimes discovered that, despite the fact that the Lord Chancellor had for a long period held shares in the canal company in his own right and as trustee, he had continued to hear matters arising out of the litigation relying on the advice of the Master of the Rolls who sat with him. Dimes appealed to the House of Lords against all the decrees made by the Lord Chancellor on the ground that he was disqualified by interest. The House of Lords set aside the decrees issued by the Lord Chancellor on the ground of pecuniary interest. In the course of his speech Lord Campbell stated:

> 'No one can suppose that Lord Cottenham could be, in the remotest degree, influenced by the interest that he had in this concern; but, my Lords, it is of the last importance that the maxim that no man is to be a judge in his own cause should be held sacred. And that is not to be confined to a cause in which he has an interest. Since I have had the honour to be Chief Justice of the Court of Queen's Bench, we have again and again set aside proceedings in inferior tribunals because an individual, who had an interest in a cause, took a part in the decision. And it will have a most salutary influence on these tribunals when it is known that this High Court of last resort, in a case in which the Lord Chancellor of England had an interest, considered that his decree was on that account a decree not according to law, and was set aside. This will be a lesson to all inferior tribunals to take care not only that in their decrees they are not influenced by their personal interest, but to avoid the appearance of labouring under such an influence.'

More difficult are those cases where there is a non-pecuniary link between a judge and the parties appearing before him. The test that will be applied in determining whether such proceedings are vitiated by the appearance of bias is that laid down by the House of Lords in *R* v *Gough* [1993] 2 WLR 883. Three types case were identified by the House of Lords. First, those cases where actual bias was alleged. In such cases the proceedings would be invalidated upon proof of bias. Second, as outlined above, there were cases where the allegation of bias rested upon a pecuniary or proprietary interest – the proceedings being invalidated upon proof of the pecuniary or proprietary interest. Third, in cases of apparent bias, where there was no pecuniary or proprietary interest, the correct test was that of whether or not there was a real danger of bias, the test being seen as equally applicable to arbitrators and members of inferior tribunals. The term 'real danger' was preferred to real likelihood because of the desire to emphasis that the possibility of bias should be enough to impugn the validity of proceedings, as opposed to proof of probability.

There are many well known examples of the decisions of lower courts being set aside on the basis that justice did not appear to have been done because of the existence of links between adjudicators and the parties. In *R* v *Sussex Justices, ex parte McCarthy* [1924] 1 KB 256 a solicitor who was representing a client against McCarthy in a motoring accident also worked as a clerk to the Sussex justices who were trying McCarthy on a criminal charge arising out of the same motoring incident. When the justices retired to consider their verdict, the clerk retired with them and they convicted the defendant of dangerous driving. Quashing the conviction on the ground that the appearance of bias was fatal, Lord Hewart CJ uttered his famous dictum to the effect that justice not only had to be done, but had to be seen to be done. Similarly, in *R* v *Altrincham Justices, ex parte Pennington* [1975] QB 549 the conviction of the defendant for selling underweight quantities of vegetables to various schools was quashed on discovery that the chairman of the court was also a co-opted member of the local authority's education committee.

Dramatic evidence that the principle applies equally to the highest court in the land was provided in December 1998 when the House of Lords announced that it had acceded to a petition to set aside its ruling in *R* v *Bow Street Metropolitan Stipendiary Magistrate, ex parte Pinochet Ugarte* (above) where it had held by a majority of three to two that the former Chilean dictator Augusto Pinochet could be made the subject of extradition proceedings. Although full reasons for the decision were not available at the time of writing, it was made clear that the principle ground of challenge, namely that Lord Hoffmann should not have taken part in the hearing because of his links with Amnesty International, one of the parties appearing in the case, had been accepted.

Independence distinguished from neutrality

The fact that judges enjoy a degree of independence from the government of the day does not necessarily mean that they are 'neutral' in their decision-making. Judges are human – they have preferences and prejudices. The key question is the extent to which these private views influence public decision-making, or at least appear to do so. In the course of his speech in the *Duport Steels* case (above), Lord Diplock observed that:

> 'It endangers continued public confidence in the political impartiality of the judiciary, which is essential to the continuance of the rule of law, if judges, under the guise of interpretation, provide their own preferred amendments to statutes which experience of their operation has shown to have had consequences that members of the court before whom the matter comes consider to be injurious to the public interest.'

In his book *The Politics of the Judiciary* Professor J A G Griffith sought to expose what he saw as 'the myth of judicial neutrality'. This 'myth' is the theory that a court ruling is a product of the law and only marginally of the judicial mind. In practice, as Griffith pointed out, judges are faced with cases involving questions regarding the powers of government or the right of individuals – essentially political questions in the eyes of most people – and the guidance given to the judges by statute and common law is inadequate and imprecise. They must, however, give a decision; they cannot remain silent.

Griffith conceded that judges in the United Kingdom are not beholden politically to the government of the day. He accepted that they seek to give decisions which accurately apply the law and, where the law leaves some latitude as to what the decision in a particular case should be, seek to give decisions which serve the public interest as they perceive it. However, as Griffith observed, what is or is not in the public interest is a political question that admits of a great variety of answers. The judicial concept of the public interest, at least seen in the cases discussed by Griffith, comprised three elements: the interests of the state and the preservation of law and order broadly interpreted; the protection of property rights; and the promotion of certain political views normally associated with the Conservative Party.

The first point Griffith illustrated by reference to such decisions as *Liversidge* v *Anderson* (above) and *R* v *Secretary of State for the Home Department, ex parte Hosenball* [1977] 1 WLR 766. In both cases the interests of the state were seen to outweigh the interests of the individual. On the law and order matter, Griffith claimed that in perhaps the most important area of all, that of police powers, the judges have left largely unfulfilled their self-styled role as protectors of the individual. He claimed that the (sometimes illegal) practices of the police in relation to questioning, search and seizure had been generally supported by the judiciary. As far as the protection of property rights is concerned, Griffith claimed that, apart from a brief period during and after the Second World War, the courts have continuously intervened to limit and curtail the powers of government to interfere with property rights, and have been far more assiduous in this than in the protection of civil rights and liberties. He referred, for example, to squatters' cases and cases involving governmental power of compulsory purchase.

Concerning the promotion of certain political views normally associated with the Conservative Party, Griffith commented that the attitude of the courts to trade union members who incur the displeasure of the union officials is one of considerable sympathy. He commented to the same degree on those who claim that their companies have unjustly dismissed them. He concluded that the suspicion arises that the courts in protecting the individual trade unionist are motivated more by their dislike of organised trade unions than by their wish to advance the personal rights of individuals. It is trade union cases that Griffith selected to illustrate most strongly his point that judicial decisions are affected by the judge's view of what will best serve the public interest. He selected the case in 1972 when five dockers, who had been imprisoned for disobedience to an order of the National Industrial Relations Court, were released from prison following the House of Lords' judgment in *Heaton's Case*. Griffith claimed that the decision in *Heaton's Case* did nothing to change any law that was relevant to the dockers' imprisonment for contempt of the National Industrial Relations Court. He saw the decision of the National Industrial Relations Court to release the dockers, following *Heaton's Case*, as using a flimsy justification for their release, which the court regarded as essential if a general strike was to be avoided. Whereas the courts had previously regarded the upholding of the rule of law as being in the public interest, they now saw the avoidance of this general strike as being most forcibly in the public interest. Griffith saw the House of Lords as being involved in this matter as well, and it is true that judgment in

Heaton's Case was given one week after the hearing. In other words the giving of the judgment was expedited.

Griffith took the view that in our society political power and the power of government are exercised by a relatively small number of people, and that the senior judges are undeniably among those few. They are bound therefore to protect the social order that allows them a position of power from threats to its stability or to the existing distribution of political and economic power. He concluded:

> 'It is not the politics of the extreme right ... but is it demonstrable that on every major social issue which has come before the courts during the last thirty years – concerning industrial relations, political protests, race relations, government secrecy, police powers, moral behaviour – the judges have supported the conventional, established and settled interests. This conservatism does not necessarily follow the day-to-day political policies currently associated with the party of the same name. But it is a political philosophy nonetheless.'

Griffith also carried out his own analysis of the sort of decisions judges were likely to give and sought to identify the sort of factors that were likely to influence those decisions. This investigation involved surveying the social and educational background of those appointed to senior judicial posts during the twentieth century. It emerged that 70 per cent of the judiciary were products of Oxford or Cambridge Universities and about 75 per cent to 80 per cent had attended public school. He also observed that in 'political' cases there was:

> '... a remarkable consistency of approach ... concentrated in a fairly narrow part of the spectrum of political opinion. It spreads from that part of the centre which is shared by right wing Labour, Liberal and Progressive Conservative opinion to that part of the right which is associated with traditional Toryism ... but not beyond it into the reaches of the far right.'

To some extent Griffith's thesis is a product of its time. The trade union disputes of the 1970s coupled with the litigation initiated by those opposed to Labour government policies (such as comprehensivisation of secondary schooling) undoubtedly resulted in a number of apparently 'pro-Tory' decisions. The experience of the latter years of the twentieth century suggests that Griffith's arguments might now be too simplistic. The Conservative administrations of Margaret Thatcher and John Major both suffered many significant defeats at the hands of the judiciary during the 1980s and 1990s – see for example the GCHQ case, and the succession of defeats suffered by the Conservative Home Secretary, Michael Howard. Most would agree that today's judges are generally a more humane and liberal breed than their predecessors – as evidenced by widespread support amongst the senior judiciary for the incorporation of the European Convention on Human Rights. Politics too has ceased to be a simple matter of adherence to left-wing or right-wing views. There are many contentious issues in relation to which opposing views can be found within the same political camp – for example animal rights, European integration, euthanasia, homosexual rights, censorship, legalisation of drugs and blood sports.

The incorporation of the Convention by means of the Human Rights Act 1998 will undoubtedly result in judges having to consider more politically sensitive cases, thus raising questions regarding their ideological impartiality. Some have suggested that, in light of this, it might be appropriate to create a judicial appointments commission to vet prospective judges, with a view towards ensuring a balanced range of opinions. By this means the views of judges on key issues (eg such as abortion) would be known in advance, and a balance achieved.

4

The Sovereignty of Parliament

4.1 Introduction

4.2 Challenging the validity of Acts of Parliament on procedural grounds

4.3 Would a substantive challenge to the validity of an Act of Parliament succeed in the courts?

4.4 Can Parliament bind its successors?

4.5 EC law in the United Kingdom

4.6 EC law and United Kingdom sovereignty

4.7 Conclusion

4.1 Introduction

The traditional analysis of the United Kingdom's constitution identifies, as one of its key features, the notion that Parliament, as the legislature, is sovereign, by which is meant the absence of any legal restraint on the legislative powers of the United Kingdom Parliament. This sovereignty is the product of the historical struggle between Parliament and the Crown that culminated, in 1689, with the Bill of Rights, the flight of James II, and Parliament's invitation to William of Orange to assume the throne. From that time onwards, the accepted legal order has been that Parliament enacts legislation, with the formal assent of the Crown, that is enforced by the judiciary.

This doctrine of parliamentary sovereignty manifests itself in a number of ways. For example, it is assumed that Parliament is legally competent to legislate upon any subject matter; it is assumed that no Parliament can bind its successors or be bound by its predecessors; and it is assumed that once Parliament has legislated no court or other person can pass judgment upon the validity of the legislation. In effect, it means that Parliament has competence to alter any aspect of the constitution, and interfere in all matters relating to individual constitutional rights.

The power of Parliament to determine key aspects of the constitutional framework is illustrated by legislation such as the Act of Settlement 1700 and His Majesty's Declaration of Abdication Act 1936. Although in 1700 Parliament laid down in the Act of Settlement the law governing accession to the English throne, Parliament was legally competent to alter the right of succession by the later Act of 1936 which provided that Edward VIII, his issue, if any, and the descendants of that issue, should not thereafter have any right to the succession. Arguably Parliament used its sovereignty in the early eighteenth century to 'reconstitute' itself as the Parliament of England and Scotland with the enactment of the Union with Scotland Act 1706. Many would argue that Parliament divested itself of a large portion of its sovereignty in 1972 with the enactment of the European Communities Act of that year, which provided that EC law should take precedence over domestic legislation.

The doctrine of parliamentary sovereignty means that Parliament can legislate to nullify rulings of the courts, even where the effect of the ruling would be retrospective. Hence in *Burmah Oil Co* v *Lord Advocate* [1965] AC 75 the House of Lords held that where private property was taken or destroyed (except by battle damage) under the royal prerogative, the owner was entitled at common law to compensation from the Crown. Parliament, however, reversed the effect of this decision by enacting the War Damage Act 1965, which retrospectively provided that no person should be entitled at common law to receive compensation in respect of damage to or destruction of property caused by lawful acts of the Crown during, or in contemplation of the outbreak of, a war in which the Sovereign is or was engaged. This Act effectively removed Burmah Oil's common law right to compensation. Such retrospective legislation is rare but quite within Parliament's competence: see further the War Crimes Act 1991.

Subject to what follows, the position today is that the courts acknowledge that they must apply the law as laid down by Parliament, but it is only Acts of Parliament which are recognised by the courts as having the attributes of legal sovereignty. The courts will not allow a mere resolution of the House of Commons, for example, to alter the existing law of the land.

4.2 Challenging the validity of Acts of Parliament on procedural grounds

Since there is no statutory definition of an Act of Parliament, what constitutes an Act of Parliament is primarily a matter of common law. At common law, a Bill becomes an Act of Parliament when it has been approved by the House of Lords and the House of Commons and has received the Royal Assent. Standing orders of each House of Parliament, together with other conventions and practices, govern the procedure on the passage of a Bill through each House. The enforcement of these procedural rules is entirely a matter for the House concerned, and the courts refuse even to consider the question as to whether there have been any procedural defects in the passage of a Bill through Parliament.

In *Edinburgh and Dalkeith Railway* v *Wauchope* (1842) 8 Cl & F 710 the respondent claimed that under the private Act of Parliament incorporating the railway company he was entitled to payment for every carriage loaded with passengers which passed over his land. The appellants argued that this provision had been repealed by a later private Act. (Note: a private Act of Parliament is one that only affects the legal rights and liabilities of certain persons or bodies and not those of the whole community.) The respondent countered with the argument that this later Act was invalid since it adversely affected his rights and according to the standing orders of the House of Commons, should not have been introduced without his having been given notice, and he had not been given such notice. The respondent had abandoned this argument by the time the case reached the House of Lords but, as it had found some support in the lower court, the House of Lords considered the argument and rejected it. As Lord Campbell observed:

> 'All that a Court of Justice can do is look to the parliamentary roll; if from that it should appear that a Bill has passed both Houses and received the Royal Assent, no Court of Justice can inquire into the mode in which it was introduced into Parliament, nor into what was done previous to its introduction, or what passed in Parliament during its progress in its various stages through both Houses. I trust therefore, that no such inquiry will again be entered upon in any court ... but that due effect will be given to every Act of Parliament, private as well as public, upon what appears to be the proper construction of its existing provisions.'

It should be noted that, since 1849, the practice has been for the Queen's printer to make two copies of each Act of Parliament which are duly authenticated by the proper officers of each House; one is then kept in the Public Record Office, and the other in the House of Lords. Inspection of these Queen's printer's copies would today be equivalent to inspection of the parliamentary roll before 1849.

The courts confirmed this strict approach to challenges based upon procedural improprieties in *Lee* v *Bude and Torrington Junction Railway Co* (1871) LR 6 CP 577. One of the arguments of the defendant was that the plaintiff company was a legal nonentity because Parliament was induced to pass the Act forming the company by fraudulent recitals on the part of the plaintiffs. Again the court refused to question any of the matters which had led to the passing of the Act. Willes J, with whom the other two members of the court agreed, stated:

> 'I would observe, as to these Acts of Parliament, that they are the law of the land ... We sit here as servants of the Queen and the Legislature. Are we to act as Regents over what is done by Parliament with the consent of the Queen, Lords and Commons? I deny that any such authority exists. If an Act of Parliament has been obtained improperly, it is for the legislature to correct it by repealing it: but, so long as it exists as law, the courts are bound to obey it.'

The modern authority that encapsulates these principles is the House of Lords' decision in *Pickin* v *British Railways Board* [1974] AC 765. By s259 of a Private Act of Parliament of 1836 setting up a railway line, it was provided that, if the line should be abandoned, the lands acquired for the track should vest in the owners of the adjoining lands. Subsequently the line became vested in the British Railways

Board who promoted a private Bill, which was unopposed, and became the British Railways Act 1968. The effect of s18 of this Act was to cancel the effect of s259 of the 1836 Act and to vest in the Board instead any land over which abandoned tracks of lines passed. The plaintiff owned land adjoining an abandoned track. He brought an action against the Board claiming that by virtue of s259 of the 1836 Act he was the owner of the land under the track to mid-track. The Board claimed that, by virtue of s18 of the 1968 Act, the land under the track had vested in the Board. The plaintiff argued that the Board had obtained the unopposed passage of the 1968 Bill, by misleading Parliament by a false recital in the preamble to the Bill that the requisite documents had been deposited with the local authority as required by standing orders. In fact, the plaintiff claimed, all the requisite documents had not been deposited and he, as owner of the land affected, had not been given notice of the intention to promote the Bill, which he would have opposed. Thus, he argued, the 1968 Act was ineffective to modify his legal rights.

Predictably it was held that the function of a court was to apply the enactment of Parliament. As Lord Reid explained:

'The idea that a court is entitled to disregard a provision in an Act of Parliament on any ground must seem strange and startling to anyone with any knowledge of the history and law of our constitution. ... The function of the court is to construe and apply the enactments of Parliament. The court has no concern with the manner in which Parliament or its officers carrying out its standing orders perform these functions. Any attempt to prove that they were misled by fraud or otherwise would necessarily involve an inquiry into the manner in which they had performed their functions in dealing with the Bill which became the British Railways Act 1968. ... For a century or more both Parliament and the courts have been careful not to act so as to cause conflict between them. Any such investigations as the respondent seeks could easily lead to such a conflict, and I would only support it if compelled to do so by clear authority. But it appears to me that the whole trend of authority for over a century is clearly against permitting any such investigation ...'

Note that nothing in these cases denies the principle that a Bill must receive the approval of both Houses and the Royal Assent before it becomes an Act of Parliament (unless it is a measure passed under the provisions of the Parliament Acts 1911– 49 which dispense with the need for the consent of the House of Lords in certain circumstances). However, if it appeared from the Queen's printer's copy of an Act that such approval and assent had been given, the approach of the courts in the above cases shows that a court will not be prepared to consider extraneous evidence that such approval or assent had not in fact been given: see further *Murray* v *Rogers* 1992 SLT 221.

Can Parliament bind its successors as to the manner and form of future legislation?

Entrenchment is the term used to describe a legislative device inserted into an Act of Parliament in order to make it more difficult, or even impossible, for a successor Parliament to amend or repeal an that Act. There are a number of such devices, their effectiveness depending principally on the nature of the constitutional arrangements within which the legislature operates.

The legislature might seek to protect a statute from amendment or repeal in future by providing that no subsequent provision is to be construed as having the effect of altering the earlier legislation unless it is clearly provided (in the later Act) that such was the intention of the legislature when enacting the later Act. This is the weakest form of entrenchment, with success depending on the willingness of the courts to exercise some flexibility by not applying the doctrine of implied repeal. For example, s4 of the Statute of Westminster 1931 provides:

> '[N]o Act of the Parliament of the United Kingdom shall extend to a Dominion as part of the law of that Dominion unless expressly requested and consented to by the Dominion.'

By this means the 1931 Act was seeking to establish a precondition that had to be met before any later legislation could operate within a dominion territory. In *Manuel v Attorney-General* [1983] Ch 77 the court had to consider a challenge to the validity of the Canada Act 1982 based on the assertion that the consent required as a precondition to its enactment had not been secured. The 1982 Act had the effect (inter alia) of empowering the Canadian legislature to amend the Canadian constitution without, in future, having to seek the approval of Parliament at Westminster. The plaintiff represented a number of Canadian indians who sought declarations to the effect that the United Kingdom Parliament, under the terms of the Statute of Westminster 1931 and the British North America Acts 1867 to 1964, had no power to amend the constitution of Canada so as to prejudice the Canadian indian nations without their consent. Such consent not having been obtained, the plaintiff sought a declaration to the effect that the Canada Act 1982 was ultra vires. Refusing the declarations sought the Court of Appeal held that the Canada Act 1982 had been duly enacted and the courts could not question its validity. The existence of a convention that Parliament would not legislate for the Dominion without consent would not prevent the courts from nevertheless giving effect to any such legislation so enacted, regardless of consent. To the extent that the Statute of Westminster 1931 purported to create preconditions for any future legislation affecting Canada, s4 was not to be read as providing that no Act of the United Kingdom Parliament could extend to a Dominion as part of the law of that Dominion unless the Dominion had in fact requested and consented to the enactment thereof. The condition that had to be satisfied was that it should be 'expressly declared in that Act that that Dominion has requested, and consented to, the enactment thereof'. It was not possible to read into this a requirement that this meant a declaration of an independently ascertainable consent. The legislature had thus reserved to itself the sole function of deciding whether the requisite request and consent had been made and given. That it had been so satisfied was indicated in the preamble of the Canada Act 1982, which stated 'Whereas Canada has requested and consented to the enactment of an Act of the Parliament of the United Kingdom to give effect to the provisions hereinafter set forth'. In the light of this the proposition that the 1982 Act was ultra vires was unarguable.

A stronger form of entrenchment is to require a certain procedure to be followed if legislation is to be effectively amended or repealed by later legislation, for example: requiring a two-thirds majority on any vote for change; the issuing of a Speaker's certificate confirming that an earlier piece of legislation has been amended by a later one; or a vote in favour of change expressed in a referendum prior to the enactment of a piece of legislation. There are three key cases that illustrate the operation of such devices.

The first is the decision of the Privy Council in *Attorney-General for New South Wales* v *Trethowan* [1932] AC 526. Under the Colonial Laws Validity Act 1865 the legislature of New South Wales had full power to make laws regarding its own constitution, powers and procedures, provided such laws were passed in such manner and form as might be required from time to time by any Act of Parliament or other law for the time being in force. One such provision, s7(A) of the Constitution Act 1929, provided that the Upper House of the legislature should not be abolished until a Bill passed by both Houses had been approved by a referendum. Any amendments to the 1929 Act also required a referendum. Subsequently a Bill was passed by both Houses seeking to abolish both the Upper House and the referendum requirement. An injunction was granted by the New South Wales Court to restrain the government of New South Wales from presenting the Bill for Royal Assent until a referendum had been held as required. On appeal, the Judicial Committee of the Privy Council held that the requirement of a referendum was binding on the legislature until it had been abolished by a law passed in the 'manner and form' required by the law for the time being, ie with the approval of the voters as expressed in a referendum. The 'manner and form' provision in question was entrenched in that it was imposed on the New South Wales legislature by a higher authority: the United Kingdom Parliament.

Second, in *Bribery Commissioner* v *Ranasinghe* [1965] AC 172, the appellant was the Bribery Commissioner of Ceylon (now Sri Lanka) whose was under a duty to bring prosecutions before the Bribery Tribunal, which was created by the Bribery Amendment Act 1958. The respondent, having been prosecuted for a bribery offence before that tribunal, was convicted and sentenced to a term of imprisonment and a fine. On appeal, the Supreme Court declared the conviction and orders made against him null and inoperative on the ground that the persons composing the Bribery Tribunal which tried him were not lawfully appointed to the tribunal. The Supreme Court had taken the view that the method of appointing persons to the panel from which the tribunal was drawn offended against an important safeguard in the Constitution of Ceylon, contained in the Ceylon (Constitution) Orders in Council 1946 and 1947, and to the extent of that inconsistency purported to amend the constitution. There was no evidence that the constitutional requirements relating to amendments (a two-thirds majority in the House of Representatives, and the endorsement of a Speaker's certificate) had been complied with in respect of the 1958 Act. The question before the Privy Council, therefore, was whether the statutory provisions for the appointment of members of the panel of the Bribery Tribunal, otherwise than by the Judicial Service Commission, conflicted with s55 of the Constitution, and, if so, whether those provisions were valid. The Privy Council held that the legislature of Ceylon was bound by the terms of the Constitution, and the courts would not uphold legislation that had not been enacted in accordance with that Constitution. When a constitution laid down that, in respect of compliance with procedures for constitutional amendment, a Speaker's certificate would be conclusive for all purposes and would not be questioned in any court of law, it was clearly intended that courts of law would look to the certificate but look no further. The courts therefore had a duty to look for the certificate in order to ascertain whether the Constitution had been validly amended. Where the certificate was not apparent, there was lacking an essential part of the process necessary for amendment. Once it was shown that an Act conflicted with a provision in the Constitution, as was the case here, the certificate became an essential part of the legislative process. Turning to the narrow point in this case, the question of whether sovereignty of Parliament necessarily required its legislation to be of incontestable validity, Lord Pearce explained the concept of limited sovereignty in the following terms:

> '[A] legislature has no power to ignore the conditions of law-making that are imposed by the instrument which itself regulates its power to make law. This restriction exists independently of the question whether the legislature is sovereign, as is the legislature of Ceylon, or whether the Constitution is "uncontrolled". ... [S]uch a Constitution can, indeed, be altered or amended by the legislature, if the regulating instrument so provides and if the terms of those provisions are complied with: and the alteration or amendment may include the change or abolition of those very provisions. But the proposition which is not acceptable is that a legislature, once established, has some inherent power derived from the mere fact of its establishment to make a valid law by the resolution of a bare majority which its own constituent instrument has said shall not be a valid law unless made by a different type of majority or by a different legislative process. And this is the proposition which is in reality involved in the argument. ... [N]o question of sovereignty arises. A Parliament does not cease to be sovereign whenever its component members fail to produce among themselves a requisite majority, eg when in the case of ordinary legislation the voting is evenly divided or when in the case of legislation to amend the Constitution there is only a bare majority if the Constitution requires something more.'

The third authority on the operation of 'manner and form' requirements is *Harris v Minister for the Interior* (1952) (2) SA 428. The South Africa Act 1909, by s152, provided that:

> '... [the Union Parliament of South Africa] may by law repeal or alter any of the provisions of this Act: Provided that no repeal or alteration of the provisions contained in this section, or in sections 35 and 137, shall be valid unless the Bill embodying such repeal or alteration shall be passed by both Houses of Parliament sitting together, and at the third reading be agreed to by not less than two-thirds of the total number of members

ot both houses. A Bill so passed at such joint sitting shall be taken to have been duly passed by both Houses of Parliament.'

Section 35 of the 1909 Act dealt with the voting rights of so-called 'Cape coloured' voters. The Separate Representation of Voters Act 1951, which sought to amend s35 of the 1909 Act by introducing racially segregated representation, was passed on a bare majority by both chambers of the South African legislature (the House of Assembly and the Senate) sitting separately. The Appellate Division of the Supreme Court of South Africa upheld the challenge to the validity of the 1951 Act based on the contention that it had not been enacted in accordance with ss35(1) and 152 of the South Africa Act 1909. Centlivres CJ noted that, given the enactment of the Statute of Westminster 1931, the Union Parliament in South Africa was free to make law repugnant to a British Act of Parliament in so far as that Act extended to the Union, and that no law made after 11 December 1931 by the Parliament of the Union was to be void or inoperative on the ground that it was repugnant to the provisions of any existing Act of Parliament of the United Kingdom. As he explained, however:

> 'The words "Parliament of a Dominion" in the Statute of Westminster must, in my opinion, be read, in relation to the Union, in the light of the South Africa Act. It is implicit in that Act that the Parliament of the Union must function bicamerally, save in the cases excepted by ss35, 63 and 152. In my opinion one is doing no violence to language when one regards the word "Parliament" as meaning Parliament sitting either bicamerally or unicamerally in accordance with the requirements of the South Africa Act. There is, in my opinion, no justification for reading the words "Parliament of a Dominion" in the Statute as meaning, in relation to the Union, Parliament functioning only bicamerally.'

In his view the Statute of Westminster 1931 had not, by mere implication, altered the South African constitution (as contained in the 1909 Act) in such a radical way as to permit the Union Parliament to fundamentally alter that country's constitution on a bare majority vote, sitting bicamerally, as it saw fit.

As to the nature of the 'limited' sovereignty enjoyed by states where the legislature operated subject to a 'higher' form of law in the form of a binding constitutional document, he observed:

> '[It has been contended that] no country which, like the Union, emerged from a Colony into a Dominion within the framework of the British Constitution can be a sovereign state unless it has a sovereign Parliament functioning bicamerally in the same manner as the British Parliament – I cannot agree with this contention. It seems to be based on the fallacy that a Dominion Parliament must necessarily be a replica of the British Parliament despite the fact that all Dominion Parliaments have constitutions which define the manner in which they must function as legislative bodies. There is nothing in the Statute of Westminster which in any way suggests that a Dominion Parliament should be regarded as if it were in the same position as the British Parliament. ... A State can be unquestionably sovereign although it has no legislature which is completely sovereign. As Bryce points out in his *Studies in History and Jurisprudence* (1901 edn, vol II, p53) legal

sovereignty may be divided between two authorities. In the case of the Union, legal sovereignty is or may be divided between Parliament as ordinarily constituted and Parliament as constituted under s63 and the proviso to s152. Such a division of legislative powers is no derogation from the sovereignty of the Union and the mere fact that that division was enacted in a British Statute (viz the South Africa Act) which is still in force in the Union cannot affect the question in issue. ... To say that the Union is not a sovereign state, simply because its Parliament functioning bicamerally has not the power to amend certain sections of the South Africa Act, is to state a manifest absurdity. Those sections can be amended by Parliament sitting unicamerally. To go further afield, it would be surprising to a constitutional lawyer to be told that that great and powerful country, the United States of America, is not a sovereign independent country simply because its Congress cannot pass any legislation which it pleases ...'

Would the 'manner and form' devices work in the United Kingdom?

The conventional view is that the 'manner and form' devices, such as those considered above, would not be binding on the United Kingdom Parliament at Westminster because it does not have 'limited' power in the sense that it operates subject to some overriding constitutional law. As Lord Pearce observed in *Bribery Commissioner* v *Ranasinghe* (above):

'[T]he English authorities have taken a narrow view of the court's power to look behind an authentic copy of the Act. But in the constitution of the United Kingdom there is no governing instrument which prescribes the law-making powers and the forms which are essential to those powers. There was, therefore, never such a necessity as arises in the present case for the court to take any close cognisance of the process of law-making.'

The Northern Ireland (Constitution) Act 1973 provides that the Province of Northern Ireland will remain part of the United Kingdom for as long as that remains the wish of the majority of those living there, and that this would not cease to be the case unless the contrary is shown in a referendum. Suppose Parliament enacts legislation ceding the Province to the Republic of Ireland without any such referendum having been conducted. Would the legislation be valid? The requirement that a referendum should be held prior to the status of the Province being changed could be seen as a 'manner and form' requirement such that no legislation to change the status of the Province would be valid unless such a referendum vote had taken place. It could be seen as a 'redefinition' provision – ie that only Parliament comprising the Crown, Lords, Commons and the Northern Ireland electorate could enact legislation changing the status of the Province. A more likely view is that a future Parliament could expressly or impliedly override the requirement in legislation ceding the Province to the Republic, but would have to consider the political repercussions.

The English authorities indicate that the courts would have to give effect to the later Act regardless of whether the requirement regarding the referendum had been complied with, although Dixon J in *Attorney-General for New South Wales* v *Trethowan* (above) suggested, albeit obiter, that the situation may not be so clear cut:

'The incapacity of the British legislature to limit its own power otherwise than by transferring a portion or abdicating the whole of its sovereignty has been accounted for by the history of the High Court of Parliament, and has been explained as a necessary consequence of a true conception of sovereignty. But in any case it depends upon considerations which have no application to the legislature of New South Wales, which is not a sovereign body and has a purely statutory origin. It must not be supposed, however, that all difficulties would vanish if the full doctrine of parliamentary supremacy could be invoked. An Act of the British Parliament which contained a provision that no Bill repealing any part of the Act including the part so restraining its own repeal should be presented for the Royal Assent unless the Bill were first approved by the electors, would have the force of law until the sovereign actually did assent to a bill for its repeal. In strictness it would be an unlawful proceeding to present such a bill for the Royal Assent before it had been approved by the electors. If, before the Bill received the assent of the Crown, it was found possible, as appears to have been done in this appeal, to raise for judicial decision the question whether it was lawful to present the Bill for that assent, the courts would be bound to pronounce it unlawful to do so. Moreover, if it happened that, notwithstanding the statutory inhibition, the Bill did receive the Royal Assent although it was not submitted to the electors, the courts might be called upon to consider whether the supreme legislative power in respect of the matter had in truth been exercised in the manner required for its authentic expression and by the elements in which it had come to reside. But the answer to this question, whether evident or obscure, would be deduced from the principle of parliamentary supremacy over the law. This principle, from its very nature, cannot determine the character or the operation of the constituent powers of the legislature of New South Wales which are the result of statute.'

4.3 Would a substantive challenge to the validity of an Act of Parliament succeed in the courts?

Prior to the great constitutional resettlement of the seventeenth century, the courts claimed the right to challenge Acts of Parliament. In the *Case of Dr Bonham* (1610) 8 Co Rep 113b Coke CJ stated:

'And it appears in our books, that in many cases, the common law will control Acts of Parliament, and sometimes adjudge them to be utterly void: for when an Act of Parliament is against common rights or reason, or repugnant, or impossible to be performed, the common law will control it and adjudge such Act to be void.'

Lord Reid in *Pickin* v *British Railways Board* [1974] AC 765 was careful to point out that the House of Lords was there concerned with the effect of a procedural irregularity on the validity of an Act. That case, and the earlier 'procedure' cases, did not actually involve any challenge to the general supremacy of Parliament.

In what circumstances therefore, if any, can a plaintiff challenge the validity of an Act of Parliament on the basis that, despite the absence of any procedural irregularity, the Act is nevertheless invalid because of its effect? In other words, would the courts be willing to countenance a challenge to the substance of a primary Act, for example because it was incompatible with basic human rights or incompatible with other international obligations of the state?

Just such an argument was raised in *Cheney* v *Conn* [1968] 1 WLR 242. A taxpayer challenged his assessments of tax liability on the basis that the Finance Act 1964 contravened international law, in that it permitted the spending of taxpayers' money on weapons of mass destruction despite the outlawing of genocide in the Geneva Conventions (as ratified by Parliament in the Geneva Convention Act 1957). Ungoed-Thomas J, confirming that the 1964 Act was valid and that it would be applied by the courts, observed (at p247):

'... if [the taxpayer's] argument were correct it would mean that the supremacy of Parliament would, in effect, be overruled. If the purpose to which a statute may be used is an invalid purpose, then such remedy as there may be must be directed to dealing with that purpose and not to invalidating the statute itself. What the statute itself enacts cannot be unlawful, because what the statute says and provides is itself the law, and the highest form of law that is known to this country. It is the law which prevails over every other form of law, and it is not for the court to say that a parliamentary enactment, the highest law in this country, is illegal. The result therefore is that on this ground, also, the taxpayer's case fails. ... The terms of the statute in this case are perfectly clear and are binding upon the courts of this country.'

The earlier decision in *Mortensen* v *Peters* 1906 14 SLT 227, albeit one concerned with the validity of a bye-law issued by the Fishery Board for Scotland under the Herring Fishery (Scotland) Act 1889, similarly confirms that the courts will not question the validity of an Act of Parliament on the basis that it is incompatible with international law.

Would the judges therefore have no choice but to give effect to an Act that was found to have been enacted with complete disregard for basic human rights? The question is, one hopes, of academic interest only, not least because of the impact upon parliamentary sovereignty of membership of the European Community (as to which see below, and the incorporation of the European Convention on Human Rights, dealt with in Chapter 9). Comments made by Lord Scarman in *Duport Steels Ltd* v *Sirs* [1980] 1 WLR 142, however, seem to suggest that the hands of the judges would be tied. As he saw it:

'... in the field of statute law the judge must be obedient to the will of Parliament as expressed in its enactments. In this field Parliament makes, and un-makes, the law: the judge's duty is to interpret and to apply the law, not to change it to meet the judge's idea of what justice requires. Interpretation does, of course, imply in the interpreter a power of choice where differing constructions are possible. But our law requires the judge to choose the construction which in his judgment best meets the legislative purpose of the enactment. If the result be unjust but inevitable, the judge may say so and invite Parliament to reconsider its provision. But he must not deny the statute. Unpalatable statute law may not be disregarded or rejected, merely because it is unpalatable. Only if a just result can be achieved without violating the legislative purpose of the statute may the judge select the construction which best suits his idea of what justice requires. Further, in our system the rule "stare decisis" applies as firmly to statute law as it does to the formulation of common law and equitable principles. And the keystone of "stare decisis" is loyalty throughout the system to the decisions of the Court of Appeal and this House.'

Against this could be put the argument that the courts will only give effect to those aspects of an Act of Parliament that conform to the rule of law, in the sense that they display the quality of 'legality'. In *R* v *Secretary of State for the Home Department, ex parte Pierson* [1997] 3 WLR 492 the House of Lords considered the Home Secretary's contention that he had the power, under s35 of the Criminal Justice Act 1991, to retrospectively increase the penal element in the applicant's sentence of life imprisonment. Counsel for the Home Secretary had tried to argue that the matter should be looked at from the point of view of the legitimate expectations of a life-sentence prisoner, and that such a prisoner would only have a legitimate expectation of procedural fairness, ie the way in which decisions were made, not of substantive fairness, ie the merits of the decision itself. In response to this Lord Steyn observed:

> 'This is a controversial question. ... I will assume that counsel for the Home Secretary's proposition about the doctrine of legitimate expectations is correct. But counsel addressed the wrong target. The correct analysis of this case is in terms of the rule of law. The rule of law in its wider sense has procedural and substantive effect. While Dicey's description of the rule of law is nowadays regarded as neither exhaustive nor entirely accurate even for his own time, there is much of enduring value in the work of this great lawyer. Dicey's famous third meaning of the rule of law is apposite. He said:
>
>> "The 'rule of law', lastly, may be used as a formula for expressing the fact that with us the law of constitution, the rules which in foreign countries naturally form part of a constitutional code, are not the source but the consequence of the rights of individuals, as defined and enforced by the courts; that, in short, the principles of private law have with us been by the action of the courts and Parliament so extended as to determine the position of the Crown and its servants; thus the constitution is the result of the ordinary law of the land."
>
> This was the pivot of Dicey's discussion of rights to personal freedom, to freedom of association and of public meeting. ... It is clear therefore that in the relevant sense Dicey regarded the rule of law as having both procedural and substantive effect. ... Unless there is the clearest provision to the contrary, Parliament must be presumed not to legislate contrary to the rule of law. And the rule of law enforces minimum standards of fairness, both substantive and procedural.'

Lord Steyn is not here claiming any right to declare primary legislation to be invalid, but is indicating that the powers of statutory interpretation vested in the judiciary should be used to nullify, so far as is possible, legislative provisions that offend against basic principles of fairness.

These sentiments were echoed by Lord Hoffmann in *R* v *Secretary of State for the Home Department, ex parte Simms; R* v *Secretary of State for the Home Department, ex parte O'Brien* [1999] 3 All ER 400, where the House of Lords was considering the validity of administrative measures curtailing the rights of convicted prisoners to discuss the safety of their convictions with journalists. He observed (at pp412g–413d):

'Parliamentary sovereignty means that Parliament can, if it chooses, legislate contrary to fundamental principles of human rights. The Human Rights Act 1998 will not detract from this power. The constraints upon its exercise by Parliament are ultimately political, not legal. But the principle of legality means that Parliament must squarely confront what it is doing and accept the political cost. Fundamental rights cannot be overridden by general or ambiguous words. This is because there is too great a risk that the full implications of·their unqualified meaning may have passed unnoticed in the democratic process. In the absence of express language or necessary implication to the contrary, the courts therefore presume that even the most general words were intended to be subject to the basic rights of the individual. In this way the courts of the United Kingdom, though acknowledging the sovereignty of Parliament, apply principles of constitutionality little different from those which exist in countries where the power of the legislature is expressly limited by a constitutional document.

The Human Rights Act 1998 will make three changes to this scheme of things. First, the principles of fundamental human rights which exist at common law will be supplemented by a specific text, namely the European Convention. But much of the Convention reflects the common law ... That is why the United Kingdom government felt able in 1950 to accede to the Convention without domestic legislative change. So the adoption of the text as part of domestic law is unlikely to involve radical change in our notions of fundamental human rights. Secondly, the principle of legality will be expressly enacted as a rule of construction in s3 and will gain further support from the obligation of the minister in charge of a Bill to make a statement of compatibility under s19. Thirdly, in those unusual cases in which the legislative infringement of fundamental human rights is so clearly expressed as not to yield to the principle of legality, the courts will be able to draw this to the attention of Parliament by making a declaration of incompatibility. It will then be for the sovereign Parliament to decide whether or not to remove the incompatibility.'

In *R (On the Application of International Transport Roth GmbH)* v *Secretary of State for the Home Department* (2002) The Times 26 February Laws J reflected on the extent to which the development of a 'human rights culture' in domestic law had altered the nature and understanding of parliamentary sovereignty, in particular the move towards what he described as an intermediate position somewhere between pure parliamentary sovereignty on the one hand and constitutional sovereignty on the other. As he put it:

'Not very long ago, the British system was one of parliamentary supremacy pure and simple. Then, the very assertion of constitutional rights as such would have been something of a misnomer, for there was in general no hierarchy of rights, no distinction between "constitutional" and other rights. Every Act of Parliament had the same standing in law as every other, and so far as rights were given by judge-made law, they could offer no competition to the status of statutes. The courts evolved rules of interpretation which favoured the protection of certain basic freedoms, but in essence Parliament legislated uninhibited by claims of fundamental rights.

In its present state of evolution, the British system may be said to stand at an intermediate stage between parliamentary supremacy and constitutional supremacy, to use the language of the Canadian case [*Re Amendment of the Constitution of Canada* (1982) 125 DLR (3d) 1]. Parliament remains the sovereign legislature; there is no superior text to which it must defer (I leave aside the refinements flowing from our membership of the European Union); there is no statute which by law it cannot make. But at the same time, the common law has come to recognise and endorse the notion of constitutional, or fundamental rights. These are broadly the rights given expression in the European Convention on Human Rights and Fundamental Freedoms (ECHR), but their recognition in the common law is autonomous. ... The Human Rights Act 1998 (HRA) now provides a democratic underpinning to the common law's acceptance of constitutional rights, and important new procedural measures for their protection. Its structure, as has more than once been observed, reveals an elegant balance between respect for Parliament's legislative supremacy and the legal security of the Convention rights.

This being our constitution's present nature, there exists a tension between the maintenance of legislative sovereignty and the vindication of fundamental, constitutional rights. How are their respective claims to be reconciled? Where is the point of escape if the legislature tramples on the territory of rights? This tension is hardly to be found in a system of pure parliamentary supremacy, and is less acute in a system of constitutional supremacy. In the former, fundamental rights are not recognised as such. The majoritarian principle, expressed and made good by a sovereign Parliament, comes first. In the latter, the majoritarian principle gives way to fundamental rights. In practice, the constitutions and jurisprudence of sovereign states in the civilised world show that this distinction is by no means always clear-cut; and to the extent in any concrete instance that it is not clear-cut, the tension to which I refer will arise. Moreover, although it may create difficulties, and its resolution case by case requires firmness of purpose and good judgment, this tension is a welcome inhabitant of a democratic state. ...

In the British state, there are at least two means by which the courts seek to resolve this tension. The first ... arises where it is suggested that a statute has effected or authorised what would undoubtedly amount to a violation of a fundamental or constitutional right. Here the courts protect the right in question, while acknowledging the legislative supremacy of Parliament, by means of a rule of construction. The rule is that while the legislature possesses the power to override fundamental rights, general words will not suffice. It can only be done by express, or at any rate specific, provision. ...

The second means by which constitutional rights are recognised consistently with the sovereignty of Parliament is engaged where a statute admittedly travels in the field of a constitutional right, and the issue is whether the right is violated, or if it is whether the extent of the statute's intrusion is acceptable or justified. Such questions characteristically arise where the right is one guaranteed by the ECHR, and the court acts pursuant to its duty under the HRA. Where one of the political rights is under consideration (that is, any of those guaranteed by ECHR arts 9 to 11), the issue most often falling for decision is whether there is shown sufficient justification, under paragraph 2 of the article in question, for the right's infringement. But the question may be, whether there has been a violation at all; and that question may of course arise in the context of Convention rights as regards which the ECHR provides no express exceptions or qualifications. ...

In this second area the court's task is quite unlike its duty in deciding whether on its true construction a statute allows or perpetrates an undoubted violation of a constitutional right. The rule of construction, that only express or at least specific words will suffice to effect such a result, is a brightline rule whose edge is sharp. In this present context, there is no brightline rule. It is because here, the court has to strike a balance between the claims of the democratic legislature and the claims of the constitutional right. Sometimes, of course, it will be plain and obvious which way the scales fall. In the field of ECHR art 10, the justification of certain specified restrictions upon the right of free expression may be clear beyond argument in time of war or other national emergency. On the other hand, an attempt to curtail free speech merely to avoid embarrassment to the Government would, no less obviously, lack any colour of justification. In the far more frequent case where the answer is by no means so plain, and a balance has to be struck between contradictory interests each possessing some substance of legitimacy, a critical factor in the court's appreciation of the balance will be the degree or margin of deference it pays to the democratic decision-maker. This deference – and its limits – have to be fashioned in a principled but flexible manner, sensitive to the particular case and its context. In some contexts the deference is nearly absolute. In others it barely exists at all. The development of principle in this field is one of the most important challenges which the common law must meet, in face of the provisions of the HRA and our own domestic acceptance of the idea of constitutional rights. The reach of the deference which the judges will pay to the democratic decision-maker, the giving and withholding of it, is the second means by which the courts resolve the tension between parliamentary sovereignty and fundamental rights in our intermediate constitution.'

That judges can exercise their powers of statutory interpretation so as to exert a very marked influence over the way in which legislation actually operates, even to the extent of producing an outcome completely contrary to that intended by Parliament, is evidenced by decisions such as *Anisminic* v *Foreign Compensation Commission* [1969] 2 AC 147, where a provision, stating that no determination of the FCC was to be questioned in any court of law, was overturned following the House of Lords' ruling that this only prevented the courts from examining 'valid' determinations (ie not a determination the courts considered to be invalid).

Beyond the law reports there is evidence that today's judges may not be willing to blindly accept the notion that they are simply in office to do Parliament's bidding. If one accepts that the doctrine of the rule of law takes priority over the doctrine of parliamentary sovereignty, on the basis that even Parliament must act subject to a 'higher' natural law, one can accept that the judges could refuse to apply an Act that sought to undermine contemporary political morality – it would not be recognised as 'law'. In his article 'Droit Public – English Style' [1995] PL 57, Lord Woolf MR identifies parliamentary sovereignty and the right of the courts to be the ultimate arbiters of what law means as the two key pillars of the rule of law. Were Parliament to legislate to abolish the role of the courts in, for example, reviewing the legality of executive action (ie judicial review), he contends that the courts would have to resist it because it would be seen as a measure designed to subvert the rule of law. He further argues that there are certain limits on parliamentary sovereignty that it is the duty of the courts to uphold – either by powers of interpretation (ie resort to irrebuttable presumptions) or outright rejection of legislation. Laws LJ, writing in 'Law and Democracy' [1995] PL 74, argues that certain rights are so basic and unalienable that they should not be at the mercy of any government, democratically elected or otherwise. Rights such as freedom of expression, even in an unwritten constitution, are so fundamental that it is not for Parliament to abrogate them. If fundamental rights subsist only by virtue of their not being voted out of existence in the legislature they are not, in his view, really rights but only privileges allowed by the legislature. He stresses the need for a 'higher law' to protect fundamental rights. He accepts that it is for governments to determine questions of policy – as governed by the conventions of the constitution – and that it is not for the judges to question that policy. However, he rejects the notion that this means Parliament is therefore constitutionally sovereign. He sees the judges as having the role of protecting basic human rights – those rights that are accepted by all politicians subscribing to the rule of law – rights so basic they are not matters of debate amongst the broad sweep of political opinion.

4.4 Can Parliament bind its successors?

A key aspect of the theory of parliamentary sovereignty is the contention that Parliament cannot bind its successors. Professor E C S Wade has encapsulated this aspect of the doctrine of parliamentary sovereignty in his observation that:

> 'There is one, and only one, limit to Parliament s legal power: it cannot detract from its own continuing sovereignty.'

This was echoed by Sir Robert Megarry V-C, at first instance in *Manuel* v *Attorney-General* [1983] Ch 77, where he observed:

> 'In my view, it is a fundamental of the English constitution that Parliament is supreme. As a matter of law the courts of England recognise Parliament as being omnipotent in all save the power to destroy its own omnipotence.'

The doctrine of implied repeal

Where it intends to repeal legislation enacted by a previous administration Parliament normally does so by means of an express clause to that effect in an Act. In some cases legislation is enacted that is simply inconsistent with earlier legislation, ie it makes no express reference to the earlier legislation but is inconsistent with it to the point where only one of the enactments can prevail. In order to deal with such cases the courts have developed a doctrine of implied repeal whereby the earlier Act is impliedly repealed to the extent that it is inconsistent with the later Act.

Two cases illustrate this point. In *Vauxhall Estates Ltd* v *Liverpool Corporation* [1932] 1 KB 733 the Corporation of Liverpool proposed a scheme for the improvement of a certain area of the city. The Minister of Health confirmed the scheme in an order that incorporated the provisions of the Acquisition of Land (Assessment of Compensation) Act 1919 and the Housing Act 1925. These two Acts each provided a different scheme of compensation for compulsorily acquired land. The 1919 Act provided in s7(1):

'The provisions of the ... order by which the land is authorised to be acquired, or of any Act incorporated therewith, shall in relation to the matters dealt with in this Act, have effect subject to this Act, and so far as inconsistent with this Act those provisions shall ... not have effect.'

The question arose as to whether the compensation due to the appellants should be calculated in accordance with the 1919 Act or in accordance with the 1925 Act. The appellants argued that, because of s7(1) of the 1919 Act, it must be calculated in accordance with that Act. It was held that the compensation should be assessed in accordance with the later Act. Parliament had exercised its power of overriding the provisions of s7(1) of the 1919 Act by enacting in the later Act of 1925 a set of provisions totally inconsistent with those of the 1919 Act. As Avory J stated:

'We are asked to say that by a provision of the Act of 1919 the hands of Parliament were tied in such a way that it could not by any subsequent Act enact anything which was inconsistent with the provisions of the Act of 1919. It must be admitted that such a suggestion as that is inconsistent with the principle of the constitution of this country. Speaking for myself, I should certainly hold until the contrary were decided, that no Act of Parliament can effectively provide that no future Act shall interfere with its provisions.'

Similarly, in *Ellen Street Estates Ltd* v *Minister of Health* [1934] 1 KB 590, the material facts of which were identical to those in *Vauxhall Estates*, counsel for Ellen Street Estates Ltd argued that although the provisions of the 1919 Act could be repealed by express words in a later Act, they could not, because of s7(1), be repealed by implication by provisions in a later Act which were inconsistent with those in the 1919 Act.

It was held that the provisions of an earlier Act could always be repealed, by implication, by provisions in a later Act that were inconsistent with those in the earlier Act. Parliament could not, by a statement in an earlier Act, effectively provide that the provisions of that Act could not be repealed by implication by inconsistent provisions in a later Act. As Scrutton LJ observed:

'Parliament can alter an Act previously passed, and it can do so by repealing in terms the previous Act ... and it can do so in another way namely, by enacting a provision which is clearly inconsistent with the previous Act.'

Maugham LJ added that, in his view, the legislature could not bind itself as to the form of subsequent legislation, and it was impossible for Parliament to enact that in a subsequent statute dealing with the same subject–matter there could be no implied repeal. For the impact of European Union membership on the doctrine of implied repeal, see section 4.5 below.

The application of the doctrine of implied repeal is not automatic. As a number of recent cases illustrate the courts will have regard to the nature of the earlier statute, in particular its constitutional significance, before determining whether or not the doctrine applies. Essentially, if the earlier statute is regarded as being 'constitutional' in nature (ie it deals with fundamental aspects of the constitution or the relationship between the individual and the state) a later inconsistent statutory provision will not be read as impliedly repealing an earlier provision unless the later provision expressly provides that this was the intention of Parliament. In *Thoburn* v *Sunderland City Council; Hunt* v *Hackney London Borough Council; Harman and Another* v *Cornwall County Council; Collins* v *Sutton London Borough Council* (2002) The Times 22 February the court had to consider an argument that the Weights and Measures Act 1985 had impliedly repealed s2 of the European Communities Act 1972 in so far as the 1985 Act appeared to preserve the rights of retailers to sell fresh produce in imperial units as opposed to metric. The court rejected the contention that there was any inconsistency, hence the comments of Laws LJ on the suspension of the doctrine of implied repeal were, strictly speaking, obiter. They are none the less instructive. In his view the European Communities Act 1972 belonged to a category of 'constitutional' statutes that could not be impliedly repealed. As Laws LJ observed:

'The common law has in recent years allowed, or rather created, exceptions to the doctrine of implied repeal: a doctrine which was always the common law's own creature. There are now classes or types of legislative provision which cannot be repealed by mere implication. ... In the present state of its maturity the common law has come to recognise that there exist rights which should properly be classified as constitutional or fundamental. ... And from this a further insight follows. We should recognise a hierarchy of Acts of Parliament: as it were "ordinary" statutes and "constitutional" statutes. The two categories must be distinguished on a principled basis. In my opinion a constitutional statute is one which (a) conditions the legal relationship between citizen and state in some general, overarching manner, or (b) enlarges or diminishes the scope of what we would now regard as fundamental constitutional rights. (a) and (b) are of necessity closely related: it is difficult to think of an instance of (a) that is not also an instance of (b). The special status of constitutional statutes follows the special status of constitutional rights. Examples are the Magna Carta, the Bill of Rights 1689, the Act of Union, the Reform Acts which distributed and enlarged the franchise, the HRA, the Scotland Act 1998 and the Government of Wales Act 1998. The ECA [European Communities Act 1972] clearly belongs in this family. It incorporated the whole corpus of substantive Community rights and obligations, and gave overriding domestic effect to the judicial and administrative machinery of Community law. It may be there has never been a statute having such profound effects on so many dimensions of our daily lives. The ECA is, by force of the common law, a constitutional statute.

Ordinary statutes may be impliedly repealed. Constitutional statutes may not. For the repeal of a constitutional Act or the abrogation of a fundamental right to be effected by statute, the court would apply this test: is it shown that the legislature's actual – not imputed, constructive or presumed – intention was to effect the repeal or abrogation? I think the test could only be met by express words in the later statute, or by words so specific that the inference of an actual determination to effect the result contended for was irresistible. The ordinary rule of implied repeal does not satisfy this test. Accordingly, it has no application to constitutional statutes. ... A constitutional statute can only be repealed, or amended in a way which significantly affects its provisions touching fundamental rights or otherwise the relation between citizen and state, by unambiguous words on the face of the later statute.

This development of the common law regarding constitutional rights, and as I would say constitutional statutes, is highly beneficial. It gives us most of the benefits of a written constitution, in which fundamental rights are accorded special respect. But it preserves the sovereignty of the legislature and the flexibility of our uncodified constitution. It accepts the relation between legislative supremacy and fundamental rights is not fixed or brittle: rather the courts (in interpreting statutes, and now, applying the HRA) will pay more or less deference to the legislature, or other public decision-maker, according to the subject in hand. Nothing is plainer than that this benign development involves, as I have said, the recognition of the ECA as a constitutional statute.'

Practical and political limitations on the exercise of parliamentary sovereignty

Whatever lawyers may say about the legal effect of the doctrine of parliamentary sovereignty it does not operate in a political vacuum. There are clear practical limitations.

1. The United Kingdom has international obligations. Were Parliament to enact legislation contravening those obligations (eg removing diplomatic immunity, undermining human rights) action would be taken against the United Kingdom on the international plane. This could involve exclusion from international decision-making bodies. Such moves could also have adverse economic consequences in terms of trade barriers, boycotts and seizure of assets overseas. Failure to conform to the rulings of the European Court of Human Rights could, for example, result in expulsion from the Council of Europe: see further Chapter 9.

2. The United Kingdom Parliament could legislate for a foreign sovereign state, for example by banning smoking in restaurants in Turkey, but the legislation (even though technically valid) would have little effect, as the Turkish courts would ignore it. The same would apply if Parliament were to pass an Act reclaiming the territory of a former colony. As Sir Robert Megarry V-C explained at first instance in *Manuel* v *Attorney-General* (above):

   'I do not think that, as a matter of law, it makes any difference if [an] ... Act ... purports to apply outside the United Kingdom ... [or] ... to other countries. If that other country is a colony, the English courts will apply the Act even if the colony is in a state of revolt against the Crown and direct enforcement of the decision may be impossible: see *Madzimbamuto* v *Lardner-Burke*. ... [S]imilarly if the other country is a foreign state which has never been British. I do not think that any English court would or could declare the Act ultra vires and void. No doubt the Act would normally be ignored by the foreign state and would not be enforced by it, but that would not invalidate the Act in this country. Those who infringed it could not claim that it was void if proceedings within the jurisdiction were taken against them. Legal validity is one thing, enforceability is another. Parliament in fact legislates only for British subjects in this way; but if it also legislated for others, I do not see how the English courts could hold the statute void, however impossible it was to enforce it, and no matter how strong the diplomatic protests. I do not think that countries which were once colonies but have since been granted independence are in any different position. Plainly once statute granted independence to a country, the repeal of the statute will not make the country dependent once more; what is done is done, and is not undone by revoking the authority to do it.'

Section 27(8) of the Scotland Act 1998 expressly provides that the power of the Parliament of the United Kingdom to make laws for Scotland remains unaffected by the terms of the 1998 Act, but it is submitted that a convention will be recognised whereby Parliament at Westminster will not legislate for Scotland without the consent of the Scottish Parliament. It is also unlikely that any move would be made to abolish the Scottish Parliament without a clear electoral mandate to do so.

3. There is a convention that a government will put forward a legislative programme that broadly reflects the manifesto on which it was elected. The legislation thus presented to Parliament derives its legitimacy from the fact that it has been endorsed by a majority of the electorate (notwithstanding the shortcomings of the electoral process). The doctrine is subject to two important modifications. First, a government is expected and required to deal with situations that arise during its lifetime and some of these will not have been foreseeable at the time of the general election. Second, a government is not expected to mark time because it has carried out all its manifesto commitments. The corollary of this is that a government ought not to force through legislation for which it has no electoral mandate, although there is clearly no legal sanction to prevent this. The practical limitation over sovereignty in this regard will be the pressure of public opinion and political opposition, and the desire of a government party to be re-elected at the next general election. At a more dramatic level, legislation that is seen to be outrageous in the extent to which it contravenes notions of fairness etc is likely to provoke civil disorder and unrest.

4.5 EC law in the United Kingdom

The United Kingdom became a member of the European Communities with effect from 1 January 1973, by virtue of the Treaty of Accession 1972. Given the dualist nature of the United Kingdom's legal system it was necessary for the Treaty of Accession and the Community treaties to be incorporated into domestic law in order for them to have effect in the domestic courts. This was achieved by the European Communities Act 1972, as amended.

With the benefit of hindsight it might be said that what the politicians of the day, and most voters, thought that they were agreeing to was membership of an enlarged free trade area. It is clear that the true legal implications of membership were not grasped at the time, in particular the consequences for parliamentary sovereignty. The level playing field required for fair competition between manufacturers and suppliers in Member States brings with it many restraints that go beyond the prohibition of anti-competitive tariffs. The institutions of the European Union have turned their attentions to related matters such as conditions of working, equal opportunities, sex discrimination, pollution, etc. As will have been seen from Chapter 2, a central tenet of the European Union's philosophy is that EC law should apply to the same extent within each Member State. Inevitably, therefore, situations have arisen where the United Kingdom's domestic law has been found to be in conflict with the provision of EC law. Given the provisions of the European Communities Act 1972 (considered below), the courts have had to try and resolve these conflicts, constrained by the doctrine of parliamentary sovereignty on the one hand and the realities of EU membership on the other.

What the European Communities Act 1972 provides

Section 1 of the 1972 Act defines the Community treaties to which the Act relates and includes the treaties entered into by the Communities prior to 22 January 1972. Any subsequent treaties entered into by the Communities may be incorporated into United Kingdom law by Order in Council. Section 2(1) is arguably the most important provision of the Act in that it provides that:

> 'All such rights, powers, liabilities, obligations and restrictions from time to time created or arising by or under the treaties, and all such remedies and procedures from time to time provided for by or under the treaties, as in accordance with the treaties are without further enactment to be given legal effect or used in the United Kingdom shall be recognised and available in law, and be enforced, allowed and followed accordingly; and the expression enforceable Community right and similar expressions shall be read as referring to one to which this subsection applies.'

The effect of this subsection is that all the provisions of EC law which are, in accordance with EC law, intended to take direct effect in the United Kingdom, are given the force of law. This applies to EC law made both before and after the coming into force of the Act. Section 2(2) provides that where EC law requires legislative implementation in the United Kingdom, for example, directives, this may be achieved by means of delegated legislation.

Section 2(4) addresses the issue of conflict between domestic legislation and EC law by providing that:

> 'The provision that may be made under subsection (2) ... includes, subject to Schedule 2 to this Act, any such provision (of any such extent) as might be made by Act of Parliament, and any enactment passed or to be passed, other than one contained in this Part of this Act, shall be construed and have effect subject to the foregoing provisions of this section; but, except as may be provided by an Act passed after this Act, Schedule 2 shall have effect in connection with the powers conferred by this and the following sections of this Act to make Orders in Council and regulations.'

The 'foregoing provisions' for these purposes include s2(1), which states that directly applicable EC law shall have effect in the United Kingdom. Therefore, s2(4) seems to amount to a statement that United Kingdom Acts of Parliament shall be construed and have effect subject to directly applicable EC law.

Section 3(1) provides that, for the purposes of all legal proceedings, any question as to the meaning or effect of any of the treaties or as to the validity, meaning or effect of any Community instrument, shall be treated as a question of law (and if not referred to the European Court of Justice) be for determination as such in accordance with the principles laid down by the European Court of Justice.

4.6 EC law and United Kingdom sovereignty

Despite Lord Denning's words in *Bulmer* v *Bollinger* [1974] Ch 401, to the effect that:

> '... when we come to matters with a European element the [T]reaty is like an incoming tide. It flows into the estuaries and up the rivers. It cannot be held back ...'

there are several possible interpretations of s2(4) European Communities Act 1972.

It can be argued that it amounts to a statement that United Kingdom legislation will only take effect to the extent that it is consistent with EC law, however clearly it may appear from the United Kingdom legislation that it is intended to have effect notwithstanding any EC law to the contrary.

It is clear both from the EC Treaty and from statements made by the European Court of Justice, that the Community view is that EC law should prevail over the domestic law of Member States in all circumstances. The European Court of Justice, in *Costa* v *ENEL* [1964] CMLR 425, stated that accession to the European Communities has, as a corollary, the impossibility for the Member State to give preference to an unilateral and subsequent measure against a legal order accepted by them on a basis of reciprocity. In *Re Export Tax on Art Treasures (No 2)* [1972] CMLR 699 the European Court of Justice stated:

> 'The grant to the Community by the Member States of the rights and powers envisaged by the provisions of the Treaty implies in fact a definitive limitation of their sovereign powers over which no appeal to provisions of international law of any kind whatever can prevail.'

This makes it clear that, as far as the European Court of Justice is concerned, any United Kingdom constitutional law doctrine of the legislative sovereignty of Parliament is either 'in suspension' or has been abandoned in favour of a new legal order.

The approach of the European Court of Justice runs contrary to the traditional doctrine of implied repeal as enunciated in *Vauxhall Estates Ltd* v *Liverpool Corporation* [1932] 1 KB 733 and *Ellen Street Estates* v *Minister of Health* [1934] 1 KB 590. The strict traditionalist, who insists on the retention of the doctrine of implied repeal as set out in *Ellen Street Estates*, would refuse to give full effect to s2(4) as regards any post-1972 domestic legislation that was inconsistent with EC law, insisting that later United Kingdom legislation always, by implication, repeals earlier legislative provision with which it is inconsistent. Note that this contention was rejected by the court in *Thoburn* v *Sunderland City Council; Hunt* v *Hackney London Borough Council; Harman and Another* v *Cornwall County Council; Collins* v *Sutton London Borough Council* (above).

A third approach to s2(4) is to treat it as amounting to a rule of interpretation that there shall be a presumption that the United Kingdom Parliament, in passing legislation, intends to legislate consistently with EC law. This approach differs from the first since it allows that if the United Kingdom Parliament were to make it clear in an Act that it intended to legislate contrary to EC law, or that it intended legislation to take effect notwithstanding any provision of EC law to the contrary, then the United Kingdom legislation would prevail to the extent that it was in conflict with EC law. This is the approach that was favoured by the Court of Appeal in *Macarthys Ltd* v *Wendy Smith* [1979] 3 All ER 325. A man had been employed as a stockroom keeper at £60 per week. Subsequently a woman was employed in this position at £50 per week. She took the matter to an industrial tribunal on the grounds that this was contrary to law. Three main questions arose; first, was this arrangement contrary to the Equal Pay Act 1970 as amended by the Sex Discrimination Act 1975?; second, if it was not, was it contrary to art 119 of the Treaty of Rome (now art 141 EC Treaty) which provides: 'Each Member State shall … ensure and … maintain the application of the principle that men and women should receive equal pay for equal work'?; third, in the event of a conflict between the United Kingdom legislation and art 119 (now art 141 EC Treaty), which should prevail in the United Kingdom courts? The Employment Appeal Tribunal held that the 1970 Act provided Ms Smith with the right to equal pay where she had performed identical duties in succession to a male employee. The employers appealed to the Court of Appeal. It was held (per Lawton and Cumming-Bruce LJJ) that the Equal Pay Act 1970, as amended by the Sex Discrimination Act 1975, only required equal pay for men and women employed in like work contemporaneously, and thus afforded no protection for the female plaintiff in the present case. There was uncertainty, however, as to whether or not art 119 (now art 141 EC Treaty) covered the situation where a woman was employed on certain work that had previously been performed by a man. Since the proper interpretation of art 119 (now art 141 EC Treaty) was uncertain, the matter was referred to the European Court of Justice under art 234 EC Treaty (formerly art 177) for a preliminary ruling.

It is interesting to note the views that were expressed by Lord Denning MR regarding the primacy of EC law:

'It is unnecessary, however, for these courts to wait until all that procedure has been gone through. Under ss2(1) and (4) of the European Communities Act 1972 the principles laid down in the Treaty are without further enactment to be given legal effect in the United Kingdom; and have priority over any enactment passed or to be passed by our Parliament.

So we are entitled and I think bound to look at art 119 [now art 141 EC Treaty] ... because it is directly applicable here; and also any directive which is directly applicable here: see *Van Duyn* v *Home Office (No 2)*. We should, I think, look to see what those provisions require about equal pay for men and women. Then we should look at our own legislation on the point, giving it, of course, full faith and credit, assuming that it does fully comply with the obligation under the Treaty. In construing our statute, we are entitled to look to the Treaty as an aid to its construction, but not only as an aid but as an overriding force. If on close investigation it should appear that our legislation is deficient or is inconsistent with [EC law] by some oversight of our draftsmen then it is our bounden duty to give priority to [EC law]. Such is the result of ss2(1) and (4) of the European Communities Act 1972 ... I pause here, however, to make one observation on a constitutional point. Thus far I have assumed that our Parliament, whenever it passes legislation, intends to fulfil its obligations under the Treaty. If the time should come when our Parliament deliberately passes an Act with the intention of repudiating the Treaty or any provision in it or intentionally of acting inconsistently with it and says so in express terms then I should have thought that it would be the duty of our courts to follow the statute of our Parliament. I do not however envisage any such situation.'

Thus Lord Denning put forward the view that if Parliament in an Act stated an express intention to legislate contrary to EC law or notwithstanding EC law, then in that one situation the United Kingdom court would give preference to the United Kingdom legislation over the EC law. The other members of the court expressed the same view, Lawton LJ saying:

'... I can see nothing in this case which infringes the sovereignty of Parliament ... Parliament by its own act in the exercise of its sovereign powers has enacted and followed in the United Kingdom (s1(1) European Communities Act 1972) and that any enactment passed or to be passed ... shall be construed and have effect subject to (s2 in accordance with s2(4) of the Act). Parliament's recognition of [EC law] and the jurisdiction of the European Court of Justice by one enactment can be withdrawn by another. There is nothing in the Equal Pay Act 1970 as amended by the Sex Discrimination Act 1975, to indicate that Parliament intended to amend the European Communities Act 1972, or to limit its application ...'

On the reference under art 177 (now art 234), the European Court of Justice ruled that art 119 (now art 141 EC Treaty) did not require contemporaneous employment (*Macarthys Ltd* v *Smith* [1980] ECR 1275), and the case was referred back to the Court of Appeal for the implementation of this interpretation: *Macarthys Ltd* v *Smith* [1981] QB 180. Although his comments were obiter Lord Denning took the opportunity afforded by the second hearing to state the following view:

'Art 119 [now art 141 EC Treaty] now takes priority over our English statute ... [EC law] is now part of our law; and, whenever there is any inconsistency, [EC law] has priority. It is not supplanting English law. It is part of our law which overrides any other part which is inconsistent with it.'

This 'rule of construction' approach, whereby domestic law is always interpreted in a manner that ensures its compliance with EC law, amounts to a retention of the doctrine of express repeal of earlier law by later legislation, but involves the abandonment of the doctrine of implied repeal as far as EC law is concerned. In this approach it is neither consistent with the traditional United Kingdom doctrine of the sovereignty of Parliament, nor with the Community doctrine of the supremacy of EC law over national law.

The matter was considered further by the House of Lords in *Garland* v *British Rail Engineering Ltd* [1983] 2 AC 751. The appellant was a female employee of the respondent company. Employees enjoyed (ex gratia) free travel on British Rail. Upon retirement male employees continued to enjoy this benefit for themselves and their families. In the case of retiring female employees, the benefit did not extend to their families. The appellant contended that this discrimination was not permitted by s6(4) of the Sex Discrimination Act 1964, and was in breach of art 119 (now art 141 EC Treaty). The complaint was dismissed by an Industrial Tribunal, allowed on appeal to the Employment Appeal Tribunal, and the respondent employers appealed successfully to the Court of Appeal. On appeal to the House of Lords, the issue was referred to the European Court of Justice, which held that the discrimination was in breach of art 119 (now art 141 EC Treaty), which was directly applicable where a domestic court found such discrimination to exist. On reference back to the House of Lords the decision of the Employment Appeal Tribunal was restored. Lord Diplock observed that:

> '... it is a principle of construction of United Kingdom statutes, now too well established to call for citation of authority, that the words of a statute passed after the Treaty has been signed and dealing with the subject matter of the international obligation of the United Kingdom, are to be construed, if they are reasonably capable of bearing such a meaning, as intended to carry out the obligation, and not to be inconsistent with it. A fortiori is this the case where the Treaty obligation arises under one of the Community treaties to which s2 of the European Communities Act 1972 applies ...'

As will have been seen in Chapter 2, the growing influence of the doctrine of indirect effect means that domestic courts are now expected to interpret domestic law to achieve conformity with EC law, regardless of whether the measure in question is directly applicable or of direct effect: see again *Von Colson* v *Land Nordrhein-Westfalen* [1984] ECR 1891, *Harz* v *Deutsche Tradex GmbH* [1984] ECR 1921 and *Marleasing SA* v *La Comercial Internacional de Alimentacion SA* [1992] 1 CMLR 305. These decisions have had some influence on the courts of the United Kingdom, as evidenced by their willingness to interpret domestic legislation to ensure compliance with directives, even if this means straining the natural language of the domestic law: see further *Pickstone* v *Freemans plc* [1989] 1 AC 66; *Lister* v *Forth Dry Dock & Engineering Co. Ltd* [1990] 1 AC 546; and *Webb* v *EMO Air Cargo Ltd (UK) (No 2)* [1995] 1 WLR 1454. Where the United Kingdom courts have drawn the line is in refusing to give retrospective effect to domestic law enacted to give effect to a directive, in the absence of clear evidence that Parliament intended the domestic law to operate retrospectively: see *Duke* v *GEC Reliance Ltd* [1988] 1 All ER 626.

A situation where there is an irreconcilable conflict between domestic law and EC law, in the sense that there has been a deliberate attempt by the United Kingdom legislature to repudiate its international obligations under EC law, may seem a remote possibility, but where a conflict arises that cannot be resolved by means of an 'elastic' approach to the interpretation of domestic law to ensure compliance, the United Kingdom courts will have little option but to refer the matter to the European Court of Justice under art 234 EC Treaty (formerly art 177). Pending the consideration of the reference by the European Court of Justice, questions arise as to the legal position of those litigants who claim that their rights under EC law are being infringed by the courts giving effect to domestic law. If domestic law is applied until the European Court of Justice rules that it is in conflict with the proper application of EC law, the litigant may have suffered financial loss. If such loss is to be prevented, the operation of the domestic law will have to be suspended by the domestic court pending the European Court of Justice's ruling.

Such a situation arose in *R v Secretary of State for Transport, ex parte Factortame Ltd (No 2)* [1990] 3 WLR 818. Fishing quotas were introduced by the EC to prevent over-fishing. The United Kingdom Parliament enacted the Merchant Shipping Act 1988 (Part II) to protect British fishing interests by restricting the number of vessels whose catch could be counted against the British quota. The Secretary of State issued regulations under the Act that required any vessel wishing to fish as part of the British fleet to be registered under the 1988 Act. Registration was contingent upon a vessel's owner being a British citizen or domiciled in Britain. In the case of companies, the shareholders would have to meet these requirements. The applicants were British registered companies operating fishing vessels in British waters. These companies now found it impossible to obtain registration because their shareholders and directors were Spanish. The applicants contended that the regulations effectively prevented them from exercising their rights under EC law to fish as part of the British fleet. The Secretary of State contended that EC law did not prevent the United Kingdom from introducing domestic legislation determining which companies where 'British nationals' and which were not.

The applicants sought judicial review of the minister's decision that their registration should cease; the minister's determination that they were no longer 'British' ships; and the relevant parts of the Act and regulations that would have the effect of preventing them from fishing. In terms of remedies the applicants sought a declaration that the minister's decision should not take effect because of its inconsistency with EC law; an order of prohibition to prevent the minister from regarding the ships as de-registered; damages under s35 of the Supreme Court Act 1981; and an interim injunction suspending the operation of the legislation pending the ruling of the European Court of Justice.

As regards the interpretation of EC law, the Divisional Court requested a preliminary ruling under art 234 (formerly art 177) so that the questions relating to the applicant's rights could be resolved. Pending that ruling, the court granted the applicants interim relief in the form of an injunction to suspend the operation of the legislation by restraining the minister from enforcing it, thus enabling the applicants to continue fishing. The Secretary of State sought to challenge the order for interim relief, which was set aside by the Court of Appeal. On appeal the House of Lords held that domestic courts had no power to grant interim relief to prevent the operation of a statute passed by Parliament, unless it could be shown that there was some overriding principle of EC law which provided that member states must provide such relief. The question of whether such a principle existed was referred to the European Court of Justice under art 234 EC Treaty.

In responding to the House of Lords' reference, the European Court of Justice held that EC law required the courts of member states to give effect to the directly enforceable provision of EC law, such EC laws rendering any conflicting national law inapplicable. A court that would grant interim relief, but for a rule of domestic law, should set aside that rule of domestic law in favour of observing EC law. On the reference back, the House of Lords held that, in determining whether interim relief by way of an injunction should be granted, the determining factor should not be the availability of damages as a remedy, but the balance of convenience, taking into account the importance of upholding duly enacted laws. Damages are not available against a public body exercising its powers in good faith. The court should not restrain a public authority from enforcing an apparently valid law unless it is satisfied, having regard to all the circumstances, that the challenge to the validity of the law is prima facie so firmly based as to justify so exceptional a course being taken. On the significance of this litigation, Lord Bridge observed (at p857):

'Some public comments on the decision of the European Court of Justice, affirming the jurisdiction of the courts of member states to override national legislation if necessary to enable interim relief to be granted in protection of rights under [EC law], have suggested that this was a novel and dangerous invasion by a Community institution of the sovereignty of the United Kingdom Parliament. But such comments are based on a misconception. If the supremacy within the European Community of [EC law] over the national law of member states was not always inherent in the EEC Treaty (Cmnd 5179–11) it was certainly well established in the jurisprudence of the European Court of Justice long before the United Kingdom joined the Community. Thus, whatever limitation of its sovereignty Parliament accepted when it enacted the European Communities Act 1972 was entirely voluntary. Under the terms of the Act of 1972 it has always been clear that it was the duty of a United Kingdom court, when delivering final judgment, to override any rule of national law found to be in conflict with any directly enforceable rule of [EC law]. Similarly, when decisions of the European Court of Justice have exposed areas of United Kingdom statute law which failed to implement Council directives, Parliament has always loyally accepted the obligation to make appropriate and prompt amendments. Thus there is nothing in any way novel in according supremacy to rules of [EC law] in those areas to which they apply and to insist that, in the protection of rights under [EC law], national courts must not be inhibited by rules of national law from granting interim relief in appropriate cases is no more than a logical recognition of that supremacy.'

The limits of applicability

It should be obvious from the foregoing that domestic courts will only have to apply EC law in the form of treaty provisions, regulations or directives where it is relevant to the issue that is the subject of the litigation. The more subtle question of whether the fundamental principles of EC law, such a proportionality, equal treatment and non-discrimination are of general application in domestic law was considered by the Divisional Court in *R* v *MAFF ex parte First City Trading and Others* [1997] 1 CMLR 250. Following the ban placed on the export of British beef by the European Commission, the Ministry of Agriculture Food and Fisheries (MAFF) had introduced a scheme of financial aid – the Slaughtering Industry (Emergency Aid) Scheme 1996 – to assist exporters who had been adversely affected. The applicants sought, unsuccessfully, to challenge the legality of the scheme on the basis that it discriminated against those exporters who lacked their own slaughtering and cutting up facilities, and was thus in breach of fundamental principles of EC law, namely the principles of equal treatment and non-discrimination. In dismissing the application Laws J observed that the fundamental principles of EC law referred to had been developed by the European Court of Justice in the course of deciding cases raising issues regarding the interpretation of the key Community treaties. Hence they were only relevant where an issue of EC law was under consideration. EC law might be under consideration where a Member State took action required by EC law, or acted under domestic law in an area that fell within the scope of the EC law. The scheme in question, however, had not been implemented at the behest of the European Community and the United Kingdom government had not had to seek the permission of the European Community prior to its implementation. The fact that the scheme had been introduced in response to action taken by the European Commission was irrelevant. Hence the principles evolved through the case law of the European Court of Justice were not binding upon a domestic court assessing the legality of the scheme.

4.7 Conclusion

Has Parliament retained sovereignty to the extent that it can enact legislation that prevails over EC law? In *Stoke-on-Trent City Council* v *B & Q plc* [1991] 2 WLR 42 Hoffmann J expressed the view that, subject to Parliament's 'undoubted but probably theoretical right to withdraw from the Community altogether', membership of the EC meant that Parliament had surrendered its sovereign right to legislate contrary to the provisions of the EC Treaty. Lord Diplock, in *Garland* v *British Rail Engineering Ltd* (above), side-stepped this key question, expressing the view that:

> 'The instant appeal does not present an appropriate occasion to consider whether, having regard to the express direction as to the construction of enactments to be passed which is contained in s2(4), anything short of an express positive statement in an Act of Parliament

passed after 1 January, 1973, that a particular provision is intended to be made in breach of an obligation assumed by the United Kingdom under a Community treaty, would justify a [domestic] court in construing that provision in a manner inconsistent with a Community treaty obligation of the United Kingdom, however wide a departure from the prima facie meaning of the language of the provision might be needed in order to achieve consistency.'

In *Thoburn* v *Sunderland City Council; Hunt* v *Hackney London Borough Council; Harman and Another* v *Cornwall County Council; Collins* v *Sutton London Borough Council* (above) Laws LJ considered a submission by counsel for one of the respondent local authorities to the effect that the legislative and judicial institutions of the EU could set limits to the power of the United Kingdom Parliament to make laws regulating the legal relationship between the EU and the United Kingdom. Rejecting this contention, he observed:

'... [this submission forgets] ... the constitutional place in our law of the rule that Parliament cannot bind its successors, which is the engine of the doctrine of implied repeal. Here is [the] argument's bare logic. (1) The ECA [European Communities Act 1972] incorporated the law of the EU into the law of England. (2) The law of the EU includes the entrenchment of its own supremacy as an autonomous legal order, and the prohibition of its abrogation by the Member States: *Van Gend en Loos* and *Costa* v *ENEL*. Therefore (3) that entrenchment, and that prohibition, are thereby constituted part of the law of England. The flaw is in step (3). It proceeds on the assumption that the incorporation of EU law effected by the ECA (step (1)) must have included not only the whole corpus of European law upon substantive matters such as (by way of example) the free movement of goods and services, but also any jurisprudence of the Court of Justice, or other rule of Community law, which purports to touch the constitutional preconditions upon which the sovereign legislative power belonging to a Member State may be exercised.

Whatever may be the position elsewhere, the law of England disallows any such assumption. Parliament cannot bind its successors by stipulating against repeal, wholly or partly, of the ECA. It cannot stipulate as to the manner and form of any subsequent legislation. It cannot stipulate against implied repeal any more than it can stipulate against express repeal. Thus there is nothing in the ECA which allows the Court of Justice, or any other institutions of the EU, to touch or qualify the conditions of Parliament's legislative supremacy in the United Kingdom. Not because the legislature chose not to allow it; because by our law it could not allow it. That being so, the legislative and judicial institutions of the EU cannot intrude upon those conditions. The British Parliament has not the authority to authorise any such thing. Being sovereign, it cannot abandon its sovereignty. Accordingly there are no circumstances in which the jurisprudence of the Court of Justice can elevate Community law to a status within the corpus of English domestic law to which it could not aspire by any route of English law itself. This is, of course, the traditional doctrine of sovereignty. If is to be modified, it certainly cannot be done by the incorporation of external texts. The conditions of Parliament's legislative supremacy in the United Kingdom necessarily remain in the United Kingdom's hands. But the traditional doctrine has in my judgment been modified. It has been done by the common law, wholly consistently with constitutional principle.'

The enacting of the European Communities Act 1972 should, therefore, be seen as an exercise of sovereignty. True, it provides for the direct applicability of EC law in the United Kingdom and the enforceability of rights arising under EC law before United Kingdom courts. This apparent forfeiture of sovereignty is, in reality, limited and partial. The European Communities Act 1972 is not entrenched. Parliament can, in theory, repeal the Act at any time and thus regain its full supremacy as a sovereign legislature.

With the passage of time, however, this regaining of sovereignty becomes more theoretical and less practical. The political realities of the situation will dictate that the greater the degree of integration in terms of economic, monetary and commercial union, the more difficult it will be for any United Kingdom government to extricate itself from the European Union. As successive generations grow up not having known anything of life prior to membership, it may be unlikely that any prospective United Kingdom government would receive a mandate for withdrawal. Monetary union in particular marks something of a political and economic 'point of no return'.

5

The Electoral System

5.1 Political parties in the United Kingdom

The origin of the Conservative and Liberal Parties

During the constitutional conflicts of the seventeenth century there emerged in Parliament two main groups: the Royalist or Court group (Tories); the Parliamentary or Country group (Whigs). These names were retained throughout the eighteenth century but group organisation in Parliament in the eighteenth and early nineteenth centuries consisted of little more than informal meetings. The late eighteenth century saw the emergence of whips to organise MPs for voting purposes, and bitter controversies over the 1832 Reform Bill led to a hardening of party lines. Following Sir Robert Peel's declaration in his 1834 election address that the Tory policy was to conserve all that was good in existing institutions, the Tory Party became generally known as the Conservative Party. The repeal of the Corn Laws in 1845 split the Conservative Party. One group, the Protectionists, led by Disraeli, opposed the repeal, and another, the Peelites, supported Peel's free trade policy. The Peelites gradually merged with the Whigs and Radicals during the 1850s and 1860s to form the new Liberal Party. The Reform Act 1832 widened the franchise considerably. After 1832 the political clubs, particularly the Tory Carlton Club and the Whig Reform Club, became centres of party loyalties. Various local Registration Societies were also formed after 1832 to persuade new voters to support particular party candidates. The further extension of the franchise in 1867 led to the main developments in local party organisation outside Parliament. With a larger electorate, the need arose for machinery to distribute party propaganda and the national organisations of the Liberal and Conservative Parties both date from this period.

The origins of the Labour Party

At the beginning of the nineteenth century, in an attempt to secure working class representation in Parliament, the Labour Representations Committee was formed by an alliance between various trade unions and socialist societies. In 1906 the name of the Labour Representation Committee was changed to the Labour Party. By 1922, when 142 Labour members were returned to Parliament, the Labour Party had replaced the Liberals as one of the two major parties. In the early 1980s, during a period of much internal strife within the Labour Party concerning its future policy directions, a group of MPs broke away to form a new centre-ground Social Democratic Party (SDP). With the election of Tony Blair as leader, the Labour Party has increasingly been marketed as 'New Labour', a party of the centre left, although for the time being it retains its long standing name.

The origins of the Liberal Democratic Party

In 1988, following the demise of the SDP led by Dr David Owen, the bulk of its members agreed to merge with the Liberal Party to form a new centre party, the Liberal Democrats.

Other parties

The other parties of any importance are, on the whole, parties whose support is concentrated in some particular geographical area of the British Isles, or whose supporters have come together on some single specific issue. Thus the Scottish Nationalist Party (SNP) and Plaid Cymru (Welsh Nationalist Party) command some support in Scotland and Wales respectively. In Northern Ireland the Official Unionist Party and the Ulster Unionist Party are both predominantly Protestant and in favour of Northern Ireland continuing as a part of the United Kingdom. The Social Democratic and Labour Party is Roman Catholic-based and favours, at the very least, reforms which would give the Roman Catholics in Northern Ireland a greater say in government affairs. In the 1997 general election, which saw a record number of candidates putting themselves forward, the issue of the United Kingdom's relationship with Europe gave rise to the emergence of the Referendum Party, fielding 543 candidates, and the UK Independence Party with 194 candidates. Independent MPs have almost disappeared from the political landscape, given the difficulty of mounting a campaign without party backing, but the election of the former BBC journalist Martin Bell to represent the constituency of Tatton in the 1997 general election campaign is a recent exception to this trend. Both the Labour Party and the Liberal Democrats agreed not to field candidates against him so that the voters would have a straight choice between Bell and the incumbent Conservative MP Neil Hamilton, who was, at the time, the subject of allegations of having received corrupt payments whilst an MP. In the event, Bell emerged with a majority of 7,000, compared with a Conservative majority of 12,000 at the 1992 election.

Registration under the Registration of Political Parties Act 1998

The Registration of Political Parties Act 1998 was enacted primarily to allow political parties to register their names and emblems so as to eliminate the use of potentially confusing party names by rival candidates at elections. The main provisions of the 1998 Act relating to registration have since been repealed and re-enacted as Part II of the Political Parties, Elections and Referendums Act 2000. Registration under the 2000 Act has been made a prerequisite for any political party seeking to play any significant role in contesting national, regional, local and European elections. In order to submit a valid nomination at a relevant election, a candidate must be standing for election in the name of a qualifying registered party; be a candidate who does not purport to represent any party (ie an independent candidate, or one not indicating any party name); or be a qualifying registered party, where the election is one for which registered parties may be nominated (ie where the 'party list' system is in operation). Under s23 the register of political parties maintained by the registrar of companies under the Registration of Political Parties Act 1998, is replaced by the new registers maintained by the Electoral Commission.

Certain office holders must be listed in the registry entry: these include a person registered as the party's leader; a person registered as the party's nominating officer; and a person registered as the party's treasurer. The person registered as a party's nominating officer must be the person having responsibility for the arrangements for the submission, by representatives of the party, of lists of candidates for the purpose of elections. The person registered as a party's treasurer is responsible for compliance with the accounting and reporting regime laid down in the Political Parties, Elections and Referendums Act 2000. A further requirement of registration, under s26, is that a party must show that it has adopted a scheme setting out the arrangements for regulating the financial affairs of the party for the purposes of the Act.

The technical requirements regarding registration are provided for by s28 and Pt I of Sch 4. In particular, the Act provides measures designed to prevent parties registering names similar to other parties that might cause confusion amongst voters. At the 1997 general election there were candidates standing for 'New Labour', 'Literal Democrats' and the 'Conversative Party'. Where the contest in a constituency is evenly balanced between candidates of the mainstream parties, the effect of votes being cast in error for independent candidates seeking to cause confusion can be significant. Similarly, the Commission can refuse to register offensive or inappropriate names. The registration may also encompass up to three emblems to be used by the party on ballot papers. The right to have party political broadcasts carried by broadcasters is limited to registered political parties by s37. Parties have to be registered if they are to submit lists for the additional member aspect of elections to the Scottish Parliament, Welsh National Assembly, the Assembly for London and the elections to the European Parliament.

By March 1999 almost 50 parties had registered in the run-up to the European Parliament elections of that year. Note that the Conservative Party was unsuccessful in its attempts to prevent disaffected Conservative MEPs registering a party with the title 'Pro-Euro Conservative Party'.

The funding of political parties

Following the two general elections of 1974, and the consequent strain placed on the finances of the major parties, the Houghton Committee investigated the issue of state funding for political parties and recommended a scheme based upon exchequer grants, the size of which would reflect the electoral support for a party at the previous general election (see Cmnd 6601, 1976). Its proposals were, however, not implemented. The topic raises two issues of constitutional significance. The first is the extent to which the source of party political funding should be disclosed. The second is the paradox whereby constituency related expenditure for parliamentary elections is closely controlled and scrutinised, whilst the spending on national campaigns is unregulated. In theory the party with the largest budget can mount the most effective campaign and thereby increase its chances of election, although the May 1997 general election campaign, during which the Conservative Party spent far more than the Labour Party, proves that money is not the only factor.

The danger is that if political parties accept large donations from any private source, suspicions will be aroused that some influence must be acquired in the process. The absence of any state funding exacerbates the problem, leaving parties at the mercy of private donors. The more egalitarian proponents of state funding also point out that it could be used to redress the imbalance in resources enjoyed by the various parties.

Proposals for state funding, on the other hand, do raise a number of problems, not least that it is MPs themselves who will be able to determine the level of support that the taxpayer is to provide for their own parties. Further, if funding were to be based on the number of seats contested, controversy would inevitably be caused by funds being given to fringe and extremist groups. Even if direct funding by way of voluntary contribution is prohibited, there may be other less obvious ways in which support can be afforded, such as by the loan of facilities, or favourable terms being offered in commercial transactions.

In October 1998 the Committee on Standards in Public Life (Neill Committee) published its findings in its report *Reform of Party Funding in the United Kingdom.* That inquiry into party funding was prompted by growing concern about:

1. the extent to which those willing to make large financial donations to political parties appeared to be able to buy influence and status (by way of honours); and
2. the effect on the democratic process of parties formed to fight on single issues, such as opposition to further European integration.

The Committee also carried out its investigations conscious of the changing political landscape, with moves towards devolution and regionalism, possible reforms of the voting system, and a possible increase in the use of referendums to secure political mandates on key issues. The Committee was concerned about what it saw as an escalating 'arms race' in election expenditure between the two main political parties, thus increasing their reliance on major donors. Overall, it saw the purpose of its proposals as being to introduce greater openness regarding the sources and use of party funds; to encourage greater public confidence that individuals and organisations are not buying influence with political parties; and to encourage individual parties to seek out many more small to medium-sized donations to their funds. Whilst the report sided against the idea of the state being obliged for the indefinite future to provide financial support for the political parties, it did recommend the establishment of a Policy Development Fund (see now s12 of the Political Parties, Elections and Referendums Act 2000).

Reflecting the concerns expressed by the Neill Committee, Part III of the Political Parties, Elections and Referendums Act 2000 lays down various accounting requirements whereby the treasurer of a registered party must keep proper records of the party's finances, and must prepare a statement of accounts in respect of each financial year. Any party with income or expenditure in excess of £250,000 pa must have its accounts audited within six months of the end of the financial year. A statement of account must be submitted to the Electoral Commission annually.

The issue of donations to party funds, and the extent to which such donations might be made to exercise influence over party policy, has been a feature of the political landscape in recent years. The 2000 Act seeks to introduce a regime that ensures greater accountability and transparency as regards such donations. A donation for these purposes includes (inter alia) any gift to a party of money or other property; any sponsorship; any subscription or other fee paid for affiliation to, or membership of, the party; any money spent (otherwise than by or on behalf of the party) in paying any expenses incurred directly or indirectly by the party; any money lent to the party otherwise than on commercial terms; and the provision otherwise than on commercial terms of any property, services or facilities for the use or benefit of the party (including the services of any person). Single donations of less than £200 in any financial year fall outside the scope of these restrictions. A registered political party may only accept donations from individuals who are registered as voters in the United Kingdom (donations cannot be accepted if they are anonymous), or from companies registered in the United Kingdom. The

Commission may order the forfeiture of donations received in circumstances where the requirements of the Act are not met. Sections 62–69 of the Act provide for a reporting regime as regards donations received by registered parties. Quarterly reports have to be provided detailing donations in excess of £5,000, along with information about the donor. During the run-up to a general election more regular (ie weekly) reports may be required.

Under ss139 and 140 directors proposing that their companies should make donations to political parties or organisations for political purposes in excess of £200 are required to seek the approval of the company in a general meeting. Any such payments must be disclosed in the relevant directors' annual report.

5.2 The Electoral Commission

Part I of the Political Parties, Elections and Referendums Act 2000 establishes the Electoral Commission (the Commission) and the Speaker's Committee. The Commission comprises between five and nine members referred to as 'Electoral Commissioners' appointed by the Queen. The power of appointment is exercisable on an Address from the House of Commons (s3(1)), and no motion shall be made for such an Address except with the agreement of the Speaker of the House of Commons, and after consultation with the registered leader of each registered party to which two or more Members of the House of Commons then belong. Members are appointed for up to ten years. Members of registered parties and donors to party funds are not eligible for appointment. An Electoral Commissioner may be removed from office by the Queen in pursuance of an Address from the House of Commons. Additional Deputy Electoral Commissioners may be appointed for the sole purpose of serving on electoral boundary committees (see below).

By virtue of s5 the Commission is placed under a duty, following each election or referendum to which the Act applies, to publish a report on the administration of the election or referendum. The Commission is also required, under s6, to keep under review, and from time to time submit reports to the Secretary of State on, matters relating to local, regional and national elections; referendums; the redistribution of seats at parliamentary elections; the registration of political parties; the regulation of their income and expenditure; and political advertising in the broadcast and other electronic media. The Commission may be required to conduct reviews into specific aspects of the electoral process as determined by the Secretary of State.

Sections 7–9 provide for the Commission to be consulted on any proposed changes to certain aspects of electoral law; for certain powers to be exercisable only with the recommendation of the Commission; and for the involvement of the Commission in changes to electoral procedures, such as the pilot scheme instituted under s10(1) of the Representation of the People Act 2000.

The Commission may, at the request of any relevant body, provide the body with advice and assistance as regards any matter in which the Commission has the relevant skill and experience (s10). Under s11 broadcasters are required to have regard to the views of the Commission as regards party political broadcasts. Under s104 of the Act the Commission is required to consider the wording of any proposed referendum question, and to publish a statement of its views as to the intelligibility of that question.

A duty to promote public awareness of current national and local electoral systems in the United Kingdom, and any such pending systems, together with matters connected with any such existing or pending systems as the Commission may determine, is placed on the Commission by s13. The Commission is also given, by virtue of s145, the general function of monitoring compliance with the financial regimes regarding funding and expenditure introduced by the 2000 Act. These supervisory functions are underpinned by the granting to the Commission of additional powers to inspect records and documents of political parties and other relevant organisations for evidence relating to income and expenditure.

The role of the Speaker's Committee is to oversee the operation of the Commission, both in terms of its use of resources and in terms of approving the Commission's 'five-year plan': see further Sch 1. The Committee is chaired by the Speaker of the House of Commons; the Chairman of the Home Affairs Select Committee of the House of Commons; the Secretary of State for the Home Department (whether or not a Member of the House of Commons); a Member of the House of Commons who is a Minister of the Crown with responsibilities in relation to local government (appointed by the Prime Minister); and five Members of the House of Commons who are not Ministers of the Crown (appointed by the Speaker). Under Sch 2 the Committee is required to report annually to the House of Commons on the exercise by the Committee of its functions. Under s15(2) the Speaker's Committee may determine, in liaison with the Commission, the number of Deputy Electoral Commissioners to be appointed.

Section 4 of the Act provides for the creation of a Parliamentary Parties Panel, comprising representatives of qualifying parties. The Panel has the function of submitting representations or information to the Commission about such matters affecting political parties as the Panel thinks fit. Each qualifying party is represented on the Panel by a person appointed to it by the treasurer of the party: s4(4). For these purposes, a qualifying party is a registered party with at least two MPs.

5.3 Constituencies

The electoral system that operates in respect of parliamentary elections to the House of Commons is based on the constituency model. The United Kingdom is divided into 659 constituencies, each returning one Member of Parliament elected on the basis of having secured the largest number of votes cast by the registered electors in the constituency. Although the Speaker of the House of Commons is a Member of

Parliament he, or she, is normally returned unopposed, at least by the major parties. The theory is that Members of Parliament hold office as representatives of the voters in their constituencies, thus ensuring that voters have a voice in the legislature.

The delimitation of constituency boundaries

Under the House of Commons (Redistribution of Seats) Acts 1949 and 1958, four permanent Boundary Commissions, for England, Wales, Scotland and Northern Ireland, were created to undertake a review of constituencies at intervals of not less than ten or more than 15 years, and report to the Secretary of State any redistribution of seats necessary to ensure, as far as possible, equal electorates. The increase in the number of constituencies from 651 to 659 followed the report of the Boundary Commission, which was approved by the House of Commons in June 1995.

Under ss16–20 of the Political Parties, Elections and Referendums Act 2000 the functions of the various Boundary Commissions have been transferred to the Electoral Commission, which is required by s14 to establish four Boundary Committees, one each for England, Scotland, Wales and Northern Ireland. Each Committee comprises between two and four members – only an Electoral Commissioner or a deputy Electoral Commissioner may be appointed a member of a Boundary Committee.

The principle underlying the redistribution of seats

As a basic principle each constituency should have the same number of voters within it to ensure that all votes have equal value. However, a Boundary Committee is entitled to depart from the strict application of this principle if special geographical considerations, including in particular the size, shape and accessibility of a constituency, so require. Parliamentary constituencies should, as far as practicable, follow local government boundaries and local ties and any inconvenience caused by a proposed alteration must also be considered. The ideal size for each constituency is found by dividing the total electorate in each Committee area by the number of constituencies in that area. Because of population distribution as in, for example, the Highlands of Scotland or rural Wales, this formula may be departed from. A constituency in the Scottish Highlands would be so large as to be unworkable if constituencies were arranged on the equal average population basis. In practice this means that an individual vote in Scotland or Wales is more powerful than an individual vote in other parts of the United Kingdom, as (because of the smaller constituency population) fewer votes are required to elect a Member. In other words, the weight which a vote carries varies according to where the voter lives. The essence of democracy is the principle of 'one man, one vote, one value', but in the United Kingdom it appears that, since not all votes have the same value, some electors are more equal than others. Section 86 of the Scotland Act 1998 does provide for a reduction in the number of Scottish constituencies consequent upon the introduction of the Scottish Parliament. This should lead in due course to a more balanced allocation of parliamentary seats for the Westminster Parliament.

If a Boundary Committee determines that changes are necessary notice must be given in the constituencies affected and representations must be invited. A local inquiry may also have to be held. The Committee must then submit its report to the Secretary of State, who must lay it before Parliament together with a draft Order in Council for giving effect, with or without modifications, to its recommendations. The draft Order must then be approved by resolutions of each House before the final Order is made by the Queen in Council.

Challenging the redistribution of constituencies

Those involved in the redistribution of parliamentary constituencies, such as the Boundary Committee and the Home Secretary, are, in theory, subject to control by the courts if they act unlawfully in the discharge of their functions. In practice, litigants were largely unsuccessful in challenging decisions of the Boundary Commissioners. In *Harper* v *Secretary of State for the Home Department* [1955] 1 Ch 238 the court rejected the contention that it had any jurisdiction to comment on the validity of Commissioners' reports placed before Parliament by the Home Secretary in the form of a draft Order. Lord Evershed MR commented that, in his view, if the courts were competent to pass judgment on the reports there might be no end to the process of challenge.

There are clearly constitutional difficulties in delaying any legal challenge to the process until the report is before Parliament. Hence in the most significant case to come before the courts on this issue, *R* v *Boundary Commission for England, ex parte Foot* [1983] QB 600, the Labour Party leader, who believed that the Commission had acted unreasonably in compiling its report, sought an order to prevent the report being put before Parliament. On the facts the Court of Appeal felt there was insufficient evidence to show that in compiling its report the Commission had failed to take into account relevant considerations, or conversely had taken into account irrelevant considerations.

5.4 The franchise

The law relating to the franchise is now largely contained in the Representation of the People Acts 1983–2000. In order to vote in a parliamentary election a person must be included in the electoral register for a parliamentary constituency. To qualify for inclusion in the register, a person must be:

1. eighteen years of age (or be due to attain his 18th birthday within 12 months of the publication of the register);
2. a British subject or a citizen of the Republic of Ireland;
3. not subject to any legal incapacity; and
4. resident in the constituency on the 'relevant date' (as defined by the revised s4(6) of the Representation of the People Act 1983 introduced by the Representation of the People Act 2000) for compiling the register.

The register of electors is prepared by the registration officer appointed for each constituency. To be included in the register, a person must be resident at an address in the constituency on the relevant date – essentially the date of the application to be placed on the register. Hence the 2000 Act introduces the concept of 'rolling registration' in place of the old system, whereby an elector had to be registered by a 'qualifying date' (10 October) in order to be eligible to vote at any subsequent local or parliamentary election.

The Representation of the People Act 2000, enacted to give effect to certain of the recommendations made by the Working Party on Electoral Procedures (chaired by George Howarth, which published its final report in October 1999) introduces changes to the system of registering voters, with particular emphasis on enabling traditionally excluded groups, such as the homeless, remand prisoners and mental patients, to register as voters. Section 4(1) provides that a person who is detained in a mental hospital as a voluntary patient, or otherwise than within the terms of disenfranchisement set out in s2, may be registered as a voter provided his stay is sufficient in length for him to be regarded as resident in the mental hospital. Similarly, under the 1983 Act a remand prisoner might have been disenfranchised if held in prison on the qualifying date for registering as a voter. Section 5 now permits such a prisoner to register as a voter if the length of time spent on remand in prison is sufficient for him to be regarded as a 'resident'. Alternatively, under s7 a declaration of local connection can be made by a person who is homeless, on remand, or a mental patient (other than one falling within s2), with the effect that they can register as a voter, provided certain procedural requirements are met.

The prohibition on convicted prisoners voting in local or general elections imposed under s3(1) of the Representation of the People Act 1983 was the subject of an unsuccessful challenge on human rights grounds in *R (Pearson and Another)* v *Secretary of State for the Home Department* (2001) The Times 17 April.

The meaning of 'residence' for electoral purposes was considered by the Court of Appeal in *Fox* v *Stirk* [1970] 2 QB 463, where the question before the Court was whether two students who took up residence in their university towns a few days before the qualifying date, and who might spend as little as 26 weeks a year in residence in those towns (spending the rest of their time at their parents' home in another part of the country), could be regarded as ordinarily resident in their university town for the purpose of the electoral register. Holding that there was a sufficient degree of permanence in the students' residence in their university towns for them to be placed on the electoral register, the Court held further that a person could, for these purposes, be regarded as resident in more than one place at any one time. It is an offence, however, for a person to vote in more than one constituency, even though his name appears on the electoral register for each constituency.

The residence requirements considered by registration officers when deciding whether or not to register a person as a voter are now to be found in s3 of the 2000 Act (formerly s5 of the 1983 Act). In determining whether a person is resident at a particular address the officer must have regard to the purpose and other circumstances, as well as to the fact, of his presence at, or absence from, the address on the 'relevant date'.

Service voters – members of the armed forces (whether serving at home or abroad), Crown servants and British Council staff overseas (and their spouses) can be registered as if they were living at the address at which, but for the service, they would normally be resident – this matter is now governed by s7 of the 2000 Act.

Under art 3 of the First Protocol to the European Convention on Human Rights, contracting states undertake to ensure that citizens enjoy the right to vote for members of the legislature.

In *R (Robertson)* v *Wakefield MDC* (2001) The Times 27 November the Divisional Court held that this right had been violated where domestic law provided that electors could only register if they were willing to allow their electoral registration details to be sold to direct marketing organisations on request. Note that the court also found this practice to be a violation of the right to privacy under art 8 of the Convention and contrary to Community law provisions relating to data protection.

In *R (Pearson and Another)* v *Secretary of State for the Home Department* (above) the First Protocol was invoked as the basis for the challenge to s3(1) of the 1983 Act brought by convicted prisoners denied the right to vote. The court took the view that although, following *Raymond* v *Honey* [1983] AC 1, convicted prisoners still retained their civil rights, the implied right to vote enshrined in art 3 was not absolute and there was room for implied limitations. Section 3(1) of the 1983 Act satisfied the requirements under the European Convention that any restrictions on the right to vote should not be such as to impair the essence or remove the effectiveness of that right, should be imposed in pursuit of a legitimate aim, and the means employed should not be disproportionate or thwart the free expression of the opinion of the people in the choice of the legislature. In assessing whether restrictions imposed met these criteria the court would bear in mind that contracting states had a wide margin of appreciation in subjecting the right to conditions. The court noted that Parliament, following careful consideration of the issues, had determined by means of primary legislation that prisoners being detained for preventative purposes should still be denied the right to vote. Deference would be given to the will of the legislature on this point.

The First Protocol was also considered in *Matthews* v *United Kingdom* (1999) 28 EHRR 361 where the applicant, a British citizen living in Gibraltar, applied to be registered as a voter for the elections to the European Parliament held in 1994 but was refused on the basis that Gibraltar was not included in the franchise for those elections.

The European Court of Human Rights held (by 15 votes to two) that the Protocol had been violated. Even though the absence of any right to vote in Gibraltar was the result of the system introduced under Community law by the EC, and accepting that the EC could not be a party to proceedings under the Convention (it is obviously not a signatory state), the Court held that there was no reason why the United Kingdom should nevertheless not be required to secure the rights provided for in the First Protocol in respect of those citizens for whom it was responsible in Gibraltar. Community law could take precedence over any local laws in Gibraltar and it was wrong that the applicant had been denied the opportunity to express a choice in respect of the legislative body that might be a party to such legislation. The European Parliament was a 'legislature' for the purposes of the Protocol as the term did not relate solely to the national legislature of a signatory state. The term could apply to a supranational body such as the European Parliament, especially given the extent to which EC law could be directly applicable in, and take precedence over, the domestic law of Member States. The Court also felt that the role of the European Parliament was sufficiently 'legislative' given its involvement in the law-making processes of the EC. The decision raises problems for the United Kingdom as it cannot, of its own volition, change the rules relating to the election of MEPs by providing Gibraltarians with the right to vote. Any such change will require a unanimous vote in favour by the EC Council of which Spain is a member. As is well known, Spain is likely to resist the extension of this franchise to Gibraltarians.

Disqualification

The following persons are not entitled to vote, even if their names appear on the electoral register: aliens, excluding citizens of the Republic of Ireland; minors; convicted persons undergoing sentences in penal institutions (save for remand prisoners as noted above); and persons convicted of corrupt or illegal practices at elections (the former are disqualified from voting for five years, the latter for five years in the constituency in question). Section 2 of the 2000 Act adds a new section to follow s3 of the 1983 Act to the effect that persons detained in mental hospitals pursuant to orders made by the criminal courts (eg under the Mental Health Act 1983 or s5(2)(a) of the Criminal Procedure (Insanity) Act 1964) are not entitled to vote in local or parliamentary elections. Others may be disqualified if the presiding officer at the polling station determines that they lack capacity at the moment of voting to understand what they are about to do, for example those who are intoxicated.

5.5 Parliamentary candidates

In principle any person can put themselves forward as a candidate in a parliamentary election, provided they can find ten persons willing to sign the nomination papers and they are willing to lodge £500 as a deposit that is forfeited if they fail to poll at least 5 per cent of the total number of votes cast. Certain categories of persons and office holders are, however, disqualified from sitting and voting in the House of Commons.

Amongst those subject to disqualification are: aliens, not including citizens of the Republic of Ireland or citizens of Commonwealth countries; persons under 21 years of age; and persons suffering from mental illness. Under the Mental Health Act 1983 the Speaker must be notified when a Member is detained as a person suffering from mental illness, whereupon the Speaker must obtain a medical report. If the detention is confirmed by this report and the Member is still detained as a mental patient according to a second report six months later, his seat is vacated.

Under the House of Commons (Clergy Disqualification) Act 1801 and s9 of the Roman Catholic Relief Act 1829 certain clergy were disqualified from becoming members of the House of Commons, namely 'person[s] having been ordained to the office of priest or deacon, or being a minister of the Church of Scotland' and 'person[s] in holy orders in the Church of Rome'. The Clergy Disqualification Act 1870 provided that Church of England clergy could only be freed from this disqualification six months after relinquishing their clerical positions. Following growing pressure for change Parliament has now enacted the House of Commons (Removal of Clergy Disqualification) Act 2001.

As the short title of the Act suggests, it provides that a person is not disqualified from being or being elected as a member of the House of Commons merely because he has been ordained or is a minister of any religious denomination. This is qualified by s1(2), which maintains the prohibition on House of Common membership for Lords Spiritual.

A person convicted of treason is disqualified from membership until receipt of a Royal Pardon or expiry of the sentence. It was previously the case that if a Member of Parliament was convicted of any crime other than treason, and was sentenced to imprisonment, the Speaker was to be informed of the nature of the offence and the sentence; but the prisoner remained a Member unless a motion was passed by the House of Commons to expel him. Under the Representation of the People Act 1981, however, a person who has been sentenced to one year's imprisonment or more is disqualified from membership of the House of Commons during his period of detention. A Member of Parliament who is sentenced to one year's imprisonment or more must vacate his seat. Bankrupts are disqualified and remain disqualified until five years after discharge, unless discharged with a certificate that bankruptcy was a result of misfortune and not misconduct. A Member who becomes bankrupt may continue to sit until the House takes notice of his bankruptcy and orders him to withdraw.

Persons convicted of corrupt and illegal practice at elections are disqualified; such corrupt practices include impersonation, bribery, treating and applying undue influence. Illegal practices include making false statements as to candidates; corruptly inducing a person's withdrawal from candidature; making payments for exhibition of election notices, except to a commercial advertising agent; employing paid canvassers; and making any other payments contrary to, or in excess of, those allowed by the Representation of the People Acts: see below at section 5.6. On the basis of s159(1) Representation of the People Act 1983, if a candidate who has been elected is reported by an election court to be guilty, either personally or through his agents, of any corrupt or illegal practice, his election is void. If he has been reported personally guilty he is incapable of being elected for the constituency concerned for ten years in the case of a corrupt practice and seven years in the case of an illegal practice. If guilty by his agents, the incapacity is for seven years in the case of a corrupt practice, and the duration of that Parliament in the case of an illegal practice. A candidate reported personally guilty of corrupt practice is also incapable of being elected to the House of Commons in any constituency for five years.

Disqualification of office-holders

The four main reasons for the disqualification of certain office-holders from membership of the House of Commons are: the risk of patronage; the physical impossibility of certain office-holders being able to attend Parliament; the conflict of constitutional duties; and the need for political impartiality in certain offices. Disqualifying offices are now set out in the House of Commons Disqualification Act 1975, as amended by the Disqualifications Act 2000. They can be summarised as follows.

1. Judicial offices. No person may hold a full-time judicial appointment and at the same time serve as a Member of Parliament. Lay magistrates are not affected.
2. Civil servants. Full-time or part-time civil servants who wish to stand as parliamentary candidates must first resign the service.
3. Members of the regular armed forces. Retired officers and members of the Territorial Army and other reserve or auxiliary forces are not disqualified.
4. Full-time members of any police force.
5. Members of the legislatures of non-Commonwealth countries other than the Irish Republic.
6. Members of certain commissions, tribunals and other bodies listed in the first Schedule to the Act – this Schedule may be amended by Order in Council.

5.6 The conduct of elections

National campaigns

In 1998 the Committee on Standards in Public Life (Neill Committee), in its report *Reform of Party Funding in the United Kingdom*, expressed the view that there ought to be an upper limit on the campaign spending of political parties. The report stated (at p126):

> 'On the assumption that a national spending limit is in place for the next general election, the limit for parties that contest more than 600 seats at that election should be set at £20 million. That limit should then be index-linked. It should not be varied in future except on the recommendation of the Election Commission [see above, section 5.2]. The limits in a general election for parties that contest fewer than 600 seats should be lower and should be based on a formula taking account of the number of seats they are contesting. Expenditure limits should continue to be set in terms of the purposes for which expenditure is incurred rather than in terms of any specified time period. Expenditure limits, at both national and local level, should be rigorously enforced. The national expenditure limits should cover benefits in kind as well as cash expenditure. Parties' accounts should itemise benefits in kind separately from cash expenditure and should indicate both the nature of each benefit in kind and its true market value.'

The Political Parties, Elections and Referendums Act 2000 addresses the issue of campaign expenditure, reflecting to some extent concern that the party with access to the most funds might be able to 'buy' success at an election. The Act also reflects that fact that, whilst during the nineteenth century concern was correctly directed at corrupt and illegal electoral practices at the constituency level (such as the bribing and treating of voters), in more recent years, particularly with the advent of mass telecommunications, the emphasis has shifted to the national campaign during general elections. The Act imposes limits on campaign expenditure which, for these purposes, is defined in s72 as expenses incurred by or on behalf of the party for election purposes, falling within those matters listed in Pt I of Sch 8 to the Act (eg party political broadcasts, manifestos, rallies, transport and advertising). The restrictions apply to general election campaigns and those for the European and regional parliaments. Expenditure on local government election campaigns is not included for these purposes. Section 72(7) expressly excludes from the scope of the definition any expenditure that is included in a return as to election expenses in respect of a candidate or candidates at a particular election.

The term 'for election purposes' is further defined in s72(4) as for the purpose of, or in connection with, promoting or procuring electoral success for the party at any relevant election. This includes the election of the party's candidates standing in the name of the party, or included in a list of candidates submitted by the party in connection with the election, or otherwise enhancing the standing of the party or of any such candidates with the electorate, in connection with future relevant elections (whether imminent or otherwise. Expenditure will also be for election purposes if it is the purpose of the expenditure to prejudice the standing with the electorate of other parties or candidates. Under s75 it is a criminal offence to incur, without reasonable excuse, campaign expenditure by, or on behalf of, a registered party without the authority of the treasurer of that party.

Section 79 and Sch 9 impose limits on campaign expenditure incurred by or on behalf of registered parties. It is an offence for the treasurer of a registered party to authorised expenditure to be incurred by or on behalf of the party where he knows, or ought reasonably to have known, that the expenditure would be incurred in excess of the statutory limit. In general terms the limit imposed by the Act is £30,000 multiplied by the number of constituencies contested by a party. Sections 80–84 provide for the auditing of party treasurer returns in respect of campaign expenditure and the delivery of returns to the Election Commission. In practical terms this means that the Labour and Conservative parties would not be permitted to spend more that £20 million each at any forthcoming general election. This compares with expenditure of £26 million and £28 million respectively in the run up to the May 1997 general election.

Expenditure by third parties during a national election campaign, aimed at securing the election of a particular party, is dealt with by Chapter I of Part VI of the Act. A third party for these purposes is any individual or organisation intending to incur controlled expenditure in excess of £10,000 during a regulated period, effectively the period of the election campaign. Any such third party must comply with the registration, notification and accounting requirements of the Act. Controlled expenditure is defined by s85 as including expenditure incurred by or on behalf of the third party in connection with the production or publication of election material that is made available to the public at large or any section of the public. Election material includes any material which can reasonably be regarded as intended to promote or procure electoral success at any national or regional election for a registered party or candidates who hold (or do not hold) particular opinions or who advocate (or do not advocate) particular policies. The provisions would thus cover money incurred in distributing publicity encouraging voters to support candidates with pro-abortion views. The provisions are also wide enough to encompass expenditure on publicity aimed at preventing the election of a candidate or party. Mindful of the fact that newspapers usually demonstrate support for one of the major political parties during election campaigns, s87 provides that the publication of any matter relating to an election, other than an advertisement, in a newspaper or periodical will be regarded as falling outside the definition of controlled expenditure. The maximum amount of money that can be spent by way of controlled expenditure is determined by s94 and Sch 10. Donations to third parties are subject to a similar control regime as that applicable to donations to registered parties: see further s95.

Television coverage

Whilst most newspapers adopt an overtly partisan approach in supporting one of the major political parties, it is widely acknowledged that television is the most powerful medium for influencing voters in respect of their choice of party in the period leading up to a general election. As a consequence measures exist to ensure that the coverage of political matters in terms of news reporting is impartial, and that the parties have access to television coverage that is broadly commensurate with their support and representativeness: see the Broadcasting Act 1990 s6(1)(b) and (c) as regards the duties imposed on independent television companies. The BBC has similar obligations arising from its agreement entered into with the Secretary of State for Culture, Media and Sport: see Cmnd 3152 (1996). An informal body, the Committee on Party Political Broadcasting, determines the allocation of time for party political broadcasts, based on the number of candidates being fielded by each party. Normally a party has to field at least 50 candidates in order to qualify for any party political broadcasts, and as noted above the s37 of the Political Parties, Elections and Referendums Act 2000 restricts the allocation of airtime to registered parties. Beyond this, the allocation of additional party political broadcasts will be based on factors such as proven electoral support. In *R* v *British Broadcasting Corporation and Another, ex parte Referendum Party* [1997] EMLR 605 the applicants were unsuccessful in attempting to seek review of this policy on the basis that it was irrational in not taking into account the fact that a newly formed political party would, of necessity, not be able to demonstrate a record of electoral support.

The ratio of time agreed upon for the allocation of party political broadcasts between the main parties is also used to determine the time allocated to news coverage of the parties during the election campaign. Between the main parties this usually translates into five broadcasts for both the Labour and Conservative Parties and four for the Liberal Democrats.

Even where time is allocated for party political broadcasts there may still be some dispute as to whether or not a broadcaster is required to transmit them in an unedited form. During the run-up to the 1997 general election campaign Channel 4 made alterations to a party political broadcast prepared by the British National Party on the basis that it might involve incitement to racial hatred: see ss17–22 of the Public Order Act 1986. Since then, of course, the Human Rights Act 1998 has come into force, providing for an enforceable right to freedom of expression. The impact of this can be seen in the way that the courts dealt with the refusal of various broadcasters to transmit a party political broadcast prepared by Pro-Life groups during the campaign for the 2001 general election. In its original form the film contained scenes involving the disposal of a foetus following an abortion. The BBC refused to broadcast the film on the grounds that its charter required it not to broadcast any material that would 'offend against good taste and decency ... encourage disorder ... or be offensive to public feeling.' In *R (On the Application of Quintavalle)* v *BBC* (2002) The Times 16 March the Court of Appeal ruled that the freedom of political speech to be enjoyed by an accredited party at a general election was not to be interfered with save on the most pressing grounds. Laws LJ expressed the view that the courts owed a special responsibility to the public as the constitutional guardian of the freedom of political debate, especially in the context of a general election. This role had its origins in a deeper truth, ie that the courts were ultimately the 'trustees of democracy's framework'. In his view the court's duty was to decide for itself whether or not the censorship being imposed by the broadcasters was justified. It was likely that, subject to express statutory prohibitions on certain types of material being broadcast, the courts would only uphold the censorship of party political broadcasts by the media where the content was gratuitously sensationalist and dishonest. As regards the Pro-Life broadcasts the broadcasters were held to have failed to give sufficient weight to the pressing imperative of free political expression, which had to give way, on this occasion, to considerations of taste and decency.

In April 1995, the Labour Party was successful in bringing an action to prevent a Panorama broadcast of an interview with the then Prime Minister, John Major, that was scheduled for the eve of the Scottish local elections. The basis for the court's granting of the injunction would appear to have been the apparent unfairness that would have been caused to opposing parties by allowing the broadcast to go ahead: see *Houston* v *BBC* 1995 SLT 1305. The case raised the important question of who the BBC owes its duty of impartiality to, given that the agreement under which it is empowered to broadcast is entered into with the Secretary of State. Although not decisive on this point, comments made by Lord Eassie in *Scottish National Party* v *Scottish Television plc and Grampian Television plc* (1997) (unreported) cast doubt on the proposition that only the Independent Television Commission was empowered to invoke the licensee television companies' obligations of political impartiality in that case. The Scottish National Party (SNP) had sought an interim interdict (injunction) to prevent the two independent television companies from broadcasting, in Scotland, a 'head-to-head' debate between the main party leaders that did not include a platform for the leader of the SNP. The SNP contended that such a broadcast would breach the television companies' obligations to observe due impartiality in the coverage of political affairs. Refusing the motion, the Court of Session ruled that the legal action had been premature, as no final decision had yet been made relating to any such broadcast, hence the issue was a hypothetical one on which the Court declined to venture an opinion. What was significant, however, was the Court's finding that the impartiality to be observed by a broadcaster under the relevant legislation was not to be judged on the basis of one programme alone, but was to be viewed 'in the round' taking into account the totality of coverage.

Constituency expenditure authorised by the candidate

The conduct of elections is regulated by the Representation of the People Act 1983, as amended by the Political Parties, Elections and Referendums Act 2000. The aim of these legislative provisions is to eliminate, as far as possible, corrupt and illegal electoral practices and other unfair methods. Each candidate must appoint an election agent, although he may act for himself in this capacity, and all campaign expenditure must be authorised by the candidate or his agent. A maximum limit is imposed on election expenditure and it is an illegal practice for the candidate or his agent to knowingly exceed this limit. That figure is calculated on the basis of £4,965 plus 5.6p per elector in county constituencies, and 4.2p per elector in borough constituencies. The legislation lays down strict requirements in respect of record keeping and expenditure. Under s132(6) of the 2000 Act, however, the maximum expenditure that may be incurred by a candidate contesting a constituency at a parliamentary by-election is increased to a flat rate £100,000, reflecting the fact that many by-elections are keenly fought contests attracting national interest.

Bribery, cheating and the use of fraudulent devices would also constitute election offences. In *R v Rowe, ex parte Mainwaring and Others* [1992] 1 WLR 1059, the appellants were successful candidates for the Liberal Democrats at local government elections. The respondents, unsuccessful Labour Party candidates, presented election petitions claiming that the appellants had engaged in corrupt electoral practices, namely the publication of a leaflet, designed to appear as if it was an official Labour Party leaflet, containing factually accurate but politically contentious accounts of Labour Party policies that might not have been popular with the Labour Party voters in the areas in which it was distributed. The leaflet complied with the requirement that it should carry the details of the distributing party's agent, but this was in minuscule print. The Court of Appeal found that a leaflet issued by one political party designed so as to appear as if it had been issued by a rival party could be a fraudulent device, notwithstanding that the contents were factually correct. For an offence to be established, however, it had to be shown that an elector had in fact been impeded or prevented in the free exercise of the franchise, and evidence of this was lacking in the present case. The result induced Nolan LJ to express the view that s115(2)(b) of the Representation of the People Act 1983 should be replaced by a more effective provision that could deal with less blatant and less easily detected, but no less effective, methods of exerting influence.

Section 136 of the Political Parties, Elections and Referendums Act 2000 clarifies the uncertainty created by the problem that arose in *Attorney-General v Jones* [1999] 3 All ER 436, where the Divisional Court was asked to rule upon whether an MP who had vacated her seat following a conviction for electoral fraud was entitled to resume her seat once her conviction had been quashed on appeal. In seeking to give effect to the ruling of the Court in that case, s136 provides that a person convicted of a corrupt or illegal practice, if already elected to a seat in the House of Commons, would have to vacate the seat from within three months of the date of the conviction (or at the time for lodging any appeal, whichever is the earlier), for five years in the case of a person convicted of a corrupt practice or, in the case of a person convicted of an illegal practice, three years. Section 136(3), however, recognises that if a court determines on an appeal that the conviction should not be upheld, the period during which the seat has to be vacated ends at that point. If the seat has not been filled in the interim the successful appellant would be able to resume his or her seat.

Unauthorised constituency expenditure incurred by third parties

Under s75 of the 1983 Act as it stood prior to the amendments introduced by the Political Parties, Elections and Referendums Act 2000 very strict limits were imposed on unauthorised third party expenditure incurred with the view of promoting or procuring the election of a candidate at constituency level. These limits were successfully challenged in *Bowman* v *United Kingdom* (1998) 26 EHRR 1. The applicant was an anti-abortion campaigner. During the 1992 general election she had distributed 25,000 leaflets, at a cost of £10,000, in the Halifax parliamentary constituency outlining the views of the various parliamentary candidates on abortion. She was, in due course, charged under s75 (which imposes a limit of £5 on such unauthorised expenditure). As a result of the summons being issued out of time the applicant was in fact acquitted of the s75 charges, but she nevertheless lodged an application with the European Commission on Human Rights. By a majority of 14 votes to six, the European Court of Human Rights ruled that the operation of s75 did amount to a violation of the applicant's rights under art 10 European Convention on Human Rights. The provision did restrict freedom of expression in a manner that was prescribed by law, and was introduced to secure a legitimate aim, namely equality between candidates seeking election, but could not be justified as 'necessary in a democratic society'. The Court noted that it was important to ensure that views could be freely expressed in the period leading up to elections, in order to ensure the proper functioning of the democratic process. Similarly it was important to ensure the free expression of the opinion of the people in choosing the legislature, and this might mean restricting the right to freedom of expression. In striking the balance between these two considerations a margin of appreciation would be allowed to contracting states. In the circumstances, however, the Court concluded that s75 effectively imposed a complete ban on the applicant disseminating her views effectively in the pre-election period, as the spending limit was so low and she had no access to other forms of broadcasting. The Court also noted that the spending restrictions were difficult to justify given that (at the time) they operated in the context of national and regional political advertising that was not subject to any financial limit provided it was not designed to ensure the election of a particular candidate in a particular constituency.

In response to this ruling s131 of the Political Parties, Elections and Referendums Act 2000 amends s75 of the 1983 Act by increasing the expenditure that may be incurred in meeting election expenses not authorised by the candidate or his agent from £5 to £500 for a parliamentary election. For local government elections the maximum figure is £50 plus 0.5p for every entry in the register of local government electors for the electoral area in question.

The prohibition on election expenditure without the consent of the candidate extends equally to expenditure designed to prevent the election of other competing candidates. Hence in *DPP* v *Luft* [1977] AC 962, the House of Lords upheld the convictions of the respondents who, without the authority of any of the candidates, had distributed leaflets urging voters not to support National Front candidates.

The regime introduced by the Political Parties, Elections and Referendums Act 2000 to regulate donations to registered political parties and third parties (considered below) is extended to cover donations to individual candidates with appropriate modifications. In any event a candidate will only be able to spend money so donated for election purposes within the limits outlined above.

Contested election results: election petitions

Since 1868 Parliament has entrusted the duty of hearing petitions against the validity of elections to an election court consisting of two judges of the Queen's Bench Division in England, or of the Court of Session in Scotland. An election petition complaining of illegal or corrupt practices or other irregularities must be presented within 21 days of the official return of the result. The court, which usually sits in the constituency concerned, determines whether the candidate in question was duly elected and whether any illegal, corrupt or other irregular practices have been proved. If the petition alleges that the successful candidate was subject to a legal incapacity, and this is proved, the court may either declare the election void or award the seat to the runner-up. The decision of the court is notified to the Speaker of the House of Commons and is recorded in the journals of the House. Such petitions are now extremely rare, perhaps the most celebrated example being provided by the challenge to Tony Benn's election as an MP following his inheritance of his father's viscountcy: see *Re Parliamentary Election for Bristol South-East* [1964] 2 QB 257.

More recently, in October 1997, the High Court set aside the result in the Winchester constituency where, at the May 1997 general election, the Liberal Democrat candidate Mark Oaten had defeated the incumbent Conservative minister, Gerry Malone, by just 2 votes. The result was set aside on the ground that there had been an error in the counting of the votes (the returning officer had wrongly disqualified 55 unstamped ballot papers), the first time such an order had been made since 1910.

5.7 Alternative electoral systems

By virtue of s7 of the Parliament Act 1911, a general election to determine the membership of the House of Commons must be held at least every five years. An incumbent Prime Minister can, in theory, seek a dissolution of Parliament at any time and thus bring about a general election. This is, potentially, a very powerful weapon in that it can be used to call an election at a time that is likely to be advantageous for the government. Alternatively, a government that loses a vote of confidence in the House of Commons would normally be expected to seek a dissolution on the basis that it can no longer command a majority of support in the House, and thus cannot govern effectively.

At present Members of Parliament are elected under the 'relative majority' or 'first past the post' system, with each parliamentary constituency returning a single member. Each elector can vote for one candidate only, and the candidate who polls the most votes within a given constituency wins that seat. It is a 'winner takes all' system. If a vote is cast for the candidate who comes second in the poll, it will not count in terms of influencing the eventual composition of the House of Commons. In this unsophisticated system there will not necessarily be any close correlation between the number of votes cast nationally for a particular party and the number of seats allocated to that party in the House of Commons. In practice the system tends to produce exaggerated majorities for the two major parties and discriminates against the minority parties. An analysis of the results in the two most recent general elections illustrates the point.

The result of the April 1992 general election

Party	Actual seats	% Seats	% Popular vote
Conservative	336	51.7	43
Labour	271	41.6	35
Liberal Democrats	20	3	18
Others	24	3.7	4

The result of the May 1997 general election

Party	Actual seats	% Seats	% Popular vote
Conservative	165	25	31
Labour	419	64	45
Liberal Democrats	46	7	17
Others	29	4	7

By dividing the number of votes cast for each party by the number of seats won it can be seen that, in the 1997 general election, it took 58,124 votes to elect each Conservative MP; 32,342 votes to elect each Labour MP; 113,985 votes to elect each Liberal Democrat MP; and 108,049 votes to elect each 'minor party' MP.

The result of the 1997 general election is commonly referred to as a landslide victory for the Labour Party, but the statistics reveal that it polled only 1.9 million votes more than it had in 1992. The problem for the Conservative Party appeared to be defections to the Liberal Democrats and abstentions by those who would normally have supported the party. The curious variable geometry of the electoral system ensures that any party thus squeezed suffers disproportionately.

The June 2001 general election produced the following results (see overleaf), which were remarkably close to the 1997 figures:

Party	Actual seats	% Seats	% Popular vote
Conservative	166	25.2	32
Labour	412	62.5	41
Liberal Democrats	52	7.9	18
Others	29	4.4	9

Proponents of the present system would contend that the following are reasons for retaining it.

1. The voting procedure is simple and the results may be quickly and easily calculated.
2. There is a link between the Member and his constituency.
3. One party usually obtains an absolute majority of seats in the House of Commons thus leading to strong government. There is no coalition government with minor parties holding the balance of power and thus being able to exert influence out of all proportion to their popular support in the country.
4. A result can normally be announced within a few hours of the polls closing.
5. Voters vote for parties not coalitions.

Against this, it can clearly be seen from the above that there is only a weak correlation between votes won nationally and representation in the House of Commons. The figures also starkly illustrate that each vote is not of equal value; compare the number of votes required to elect each Labour MP, compared with the number required to elect each Liberal Democrat. When the results of the 1997 election are broken down on a regional basis, the anomalies become even more stark. The Conservative Party won 34 per cent of the popular vote in English constituencies and won 31 per cent of English seats. Meanwhile the Labour Party won 44 per cent of the popular vote in England but secured 62 per cent of the seats. For the Liberal Democrats the figures were 18 per cent and 6 per cent respectively. In Scotland the Conservatives polled 18 per cent of the popular vote, but did not win a single seat. By contrast the SNP polled only 6 per cent of the popular vote but won 6 seats. Similarly in Wales, the Conservatives won 20 per cent of the popular vote without managing to retain a single seat, whilst Plaid Cymru won 4 seats with just 10 per cent of the popular vote. At the 1997 general election 48.2 per cent of votes cast (over 14 million votes) did not count towards electing an MP, and 50 per cent of MPs were elected by less than half their constituency – one MP being elected by just 33 per cent of those who voted.

The key problem with reforming the electoral system is that a party has to win power in order to do so. It will then be in the odd position of seeking to reform a system that has delivered its election victory. The system could thus be seen to be self-perpetuating. A Royal Commission on Electoral Systems was appointed in 1900 and reported in favour of changing to a system known as the alternative vote (see below) in 1910. In the Representation of the People Act 1918, Parliament began to pave the way towards a system of proportional representation by single transferable vote (see below) when it introduced that system for the university constituencies. The university vote was, however, abolished in 1948. In 1930 a Bill which sought to introduce the alternative vote passed the Commons but was lost, never to be revived, when the Labour government fell in 1931. Thereafter the climate of opinion changed and in 1944 a Speaker's Conference rejected the idea of proportional representation. The Labour Party expressed its broad support for the notion of electoral reform following its fourth successive election defeat in 1992, and invited Professor Raymond Plant to head an inquiry on the issue. The party's annual conference in October 1995 reaffirmed the commitment to investigate the possibility of reform, and the manifesto on which it fought and won the 1997 general election confirmed that the party was 'committed to a referendum on the voting system for the House of Commons' involving 'an independent commission ... appointed ... to recommend a proportional alternative to the first-past the post system': see the details of the Jenkins Commission, and the reform of the electoral system for the election of MEPs, below.

Alternatives: the alternative vote system

Under this system the voter is asked to list the candidates within the constituency in order of preference. If no candidate gains an absolute majority of first preference votes then the lowest candidate is eliminated and his second preference votes are distributed amongst the other candidates. The process may be repeated until a candidate emerges who has an absolute majority of more than half the votes. This system is used to elect the Australian Lower House. It is not a proportional system, but it does reduce the number of wasted votes and has the advantage of being easy to understand and administer.

Alternatives: the party list system

The ultimate and only precise means of achieving direct proportionality is to have only one constituency, composed of the whole country, with the parties presenting lists of candidates and electors voting not for individual candidates, but for the whole party list. Seats are then allocated to the parties in proportion to the votes received by each party list. However, difficulties may be encountered in drawing up the list and in particular determining the order of candidates. It would also destroy the territorial constituency system with its strong link between one MP and one constituency.

As a variant upon this it is possible to combine a first past the post or alternative vote system with a limited party list system, ie the total number of MPs comprises a mixture of constituency and party list representatives. A version of this system is used for elections to the Bundestag in Germany, a procedure under which no party gets any members from the party list unless it polls at least five per cent of the national vote.

Reflecting in part its support for electoral reform, but also in response to moves within the EC to make proportional representation the norm for EC elections, the Labour government introduced its European Parliamentary Elections Act 1999 making provision for elections to the European Parliament using the regional list electoral system in England, Wales and Scotland. The 1999 Act amended the European Parliamentary Elections Act 1978 by moving from a system based on the division of Great Britain into 78 constituencies, towards one that saw England divided into nine electoral regions returning a total of 71 MEPs. Scotland, Wales and Northern Ireland are each classified as a single region returning eight, five and three MEPs respectively.

This form of the party list system involves each registered party drawing up a list of potential MEPs. Normally, all the major parties compile lists with enough names to fill all the vacant seats should they be so successful. Section 3(3)–(6) indicate the manner in which seats are allocated:

> '(3) The first seat shall be allocated to the party or individual candidate with the greatest number of votes.
>
> (4) The second and subsequent seats shall be allocated in the same way, except that the number of votes given to a party to which one or more seats have already been allocated shall be divided by the number of seats allocated plus one.
>
> (5) In allocating the second or any subsequent seat there shall be disregarded any votes given to – (a) a party to which there has already been allocated a number of seats equal to the number of names on the party's list of candidates, and (b) an individual candidate to whom a seat has already been allocated.
>
> (6) Seats allocated to a party shall be filled by the persons named on the party's list of candidates in the order in which they appear on that list.'

As an illustration of how the system might operate consider the following example. Suppose that the Labour Party, the Conservative Party, the Liberal Democrats and Plaid Cymru contest the five seats available in Wales, with the following results: Labour Party 800,000 votes; Conservative Party 300,000 votes; Liberal Democrats 120,000 votes; Plaid Cymru 100,000 votes.

A total of 1,320,000 votes will have been cast. The Labour Party has the highest number of votes and is thus allocated the first seat. The Labour total would then be divided by 2 (the number of seats won plus 1), giving a total of 400,000. As it would still have the most votes the second seat would go to Labour, reducing its vote to 266,000 (800,000 divided by 2 seats won, plus 1). The third seat would be allocated to the Conservative Party, as it polled 300,000 votes. The fourth seat would be allocated to Labour (given its 266,000 vote), and the last seat would go to the Conservatives (300,000 votes divided by 1 seat won plus 1, giving it 150,000, ahead of the Liberal Democrats). It should not be assumed, therefore, that the smaller parties will necessarily benefit from the introduction of proportional representation. Under this scheme voters do not have a choice between candidates selected by the parties. Voters can, of course, vote for independent candidates, but the chances of any such candidates succeeding are slim. It is the 'closed list' aspect of these proposals that has attracted so much criticism, from both left and right. Critics argue that power is being transferred from the electorate to a 'selectorate' of party managers.

Party list systems are also used to select the 'additional members' to the Scottish Parliament and the Welsh Assembly. The Scottish Parliament comprises 73 constituency members (elected on the first past the post basis) and 56 party list members. The Welsh Assembly has 40 constituency members and 20 party list members. Following the May 1999 elections no single party gained an overall majority in the Scottish Parliament or the Welsh Assembly – immediately calling into question the merits of this form of proportional representation, not least because those parties seeking to form coalition governments are forced to renege on manifesto commitments as the price for entering into a deal with other minority parties. The experience may make the introduction of electoral reform for elections to the House of Commons a more distant prospect.

Alternatives: the single transferable vote system

The single transferable vote system is an alternative to the party list system. It requires multi-member constituencies of between five and seven members. Voters list the individual candidates in order of preference. In counting the votes, the principle that applies is that the candidate only needs a certain number, or quota of votes, to be elected, and any votes that he receives beyond this figure are surplus and serve only to build up an unnecessary majority. So, once the candidate has received the quota necessary to secure his election, the 'surplus' votes are redistributed among the other candidates according to second preferences.

There are several variations based on the procedures used to determine the quota, count the votes, and redistribute the surplus votes, but the quota is generally established by the following formula: divide the number of votes cast plus 1, by the number of seats plus 1.

The single transferable vote system has been used for European Parliament elections in Northern Ireland since 1978 and the European Parliamentary Elections Act 1999 retains that system for the Province.

The Report of the Jenkins Commission

The Labour Party pledged, in the manifesto on which it fought and won the 1997 general election, that it would establish an independent body to propose an alternative to the current voting system used at general elections, and hold a referendum at which voters could express their preferences. Once elected the Labour government appointed Lord Jenkins of Hillhead to head the Commission of inquiry into the voting system and it produced its Report at the end of October 1998.

The Commission's key proposal is that the current 'first past the post' system should be replaced by an enhanced alternative vote system. Approximately 80 per cent of MPs would be elected on a constituency basis – the number of constituencies being reduced to around 525. The remaining MPs would be drawn from party lists and would represent other geographical areas such as cities and counties. Electors would cast two votes in order to elect a constituency MP, numbering the candidates in their order of preference. If a candidate secured a 50 per cent share of the votes on the first count he or she would be elected as the MP for that constituency. If no candidate secured 50 per cent of the votes on the first count, the candidate with the lowest number of first preference votes would be eliminated and his or her second preference votes would be redistributed amongst the candidates. The process of eliminating lowest scoring candidates would continue until a candidate achieved 50 per cent of the first preference and redistributed second preference votes.

Voters would also cast a party list, or 'top-up' vote, for MPs who would represent cities or counties. The proposal is that this vote could simply be for a party, or for a specific candidate appearing on the party list. Votes for this category of candidate or party would be cast by placing a single cross against the party's name or that of the party's list candidate. Both votes (those for the list candidate and those for the party in general) would be added to make up a party's total vote and determine whether or not it wins a seat. The purpose of this top-up system would be to help ensure that there was a closer correlation between the total number of votes cast and the allocation of seats to parties at Westminster, and to prevent the creation of 'electoral deserts' whereby the Conservative Party tends to be under-represented in Wales and Scotland, and the Labour Party (arguably) under-represented in the south-east of England. Candidates elected on a constituency basis and those elected on the party list basis would have equal status at Westminster. The Committee also recommends the creation of an independent Electoral Commission to oversee the referendum on whether the voting system should be changed.

If the two most recent general elections had been conducted using the enhanced alternative vote system proposed by the Jenkins Commission the allocation of seats would have been as follows: 1997: Conservatives 167 seats; Labour 367 seats; Lib Dem 92 seats; Nationalists 14 seats, 1992: Conservative 316 seats; Labour 240 seats; Lib Dem 74 seats; Nationalists 11 seats. Given that the reforms proposed in the Jenkins Report involve significant changes to the House of Commons there would seem little immediate prospect of the government moving to implement them.

5.8 Referendums

A referendum is a vote, in which all voters (or all voters within a particular area) can participate, on a single issue or a series of linked issues. Dicey observed that 'the main use of the referendum is to prevent the passing of any important Act which does not command the sanction of the electors', and that '[t]he referendum supplies ... the best, if not the only possible, check upon ill-considered alterations in the fundamental institutions of the country.'

The reality is that, to date, little use of referendums has been made, and it has still to emerge as a traditional feature of the British constitution. The reluctance to make use of referendums may be related to the convention of the electoral mandate, whereby a government is elected on the basis of its election manifesto, and thus has a mandate to implement the policies on which it was elected. It does not have to obtain a majority of support in a further popular vote for its actions to obtain legitimacy.

Since 1973 there have been six referendums; the Northern Ireland Border Poll (1973); the referendum on UK membership of the EEC (1975); the two devolution referendums held in Wales and Scotland (1979); and the two devolution referendums held in Wales and Scotland (1997). The circumstances in which referendums have been held suggest, therefore, that Dicey's observations were to some extent correct, in that all of the issues referred to above could be described as involving fundamental constitutional matters. This view is further supported by the evidence contained in the manifestos upon which the three main political parties fought the 1997 general election, for example the pledges from both the Conservative and Labour Parties to the effect that they would hold a referendum before the United Kingdom joined a single European currency.

A number of fundamental questions remain unanswered, however. Why should any government agree to a referendum, and what is the constitutional significance of the result? Cynics would suggest that no sensible politician would agree to a referendum unless he or she is already confidant that the outcome will endorse the course of action that they want to take anyway. The paradox, of course, is that if a politician feels that a policy has popular support, there is no purpose to be served in proving this by holding a referendum. Conversely it could be argued that a referendum could help a party that is divided on a key issue, as the Labour government was over EEC membership in the mid-1970s. Similarly, Labour's enthusiasm for referendums on devolution in the run-up to the 1997 general election may have been inspired by a desire to prevent breakaway groups campaigning for devolution in Wales and Scotland.

A Prime Minister can to some extent absolve himself of responsibility for the outcome by saying that he is merely giving effect to the will of the people – an argument that assumes that the referendum will produce a decisive result. It might also be argued that there are some fundamental constitutional reforms that cut across traditional party boundaries and as such are highly suitable for resolution by means of a referendum, eg abolition of the monarchy, abolition of the House of Lords, adoption of a Bill of Rights, adoption of a written constitution, electoral reform, etc.

Where a referendum has been held, what is the constitutional significance of the result? Much will depend on the wording of the legislation that has been enacted to provide for the holding of the referendum: see Chapter 1 for a consideration of the referendums held on devolution of power to Wales and Scotland. The key question concerns parliamentary sovereignty. Can an Act bind Parliament to pass legislation giving effect to the wishes of the voters as expressed through a referendum? On the basis that Parliament cannot bind its successors the answer would have to be in the negative – referendums should be seen as advisory only in terms of the majority preference. The enabling Act may state that a Bill to give effect to the result will be introduced into the House of Commons, but there can be no guarantee that it would be passed. Indeed, it seems unlikely that the courts could force the government of the day to introduce such a Bill if, notwithstanding the outcome of a referendum, it decided not to. Perhaps the most that can be said is that there is an embryonic convention that the government of the day will comply with the wishes of the electorate as expressed via the vote in a referendum.

Another issue that may receive more attention should there be an increasing reliance on the use of referendums is whether the outcome should be determined on the basis of the majority of votes cast, or whether a proposition would have to have the support of a majority of those registered to vote. The use of a threshold requirement for constitutional change, as was the case with the devolution referendums in 1978 when 40 per cent of those eligible to vote had to be in favour of change for it to be taken further, is valid only if the system for registering eligibility is accurate. The current system is likely to contain a six per cent inaccuracy. It is submitted that, for as long as referendums remain advisory, Parliament ought to take the size of the turnout and the decisiveness of the result into account when determining how to proceed.

The funding of political campaigns during referendums was considered in the report of the Neill Committee on party funding. The report contains a number of proposals aimed at ensuring that referendums are conducted on a 'level playing field'. To this end it recommended that each 'side' should be given equal access to an amount of core funding sufficient to enable it to mount at least a minimal campaign and to make its views widely known. The matter has now been put on a statutory footing by Part VII of the Political Parties, Elections and Referendums Act 2000. The controls relate to any referendum held throughout the United Kingdom; one or more of England, Scotland, Wales and Northern Ireland; or any region in England specified in Sch 1 to the Regional Development Agencies Act 1998. A referendum for these purposes is a referendum or other poll held in pursuance of any provision made by or under an Act of Parliament, on one or more questions specified in or in accordance with any such provision. Under s106 of the 2000 Act those parties and organisations that wish to campaign in respect of the referendum question must register with the Commission in order to become 'permitted participants'. Registration involves providing an indication of the outcome or outcomes for which the party, individual or organisation proposes to campaign. Organisations and individuals are also required to provide the Commission with information as to how the accounting requirements regarding campaign expenditure during the referendum period will be met. Campaign expenditure as regards referendums has essentially the same meaning as campaign expenditure in respect of national and regional elections. It is a criminal offence for any person to incur expenditure in excess of £10,000 in a referendum campaign unless they are registered as a participant under s106, and expenditure by permitted participants must be authorised by the relevant person within the participating organisation. The Act provides for limits on referendum campaign expenditure by permitted participants, currently £5,000,000 for organisations or groups of organisations, and a variable sum for registered parties related to the percentage of the popular vote secured by that party at the most recent general election. Broadcasters are only permitted to transmit referendum broadcasts by organisations designated by the Commission.

Restrictions regarding donations to permitted participants are imposed by s119, similar in terms to those applying to donations to registered political parties and third parties. Section 125 prohibits the publication (whether by local or central government) during the referendum campaign of any material that deals with any of the issues raised by any question on which a referendum is being held, or puts any arguments for or against any particular answer to any such question, or is designed to encourage voting at such a referendum. This effectively means that the government of the day will have up until 28 days before a referendum is held to use the Whitehall machinery to campaign for a particular outcome.

6

The House of Commons

6.1 Introduction

The United Kingdom Parliament sits at Westminster in London. It is a bicameral parliament, comprising the House of Commons and the House of Lords. In historical terms it is the House of Commons that is the younger of the institutions but, given the growth in universal adult suffrage, and the acquisition of almost exclusive jurisdiction over the raising of revenue, it is the House of Commons that is the more powerful legislative body within the constitution. The purpose of this chapter is to examine how the House of Commons operates, and to examine some arguments and proposals for reform. Following the enactment of the Scotland Act 1998 and the Government of Wales Act 1998 regional legislatures have been established in those countries.

Membership of the House of Commons

Each of the 659 Members of Parliament represents a parliamentary constituency. MPs are elected as individuals to represent their constituencies in the House of Commons, but the organisation of that chamber reveals that members rarely, if ever, sit as independents. By convention members are bound together in party groupings, and the convention is that the party having an overall majority of members forms the government of the day. Like many conventions, this reflects practical politics, as the party with the overall majority is the one that will be able to successfully enact legislation, and hence implement its policies. To some extent the law recognises the existence of this party political alignment of members, for example the statutory recognition of the role of 'Leader of the Opposition'. Occasionally members will change their party allegiances during the life of a parliament, a process known as 'crossing the floor'. In 1977 a Labour Cabinet minister, Reg Prentice, defected to the Conservative Party, eventually becoming a minister in Mrs Thatcher's first government. Alan Howarth, a former Conservative Party Vice-Chairman made a similar crossing, in the opposite direction, in 1995. Such defections take on a greater significance when a government has a small majority. Once a government loses its overall majority it can remain in power only by calling upon the support of minority parties, in effect forming a loose coalition, as the Labour and Liberal parties did from 1977–79. By convention, a government that can no longer command the support of the majority of the House must seek a dissolution of the House so that an election can be held.

Devolution and Westminster representation

Given the range of topics in relation to which power has been devolved to the Scottish Parliament and a Welsh Assembly there have inevitably been questions asked about the proper role to be played by Scottish and Welsh backbenchers who continue to sit at Westminster. The argument is that many of their constituents' concerns will henceforth be raised in the regional bodies, rather than at Westminster. It might also be seen as logical to dispense with Question Time sessions for Welsh and Scottish Secretaries of State, and to wind up the activities of the relevant regional committees at Westminster.

One of the intractable problems arising in the devolution debate is the so-called 'West Lothian Question', so named after the MP for that area, Tam Dalyell, who persistently raised the issue in the House of Commons. With significant power being devolved to the Scottish Parliament, in particular the power to increase levels of taxation, what should be the role of Scottish MPs at Westminster? If their powers and rights are to continue unabated, a situation could be created whereby English MPs would not be able to vote upon matters directly affecting Scotland, but Scottish MPs would be able to vote on matters directly affecting England, Wales and Northern Ireland. The irony in such an arrangement is, of course, that it turns the moral justification for devolution, the unfairness of an unrepresentative English majority legislating for regional minorities, on its head. The Scottish MPs would be wholly unaccountable in terms of their voting on matters relating to England alone.

The problem is particularly acute for a Labour government, given the current distribution of parliamentary seats, as the Scottish constituencies primarily return Labour candidates. The logical response to the 'West Lothian Question' would be for Scottish MPs to cease to have the right to vote at Westminster on matters exclusive to other regions. A Labour government could find itself in the uniquely uncomfortable position of having an overall majority in the House of Commons, but only when the Scottish and Welsh MPs were included in the total. Only on a handful of occasions has the Labour Party won a majority of English seats at a general election. For the time being dual membership of both the Scottish and Westminster Parliaments will be possible. The Scotland Act 1998 and the Government of Wales Act 1998 do not directly address the 'West Lothian' question, but s86 of the Scotland Act 1998 does remove the requirement contained in rule 1(2) of Sch 2 to the Parliamentary Constituencies Act 1986 to the effect that Scotland is to have not less than 71 constituencies for the purposes of elections to the Westminster Parliament. This opens the way for the number of Scottish constituencies to be reduced, thus deflecting some criticisms regarding over-representation. Note however, that if the number of constituencies in Scotland is reduced, there could be a consequent reduction in the membership of the Scottish Parliament itself to maintain the balance between the constituency and part list members.

The reality, it is submitted, is that it is not possible to tamper with one aspect of Parliament's powers, for example by devolving power to Scottish and Welsh assemblies, without also looking at what reforms this would necessitate as regards the 'rump' of the Parliament that would remain to govern England.

Resignation from the House of Commons

In law, a member of the House of Commons is unable to resign his seat. The only way to be released from membership is to accept a disqualifying office. Traditionally the offices of Steward or Bailiff of the Chiltern Hundreds or of the Manor of Northstead were used for this purpose. They are expressly preserved as a ground of disqualification by s4 of the 1975 Act.

Ministers of the Crown

Not more than 95 holders of specified ministerial offices may sit and vote at any one time in the House of Commons: House of Commons Disqualification Act 1975, s2(1). Additional appointments must therefore be made from the House of Lords.

Oath of allegiance

Members of Parliament are required to swear an oath of allegiance to the Crown at the start of any new Parliament as a pre-condition to discharging their functions fully as representatives of their constituents: see s1 Oaths Act 1978. Those wishing to do so can affirm under s5. It is an offence to sit and vote in the House of Commons without having been sworn as required: see the Parliamentary Oaths Act 1866. Gerry Adams and Martin McGuiness, Sinn Fein MPs elected in May 1997, could not take their seats at Westminster because they refused to take the oath or affirm. They refused to comply with the swearing requirement because it involved swearing allegiance to the British Crown. They did however obtain passes to tour the building and use some of the facilities. In June 1997 the Speaker ruled that the two MPs were not entitled to office facilities in the House of Commons, but would be allowed free stationery and postage in taking up constituency issues. The MPs indicated that they intended to challenge the ruling before the European Court of Human Rights in Strasbourg.

6.2 The Speaker of the House of Commons

History of the Speakership

The Speakership dates back under its present title to 1377 when Sir Thomas Hungerford was appointed. Up to the seventeenth century the Speaker was often an agent of the King. By the Civil War the Speaker's duty to the House of Commons had been recognised, as illustrated by Speaker Lenthall's reply in the House to King Charles I who had come to arrest five members for treason:

> 'May it please Your Majesty, I have neither eyes to see nor tongue to speak in this place, but as the House is pleased to direct me, whose servant I am here, and I humbly beg Your Majesty's pardon that I cannot give any other answer than this to what Your Majesty is pleased to demand of me.'

Election of the Speaker

The Speaker is elected at the beginning of every new Parliament or when the previous Speaker dies or retires. He does not generally change with a change of government. In the past when a new Speaker has been required, the practice has been for the longest serving member of the House to move the election of the member, selected from the government party, whose name has been previously agreed between the party leaders in consultation with backbenchers. The House then votes for this member. Since 1992 there have been two contested elections for the Speakership.

Duties of the Speaker

The Speaker must be seen to be completely impartial and be above party politics and preserve the rights of minorities in the House, hence the requirement that on taking office he should sever his party connections. While the Speaker must continue as a Member of Parliament, he does not speak in debate or vote in the House, and is usually returned unopposed at general elections. Although unable to represent his constituents' interests in the House, he is able to deal with their individual grievances privately with the government departments concerned.

The Speaker acts as chairman during debates and generally presides over the House, except when it is in committee. It is the Speaker who calls members to speak and decides how many supplementary questions shall be allowed at Question Time. He is responsible for the maintenance of order and the general conduct of debates. He can request members using unparliamentary language or behaviour to withdraw. In cases of grave general disorder he may suspend the sitting. If a member is wilfully disobedient to a ruling the Speaker can 'name' the member, thereby suspending him from the House. He guides the House on all questions of procedure and privilege. He will rule as to whether a certain matter is in accordance with the rules and precedents of the House. It is the Speaker who reprimands on behalf of the House offenders brought to the Bar. The Speaker does not vote in division unless there is a tie, in which case, according to the ruling of Speaker Addington (1796), 'the Speaker should always vote for further discussion where this is possible'.

For example, in July 1993, during the passage of what was to become the European Communities (Amendment) Act 1993 (the Bill to ratify the Maastricht Treaty), the House of Commons had to consider an opposition amendment that called for the adoption of the Protocol on Social Policy. The vote on the opposition motion produced an apparent dead heat, the Speaker exercising her casting vote in the government's favour.

The Speaker will usually give his casting vote in favour of the introduction of a Bill, in favour of a Bill being given its Second Reading, or against a guillotine motion. He also decides which of the amendments proposed at the Report Stage of legislation shall be debated. This is an important power. The Speaker's decision to allow debate on a long list of proposed amendments obviously affects the speed with which a Bill is passed, and may even result in the Bill not completing all of its stages in both Houses before the end of the session. This is particularly relevant in the case of Private Members' Bills for which there is in any case little time made available for debate.

The Speaker also determines whether a Bill is a 'money Bill' within the meaning of the Parliament Act 1911. He decides as to whether an application for an emergency debate under Standing Order No 10 is proper to be put to the House. He is partially responsible for the selection of the topic for the daily adjournment debate on Thursdays. The Speaker also decides whether to put a closure motion proposed during the passage of legislation to the House. A closure motion occurs where an MP, usually a government Whip, moves 'that the question be now put', that is, that the debate terminate and that a vote be taken immediately. If a closure motion is put and the House passes it, with at least 100 members voting in favour, then there can be no further debate and the question must immediately be put to the vote. The Speaker may refuse to put the closure motion on the grounds that it is an abuse of the rules of the House or an infringement of the rights of minorities. It is for the Speaker to decide whether the termination of debate at that point would involve too drastic a curtailment of the rights of MPs to debate proposed legislation. Because of the lack of parliamentary time and the rule that a Bill must go through all its stages in both Houses within one session of Parliament, the exercise of the Speaker's discretion on the question of a closure motion can be of great significance.

The Speaker is also chairman of the Boundary Commissions, which review the distribution of seats, and represents the Commons in its relations with the Lords and the Sovereign.

6.3 The legislative process

Introduction

A proposed piece of legislation is called a Bill. It becomes an Act when it has been passed by Parliament and has received the Royal Assent. A distinction must be drawn between Public and Private Bills. Public Bills seek to alter the general law and concern the whole community. They are introduced into Parliament under the Standing Orders of the two Houses relating to public business. Private Bills affect only a section of the community and relate to matters of individual corporate or local interest. They are promoted by interested persons or bodies outside Parliament and are subject to separate Standing Orders relating to private business.

Hybrid Bills are Public Bills that are classified by the Speaker as having a particular effect on one section of the community. They are defined by Erskine May as 'a Public Bill which affects a particular private interest in a manner different from the private interests of other persons or bodies of the same category or class'.

Public Bill procedure

Most Public Bills are government Bills introduced and promoted by the government; but some may be Private Members' Bills introduced by backbench Members of Parliament. Bills may be introduced into either House, but politically controversial legislation, financial legislation, and electoral legislation will be introduced in the House of Commons. In the case of a government Bill, introduced in the House of Commons, the procedure for enactment is as outlined below.

First Reading

A 'dummy' copy of the Bill is placed on the table on the day of presentation; when the moment of presentation is reached, after questions, the Speaker calls the sponsoring minister, the Clerk reads the short title of the Bill and the minister, or a Whip acting on his behalf, names a (notional) day for the Bill's Second Reading. No debate takes place at the First Reading. The Bill is then printed and published and the opposition, particularly, can study it with a view to criticism and amendment.

Second Reading

When the Bill is printed it can proceed after examination for compliance with the House's rules, to its first substantive stage, which is called the Second Reading. The date on which the debate is to take place will be announced by the Leader of the House. Wherever possible the government aims to leave two weekends between the printing and Second Reading of a Bill. The Second Reading is the time at which the House considers the principle and merits of the Bill, and a vote is taken on whether to give the Bill a Second Reading. It is rare however for a government Bill to be denied a Second Reading. Under Standing Order No 90 a Bill can be considered by a Second Reading Committee, in which case the formal question on Second Reading can be voted upon without debate in the House. Although little used, this procedure is suited to non-controversial Bills not involving substantial issues of principle. Under s19 of the Human Rights Act 1998 the minister in charge of a Bill is under a duty to make a statement, prior to the Second Reading, to the effect that in his view the provisions of the Bill are compatible with the Convention rights as protected by the 1998 Act. Alternatively he must make a statement explaining that, although he is unable to make a statement of compatibility, the government nevertheless wishes the House to proceed with the Bill.

Committee stage

After Second Reading, a Bill is normally referred to a standing committee consisting of between 16 and 50 members nominated by a committee of selection and reflecting party strength in the House. Standing committees are constituted to deal with Bills as and when necessary, and there have been up to ten sitting at one time. They are designated by letters – eg Standing Committee 'A', Standing Committee 'B'. Standing committees will normally be divided on party grounds, mirroring the House itself. Bills relating exclusively to Wales may be referred to the Welsh Grand Committee

The committee stage involves detailed clause by clause consideration of the Bill. The committee may generally amend the Bill as it thinks fit, provided that the amendments made are relevant to the subject matter of the Bill. Amendments and new clauses may be moved by the minister, the opposition spokesmen, or by any member of the committee. Provision also exists for non-party political Bills to be referred to special standing committees, where a more informed discussion can take place and evidence can be taken, but this procedure has only rarely been on used, not least because of the delay that would ensue in the passage of the legislation. The quinquennial Armed forces Bill is usually considered by an ad hoc select committee, utilising the expertise of the Defence Select Committee.

Instead of referring a Bill to a standing committee the Bill may be considered by a committee of the whole House. In general, this procedure will be used for Bills of first class constitutional importance, those requiring a very rapid passage, and certain financial measures, including at least part of each year's Finance Bill. Exceptionally, Bills may be referred to a select committee, in which case evidence may be taken and a report made. There is no settled definition of what constitutes a Bill of first class constitutional importance, but examples might include the Parliament Acts 1911 and 1949, the Statute of Westminster 1931, and any legislation designed to achieve significant reforms of the House of Lords or the electoral system. In addition, consideration of the clauses in some Bills may be divided between standing committees and a committee of the whole House, the more sensitive or controversial aspects being considered by the committee of the whole House (eg Sunday trading hours, or the age of consent for homosexual acts).

Report stage
When a Bill has completed its committee stage, it is reported as amended to the whole House. Further amendments, alteration of amendments made by the committee, and new clauses, may be made at this stage. All members may speak and vote at this stage, unlike in a standing committee. In theory, a Bill that has been considered by a Second Reading committee can be referred to a committee for its report stage, but this rarely occurs in practice.

Third Reading
The final Commons stage of the Bill is the Third Reading. The Bill is debated once more in general terms with only verbal amendments allowed. Except for Bills of major political or constitutional importance the Third Reading is usually brief and formal.

House of Lords stages and amendments
After its Third Reading, the Bill is sent to the House of Lords where it goes through stages similar to those in the Commons. The House of Lords has no standing committees and the committee stage is usually taken by a committee of the whole House. If the Lords amend the Bill, their amendments are printed and considered by the Commons and agreed to, amended, or disagreed to. If they are disagreed to, the Commons send to the Lords a note of the reasons for the disagreement and the Lords consider the matter further. In the case of an impasse between the Houses, the Parliament Act 1949 provides for the will of the Commons to prevail. The Lords have no power to amend a Money Bill.

The Parliament Act 1911 annulled the power of the Lords over Money Bills, reducing it to a delaying power of one month only, after which a Money Bill sent up from the Commons may receive the Royal Assent even if it has not been approved by the House of Lords. The Lords power over all other Public Bills (except a Bill to extend the maximum life of a Parliament beyond five years) was reduced by the 1911 Act to a mere delaying power, the power to delay being further reduced by the Parliament Act 1949. The position now is that a Bill which the Lords refuse to pass within one month may nevertheless receive the Royal Assent provided that it has been passed by the House of Commons in two successive sessions, and one year has elapsed between the date of the Bill's Second Reading in the House of Commons in the first session and its Third Reading in the House of Commons in the second session.

Royal Assent

The assent of the Sovereign is required after a Bill has passed through both Houses for it to pass into law. Such assent has not been withheld since 1707, but every Bill is still required to go through the procedure appointed. After the Royal Assent has been given the Bill becomes an Act.

Commencement Orders

Some Acts are brought into force immediately, some at a date specified in the Act and others by Commencement Orders, which may activate all or part of the Act at a date determined by the government by Order in Council or a minister by statutory instrument. In this respect it should be noted that special measures apply to so-called Budget resolutions, announced in the course of the Chancellor's Budget speech. Under s5 of the Provisional Collection of Taxes Act 1968, Budget resolutions coming into immediate effect have to be passed within 25 days of the House approving the resolution. Where the relevant Finance Bill (which gives effect to the Budget proposals) is not given a Second Reading within 30 sitting days from the date they are announced, they cease to have effect; the same applies if the Finance Bill is not enacted within four months of the resolutions coming into effect. In any event, a government unable to get its Finance Bill through the House of Commons is likely to resign, thus prompting a general election.

Private Members' Bills procedure

Although the bulk of the legislative programme is taken up by government Bills, there are a number of procedures under which private members may initiate Bills. The relatively small amount of time available for consideration of private Members' Bills is allocated by means of a ballot drawn on the second Thursday the House sits in each session. The ten members placed highest in the ballot may claim some of the expenses incurred in drafting their Bills.

Standing Order No 6 relating to the precedence of government business lays down that ten Fridays be set aside for Private Members' Bills and ten Fridays for private members' motions. Time for debate on Private Members' Bills is therefore severely restricted. Members may nominate a day for the Second Reading of their Bill, and it is obviously to the advantage of the member drawn first in the ballot to nominate the first Friday available, for the second member to nominate the second Friday, and so forth. But on only six Fridays is precedence given to Second Readings. Since debate on an important or contentious Bill can be expected to last for nearly the whole of the short Friday session, not all, even of the ballot Bills, will be debated. On the remaining four Fridays, precedence is given to the later stages of those Bills that received their Second Readings earlier in the session.

A member who is low down in the ballot may nevertheless succeed. If he puts his Bill down for the first Friday, for example, he may hope for two courses of action. Firstly, if the Bill named first is not particularly controversial, and few members wish to speak on it, he may hope to get a debate during part of the remaining time left available. Otherwise he may hope to have his Bill given a Second Reading without debate at 2.30pm, when the Clerk reads out the titles of Bills that are on the order paper, in their order of precedence. But if a member should shout 'object', the Bill is not given a Second Reading and the member in charge of the Bill must nominate another day, failing which the Bill is regarded as dropped. A Bill whose sponsoring member is placed very low in the ballot, or one introduced under the Ten Minute Rule or Standing Order 39 (see below), is bound to have to take its chance at 2.30pm. It follows that such a Bill is very unlikely to make any further progress unless its contents are such as to arouse absolutely no dissent. A Bill that gets read a second time on a Friday is usually then committed to a standing committee, but it may go to a committee of the whole House if the member so moves after Second Reading. There is a single Standing Committee for all Private Members' Bills (except Scottish Bills) that have been read a second time. The same queuing system applies here as at the other stages, and this is a substantial impediment to the passage of Bills, particularly long and complex ones.

Another impediment to a Bill getting a Second Reading, or negotiating its report stage in time, is the necessity to secure the closure. Many Private Members' Bills are 'talked out'; in other words, the debate on them has not been concluded when the available time is exhausted. This occurs more frequently than is the case with government Bills, not only because less time is available, but also because the 'guillotine' (ie a time allocation order whereby debate on a particular matter can be brought to a close once the time limit is reached) is not used on Private Members' Bills. If opponents of the Bill, therefore, are still speaking just before 2.30pm, its sponsor or a colleague must seek to move 'that the question be now put', otherwise the debate would be interrupted and stand adjourned without the question having been put. The Chair will not permit the closure to be moved if insufficient debate has taken place. In addition a motion of closure requires the support of 100 votes if it is to be carried, and this is difficult to achieve on a Friday when attendance at the House is low.

Private Members' Bills cover a variety of subjects, often controversial matters such as divorce law reform, banning blood sports, abortion and homosexuality, for which the government chooses not to allocate time, or is disinclined to introduce itself because of adverse public opinion. A private member may not propose a Bill the main object of which is the creation of a charge on the public revenue. Not surprisingly, given the above, relatively few Private Members' Bills succeed in terms of becoming Acts of Parliament. In most sessions approximately 100 Bills will be introduced, of which one could expect 15 to become law.

The Ten Minute Rule

Bills introduced under the Ten Minute Rule are not, in general, serious attempts at legislation. The procedure is mainly used as a means of drawing attention to a particular subject or testing parliamentary opinion on a subject. Members wishing to present a Ten Minute Rule Bill must give notice of a motion for leave to bring in a Bill at 10.00am every Tuesday and Wednesday, for a Tuesday or Wednesday three weeks ahead. The member may speak briefly in support of the Bill and an opponent may reply. The House may then decide on whether the Bill should be introduced. Upon occasion such Bills do become law through general consent, though there is rarely time for debate after the introduction.

Standing Order No 39

Standing Order No 39 allows every member the right to introduce a Bill after due notice. The Bills introduced under this procedure cannot be high on the list on Second Reading Fridays and there is little practical likelihood of their being debated, unless the government makes time available on other days in the week. However, Bills that are totally non-controversial are sometimes introduced under this system, and these have occasionally passed into law.

Private Bill procedure

A Private Bill is a Bill seeking to alter the law relating to a particular locality (Local Bill) or seeking to confer rights on or absolve from liability a particular person or body of persons (Personal Bill). The procedure for private legislation is regulated by standing orders of each House relating to private business. They are initiated by petition from persons or bodies (promoters) outside Parliament. The standing orders require that full notice shall be given to persons and bodies where legal rights may be affected by the proposed legislation, so that they may, if necessary, oppose it. In the House of Commons the Bill is introduced by being presented at the table by the clerk of the Private Bill office. It is then deemed to have been read for a first time. At the Second Reading debate, the House determines whether, assuming the facts stated in the preamble to the Bill to be true, the Bill is unobjectionable from the point of view of national policy. If read a second time, the Bill is committed to a committee of four members in the Commons (or five members in the Lords).

The committee stage of a Private Bill has some of the features of a quasi-judicial proceeding. The promoters and the opponents of the Bill are often represented by counsel and may call evidence. The Committee first considers the preamble of the Bill. If the preamble is accepted the clauses are then considered and may be amended. If the preamble is rejected the Bill falls. After Committee stage the Bill is reported to the House. It then follows a procedure similar to that of a Public Bill.

Hybrid Bill procedure

The standing orders for private business apply to a hybrid Bill so that, if opposed after its Second Reading, it goes before a select committee where those whose legal rights are affected by the Bill may raise their objections and petition against it. After the petitioners have been heard by the select committee, the Bill then passes through its committee stage and later stages as if it were an ordinary Bill.

6.4 Opportunities for debate in the House of Commons

Apart from the opportunities for debate during the legislative process, there are various other opportunities for debate in the House of Commons.

Adjournment debates

At the end of every day's business, when the adjournment of the House is formally moved, half an hour is made available for a private member to raise a topic in debate and for a ministerial reply to be given. Members with topics they want debated enter a ballot. The ballot determines what the topic is going to be on Monday, Tuesday, Wednesday and Friday. For Thursday the Speaker selects one of the submitted topics. Usually, adjournment debates are on some matter of local interest, so the debates tend to be constituency orientated. Often, if a member is dissatisfied with an answer he has received in correspondence with a minister or in answer to a parliamentary question, he may raise the matter on the adjournment. However, adjournment debates usually take place in an almost empty House and at an inconvenient time for press coverage. Such debates are not followed by a vote of the House.

Standing Order No 10 – motion to adjourn

Standing Order No 10 allows members to suggest that a specific and important matter should have urgent consideration and that an emergency debate be held upon it. It is for the Speaker to decide whether the matter is sufficiently important and urgent to warrant giving it precedence; the Chair in general gives leave very seldom. If leave is granted, and if the motion is approved by the House or supported by 40 members, the motion will be debated either that evening or the following day.

The final day before each of the four parliamentary recesses is also devoted to a series of private members debates and ten Fridays per session are also set aside for private member motions. Other opportunities for debate occur in the debate on the address in reply to the Queen's Speech, the debate on the Budget, debates on motions of censure, the 19 Opposition Days, the three Estimate Days and on the Second Reading of Consolidated Fund Bills.

Devices for curtailing debate

Delay of Bills in the House of Commons is a threat to the government's legislative programme. The more time which one Bill takes, the less time is available for other legislation, and a government with a heavy legislative programme may find its plans frustrated by the opposition or individual members seeking to prolong proceedings. To overcome this threat, various methods of curtailing debate have been adopted by the House.

Standing Order 22
The Speaker or chairman may require a member to discontinue his speech if he persists in irrelevance or tedious repetition.

The closure
Under Standing Order 30 any member, either in the House or in committee, may move 'that the question be now put'. If the chairman finds the application in order the closure motion must be put forthwith and voted upon without debate. Not fewer than 100 members must vote for the motion. If carried the debate ceases and the motion under discussion must be voted upon.

The kangaroo
This is the power of the Speaker at the Report stage (or the chairman at the Committee stage) to select from among the various proposed amendments those that are to be discussed.

The guillotine motion
The term 'guillotine motion' is a colloquial expression for an allocation of time motion. The purpose of such a motion is to provide that one or more stages of a Bill be disposed of either by a fixed date, or by a fixed number of sittings of the House, or a committee, or both. Each guillotine motion is specific, and devised by the government for the particular Bill or Bills to which it applies. The guillotine motion may be debated for no more than three hours. If a Bill before a standing committee is the subject of an 'allocation of time order', a detailed timetable is recommended to the standing committee. Some or all of the details of the timetable may be prescribed in the allocation of time order itself, or left to the Business Committee to recommend.

The Business Committee, set up under Standing Order No 45, consists of the

Chairman of Ways and Means (the Deputy Speaker) who acts as chairman, and no more than eight MPs nominated by the Speaker in respect of each Bill. The function of the Committee is to divide the Bill into various parts and allot time to each part. The effect of the order is that at the end of each allotted period the part of the Bill in question is voted upon forthwith, although substantial parts of the Bill may not yet have been discussed at all.

The guillotine is not lightly used and is not applied without reason, for instance, in the face of delaying tactics amounting to obstruction. In other cases the guillotine could not be applied because the government could not be sure of carrying the necessary motion.

On the whole, these devices are unpopular with parliamentarians because they can restrict valuable criticism and amendment of legislation. If used extensively – and they are being used increasingly – it can be argued that they deny the legislative role of Parliament.

6.5 Parliamentary questions

Since the late seventeenth century it has been the practice to question ministers in Parliament. There are three categories of question:

1. Question for oral answer, which is intended to be given an oral answer in the House during Question Time.
2. Private notice question which can be asked if the Speaker judges its subject matter to be urgent and important. These are take orally in the House at the end of Question Time.
3. Question for written answer, which is not taken orally in the House but is printed in the Official Report (Hansard).

Parliamentary question procedure

The process for asking a question in the Chamber is fairly lengthy. The member must first give notice of his question by handing it to the clerks in the Table Office not more than ten sitting days and not less than two sitting days before it is to be asked. The question, either seeking information or pressing for action, must be addressed to a specific minister and must concern a matter for which he is responsible as a minister. A question addressed to the wrong minister may be transferred to the minister actually responsible. Ministers are questioned on a rota basis, each department being allocated particular days of the week. Prime Minister's questions used to be scheduled for each Tuesday and Thursday from 3.15 to 3.30pm. Since May 1997 Prime Minister's questions have been scheduled for a 30-minute slot on a Wednesday. No member may ask more than eight questions in every ten sitting days, with a maximum of two questions on any one day. Only one question may be put to each minister on any day. Answers to questions are drafted in the appropriate department. They provide not only an answer for the particular question asked, but also prepare sufficient background material to enable the minister to deal with any supplementary questions that may be asked. Ministers may refuse to answer questions affecting state security, or which touch on matters that are sub judice.

Procedure at Question Time

Question Time takes place on Monday, Tuesday, Wednesday and Thursday, after prayers from 2.35 to 3.30pm. The Speaker calls the member whose question stands first on the Order Paper. The minister reads out his prepared answer. Supplementary questions may then be asked which must relate to the original question. These will be unscripted and contain an element of surprise. When the Speaker considers that enough supplementaries have been asked he calls question number two on the Order Paper, and so on until the time allocated to questions has expired. Any oral questions that have not been answered by then will receive a written answer printed in the next issue of Hansard.

Private notice questions

Questions concerning sudden emergencies or developments that require immediate attention may be raised with the appropriate minister by means of the private notice question. To ask a question by private notice, a member must apply to the Speaker before 12 noon on the day on which an answer is required. Private notice is given to the minister concerned and his department is immediately informed. Besides being subject to the same rules as to form and content as ordinary questions, a private notice question must satisfy two additional criteria – it must be urgent, and it must be of public importance. If the Speaker allows a private notice question it will be answered immediately after Question Time.

Questions for written answer

There is no limit to the number of questions for written answer that may be tabled and these form the majority of questions answered in each session. Written questions are subject to the same rules of order as oral questions. Usually written questions are answered within seven days of being tabled. If an earlier answer is required a priority written answer may be requested provided a minimum of two sitting days notice is given.

Reform of Question Time

Does the Question Time procedure actually achieve anything worthwhile? It is suggested in some quarters that the effectiveness of Question Time as a method of securing control of the executive by Parliament is limited, partly because it is an unequal struggle between the minister, with vast library and research facilities available through his department, and the backbencher, who has only modest facilities available. Indeed, the reticence of the department in giving information may mean that the backbencher is not even aware of difficult and pertinent questions which he could and should be asking. When a parliamentary question is submitted it is passed immediately to the relevant government department and the officials in that department will give priority to preparing a brief for the minister enabling him to answer not only that question, but also any supplementary questions that the officials anticipate. The department knows by whom the question is asked, and in preparing the brief will bear in mind the interest and concerns of the questioner and other MPs who are similarly interested and likely to put supplementary questions. Generally, therefore, the private member is no match for the minister with his Civil Service brief.

The opposition parties ask more questions than the government party, but because there are more government backbenchers they may catch the Speaker's eye and ask more supplementary questions. Some questions are 'arranged' by the government so that it can publicise or emphasise a particular matter, especially government success. Government policy is not often changed by a question but it can be pushed faster in a particular direction. Questions very often uncover some administrative flaw and secure a remedy because of the publicity given the matter. Ministers rarely gain or lose in reputation at Question Time. Most of them can cope quite satisfactorily with it having risen through the House themselves. Often a minister will deal with a question simply by resorting to a party political gibe, stonewalling or evasion.

During 1995 the House of Commons Procedure Committee considered the case for reforming the Question Time procedure (*Prime Minister's Questions*, Select Committee on Procedure, 7th Rep. HC 555), and recommended that a number of changes should be introduced on an experimental basis. The Committee observed that:

> 'It could be said that Prime Minister's Questions have developed from being a procedure for the legislature to hold the executive to account into a partisan joust between the noisier supporters of the main political parties.'

The Committee proposed that questions at the Thursday session should be on specific issues notified in advance (the day before). Supplementary questions would have to be linked to the main question in terms of subject matter. Backbenchers' names would be drawn by ballot, but the Leader of the Opposition would always be permitted the second question, of which he would have to give notice by noon on Thursday. The aim of these reforms would be to move away from the ritualised and time-consuming process of the 'open' question, towards a more structured and orderly debate. Critics have observed that a key advantage of the existing procedures is that a member can effectively ambush the Prime Minister, thus securing maximum political advantage.

As indicated above, one of first changes introduced by Prime Minister Blair was the longer weekly Wednesday session of Prime Minister's questions, in place of the twice-weekly sessions. His aim was for a more informative and less adversarial exchange with MPs.

6.6 Parliamentary committees

The committees of the House of Commons fall into two main categories:

1. standing committees; and
2. select committees.

As explained above standing committees are appointed to deal with the Committee stage in the passing of Bills. In addition, there are the Grand Committees for Scotland, Wales and Northern Ireland, standing committees appointed to deal with delegated legislation and those appointed to consider European Community documents. The standing committees on delegated legislation consider most statutory instruments and other orders subject to the affirmative resolution procedure, and those measures subject to the negative resolution procedure in relation to which a prayer has been tabled (ie objections have been raised). The findings of the committee are reported to the House and a vote is taken on the measures in question 'forthwith', ie without further debate in the House. Draft EC legislation is considered by the Select Committee on European Legislation. If further scrutiny is felt to be appropriate the EC measures can be referred to one of the two European Standing Committees ('A' and 'B'). The role of the Scottish and Welsh Grand Committees has been expanded in recent years, reflecting the move towards the devolution of power to these regions. In addition to considering proposals for legislation the Grand Committees can question ministers and debate motions relevant to their respective regions. The Scottish and Welsh Grand Committees also regularly sit away from Westminster.

Select committees of the House of Commons can be sub-divided into three main categories:

1. Ad hoc select committees;
2. sessional select committees; and
3. departmental select committees.

Where select committees are designated as 'joint committees' they include members of the Lords and Commons sitting together. Ad hoc select committees are set up for a specific purpose when the need arises. Their inquiries are specified and limited in their extent and they are dissolved when their inquiries are concluded. Examples include the Committee on Standards in Public Life set up in 1994, and the Joint

Committee on Parliamentary Privilege appointed in 1997–98. A joint committee was also appointed to consider options for reform of the House of Lords during 2002.

Sessional select committees are those set up at the beginning of the session and remaining throughout the session. They comprise those committees concerned with the domestic running of the House, and those concerned with the scrutiny of some aspects of government activity, with the latter to some extent complementing the work of the departmental select committees considered below.

Domestic select committees

The domestic select committees of the House of Commons have their work allocated as follows:

1. Accommodation and Works (nine members, quorum of three);
2. Administration (nine members, quorum of three);
3. Catering (nine members, quorum of three);
4. Information (nine members, quorum of three);
5. Finance and Services (11 members, quorum of three);
6. Broadcasting (11 members, quorum of three);
7. Liaison (31 members, quorum of six) – formally established in 1980, having existed on an ad hoc basis from 1967 to co-ordinate the work of the select committees, consider general matters relating to the work of select committees, and to advise the House of Commons Commission on the work of select committees as appropriate.
8. Standards and Privileges (11 members, quorum of five) – this Committee now combines the work of the disbanded Select Committee on Members' Interests and the Select Committee on Privileges. The Committee also oversees the work of the Parliamentary Commissioner for Standards (see section 6.10 below);
9. Procedure (17 members, quorum of five);
10. Selection (nine members, quorum of three) – appoints members to standing committees and proposes membership of select committees;
11. Standing Orders (18 members, quorum of three);
12. Modernisation (15 members, quorum of three) – created in June 1997.

Select committees and legislative proposals

Four select committees exist to scrutinise proposed legislation, organised as follows:

1. Deregulation (18 members, quorum of five) – considers proposals from ministers under the Deregulation and Contracting Out Act 1994. The Committee considers the proposals and whether or not they should be laid before Parliament. At the end of the 60-day laying process the Committee can make its recommendation to the House regarding approval or rejection.
2. European Legislation (16 members, quorum of five) – considers draft EC

legislation and documents submitted by one EU institution to another, such as draft Council recommendations and resolutions. The Committee can recommend further scrutiny by the standing committees dealing with EC legislation.

3. Joint Committee on Statutory Instruments (14 members – seven from each House – quorum of two from each House) – considers whether statutory instruments are properly drafted and within the powers of the relevant parent Act. Cannot question the merits of a measure. Where delegated legislation deals with financial matters only the Commons members take part.

4. Consolidation Bills Joint Committee (24 members – 12 from each House – quorum of two from the Commons and three from the Lords) – looks at proposals to draw together provisions in existing legislation for inclusion in consolidating Bills.

Other non-departmental select committees

Three other select committees examine external matters, they are:

1. Committee of Public Accounts (16 members, quorum of four) – considers value for money audits prepared by the Comptroller and Auditor General and the accounts detailing public expenditure approved by Parliament.

2. Committee on Public Administration (11 members, quorum of three) – oversees the work of the Parliamentary Commissioner for Administration (ie the 'Ombudsman') and the standard of administration provided by the Civil Service.

3. Environmental Audit Committee (15 members, quorum of four) – established in 1997, this Committee oversees the extent to which government departments and other public bodies achieve targets set in relation to pollution control and sustainable development.

4. Human Rights (Joint Committee) (six members from each House, quorum three from each House) – considers and report on matters relating to human rights in the United Kingdom and proposals for remedial and draft remedial orders made under the Human Rights Act 1998.

Departmental select committees

On 25 June 1979 the House of Commons considered several motions relating to the structure and scope of its own departmental select committee system, based upon proposals for reform contained in the first report from the Select Committee on Procedure, Session 1977–78. After debate, the House approved a package of reforms amounting to the establishment of a system of new departmental committees to replace the rather ad hoc system that had been developing piecemeal since the 1960s. The reform left untouched many of the (then) existing committees. Those that closely resembled the new departmentally based committees were abolished so as to avoid confusion, duplication of effort and unnecessary cost.

The departmental select committees are currently organised as follows:

1. Agriculture (maximum number of members 11, quorum three);
2. Defence (maximum number of members 11, quorum three);
3. Culture, Media and Sport (maximum number of members 11, quorum three);
4. Education and Skills (maximum number of members 11, quorum three);
5. Environment, Food and Rural Affairs (maximum number of members 17, quorum five);
6. Foreign Affairs (maximum number of members 11, quorum three);
7. Health (maximum number of members 11, quorum three);
8. Home Affairs (maximum number of members 11, quorum three);
9. International Development (maximum number of members 11, quorum three);
10. Northern Ireland Affairs (maximum number of members 13, quorum four);
11. Science and Technology (maximum number of members 11, quorum three);
12. Scottish Affairs (maximum number of members 11, quorum three);
13. Trade and Industry (maximum number of members 11, quorum three);
14. Transport, Local Government and the Regions (maximum number of members 17, quorum five);
15. Treasury (maximum number of members 11, quorum three);
16. Welsh Affairs (maximum number of members 11, quorum three);
17. Work and Pensions (maximum number of members 11, quorum three).

The Foreign Affairs Committee, the Home Affairs Committee and the Treasury Committee each have the power to appoint one sub-committee, eg the Sub-Committee on Immigration Advice.

The select committees on Education and Skills and Environment, Food and Rural Affairs can each appoint two sub-committees

Membership and staffing

The arrangements for membership of select committees are provided in the standing orders of the House. By convention government ministers, parliamentary private secretaries and prominent front-bench spokesman are not nominated. The chairman of each committee is chosen by the members of that committee, although party whips have in the past exercised considerable influence in this regard. In July 2001 government whips intervened to remove two 'non-Blairite' Labour MPs, Gwyneth Dunwoody and Donald Anderson as chairs of the Transport and Foreign Affairs select committees respectively. Faced with a backbench revolt the government eventually reinstated both MPs as committee chairs and suggested that the Modernisation Committee should review the issue of select committee membership. Whilst the balance of the parties in the House of Commons will be reflected in the composition of each committee, the chair may be drawn from the opposition. The maximum number of members for each committee is laid down in standing orders. Members are nominated or discharged on a motion tabled by the Committee of

Selection. The House of Commons Commission is responsible for the provision of adequate support staff for committee work. Under Standing Order No 99 each committee has the power to appoint persons with technical knowledge either to supply information that is not readily available, or to elucidate matters of complexity within the committee's order of reference. The numbers and distribution of these specialist advisers will vary according to the needs of each committee and the particular inquiry undertaken, but it has become possible for a pool of expertise to be permanently available, unlike the old system where advisers were appointed only for specific inquiries. Most committees have appointed specialist advisers, and also full-time researchers known as select committee temporary assistants. Each select committee is supported by staff from the Committee Office and has a clerk.

Scope of enquiries

The departmental select committees are appointed to examine the expenditure, administration and policy of the principal government departments and associated public bodies. Norman St John-Stevas, the then Leader of the House, explained this as follows:

> 'The objective of the new committee structure will be to strengthen the accountability of ministers to the House for the discharge of their responsibilities. Each committee will be able to examine the whole range of activity for which its minister or ministers have direct responsibility. The government also accepts the Procedure Committee's view that the committees must be able to look at the activities of some public bodies that exercise authority of their own and over which ministers do not have the same direct authority as they have over their own departments. The test in every case will be whether there is a significant degree of ministerial responsibility for the body concerned. (HC Deb, Vol 969 c44, 25 June 1979.)

Powers

Under the terms of the motion approved on 25 June 1979 the departmental select committees have the following powers:

> '(a) To send for persons, papers and records, to sit notwithstanding any adjournments of the House, to adjourn from place to place and to report from time to time.
> (b) To appoint persons with technical knowledge either to supply information which is not readily available or to elucidate matters of complexity within the committee's order of reference.
> (c) To report from time to time the minutes of evidence taken before sub-committees; and the sub-committees appointed under this Order shall have power to send for persons, papers and records, to sit notwithstanding any adjournment of the House, and to adjourn from place to place, and shall have a quorum of three.'

These powers are essentially the same as those granted to the old select committees. Whilst there was, perhaps, an assumption that those called to give evidence before select committees would be co-operative, experience has shown that this cannot be relied upon, notwithstanding the assurance given by the Leader of the House, on behalf of the government, that:

'... every minister from the most senior Cabinet minister to the most junior under secretary will do all in his or her power to co-operate with the new system of committees and to make it a success. I believe that declaration of interest to be a better guarantee than formal provisions laid down in standing orders.'

Select committees cannot compel the attendance of members of either House. When questioned, in 1986, by the Defence Select Committee in connection with the Westland Affair, and in particular about the decision to publish a letter written by the Attorney-General, Leon Brittan simply refused to answer. Similarly, in 1992, the two sons of the late Robert Maxwell refused to answer questions put by members of the Select Committee on Social Security. This was in fact referred to the House of Commons as a possible contempt, but the Maxwell brothers, who initially refused to attend, claimed privilege against self-incrimination.

Similarly, in February 1998 the House of Commons Home Affairs Select Committee had to order the Commander of the United Grand Lodge of England to hand over the names of freemasons who were allegedly involved in the John Stalker affair, the investigation into the Birmingham pub bombings and allegations of corruption made against members of the West Midlands serious crime squad. Initially the request was refused, but was eventually acceded to when it was made clear that failure to supply the names could result in a charge of contempt of Parliament, and possibly imprisonment.

Appearances by civil servants before select committees were governed by what were know as the 'Osmotherly rules'. Guidance is now to be found in the Cabinet Office publication *Departmental Evidence and Response to Select Committees* (1994). Paragraphs 38–41 provide:

'Officials who give evidence to select committees do so on behalf of their ministers and under their direction ... it is customary for ministers to decide which official or officials should represent them. Select committees have generally accepted this position. Should a committee invite a named official to appear, and the minister concerned did not wish to be represented by that official, the minister might suggest to the committee that another official could more appropriately do so. If a committee insisted on a particular official appearing before them, they could issue a formal order for attendance, and request the House to enforce it. In such an event the official would have to appear before the committee but, in all circumstances, the official would remain subject to ministerial instruction on how to answer questions and on what information to disclose.'

In effect this means that a civil servant can be instructed to remain silent under questioning. The position as regards former civil servants is perhaps more contentious. When the Select Committee on Trade and Industry was investigating the 'Iraqi Supergun' affair, the Secretary of State for Defence refused to liaise with two key civil servants who had retired after the events in question had occurred. The reason given was that former civil servants would not have access to departmental papers and could not be said to represent the minister in question, no longer being responsible to him. This attitude suggests that ministers see appearances before select committees as perhaps more adversarial than inquisitorial. Further, the 'Supergun' affair suggests that, whilst ministers see civil servants as owing responsibility to ministers, a minister is perhaps less accountable to Parliament: see further Chapter 7, section 7.3, and comments arising from the Scott Report.

Certain select committees were granted an increase in their powers following the second Report of the House of Commons Select Committee on Procedure (Cmnd 1532). The Home Affairs Select Committee has been given power to examine the work and spending of the Lord Chancellor's Department, the Attorney-General's Office, the Treasury Solicitor's Department, the Crown Prosecution Service and the Serious Fraud Office. The Committee will be allowed to examine the judicial appointments system but not individual judicial appointments. It will not have power to consider court cases or the confidential advice given by the Law Officers to the Crown.

Reports

Departmental committees have the power to report to the House. Standing Order No 81 provides that every select committee has the power to submit a report to the House detailing its opinion and observations upon any matter referred to them for their consideration, together with the minutes of the evidence taken before them, and also to make a special report of any matters which they may think fit to bring to the notice of the House. Approximately one-third of select committee reports are debated on the floor of the House. In any event the government is expected to reply to a select committee's recommendations within two months of a report being laid before the House. Provision is now made for select committee reports to be debated on three Wednesday mornings in each session.

An assessment of the present select committee system and possible reforms

Notwithstanding the important contribution made by select committees in ensuring a degree of scrutiny of the executive by the legislature, and the effectiveness of the post-1979 reforms, there are still a number of issues related to their powers and procedures that cause concern. Although the House of Commons Committee of Selection formally makes appointments to the committees, the party whips have considerable influence over who is chosen. This enables the front bench of a party to exclude from a committee any MP whose contribution to the work of a select committee is likely to be contrary to the policy of the front bench. Thus the government may attempt to exclude from a committee MPs of its own party who are likely to join with those from the opposition to produce a report highly critical of the government.

The effectiveness of select committees can be hampered by inadequate resourcing that prevents the enlisting of sufficient numbers of support staff, such as secretaries, researchers and technical experts. Some of these problems were highlighted in the report published by the Liaison Committee of Chairs of Select Committees (*Shifting the Balance*) in March 2000. The report also highlighted problems of committee members not turning up for meetings, and of reports being ignored.

MPs themselves have only a limited amount of time to devote to committee work and, if an MP is a careerist, he or she will want to devote energy to those activities that may lead to appointment to a ministerial or 'shadow' post. Worthy contribution to the work of committees may not be the most effective way of ensuring this.

It should also be noted that there are some aspects of central government work that are not shadowed by a select committee, notable the Prime Minister's Office (although the Committee on Public Administration has attempted to address this).

At present select committees choose for themselves the issues to be investigated. They could be made more effective if they were given specific responsibilities to report on the work of various agencies such as regulators and quangos. It has been suggested (see *Reinventing Westminster – Charter 88*, published October 1996) that select committees could be involved in the examination of draft Bills prior to their being introduced into the Commons, but there are clear dangers here of a blurring of the distinctions between select and standing committees.

Regarding the operation of select committees, an undoubted weakness is that there is still no effective sanction available against a minister who refuses to appear, or refuses to allow civil servants to appear to give evidence or face questioning. The Procedure Committee had suggested stronger powers, particularly to order the attendance of ministers:

> 'Select committees should be empowered to order the attendance of ministers to give evidence to them ... and to order the production of papers and records by ministers, including secretaries of state. In the event of a refusal by a minister to produce papers and records required by a select committee the committee should be empowered to claim precedence over public business for a debate on a Motion for an Address or for an Order for the Return of the Papers ...'

The government raised three main objections to these proposed powers: first that it was not appropriate for a select committee to order about members of the House – only the House as a whole had such a constitutional power. Second, that it was not appropriate for the committee to have procedure for a debate unless it was shown that the matter was one of general concern to the House as a whole. Third, the whole question was one of judgment sometimes involving public interest and not amenable to hard and fast rules.

Select committees have been remarkably successful in producing 'non-partisan' reports rather than dividing down party lines and producing a majority report by the government party and a minority report by the other parties. The extent to which such reports will influence the executive while there continues to be among MPs, particularly those on the front benches, such a strong belief in the notion and practice of party government, with a single party having the right to formulate policy, is questionable. The impact of any select committee finding may also be undermined by the fact that there is no guaranteed time set aside for debating committee reports (other than those of the Public Accounts Committee).

6.7 Parliamentary control of national finance

Parliamentary scrutiny of national finance can be divided into scrutiny of revenue raising and expenditure, and examination of the latter further subdivided into that which is prospective and that which is retrospective.

Taxation and borrowing

Taxation and borrowing must be authorised by statute. The power to levy taxes is found in an enabling Act, but the precise rates that will apply in any given financial year will be determined in the Budget. Traditionally the Budget was announced in March, but since 1994 consideration of both taxation and spending proposals has been combined and these issues are debated together in the autumn. The presentation of the Budget is followed by the introduction of the Finance Bill designed to give effect to the Budget proposals. Assuming the government of the day has a reliable working majority in the Commons there is little prospect of the opposition being able to influence the contents of the Finance Bill. Indeed, for a government to lose the vote on a Finance Bill would be tantamount to a vote of no confidence. Several days are set aside for debate on the Budget proposals but, given that the contents of the Budget is always a closely guarded secret, the reply to the Budget by the Leader of the Opposition has to be largely extempore, based on what he or she can prepare as the budget speech is progressing. Inevitably the debate normally focuses on a broad attack on government economic policies, rather than issues of detail.

Despite its significance in terms of the effect on the economy, there are few formal parliamentary controls over government borrowing as expressed in the Public Sector Borrowing Requirement (PSBR).

Expenditure

A charge on the public purse can only be incurred following a request by the Crown. Parliament responds to these requests by granting expenditure. Hence opposition parties cannot make formal demands for money to be spent on alternative projects. As far as parliamentary control over expenditure is concerned supply is granted by Parliament annually in the Appropriation Act, and the Consolidated Fund Acts.

Following reforms introduced in 1983, there are three annual 'estimate days' devoted to consideration of the main and supplementary estimates of spending, enabling the House of Commons to debate and vote on the details of public expenditure. What were formerly known as 'supply days' and used for consideration of spending plans by the opposition, have become 'opposition days'. Seventeen of these days are at the disposal of the Leader of the Opposition, and matters selected by him take precedence over government business. The three remaining days are allotted to the leader of the second largest opposition party, which is defined as the party of those not represented in the government which has the second largest number of members elected to the House as members of that party.

Since the setting up of the specialist select committee system in 1979, government estimates have been laid before the appropriate committee according to department, but there is no time guaranteed for the House to debate the reports of these committees, and certainly not before it has to vote the authorisation of the expenditure proposed. The degree of control exercised by these committees over government expenditure must therefore be regarded as quite limited.

Auditing of expenditure

The National Audit Act 1983 was introduced to strengthen parliamentary control and supervision of expenditure of public money by making new provision for the appointment and status of the Comptroller and Auditor General, establishing a Public Accounts Commission and a National Audit Office, and making new provision for promoting economy, efficiency and effectiveness in the use of public money by government departments and other authorities and bodies.

The Comptroller and Auditor General, appointed by the Prime Minister acting with the agreement of the chairman of the Public Accounts Committee, becomes, by virtue of his office, an officer of the House of Commons, having complete discretion in the discharge of his functions and as to the manner in which any examinations are carried out. In determining whether to carry out any such examinations, he shall take into account any proposals made by the Public Accounts Committee. The Comptroller and Auditor General may carry out examinations into the economy, efficiency and effectiveness with which any department, authority or other body (as prescribed by the Act) has used its resources in discharging its functions. He may not question the merits of the policy objectives of any department, authority or body in respect of which an examination is carried out. In conducting his investigations the Comptroller and Auditor General has a right of access to all such documents as he may reasonably require for discharging his functions. His reports are considered by the Public Accounts Committee.

The Public Accounts Committee was established in 1861 and has been re-appointed annually since then. It has 16 members, all backbenchers, selected so as to represent the composition of the House. The chairman is always a member of the opposition, usually with ministerial experience in finance. The Committee is generally regarded as one of the most successful select committees. It is concerned with accounts of money already spent, not with estimates of proposed expenditure. Its brief is to see that public money has been spent economically, and not wastefully. It has the power, under standing orders, to call for papers and civil servants and ministers for questioning. It reports to the Treasury and to the department concerned, as well as to Parliament. A day in each session is reserved for debating the Committee's reports. The reports may also prompt the questioning of ministers.

It is generally acknowledged that these reforms have helped to strengthen parliamentary scrutiny of public spending in terms of uncovering and highlighting serious financial mismanagement and inefficiency. Once the report is before Parliament the burden is on the government of the day to respond. It may be that the very existence of these procedures has a salutary effect on those responsible for spending taxpayers' money.

6.8 Reform of House of Commons procedures

The process by which Public Bills make the transition from statements of government policy to Acts of Parliament was considered by the House of Commons Modernisation Committee in its report published in July 1997. The Committee usefully summarised what it saw as the requirements of a proper legislative process:

> '(a) The government of the day must be assured of getting its legislation through in reasonable time (provided that it obtains the approval of the House).
> (b) The opposition in particular and Members in general must have a full opportunity to discuss and seek to change provisions to which they attach importance.
> (c) All parts of a Bill must be properly considered.
> (d) The time and expertise of Members must be used to better effect.
> (e) The House as a whole, and its legislative committees in particular, must be given full and direct information on the meaning and effect of the proposed legislation from those most directly concerned, and full published explanations from the government on the detailed provisions of its Bill.
> (f) Throughout the legislative process there must be greater accessibility to the public, and legislation should, so far as possible, be readily understandable and in plain English.
> (g) The legislative programme needs to be spread as evenly as possible throughout the session in both Houses.
> (h) There must be sufficient flexibility in any procedures to cope with, for example, emergency legislation.'

The Committee highlighted a number of areas where it felt that changes could and should be made.

Pre-legislative consultation

The Committee noted that the House of Commons does not currently undertake any systematic consideration of draft Bills, and that consultations between the government and those outside Parliament who might have a legitimate interest in the legislation was 'patchy and spasmodic'. This failure to consult is exacerbated by a culture amongst government ministers of presenting draft legislation to the House of Commons as a fait acompli, resisting any proposals for significant change for fear that this might be taken as evidence of political weakness.

The report concluded in favour of pre-legislative scrutiny by a committee of the House of Commons, but was not specific as to what form the committee should take. Having considered the pros and cons of using the existing departmentally related select committees, a new permanent structure of legislative committees, ad hoc select committees of the House, and joint committees of both Houses for individual draft Bills, the report notes:

> 'While the actual route to be followed for any particular draft Bill will depend on a whole range of circumstances and will in any case be a matter for consultation, we believe that in general, unless there are unusual circumstances, there are significant benefits in draft Bills being considered by a committee of the House. We cannot on the one hand complain at the absence of consultation before the introduction of legislation and the unwillingness of ministers to countenance amendment once it is introduced, while on the other hand neglecting opportunities to contribute at the consultative stage.' (para 30)

It concludes by recommending that the House should use one of the following (para 91):

> '(i) an ad hoc select committee to consider a particular draft bill: or
> (ii) following a discussion with the House of Lords, an ad hoc joint select committee to consider a particular draft Bill: or
> (iii) consideration of a particular draft bill by the appropriate departmental select committee.'

First Reading and presentation of Bills

As an alternative to pre-legislative scrutiny the report suggests that Bills might be subjected to scrutiny by First Reading committees. As the report states:

> 'One advantage of committee scrutiny before rather than after Second Reading is that ministers should be more receptive to possible changes and suggested improvements at this stage, particularly on matters of detail … such a committee would be particularly useful for single-purpose bills, where detailed scrutiny after approval of the principle of the Bill at Second Reading might be less fruitful.' (para 32)

The Committee observed that, in most cases, it was not government practice to provide a simple non-technical explanation of the intended effects of a Bill to those potentially affected by its provisions. Whilst accepting the submission of First Parliamentary Counsel to the effect that:

> '… a Bill is not there to inform, to explain, to entertain or to perform any of the other usual functions of literature. A Bill's sole reason for existence is to change the law. The resulting Act is the law. A consequence of this unique function is that a Bill cannot set

about communicating with the reader in the same way that other forms of writing do. It cannot use the same range of tools. In particular, it cannot repeat important points simply to emphasise their importance or safely explain itself by restating a proposition in different words. To do so would risk creating doubts and ambiguities that would fuel litigation. As a result, legislation speaks in a monotone and its language is compressed.' (para 35)

The Committee resolved in favour of government departments producing guides to the main provisions of the Bills they were promoting, with the emphasis being placed on the use of plain English. Questions might remain, however, as to the status of such guidance in relation to the task of statutory interpretation.

Committee stage

The Modernisation Committee characterised the proceedings of standing committees as:

'... often ... devoted to political partisan debate rather than constructive and systematic scrutiny ... where policy differences are great, the role of government backbenchers on a standing committee has been primarily to remain silent and to vote as directed. By contrast the opposition has often set out to devise methods designed simply to extend debate.' (para 8)

The result of these tactics is that important sections of Public Bills sometimes receive little or no scrutiny at the committee stage because of the imposition of time allocation orders (ie 'the guillotine') that bring deliberations to an end at a specified point in time.

Noting that reform of the committee stage would have to address not only the procedural issues, but also the practices and culture of the House of Commons, the report suggested the following:

1. all members of standing committees to be provided with notes on clauses produced at the time of presentation of a Bill;
2. clauses should be considered as a whole, before amendments, so as to isolate common points of agreement and criticism (the rationale being that ministers who knew that the principle of the clause was agreed might 'approach amendments in a more constructive frame of mind');
3. allowing standing committees to meet during the parliamentary recess;
4. permitting standing committees to consider the technical details of Bills of first class constitutional importance, once the issues of principle have been considered by a committee of the whole House.

Report stage

The weaknesses outlined in the Modernisation Committee's report were the exploitation of the report stage, by the opposition, as an opportunity to raise party political points not always sufficiently closely related to the subject matter of the

Bill, and the tendency of the government to use to report stage to introduce large numbers of amendments consequent upon the committee stage.

The report noted the suggestion that the report stage could be divided so that detailed matters were committed to a standing committee, with matters of principle being debated on the floor of the House, but doubted the practicality of the proposal.

Post-legislative scrutiny

The Committee noted the value of a systematic post-legislative scrutiny of legislation, carried out via departmental select committees, and undertook to consider the matter in more detail in a subsequent report.

The legislative cycle

A Bill cannot be introduced twice in a parliamentary session. Hence the government will want to force a Bill through before the end of a session to ensure that it is not lost, possible resorting to devices that limit proper scrutiny. The opposition, aware of the time pressure on the government, has a vested interest in delaying consideration of legislation until the later stages of the session when perhaps some concessions can be wrung from the government.

As the report highlighted, the problems caused by the current legislative cycle are such that early on in the parliamentary year:

> '... the House is usually swamped with major Bills in committee as ministers seek to get a head start for their own measures ... By contrast the House of Lords is under extreme pressure at the latter end of the session as it receives the major Commons Bills. ... This pattern, combined with the absolute cut-off imposed by prorogation, frequently makes the last few days of a session particularly chaotic as attempts are made to complete the government's legislative programme. Bills go to and fro between the Houses, both of which are asked to agree (or disagree) usually with minimal notice to a large number of amendments. Few, if any Members, are able to know what is going on, and there is potential scope for error. The House has in the past even been asked to debate Lords amendments of which there has been no available text.' (paras 11–12)

The report recommended that:

> '... in defined circumstances and subject to certain safeguards, government Bills may be carried over from one session to the next in the same way as hybrid and private Bills. Discussions should begin between the appropriate authorities in both Houses to determine how this might best be achieved, without infringing the constitutional implications of prorogation. In drawing up detailed proposals the appropriate authorities should consider in particular the need to ensure (a) the identification by the government as early as possible of any Bill it wished to be subject to a carry-over procedure, (b) that the procedure should only be used for Bills which are either to be subject to select committee type scrutiny or are introduced after a certain period in the session and (c) that no Bill should be carried over more than once.' (para 102)

The programming of legislation

With non-contentious legislation a programme for the legislative process can be agreed 'through the usual channels' (ie via the Whips' Office), but this is not an open process and can break down were politically controversial legislation is under consideration. In some legislatures a 'Legislative Business Committee' recommends procedures for dealing with specific Bills, but this does add another layer of bureaucracy to the process. The Modernisation Committee recommendation was that, for a trial period, and in respect of a selected number of Bills, there should be consultation leading to the presentation of 'an amendable programme motion' directly after Second Reading, which would indicate: 'the committee option to be followed; the date by which the Bill should be reported from committee ... the amount of time proposed for Report Stage and Third Reading ... [and] in defined circumstances, provisions for carry-over to a subsequent session.' Were such a programme to be agreed no subsequent Time Allocation Order could be made.

The 'Cook' reforms

In October 2002 MPs voted on a series of reform proposals introduced by Robin Cook as Leader of the House. The following changes were supported:

1. changing Commons sitting times and introducing an earlier start and finish of 11.30am–7pm Tuesday and Wednesday, and 11.30am–6pm Thursday – with the result that Prime Minister's Question Time moves to lunchtime instead of mid-afternoon;
2. starting the summer recess two weeks earlier, with MPs returning for two weeks in mid-September before a break for party conferences;
3. permitting the carrying over of government Bills from one session to the next, rather than Bills falling after a single session, providing the Bill completes its passage in a year;
4. reducing the deadline for applying to raise a subject at Question Time from ten days to three;
5. more legislation to be published in draft form.

6.9 Parliamentary privilege

Parliamentary privilege is part of the law and custom of Parliament. It allows Parliament to conduct its affairs without improper interference by the Sovereign, the courts or other bodies or persons outside Parliament. Privilege, unless created by statute, forms part of the common law. It is defined in Erskine May as:

> '... the sum of the peculiar rights enjoyed by each House collectively as a constitutional part of the High Court of Parliament and by members of each House individually,

without which they could not discharge their functions, and which exceed those possessed by other bodies or individuals.'

At the opening of each Parliament, the Speaker formally claims from the Crown for the Commons 'their ancient and undoubted rights and privileges'. These are:

1. freedom of speech in debate;
2. freedom from arrest;
3. freedom of access to Her Majesty whenever occasion shall require; and that the most favourable construction should be placed upon all their proceedings.

The other privileges of the House of Commons, not expressly claimed by the Speaker, include:

1. the right of the House to regulate its own composition;
2. the right to take exclusive cognisance of matters arising within the precincts of the House;
3. the right to punish both members and non-members for breach of privilege and contempt;
4. the right of impeachment.

Freedom of speech

The right is guaranteed by art 9 of the Bill of Rights 1689 which provides:

'... the freedom of speech and debates or proceedings in Parliament ought not to be impeached or questioned in any court or place out of Parliament.'

The effect of art 9 is that no member may be made the subject of an action in the courts on the basis of statements made in the course of Parliamentary proceedings. The rationale for the privilege is that members should not be inhibited in representing their constituents, challenging the executive, or discharging their legislative functions by the threat of possible legal action. If a member is sued for defamation in respect of something said during the course of parliamentary proceedings, the writ should be struck out as disclosing no cause of action. Were the matter to come to trial the court would presumably hold that the defendant's comments were protected by absolute privilege.

Even where an action in defamation is brought against a Member of Parliament in respect of statements made other than in parliamentary proceedings, the action cannot normally be supported by reference to other non-defamatory statements made in the course of parliamentary proceedings. In *Church of Scientology* v *Johnson-Smith* [1972] 1 QB 522, where the defendant MP, who was being sued for a libel in respect of comments alleged to have made during a television interview, raised the defence of fair comment, it was held that the plaintiff, who needed to prove malice on the defendant's part, could not use speeches made by the defendant in the House of Commons as evidence to substantiate his allegation of malice.

Whilst issues of privilege, as regards freedom of speech, are usually associated with MPs being immune from suit, a corresponding issue arises where an MP seeks to rely on statements made during proceedings in Parliament in order to initiate an action for defamation. The corollary of the right to free speech has traditionally been that if an MP has sought to bring proceedings for defamation in the courts he has not been permitted to adduce as evidence statements made during parliamentary proceedings, as this too would raise the possibility of those proceedings being questioned in court. The issue has been addressed by the courts on a number of occasions and, as will be seen below, has now been resolved by means of amending legislation.

In *Prebble* v *Television New Zealand Ltd* [1994] 3 WLR 970 the defendant television company broadcast a programme in which allegations were made of impropriety on the part of the Labour government. The plaintiff, the minister for state-owned enterprises, alleged that the programme had defamed him by implying, inter alia, that he had misled the House of Representatives concerning the government's policy on the sale of state-owned industries. The defence contended that either the programme had not conveyed any defamatory meaning, or to the extent that it had its contents were true. At first instance those elements of the defence statements that sought to rely on statements made in proceedings in Parliament in order to refute the plaintiff's claim were struck out, on the basis that reliance on them infringed art 9 of the Bill of Rights 1689. The decision was upheld by the Court of Appeal, but in addition a majority of the court held that the plaintiff's action should be stayed unless and until privilege in respect of the statements relied upon was waived by the House of Representatives. The Privileges Committee of the House of Representatives having concluded that it did not have the power to waive the privilege, the plaintiff appealed to the Board against the stay of his action, and the defendants sought to appeal against the upholding of the first instance decision to strike out parts of the defence submission. The Privy Council, allowing the plaintiff's appeal, and dismissing the defendant's, held that the fact that the person making the impugned statement in Parliament was also the initiator of the legal proceedings did not justify any departure from the principle enshrined in art 9 of the Bill of Rights 1689. The privilege in question belonged to Parliament, not to individual members. Whether or not a member had misled Parliament was a matter to be dealt with by Parliament and fell outside the jurisdiction of the courts. If the defendant had intended to adduce evidence of proceedings in Parliament simply to prove what had been said or decided, there would have been no objection. On the facts, however, the defendant sought to adduce the evidence in order to prove that the House had been misled. The Privy Council accepted that, whilst there might be cases where justice demanded a stay of proceedings, where for example the majority of the evidence relied upon by the defendant was protected by privilege and it would be impossible for him to defend a libel action unless that privilege was waived, and that failure to grant a stay in such cases could result in a significant restriction on the freedom of the press to comment on political affairs, the present case did not fall within that category. The majority of the statements relied upon by the defence were not protected by privilege and it was not unjust in the circumstances to allow the action to proceed.

In July 1995, May J, sitting in the High Court, halted a libel action brought by the Conservative MP Neil Hamilton against *The Guardian* newspaper, on the grounds that to admit as evidence the material that *The Guardian* sought to rely on by way of defence (which related to cash for questions allegations) would infringe art 9 of the Bill of Rights. The decision was criticised as effectively preventing the MP concerned from clearing his name (see further *Allason* v *Haines* (1995) 145 NLJ 1576; The Times 25 July), and was the main impetus behind a change in the law relating to parliamentary privilege effected by the enactment of s13 of the Defamation Act 1996. That section provides:

'(1) Where the conduct of a person in or in relation to proceedings in Parliament is in issue in defamation proceedings, he may waive for the purposes of those proceedings, so far as concerns him, the protection of any enactment or rule of law which prevents proceedings in Parliament being impeached or questioned in any court or place out of Parliament.

(2) Where a person waives that protection –

(a) any such enactment or rule of law shall not apply to prevent evidence being given, questions being asked or statements, submissions, comments or findings being made about his conduct, and

(b) none of those things shall be regarded as infringing the privilege of either House of Parliament.

(3) The waiver by one person of that protection does not affect its operation in relation to another person who has not waived it.

(4) Nothing in this section affects any enactment or rule of law so far as it protects a person (including a person who has waived the protection referred to above) from legal liability for words spoken or things done in the course of, or for the purposes of or incidental to, any proceedings in Parliament.'

An opposition amendment, which was defeated, would have narrowly defined the situations where the privilege could be waived, and would have given the House the right to determine whether the privilege should be waived. Opponents of the change also warned against upsetting the delicate balance of the unwritten constitution, pointing out that it might result in Parliament surrendering its collective privilege at the behest of one member (a sentiment echoed by the Privy Council in *Prebble* v *Television New Zealand Ltd*, above). These critics have, to some extent, been vindicated by comments made by Lord Browne-Wilkinson in the course of his speech in *Hamilton* v *Al Fayed* [2000] 2 All ER 224. He rejected the contention that, so far as s13 of the 1996 Act was concerned, there was a distinction to be drawn between the privileges of an individual MP and the privileges of the House of Commons as a whole. In effect the waiver of privilege by one MP overrode the privilege belonging to Parliament.

The Hamilton/Fayed libel case that was permitted to proceed following the House of Lords' ruling that s13 permitted the consideration of evidence given to parliamentary committees if an MP exercised his right of waiver under s13, also raised the spectre of conflicts between Parliament and the courts arising where it was alleged in the course of an MP being cross-examined that he or she had lied to the House of Commons.

Despite the changes introduced by s13, Neil Hamilton decided not to pursue his action against *The Guardian*, and famously lost his libel action against Al Fayed.

Essentially the debate is between those who believe that MPs may be denied justice by not being permitted to waive privilege and bring proceedings for libel, and those who believe that the changes curtail freedom of speech by inhibiting those who comment critically in the media on parliamentary proceedings. As Lord Hoffmann observed, whilst there is an obvious public interest in maintaining absolute privilege in respect of proceedings in Parliament, there is (arguably) no obvious corresponding public interest in allowing absolute privilege to those commenting upon the way in which members discharge their functions in the House.

The House of Lords has stressed that the ruling in *Pepper (Inspector of Taxes)* v *Hart* [1993] 1 All ER 42, to the effect that extracts from Hansard can be cited to assist a court in interpreting legislation, should not be seen as undermining the parliamentary privilege enshrined in art 9. Lord Browne-Wilkinson expressed the view of the majority in observing that there could be sound reasons for departing from the long standing rule that no account should be taken of extracts from Hansard in construing Acts of Parliament, where the legislation in question was ambiguous or obscure, or where adherence to the literal rule produced an absurd result and there was evidence in Hansard that would reveal the mischief aimed at by the legislation, or where the very question before the court had been considered in Parliament. It was envisaged that, provided only comments made by a minister or other person promoting a Bill were taken into account under this exception, the courts would be giving effect to Parliament's intentions, rather than undermining the independence of MPs.

Proceedings in Parliament

The term 'proceedings in Parliament' is not defined in the Bill of Rights. As Lord Woolf MR observed in *R* v *Parliamentary Commissioner for Standards, ex parte Al Fayed* [1998] 1 All ER 93, the question should be 'approached by consideration of the broader principles which underline the relationship between Parliament and the court. That relationship was elegantly described by Sedley J [refusing leave in this case] as "a mutuality of respect between two constitutional sovereignties".'

It would seem that remarks made in debate, discussions in committee, parliamentary questions and answers, and votes are clearly within the concept of proceedings in Parliament. For example, Neil Hamilton, the former Conservative MP who lost his seat in the 1997 general election amid allegations concerning his accepting cash for asking questions in the House of Commons, used the protection offered by parliamentary privilege to allege that Mohamed Fayed, the owner of Harrods, had ordered a member of his staff to open a customer's safe deposit box.

His comments were made in the course of giving evidence before the House of Commons Select Committee on Standards and Privileges

Similarly, in *Hamilton* v *Al Fayed* [1999] 3 All ER 317, the Court of Appeal held that investigations by the Parliamentary Commissioner for Standards, and the deliberations of the Committee on Standards and Privileges constituted 'proceedings in Parliament' and were thus protected by art 9 of the Bill of Rights.

Other words spoken within the precincts of Parliament unconnected with parliamentary proceedings are unlikely to be so protected, for example, in *Rivlin* v *Bilainkin* [1953] 1 QB 485 the posting of libellous material in the House of Commons post box to members was held to be insufficient in itself to render the communications the subject of parliamentary privilege.

Between these two extremes lies a grey area. In particular, problems have frequently arisen regarding the status of communications between constituents and their MPs and between members and ministers. An instructive illustration is provided by the 'Strauss affair'. Strauss, a Labour MP, wrote to the Paymaster General complaining about the way in which the London Electricity Board disposed of their scrap cable. The Paymaster General denied responsibility on the ground that the matter concerned day-to-day administration rather than policy, and he passed the letter to the board. The board took exception to Strauss' allegations and threatened to sue him for libel unless he withdrew and apologised. Strauss raised the threat as a question of privilege and the matter was referred to the Committee of Privileges. The Committee reported that in writing his letter Strauss was engaged in a proceeding in Parliament for the purposes of art 9 and that the board, in threatening to sue, were in breach of parliamentary privilege. However, when the report of the Committee was debated in the House, on a free vote it rejected the findings of the Committee. The House resolved that the 'Strauss' letter was not a proceeding in Parliament.

The decision in Strauss is not binding on the House in future cases, and the Select Committee on Parliamentary Privilege recommended in 1967 that the decision of the House in Strauss should be reversed by legislation. Communications between members and ministers, while not perhaps covered by parliamentary privilege, may however be protected by qualified privilege in the law of defamation: see further Chapter 12.

In *Beach* v *Freeson* [1972] QB 14 qualified privilege was held to attach to the sending of a letter from a member to the Lord Chancellor containing the complaints made by a constituent about the plaintiff's firm of solicitors. The Lord Chancellor's responsibility for the courts and the fact that solicitors are officers of the court were sufficient to bring the case within the general common law rule under which, where both sender and recipient have a special interest, a duty respectively to send and receive the communications, the publication is protected by qualified privilege. Letters from members of the public to MPs enjoy only qualified privilege.

In *R* v *Rule* [1937] 2 KB 375 qualified privilege was held by the Court of Criminal Appeal to attach to the sending of two letters from a constituent to his MP containing complaints about the conduct of a detective sergeant and a justice of the peace. Lord Hewart CJ said:

> 'A Member of Parliament to whom a written communication is addressed by one of his constituents asking for his assistance in bringing to the notice of the appropriate minister a complaint of improper conduct on the part of some public official acting in that constituency in relation to his offices, has sufficient interest in the subject-matter of the complaint to render the occasion of such publication a privileged occasion.'

In *Rost* v *Edwards* [1990] 2 WLR 1280 the plaintiff, an MP, sued the defendants for libel. He had been the subject of an art in *The Guardian* newspaper that allegedly implied that he had used his membership of the House of Commons Select Committee on Energy to acquire information, which he in turn sold to companies overseas. As a result, so the plaintiff claimed, he had been de-selected from membership of the Standing Committee of the Electricity Privatisation Bill and had not been appointed as Chair of the Energy Select Committee. To support these claims the plaintiff sought to adduce evidence of the appointment procedures of the House of Commons committees. In relation to his failure to register his business interests, the plaintiff further sought to adduce evidence as to the criteria for registration in the Register of Members' Interests and his reasons for non-registration. The question arose during the trial as to whether or not the evidence the plaintiff sought to adduce was inadmissible on the ground that it was protected by parliamentary privilege as it related to proceedings in Parliament. Popplewell J held that the evidence relating to appointments to committees could not be adduced, but that relating to the Register of Members' Interests could.

In the course of his decision Popplewell J expressed some sympathy with the plaintiff's contention that no breach of privilege arose in this case because he sought only to ascertain what had happened in the House of Commons, as opposed to wanting to question the propriety of the proceedings, but felt that the weight of authority prevented him from accepting the submission. In the circumstances the only option open to the plaintiff seeking to adduce such evidence was to petition the House for permission to do so. In relation to the Register of Members' interests he observed:

> 'There are clearly cases where Parliament is to be the sole judge of its affairs. Equally there are clear cases where the courts are to have exclusive jurisdiction. In a case which may be described as a grey area a court, while giving full attention to the necessity for comity between the courts and Parliament, should not be astute to find a reason for ousting the jurisdiction of the court and for limiting or even defeating a proper claim by a party to litigation before it. If Parliament wishes to cover a particular area with privilege it has the ability to do so by passing an Act of Parliament giving itself the right to exclusive jurisdiction. Ousting the jurisdiction of the court has always been regarded as requiring the clearest possible words. Nothing in the authorities, as I have indicated, in any way covers the instant situation. It is true that courts have over the years enlarged the definition of "proceedings" from the formal speeches in the House to other matters, as appears from the various authorities to which I have been referred ... but ... there are

plenty of areas which are not covered by proceedings in Parliament. It is clearly not possible to arrive at an exhaustive definition. ... A line has to be drawn somewhere. As Lord Pearce once said: "I do not know, I only feel." In the result, I conclude that claims for privilege in respect of the Register of Members' Interests does not fall within the definition of "proceedings in Parliament" ...'

The Parliamentary Commissioner Act 1967, s10(5) accords absolute privilege to communications between MPs and the Parliamentary Commissioner for Administration.

It is interesting to note that, in respect of the right granted to an MP to waive parliamentary privilege under s13 of the Defamation Act 1996, considered above, subs(5) provides that the term 'proceedings in Parliament' applies to:

'(a) the giving of evidence before either House or a committee;
(b) the presentation or submission of a document to either House or a committee;
(c) the preparation of a document for the purposes of or incidental to the transacting of any such business;
(d) the formulation, making or publication of a document, including a report, by or pursuant to an order of either House or a committee; and
(e) any communication with the Parliamentary Commissioner for Standards or any person having functions in connection with the registration of members' interests.'

For these purposes 'a committee' means a committee of either House or a joint committee of both Houses of Parliament.

Hamilton v *Al Fayed* (above) makes it clear that an MP's right to waive parliamentary privilege under s13 of the 1996 Act holds good even where there had been a parliamentary inquiry into the matters complained of.

Reports of parliamentary proceedings

The House has persistently claimed the right to prevent or limit reporting of its deliberations, but it resolved in 1971 to entertain complaints of breach of privilege or contempt in relation to such reports only where the sitting of the House or committee in question was in private. At common law the fair and accurate reporting of parliamentary debates is protected by qualified privilege (see *Wason* v *Walter* (1869) LR 4 QB 73). This privilege was confirmed by the Court of Appeal in *Cook* v *Alexander* [1974] QB 279, a case which also established qualified privilege for the parliamentary 'sketch' or summary of debate – so long as it is fair and accurate. This privilege holds notwithstanding notice on the part of a participant in the debate. See further Sch 1 of the Defamation Act 1996.

Parliamentary papers

The Parliamentary Papers Act 1840, at s1, provides that any civil or criminal proceedings arising out of the publication of any papers or reports made by the authority of either House must be stayed on the production of a certificate to that effect from an officer of the House. By s3 of the Act, qualified privilege attaches to fair and accurate extracts from, or abstracts of, papers published under the authority of Parliament.

Freedom from arrest

Immunity from arrest is now of little importance and in 1967 the Committee on Parliamentary Privilege appointed to review the law of parliamentary privilege recommended its abolition. The immunity only applies to civil arrest and extends not only while Parliament sits, but also for 40 days before and after. In *Stourton* v *Stourton* [1963] P 302, which concerned the Baron and Baroness Mowbray, the Baroness issued a summons for leave to issue a writ of attachment because the Baron was in breach of an order made under s17 of the Married Women's Property Act 1882. Parliament was sitting. Scarman J held that the Baron was protected from arrest by parliamentary privilege because the writ of attachment was to compel performance of acts required by civil process and not for a criminal contempt of court.

The immunity does not protect members from arrest on criminal charges, nor from detention under regulations made under the Defence of the Realm Acts in time of war. In 1940, for example, the Commons Committee of Privileges was of opinion that there had been no breach of privilege when Captain Ramsay, a member, had been detained under regulations made under the Emergency Powers (Defence) Act 1939. It is a contempt of the House for any person to seek to serve a writ or other legal process upon a member within the precincts of the House.

The right of the House to regulate its own composition

The House used to have the right to determine disputed elections. This is now regulated by statute, the matter being committed to an election court consisting of two judges of the Queen's Bench Division. Subject to provisions applying where the judges disagree, the determination certified by the court 'shall be final to all intents and purposes'. The House of Commons, on being informed by the Speaker of a certificate of the court, shall order it to be entered in their journals and shall give the necessary direction for confirming or altering the return, or for issuing a writ for a new election, or for carrying the determination into execution as the circumstances may require.

The House still retains the exclusive right to determine by resolution when a writ for the holding of a by-election shall be issued. The House also maintains the right to determine whether a member is qualified to sit in the House, and can declare a member's seat vacant on grounds of legal disqualification or for any other reason it thinks fit. Legal disqualification may be determined by an election court or the Judicial Committee of the Privy Council.

The right of the House to expel a member whom it considers unfit to sit has been used sparingly. One example is that of Gary Allighan MP who in 1947 was expelled from the House for contempt. He had falsely alleged that MPs had given details of parliamentary party meetings held within the Palace of Westminster to journalists in return for money or while under the influence of drink. He was himself guilty of this behaviour and his contempt was compounded by his lying to the Committee of Privileges. The House voted to expel him.

The right to take exclusive cognisance of matters arising within the precincts of the House

Proceedings in Parliament cannot be called in question in any court. The House maintains the right to control its own proceedings and regulate its internal affairs without interference from the courts. The leading case is *Bradlaugh* v *Gossett* (1884) 123 QBD 271. Charles Bradlaugh was elected as Member of Parliament for Northants. He was an atheist and refused to take the oath. Eventually the House allowed him to make an affirmation of allegiance under the Parliamentary Oaths Act 1866, in lieu of taking an oath. A common informer then sued Bradlaugh for penalties on the ground that he did not come within the classes of persons permitted by the statute to affirm instead of taking an oath, and therefore he was not qualified to sit and vote in the House. The court held that Bradlaugh was not entitled to affirm and his seat was declared vacant. He was re-elected and rather than be excluded again he sought to take the oath. The House would not allow him to do so, and in July 1883 they passed a resolution: 'That the Serjeant-at-Arms do exclude Mr Bradlaugh from the House until he shall engage not further to disturb the proceedings of the House.' In August 1881 Bradlaugh tried to enter the House and was forcibly ejected by the Serjeant-at-Arms (Gossett). Bradlaugh claimed an injunction to restrain the Serjeant-at-Arms from excluding him, and a declaration that the resolution was void. The court held that it had no jurisdiction to interfere.

As Lord Coleridge CJ observed:

'What is said or done within the walls of Parliament cannot be inquired into in a court of law. On this point all the judges in the two great cases which exhaust the learning on the subject – *Burdett* v *Abbott* 14 East 1, 148 and *Stockdale* v *Hansard* 9 Ad & E 1 – are agreed, and are emphatic. The jurisdiction of the Houses over their own members, their right to impose discipline within their walls, is absolute and exclusive. To use the words of Lord Ellenborough, "They would sink into utter contempt and inefficiency without it ..."'

Stephen J said:

'I think that the House of Commons is not subject to the control of Her Majesty's Courts in its administration of that part of the statute-law which has relation to its own internal proceedings, and that the use of such actual force as may be necessary to carry into effect such a resolution as the one before us is justifiable. Many authorities might be cited for this principle; but I will quote two only. The number might be enlarged with ease by reference to several well-known cases. Blackstone says 1 Com 163: "The whole of the law and custom of Parliament has its original from this one maxim, that whatever matter arises concerning either House of Parliament ought to be examined, discussed, and adjudged in that House to which it relates, and not elsewhere." This principle is re-stated nearly in Blackstone's words by each of the judges in the case of *Stockdale* v *Hansard* 9 Ad & E 1. As the principal result of that case is to assert in the strongest way the right of the Court of Queen's Bench to ascertain in case of need the extent of the privileges of the House, and to deny emphatically that the Court is bound by a resolution of the House declaring any particular matter to fall within their privilege, these declarations are of the highest authority. Lord Denman says 9 Ad & E at p114: "Whatever is done within the walls of either assembly must pass without question in any other place." Littledale J says at p162: "It is said the House of Commons is the sole judge of its own privileges; and so I admit as far as the proceedings in the House and some other things are concerned." Patteson J said at p209: "Beyond all dispute, it is necessary that the proceedings of each House of Parliament should be entirely free and unshackled, that whatever is said or done in either House should not be liable to examination elsewhere." '

Rejecting the application, Stephen J said he did so even assuming that the resolution was inconsistent with the Parliamentary Oaths Act. It seemed to follow, in his view, that the House of Commons has the exclusive power of interpreting the statute, so far as the regulation of its own proceedings within its own walls was concerned. The court also expressed extreme reluctance in any case to declare a resolution of the House void. The injunction was refused because reasonable force could be used to exclude any person from premises where he would be a trespasser.

If a statute is to bind the House it must do so clearly. In *R* v *Graham-Campbell, ex parte Herbert* [1935] 1 KB 594 A P Herbert, an Independent MP, applied for summonses against the members of the House of Commons Kitchen Committee for selling drinks in the members' bar without a justices' licence. The Chief Metropolitan Magistrate refused to issue the summonses and the Divisional Court of the King's Bench Division held that he had been right to decline jurisdiction because of parliamentary privilege.

The House does not generally assert jurisdiction over matters arising within its precincts if they have no direct connection with its proceedings. The penal powers of the House are inadequate to deal with ordinary crimes and these are usually left to the criminal courts.

The Scottish Parliament, by contrast, is subject to the orders of the courts, save only to the extent that this power is limited by statute. Hence s40(3) of the Scotland Act 1998 provides, inter alia, that in any proceedings against the Scottish Parliament the court shall not make an order for suspension, interdict, reduction or specific performance (or other like order) but may instead make a declarator (ie grant declaratory relief). The Court of Session in *Whalley and Others* v *Watson* (2000) The Times 21 March confirmed that, in terms of its relationship with the courts, the Scottish Parliament owed its powers to statute and was subject to the law and the courts.

The right to punish for breach of privilege and contempt

The House has the power to maintain its privileges and to punish those who break them or commit contempt of the House. All breaches of privilege are contempts of the House, but not all contempts involve the infringement of the privileges of the House. Contempt of the House is a very wide concept. Erskine May describes it as:

'... any act or omission which obstructs or impedes either House of Parliament in the performance of its functions, or which obstructs or impedes any member or officer of such House in the discharge of his duty, or which has a tendency, directly or indirectly, to produce such results, may be treated as a contempt even though there is no precedent of the offence.'

While the House cannot create new privileges, except by statute, there is no complete list of behaviour which constitutes contempt, though the following are examples: attempting to disrupt the proceedings of the House; attempting to bribe members; casting imputations reflecting upon the dignity of the House; refusing to give evidence, or giving false evidence, or tampering with witnesses before a committee of the House; the service of writs on members within the precincts of the House; and obstructing an Officer of the House while in the execution of his duty.

Complaints of breach of privilege may be raised by a member or in the House by the Speaker. If the Speaker rules that a prima facie case has been made out, a motion is proposed, by the Leader of the House or the member who raised the matter, that the matter be referred to the Committee of Standards and Privileges. The motion may then be debated and voted upon. The committee, comprising 11 senior MPs is the master of its own proceedings. It can compel the attendance of witnesses and the production of document, failure to comply being a contempt. There is no requirement of legal representation, indeed the 'defendant' may not be given any hearing at all. At the conclusion of its investigation the committee reports its findings to the House and may recommend the action that the House should take. The House need not accept the committee's findings or recommendations, but it almost always does. This procedure has been criticised. The Select Committee on Parliamentary Privilege in 1967 recommended that persons directly concerned in the Committee's investigations should have the right to attend its hearings, make submissions, call, examine and cross-examine witnesses, and, with leave of the committee, be legally represented and apply for legal aid. These recommendations were not adopted.

If the House finds that a breach of privilege or a contempt of the House has been established it may adopt one of several courses of action. It may order the offender to be reprimanded or admonished by the Speaker at the Bar of the House. A member may be suspended or expelled from the House. Although the House no longer has the power to impose a fine, it may commit a person to prison. The commitment cannot last beyond the end of the session and the prisoner must be released upon the prorogation or dissolution of Parliament. Officials of the House may be dismissed and persons such as lobby correspondents, who are granted special facilities in the Palace of Westminster, may have those facilities withdrawn.

It is interesting to speculate upon the possible repercussions of the decision of the European Commission on Human Rights in *Application No 13057/87* v *Malta*, in which it was held that the jurisdiction of the Maltese House of Representatives, to punish those alleged to have been in breach of its privileges contravened art 6(1) of the European Convention on Human Rights, because such proceedings involved the House as victim, prosecutor and judge. In theory the same objections could be raised to the jurisdiction of the House of Commons to deal with breaches of its privileges and contempt.

The courts and parliamentary privilege

The House of Commons claims to be the absolute and sole judge of its own privileges and maintains that its judgment cannot be called into question by any other court. The courts do not agree. They maintain the right to determine the nature and extent of parliamentary privilege when adjudicating upon the rights of individuals outside the House. This disagreement has given rise to constitutional conflict, as evidence by decisions such as *Stockdale* v *Hansard* (1839) 9 Ad & E 1. Stockdale published an illustrated treatise on the reproduction system. A copy was found in possession of a prisoner in Newgate and was described by the inspectors of prisons in a report to the government as 'disgusting and obscene'. The report was printed by order of the House of Commons and was sold by Hansard, the parliamentary printers. The plaintiff brought an action for libel against Hansard. The defendants, acting under the direction of the House of Commons, pleaded that the publication was covered by parliamentary privilege. The Court of Queen's Bench rejected this plea and awarded damages to Stockdale. Regarding the power of the House of Commons to create new privileges by resolution, Lord Denman CJ commented:

> 'The supremacy of Parliament, the foundation on which the claim is made to rest, appears to me completely to overturn it, because the House of Commons is not Parliament, but only a co-ordinate and component part of the Parliament. That sovereign power can make and unmake the laws; but the concurrence of the three legislative estates is necessary; the resolution of any one of them cannot alter the law, or place anyone beyond its control. The proposition is therefore wholly untenable, and abhorrent to the first principles of the constitution of England.'

Stockdale then brought another action against Hansard. On the instructions of the House the defendants entered no plea, and the plaintiff was again awarded damages. In the subsequent action, *Case of the Sheriffs of Middlesex* (1840) 11 Ad & E 273, the Sheriff of Middlesex, in pursuance of a writ from the Court of Queen's Bench, levied execution upon property of Hansard. The House of Commons thereupon committed the Sheriffs for contempt, and breach of privilege. A writ of habeas corpus was applied for on the ground that the Sheriffs were unlawfully detained. Upon motion to discharge the Sheriffs from custody, the Court of Queen's Bench held that the court had no jurisdiction to interfere.

In 1840 the House of Commons secured the passing of the Parliamentary Papers Act, conferring absolute privilege on matters contained in parliamentary papers. There is therefore in effect a dualism:

> '... there may be at any given moment two doctrines of privilege, the one held by the courts, the other by either House, the one to be found in the Law Reports, the other in Hansard.'

However, in allowing the House to enforce its own view of privilege and commit the Sheriffs of Middlesex, the courts have perhaps recognised their subordination to Parliament.

6.10 MPs as representatives of outside interests

Whilst in theory MPs are elected as independent Members of Parliament to represent their constituents, it is an obvious truth that in the majority of cases they will also be members of a political party, and will act in accordance with the agreed party line in terms of questions, debates and votes in the House of Commons. The fact that MPs may be told by the party hierarchy how they must vote on a given issue, and even punished if they do not, is not seen as in any way improper.

A distinction may, however, be drawn between internal party pressure, and a situation where a member's actions are the consequence of influence and pressure from outside the House of Commons. Where the external pressure takes the form of duress or blackmail, it will be considered a serious contempt of the House, but the position as regards the mere threat of financial loss, for example through the loss of a consultancy, has always been less clear. In the case of *W J Brown* (1947), Brown, an Independent MP, agreed to become the salaried parliamentary general secretary of the Civil Service Clerical Association. Disagreement arose between Brown and the association over his political attitudes and the latter proposed the termination of the agreement. Brown claimed the proposal was a breach of parliamentary privilege as it was calculated to influence him in his conduct as an MP. The Committee of Privileges reported that on the particular facts no breach of privilege had been committed. Commenting generally on such agreements, the committee was of opinion that it would be improper for a member to enter into any arrangement fettering his complete independence by undertaking to press some particular point of view on behalf of an outside interest, whether for reward or not. The committee refused to condemn contractual relationships, recognising that many members received financial assistance from outside bodies. The payments in themselves did not involve a breach of privilege and the committee concluded that if the contract itself were not a breach, then neither was a legitimate decision to terminate it.

It is an accepted feature of the proceedings of the House of Commons that members should not take part in debates in Parliament on matters in which they have a financial interest unless that interest is first disclosed. To this end the House of Commons has, since the mid-1970s, maintained a voluntary Register of Members' Interests, in which members are expected to give details of relevant paid directorships and consultancies.

The issue of MPs engaging in extra-parliamentary activities for which they receive payment has, however, traditionally been a source of friction between Labour and Conservative MPs. The view held by many Labour MPs is that MPs should regard themselves as being required to work full-time for their constituents, and that to take on other remunerative work might result in a conflict of interests. By contrast, many Conservatives argue that the salary paid to MPs is too low to attract enough capable candidates, that outside interests help the MP have a better understanding of the world of commerce and finance, and that, in any event, many Labour MPs effectively have financial interests outside Parliament by virtue of being sponsored by various trade unions.

The Nolan Committee Report and its consequences

In October 1994, in response to growing concerns as to the effectiveness of voluntary controls over MPs regarding their business interests, allegations that a number of MPs had accepted offers of cash in return for agreeing to ask specific questions in the House of Commons, concerns over the actions of ministers in the Matrix Churchill affair, and the issue of ministers resigning to take up business positions in which their ministerial experience could be of commercial advantage, the Conservative government instituted an 'Inquiry into Standards in Public Life' chaired by Lord Nolan. The Nolan Committee, technically a standing committee, was established initially for three years, with a brief to inquire into standards of propriety in public life. It published its first report in May 1995 (Cmnd 2850).

The Report made grim reading for many MPs, concluding that the self-regulatory mechanisms of Parliament had not been sufficient to prevent bad practices from developing, in particular noting that:

> '... a fall in public confidence in the financial probity of MPs has coincided with an increase in the number of MPs holding paid consultancies which relate to their Parliamentary role.'

In relation to the activities of MPs and the need for regulation, the Report observed:

> 'Some 30 per cent of backbench MPs now hold such consultancies. The House of Commons would be less effective if all MPs were full-time professional politicians, and MPs should not be prevented from having outside employment. It reduces the authority of Parliament if MPs sell their services to firms engaged in lobbying on behalf of clients. This should be banned. Other parliamentary consultancies and the fact that some MPs have more than one are also a cause for concern. It is impossible to be certain that MPs

with such consultancies never allow their financial interests to affect their actions in Parliament, yet this would clearly be improper. Guidance associated with the Register of Members' Interests has led to some confusion among MPs as to what conduct is acceptable. The long-established law of Parliament in this area should be reaffirmed. Full disclosure of consultancy agreements and payments, and of trade union sponsorship agreements and payments, should be introduced immediately ... Parliament should review the merits of allowing MPs to hold consultancies, taking into account the wider implications of greater restrictions. The Register of Interests should be more informative. The rules on declaring interests, and on avoiding conflicts of interest, should be set out in more detail. A Code of Conduct for MPs should be drawn up. We have set out a draft. The Code should be restated at the start of each new Parliament. More guidance for MPs, including induction sessions, should be available. The public needs to know that the rules of conduct governing MPs' financial interests are being firmly and fairly enforced. There have been calls for these rules to be put into statute law and enforced by the courts. We believe that the House of Commons should continue to be responsible for enforcing its own rules, but that better arrangements are needed. By analogy with the Comptroller and Auditor General, the House should appoint as Parliamentary Commissioner for Standards, a person of independent standing who will take over responsibility for maintaining the Register of Members' Interests; for advice and guidance to MPs on matters of conduct; for advising on the Code of Conduct; and for investigating allegations of misconduct. The Commissioner's conclusions on such matters would be published. When the Commissioner recommends further action, there should be a hearing by a sub-committee of the Committee of Privileges, comprising up to seven senior MPs, normally sitting in public, and able to recommend penalties when appropriate. MPs who are being heard should be entitled to be accompanied by advisers.'

The specific proposals were as follows:

1. Members of Parliament should remain free to have paid employment unrelated to their role as MPs.
2. The House of Commons should restate the 1947 resolution which places an absolute bar on Members entering into contracts or agreements which in any way restrict their freedom to act and speak as they wish, or which require them to act in Parliament as representatives of outside bodies.
3. The House should prohibit Members from entering into any agreements in connection with their role as parliamentarians to undertake services for or on behalf of organisations which provide paid parliamentary services to multiple clients or from maintaining any direct or active connections with firms, or parts of larger firms, which provide such parliamentary services.
4. The House should set in hand without delay a broader consideration of the merits of parliamentary consultancies generally, taking account of the financial and political funding implications of change.
5. The House should: require agreements and remuneration relating to parliamentary services to be disclosed; expand the guidance on avoiding conflicts of interest; introduce a new Code of Conduct for Members; appoint a Parliamentary Commissioner for Standards; and establish a new procedure for investigating and adjudicating on complaints in this area about Members.

6. On disclosure of interests: the Register should continue broadly in its present form, and should be published annually. However, the detailed entry requirements should be improved to give a clearer description of the nature and scope of the interests declared; updating of the Register should be immediate. The current updated version should be made more widely available electronically. Members should be required to deposit in full with the Register any contracts relating to the provision of services in their capacity as members, and such contracts should be available for public inspection; from the same time, members should be required to declare in the Register their annual remuneration, or estimated annual remuneration, in respect of such agreements. It would be acceptable if this were done in bands: eg under £1,000; £1,000–5,000; £5,000–10,000; then in £5,000 bands. An estimate of the monetary value of benefits in kind, including support services, should also be made; Members should be reminded more frequently of their obligations to Register and disclose interests, and that Registration does not remove the need for declaration and better guidance should be given, especially on first arrival in the House.

7. Members should be advised in their own interests that all employment agreements which do not have to be deposited should contain terms, or be supported by an exchange of letters, which make it clear that no activities relating to Parliament are involved.

8. The rules and guidance on avoiding conflict of interest should be expanded to cover the whole range of business pertaining to Parliament, and particular attention should be paid to standing committees.

9. The House should draw up a Code of Conduct setting out the broad principles that should guide the conduct of Members; this should be restated in every new Parliament.

10. The government should take steps to clarify the law relating to the bribery of or the receipt of a bribe by a Member of Parliament.

In terms of enforcement procedure the Report recommended that the House of Commons should appoint a person of independent standing as a Commissioner with the same ability to make findings and conclusions public as is enjoyed by the Comptroller and Auditor General and the Parliamentary Commissioner for Administration, sufficient independent discretion to decide whether or not a complaint merited investigation or to initiate an investigation, and the power to send for persons, papers and records. The Report envisaged this Commissioner being supported by the authority of a select committee with the necessary powers.

Following debate in the House of Commons in May 1995, the Report was referred to a House of Commons Select Committee on Standards in Public Life, which reported in July 1995. The Committee:

1. rejected as unworkable the Nolan recommendation that, whilst MPs should be banned from working for multi-client lobbyists, they should still be permitted to

have contracts with single clients. Instead the Select Committee adopted the view that all paid advocacy should be prohibited;

2. endorsed the proposal that all new MPs should be required to undergo a training course in ethics, offered under the auspices of the newly created Parliamentary Commissioner for Standards;
3. rejected proposals that the new Commissioner should have the independence enjoyed by the Parliamentary Commissioner for Administration, preferring instead to adopt a model that made the Parliamentary Commissioner for Standards accountable solely to the House of Commons;
4. called for all agreements entered into by MPs with outside clients to be notified to the Parliamentary Commissioner for Standards and registered in the Register of Members' Interests.

The result of the Nolan Committee's labours is a new self-regulatory regime for the House of Commons and its members. Sir Patrick Downey was appointed as the first Parliamentary Commissioner for Standards, responsible for maintaining the Register of Members' Interests, advising MPs on a confidential basis regarding possible conflicts of interest and investigating complaints from MPs and members of the public regarding the Register of Members' Interests and the propriety of MPs' conduct. The operation of this new regime is scrutinised by the Select Committee on Standards and Privileges (replacing the Privileges and Members' Interests Committee).

The ensuing Code of Conduct for Members of Parliament was prepared following a resolution of the House on 19 July 1997, its stated purpose being to 'assist Members in the discharge of their obligations to the House, their constituents and the public at large.' Its preamble provides that Members have a duty to uphold the law, act in accordance with the trust that the public has placed in them, and have a duty to act in the interests of their constituents and the nation as a whole. Regarding personal conduct the Code provides that Members should observe the general principles of conduct identified by the Committee on Standards in Public Life, namely:

1. Selflessness: holders of public office should take decisions solely in terms of the public interest. They should not do so in order to gain financial or other material benefits for themselves, their family or their friends.
2. Integrity: holders of public office should not place themselves under any financial or other obligation to outside individuals or organisations that might influence them in the performance of their official duties.
3. Objectivity: in carrying out public business, including making public appointments, awarding contracts, or recommending individuals for rewards and benefits, holders of public office should make choices on merit.
4. Accountability: holders of public office are accountable for their decisions and actions to the public and must submit themselves to whatever scrutiny is appropriate to their office.

5. Openness: holders of public office should be as open as possible about all the decisions and actions that they take. They should give reasons for their decisions and restrict information only when the wider public interest clearly demands.
6. Honesty: holders of public office have a duty to declare any private interests relating to their public duties and to take steps to resolve any conflicts arising in a way that protects the public interest.
7. Leadership: holders of public office should promote and support these principles by leadership and example.

The Code goes on to provide, inter alia, that:

> 'Members shall base their conduct on a consideration of the public interest, avoid conflict between personal interest and the public interest and resolve any conflict between the two, at once, and in favour of the public interest.'

The acceptance of a bribe to influence conduct as a member is declared to be contrary to the law of Parliament. For these purposes 'bribe' is construed to include any 'fee, compensation or reward in connection with the promotion of, or opposition to, any Bill, motion, or other matter submitted, or intended to be submitted to the House, or to any Committee of the House.'

The Code also seeks to emphasise the importance of disclosure of Members' interests, and states categorically that 'no Member shall act as a paid advocate in any proceeding of the House.'

On present evidence it would appear that further reforms and refinements may still be necessary. Notwithstanding the conclusion reached by the Parliamentary Commissioner for Standards, to the effect that there was compelling evidence that former MP Neil Hamilton had accepted £25,000 in return for asking parliamentary questions on behalf of Mr Al Fayed, the House of Commons Standards and Privileges Committee concluded, in its report published in November 1997, that there was no absolute proof that such payments were made or were not made. It did conclude, however, that Mr Hamilton's conduct fell seriously below that required of MPs, in particular his failure to disclose payments from lobbyists, his deliberate misleading of the then President of the Board of Trade, Michael Heseltine, regarding his links with lobbyists, and his acceptance of gifts from business contacts.

The outcome prompted calls for a review of the system of parliamentary self-regulation, in particular the need for a clearer set of rules determining the respective roles of the Standards and Privileges Committee and the Parliamentary Commissioner for Standards.

By way of response the Committee on Standards in Public Life, chaired by Lord Neill, reviewed the procedures for dealing with complaints against MPs and published a report in January 2000 proposing a number of significant reforms. It suggested that MPs accused of serious misconduct falling short of bribery should be able to challenge the findings of the Parliamentary Commissioner before a tribunal comprising up to four senior MPs chaired by a lawyer. The tribunal would have the power to reassess the facts alleged and the MP would be entitled to legal aid for representation. The report also recommended that the Standards and Privileges Committee should be reformed so as to comprise more senior MPs, and that the chair should be occupied by a member of the opposition parties. For more serious cases of misconduct the report urged the government to consider the introduction of new bribery offences that might applied to MPs.

The courts have made it clear that, unlike the position taken in respect of the Parliamentary Commissioner for Administration, the decisions of the Parliamentary Commissioner for Standards are not normally amenable to judicial review: see *R* v *Parliamentary Commissioner for Standards, ex parte Al Fayed* (above). The Master of the Rolls emphasised that the distinction between the two Commissioners was that, whilst the Ombudsman was concerned with the administrative process outwith Parliament, the Parliamentary Commissioner for Standards was concerned with the activities and events within Parliament. Thus the matters with which the Ombudsman dealt were very much the staple fare of judicial review. By contrast, the courts had always been careful not to trespass on the jurisdiction of Parliament to regulate its own procedure where the subject matter was something wholly concerned with proceedings in Parliament. Lord Woolf MR was further encouraged to this conclusion by the fact that the Parliamentary Commissioner for Standards operated within a framework that (at the time) included the Committee on Standards in Public Life and the Select Committee on Standards and Privileges, thus indicating that the way in which he discharged his functions was a matter for scrutiny by Parliament rather than the courts.

6.11 The House of Lords

Most legislatures are bicameral, meaning they are comprised of two 'houses' or bodies; for example Congress and the Senate in the United States. The purpose of a second chamber is typically to provide for further, often specialised, scrutiny of legislative proposals, and to widen the range of those allowed to play some part in the legislative process. In the United Kingdom Parliament has, since the middle ages, been divided into two bodies, the House of Lords and the House of Commons. The origins of the House of Lords can be traced back to the council of clergy and noblemen summoned to advise the King in the eleventh and twelfth centuries. Although reform of the House of Lords is very much a current political debate, it should be recalled that there has been a steady erosion of its powers for over 600 years. In 1407 Henry IV accepted that money grants had to be initiated by the Commons, and in 1678 the exclusive control of taxation passed effectively to the House of Commons. Since the revolution of the seventeenth century it is the House of Commons that has become the dominant chamber. This is reflected in its control over financial matters and its stronger claim to legitimacy, being the elected chamber. The Parliament Acts 1911 and 1949 further regulate the relationship between the two Houses, again making it clear that, save for a number of important exceptions (such as legislation to extend the life of a Parliament), ultimate power rests with the House of Commons. As a legislative body the House of Lords was, until 1999, unique in being composed of nominated members and those whose right it was to sit in the House on the basis of having inherited titles from their forebears. As outlined below, hereditary membership has ceased but the debate continues as to how membership of the second chamber should be determined.

What is a second chamber for? The 1968 White Paper *House of Lords' Reform* (Cmnd 3799) outlined seven key functions of the House of Lords.

Provision of the highest court of appeal

The House of Lords acts as the final court of appeal for the whole of the United Kingdom in civil cases and for England, Wales and Northern Ireland in criminal cases. The House may also hear certain other appeals, including those from the Courts-Martial Appeal Court. The judicial work of the House is separate from its other functions. The only peers who participate are the Lord High Chancellor, the Lords of Appeal in Ordinary, who are expressly appointed for the purpose, and Lords who hold or have held high judicial office.

Provision of a forum for free debate on matters of public interest

In the House of Lords Wednesday is traditionally set aside for special debates on a wide range of subjects. Debates may be initiated by the government, opposition, backbench or independent members. Once a month, from the beginning of the Session until the Spring Bank Holiday recess, there are two Short Debates, limited to two-and-a-half hours each. The right to initiate such debates is confirmed to backbenchers and crossbenchers, and the subjects for debate are chosen by ballot.

The revision of Public Bills brought from the House of Commons

About one half of the time of the House of Lords is devoted to the consideration of Public Bills. Most of this time is spent on revising Bills that have already passed the Commons, where most of government legislation is introduced. There are four main reasons why most legislation is introduced in the House of Commons:

1. In most cases the relevant departmental minister is a member of the House of Commons;
2. The House of Commons, as the elected chamber, is the political forum in the legislature;
3. Many Bills have a significant financial content even if they are not strictly Money Bills;
4. The provisions of the Parliament Acts (considered below) are only available to enforce the will of the Commons in respect of Bills introduced in that House.

Whilst the procedure of the two Houses for considering Public Bills is very similar, there are some significant differences. It is an established convention that the Lords do not ordinarily divide upon the Second Reading of a government Bill, which usually goes to committee. While in the Commons Public Bills usually go to a standing committee, in the Lords they are normally considered by a committee of the whole House. The Lords, unlike the Commons, allow amendments to be tabled at Third Reading.

The Lords have nothing corresponding to the Commons 'guillotine motion' and there is no effective machinery for curtailing debate. Nor is there provision for the selection of amendments for debate and all amendments tabled may be debated. An amended Bill is returned from the Lords to the Commons for consideration of the Lords' amendments. Usually most Lords' amendments are accepted, but if the Commons rejects them, the Lords will not normally insist on them. Under the 'Salisbury Convention' the House of Lords will not use its power to veto or amend legislation in order to bar the progress of any Bill that the government of the day claims embodies a manifesto commitment upon which it was elected.

If Lords' amendments to a Bill are rejected by the Commons, and should no compromise solution be found, or should the Lords reject a Commons Bill altogether, then, unless it is a Money Bill, it cannot become law during that session. Parliamentary sessions last about a year and normally begin in October or November. Bills that are not enacted in the course of a session are lost at the end of the session. A Bill can only introduced once in any parliamentary session. A good illustration of how the House of Lords can impede the government's legislative programme in this way is provided by the passage of the European Parliamentary Elections Bill. In November 1997 it was given a second reading by the House of Commons. When the Bill reached the House of Lords a large number of peers objected to the provisions in the Bill to introduce a 'closed' party list form of proportional representation for the election of MEPs (see further Chapter 5). The Lords' amendments were sent back to the House of Commons and rejected. By November 1998 the Bill had gone to the Lords and been rejected for a fifth time. Because the parliamentary session had come to an end the government had to concede defeat and introduce the Bill in the following parliamentary session. The Bill was rejected yet again by the House of Lords and the Bill was sent for the Royal Assent without Lords' approval. It can be argued that the Lords' opposition to the Bill was not a breach of the Salisbury Convention because, although the manifesto on which the Labour Party fought and won the 1997 election indicated that, if elected, it intended to introduce proportional representation for elections to the European Parliament, it did not indicate that it would be proposing the use of closed lists.

A Commons Bill lost because it is not accepted by the Lords can be passed in the following session, without the Lords' consent, if the provisions of the Parliament Act 1911, as amended by the Parliament Act 1949, apply.

This shift in power from the Lords to the Commons originated in 1909 when the

Lords rejected the Budget that Lloyd George had presented to the Commons. The Liberal government, once re-elected, introduced a Parliament Bill to restrict the powers of the House of Lords. This Bill (which became the Parliament Act 1911) was passed by the House of Lords in August 1911, under the threat that sufficient Liberal peers would be created to ensure its passage should the Bill be rejected. The Parliament Act 1911 made a number of significant changes, inter alia:

1. A Bill certified by the Speaker as a Money Bill should receive the Royal Assent and become an Act of Parliament without the consent of the House of Lords if, having been sent up from the House of Commons at least one month before the end of the session, it had not been passed by the Lords without amendment within one month of its being sent up;
2. Any other Public Bill, except one for extending the life of a Parliament, could become an Act of Parliament without the consent of the House of Lords if it had been passed by the House of Commons in three successive sessions, two years having elapsed between its first Second Reading and its final passing in the House of Commons, and if it had been sent up to the House of Lords at least one month before the end of each of the three sessions.

In 1947 the Labour government introduced a Bill designed to amend the 1911 Act by means of further reducing the delaying power of the House of Lords to 12 months. The House of Lords refused to pass the Bill, with the result that it was presented for the Royal Assent without having been passed by the House of Lords, and became the Parliament Act 1949.

In summary, the effect of the Parliament Acts is that the Lords have power to delay a Public Bill brought from the House of Commons until the session after that in which it was first introduced, and until not less than 13 months have elapsed from the date of the Second Reading in the Commons in the first session. The Parliament Acts procedure does not apply to Bills introduced in the House of Lords; Bills to extend the life of a Parliament beyond five years; Provisional Order Bills; Private Bills; or delegated legislation. The three Acts passed under the Parliament Act 1911 are the Welsh Church Act 1914 disestablishing the Church of Wales, the Government of Ireland Act 1914, providing for Irish home rule, and the Parliament Act 1949.

Some constitutional lawyers (notably Hood Phillips and Zellick) have questioned the validity of the 1949 Act, arguing that as the House of Lords was not involved in enacting the 1949 Act it is not an Act of Parliament (because it was not agreed by the Crown, Lords and Commons acting together), but merely delegated legislation granting power to the Commons and the Crown acting in concert for certain purposes. The argument concludes that the power was not delegated so that it could be used to enlarge the powers of the House of Commons, hence the 1949 Act is ultra vires. Interesting as this may be as an academic argument, it has not prevented reliance on the 1949 Act to ensure the enactment of the War Crimes Act 1991 and the European Parliamentary Elections Act 1999. On its first journey through the

House of Lords, the War Crimes Bill (which proposed changes in English law to enable the prosecution in English courts of Nazi war criminals living in the UK) was defeated at Second Reading by 207 votes to 74. Utilising the procedures of the 1911 and 1949 Acts the government decided to re-introduce the Bill. On the second journey through the House of Lords the Bill was again defeated at Second Reading, this time by 131 votes to 109. The Bill was sent direct to the Queen for Royal Assent, which was granted in the summer of 1991. One might ask whether it was legitimate for the House of Lords to reject the principles of the Bill at Second Reading when the House of Commons had indicated its view (on both occasions) by overwhelmingly voting in favour of those principles? Further, if the Hood Phillips and Zellick argument is correct, can the War Crimes Act 1991 be regarded as an Act or, again, as merely a special species of delegated legislation authorised by the 1911 Act – in which case the courts could question its validity?

The initiation of Public Bills

The more important and controversial Bills almost invariably begin in the House of Commons. However, Bills that are relatively uncontroversial in party political terms will often be introduced in the House of Lords. By convention all Consolidation Bills (Bills which do not alter the law but replace a number of Acts dealing with a particular subject by a single Act), and most Bills to give effect to changes in the law proposed by the Law Commission, are introduced in the Lords. Unlike members of the House of Commons, members of the Lords are free to introduce Private Members' Bills, and there is usually sufficient time for them to be debated. However, if they are passed there is no guarantee that time will be found for them in the House of Commons. The fact that the Lords have no constituents makes it easier for them to discuss measures proposing controversial changes, and they played a significant part in reforming the law relating to homosexuality and abortion.

The consideration of subordinate legislation

Subordinate or delegated legislation is made by ministers under powers conferred upon them by statute. There are three main categories. First, affirmative instruments, which require the approval of both Houses of Parliament before they can come into or remain in force. Second, negative instruments, which may be annulled by resolution of either House. Third, general instruments, which are not subject to any parliamentary proceedings. The powers of the House of Lords over delegated legislation were not curtailed by the Parliament Acts and are the same as those enjoyed by the House of Commons. When a resolution of each House approving the instrument is required, the House of Lords always has an opportunity to debate it. In the case of a negative instrument, any member may move a motion to annul it, and while in the Commons time often cannot be found to debate such motions, in the Lords there is no such difficulty. Members of the Lords also sit on the Joint Committee on Delegated Legislation (see section 6.6).

The scrutiny of the activities of the executive

There are several means of questioning ministers in the House of Lords about government policy in addition to those provided by general debates. Each day up to four oral or 'starred' questions may be asked of the government and are taken as first business. No Lord may ask more than two questions on any day nor may he have more than three questions on the order paper at any time. Supplementary questions may be asked by any member, but there may not be a debate. Unstarred questions are taken at the end of business. The member asking the question makes a speech, and a debate may take place before the minister's reply, which concludes the proceedings. Private Notice Questions may be asked on matters of urgency. It is for the Leader of the House or as a last resort for the House itself, to decide what constitutes a matter of urgency. Questions for Written Answers may be placed on the Order Paper. They are normally answered within a fortnight, and the answers are printed in the Official Report (Hansard). In all cases questions are addressed to Her Majesty's government and not to individual ministers.

The scrutiny of private legislation

Unlike Public Bills, which are introduced by members, Private Bills originate outside Parliament and are promoted by bodies and individuals seeking special powers not available under the general law. The powers of the House of Lords in relation to private legislation were not limited by the Parliament Acts and are the same as those of the House of Commons. The procedure for considering Private Bills is generally the same in both Houses. They are subject to consideration by counsel to the Chairman of Committees in the Lords and counsel to the Speaker in the Commons. For the most part their consideration takes place in committee.

6.12 Membership and privileges of the House of Lords

Hereditary and life peers

From the fifteenth century until the enactment of the House of Lords Act 1999, a large proportion of the 'Lords Temporal' (as opposed to the 'Lords Spiritual' who were member of the House of Lords by virtue of being holders of certain religious posts) were members of the House of Lords by virtue of the hereditary principle. Titles were bestowed by the Crown on certain families, either as rewards for services rendered or simply for cash, and the right to sit in the House of Lords was handed down through the family rather as a piece of property would be.

From 1707 until the Peerage Act 1963 there were 16 representative peers for Scotland elected by the Scottish peers for the duration of a Parliament. From 1963 until 1999 all holders of peerages of Scotland had the right to be admitted to the House of Lords. Peers of Ireland did not have any right to sit in the Lords but could be elected to the Commons. The conventional view as to the nature of an hereditary peerage (obviously prior to the enactment of the House of Lords Act 1999) was summarised by Gorman J in *Re Parliamentary Election for Bristol South-East* [1964] 2 QB 257, where he observed:

'The hereditary principle is still firmly embodied in the Constitution. Though by legislation starting with the Parliament Act 1911, the powers of the House of Lords have been curtailed, it still remains the law that the composition of the House of Lords is largely based on the hereditary principle, namely, that persons of a certain class, that is to say, persons who by creation by letters patent or by succession have become peers of the realm, have the right and duty to sit in the House of Lords. A peerage (and for this purpose we confine our consideration to United Kingdom peers) constitutes a complex of rights, privileges and duties. As [Lord Wrenbury] stated ... in *Viscountess Rhondda's Case* [1922] 2 AC 339 ... "A peerage is an inalienable incorporeal hereditament created by the act of the Sovereign which, if and when he creates it, carries with it certain attributes which attach to it not by reason of any grant of those attributes by the Crown, but as essentially existing at common law by reason of the ennoblement created by the grant of the peerage." '

That a hereditary title should enable a person to be a member of the legislature, albeit the less powerful chamber, has always seemed out of step with the concept of a mature liberal democracy. The Labour Party also consistently opposed the notion of hereditary membership on the basis that the majority of hereditary peers were natural supporters of the Conservative Party, thus giving it an in-built majority in the second chamber, regardless of the views of the voting public as expressed through the ballot box.

The Parliament Act 1911 (considered above) was regarded as a temporary measure pending further reform of the composition of the Lords and the relationship between the two Houses of Parliament. In 1917 a conference consisting of 15 members of each House, and chaired by Viscount Bryce, was appointed to consider both the composition and powers of a reformed Second Chamber. The conference reported in 1918. It saw the primary functions of a Second Chamber as including: the examination and revision of Commons Bills; the initiation and discussion of non-controversial Bills; the interposition of so much delay (and no more) in the passing of a Bill into law as might be needed to enable the opinion of the nation to be adequately expressed upon it; and the discussion of general questions of policy.

The conference recommended, in its majority report, that the House of Lords should consist of 246 members indirectly elected by MPs representing regional units. A further 81 members would be chosen by a Joint Standing Committee of both Houses. The 81 were to be hereditary peers and bishops, and the number was to be gradually reduced to 30 hereditary peers and bishops and 51 others. The Law Lords were to sit ex-officio. With the exception of those sitting ex-officio, all members would hold seats for 12 years, one-third retiring every fourth year. The reformed second chamber was to have full powers over non-financial legislation. Any differences between the two Houses was to be resolved by a Free Conference Committee consisting of up to 30 members of each House. A Bill that had been passed by the House of Commons and agreed to by a majority of the Free Conference might, in certain circumstances, become law without the agreement of the second chamber. No action was ever taken to implement the Bryce Report.

The Parliament Bill (that was to become the Parliament Act 1949) was introduced by the Labour government in the House of Commons in 1947 to further regulate the powers of the House of Lords. Under pressure from the Conservatives and Liberals the Second Reading of the Bill in the House of Lords was adjourned to enable a conference of party leaders to take place. Agreement was reached on certain principles regarding the role and composition of a reformed House, such as the need for the second chamber to be complementary to, and not a rival to, the Lower House; that no one political party should have a permanent majority; that heredity should not by itself constitute a qualification for admission; and that women should be admitted. In April 1949 the conference broke down following disagreement over the period of the Lords' delaying powers. The House of Lords then rejected the Parliament Bill on Second Reading, and it was passed into law under the provisions of the 1911 Act. The Parliament Act 1949 amended the Parliament Act 1911 by reducing from three to two the number of sessions in which a Bill must be passed by the Commons, and reducing the period between the first Second Reading and final passing in the House of Commons from two years to one.

The desire for change was to some extent reflected in the enactment of the Life Peerages Act 1958 whereby the composition of the House of Lords was significantly altered. Under the 1958 Act it became possible for the Sovereign, on the advice of the Prime Minister, to appoint, by way of Letters Patent, baronies for life, without limit of number, to persons of either sex. The object was to strengthen and broaden the composition of the House by securing the experience of distinguished men and women without conferring the right of succession upon their issue.

Many would argue that this has been the most successful reform, allowing those who have been successful in the arts, industry and the public service to contribute to the political process. It has also served as a useful power of patronage in the hands of Prime Ministers. Senior politicians retiring from the House of Commons or who lose their seats at elections are normally offered life peerages as a means of remaining in politics.

A further reform was introduced in 1963 in the form of the Peerage Act, a measure that enables hereditary peers, other than those of the first creation, to renounce their titles for life by disclaimer. The peerage remains dormant and devolves upon the heir in the normal manner on the renouncer's death. Under the Act, if a sitting member of the House of Commons succeeds to a title, he has one month after the death of his predecessor in which to disclaim, or, if the death occurs during an election campaign, one month from the declaration of the poll in favour of a successful peer. Existing peers had 12 months from the Royal Assent to the Act on 31 July 1963 in which to disclaim. Peers who succeed thereafter have 12 months from succession or their coming of age. A person who has disclaimed a peerage is entitled to vote in parliamentary elections and is eligible for election to the House of Commons.

The issue of Lords' reform continued to be a matter of heated political debate throughout the 1960s. The Queen's Speech for the 1967–68 session contained the following provision:

> 'Legislation will be introduced to reduce the powers of the House of Lords and to eliminate its present hereditary basis, thereby enabling it to develop within the framework of a modern parliamentary system. My government are prepared to enter into consultations appropriate to a constitutional change of such importance.'

The measure in question was the Parliament (No 2) Bill 1969. Inter-party talks on Lords' reform took place at a conference between party leaders from 8 November 1967 to 20 June 1968, when talks were broken off by the government following the rejection by the House of Lords of a Government Order continuing sanctions against the government of Rhodesia. In November 1968 the government published its White Paper *House of Lords' Reform*, which was later embodied in the Parliament (No 2) Bill 1968–69. Its main proposals were that:

1. The reformed House of Lords was to be a two-tier structure comprising voting peers and non-voting peers.
2. Succession to a hereditary peerage was no longer to carry the right to a seat in the House of Lords, but existing peers by succession would have the right to sit as non-voting members during their lifetime, or might be created life peers to enable them to continue in active participation as voting members.
3. Voting peers would be expected to play a full part in the work of the House, would be required to attend at least one-third of the sittings, and would be subject to an age of retirement. Non-voting peers would be able to play a full part in debates and in committees but would not be entitled to vote.
4. The voting House would initially consist of about 230 peers, distributed between the parties in such a way as to give the government a small majority over the opposition parties, but not a majority of the House as a whole when those without party allegiance were included.
5. The reformed House would be able to impose a delay of six months from the date of disagreement between the two Houses on the passage of non-financial public legislation. After this delay a Bill could be submitted for Royal Assent by resolution of the House of Commons.
6. The Lords would be able to require the House of Commons to reconsider subordinate legislation, but would not be able to reject it outright.

7. A review would be made of the functions and procedures of the two Houses once the main reform had come into effect.

The White Paper was debated in both Houses. In the Lords it was approved by 251 votes to 56. In the Commons more criticism was raised, particularly because of the extension of patronage that a nominated and paid Upper Chamber would produce, and because of the political power that the proposals would place in the hands of cross-bench voting members. With the imposition of a three-line whip by the government, and on a free vote by the Conservative and Liberal parties, the motion to reject the White Paper was defeated by 270 votes to 159.

Despite the Commons' opposition to the White Paper, the government decided to honour its pledge in the Queen's Speech and implement the proposals. Accordingly the Parliament (No 2) Bill was introduced in 1968. As this was a 'constitutional' Bill, its committee stage was taken on the floor of the House of Commons, giving opponents the opportunity to prolong proceedings and table a large number of amendments. After the House had spent 11 days in committee and only the preamble and the first five clauses out of 20 had been considered, the Prime Minister announced the abandonment of the Bill on 17 April 1969.

As outlined below, it was not until May 1997 that a Labour government committed to radical reform of the House of Lords was returned to power with a large enough majority to be confident of being able to effect the necessary legislation without becoming mired in lengthy constitutional wrangles. By way of providing a context in which to consider those changes it is instructive to consider the statistics for membership of, and party allegiance in, the House of Lords shortly before the House of Lords Act 1999 came into force. They were as follows:

Composition of the House of Lords by rank as of 1 December 1998

Rank	Number
Prince	1
Archbishops	2
Dukes (and Dukes of the Blood Royal)	25 + (3)
Marquesses	34
Earls (and Countesses)	169 + (5)
Viscounts	103
Bishops	24
Barons/Lords	833
Baronesses	95
Ladies	3
TOTAL	1,297

Composition of the House of Lords by peerage type as of 1 December 1998

Type of peerage	Number
Archbishops and bishops	26
Peers by succession	750 (of whom 16 were women)
Hereditary peers of the first creation	9
Life peers under the Appellate Jurisdiction Act 1876	28
Life peers under the Life Peerages Act 1958	484 (of whom 87 were women)
TOTAL	1,297

Composition of the House of Lords by party allegiance as of 1 December 1998

Party	Life peers	Hereditary peers of first creation	Hereditary peers by succession	Lords Spiritual	Total
Conservative Party	173	4	298		475
Labour Party	158	1	17		176
Liberal Democrat	45	0	24		69
Crossbenchers	120	4	198		322
Others	9	0	89	26	124
TOTAL	505	9	626	26	1,166

The figures for party allegiance reflect those peers eligible to vote. As of 1 December 1998 there were 68 peers without a Writ of Summons and 66 peers who had taken leave of absence. The working peers (those attending on a regular basis) number between 350–400, the majority of whom were life peers.

Composition after the House of Lords Act 1999

The House of Lords Act 1999, which has the effect of removing the rights of hereditary peers to sit and vote in the House of Lords, received the Royal Assent on 11 November 1999. Section 1 of the Act provides that 'No-one shall be a member of the House of Lords by virtue of a hereditary peerage.' Section 2 of the Act goes on to provide for 92 hereditary peers to remain as members of the House of Lords, but only as life peers. With the exception of the holder of the office of Earl Marshal, and the holder of the office of Lord Great Chamberlain, those hereditary peers wishing to remain as life peers were required to put themselves forward for selection by their fellow peers. Under Standing Orders of the House 15 peers were selected by the whole House to serve as deputy speakers or in any other office required by the House. The remaining 75 (42 Conservative, 28 crossbenchers, three Liberal democrat and two Labour) were selected by a ballot conducted amongst the hereditary peers.

As a consequence of their being removed from the House of Lords hereditary peers regain various civic rights. In particular the right to vote at elections to the House of Commons, and to be elected as a member of that House. Those hereditary peers remaining in the House of Lords as 'excepted peers' under s2 of the 1999 Act remain disqualified from these activities.

For the avoidance of doubt s5 provides that 'any writ of summons issued for the present Parliament in right of a hereditary peerage shall not have effect after that session unless it has been issued to a person who, at the end of the session, is excepted from s1 by virtue of s2.' This provision was included to deal with the contention raised by some hereditary peers that, having received a writ of summons to attend Parliament, they should be allowed to sit and vote in the House of Lords until the dissolution of Parliament. That s5 prevents hereditary peers from sitting after the end of the session in which the House of Lords Act 1999 was passed was confirmed by the Committee for Privileges of the House of Lords: see further *Lord Mayhew of Twysden's Motion* [2000] 2 WLR 719.

Under the Peerage Act 1963 a hereditary peer applying for a writ of summons to the House of Lords lost the right to disclaim his title. The right to disclaim remains unaffected by the House of Lords Act 1999, but references to writs of summons have been removed, as hereditary peers (unless excepted under s2) will not be entitled to receive a writ of summons. Hereditary peers excepted under s2 will not be permitted to disclaim.

As part of the drive to increase the representativeness of the House of Lords members of the public were invited, during 2000, to apply for one of up to ten life peerages simply by requesting and completing an application form. Approximately 2,000 applications were received. The criteria for selection provided that candidates should be persons of integrity, independence, able to demonstrate objectivity, openness, and with the ability to contribute to the working of the House. Successful candidates sit as crossbenchers.

The early evidence of voting patterns in the revised House of Lords indicates that if the Labour government was hoping to 'tame' the second chamber by removing the large pro-Conservative lobby it is likely to be disappointed. The first Mode of Trial Bill, by which the government sought to restrict the right to trial by jury, was defeated in January 2000 by 222 votes to 126 – the first outright defeat for a government Bill since the Sunday trading legislation in 1990. Between January and April 2000 the Labour government suffered a further ten defeats in various votes on amendments in the Lords.

Composition of the House of Lords by peerage type as of 1 May 2003

Type of peerage	Number
Archbishops and bishops	25
Peers under the House of Lords Act 1999	92 (of whom 4 are women)
Life peers under the Appellate Jurisdiction Act 1876	27
Life peers under the Life Peerages Act 1958	545 (of whom 109 are women)
TOTAL	689

Composition of the House of Lords by party allegiance as of 1 May 2003

Party	Life peers	Hereditary: elected by party	Hereditary: elected office holders	Hereditary: Royal office holders	Lords Spiritual	TOTAL
Conservative Party	163	41	9	0	0	213
Labour Party	182	2	2	0	0	186
Liberal Democrat	60	3	2	0	0	65
Crossbenchers	146	29	2	2	0	179
Lords Spiritual	0	0	0	0	25	25
Others	7	0	0	0	0	7
TOTAL	558	75	15	2	25	675

The Lords Spiritual

These are the Archbishops of Canterbury and York, the Bishops of London, Durham and Winchester, and the next 21 diocesan bishops of the Church of England according to the seniority of their appointment. When such a bishop dies or resigns, his seat in the House is taken by the next senior diocesan bishop. They hold their seats in the Lords until they resign from their episcopal offices.

The 'Law Lords'

The Law Lords, or Lords of Appeal in Ordinary as they are formally titled, are appointed by the Crown to perform the judicial duties of the House. A maximum of 11 may be appointed to serve in a judicial capacity at any one time. They are entitled to sit and vote for life, notwithstanding retirement from their judicial office, and may participate in general debate.

Salaries and expenses

Members of the House of Lords do not receive a salary. Salaries are paid to government ministers in the Lords, the Leader of the Opposition, Opposition Chief

Whip, the Chairman of Committees, the Principal Deputy Chairman of Committees and the Lords of Appeal in Ordinary. Members of the House are entitled to expenses incurred for the purpose of attending the sittings of the House or its committees, such as accommodation, subsistence, travel, general office expenses or secretarial or research assistance.

The privileges of the House of Lords

The privileges of the House of Lords are similar to those enjoyed by the House of Commons, as outlined at section 6.9. They include freedom of speech – art 9 of the Bill of Rights applies to the Lords as it does to the Commons. Freedom from civil arrest is also included – individual peers may claim privilege from civil arrest at any time: see *Stourton* v *Stourton* [1963] P 302. The House of Lords has the right to regulate its own composition, via its Committee of Privileges, including the determination of the right of newly created peers to sit and vote. Claims to established peerages are also determined by that Committee. It also enjoys the right to punish for contempt. The Lords can commit a person for a definite term and may also impose fines. In March 2000 the Committee on Standards in Public Life chaired by Lord Neill announced that it would investigate proposals that members of the House of Lords be subject to a compulsory disclosure of interests regime similar to that in operation in the House of Commons. Members of the House of Lords are currently governed by a voluntary scheme and are only required to disclose consultancies with lobbying companies.

In May 2002 the House of Lords Register of Members' Interests was opened for public scrutiny. The Register, which requires peers to declare company directorships, consultancies and any other interests relevant to parliamentary business, was introduced as part of the drive to ensure that the allegations of 'sleaze' that had been levelled at the House of Commons were not replicated as regards the House of Lords.

6.13 The future of the second chamber

The case for reforming the membership of the House of Lords seems to have broad popular support. Membership of the legislature based on the hereditary principle did not sit well with a modern constitution, notwithstanding that the United Kingdom has a constitutional monarch who succeeds to that position by right of birth. If the United Kingdom Parliament were unicameral, and proposals were being put forward to convert it to a bicameral body, it is very unlikely that anyone would seriously suggest that two-thirds of the members of the upper chamber should be able to pass on the right to sit and vote to their sons and daughters.

The debate, therefore, is less about whether there should be reform as opposed to preservation of the status quo, and more about what the reforms should be. The arguments in favour of abolishing the voting rights of hereditary peers were enticingly egalitarian. The task of devising a modern second chamber that has a proper working relationship with the House of Commons presents far more difficulties.

Those who argue for the outright abolition of the House of Lords, in other words those who advocate a unicameral legislature, contend that, in a unitary constitutional structure, a second chamber is redundant. Abolitionists reject the notion that the House of Lords can be justified on the basis that it acts as a necessary check on the Commons and can provide more effective scrutiny of legislative proposals. The rationale for abolition is that if there are defects with the representativeness and effectiveness of the Commons, it is the House of Commons itself that needs to be reformed so that it operates properly. They might add that the space and resources currently utilised by the House of Lords could be more effectively deployed by an expanded House of Commons. Criticisms to the effect that a unicameral legislature could aggregate unlimited power to itself are usually met with the response that the control exercise by the House of Lords under our current system is at best sporadic. Rather than being occasionally contained, obstructed or thwarted by the House of Lords, the House of Commons could be required to operate within the confines of a written constitution, if necessary with entrenched provisions, perhaps requiring a referendum for amendment. A number of countries operate on the basis of a unicameral legislature, notably New Zealand, Sweden and Denmark.

Those who advocate the retention of a second chamber tend to focus their proposals for reform either on the method of appointing its members, or on the rights of members. Those who advocate a directly elected second chamber face a number of obvious difficulties. Why duplicate the House of Commons? If the proposal is that election should be on some basis other than that used at present for parliamentary elections it is open to criticism on the grounds that it will either produce a less representative assembly, leaving it open to questions as regards its legitimacy, or that it could produce a more representative assembly, perhaps by the adoption of proportional representation, and thus represent a threat to the House of Commons. The adoption of the model based on a powerful second chamber, as can be found in federal constitutions such as those in Australia, Switzerland and the United States of America, would require some fundamental changes to the British constitution, particularly in terms of ministerial responsibility to the House of Commons.

In countries such as Iceland and Norway the second chamber is elected by the lower house, so the party political composition of second chamber will normally mirror that of the lower house. The attraction of this method is that there is still an indirect link with the democratic process, in that the membership is determined by those who have been elected, and it ensures that the second chamber is unlikely to be able to thwart the will of the democratically elected legislative body. An upper chamber that mirrors the political complexion of the lower chamber may not provide a very effective means of control, however. Where a the party of government has a large majority in the House of Commons, the House of Lords can provide a more effective bulwark against executive high-handedness than Her Majesty's loyal opposition. Notwithstanding the 'in-built' Conservative bias of the old hereditary House of Lords in the period 1979–83 the Conservative government sustained 45 defeats in the House of Lords. During 1983–87 the figure was 62 defeats, and between 1987 and May 1990 the Conservative government sustained 40 defeats.

In some countries such as France and Austria, the second chamber is elected by an electoral college, or by regional assemblies, thus ensuring that the legislature represents a wider group of interests than might otherwise be the case. Difficult questions will remain, however, as to the extent to which the indirectly elected body can be permitted to obstruct the will of the directly elected body. A further possible variant is to assemble a second chamber on a functional basis, in the sense that the membership is made up of the holders of specific posts, for example local authority chief executives, designated trade union leaders, university vice-chancellors, heads of quangos such as the Equal Opportunities Commission, English Heritage, the Countryside Commission etc. The presence in the House of Lords of the Lords Spiritual and the Law Lords to some extent provides a skeletal model of this approach. The advantage of such a model is that it brings a varied range of experience and wisdom to bear upon the legislative proposals of the House of Commons, but it also raises questions as to where the power of patronage would lie. One would also have to question the extent of the 'checking' powers to be given to such an assembly, and the extent to which individuals, holding influential and demanding posts in commerce, industry and the public sector, would be able to attend regularly to discharge their legislative duties.

The Labour government that took office in May 1997 was committed to reforming the House of Lords, initially by ending the voting rights of hereditary peers. As indicated above this was achieved by means of the House of Lords Act 1999. The more difficult task of determining how membership of the second chamber should be provided for in the future was handed over to a Royal Commission chaired by Lord Wakenham.

The Royal Commission

The Royal Commission on the House of Lords chaired by Lord Wakeham was given the following terms of reference:

'Having regard to the need to maintain the position of the House of Commons as the pre-eminent chamber of Parliament and taking particular account of the present nature of the constitutional settlement, including the newly devolved institutions, the impact of the Human Rights Act 1998 and developing relations with the European Union:

(i) To consider and make recommendations on the role and functions of the second chamber;

(ii) To make recommendations on the method or combination of methods of composition required to constitute a second chamber fit for that role and those functions ...'

The ensuing report – *A House for the Future* – came out in favour of a revised second chamber comprising some 550 members. It envisaged that the majority of these members would be appointed by an independent 'Appointments Commission' with a minority being elected (65 under model 'A'; 87 under model 'B'; 195 under model 'C'). The 92 hereditary peers spared under the House of Lords Act 1999 would be removed over a period of time. Elected members would be drawn from regional lists, such as those now used for the election of MEPs, with one-third being elected every five years. Once elected a term of office would be for 15 years. The Law Lords and Lords Spiritual would continue to enjoy membership of the second chamber by virtue of office.

The proposals placed considerable power in the hands of the Appointments Commission, which was charged with ensuring that those appointed were representative of the nation as a whole, in terms of gender, ethnicity, background and representation of the regions. It recommended that existing life peers should remain in office until death, envisaging that the change over to an appointed and/or elected chamber would take 20 to 30 years. The Appointments Commission began the task of soliciting applications in the summer of 2000. In the interim between the abolition of hereditary peers' voting rights and the more radical stage two reforms the Prime Minister began the process of appointing Labour life peers with a view to equalising party support in the House of Lords.

The Royal Commission report did not recommend any changes to the powers of the House of Lords, other than a removal of the power to veto statutory instruments. It did recommend that the House of Lords should set up a Constitutional Committee to examine more closely the constitutional implications of Bills, and a Human Rights Committee to examine the human rights implications of proposed legislation. The report made no recommendation as to the name of the revised second chamber, or the titles to be bestowed on those appointed or elected. It was felt that such matters should be the result of an evolutionary process.

The government's response

On 7 November 2001, by way of response to the report of the Royal Commission chaired by Lord Wakeham, the government published its White Paper on House of Lords' reform *Completing the Reform* (Cm 5291). The White Paper addresses three issues in particular: the functions of the second chamber; the powers of the second chamber and its relationship with the House of Commons; and the membership of the second chamber.

As a basis for its reform proposals the White Paper identifies the following principles, namely that the House of Lords should be:

'(i) A revising and deliberative assembly – not seeking to usurp the role of the House of Commons as the pre-eminent chamber;
(ii) Composed of a membership appropriate to its revising and deliberative functions, and not duplicate or clone the Commons.

(iii) Political in approach – but not dominated by any one political party.

(iv) Representative of independent expertise and of the broader community in the UK – but not disrupt the relationship between elected members of the Commons and their constituents.'

The functions of the second chamber

The White Paper sees the principle function of the second chamber as being the consideration and revision of legislation, scrutiny of the executive and the provision of a forum for the debating of, and reporting on, public issues.

In recommending that there be no significant changes in the functions of the second chamber, the White Paper observes:

'21. The House of Lords' most important function will continue to be as a revising chamber for legislation. The House of Commons will retain the primary authority for the approval of legislation. The role of the Lords is to provide further scrutiny of legislation, obliging the government to justify further its legislative proposals and examining them in a less partisan spirit than the Commons, with the perspective and expertise it is able to bring to bear from a different membership. The Lords also gives, and should continue to give, the government an opportunity to consider issues raised during debate on its legislation in both Houses and to propose suitable amendments.

22. The House of Lords also has, and should continue to have, a role to play in scrutiny. The House of Lords is a powerful deliberative assembly, both in its debates and in the work of its committees, particularly its Select Committees on Delegated Powers and Regulatory Reform and the European Union (both of which are especially strengthened by the role of independent experts who sit on the cross-benches). Reform should be geared to strengthening this capacity, without duplicating the work of the House of Commons.

23. The House of Lords plays an important role in holding the government to account. Its ability to do so is critically dependent upon the fact that many ministers sit in the Lords. Ministers should continue to be appointed from the Lords in broadly the number that obtains at present. A measure of parliamentary scrutiny would be lost if ministers were directly accountable only to the House of Commons. It is important, however, to separate holding individual ministers to account from holding the government as a whole to account. The second chamber can question and criticise individual ministers. But the power to hold the government collectively to account must remain with the House of Commons.

24. There is no case for giving specific new functions to the House of Lords. The government agrees with the Royal Commission that there is a role for the House of Lords in reviewing the impact of constitutional reform. But this is something which should develop within the existing constitutional framework.'

The powers of the second chamber and its relationship with the House of Commons

The government view, clearly stated in the White Paper, is that:

'Reform of the House of Lords must ... satisfy one key condition: it must not alter the respective roles and authority of the two chambers and their members in a way that would obscure the line of authority and accountability that flows between the people and those they elect directly to form the government and act as their individual representatives. Decisions on functions, on authority, and membership of the House of Lords need to be consistent with these settled principles of our democracy.' (para 18)

The White Paper does propose, however, that the House of Lords should lose its power to veto subordinate legislation, the power of veto being replaced with a power to delay such legislation for up to three months. As the White Paper explains (paras 32–33):

'For an affirmative instrument, this will be a delay in its coming into force [for three months]. For a negative instrument, the instrument will remain in force, but under "notice" of annulment unless the Commons (re)confirms it. During the three-month period, the government and the House of Commons will have to consider the Lords' objections to the measure. If, before the end of the period, the government decides it wishes to proceed with the instrument, and the Commons confirms its approval of that decision, the statutory instrument will become or remain law. ... The effect of this change will be to increase the influence of the Lords in relation to secondary legislation. While a reduction in the nominal power to reject statutory instruments absolutely, this change will in practice render the Lords more effective in assuring the quality of secondary legislation, since the House will be able to point out flaws and urge some recasting of the terms of a statutory instrument, without rejecting it outright. This provides a parallel power to that in main legislation enabling the Lords to ask, through delay, the government to reflect again, but ultimately not to frustrate a legislative proposal endorsed by the Commons.

The issue of reforming the delaying powers of the House of Lords as regards primary legislation was considered by the Royal Commission and the government agrees with its conclusions that any changes would be "far from simple to enact, and the practical effect insufficient to justify the parliamentary time and effort required." '

The membership of the second chamber

Under the White Paper proposals the membership of the reformed second chamber would eventually (over a ten-year period of transitional change) be capped at 600. The 92 remaining hereditary peers would be removed. Those appointed to the second chamber would not be made peers, but would be given the title 'Member of the Lords' designated 'ML'.

Whereas the Royal Commission envisaged an elected element in a reformed second chamber of 87 members, the White Paper favours an elected membership of 120. Elected members would represent constituencies based on those used for the election of members of the European Parliament, successful candidates being selected on the basis of a party-list system.

A further 120 members would be appointed by the Appointments Commission, the Commission being under a duty to ensure a balanced and representative selection of members, reflecting the demographic and ethnic mix of the populations as a whole.

The remaining 332 members would be political appointees nominated by the major political parties. The Appointments Commission would have a supervisory role in respect of such nominations in that it would be required to vet nominees for propriety, and would be required to ensure an appropriate political balance across the political parties. The right of each party to nominate members would be based on its electoral support at the most recent general election, subject to a proviso that no one political party should have an overall majority.

At least 12 Law Lords would continue to sit as members of the second chamber but the representation of Church of England bishops would be reduced from 26 to 16.

The White Paper seeks further comment on the terms of membership, particularly the length of appointment. It further provides (para 57):

> '... the government would welcome views on the length of the elected and appointed terms and whether, in each case, it should be less than 15 years. We do not believe that the two categories of members need necessarily serve terms of equivalent length. Indeed, if Lords elections are timed to coincide with general elections, and Parliaments are the unit of tenure for elected members of the Lords, it would not in any case be possible to have equivalent terms. The precise arrangement for those elected would depend on whether links with general or European or regional elections were chosen, but the realistic choice is between 5, 10 and 15 years (if to coincide with Euro elections); or between one, two or three Parliaments or electoral cycles (if to coincide with general elections or regional elections), and the government is inclined to think that on balance it lies between the shorter options in each case. The choice of terms for appointed members is also between 5, 10 and 15 years. As they will not necessarily be appointed at the beginning of a parliament, there is no need to tie them to the parliamentary cycle.'

The White Paper has been seen by many as a political fudge – especially as regards the issue of elected members for the House of Lords. Having elected members is either desirable or it is not. Critics argued that opting to have a 20 per cent elected element sends mixed messages as to the value of democratic representation. There may also be issues regarding the relative legitimacy of elected and appointed members of the second chamber. Given current levels of voter apathy questions might also be asked as to the extent to which voters might be bothered to register their preferences in elections for members of the Lords. The White Paper, perhaps wisely, envisages elections for the Lords being held on the same day as general elections thus masking what may be a high level of voter indifference regarding who their representative might be in the second chamber.

The White Paper also reflects the conflict in which any government advocating Lords' reform inevitably finds itself. It seeks to attack the iniquities of hereditary membership and the historic pro-Conservative bias, but at the same time it is fearful of creating an institution that could be said to rival the Commons in terms of power and legitimacy. Nothing short of a complete constitutional resettlement will solve this conundrum, hence the uneasy and not altogether coherent compromise offered in the White Paper.

Whilst relieving hereditary peers of their right to vote might go some way to deflecting the criticisms of the Lords on the grounds of it being an unrepresentative and undemocratic body, the question nevertheless arises as to what extent the appointed peers can claim that they have any stronger claim to vote. Critics have pointed out that this change would convert the House of Lords into a powerful quango.

In May 2002 the government indicated that it would be willing to increase the elected element to more than 20 per cent if there was sufficient support for this in the House of Commons.

The work of the Joint Committee

A Joint Committee on House of Lords Reform was established in 2002, its terms of reference being:

> '(1) to consider issues relating to House of Lords reform, including the composition and powers of the second chamber and its role and authority within the context of Parliament as a whole, having regard in particular to the impact which any proposed changes would have on the existing pre-eminence of the House of Commons, such consideration to include the implications of a House composed of more than one "category" of member and the experience and expertise which the House of Lords in its present form brings to its function as the revising Chamber; and
> (2) having regard to paragraph (1) above, to report on options for the composition and powers of the House of Lords and to define and present to both Houses options for composition, including a fully nominated and fully elected House, and intermediate options; and to consider and report on –
> (a) any changes to the relationship between the two Houses which may be necessary to ensure the proper functioning of Parliament as a whole in the context of a reformed second chamber, and in particular, any new procedures for resolving conflict between the two Houses; and
> (b) the most appropriate and effective legal and constitutional means to give effect to any new parliamentary settlement; and in all the foregoing considerations, to have regard to –
> (i) the Report of the Royal Commission on House of Lords Reform (Cm 4534);
> (ii) the White Paper *The House of Lords – Completing the Reform* (Cm 5291), and the responses received thereto;
> (iii) debates and votes in both Houses of Parliament on House of Lords reform; and
> (iv) the House of Commons Public Administration Select Committee report *The Second Chamber: Continuing the Reform*, including its consultation of the House of Commons, and any other relevant select committee reports.'

In December 2002 the Joint Committee on House of Lords Reform published its first report. The proposals for reform envisaged 'a continuation of the present role of the House of Lords, and of the existing conventions governing its relations with the House of Commons.'

The Committee identified what it saw as 'five qualities desirable in the makeup of a reformed second chamber:' These were: legitimacy; representativeness; no domination by any one party; independence; and expertise.

On the basis of a reformed second chamber of about 600 members (tenure being for 12 years), with most appointed by a new Appointments Commission (the Prime Minister of the day to retaining a power of nomination, such nominations being subject to scrutiny by the Appointments Commission), the Committee agreed in its first report that seven options regarding composition should be considered by Parliament.

The first option is that of a fully appointed second chamber. The report states (paras 63–65):

> 'A fully appointed House would most closely resemble the existing House of Lords, with the remaining hereditary element removed. Although the legitimacy of such a House would be challenged, this could be mitigated if a new independent and respected Appointments Commission was set up by statute. We have said that we consider that there is a place for political appointments to the House but, to ensure the integrity of the process, all such appointments should be scrutinised by the Appointments Commission. … It would be the responsibility of the … Appointments Commission, to ensure that … representativeness was achieved. … A fully appointed House could also provide a method for the inclusion of independent members and experts. It could continue to provide part-time members who could bring contemporary professional experience to bear on the duties of scrutiny and the passing of legislation.'

The second option is that of a fully elected second chamber. The report states (paras 67–69):

> 'The principal argument in favour of a fully elected House is that it would have greater legitimacy and accountability. That view rests upon the premise that legitimacy and accountability are conferred by election. On the other hand the existing House, in exercising independence and in applying expertise, has contributed significantly to the process of parliamentary scrutiny. That may also be considered a basis of legitimacy, important but different from legitimacy conferred by election. Legitimacy based entirely on election may well result in a House which is more assertive. While a reformed second chamber could not unilaterally increase its formal powers, it is a matter for consideration just how far it might feel disposed, by more vigorous use of its existing powers, to challenge the House of Commons and the government. Such developments could represent a significant constitutional change. … An elected House is also likely to have few if any independent members … the domination of the House by elected party politicians would irrevocably change the nature of the House and the attitude and relationship of the House to the Commons and to the government. In a fully elected House there could be no question of continuing membership for the law lords or Church of England bishops … the cost is likely to be greater because elected members will expect to be salaried and will expect facilities on a par with those in the House of Commons.'

The third option is to have an 80 per cent appointed/20 per cent elected second chamber. Of this the report observes (para 70):

> 'We do not share the view that a House of mixed composition is necessarily undesirable. Indeed, in certain senses the House of Lords has always been a mixed House (comprising hereditary peers by succession, hereditary peers of first creation, ex officio members, and in recent times life peers). However, although this model would ensure the entry to the House of a sufficient number of independents, we can foresee difficulties in holding a

direct election for only twenty per cent of the second House. Turnout in all elections has fallen to a worryingly low level. We cannot see an election for a small proportion of the new House raising any enthusiasm or contributing to a sense of the importance of the reformed House in the eyes of the electorate.'

The remaining options for reformed compositions are variations on the third, namely: an 80 per cent elected/20 per cent appointed second chamber; a 60 per cent appointed/40 per cent elected second chamber; a 60 per cent elected/40 per cent appointed second chamber; a 50 per cent appointed/50 per cent elected second chamber. Of these variations the report states (paras 71–74):

'... if the appointed element is pitched as low as 20 per cent, difficulties will arise. The current working House consists of 300 or so members but it is a frequently changing 300, depending on the business being considered. The independent element and the element of expertise need to have a sufficiently wide base to provide opinion on a vast range of subjects as they arise in the course of the House's business. With a smaller appointed element in an elected House of reduced size, that provision is unlikely to be sufficient or satisfactory. The law lords and the bishops (or other religious representatives) could not easily be retained. Moreover, a House of largely elected members is bound to change the culture of the second House, making it less attractive for those who wish to remain unaffiliated to party. ... [a 60 per cent appointed/40 per cent elected mix] ... would provide a more reasonable basis of independent members and experts who do not wish to stand for election. It would, on the other hand, provide a significant elected element, to go some way to meet the demands of legitimacy. ... [a 60 per cent elected/40 per cent appointed split] ... retains the advantages of a mixed House. Nevertheless, it is a matter of judgement as to whether a 40 per cent appointed House is sufficient to provide the necessary diversity of expertise. ... The above arguments broadly apply to [the 50 per cent elected/50 per cent appointed option]. ... However, the exact half-way House may have some appeal on grounds of mathematical neatness. It would provide an apparently sufficient balance of electoral legitimacy on the one hand and of independence and expertise from appointment on the other.'

Regarding the method used to elect any members to the second chamber, the report observes (para 53):

'Most opinion concludes that, if the second chamber is to be different from the first ... the method of election needs to be different, and elections should be held on different dates from general elections. The context should not be the election of a government, and, in any case, without fixed-term Parliaments there would be practical difficulties ... the electoral systems recommended by the Commons Public Administration Committee (open regional lists or Single Transferable Vote) both have the advantages that they provide for much larger constituencies than for MPs, minimising the risk of overlap. "First-past-the-post", especially if applied to a smaller percentage of a smaller sized House, would both rule out minor parties and independents, and give an undue preponderance to the largest party.'

It is envisaged that the options will be voted on once both Houses have had the opportunity to consider the report in detail.

Once Parliament has made a decision regarding the composition of the second chamber the committee will examine the conventions that regulate relations between the two chambers, and whether any additional powers should be given to the second chamber.

Assuming the Labour government has the will, before 2005, to introduce the legislation necessary to give effect to the White Paper proposals, a further constitutional question arises as to how such a change would be accomplished. Assuming opposition from the House of Lords, and setting aside the possible creation of hundreds of pro-reform life peers, could a Labour government push legislation through, utilising the Parliament Acts, to effect these changes without the consent of the Lords? Given that it would arguably be seen as a matter touching upon the privileges of the House of Lords, the courts might be sympathetic to an argument that ultimately it is a matter for the House of Lords itself to resolve: see further the *Bradlaugh* litigation considered above at section 6.9.

Whilst the current situation, whereby all members of the second chamber are appointed for life, is said to be 'interim', it should be remembered that the changes introduced by the Parliament Acts 1911 were similarly described. It was almost 90 years before further major changes were made.

7

The Executive

7.1 Introduction

7.2 The Prime Minister and the Cabinet

7.3 Ministerial responsibility

7.4 Ministers' powers: delegated legislation

7.5 Ministers' powers: prerogative power

7.6 Government departments

7.7 The Civil Service

7.8 Police forces

7.9 Judicial control of police forces

7.1 Introduction

The term 'the executive' has no legal status as such but is generally seen, along with the legislature and the judiciary, as comprising one of the three key branches of government. As has been seen in Chapter 3, the doctrine of the separation of powers holds that, in an ideal constitutional arrangement, those forming the executive should not discharge legislative or judicial functions, and should be subject to controls exercised by the judiciary and legislature.

In the British constitution the executive branch of government comprises: central government, in the form of ministers and their departments; local government; the police; and various other administrative bodies, such as tribunal and commissions created to give effect to government policy. This Chapter will examine the executive in so far as that term relates to central government and the control of police forces. For coverage of local government and the tribunal system: see Molan, *Administrative Law* (4th ed, Old Bailey Press), Chapters 3 and 4.

7.2 The Prime Minister and the Cabinet

Whilst a party is able to remain in government because it commands an overall majority of seats in the House of Commons, even a cursory examination of the exercise of power would reveal that, in reality, the key policy decisions and legislative proposals are generated by the Prime Minister and Cabinet ministers. Given that the Prime Minister effectively appoints his Cabinet members, and many more who hold more junior ministerial posts, his grip on power is considerable. Significantly, however, much of this is the result of historical accident and convention.

Formal position of the Prime Minister

The office of Prime Minister is a de facto institution recognised by statute but governed mainly by convention. It is invariably held together with the office of First Lord of the Treasury. In the eighteenth and nineteenth centuries, when Walpole, William Pitt the Younger, Disraeli and Gladstone were shaping the Prime Ministerial role into its present form, the holder of the office of First Lord of the Treasury had powers of patronage which enabled him to control departmental appointments so as to secure advantage for his party. The title Prime Minister only dates from 1905 and before 1937 the salary of the Prime Minister was derived from holding the office of First Lord of the Treasury.

The Ministerial and Other Salaries Act 1975 and the Parliamentary and Other Pensions Act 1972, now refer to the 'Prime Minister and First Lord of the Treasury' and it seems unlikely therefore that the two offices will become separated again. The last occasion on which they were separated was between 1895 and 1902, when Lord Salisbury was Prime Minister and Balfour was First Lord of the Treasury. Although the First Lord of the Treasury ceased to have responsibility for Civil Service affairs on the creation of the Civil Service Department in 1968, the Prime Minister is now titled Minister for the Civil Service as well as First Lord of the Treasury, and so retains ultimate responsibility for the Civil Service. With this responsibility go certain rights of patronage, as the appointment of senior civil servants is made on the Prime Minister's recommendation. On the abolition of the Civil Service Department in 1981 the Prime Minister retained overall responsibility for the Civil Service, but functions relating to conditions of service and pay were transferred to the Treasury, and other matters of management and efficiency to a new Management and Personnel Office, which is run on a day-to-day basis by another Cabinet minister.

The Prime Minister is, in theory, answerable to Parliament for the way in which he exercises his powers. In reality it has become more difficult for Parliament to exercise any effective scrutiny given the increasingly 'presidential' style of politics practised by successive Prime Ministers in recent years. In an attempt to counter these criticisms Tony Blair agreed, in April 2002, to appear before the House of

Commons Liaison Committee twice a year. The Committee is comprised of select committee chairs and its meetings with the Prime Minister are televised. Although an agenda is issued there is no requirement that questions are limited to agenda topics. Special advisers to the Prime Minister cannot be compelled to appear before the Committee.

From time to time politicians have been appointed to the post of Deputy Prime Minister, although in constitutional terms there is no such office, as the Crown does not appoint to that position. During the Second World War Clement Atlee served as Deputy Prime Minister to Winston Churchill, principally to take charge of government on the 'Home Front', although there was no agreement that he would have replaced Churchill had the latter been unable to continue in office. In modern times the appointment of a senior Cabinet figure as Deputy Prime Minister has found favour with a number of Conservative administrations, but it is far from clear what purpose such appointments have served, other than to cement political allegiances, or prevent splits within the party. Margaret Thatcher appointed Geoffrey Howe as her deputy in 1989. In July 1995, following his re-election as Conservative Party leader, John Major appointed Michael Helsetine as his deputy. Following the election of a Labour government in May 1997, Tony Blair appointed John Prescott as his deputy.

Choosing a Prime Minister

As a matter of constitutional theory the choice of Prime Minister is that of the Queen alone in the exercise of the Sovereign's personal prerogative. In practice the person in whose favour that prerogative must be exercised is known in advance by the Sovereign. Generally, in appointing a Prime Minister, the Queen should choose that person who is able to command the support of the majority in the House of Commons – usually the leader of the party with the majority of seats. The Sovereign no longer has a personal discretion as to whom she appoints except in certain unusual circumstances.

The office of Prime Minister may become vacant on the dismissal, death or resignation of the holder. In modern constitutional practice the dismissal of a Prime Minister is unlikely to arise except in the most extreme circumstances. Since the Victorian era all new appointments have been made necessary by death or resignation. Resignation may be personal, for example on grounds of ill-health (akin to death in office). Alternatively, the entire executive or ministry may resign with the Prime Minister when the governing party is defeated on a motion of non-confidence or at a general election.

Before the Conservative Party adopted a ballot system for the election of its leader in 1964, the resignation or death of a Conservative Prime Minister left some discretion to the Sovereign in the choice of a successor. All the major parties now elect their leader by ballot, although the electoral colleges that make the choice are differently constituted. Conservative MPs alone elect their leader, whereas the

Labour leader is elected on a 'one member one vote' basis. It seems that the proper course for the Sovereign to take on the death or resignation of a Prime Minister is to wait until the governing party has elected its new leader and then invite that person to take office. This is what happened in 1976 when Wilson announced his intention to resign and Callaghan was elected as the new leader of the Labour Party. The appointment of John Major as Prime Minister in 1990 arose as a result of Margaret Thatcher's resignation, following her decision not to contest the election for the Conservative Party leadership beyond its second round. As she later pointed out, even though she lost the leadership contest, she remained Prime Minister until her resignation was accepted by the Queen. Similarly, when John Major announced his resignation as leader of the Conservative party in June 1995, thus sparking a leadership contest, he remained as Prime Minister and, by convention, would have only had to resign if he had been defeated in that contest.

Following defeat on a motion of no confidence in the House of Commons, the proper course is for the Prime Minister and the entire government to resign. The Prime Minister may then either advise the monarch to invite the Leader of the Opposition, which is a recognised position having a statutory salary, to form a Government or request a dissolution. The latter course was favoured by Callaghan when his minority Labour government was defeated on an Opposition motion of no confidence in 1979.

If the Prime Minister judges that the time is advantageous he may request a dissolution with a view to causing a general election to be held. If the government is defeated decisively at the subsequent election, modern constitutional convention requires the Prime Minister and entire government to resign before the new Parliament meets. The Leader of the Opposition will usually have an overall majority in the Commons if the government has been defeated, and will be the person invited to form a new ministry. Where no one party secures an overall majority at a general election the Prime Minister need not resign immediately, but may wait to see if he can obtain a majority in the new House with support from another party.

Functions of the Prime Minister

The primary functions of a Prime Minister are the formation of a government and providing political leadership for his party. A list of proposed ministerial appointments is presented to the Queen for her approval. The Queen may make observations, suggestions and objections, but she cannot disapprove the appointment of a particular minister if the Prime Minister insists on that choice. Junior ministers are chosen by the Prime Minister without consulting the Sovereign. In appointing ministers the Prime Minister is bound by certain conventions. A minister must be, or become, a member of one or other of the Houses of Parliament, each department must have a ministerial spokesman in the Commons and the Chancellor of the Exchequer must be a member of the House of Commons. Under the House of

Commons Disqualification Act 1975, s2, there may be up to 95 holders of ministerial office in the Commons. Additional ministers may be appointed from the House of Lords. The Prime Minister may require a minister to resign at any time: see ministerial responsibility, considered below at section 7.3.

By means of conference speeches, performances at the despatch box during debates and Prime Minister's Question Time in the House of Commons, appearances in the media and on the international stage, the Prime Minister can help to communicate government policy and convey a particular public image of his party.

Beyond these key functions it should be noted that the Prime Minister also enjoys substantial powers of patronage in relation to posts going beyond his immediate government. He advises the Queen on the granting of peerages and other honours and on appointments to certain high offices of state, including bishops, Lords of Appeal and senior members of the armed forces. Senior appointments in the Civil Service must be approved by the Prime Minister.

The origins of Cabinet government

At the close of the seventeenth century, Trenchard wrote in his *Short History of Standing Armies*:

> 'Formerly all matters of state and discretion were debated and resolved in Privy Council, where every man subscribed his opinion and was answerable for it. The late King Charles II was the first who broke this most excellent part of our constitution by setting up a cabal or cabinet council, where all matters of consequence were debated and resolved, and then brought to the Privy Council to be confirmed.'

A cabal was a club or association of intriguers; cabinet was a French word for a small private room or closet. Both words were derogatory and the whole passage illustrates the misgivings that surrounded the emergence of this new political institution, at the end of the seventeenth century. At the restoration of the monarchy in 1660 the Privy Council was involved in a large volume of political and administrative business. Charles II become frustrated with the delays occasioned by debate and began to weaken the Council by removing political power from it, preferring to consult with a small number of trusted advisers. He was able to justify this to some extent by alleging that the size of the Privy Council made it unable to act in secrecy and with sufficient speed to meet the exigencies of great affairs. Yet it was he who increased the number of Privy Councillors so as to make it unwieldy and unworkable. The use of a Cabinet vested real power in the hands of a small group of ministers who were not accountable to Parliament. Parliament complained that the Privy Council was not being consulted regularly and did not know who was responsible for the formulation of policy. Attempts were made to restore the Privy Council to its former status and in 1679 it was remodelled and the membership reduced from 50 to 30. Charles II promised to be guided by its advice but that promise was soon broken and a Cabinet, cabal or 'jurba' reappeared.

Clause 4 of the Act of Settlement 1700 would have imposed a statutory duty to govern by Council and not Cabinet. It provided that:

'... all matters and things relating to the well governing of this country which are properly cognisable in the Privy Council by the bias and customs of this Realm shall be transacted there, and all resolutions thereupon shall be signed by such of the Privy Council as shall consent to the same.'

This clause was a response to the alarm that the use of the Cabinet device had provoked, but it was repealed during the reign of Queen Anne before it came into effect. It is argued in Taswell-Longmead's *Constitutional History* that the last example of spontaneous and independent action by the Privy Council is to be found at the very end of the reign of Queen Anne, when the Council met and secured the Hanoverian succession against the Jacobites, as she lay on her death-bed.

By the middle of the eighteenth century the Cabinet had become a recognised institution, but its precise status was still uncertain. The relationship between the Cabinet and the party system was undefined, as was the broader relationship of the Cabinet with Parliament. The process that eroded the right of the King to choose his ministers was a lengthy one.

Several factors taken together indicate the manner in which political power shifted away from the monarch to the Cabinet, until eventually the effective choice of ministers passed to the Prime Minister. Firstly, the eighteenth century saw a gradual decline in the prestige of the monarchy. George I did not attend Cabinet meetings after 1717 and both he and George II were frequently absent from Britain. This shifted the emphasis within the Cabinet towards the formulation of policy as well as its execution. A period of personal direction of national policy by George III between 1763 and 1782 culminated in the loss of the American colonies and the fall of Lord North's government. This severe blow to the prestige of the monarchy was exacerbated by the onset of George III's mental illness in 1787. During his reign the Cabinet established the right to consider matters without the King's request that they should do so.

The party system was also developing in the eighteenth century and where, as under Walpole, who presided at Cabinet meetings between 1721 and 1742, the Cabinet was relatively homogeneous, its members met not only as advisers to the King, but as leaders of a party. Such a Cabinet was in a position to initiate policy and gain parliamentary support for it. Gradually it became accepted that the Cabinet and Prime Minister needed the support of a majority in Parliament, and therefore must have the same political views as that majority. After the Reform Act of 1832, which extended the franchise and reformed abuses, it became clear that influence and patronage would no longer be sufficient to secure the election of that majority. The reliance of the Cabinet on the support of a majority in the Commons meant that the choice of ministers had been greatly narrowed, if it had not yet passed completely from the monarch's hands. The increased power of the electorate meant that the executive had to be more responsive to its views. The chain of responsible government, the executive being responsible to Parliament and ultimately through the process of election of MPs to the electorate, was established.

Cabinet membership

The number of ministers in the Cabinet is in the sole discretion of the Prime Minister. Attlee thought 16 was the ideal, Churchill preferred a larger Cabinet of 22. Heath favoured a small Cabinet of 18 members while Labour Cabinets have fluctuated between 20 and 23. By convention and custom certain ministers are always members of the Cabinet. They include: the Lord Chancellor, Secretary of State for Foreign and Commonwealth Affairs, Home Secretary, Chancellor of the Exchequer, Secretary of State for Defence, Lord President of the Council, Leader of the House of Commons, Secretary of State for Scotland, together with the other secretaries of state and ministers in charge of the major departments. In addition, every Cabinet includes two or three ministers without portfolio who have no department of state but instead undertake special duties and often co-ordinate government policy. During wartime the normal Cabinet has been replaced by a small 'War Cabinet' to oversee the conduct of the war. During the First World War the War Cabinet had six members. The Second World War Cabinet had between seven and ten members. During the South Atlantic Campaign Mrs Thatcher formed an inner War Cabinet of five members: the Prime Minister, Foreign Secretary, Home Secretary, Secretary of State for Defence and the chairman of the Conservative Party. The Prime Minister presides over the allocation of functions between Cabinet committees and decides how government functions should be allocated between departments. He may, therefore create, amalgamate or abolish departments. He may take an active interest in the affairs of particular departments, especially the Treasury and Foreign and Commonwealth Office, intervene personally in major issues, and take decisions without consulting Cabinet. The Prime Minister presides over meetings of the full Cabinet and its most important committees. He decides the agenda for Cabinet meetings and controls discussion. At the end of a meeting no formal vote is taken on the policy decided; it is for the Prime Minister to sum up the consensus. Cabinet decision-making can, therefore, be dominated by the Prime Minister. Cabinet government was described by L S Amery in *Thoughts on the Constitution* (1953), in the following terms:

> 'The central directing instrument of government, in legislation as well as in administration, is the Cabinet. It is in Cabinet that administrative action is co-ordinated and legislative proposals sanctioned. It is the Cabinet that controls Parliament and governs the country.'

The special position enjoyed by the Prime Minister has led some authorities to the conclusion that Cabinet government has now given way to Prime Ministerial government. As Richard Crossman wrote: 'The post-war epoch has seen the final transformation of Cabinet government into Prime Ministerial government.'

Certainly, if a Prime Minister took full advantage of the conventional powers available he could dominate Cabinet and policy formulation. But the power of the Prime Minister relative to the Cabinet depends upon a number of factors, including his personality and the strength and standing in Parliament and in the party.

The Cabinet secretariat, headed by the Permanent Secretary to the Cabinet Office who is directly responsible to the Prime Minister, has responsibility for servicing the Cabinet and Cabinet committee meetings, taking minutes and circulate details of conclusions.

Cabinet committees

Since the end of the First World War a complicated Cabinet committee system has been established to facilitate the discussion and formulation of policy options and to co-ordinate the activities of the various government departments, with regard to policy. The existence, composition and functions of these Cabinet committees was, until recent times, kept highly secret. It is thought that Margaret Thatcher had some 25 standing Cabinet committees and about 110 ad hoc groups. In May 1992, John Major broke with tradition by making public the existence of the Cabinet committees and naming the members of the committees, a practice that has been maintained by his successor as Prime Minister, Tony Blair. The current arrangements provide for a number of committees divided into four broad areas: economic and domestic; civil contingencies; overseas and defence; and European.

The complete listing, as of November 2002, was:

Economic and domestic affairs
* Ministerial Committee on the Criminal Justice System (CJS)
* Ministerial Sub-Committee on Crime Reduction (CJS(CR))
* Ministerial Sub-Committee on Criminal Justice System Information Technology (CJS(IT))
* Ministerial Committee on the Nations and Regions (CNR)
* Ministerial Committee on Domestic Affairs (DA)
* Ministerial Sub-Committee on Adult Basic Skills (DA(ABS))
* Ministerial Sub-Committee on Active Communities and Family (DA(ACF))
* Ministerial Sub-Committee on Drugs Policy (DA(D))
* Ministerial Sub-Committee on Equality (DA(EQ))
* Ministerial Sub-Committee on Fraud (DA(F))
* Ministerial Sub-Committee on Energy Policy (DA(N))
* Ministerial Sub-Committee on Older People (DA(OP))
* Ministerial Sub-Committee on Rural Renewal (DA(RR))
* Ministerial Sub-Committee on Social Exclusion and Regeneration (DA(SER))
* Ministerial Committee on Economic Affairs, Productivity and Competitiveness (EAPC)
* Ministerial Sub-Committee on Employment (EAPC(E))

- Ministerial Committee on the Environment (ENV)
- Ministerial Sub-Committee on Green Ministers (ENV(G))
- Ministerial Committee on Local Government (GL)
- Ministerial Committee on the Legislative Programme (LP)
- Ministerial Panel on Regulatory Accountability (PRA)
- Ministerial Committee on Public Services and Public Expenditure (PSX)
- Ministerial Sub-Committee on Electronic Service Delivery (PSX(E))
- Ministerial Sub-Committee on Local PSAs (PSX(L))
- Ministerial Committee on Science Policy (SCI)
- Ministerial Sub-Committee on Biotechnology (SCI(BIO))
- Ministerial Committee on Welfare Reform (WR)
- Ministerial Group on Children and Young People's Services (MISC9)
- Ministerial Group on the Millennium Dome (MISC10)
- Ministerial Group on Wembley Stadium (MISC12)
- Ministerial Group on Animal Rights Activists (MISC13)
- Ministerial Group on the Manchester Commonwealth Games (MISC15)
- Ministerial Committee on E-Democracy (MISC17)
- Ministerial Committee on Universal Banking Service (MISC19)
- Ministerial Committee on Social and Economic Aspects of Migration (MISC20)
- Ministerial Committee on the Government's Response to Parliamentary Modernisation (MISC21)

Civil contingencies
- Ministerial Committee on Civil Contingencies (CCC)
- Central Secretariat
- Ministerial Committee on Constitutional Reform Policy (CRP)
- Ministerial Sub-Committee on Incorporation of the European Convention on Human Rights (CRP(EC))
- Ministerial Sub-Committee on Freedom of Information (CRP(FOI))
- Ministerial Sub-Committee on House of Lords Reform (CRP(HL))
- Ministerial Consultative Committee with the Liberal Democratic Party (JCC))

Overseas and defence
- Ministerial Committee on Defence and Overseas Policy (DOP)
- Ministerial Committee on Northern Ireland (IN)
- Ministerial Committee on Intelligence Services (CSI)
- Ministerial Group on the Restructuring of the European Aerospace and Defence Industry (MISC5)
- Ministerial Sub-Committee on Conflict Prevention in Sub-Saharan Africa (DOP(A))
- Ministerial Sub-Committee on Conflict Prevention outside Sub-Saharan Africa (DOP(OA))

- Ministerial Sub-Committee on International Terrorism (DOP(IT))
- Ministerial Sub-Committee on Protective and Preventive Security (DOP(IT)(T))

European
(Note: European issues also covered by DOP)

- Ministerial Sub-Committee on European Issues (EP)
- World Summit on Sustainable Development (MISC18)

Of the individual committees the most significant are those dealing with: defence and overseas policy; economic affairs; home and social affairs; public expenditure; the environment; legislation; local government; the intelligence services; Northern Ireland; constitutional reform policy; devolution; and the Queen's speech and future legislation.

Four committees that existed under the previous Conservative administration have been abolished: nuclear defence policy; competitiveness; co-ordination and presentation of government policy; and the ministerial sub-committee on terrorism. Amongst the new committees are those dealing with devolution, chaired by the Lord Chancellor; constitutional reform, chaired by the Prime Minister; and a sub-committee on the incorporation of the European Convention on Human Rights into domestic law, chaired by the Lord Chancellor. It is also noteworthy that the constitutional reform committee has, amongst its membership, the leader of the Liberal Democrat Party and five other members of that party. The only precedents for such joint committees are those dealing with a disarmament conference in 1931, and defence research between 1935 and 1937. Liberal Democrat members of the committee are bound by laws and conventions relating secrecy, but are not invited to attend full Cabinet meetings, and are still be free to oppose the government in the House of Commons.

Many of the key committees, such as those dealing with defence and overseas policy, intelligence services, and constitutional reform, are chaired by the Prime Minister. Others are chaired by the appropriate Cabinet minister, for example the Public Services and Public Expenditure Committee is chaired by the Chancellor of the Exchequer; the sub-committee on European issues is chaired by the Foreign Secretary.

The number of committees chaired by a Cabinet minister, and the number of Cabinet committees on which a minister sits, are usually taken as indications of how influential a minister is in terms of developing and directing government policy. Cabinet committees derive their authority from the Cabinet itself and their decisions have the same status as formal Cabinet decisions. The Cabinet and its committees are supported by the Cabinet Secretariat, a non-departmental body.

In addition, there is also the Prime Minister's policy unit, based at Downing Street, which is independent of the Cabinet Office.

Conventions relating to Cabinet government

The main conventions of Cabinet government are:

1. the Queen must act on the advice of her ministers;
2. the Cabinet must always tender unanimous advice;
3. the Cabinet must obtain and maintain a majority in the House of Commons on all major matters of policy;
4. the Cabinet must produce a Queen's Speech at the opening of each session, stating the legislation which it proposes during that session;
5. the mandate doctrine requires the government's statement in the Queen's Speech to be consistent with the policy on which they were elected. Latitude is allowable only in respect of issues that are unforeseeable, such as foreign affairs. Here the government must offer policies consistent with its general political philosophy.

The Privy Council

The Privy Council comprises approximately 400 members appointed for life by the Sovereign acting on the advice of her ministers. By convention all Cabinet ministers must be sworn as members of the Privy Council. Holders of certain high offices, such as the Archbishops of Canterbury and York, the Speaker of the House of Commons, the Lords of Appeal in Ordinary, the Lords Justices of Appeal, the Master of the Rolls, the Lord Chief Justice, the President of the Family Division, senior non-Cabinet ministers, distinguished politicians and eminent judges from the Commonwealth, and others who have rendered high public or political service, may also be appointed. Members must be British subjects or citizens of the Republic of Ireland. Appointment is for life. All members of the Privy Council are entitled to the prefix 'the Right Honourable'.

On appointment new Privy Councillors must swear on oath not to disclose anything said or done in Council. It was thought that this oath preserved Cabinet secrecy, but following the decision in the 'Crossman Diaries' case – *Attorney-General v Jonathan Cape Ltd* [1976] QB 752 – this is now doubtful. Privy Council members can resign if their conduct necessitates this, or in extreme cases it can be revoked. In 1921 Sir Edgar Speyer was stripped of his membership of the Privy Council on the ground that he had collaborated with the Germans. John Profumo resigned in 1963, as did John Stonehouse some years later. In June 1997 the former Conservative minister Jonathon Aitken resigned from the Privy Council following the discontinuance of his libel action against *The Guardian* newspaper. The newspaper had alleged that he had accepted financial favours in secret weapons deals with the Saudi Arabian government. Aitken was subsequently charged with having perjured himself during the course of the libel action.

Business for the Privy Council and its committees is prepared by the Privy Council Office for which the Lord President of the Council is responsible. The Clerk of the Privy Council in Ordinary is the permanent head of this office and both he and the deputy head are appointed by the Sovereign on the Lord President's recommendation. The Lord President of the Council is responsible for summoning Privy Council members and drafting the agenda. For a quorum at least three members must be present. Usually four are summoned and they will be the ministers most concerned with the business to be transacted. All formal acts of the Council are expressed either as Orders in Council which are authenticated by the signature of the Clerk of the Council, or as proclamations which are signed by the Queen personally. It is customary to make the more important executive orders by way of Order in Council, as it is felt that this gives to them an added dignity. Although the Orders issued by the Council are still expressed as being made by the Queen with the advice of her Privy Council, the Council has in fact lost its advisory role and merely records formal assent to the documents already deliberated and decided upon by Cabinet, committee of the Council or the various ministers and government departments.

Several standing committees of the Privy Council exist. These include the Political Honours Scrutiny Committee which advises on the suitability of persons to receive titles and honours at CBE level and above; the Baronetage Committee which reports on claims to baronetcies; the Universities Committee which advises on the Statute of the Universities of Oxford and Cambridge; and committees on the Isle of Man and the Channel Islands which report on Bills passed by the island legislatures. Ad hoc committees of the Privy Council may also be appointed by the Crown at any time to advise upon particular questions. In 1982 for example, members of the Privy Council, under the chairmanship of Lord Franks, were appointed to conduct an inquiry into the apparent failure of the government to respond to intelligence information in such a way as to prevent an invasion of the Falkland Islands occurring.

In 1641 the Act for Abolishing Arbitrary Courts was passed, abolishing the prerogative jurisdiction of the monarch through the Privy Council to hear civil and criminal cases that fell within the jurisdiction of the ordinary courts of equity and common law. The Privy Council was still able to hear appeals from the overseas possessions of the Crown, and as the British Empire expanded throughout the eighteenth century it became usual to provide for appeal from the decisions of the colonial courts to His Majesty's Privy Council. With the growth of the Empire the amount of judicial business coming before the Privy Council from the Colonies increased to the extent that in 1833 it became necessary for the Judicial Committee Act to be passed. This Act 'for the better administration of justice in his Majesty's Privy Council' constituted a committee of the Privy Council to be known as the Judicial Committee. Together with the Judicial Committee Act 1844, this is still the principal United Kingdom enactment regarding the Judicial Committee. The Judicial Committee comprises the Lord President of the Council (who never sits), persons who hold or have held high judicial office in the United Kingdom and are Privy Councillors, and senior members of the judiciary from certain Commonwealth countries that retain the right of appeal to the Privy Council. The quorum of the

Judicial Committee is three, but usually five members sit to hear an appeal. The Judicial Committee hears appeals from the Superior Courts of the Isle of Man, the Channel Islands, Colonies, associated States, and such independent Commonwealth countries as have retained the right of appeal from their own courts. Appeals may lie as of right, with leave of the court below, or by special leave of the Judicial Committee. The Committee will only give special leave to appeal in a criminal case if there has been such disregard of the forms of legal process or the principles of natural justice as to involve a substantial and grave injustice to the accused. Special leave will only be granted in civil cases where important points of law, matters of public importance, or substantial property are in issue. The Judicial Committee does not deliver a judgment. Its decision is still delivered in the form of an advice and the government issues an Order in Council to give effect to that advice. The Judicial Committee (Dissenting Opinions) Order 1966 now permits dissenting opinions to be delivered. The Committee is not strictly bound by its own decisions. The Judicial Committee of the Privy Council also exercises a number of functions within the United Kingdom legal system:

1. it hears appeals from various professional disciplinary bodies including the General Medical Council and other professions ancillary to medicine and also some appeals from the ecclesiastical courts;
2. under s4 of the Judicial Committee Act 1833 the Crown may refer any matter to the Judicial Committee for an advisory opinion;
3. under s7 of the House of Commons Disqualification Act 1975 any member of the public may apply to the Judicial Committee for a declaration that a member of the House of Commons is disqualified under the Act.

7.3 Ministerial responsibility

Democracy requires that those who govern should be responsible to those whom they govern. Responsibility carries with it notions of openness, honesty and accountability. Given the nature of the constitutional arrangements that pertain in the United Kingdom, not least the absence of any statutory code regulating the behaviour of ministers and their relationship with Parliament, enormous importance attaches to the convention of responsible government. The convention of ministerial responsibility has two aspects: (i) the individual responsibility of ministers to Parliament for decisions taken in their departments, whether by themselves or by their civil servants; and (ii) the collective responsibility of the government to Parliament and in particular to the House of Commons.

To some extent these convention have been supplemented by codes of practice such as *Questions of Procedure for Ministers*, a revised version of which was promulgated by Tony Blair in August 1997, shortly after becoming Prime Minister. The latest version reflects issues raised in the Nolan Report and also the Scott *good example*

Report on the 'Arms to Iraq' affair. Ministers are expected to comply with both the letter and the spirit of the Code.

The Code expressly states that ministers must 'give accurate and truthful information to Parliament, correcting any inadvertent error at the earliest opportunity', and makes clear that 'ministers who knowingly mislead Parliament will be expected to offer their resignation to the Prime Minister.'

The Code also provides that ministers should:

1. uphold the political impartiality of the Civil Service, and not to ask civil servants to act in any way which would conflict with the Civil Service Code – in particular ministers should not ask civil servants to attend part conferences or policy groups of any parliamentary party;
2. give fair consideration and due weight to informed and impartial advice from civil servants, as well as to other considerations and advice, in reaching decisions;
3. comply with the law, including international law and treaty obligations, and to uphold the administration of justice;
4. make efficient use of official cars and other publicly funded travel arrangements – air miles and other benefits earnt whilst travelling on government business should be forgone or used against official travel;
5. be scrupulous in avoiding any apparent conflict of interest between their private affairs (or those of a spouse) and their public duties, particularly in relating to financial matters;
6. report all gifts to the Permanent Secretary – those exceeding £140 in value should not be accepted.

Ministers should not:

1. use public resources for party political purposes – in particular ministers should not use government property in connection with constituency work;
2. accept payment (other than donations to an agreed charity) for public speeches of an official nature;
3. take any active part in the affairs of any union of which he might be a member;

The revised Code also reinforces the Prime Minister's control over his Cabinet colleagues by providing that the assignment of duties to junior ministers outside the Cabinet will have to have prime ministerial approval, as will the appointment of special advisers to Cabinet ministers. The importance of ensuring a co-ordinated presentation of government policy is also underlined by the requirement that all major interviews and media events, and the content of key policy speeches and press releases, should be agreed first with the Prime Minister's office.

The Nolan Committee's First Report on *Standards in Public Life* dealt in particular with the growing criticism directed at ministers taking up lucrative posts in industry immediately following resignation from ministerial office. As a result ministers are now subject to restrictions similar to those imposed on senior civil servants who resign to take up private sector employment. The Code provides that ministers wishing to take up paid employment within to years of leaving office should seek guidance from the Advisory Committee on Business Appointments. It is perhaps significant that the matter could not be left to the common sense of the ministers concerned.

The Committee on Standards on Public Life, under the chairmanship of Lord Neill, made further recommendations in its report published in January 2000, prompted in part by concerns raised by the style of government being developed under the Blair administration. The report suggested a limit on the number of special advisers appointed to assist ministers, and that the activities of these advisers should be brought within a code of conduct with legal status. Of particular concern was the emergence of a politicised civil service whose members saw political loyalty as their first concern.

Individual responsibility: for the operation of the department

In theory, ministers are responsible to Parliament for their own actions, omissions and mistakes as well as for those of the officials in their departments. In its classical form, the convention is that criticism should be directed at the minister rather than at any civil servant who may be at fault, and that in cases where there has been serious mismanagement of a department's affairs, it is the minister who resigns. This convention reflects the theory that individual civil servants are meant to remain anonymous, so as to promote the objectivity and efficiency, of the Civil Service.

Two questions arise from the minister's departmental responsibility. First, is the minister obliged to accept responsibility for every occurrence of maladministration within his department? Second, if maladministration is found to have occurred, is the minister under a duty to resign?

Scope of ministerial responsibility

The case that is regularly (and probably inaccurately, see below) cited as the classic illustration of ministerial responsibility for the workings of the department which the minister heads is that referred to as the *Crichel Down* affair. Crichel Down, an area of farmland in Dorset, had been compulsorily acquired by the Air Ministry in 1939. After the war the land was transferred to the Ministry of Agriculture. The previous owner asked to re-purchase it, but was refused. The refusal was accompanied by misleading replies and assurances from the Ministry of Agriculture and was largely based upon an inaccurate report prepared by a civil servant. Members of Parliament raised the case with the Minister of Agriculture and an inquiry found that there had been muddle, inefficiency, bias and bad faith on the part of certain officials. The report of the inquiry led to the resignation of the Minister of Agriculture, Sir Thomas Dugdale. In the debate, the Home Secretary, Sir David Maxwell-Fyfe, stated his view that:

1. a minister must protect a civil servant who has carried out his explicit orders;
2. a minister must defend a civil servant who acts properly in accordance with policy;
3. where an official makes a mistake or causes some delay, but not on an important issue of policy and not where a claim to individual rights is seriously involved, the minister should acknowledges the mistake and accept responsibility although he is not personally involved, and should state that he will take corrective action in the department;
4. where action has been taken by a civil servant of which the minister disapproves and has no previous knowledge, and the conduct of the official is reprehensible, there is no obligation on a minister to endorse what he believes to be wrong or to defend what are clearly shown to be errors of his officers. He remains, however, constitutionally responsible to Parliament for the fact that something has gone wrong, but this does not affect his power to control and discipline his staff.

In instances falling within (1) and (2) the traditional view is that the minister is personally responsible and must account for what has happened to Parliament, and can expect to have to resign if the consequences are serious. In instances falling within (3) and (4) it has been contended that the minister bears a 'constitutional responsibility' to subject himself to scrutiny by the House of Commons and account for what as happened, but that his responsibility is not personal in the sense that the failings would justify calls for the minister's resignation. As Sir Robin Butler (in his capacity as Cabinet Secretary) informed the Scott Inquiry:

> 'While ministerial Heads of Department must always be accountable for the actions of their department and its staff, neither they, nor senior officials, can justly be criticised for shortcomings of which they are not aware, and which they could not reasonably have been expected to discover, or which do not occur as a foreseeable result of their own actions … I am using "accountability" to mean that the minister must always answer questions and give an account to Parliament for the action of his department whether he is "responsible" in the sense of attracting personal criticism himself, or not. So I am using "accountability" to leave out, as it were, the blame element of it.'

On this basis Sir Robin was of the view that Lord Carrington ought not to have resigned over the invasion of the Falkland Islands by the Argentinians (see below) as he was not personally at fault.

A further political development that has had profound consequences regarding the scope of ministerial responsibility is transfer of departmental functions to the Next Steps agencies. Increasingly ministers are willing to draw a distinction between their policies and the execution of those policies by agency staff. A good example is provided by the Prison Service, which was set up as an executive agency to run prisons in the late 1980s. Following a number of high profile prison escapes, including escapes from Parkhurst, there were calls for the then Home Secretary, Michael Howard, to resign. He, however, argued that the running of prisons was now chiefly the responsibility of the Prison Service, and duly sacked its chief executive Derek Lewis, pointing out that the escapes in question were not the direct result of any Home Office policy for which the Home Secretary was responsible.

Sanctions for departmental failings

The political realities of the last 40 years indicate that there is little evidence to support the contention that it is a convention that a minister should resign in the event that there are serious failures within the department that he or she heads. Exactly why a minister resigns is always open to interpretation, but four categories of resignation can be identified. First, because of a failure by a minister to discharge his duties properly. By their very nature such resignations are rare, requiring as they do a public recognition by the minister that he has not acted properly; examples include the resignation of Hugh Dalton following his leaking of Budget details in 1945, the resignation of Nichlolas Ridley over offensive comments about the Germans (1990), arguably the resignation of Edwina Currie after her comments that most of the chickens sold in the United Kingdom were infected with salmonella, and the resignation of Estelle Morris as Education Secretary because, as she disarmingly put it, she was 'not up to the job'. Interestingly, when details of the 1996 Budget were leaked to the *Daily Mirror*, there was no suggestion that the Chancellor should resign, only a call for an inquiry into how it had happened – again an example of the minister's constitutional responsibility, rather than his ministerial responsibility. Second, where the senior civil servants in a department have not acted properly, perhaps by being negligent, dilatory, or incompetent. Examples falling within this category might include the resignations of Lord Carrington and Humphrey Atkins over the Falklands invasion (1982), the resignation of Leon Brittan over Westland (1986), and the *Crichel Down* affair itself. Third, ministers resign over policy differences. Fourth, because of indiscretions in their personal lives. These last two categories, however, are much more closely related to collective responsibility, than they are to the question of the minister's accountability to Parliament, as to which see below.

On the basis of the above, it is difficult to sustain the convention that ministerial responsibility is enforced by the prospect of resignation. Once that is accepted, the search begins for the alternative sanction. Perhaps we are moving towards a situation where it is the civil servant who becomes more accountable: see the consideration of select committee powers at Chapter 6, section 6.6. Certainly the sacking of the head of the Prison Service by the Home Secretary, following the Parkhurst escapes, suggests that the idea that Parliament can force a minister to resign is a somewhat outdated notion.

Ministerial responsibility and the Ombudsman

Reflecting in part concerns arising from the *Crichel Down* affair, Parliament enacted the Parliamentary Commissioner Act 1967 (as amended), creating the role of the

Parliamentary Commissioner for Administration (PCA) or Ombudsman to whom individual citizens could complain if they were dissatisfied about the service provided by government departments. Normally a complaint must be made by the 'person aggrieved' unless he is unable to act for himself. All complaints must be submitted via a Member of Parliament, providing for the so-called 'MP filter'. This is supposed to serve two functions: first, to the provide MP with an opportunity to deal with the complaint if he sees fit; and, second, to ensure that clearly inappropriate or unmeritorious complaints can be rejected before reaching the PCA, thus reducing his workload. In reality MPs are reluctant to reject complaints in this manner for fear of appearing unhelpful to their constituents.

Complaints must be of injustice sustained in consequence of maladministration, a term not defined in the 1967 Act, but one memorably illustrated by the late Richard Crossman in his so-called 'catalogue' as involving rudeness, ineptitude, delay, wrong advice and loss of documents. In 1994 William Reid, a serving PCA, attempted his own definition which encompassed: neglecting to inform a complainant on request of his or her rights or entitlement; ignoring valid advice or disregarding relevant considerations; failing to offer redress; failure by management to monitor compliance with adequate procedures; cavalier disregard of guidance which was intended to be followed in the interests of equitable treatment of those who use a service; and failure to mitigate the effects of rigid adherence to the letter of the law where that produces manifestly inequitable treatment.

The PCA works by investigating the complaint from within the government department. Under s7 of the 1967 Act the PCA must ensure that the principal officer of the department or authority concerned, and any other person alleged in the complaint to have taken or authorised the action complained of, has an opportunity to comment on any allegations contained in the complaint. Investigations will be conducted in private, but the PCA is at liberty to obtain information from such persons and in such manner, and make such inquiries, as he thinks fit: s7(2). He has powers similar to those of the High Court as regards securing the presence of witnesses and the production of documents. Under s8(1) the PCA may require 'any minister, officer or member of the department or authority concerned or any other person who in his opinion is able to furnish information or produce documents relevant to the investigation to furnish any such information or produce any such document.'

Under s12(3) of the Act the PCA cannot question the merits of a decision taken without maladministration by a government department or other authority in the exercise of a discretion vested in that department or authority. What this effectively means is that the PCA cannot actually question the merits of a decision taken without maladministration. He can still investigate maladministration in administrative processes and the decisions resulting therefrom.

The government departments subject to investigation by the PCA are listed in Sch 2 to the 1967 Act as amended. All the major government departments are listed, and in 1987 the PCA's jurisdiction was extended to quangos, although bodies subject to control by the Council on Tribunals are excluded. As regards those departments subject to his investigation, the PCA is limited by s5(1) to investigating: 'any action taken by or on behalf of a government department or other authority to which this Act applies, being action taken in the exercise of administrative functions of that department or authority.' The effect of this is that he cannot carry out any investigation of complaints relating to the exercise of legislative functions, such as the preparation or creation of delegated legislation, although he could investigate complaints into the way in which a scheme set up by way of delegated legislation was actually being administered.

Section 5(3) of the 1967 Act prohibits the PCA from investigating any of the matters referred to in Sch 3 to the Act, including action taken in matters certified by a secretary of state or other minister of the Crown to affect relations or dealings between the government of the United Kingdom and any other government or any international organisation of states or governments. The following matters are also excluded from his jurisdiction.

1. Action taken in connection with the administration of the government of any country or territory outside the United Kingdom which forms part of Her Majesty's dominions or in which Her Majesty has jurisdiction.
2. Action taken by the Secretary of State under the Extradition Act 1870 or the Fugitive Offenders Act 1881.
3. Action taken by the Secretary of State for the purposes of investigating crime or of protecting the security of the state, including action so taken with respect to passports.
4. The commencement or conduct of civil or criminal proceedings before any court of law in the United Kingdom, of proceedings at any place under the Naval Discipline Act 1957, the Army Act 1955 or the Air Force Act 1955, or of proceedings before any international court or tribunal.
5. Any exercise of the prerogative of mercy or of the power of a Secretary of State to make a reference in respect of any person to the Court of Appeal, the High Court of Justiciary or the Courts-Martial Appeal Court.
6. Action taken on behalf of the Minister of Health or the Secretary of State by a (regional health authority, an area health authority, a district health authority, a special health authority except the Rampton Hospital Review Board, a family practitioner committee, a health board or the Common Services Agency for the Scottish Health Service) or by the Public Health Laboratory Service Board.
7. Action taken by any person appointed by the Lord Chancellor as a member of the administrative staff of any court or tribunal, so far as that action is taken at the discretion, or on the authority of any person acting in a judicial capacity or in his capacity as a member of the tribunal. Similarly, any action taken by any member of the administrative staff of a relevant tribunal.
8. Action taken in matters relating to contractual or other commercial transactions, whether within the United Kingdom or elsewhere, being transactions of a

government department or authority to which the Act applies, not being transactions for or relating to the acquisition of land compulsorily or in circumstances in which it could be acquired compulsorily or the disposal as surplus of land acquired compulsorily.

9. Action taken in respect of appointments or removals, pay, discipline, superannuation or other personnel matters, in relation to service in any of the armed forces of the Crown, including reserve and auxiliary and cadet forces; service in any office or employment under the Crown or under any authority listed in Sch 2 of the 1967 Act; or service in any office or employment, or under any contract for service, in respect of which power to take action, or to determine or approve the action to be taken, in such matters is vested in Her Majesty, or in any minister of the Crown.

10. The grant of honours, awards or privileges within the gift of the Crown, including the grant of Royal Charters.

If the PCA finds that a government department has been at fault he will work towards securing a friendly settlement between the complainant and the department. The PCA cannot have any of his recommendations put into effect by force of law. Ultimately, if the PCA concludes that maladministration has occurred and feels that the attention of Parliament should be drawn specifically to it he can lay a special report on the matter before both Houses of Parliament.

Everything is then left to the doctrine of ministerial responsibility, the assumption being that the minister will be asked questions about the matter, and will have to taken some appropriate action. In reality such reports are not often necessary, because a mutually agreed settlement can be reached.

Amongst the high profile cases dealt with by the PCA since 1967 are the 'Sachsenhausen case', and the investigation into the 'Barlow Clowes' affair. In the former, an Anglo–German Agreement of 1964 provided for £1 million to be paid in compensation to UK citizens who suffered from Nazi persecution during the Second World War. Distribution of this money was left to the discretion of the UK government and in 1964 the Foreign Secretary (then Mr Butler) approved rules for the distribution. Later the Foreign Office withheld compensation from 12 persons who claimed to be within these rules because of their detention within the Sachsenhausen concentration camp. Pressure from many MPs failed to get this decision reversed and a complaint of maladministration was referred to the PCA. By this time the whole of the £1 million had been distributed to other claimants. After extensive investigations the PCA reported that there were defects in the administrative procedures by which the Foreign Office reached its decisions and subsequently defended them, and that this maladministration had damaged the reputation of the claimants. When this report was debated in the Commons, the Foreign Secretary (Mr George Brown) assumed personal responsibility for the decisions of the Foreign Office, which he maintained were correct. He nonetheless made available an additional £25,000 in order that the claimants might receive the same rate of compensation as successful claimants on the fund.

Similarly the Barlow Clowes investigation into the granting of credit licences by the Department of Trade and Industry lead, eventually, to the payment of compensation (over £150 million) to those who had lost their investments because of the company's fraudulent activities.

The PCA's report on the failure of the Home Office to review the convictions of over 1,500 prisoners who had been sentenced to imprisonment on the strength of the discredited evidence of Home Office forensic scientist Dr Alan Clift, included severe criticism of that department for not acting more quickly in the light of what he described as an 'unprecedented pollution of justice'.

The 1994 report included details of compensation awarded to poultry farmers following a finding of maladministration on the part of the Ministry of Agriculture and criticisms of the planning blight caused by the handling of the Channel tunnel rail link project. The operation of certain aspects of the work of the Child Support Agency has come in for strong criticism in both the 1994 and 1995 reports, the PCA highlighting maladministration in the form of the wrongful release of confidential information to potentially violent estranged husbands, the wrongful labelling of fathers as potentially violent, the failure to spot palpably false paternity claims, and misdirecting correspondence.

Even though many of the complaints investigated have resulted in only modest levels of compensation being paid, they are nevertheless important in providing the individual concerned with an assurance that his concerns are taken seriously, and can result in improvements in the way that the executive conducts its business. For example, customs officials had advised that a car could be temporarily imported into the United Kingdom without payment of purchase tax but, on arrival, the owner was made to pay the £167 purchase tax which was, in reality, due. The PCA persuaded the department, which had refused any concession, to refund the full amount. In another case a complainant, who had been encouraged by the Board of Trade to suppose that his company would be eligible for an investment grant if it installed a grain-processing plant, found that the plant was ruled ineligible after it had been installed and the expenditure incurred. The PCA persuaded the Board to pay compensation of £950. The 1995 report revealed that the Child Support Agency had been persuaded to make an ex gratia payment of £250 to a man who had been sent a child maintenance form in error.

The courts and ministerial responsibility

While the courts cannot enforce the convention of ministerial responsibility they do, from time to time, cite it as a reason for not intervening to quash a minister's decision. In particular the courts will recognise the fact that ministers will frequently have to delegate their decision-making functions. Whilst, strictly, this would be a breach of the rule against sub-delegation, the courts accept that, in theory, the minister is answerable to Parliament for the actions carried out on his behalf and with his authority by senior civil servants. In *Carltona Ltd* v *Commissioners of Works* [1943] 2 All ER 560 the appellant's food factory was requisitioned by the Commissioners. The appellants sought a declaration that the notice was invalid because of unlawful delegation of the minister's functions to a senior civil servant. Rejecting the contention that there had been an unlawful delegation of functions by the minister, Lord Greene MR observed that:

> 'It cannot be supposed that this regulation meant that, in each case, the minister in person should direct his mind to the matter. The duties imposed upon ministers and the powers given to ministers are normally exercised under the authority of the ministers by responsible officials of the department. Public business could not be carried on if that were not the case. Constitutionally, the decision of such an official is, of course, the decision of the minister. The minister is responsible. It is he who must answer before Parliament for anything that his officials have done under his authority, and, if for an important matter he selected an official of such junior standing that he could not be expected competently to perform the work, the minister would have to answer for that in Parliament. The whole system of departmental organisation and administration is based on the view that ministers, being responsible to Parliament, will see that important duties are committed to experienced officials. If they do not do that, Parliament is the place where complaint must be made against them.'

The question of what factors the court should consider when assessing the legality of the delegation of ministerial functions, in the absence of any express statutory restriction, was reviewed by the House of Lords in *R* v *Secretary of State for the Home Department, ex parte Oladehinde* [1990] 3 WLR 797, a case concerned with the delegation of powers to deport. The House of Lords held that in the absence of any statutory restrictions, the factors to which the court would have regard were the seniority of the officers to whom the power had been delegated, the possibility of any conflict with their other statutory duties, and whether they had fully considered the applicant's cases. The courts have also upheld the delegation of tasks such as the reviewing of release dates for prisoners serving life sentences. The House of Lords in *R* v *Secretary of State for the Home Department, ex parte Doody & Others* [1993] 3 All ER 92, expressly approved the comments of Staughton LJ in the court below to the effect that the Home Secretary had to deal, on average, with 130 mandatory life sentence cases each year, and that:

> 'Parliament must be well aware of the great burden that is placed on senior ministers who not only take charge of their departments but also speak for them in Parliament, attend meetings of the Cabinet and its committees, and see to their constituency affairs. ... I can see nothing irrational in the Secretary of State devolving [the consideration of minimum periods to be served by convicted murderers] upon junior ministers. They too are appointed by the Crown to hold office in the department, they have the same advice and assistance from departmental officials as the Secretary of State would have, and they too are answerable to Parliament.'

It is submitted that the judicial attitude to ministerial responsibility evidence above is more the product of constitutional expediency, rather than a reflection of any genuine belief that such conventions are any longer really effective.

The Scott Report

Following the collapse of the Matrix Churchill trial in 1992, which concerned alleged breaches of export control orders by companies supplying arms to Iraq, a committee of enquiry, chaired by Sir Richard Scott, was instituted to investigate the constitutional implications of the issues that arose during the trial. Of key significance here is the evidence to suggest that the guidelines on arms exports had been relaxed, so as to permit the export of militarily useful equipment to countries such as Iraq; that this information had been withheld from Parliament; and that the government had appeared to be willing to rely on public interest immunity certificates being granted to suppress the evidence concerning the changes to the guidelines with the possibility that innocent persons might have been convicted of breaching them.

After three years of receiving evidence from all those involved, many of them senior Cabinet figures, the Report (*Inquiry into the Export of Defence Equipment and Dual-Use Goods to Iraq and Related Prosecutions*, 1995–96, HC 115) was published as a House of Commons Paper in February 1996. What the Report revealed was that the doctrine of ministerial responsibility had not operated effectively to ensure that the House of Commons was kept aware of changes in government policy regarding arms sales. Further, the usual mechanisms for enforcing ministerial responsibility, such as parliamentary questions and hearings of select committees, had not adduced accurate answers, with the result that members of the House were misled. It was clear that Sir Richard felt that information had been withheld on grounds of political expediency, rather than to protect the public interest. Many of the ministers involved claimed that if they had misled Parliament they had done so unwittingly, suggesting that their departmental advisers were to blame. Significantly, no ministers resigned following the publication of the Report, something that Sir Richard appeared to presage in his Report where he observed (para K7.16):

> 'If ministers are to be excused blame and personal criticism on the basis of the absence of personal knowledge or involvement, the corollary ought to be an acceptance of the obligation to be forthcoming with information about the incident in question. Otherwise Parliament (and the public) will not be in a position to judge whether the absence of personal knowledge and involvement is fairly claimed or to judge on whom responsibility for what has occurred ought to be placed.'

Following a debate on the Report (which the government won by a majority of one on a technical motion), the Public Service Committee of the House of Commons launched an inquiry into ministerial responsibility. In its report, published in July 1996, it concluded that ministerial responsibility in the modern constitution was less based on a convention of resignation in the wake of departmental failings, and more on keeping Parliament fully and accurately informed, of responding to questions asked in Parliament, whether as parliamentary questions or in front of select committees, and resigning if found to have knowingly misled the House, ie where it was the minister's decision to lie. The Committee also recommended that the House of Commons pass a resolution that ministers and civil servants were under a duty not to obstruct the House in its work and should co-operate with Parliament as much as possible.

Collective responsibility

The convention of collective responsibility is traditionally evidenced by two separate conventions. First, by the convention that the government must resign if it loses the support of the House of Commons. The Prime Minister and his ministers are, in theory, collectively responsible to Parliament for the conduct of national affairs. If the Prime Minister loses the support of an overall majority of MPs in the House of Commons he will be expected to resign (if the lack of support is for reasons associated personally with the Prime Minister) or, as is more usually the case, seek a dissolution of Parliament. The rule does not mean that the government must resign whenever it is defeated; there has to be a clear-cut defeat on a matter of policy. The government may choose to treat an issue as a matter of confidence indicating that it will resign if defeated. The opposition can move a motion of no confidence that, if carried, would mean the resignation of the government. In legal terms there is nothing to stop a government that has been defeated on a motion of no confidence (eg because of the absence of a number of supporters) from ignoring the result and tabling another motion in support of the government when able to muster its full support. In terms of conventional behaviour it would be without precedent, however, and politically would be confirmation of the insecurity of the government position. The resignation convention is not always regarded as part of collective responsibility, but as a separate convention. This is because collective responsibility is seen as the day-to-day answerability of the government for policy, rather than its obligation to resign when it loses the confidence of the House. It seems more natural, however, to treat resignation for lack of the confidence of the House as the ultimate threat that gives answerability its substance.

Second, collective responsibility is evidenced by the convention that the government must speak with one voice. All members of the government share in the collective responsibility of the government, and ministers may not publicly criticise or dissociate themselves from government policy. The essence of collective responsibility is that the Cabinet should be seen to be in agreement. Any policy decision reached by the Cabinet has to be supported thereafter by all members of the Cabinet whether they approve of it or not, unless they feel compelled to resign.

The constitutional justification for the rule is that the answerability of the government to Parliament would be much impaired if individual ministers were able to say that they personally did not agree with decisions taken in Cabinet. Ministers, including non-Cabinet members, are normally bound therefore not to differ publicly from Cabinet decisions nor to speak or vote against the government in Parliament. The convention is closely related to that of Cabinet secrecy. As all ministers must support government policy, it is desirable that the process by which such policy decisions are made be kept secret. Unless the Prime Minister decides otherwise therefore, secrecy attaches to discussions in Cabinet, Cabinet papers and the proceedings of Cabinet committees. The rule increases party discipline and unity within the government, strengthens the government in Parliament and reinforces the secrecy of decision-making within the Cabinet thereby minimising public disagreement between both ministers and departments of state. It also serves to strengthen the authority of the Prime Minister in relation to his colleagues. As Lord Widgery CJ observed in *Attorney-General* v *Jonathan Cape Ltd* [1976] QB 752:

> 'I find overwhelming evidence that the doctrine of joint responsibility is generally understood and practised and equally strong evidence that it is on occasion ignored. The general effect of the evidence is that the doctrine is an established feature of the English form of government, and regarded as confidential. ... I have been told that a resigning minister who wishes to make a personal statement in the House, and to disclose matters which are confidential under the doctrine obtains the consent of the Queen for this purpose. ... I cannot accept the suggestion that a minister owes no duty of confidence in respect of his own views expressed in Cabinet. It would only need one or two ministers to describe their own views to enable experienced observers to identify the views of the others. ...The Cabinet is at the very centre of national affairs, and must be in possession at all times of information which is secret or confidential. Secrets relating to national security may require to be preserved indefinitely. Secrets relating to new taxation proposals may be of the highest importance until Budget day, but public knowledge thereafter. To leak a Cabinet decision a day or so before it is officially announced is an accepted exercise in public relations, but to identify the ministers who voted one way or another is objectionable because it undermines the doctrine of joint responsibility.'

Agreements to differ

Occasionally it may be politically impossible for the Cabinet to maintain a collective front. In 1932 the Liberal members of the National government only agreed to remain on condition that they were allowed to speak and vote against it on the question of the imposition of tariffs. The opposition attacked the government for abandoning the convention of Cabinet responsibility but the government defended itself on the ground that the National government was a constitutional phenomenon to which new considerations applied. This episode became known as the 'agreement to differ'.

In 1975, the Labour Cabinet agreed to differ on the question of the United Kingdom's continued membership of the EEC. A referendum was to be held and the Cabinet, by a majority of 16 to 7, decided to recommend continued membership of the EEC to the electorate. But it was agreed that ministers who opposed the government's policy should be free to speak and campaign against it outside Parliament.

Collective responsibility and ministerial responsibility

As noted above, it would be wrong to suggest that ministers resign simply because the departments for which they are responsible have been guilty of serious errors. Much depends upon the political support for the minister in question. If questioned about the failings of a fellow Cabinet member, a minister cannot express the view that his colleague should resign and still uphold collective responsibility by presenting a united Cabinet front, hence he will defend his colleague. If, however, the erring minister's position becomes indefensible, he will be ousted by his colleagues who are unwilling to be publicly embarrassed in the media by their increasingly unconvincing attempts to defend him. Once the support of Cabinet colleagues is withdrawn a minister's position becomes politically untenable. Private papers published after the death of Sir Thomas Dugdale indicate that it was the lack of backbench support that lead to his resignation over the *Crichel Down* affair, not simply a high regard for the niceties of constitutional convention.

Collective responsibility and individual responsibility for the personal conduct

Since 1979 the most common reason for ministerial resignation has been personal indiscretion. This trend may, in part, have been attributable to a more aggressive and intrusive stance being adopted by the tabloid press, but must also be linked to the Major government's decision to endorse a 'Back to Basics' policy on personal morality, thus inciting the press to unearth evidence that would show his ministers to be behaving hypocritically. In September 1992 David Mellor resigned as Heritage Secretary after disclosure of an extra-marital affair. Tim Yeo, an Environment Minister (1994), Hartley Booth, a parliamentary private secretary (1994), and Robert Hughes, Citizens' Charter Minister (1995), all resigned for similar reasons. In all 15 Conservative ministers and parliamentary private secretaries resigned for reasons related to personal misconduct between September 1992 and April 1995.

As with ministerial departmental responsibility, the key question is the extent to which the minister can retain the respect, confidence and support of his Cabinet colleagues and backbenchers. The greater the embarrassment caused, the more likely the individual is to resign – witness the resignation of Welsh Secretary Ron Davies over the 'Clapham Common' affair in November 1998, and the resignation of Peter Mandleson over the Hinduja passport affair in January 2001.

7.4 Ministers' powers: delegated legislation

Ministers will have vested in them many statutory powers. The usual framework is for the government of the day to adopt a particular policy, for example the granting of licences for radio broadcasts, legislation is enacted giving effect to the broad thrust of the policy, and the power to give effect to the policy will be vested in the relevant minister as appropriate. The power may, for example, be a power to grant licences. In the exercise of this power the minister will be subject to control by the courts, by means of the procedure known as the application for judicial review (see further Chapter 8) and will be answerable to Parliament through the doctrine of ministerial responsibility outlined above.

Occasionally, however, Parliament may pass an Act that actually gives a minister the power to legislate himself. Continuing with the above example, an Act providing for the licensing of radio broadcasting may provide that the minister can draw up regulations to govern the types of licence to be granted, and the procedure to be adopted in making applications. In what appears to be a contravention of the doctrine of the separation of powers, therefore, ministers frequently acquire the power to legislate by means of what is known as delegated legislation. The most common format for delegated legislation is the statutory instrument, but the term is wide enough to encompass ministerial orders, departmental circulars, guidelines and codes of conduct (although they might not all have legal effect).

Ideally all legislation should be passed by Parliament as primary legislation, subject to full debate and scrutiny. The reality in a modern government is that this is not a realistic proposition. As indicated above, primary legislation will often be generalised in nature, leaving the fine detail to be determined by the responsible minister. This has advantages in that it allows flexibility, measures can be introduced quickly where this is seen as desirable, and the minister concerned can introduce new measures to deal with unforeseen situations. Clearly this is more efficient than having to introduce a new piece of primary legislation to deal with each emergent problem in a given area.

Most important measures introduced by ministers by way of delegated legislation will take the form of statutory instruments: see s1(1) Statutory Instruments Act 1946. A statutory instrument can be regarded as having been made as soon as it drafted and signed by the appropriate minister and can become effective from that point onwards. Alternatively a statutory instrument is 'made' when signed but only comes into effect on a certain date, specified on the order itself. The most common situation is where the statutory instrument is signed by the minister and is due to come into effect on some specified date in the future, after one of the various 'laying procedures' has been complied with.

Parliamentary scrutiny

It is possible for an enabling Act to require ministerial orders to be enacted by way of statutory instrument, but not require any laying procedure at all. This is not uncommon, but obviously raises questions about opportunity of scrutiny in Parliament. Such a possibility should be raised when the enabling Act is progressing through Parliament. Where laying procedures are required there are three possible courses of action. First the enabling Act (ie the Act giving the minister the power to make the delegated legislation) might specify only a bare laying procedure – all that is required is that the measure is laid before Parliament. Second, the measure might be subject to the negative resolution procedure, where it is laid before Parliament for a specified time and becomes law if there is no vote against it during the laying period. Finally, there is the positive laying procedure whereby the measure is laid before Parliament and cannot become law unless there is a positive vote in favour of its coming into effect. Note that under the Human Rights Act 1998 ministers are given the discretion to introduce measures by way of statutory instrument or Order in Council in order to remedy defects in either primary or subordinate legislation so as to ensure compliance with the Convention rights protected by the 1998 Act.

The sheer volume of measures laid before Parliament makes it impossible for any one MP to check them all. The positive resolution procedure clearly provides a much better safeguard against abuse of power than the negative resolution procedure, but does not appear to be employed so frequently. Under the negative resolution procedure, parliamentary time may not be available for the prayers necessary to bring about the annulment of the instrument.

Since 1973 it has been the function of the Joint Committee on Delegated Legislation to scrutinise all statutory instruments, draft instruments, schemes requiring approval by way of statutory instrument, and so on. There are particular matters regarding which the attention of the House of Commons will be drawn by the Committee, as follows:

1. Where an instrument imposes a charge on public revenues or contains provisions requiring payments to be made to any public authority in consideration of any licence, or any consent, or of any services rendered.
2. Where an instrument purports to exclude the jurisdiction of the courts.
3. Where an instrument purports to have retrospective effect.
4. Where there appears to have been an unjustifiable delay in laying or publicising the instrument.
5. Where there is doubt as to whether the instrument is intra vires its enabling Act.
6. Where the terms of the instrument require elucidation.
7. Where for any other reason the drafting of the instrument appears to be defective.

It is important to bear in mind that the Committee is concerned neither with the merits of any given instrument, nor the soundness of the policy that it seeks to implement. If the Committee does report to the House of Commons on a statutory instrument for any of the reasons outlined above, reliance is placed on the principle of ministerial responsibility to actually achieve some explanation of justification for, or amendment of, the instrument.

Where there is agreement between the parliamentary parties, a minister may move that a statutory instrument be referred to one of the Standing (Merits) Committees on Statutory Instruments. The procedure can be adopted provided the instrument is one in relation to which the affirmative resolution procedure applies, or a member has given notice of a motion that it be annulled. Although the committee is able to debate the merits of an instrument, it cannot vote on the matter. The intention is that the House of Commons will take note of the points made in committee, although when the instrument returns to the House there will be no debate on it, simply a vote.

Scrutiny by the courts

Whilst the doctrine of parliamentary sovereignty restrains the courts from declaring primary legislation to be invalid, no such problems arises in respect of delegated legislation. The courts will simply look to the relevant enabling Act to see if the minister has exceeded his powers in creating the delegated legislation, either by not following the correct procedure, or by creating delegated legislation which, in terms of its contents and effect, exceeds the limits of the powers delegated to him by Parliament.

For example, in *R* v *Secretary of State for Social Security, ex parte Joint Council for the Welfare of Immigrants* [1996] 4 All ER 385 the courts refused to accept that a minister had been empowered by Parliament to create regulations relating to social security that would adversely affect certain basic human rights. The effect of the regulations was to remove from asylum seekers any entitlement to income benefit where: asylum was sought otherwise than on arrival in the United Kingdom; or an asylum seeker had been refused leave to remain and was awaiting the outcome of an appeal against that decision. Confirming that the 1996 regulations were ultra vires the Social Security (Contributions and Benefits) Act 1992, Simon Brown LJ adverted to the fact that Parliament, in enacting the Asylum and Immigration Appeals Act 1993, had given asylum seekers certain rights not to be removed pending determination of their claims to refugee status. The 1996 regulations, if effective, would have rendered the rights granted by the 1993 Act nugatory, as asylum seekers without private means would either have had to return to countries from which they had fled, or attempted to conduct their claims for asylum whilst living destitute and homeless. The court was of the view that Parliament could not have intended the Secretary of State to be vested with powers, exercisable by way of regulation, that would result in so serious an interference with the rights of asylum seekers. Simon Brown LJ described the regulations as 'uncompromisingly draconian' and likely to result in a life for asylum seekers that was 'so destitute that no civilised nation could contemplate it'.

There are a number of well-known examples of subordinate legislation being struck down for want of any clear enabling provision in the area of taxation, where the courts have traditionally adopted a restrictive approach. In *Attorney-General* v *Wilts United Dairies* (1922) 91 LJKB 897 regulations under a milk price fixing scheme, requiring producers to pay a levy to the Food Controller, were invalidated by the House of Lords as amounting to unlawful taxation, since there was no clear statutory authority for such measures. Similarly, in *Customs and Excise Commissioners* v *Cure and Deely Ltd* [1962] 1 QB 340, the Commissioners had made a regulation under which they could determine the amount of tax due from the taxpayer in the event of a tax return being submitted late. The High Court invalidated the regulations on a number of grounds, inter alia, that the Commissioners were only empowered to collect the amount of tax due at law, not the amount they thought fit. They had, therefore, purported to give themselves power by way of delegated legislation going way beyond what was envisaged by Parliament in passing the enabling Act.

Further, a statutory instrument may yet be quashed on the ground that it simply goes further than is necessary to deal with a particular mischief. In *McEldowney* v *Forde* [1971] AC 632 the House of Lords, by a majority, upheld the validity of a regulation made under emergency powers legislation prohibiting membership of republican clubs, but in the course of their speeches their Lordships made plain their view that such a measure was at the very limits of what was acceptable.

Whilst the principles upon which the courts will intervene can be broadly stated, the reality is that any party seeking to impugn the validity of delegated legislation may face difficulties peculiar to this area. Although the fact that subordinate legislation has been approved by a resolution in the House of Commons will not make it immune from judicial review, the courts will be less likely to intervene where the measure primarily gives effect to matters of policy falling within the political responsibility of the executive: see *Nottinghamshire County Council* v *Secretary of State for the Environment* [1986] AC 240.

7.5 Ministers' powers: prerogative power

As indicated above the vast majority of powers exercised by ministers are to be found in statute. This is significant, not only because there is a recognition that the minister exercises the power on trust, ie he has been granted it by the legislature to be exercised for the public good, but also because the power has to be exercised within the confines express or implied in the enabling Act – this is the basis of the ultra vires doctrine by which the courts will intervene to quash any abuse of statutory discretion by a minister.

Not all the powers exercised by ministers have a statutory basis, however. Many of the key powers are still based on the exercise of the royal prerogative. Historically the term 'prerogative' has been applied to those special rights and privileges which the King had as a feudal lord, such as, for example, the privilege that he could not be sued in his own courts and, in a more general way, to all the powers and the authority of the King, whether exercised directly by him, or through some other agency. The struggle between the Stuart monarchy and Parliament in the seventeenth century culminated in the removal of James II from the throne and his replacement by the Protestant William and Mary, who accepted the new constitutional arrangements set out by Parliament in the Bill of Rights 1689. Some of the complaints listed in the preamble and some of the articles of the Bill specifically refer to the issue of prerogative power. The most important legal change brought about by the events of 1689 was the emergence of the general principle that prerogative powers could be limited or even abolished by statute. Some powers still exist, however, that can be exercised either by the monarch in person, or on behalf of the Crown by ministers; these are what are now generically termed prerogative powers.

Instances of the exercise of prerogative power that would still involve the Sovereign personally include the appointment of a Prime Minister; the dissolution of Parliament; the granting certain honours; and, exceptionally, the dismissal of ministers. As will be seen, however, the vast majority of these prerogative powers are now exercised on the Sovereign's behalf by her ministers.

Disposition of the armed forces

Under the prerogative and statute the Sovereign is the commander-in-chief of the armed forces of the Crown. While many matters regarding the armed forces are now regulated by statute, their control, organisation and disposition is governed by the prerogative. In *China Navigation Co* v *Attorney-General* [1932] 2 KB 197, a case in which the court confirmed the right of the Sovereign to determine the military protection to be provided to British subjects overseas, Scrutton LJ observed that:

> 'The administration of the army is in the hands of the King, who unless expressly controlled by an Act of Parliament cannot be controlled by the Court.'

Similarly, in *Chandler* v *DPP* [1964] AC 763, Lord Reid observed:

> 'It is in my opinion clear that the disposition and armament of the armed forces are, and for centuries have been within the exclusive discretion of the Crown and that no one can seek a legal remedy on the ground that such discretion has been wrongly exercised.'

Today a distinction would be drawn between a legal challenge to a policy decision touching upon the conduct of warfare and foreign affairs on the one hand, and policies adopted by the military relating to the terms and conditions under which members of the armed forces serve on the other. Lord Usher's view expressed in *R* v *Secretary of State for War* [1896] 1 QB 121, to the effect that 'An officer ... cannot as between him and the Crown take proceedings in the courts of law in respect of anything which has happened between him and the Crown in consequence of his being a soldier', is no longer sustainable. Following the decision in the GCHQ case (considered below), if the matter is justiciable the courts will examine the decision to determine its legality. In *R* v *Ministry of Defence, ex parte Smith* [1996] 2 WLR 305 the applicants, one female and three male homosexuals, were administratively discharged from the armed forces pursuant to the Ministry of Defence policy (made under prerogative powers preserved by s138(1) of the Naval Discipline Act 1957 and s11(3) of the Army Act 1957 and of the Air Force Act 1955) prohibiting individuals with homosexual proclivities from serving. The applicants unsuccessfully sought judicial review of the policy, promulgated under the prerogative, on the basis that it was irrational and violated the provisions of the European Convention on Human Rights. The Court of Appeal held that the policy, whilst justiciable and thus reviewable, could not be impugned on the basis of irrationality, having been approved by, amongst others, both Houses of Parliament. Whilst the courts did have an important role to play in ensuring that the rights of citizens were not abused by the unlawful exercise of executive power, the courts could not usurp the position of the primary decision-maker in order to regulate the conditions of service of the armed forces of the Crown. The Court declined to adjudicate on the point raised concerning the incompatibility of the ban with the provisions of the European Convention on Human Rights, but the Master of the Rolls did observe that the failure of a decision-maker to advert to the Convention when exercising his discretion was not, of itself, a ground upon which the decision could be challenged by way of judicial review.

Prerogative of mercy

The courts are Her Majesty's courts and certain prerogative powers remain in relation to their work. For example, the Attorney-General in England may exercise the prerogative power to enter a nolle prosequi to stop a trial on indictment. On the advice of the Home Secretary, or the Secretary of State for Scotland, the Crown may exercise the prerogative power to pardon convicted offenders or remit or reduce a sentence. The Crown may, under the prerogative, grant leave for appeal from colonial courts to the Judicial Committee of the Privy Council, where the right still exists.

Legislative powers

In addition to the power to summon, prorogue and dissolve Parliament and to assent to Bills considered above, the Crown also has powers to legislate under the prerogative by Order in Council or by letter patent; note however the effect of the *Case of Proclamations* (1611) 12 Co Rep 74.

Powers relating to external affairs

Under the prerogative the Crown may declare war or make peace. In *R* v *Bottrill, ex parte Kuechenmeister* [1947] KB 41 a certificate from the Secretary of State denying that a state of war with Germany had ended was accepted as conclusive by the court in habeas corpus proceedings brought by a German national who had been detained as an enemy alien. The making of treaties is also governed by the prerogative. The general rule is that it is a matter exclusively for the Crown whether or not to enter into a treaty, though the treaty cannot give rise to new rights and duties in United Kingdom law unless they are given effect by legislation. The prerogative also includes the power of the Crown to recognise foreign governments, acquire territory, prevent aliens from entering the United Kingdom and to intern enemy aliens.

Emergency powers

In time of war the government (in modern times) acts under statutory powers, but the older prerogative powers remain. In the early seventeenth century it was recognised that in an emergency that threatened the realm, every man might disregard property rights in, for example, creating fortifications and digging trenches to repel the enemy. These powers were apparently not thought of as prerogatives since they were shared by the King with all his subjects. In *The Case of the King's Prerogative in Saltpetre* (1607) 12 Co Rep 12 it was held that the King had the prerogative right to mine for saltpetre on private property and to carry it away, because it was necessary for the defence of the realm. The scope of the prerogative in time of war was extensively discussed by the House of Lords in *Burmah Oil Co Ltd* v *Lord Advocate* [1965] AC 75. In 1942 the British force in Rangoon destroyed the appellant's oil installations to prevent them falling into the hands of the advancing Japanese. The preliminary question for the House was whether the appellants were entitled to compensation. The House accepted that the destruction had been carried out lawfully under the prerogative. Lord Reid stating that 'The prerogative certainly covers doing all those things in an emergency which are necessary for the conduct of war.'

Lord Reid linked this to the prerogative right to control the armed forces; the reason for leaving the waging of war to the executive, he said, was obvious. What was necessary would depend on the circumstances. Their Lordships went on to hold that although the installations had been lawfully destroyed under the prerogative, compensation was payable. The only common law exception to the rule that damage done under the prerogative in time of war gave rise to an entitlement to compensation was that of battle damage; damage actually caused by the use of weapons during conflict. The case was reversed by the War Damage Act 1965 which retrospectively provided that no person is entitled at common law to receive compensation in respect of damage caused by lawful acts of the Crown during, or in contemplation of the outbreak of, a war in which the Sovereign is or was engaged. The Act only applies where there is a war and the principle of *Burmah Oil* presumably remains intact in the case of emergencies not amounting to war. As regards the maintenance of domestic law and order, *R* v *Secretary of State for the*

Home Department, ex parte Northumbria Police Authority [1988] 1 WLR 356 confirms the existence of a residual prerogative power, vested in the Home Secretary, to provide such assistance as is required to police forces in order to enforce the law. Wide as a such a residual prerogative power might be it cannot, save for the most compelling reasons, be used to exile the Queen's subjects from territories for which the Crown has responsibility: see *R v Secretary of State for the Foreign and Commonwealth Office, ex parte Bancoult* (2000) The Times 10 November.

Prerogative and statutory powers

The common law rule is that if a prerogative power has been replaced by statute, the courts will proceed on the basis that it is the statutory power that is, and should be, exercised. Such an approach will be of more than merely constitutional significance when there is some distinction between the prerogative and statutory powers in terms of the rights and duties of citizens. The point is illustrated by the House of Lords' decision in *Attorney-General v De Keyser's Royal Hotel Ltd* [1920] AC 508, where troops had been accommodated at the plaintiff's hotel that had been requisitioned by the Crown for this purpose. There appeared to be two different powers under which this could be carried out: the royal prerogative, which was unclear as to the property owner's right to compensation in such circumstances; and the Defence Regulations of 1803 and 1842, which provided a code for the making of compensation payments in the event of property being requisitioned.

In the statute under which the Regulations were made there was no mention of the co-extensive prerogative power, and the Crown was not expressly bound by the statute. It was held that if an area of prerogative power is subsequently covered, or 'overlapped' by a statutory provision, the statutory provision should prevail. In this case compensation was, therefore, payable under the Defence Regulations. As Lord Dunedin observed:

> 'Inasmuch as the Crown is a party to every Act of Parliament it is logical enough to consider that when the Act deals with something which before the Act could be effected by the prerogative, and specially empowers the Crown to do the same thing, but subject to conditions, the Crown assents to that, and by that Act, to the prerogative being curtailed.'

Lord Atkinson added:

> '... after the statute has been passed, and while it is in force, the thing it empowers the Crown to do can thenceforth only be done by and under the statute, and subject to all the limitations, restrictions and conditions by it imposed, however unrestricted the Royal Prerogative may theretofore have been.'

A distinction will be drawn by the courts where the prerogative power is not entirely replaced by a statutory provision. In *R v Secretary of State for the Home Department, ex parte Northumbria Police Authority* (above) the Secretary of State, claiming to act either under s41 of the Police Act 1964, or under his prerogative powers, issued a circular to chief constables indicating that central government would supply them with riot equipment such as CS gas, in the event of a local police authority refusing to sanction the purchase of such equipment. The applicant authority contended that s4(4) of the 1964 Act gave police authorities the exclusive power to equip local police forces, and that this statutory power usurped any remaining prerogative power in the Secretary of State to supply such equipment. The Court of Appeal held that, notwithstanding the power granted to the Secretary of State under s41 of the 1964 Act, s4(4) of the Act had not replaced the prerogative power of the Secretary of State to maintain law and order. Crucial to this reasoning was the finding that s4(4) did not give local police authorities a monopoly over the supply of such equipment.

The correct approach to be adopted where the prerogative power is replaced with one under statute, but the statute has not yet been brought in to force, was considered by the House of Lords in *R* v *Secretary of State for the Home Department, ex parte Fire Brigades Union and Others* [1995] 2 WLR 464. A scheme existed for allocating public funds by way of compensation for the victims of crime, administered by the Criminal Injuries Compensation Board, under the prerogative. Sections 108–117 of the Criminal Justice Act 1988 sought to codify this scheme and place it on a statutory basis, leaving the quantum of any funds awarded to be determined by application of the common law principles. Section 171(1) empowered the Secretary of State to bring the scheme into effect on a day to be announced. In November 1993, in the exercise of his prerogative powers, the Secretary of State announced a new tariff scheme under which set amounts would be payable to the victims of crime, depending upon how their claims were categorised. The effect of this new tariff scheme was that much lower awards would be made in the future, resulting in a halving of the cost of the criminal injuries compensation scheme by the year 2000. The application for judicial review of: (i) the Secretary of State's failure to implement the statutory scheme under the 1988 Act; and (ii) his exercise of prerogative power in introducing the revised tariff for awards, was dismissed at first instance, and on appeal the Court of Appeal held that, whilst the Secretary of State was under no duty to introduce the statutory scheme, it was an abuse of his common law prerogative powers to introduce a compensation scheme other than that contained in the 1988 Act. The Secretary of State appealed to the House of Lords and the applicants cross-appealed, where it was held (by a majority), dismissing both the appeal and cross-appeals, that, as the Secretary of State had a discretion under s171(1) of the 1988 Act to bring the scheme into effect at some future date, the applicant's contention, to the effect that the Secretary of State had to bring the scheme into effect at some time, if correct, would mean the courts being able to grant an order of mandamus to this effect. Lord Browne-Wilkinson observed that it would be undesirable for the courts to be seen to be intervening in the legislative process to this extent, as it would involve the courts in treading 'dangerously close to the area over which Parliament enjoys exclusive jurisdiction, namely the making of legislation.' The section was to be read as conferring a discretion upon the

Secretary of State that had to be exercised (or not) according to law. In this case the House of Lords felt that the Secretary of State had acted unlawfully in determining that he would never exercise his powers under s171(1). Regarding the exercise of prerogative power, the fact that the statutory scheme had not come into effect meant that, unlike the position in the *De Keyser* case, the prerogative power continued to exist and could be invoked by the executive. The existence of the embryonic statutory scheme was, however, a factor that had to be borne in mind by a minister exercising the prerogative power, and limited the way in which that power could lawfully be used. In the present case the Secretary of State could not rely on his own act of introducing a revised scheme for compensation under the prerogative as a ground for not exercising his discretion under s171(1). Hence the introduction of the revised scheme under the prerogative, given the pre-existing statutory scheme, constituted an abuse of power and was thus ultra vires.

The constitutional significance of the case lies in the extent to which the majority was willing to provide a brake on the actions of the executive, and risk accusations of judicial supremacisim. Mindful of such criticisms, Lord Keith (dissenting) viewed the decision as to whether or not to implement the legislation as one that was essentially administrative or political, in respect of which the Secretary of State owed a duty to Parliament, not the public at large. Hence, in his view, it would have been inappropriate for the courts to intervene.

Control of prerogative power in the courts

Prior to the House of Lords' decision in *Council of Civil Service Unions* v *Minister for the Civil Service* [1984] 3 All ER 935 (the GCHQ case), the approach of the courts was that they were prepared to adjudicate upon whether or not a prerogative power existed, but having concluded that it did, they were unwilling to comment on the legality of the exercise of the prerogative power. The significance of the GCHQ case was the recognition by the House of Lords that prerogative power was, in principle, amenable to judicial review in the way that any other public law power was.

The case arose as a consequence of actual and threatened industrial action at the government's communications headquarters (GCHQ). The Minister for the Civil Service issued an oral instruction to the effect that civil servants employed there would be prohibited from membership of any trade union. The staff of GCHQ were not consulted prior to the taking of this decision, which was made pursuant to the Minister's powers, under art 4 of the Civil Service Order in Council 1982, to give instructions 'for controlling the conduct of the Service, and providing for ... the conditions of service', the Order itself being made under the royal prerogative.

The House of Lords held that simply because a decision-making power was derived from a common law and not a statutory source it should not, for that reason only, be immune from judicial review. Lord Roskill thought that the right of challenge to the exercise of prerogative power could not, however, be unqualified. In his view it depended on the subject matter of the prerogative power. Prerogative powers such as those relating to the making of treaties, the defence of the realm, the prerogative of mercy, the grant of honours, the dissolution of Parliament and the appointment of ministers were not, he thought, susceptible to judicial review because their nature and subject matter was such to render them not amenable to the judicial process. It was also pointed out that prerogative decisions would usually involve the application of government policy of which the courts were not the appropriate arbiters. According to Lord Diplock:

> '... the kind of evidence that is admissible under judicial procedures and the way in which it has to be addressed tend to exclude from the attention of the court competing policy considerations which, if the executive discretion is to be wisely exercised, need to be weighed against one another – a balancing exercise which judges by their upbringing and experience are ill-qualified to perform.'

Their Lordships agreed therefore that executive action based on common law or the use of a prerogative power was not necessarily immune from review. This was especially so in the present case where the prerogative derived from an Order in Council, which was virtually indistinguishable from an order deriving from statute. In such cases the decision might be reviewed by the courts just as it would have been if it had rested on statutory powers. In the instant case, the decision rested upon the minister's consideration of national security, a matter the House of Lords thought it was for the executive to weigh and decide. Their Lordships accepted that the overriding element of national security, in maintaining services at GCHQ, displaced any right the unions may have had to judicial review of the order.

Since the GCHQ case the courts have been willing to review the exercise of prerogative power as regards the issuing of passports – see *R* v *Secretary of State for Foreign and Commonwealth Affairs, ex parte Everett* [1989] 1 All ER 655 – and it has been held that the prerogative powers exercised by the Home Secretary in respect of immigration and deportation decisions will be subject to judicial review, but not on the grounds that, in exercising those powers, he has failed to take into account the terms of an international treaty not yet incorporated into domestic law: see *R* v *Secretary of State for the Home Department, ex parte Ahmed and Others* [1998] INLR 570. The reviewability of the exercise of the prerogative of mercy was confirmed in *R* v *Secretary of State for the Home Department, ex parte Bentley* [1994] 2 WLR 101. The applicant's brother, Derek Bentley, was convicted of the murder of a police officer in 1952 and, despite the jury's recommendation, and the advice of Home Office officials to the effect that the death penalty should not be enforced, was subsequently executed in 1953. In 1992 the Home Secretary, whilst indicating that he had some sympathy for the view that Bentley should not have been hanged, refused to grant him a posthumous pardon, on the ground that it was not Home Office policy to do so unless the defendant concerned had been proved to be both technically and morally innocent of any crime, and that following a review of his case he was satisfied that Bentley's innocence had not been established. The Divisional Court declined to make any order, but invited the Home Secretary to look again at the range of options that might permit some formal recognition to be given to the generally accepted view that Bentley should not have been hanged. Watkins LJ saw no reason why, in the light of the House of Lords' decision in the GCHQ case, the exercise of the prerogative of mercy should not be susceptible to review. Whilst the formulation of policy relating to the granting of pardons might not be justiciable, the failure by a Home Secretary to consider the variety of ways in which that prerogative might be exercised could be reviewed. In the instant case the Home Secretary should have considered whether or not the grant of a conditional posthumous pardon was appropriate as recognition that the state had made a mistake, and that Bentley should have had his sentence commuted: see further *R* v *Secretary of State for the Home Department, ex parte Harrison* [1988] 3 All ER 86 and *R* v *Solicitor-General, ex parte Taylor* [1996] COD 61 (no judicial review of decision not to institute contempt proceedings).

The Human Rights Act 1998 raises the prospect of an exercise of prerogative power being challenged on the basis that it conflicts with Convention rights protected by the Act. Section 6(1) provides that it is unlawful for a public authority to act in a way that is incompatible with a Convention right and this would certainly encompass a minister exercising prerogative power.

7.6 Government departments

Government departments, sometimes known as ministries, are, in law, part of the Crown. They are involved in the everyday process of assisting in the formulation of executive policy and executing the law. In general constitutional terms, each department is headed by a minister, sometimes known as a Secretary of State, who is answerable to Parliament for all the operations of his department. These departments are staffed by civil servants, full-time paid employees who owe their position to appointment not election and who do not lose their position when one government falls and is replaced by another.

The creation of government departments

Except for periods of wartime emergency, it is difficult to find an example of the creation of a new department in direct response to the discovery of a new need. Needs become gradually, evident and at first are usually provided for through an existing department dealing with matters which are in some way similar. For example, the nineteenth century saw the growth of the social service functions of government. Some of these functions were attached at first to the Home Office (itself set up in 1782) or Board of Trade. Others were performed by a committee of the Privy Council set up to perform the particular functions concerned. When the administrative duties of these committees became more complicated it was felt necessary that they should be entrusted to a separate department. The relevant committee of the Privy Council developed into what was called a board and eventually into a fully-fledged ministry or department. Thus, a new department is created at a point where a function becomes sufficiently important and sufficiently complex to require separate departmental organisation.

Fusion, fission and transfer

An illustration of fusion and fission is provided by the functions originally vested in the Ministry of Health when it was set up in 1917. The Ministry of Health took over from other authorities various functions concerned with the relief of poverty and the improvement of the conditions of life. Thus the ministry: took over the powers of the Local Government Board; replaced the English and Welsh Insurance Commissioners; acquired the Privy Council's powers over the midwifery service; and acquired the powers of the Home Office over infant life protection, the practice of anatomy and the treatment of lunacy and mental deficiency. In addition, a variety of other functions were transferred to the Ministry of Health from the Board of Trade, the Ministry of Agriculture and Fisheries and the Board of Education. It was also responsible in the 1920s for operating the then very rudimentary town and country planning legislation. It seemed like good policy to gather together such services in one ministry in order to ensure their proper co-ordination but the functions of the government in these fields increased, especially after the Second World War, and the ministry became unwieldy, with the danger that certain of its functions would be neglected. So the process of fission (splitting up) was put into operation and the responsibilities of the former Ministry of Health became divided between three ministries: Health; Housing and Local Government; and Ministry of Social Security. However, change occurred again in 1970 when housing, local government and planning became part of the new Department of the Environment, which also until 1976 had responsibility for transport. In 1968 Health and Social Security were fused to form the Department of Health and Social Security, a 'super department' that became too unwieldy for one Secretary of State. From June 1987 the two parts were again separated into two departments, the Department of Health and the Department of Social Security. Today there is a Department of Health and a Department for Work and Pensions. In addition to this fusion and fission process there has been, over the years, an almost continuous process of functions being transferred from one department to another. Excluding instances of creation and transfer made for purely political reasons, for example, to please a particular interest group by giving recognition to their interest by the creation of a new department, or to increase the status of one minister at the expense of another, the aim is to produce departments with what has been described as 'coherent missions'. Of course, it is impossible today to divide government functions into a series of neatly defined blocks, each to be occupied by one government department, and so the boundaries between the government departments are blurred and continually changing.

The principal departments of state

The Treasury is regarded as the most important of the departments of state and the Prime Minister is always, by convention, the First Lord of the Treasury, although the Chancellor of the Exchequer is its effective head. Its important functions place it at the centre of the administration. They include: the raising of revenue; the control of public (government) expenditure; and the overseeing of the national economy. From 1920 to 1968 and again, to a large extent, since 1982, the Treasury also managed the Civil Service. This involved the control of Civil Service promotion and appointments, especially at the highest levels, the direction of organisation and methods, and the overseeing of discipline. In 1968 the government adopted the Fulton Committee's recommendation for a Civil Service Department, and this was established, headed by the Prime Minister. It was disbanded at the end of 1981. Departmental estimates of their spending for the coming year have to be approved by the Treasury before presentation to Parliament. Whenever a department proposes action involving new expenditure or new distribution of existing expenditure the consent of the Treasury is, in effect, necessary.

While the functions of the Treasury are all closely interrelated, the Home Office, by contrast, has many very different duties involving an enormous volume of work. They include the organisation of the prison service, race relations, immigration and nationality, together with important responsibilities for the police and internal security. The Home Office has a large staff: about 25,000 compared with 1,000 in the Treasury. However, the Treasury's tasks are regarded as particularly important and so it has 25 per cent more senior civil servants than the Home Office. Ambitious civil servants covet posts in the Treasury and this would seem to be a recognition of its influential position in government structure and the power of its officials. The head of the Home Office is the Home Secretary.

The Department of Health is responsible for health services. The National Health Service Reorganisation Act 1973 provided for the establishment of 14 regional health authorities and 90 area health authorities, and smaller district authorities were also set up. In 1980 the area authorities were disbanded so that the pattern now is one of regional and district authorities only. The Department of Social Security, separated from that of Health in 1987, was responsible for social security services such as war pensions, sickness benefit, maternity allowance and supplementary benefit. It is now part of the Department for Work and Pensions.

What was the Department of the Environment, Transport and the Regions has become the Department of the Environment, Food and Rural Affairs. Many functions previously discharged by the Department of the Environment have been transferred to the Department for Transport, Local Government and the Regions. This department also has responsibility for the fire service and electoral law – matters previously within the remit of the Home Office.

The Foreign Office and the Commonwealth Office merged in 1968 under a Secretary of State for Foreign and Commonwealth Affairs. In 1975 the Ministry of

Overseas Development lost its identity as a separate government department and became a part of the Foreign and Commonwealth Office. The then Minister of Overseas Development, Mrs Judith Hart, was highly critical of this move, regarding it as an indication of the government's increasing lack of commitment to providing overseas aid to developing countries. Since May 1997 the Secretary of State for International Development has been a post of Cabinet rank in the Labour administration. The Foreign and Commonwealth Office is staffed, as are overseas missions, consular posts and delegations, by members of the Diplomatic Service. This is a body separate from the Civil Service that was formed in 1965, although even before that date the Foreign Service had an identity that was separate from the Home Civil Service.

A unified Ministry of Defence was established in 1964 by the merger of four separate departments: the Ministry of Defence, the Admiralty, the War Office and the Air Ministry. Its responsibilities include: the formulation of defence policy and the control and administration of the armed forces. The political head of the ministry is the Secretary of State for Defence.

7.7 The Civil Service

Brief history

Before the nineteenth century it was not possible to speak of a Civil Service since each department head had almost complete independence in the matter of recruitment, which was generally by patronage or purchase of a sinecure, and there were no general rates of pay applicable across department boundaries, nor indeed possibilities for movement from one department to another. In 1854 Sir Stafford Northcote and Sir Charles Trevelyan presented a commissioned *Report on the Organisation of the Permanent Civil Service*. Four main points were made in the Report:

1. for recruitment, open competitive examinations should be introduced, standardised throughout the service and conducted by a central board;
2. there should be a distinction between the 'intellectuals' and the 'mechanicals', namely, those destined for 'superior situations' and those who were to occupy the lower class of appointments, and the two classes should be recruited at two quite distinct educational levels;
3. the service should be unified by the introduction of uniform salary grades and the principle of free transferability of a civil servant from one department to another;
4. promotion should be by merit rather than by seniority and safeguards should be introduced to prevent abuses in the promotion system.

In 1855 Civil Service Commissioners were appointed by Order in Council and given the task of organising a system of examinations for recruitment. By Orders in Council in 1870, a system of open competitive examinations was introduced. The staff of all departments were unified into one Civil Service and certain general rates of pay and pensions were laid down. It will be seen that the fundamentals laid down by Northcote and Trevelyan have remained virtually unchallenged until comparatively recent times. One of the most important reviews of the civil service, in terms of actually bringing about change, was the Fulton Report of 1967. The Fulton Commission, set up in 1966, saw six major defects in the organisation. These included:

1. the service being based too much on the philosophy of the amateur, the generalist or all-rounder, rather than emphasising the need for particular skills for particular jobs;
2. the maintenance of the four-fold division of administrative class, executive class, clerical class, and clerical assistant class, each with a separate pay and career structure, which impeded the most efficient use of individuals;
3. specialists, for example the medical officer and legal classes, being denied opportunities for full administrative responsibility at the highest level;
4. inadequate personnel management and career planning.

As a result of Fulton, in 1971 the administrative, executive and clerical classes merged to form one administrative group. Since 1981 the Treasury has been responsible for determining Civil Service pay and conditions, and the Cabinet Office has been responsible for the management of the Civil Service.

Over the last decade there has been an increasing trend towards quasi-privatisation of Civil Service functions with the devolution of power to nearly 100 semi-independent agencies under the 'Next Steps' programme. Amongst the functions that have been re-allocated are passports, prisons and social security benefits. Some have been transferred to the private sector altogether, for example the work of the Chessington Computer Centre, the Occupational Health and Safety Agency, the Recruitment and Assessment Services Agency and HM Stationery Office.

Some departments are working along 'Next Steps' lines – eg Customs and Excise and Inland Revenue. On the basis of the White Paper *Continuity and Change* published in July 1994, it would appear that the trend towards de-centralisation is set to continue. Among its key proposals are the following: performance-related pay for senior civil servants; increased flexibility in pay structures for senior staff; and overall staffing levels to decline further.

In 1976 there were 751,000 civil servants, the figure for July 1997 was 472,000, with a further 19,900 staff employed on a casual basis. The White Paper does not address the implications for the working relationship between senior civil servants and ministers, and the provision of information for parliamentary questions.

In the future it may be that the role of the civil servant is extended to encompass the provision of assistance to leaders of opposition parties. In June 1997 the government announced proposals to second civil servants to the opposition to ensure that its leader and front bench spokespersons were adequately briefed to take part in debates on key issues. The desire is ensure that the opposition can perform its role properly and is borne out of Prime Minister Blair's experiences as Leader of the Opposition, where he noted the pressure placed on his private office as a result of the lack of any Civil Service support. The proposal might also be extended to minority parties. Whilst such a move would do much to help remove the information gap between government and opposition, civil servants might be concerned about their possible politicisation, in being identified as assisting one party or another, and may not see secondment as a route to rapid advancement within the government machine.

The constitutional position of the civil servant

A civil servant may be defined as a servant of the Crown employed in a civil capacity who is paid wholly and directly out of money voted by Parliament. This definition excludes the armed services who are employed in a military and not in a civil capacity and police officers. It also excludes public servants in local government and the public corporations who are not servants of the Crown, and are not paid directly from money voted by Parliament. The term 'civil' also implies a distinction from the 'political' service consisting of ministers responsible to Parliament. The Civil Service Code provides that:

> 'The constitutional and practical role of the Civil Service is, with integrity, honesty, impartiality and objectivity, to assist the duly constituted government, of whatever political complexion, in formulating policies of the government, carrying out decisions of the Government and in administering public services for which the government is responsible. ... Civil servants are servants of the Crown. Constitutionally, the Crown acts on the advice of ministers and, subject to the provisions of this Code, civil servants owe their loyalty to the duly constituted government.'

Unless statute provides otherwise, all civil servants are employed at the pleasure of the Crown. They may therefore, in law, be dismissed at pleasure and civil servants have no common law remedy for wrongful dismissal or breach of contract of employment. The civil service staff associations and the Crown have negotiated procedures for disciplining and dismissing staff, and the Employment Protection (Consolidation) Act 1978 (as amended) now gives civil servants a statutory right to appeal to an industrial tribunal in respect of unfair dismissal. In practice civil servants enjoy one of the most secure tenures of employment in the country. Under guidelines introduced in the wake of the Nolan Committee Report on *Standards in Public Life*, civil servants who feel that they are being required by ministers to act in a manner that is illegal, improper or unethical, will, as a last resort, be able to take their complaints to the Civil Service Commissioners. The guidelines also remind civil servants of their duty to preserve confidentiality, stating that they should not 'seek to frustrate or influence the policies, decisions or actions of government by the unauthorised, improper, or premature disclosure outside the government of any information to which they have access as civil servants.'

Rules affecting the political activities of civil servants

In order to preserve the appearance of political neutrality, civil servants are limited in the political activities they may undertake. No civil servant may become a Member of Parliament: House of Commons Disqualification Act 1975. A civil servant is required to resign his position before his nomination as a parliamentary candidate can be accepted: Servants of the Crown (Parliamentary Candidature) Order 1960. Beyond this, political activity is restricted according to which of three groups a civil servant is classified as belonging to.

The first is the 'restricted category'. Civil servants in senior administrative grades, and staff in executive or clerical grades whose work is associated with those in the position of giving advice to ministers, or whose work involves direct contact with the public, are barred from participation in political activities at national level. Although they may be members of a political party, they may not hold office in the party, and may not express in public any views on matters of national political controversy. With permission they may take part in local politics, associated with the work of the local council, but are obliged to act with discretion, particularly where a matter concerns the department where they are employed. In practice, it is unlikely that those in senior administrative grades would seek permission to associate themselves publicly with any particular political party.

Second, there is the 'intermediate category'. Civil servants in this category may, with the permission of their departments, take part in all political activity both local and national, except parliamentary candidature. However, they must observe a code of discretion, for example, they may discuss in public national policies, but are to avoid personal attacks on ministers, or causing embarrassment to the departments which employ them.

Finally, there is the 'politically free category'. This includes industrial civil servants and those non-industrial civil servants in the most minor grades. They may engage in all political activities whether at national or local level, other than parliamentary candidature, unless they are on duty, wearing uniform or on government premises at the time. It must be remembered, of course, that all civil servants are subject to the provisions of the Official Secrets Acts 1911–1989, which prohibit the passing on by a civil servant of any confidential information gained by him by virtue of his employment.

The relationship between ministers and civil servants

The theoretical position is that ministers, who are elected representatives, make policy decisions under the influence of a variety of factors, and civil servants, who are paid employees and non-representative, execute those decisions. However, it has long been accepted that the reality may be very far from this theoretical concept and that civil servants may play an important part in determining government policy and activity. Nevertheless, the doctrine of ministerial responsibility whereby the minister is, in theory, responsible to Parliament and ultimately to the public for all that happens within his ministry still exists, since it is accepted as an essential foundation of British democracy that those who govern the people should be answerable through Parliament to the people.

In real terms the importance of the Civil Service in the formulation of policy in any particular case is dependent upon various factors. Ministers are Members of Parliament as well as heads of government departments and will have parliamentary and constituency duties as well as ministerial responsibilities. By contrast, the civil servant spends all of his or her working time in the department. Inevitably, some decision-taking of lesser importance will fall upon the top civil servants in his department. Ministers frequently move from department to department and, when newly arrived, a minister is inevitably very reliant on his civil servants in respect of matters of detail, and the very extent of government activities today means that some decision-taking will rest with higher civil servants. Because civil servants are expected to supply ministers with the information they need in order to come to a decision on any particular matter, that decision can be influenced by the way in which the information is presented and, indeed, by what information is omitted. A minister may ask senior civil servants for advice, and even if he requests an outline of the possible alternatives with the pros and cons, there are clearly plenty of opportunities for the civil servants to influence the minister's decision.

There will be less scope for influence by senior civil servants where an experienced minister is appointed, or possibly where a government seeks to promulgate a radical policy for which it has a clear mandate. The Civil Service Code seeks to lay down some guidelines as to how civil servants should conduct themselves in this context. Reaffirming that civil servants are accountable to ministers, and that they should discharge their public law functions reasonably and according to the law, the Code stresses that civil servants should 'give honest and impartial advice to ministers, without fear or favour, and make all information relevant to a decision available to ministers', and that they should not deceive or knowingly mislead ministers, Parliament or the public. In particular the Code goes on to provide that:

'Civil servants should conduct themselves in such a way as to deserve and retain the confidence of ministers and to be able to establish the same relationship with those whom they may be required to serve in some future administration. They should comply with restrictions on their political activities. The conduct of civil servants should be such that ministers and potential future ministers can be sure that confidence can be freely given, and that the Civil Service will conscientiously fulfil its duties and obligations to, and impartially assist, advise and carry out the policies of the duly constituted government. ... [T]hey should not seek to frustrate or influence the policies, decisions or actions of government by the unauthorised, improper or premature disclosure outside the government of any information to which they have had access as civil servants.'

In situations where a civil servant feels that he is being required to act in a way which is illegal, improper, or unethical; is in breach of constitutional convention or a professional code; or may involve possible maladministration, he may, ultimately, report the matter in writing to the Civil Service Commissioners.

7.8 Police forces

Constitutionally police officers form part of the executive, giving effect to and enforcing laws passed by the legislature. There are obvious dangers, however, in police officers being identified as agents of the executive. They must be impartial in their safeguarding of law and order, and will lose the confidence of the communities they seek to police if they are perceived to be merely enforcing the diktat of whatever party is in government. This goes some way towards explaining why the police forces in England and Wales have always been organised on a local (effectively a county) basis, and why the control and supervision of police forces has always been based on the delicate tripartite relationship between chief constable, Home Secretary and local police authority. The aim is to ensure sufficient central control in order to ensure the maintenance of consistent national standards, whilst ensuring that police forces remain politically independent and answerable to locally elected representatives.

The modern statutory basis for the organisation of non-metropolitan police forces in England and Wales was originally enacted in the form of the Police Act 1964, as augmented by the Police and Criminal Evidence Act 1984 (PACE) and amended by the Police and Magistrates' Court Act (PAMCA) 1994. The law has now been consolidated in the Police Act 1996, and references below are to the provisions of the 1996 Act unless otherwise stated. The provisions of Pt I of PAMCA 1994, now re-enacted in the 1996 Act, largely give effect to the proposals for reform of the police service set out in the White Paper *Police Reform: the Government's Proposals for the Police Service in England and Wales* (Cm 2881) and aim to give more power to local police authorities and to chief constables to enable them to serve their local communities more effectively, and to instil a sense of 'business management' in the running of police forces. Under the 1996 Act provision is made for 37 police areas in England (excluding the Metropolitan District) and four in Wales, each with its own police authority.

The constitutional position of police officers

One of the better known truisms in English law is that a police constable is simply 'a citizen in uniform'. While it is true that private citizens enjoy powers of arrest, and that in exercising those powers a police constable is not above the law, there are many powers relating to law enforcement that can only be exercised by police constables. Most writers agree with the assertion that a police officer is a Crown servant, although, as observed above, not a servant of the government. For certain purposes a police officer is expressly stated to be a Crown servant: see official secrets legislation, *Lewis* v *Cattle* [1938] 2 KB 454. Police officers are appointed by the chief constable and paid out of local police authority funds. In this sense they are analogous to local government employees: see the judgment of McCardie J in *Fisher* v *Oldham Corporation* [1930] 2 KB 364.

As Lord Parker CJ observed in *Rice* v *Connolly* [1966] 2 All ER 649 (at p651):

> 'It is ... in my judgment clear that it is part of the obligations and duties of a police constable to take all steps which appear to him necessary for keeping the peace, for preventing crime or for protecting property from criminal injury. There is no exhaustive definition of the powers and obligations of the police, but they are at least those, and they would further include the duty to detect crime and to bring an offender to justice.'

Under the provisions of the Police Reform Act 2002 police support staff (ie civilians) can be designated as belonging to one of four categories (provided they have received appropriate training etc). These are: community support officers; investigation officers; detention officers; and escort officers. The purpose of this change is to allow routine police procedures to be conducted by civilians thereby releasing valuable police time.

Police forces outside London

The running of the non-metropolitan police forces is conducted under a tri-partite power-sharing arrangement where functions are divided amongst the chief constable, the police authority and the Home Secretary.

The police authority

Police authorities, constituted under s3 of the 1996 Act, as amended by the Criminal Justice and Police Act 2001, comprise 17 members, nine councillors, three magistrates and five independent members. The independent members are selected by the other members of the police authority from a short list of ten prepared by the Home Secretary. Appointment will normally be for four years, with no upper age limit for retirement.

Each authority is subject to a statutory duty (s6) to secure the maintenance of an efficient and effective police force for its area, with reference to objectives determined by the Secretary of State, objectives determined by the authority itself, performance targets determined by the authority for itself, and any local policing plan issued by the authority.

By virtue of s111 of the Local Government Act 1972 a police authority is empowered to do anything which is calculated to facilitate the discharge of its duty under s6 of the 1996 Act. This may, for example, extend to the provision of financial support for officers faced with legal costs arising out of litigation related to the discharge of their duties: see further *R* v *DPP, ex parte Duckenfield* [1999] 2 All ER 873.

Prior to the commencement of each financial year each police authority will be under a statutory duty to determine policing objectives for the year ahead, following consultation with the chief constable and to take steps to ascertain views on community policing under s106 of the Police and Criminal Evidence Act 1984. In addition each authority will be required to issue a local policing plan (prepared by the chief constable for its consideration), which should include a statement of the authority's priorities for the year ahead, resource requirement and resource allocation. If an authority proposes to issue a plan that differs from that submitted for consideration by the chief constable it must consult him first. At the end of each financial year each police authority must submit an annual report, including an assessment of the extent to which the local policing plan has been carried out: s9.

The chief constable

Section 11 of the 1996 Act, provides that each force shall have a chief constable, appointed by the police authority and subject to the approval of the Home Secretary. In discharging his functions, the chief constable will have to have regard to the local policing plan issued by the police authority. The police authority, acting with the approval of the Home Secretary, will be able to call upon the chief constable to retire in the interests of efficiency, but not before it has provided the chief constable with an opportunity to make representations. Under s42, the Home Secretary can, of his own volition, call upon the chief constable to resign, but is required to conduct an inquiry into the matter where representations are made to him to do so. The role of the Home Secretary and the police authority in respect of calling for the resignation of the chief constable were further amended by the Police Reform Act 2002.

By virtue of s10 of the 1996 Act the chief constable is given a very wide discretion as to the organisation and disposition of his officers, but he must act with due regard to the local policing plan issued by the police authority for his area.

The role of the Home Secretary

Under the 1996 Act the Home Secretary has the power to dismiss a chief constable (s42), request reports on policing matters (s43), make grants to police forces (ss46–48), order local inquiries into police matters, such as the Scarman Report on the Brixton riots (s49), make regulations concerning the administration of the police force (s51), and appoint Inspectors of Constabulary who investigate the efficiency of forces and report back to the Home Secretary: s54. Section 37 provides that the Home Secretary may determine objectives for the policing of all police areas having consulted those who represent both police authorities and chief constables. The Home Secretary may further require police authorities to establish performance targets to be aimed at in seeking to achieve his objectives. More generally, the Home Secretary may, from time to time, issue circulars to police forces. The residual prerogative power of the Home Secretary to supply equipment to chief constables, possibly against the wishes of the local police authority, was confirmed in *R* v *Secretary of State for the Home Department, ex parte Northumbria Police Authority* [1988] 1 WLR 356. Under the Police Reform Act 2002 the Home Secretary can order an inspection of a police force and, if the report is critical, he can give directions to the relevant police authority to take the necessary remedial measures in conjunction with the relevant chief constable.

The Metropolitan Police

The Metropolitan Police was established by the Metropolitan Police Act 1829. It was run by magistrates until 1866 when the first Commissioner was appointed, answerable to the Home Secretary. When the London County Council was created in 1888, moves to introduce a police authority, similar to those that existed outside London, were resisted on the grounds that it was more desirable for the policing of the capital to be under the control of central government. Following the creation of the Greater London Authority under the Greater London Authority Act 1999, the Commissioner of the Metropolitan Police must now take into account the views of the Metropolitan Police Authority and the Mayor for London. The operation of the Metropolitan Police Authority is similar to that of police authorities that exist elsewhere in the country. Of the Authority's 23 members, 12 are also members of the Greater London Assembly (including the Deputy Mayor) and are appointed to the Authority by the Mayor. The remaining members of the Authority comprise one person appointed by the Home Secretary, magistrates and other independent persons. The Authority has taken on most of the police-related functions previously discharged by the Receiver of the Metropolitan Police.

The unique constitutional position of the Metropolitan Police Commissioner was usefully summarised by Lord Denning MR in *R* v *Metropolitan Police Commissioner, ex parte Blackburn* [1968] 2 QB 118 at 135, where he stated:

'The office of Commissioner of Police within the metropolis dates back to 1829 when Sir Robert Peel introduced his disciplined force. The commissioner was a justice of the peace specially appointed to administer the police force in the metropolis. His constitutional status has never been defined either by statute or by the courts. It was considered by the Royal Commission on the Police in their report in 1962 (Cmnd 1728). I have no hesitation, however, in holding that, like every constable in the land, he should be, and is, independent of the executive. He is not subject to the orders of the Secretary of State, save that under [statute] the Secretary of State can call on him to give a report, or to retire in the interests of efficiency. I hold it to be the duty of the Commissioner of Police, as it is of every chief constable, to enforce the law of the land. He must take steps so to post his men that crimes may be detected: and that honest citizens may go about their affairs in peace. He must decide whether or not suspected persons are to be prosecuted; and, if need be, bring the prosecution or see that it is brought; but in all these things he is not the servant of anyone, save of the law itself. No Minister of the Crown can tell him that he must, or must not, keep observation on this place or that; or that he must, or must not, prosecute this man or that one. Nor can any police authority tell him so. The responsibility for law enforcement lies on him. He is answerable to the law and to the law alone. That appears sufficiently from *Fisher* v *Oldham Corporation* ([1930] 2 KB 364, [1930] All ER Rep 96), the Privy Council case of *A-G for New South Wales* v *Perpetual Trustee Co Ltd* ([1955] 1 All ER 846, [1955] AC 457).'

Note that the City of London has its own police force for which the Common Council of the City of London is the police authority.

A national police force?

The idea of a national police force has traditionally been rejected for fear that it could create the beginnings of a 'police state', with officers under the direction of politicians. The Royal Commission on the Police (1962) (Cmnd 1728) considered the issue, concluding that the ideal arrangement was to have local forces, accountable to local bodies, with a degree of centralised supervision of standards. Provision does exist for co-operation between local forces on the basis of what is known as 'mutual aid'. Under s24 of the 1996 Act a chief constable can supply manpower and equipment to another force, regardless of the view of his police authority. In addition, the Association of Chief Police Officers (ACPO) is a powerful lobby group co-ordinating the views of chief constables. The president of the association normally has some direction over the national reporting centre, which helps to co-ordinate mutual aid. There was evidence of a high level of co-operation during the miners' strikes of the 1980s.

Under s1 of the Police Reform Act 2002 the Home Secretary is under a duty to prepare an annual National Policing Plan for that year. The Plan must set out whatever the Secretary of State considers to be the strategic policing priorities generally for the police forces maintained for police areas in England and Wales. Matters to be covered in the Plan will include setting performance objectives and issuing guidance. The Plan is laid before Parliament.

A National Criminal Intelligence Service (NCIS) has existed on a non-statutory basis for some years. Since April 1998, following the enactment of the Police Act 1997, it operates under the regulatory framework provided by that Act.

The NCIS has no active policing role as such. Its main purpose is in regard to the gathering and processing of intelligence, particularly in relation to offences that concern more than one police area. Often the intelligence will concern organised criminal activities such as football hooliganism, drug dealing, pornography, fraud and car theft.

Under s2(2) of the 1997 Act the functions of the NCIS are stated as being to:

1. gather, store and analyse information in order to provide criminal intelligence;
2. provide criminal intelligence to police forces in Great Britain, the Royal Ulster

Constabulary, the National Crime Squad (NCS) (see below) and other law enforcement agencies; and

3. act in support of such police forces, the Royal Ulster Constabulary, the NCS and other law enforcement agencies carrying out their criminal intelligence activities. For these purposes 'law enforcement agency' includes, inter alia, any government department.

Within the statutory framework the NCIS operates under the supervision of the Service Authority for the NCIS, which is charged with the task of maintaining the NCIS. The Service Authority has 19 members (although more may be appointed by the Secretary of State or co-opted by NCIS itself). The membership of the Authority reflects the tripartite nature of police force regulation generally, comprising those drawn from the police, police authorities and those appointed by the Secretary of State.

Under s3(1) the NCIS Service Authority is under a duty to ensure that the NCIS operates in a manner that is efficient and effective. The Secretary of State will establish long term objectives for the NCIS: s26. It is then for the Authority, in consultation with the Director-General of the NCIS (see below), the NCS Service Authority (see below), persons whom it considers to represent the interests of the authorities who between them maintain the police forces in Great Britain and the Royal Ulster Constabulary, and the Commissioners of Customs and Excise, to set the more immediate objectives for NCIS at the beginning of each financial year.

The NCIS Service Authority is also under a duty to draft an annual plan ('the service plan') detailing how the objectives are to be maintained, and including a statement of the Authority's priorities for the year. The service plan should also include details of any objectives determined by the Secretary of State under s26; any objectives determined by the Authority under s3; and any performance targets established by the Authority, whether in compliance with a direction under s27 or otherwise. In carrying out its functions the Service Authority will have to have regard to any objectives determined by the Secretary of State under s26 of the 1997 Act, any objectives determined by the Authority under s3, any performance targets established by the Authority, whether in compliance with a direction under s27 or otherwise, and any service plan issued by the Authority under s4. In its annual report the NCIS Service Authority will assess the extent to which the service plan has been carried out.

The Secretary of State will receive copies of the service plan and annual report, and can issue directions to the NCIS Service Authority with which it must comply. The Act empowers the Secretary of State, if it appears to him to be expedient in the interests of public safety or order so to do, to order a chief constable to provide for reinforcements for another police force.

In addition to determining objectives for the NCIS, the Secretary of State may direct the NCIS Service Authority to establish levels of performance ('performance targets') to be aimed at in seeking to achieve these objectives; and can issue codes of practice relating to the discharge by the NCIS Service Authority of its functions. Section 31 also empowers the Secretary of State to order the NCIS to produce for him a report on any specific issue, and s32 grants him a similar power in relation to the Director-General of NCIS.

Following changes introduced by the Criminal Justice and Police Act 2001, the Director-General of the NCIS is appointed by the Secretary of State. In general terms a person is eligible for appointment as Director-General if he holds the rank of chief constable in a police force in Great Britain or in the Royal Ulster Constabulary, is the Commissioner, an Assistant Commissioner or a Deputy Assistant Commissioner of Police of the Metropolis. The Secretary of State may call upon the Director-General of the NCIS to retire in the interests of efficiency or effectiveness. The Secretary of State can also order an inspection of the NCIS by the inspectors of constabulary if he thinks this necessary.

After the end of each financial year, the Director-General is required to submit to the NCIS Service Authority a general report on the activities of the NCIS during that year. Section 22 of the 1997 Act specifically provides for the Director-General of the NCIS to provide for collaboration agreements between forces where it appears to him that 'any police functions can more efficiently or effectively be discharged by members of NCIS and members of their respective forces ... acting jointly'. This collaboration may extend to the sharing of premises, equipment or other material or facilities. Under s23 the Director-General also has a general power to provide constables or other assistance for the purposes of enabling a police force or the National Crime Squad to meet any special demand on its resources.

Under the terms of the Security Service Act 1996, the Security Service is given the function of acting in support of the activities of police forces and other law enforcement agencies in the prevention and detection of serious crime. The participation of the Security Services will be co-ordinated by the NCIS.

Part II of the 1997 Act provided for the establishment of a National Crime Squad (NCS), with effect from April 1998. Unlike the NCIS, the NCS is a new body that brings together the operations of six regional crime squads. In simplistic terms it might be seen as the operational arm of the NCIS in that it carries out policing activities related to tackling serious organised crime. The regulatory framework within which the NCS operates is very similar to that created for the NCIS. The day-to-day running of the NCS is under the control of a Director-General, whilst the responsibility for maintaining the NCS rests with the NCS Service Authority. Again the membership of that Authority reflects the tripartite model for the regulation of police forces generally. To ensure proper co-ordination and co-operation between the NCIS and the NCS the two service authorities share the same core membership. Under s48(3), the NCS may, at the request of a chief officer of police of a police force in England and Wales, act in support of the activities of his force in the prevention and detection of serious crime; and, at the request of the Director-General of the NCIS, act in support of the activities of the NCIS.

7.9 Judicial control of police forces

As public officers, chief constables are, in theory, subject to control by the courts through the process of judicial review. In reality, however, the courts have shown themselves reluctant to intervene and order a chief constable to exercise his discretion in respect of police policy in a particular way. In *R* v *Metropolitan Police Commissioner, ex parte Blackburn* (above) Raymond Blackburn sought an order of mandamus compelling the Commissioner to enforce the law against illegal gambling. The Court of Appeal held that while there might be extreme cases where the courts would issue orders of mandamus directed at the Commissioner, as a general rule day-to-day policing policies were a matter for the police alone. By the time this matter reached the Court of Appeal the policy of the Metropolitan Police had been altered. As Lord Denning commented (at p136):

'... it is for the Commissioner of Police of the Metropolis, or the chief constable, as the case may be, to decide in any particular case whether inquiries should be pursued, or whether an arrest should be made, or a prosecution brought. It must be for him to decide on the disposition of his force and the concentration of his resources on any particular crime or area. No court can or should give him direction on such a matter. He can also make policy decisions and give effect to them, as, for instance, was often done when prosecutions were not brought for attempted suicide. But there are some policy decisions with which, I think, the courts in a case can, if necessary, interfere.'

A similar non-interventionist approach was taken, again by a Court of Appeal led by Lord Denning MR in *R* v *Chief Constable of Devon and Cornwall, ex parte CEGB* [1981] 3 WLR 807. The case arose because the Electricity Board was unable to carry out a survey of farmland as a possible site for a nuclear power station, due to the continuing activities of objectors. In a written reply to complaints from the Board, the chief constable stated that he was unwilling to act against the objectors in the absence of stronger evidence of illegal action on their part. The Board applied for an order of mandamus to compel the chief constable to act, but this was refused by the Divisional Court. The Board appealed to the Court of Appeal. In upholding this decision Lord Denning MR stated:

'Notwithstanding all that I have said, I would not give any orders to the chief constable or his men. It is of the first importance that the police should decide on their own responsibility what action should be taken in any particular situation. ...The decision of the chief constable not to intervene in this case was a policy decision with which I think the courts should not interfere.'

The Master of the Rolls did, however, express the hope that the chief constable would decide to use his men to clear the obstructors off the site or at any rate help the Board to do so.

In *R* v *Chief Constable of Sussex, ex parte International Trader's Ferry Ltd* [1999] 1 All ER 129, which concerned large-scale public demonstrations, by individuals opposed to the export of livestock for slaughter on the continent, circumstances had necessitated the deployment of considerable police manpower in order to maintain order and ensure that the trade could continue unhindered. The chief constable gave notice that, in the interests of the efficient use of resources, he was only prepared to provide police protection to such shipments on two consecutive days per week, or four consecutive days per fortnight. Without police intervention the demonstrators would effectively prevent the export of livestock from the ports affected. The applicant company contended that the decision of the chief constable regarding the deployment of resources was unreasonable as that term is understood in domestic administrative law, and also that it amounted to a violation of the right to free movement of goods under the EC Treaty. Rejecting these arguments Lord Slynn observed that the chief constable had the power to deploy his resources as he saw fit, including the taking of action that impinged on the rights of citizens to pursue ostensibly lawful activities. He continued:

'In a situation where there are conflicting rights and the police have a duty to uphold the law the police may, in deciding what to do, have to balance a number of factors, not the least of which is the likelihood of a serious breach of the peace being committed. That balancing involves the exercise of judgment and discretion. The courts have long made it clear that, though they will readily review the way in which decisions are reached, they will respect the margin of appreciation or discretion which a Chief Constable has. He knows through his officers the local situation, the availability of officers and his financial resources, the other demands on the police in the area at different times. ... It is my opinion wrong to over-emphasise particular areas where he might have done more or, as the Divisional Court said, where other chief constables might have reacted in a somewhat different way to particular aspects of the problem. The overall picture must be regarded. ... Here he did carry out a balancing exercise as he was required to do. He allocated his men on a carefully considered basis. He has not been shown to have ignored relevant facts or taken account of irrelevant factors in a way which vitiates his overall decisions. These decisions have not been shown to be unreasonable in a *Wednesbury* sense.'

Lord Hoffmann, commenting upon the need for the chief constable to take a balanced view of the needs of the area for which he was responsible, added:

'The fact that a chief constable considers that certain resources would be needed to prevent some kind of criminal behaviour does not entail that he is obliged to provide them. He might, for example, decide that the only way to eliminate muggings on the streets of Brighton or burglaries in Rottingdean would be to have many more constables on patrol and spend large sums on vehicles and communication equipment. This cannot create a duty to find the resources at the expense of other policing activity. I can see no distinction between the interests of ITF in obtaining protection from demonstrators and those of the citizens of Brighton and Rottingdean in obtaining protection from muggers and burglars.'

Reluctance has also been shown as regards intervening in matters of internal management. In *Vince and Another v Chief Constable of Dorset Police* [1993] 1 WLR 415 the plaintiffs sought a declaration that the chief constable of Dorset was, by virtue of s36(1) of the 1984 Act, under a duty to appoint a sufficient number of custody officers so as to ensure that there would always be one available at each designated station. The plaintiffs also sought a declaration that it would be unlawful for the chief constable to appoint an acting sergeant as a custody officer under s36(3) of the 1984 Act. At first instance the first declaration in relation to s36(1) was granted, but not that in relation to s36(3). On appeal by the chief constable and cross-appeal by the plaintiffs, the Court of Appeal held, allowing the appeal and (by a majority) dismissing the cross-appeal, that whilst s36(1) created a duty to appoint a custody officer at each designated station, the chief constable had a discretion as to the number of additional officers to be appointed. The cross-appeal was dismissed on the ground that the plaintiffs had not produced evidence of an acting sergeant being appointed as a custody officer, hence the question was academic, and the Court would not express a final opinion. Steyn LJ (dissenting) expressed the view that the Royal Commission on Criminal Justice ought to consider the implications of the decision given the crucial role played by custody officers. In particular he felt that the Court should have indicated its view that acting sergeants should not be appointed to such a position. See *R* v *Oxford, ex parte Levey* (1986) The Times 1 November; *Hill* v *Chief Constable of West Yorkshire* [1988] 2 All ER 238.

8

Judicial Review of Executive Action

8.1 Introduction

As will have been seen from Chapter 3 two of the key principles underpinning constitutional law are the doctrine of the separation of powers and the concept of the rule of law. An examination of judicial review of executive action provides an opportunity to see both of these principles in operation. Historically the High Court has always claimed the right at common law to review the legality of action taken by 'inferior bodies' or bodies of limited jurisdiction. In the past this would typically have involved judicial review of the decisions of Justices of the Peace where it was claimed that they had exceeded their powers. The High Court developed this jurisdiction to encompass review of other administrative agencies, such as local commissioners, boards of works, education boards, tribunals and local authorities. During the twentieth century the jurisdiction has been extended significantly to encompass ministers exercising both statutory and prerogative powers, and regulatory bodies acting in the public interest, notwithstanding their lack of statutory underpinning. These developments have given rise to a body of principles that, collectively, are known as administrative law.

   The essence of the jurisdiction is that the High Court has the power to review the actions of an executive or public law body to determine whether or not that body has acted within the scope of its powers (ie acted 'ultra vires'). Where it is found to have exceeded its powers its determination (or more accurately its purported determination) can be quashed by the court granting one of the special public law remedies such as a quashing order, formerly known as an order of certiorari.

The link with basic constitutional principles should be apparent. By the process of judicial review the courts are acting as a check upon the executive – providing a stark and practical illustration of the separation of powers in operation. By ensuring that executive bodies act within the scope of their powers the courts are also upholding the rule of law, ensuring that the executive cannot act in a manner that is arbitrary and without any legal justification, and ensuring that they are not 'above the law'. It is also possible to discern a link with parliamentary sovereignty in as much as most executive bodies will be exercising statutory powers and the reviewing court will be seeking to ensure that Parliament's will is being carried out by the executive body. For an executive body to assume a power not granted by Parliament, or to exercise such a power in a manner not intended by Parliament, would be to call into question the ultimate authority vested in the legislature by the British constitution.

The actual procedure to be followed by a person seeking to invoke the aid of the courts by way of an application for judicial review, and the remedies available thereby, are considered later in this chapter. For the moment our concern is with the grounds upon which an application might be made. On what basis can it be alleged that an executive body has acted ultra vires?

The ultra vires doctrine

In very general terms action can be ultra vires because it is incompatible with the express limits laid down in an enabling Act, or because it is incompatible with the implied limits that attach to the power provided for in the enabling Act. Of the implied limits there are some that relate to the way in which a decision is made (ie the procedure leading up to the decision) and others that relate to the actual decision itself (ie the reasonableness of the decision), although it would be inaccurate to suggest that the two types of implied limit were mutually exclusive.

In considering what follows it is important to bear in mind that the purpose of judicial review is not to provide some sort of appeal from the decisions taken by the executive. The courts are not there to provide a second opinion. Judicial review is concerned with the legality of executive action. If an executive decision is vitiated by illegality, whether procedural or substantive, it can be struck down. A court exercising its power of judicial review should not be concerned with the merits of the executive action in question (ie whether or not it was a 'good' decision). Further, it should be borne in mind that even if an applicant succeeds in persuading a court that, for example, a minister has exceeded his powers in making a particular decision, the court will simply quash the decision. It does not substitute its own decision for that of the minister. The minister remains free to determine the issue again. He might still find against the interests of the applicant. Provided, on this second occasion, he acts within the limits of his powers the courts will not have any basis on which to intervene.

8.2 Breach of express statutory requirements

In administrative law the term jurisdiction can most readily be equated with power. Inferior bodies, created by statute, are bodies of 'limited jurisdiction' because they can only do what they are empowered to do by the terms of their enabling Acts. An Act may provide a tribunal with the power to determine the rent to be paid for furnished accommodation in the city of Coventry. If one examines that provision it will be apparent that the statute has in fact imposed three express limits on the power of the tribunal. The first is that its power relates to the setting of rent levels; the second is that it is a power only to be applied in respect of furnished accommodation; the third is the geographical limitation to properties lying within the city boundaries of Coventry. The tribunal could act ultra vires if it failed to observe any one of these express limits. Hence if it determined that a dwelling in Wolverhampton was actually within the city of Coventry and proceeded to determine the level of rent to be paid it would clearly be usurping a power that it does not have. The property owner could (in the absence of any statutory right of appeal) apply for judicial review of the decision on the basis that it was ultra vires the enabling Act.

As noted above judicial review is concerned with legality, not merits, hence the courts would not normally review a tribunal's findings of fact, but in the example given the types of error illustrated are sometimes called 'jurisdictional' because they relate to facts upon which the jurisdiction of the tribunal or decision-maker depends. The courts will not allow an inferior body to make a mistake of fact that results in it purporting to exercise a jurisdiction it does not possess. In *R* v *Fulham, Hammersmith and Kensington Rent Tribunal, ex parte Zerek* [1951] 2 KB 1 a rent tribunal was empowered to assess the correct level of rent payable for unfurnished lettings, and proceeded to reduce the rent payable to a landlord, who contested its decision on the basis that it had no jurisdiction to set a rent because the letting was in fact furnished. The Divisional Court refused his application for certiorari to quash the tribunal's determination, but in the course of so doing Lord Goddard CJ stated:

> '... if a certain state of facts has to exist before an inferior tribunal have jurisdiction, they can inquire into the facts in order to decide whether or not they have jurisdiction, but cannot give themselves jurisdiction by a wrong decision upon them; and this court may, by means of proceedings for certiorari, inquire into the correctness of the decision.'

Again in *White and Collins* v *Minister of Health* [1939] 2 KB 838, the Court of

Appeal considered the power of a local authority to exercise compulsory purchase powers over land not forming 'part of any park, garden, or pleasure ground'. The Court concluded that the question of whether an area of land did, or did not, compromise part of a park or pleasure ground was one of jurisdictional fact. The local authority's decision on such a matter had to be open to challenge in the courts, otherwise it would have been able to exercise its powers of compulsory purchase over any land it chose to, simply by determining that the land did not, in its view, comprise any part of a park etc.

By contrast, if a tribunal sets a particular level of rent for furnished accommodation and the landlord's only objection is the fact that he thinks it is too low in light of the quality of the furnishings provided, the courts will not intervene, unless the rent set is so low as to amount to an unreasonable decision. In setting the rent the tribunal has exercised its powers as required by statute. The fact that the court might think the rent level a little too high or low would not of itself render the tribunal's decision unlawful – again its is a question of legality, not merits.

Other express limits in statutes may be far more straightforward to deal with. If a statute provides that a tribunal can make awards of compensation up to £1,000, an award in a single case of £3,000 will clearly be ultra vires. The tribunal simply does not have the power to make any such award.

8.3 Natural justice

For centuries, at common law, the courts have developed and applied the rules of natural justice, traditionally seen as encompassing two propositions: audi alteram partem – no man is to be condemned without a hearing; and nemo judex in causa sua – no man should sit as a judge in his own case. What has been of particular significance since the late nineteenth century is the willingness of the courts, albeit hesitantly at times, to apply these principles to public bodies making decisions affecting citizens, whether in connection with their private property rights, or their public law rights arising under statutes.

The aim of the courts has been to try to ensure that public bodies adopt fair procedures, although as will be seen the questions of when natural justice should be observed and what observance requires in practical terms have proved problematic. Underpinning the issue of natural justice is the ultra vires doctrine. Subject to any express procedural requirements laid down by statute, the courts will assume that statutory powers are to be exercised on the basis of a fair procedure having been followed. The requirement of a fair procedure can almost be seen as jurisdictional. Unless a fair procedure has been followed the decision-making body does not have the power to make a decision – the fair procedure is a pre-condition to the exercise of discretion.

The emergence of a duty to act fairly

The decision often cited as the basis for the modern law relating to fairness in executive decision-making is that of the House of Lords in *Ridge* v *Baldwin* [1964] AC 40. Charles Ridge had been dismissed from his position as chief constable of the County Borough of Brighton by the local watch committee. He contended before the House of Lords that the principles of natural justice applied to the exercise of powers to dismiss him, and that these principles had been breached by not allowing him to know the full case against him, and by not allowing him to put his case properly. The House of Lords allowed his appeal, holding that natural justice did apply and had not been observed. Lord Reid identified three types of case involving dismissal from a position, and explained the way in which the rules of natural justice might, or might not, apply in each case.

First, there were what he described as 'master and servant' cases where natural justice did not really have any relevance. A master was free to dispense with a servant's services as he wished, without granting the latter any hearing. The servant's remedy lay in an action for breach of contract (hence the creation of industrial tribunals). Second, there were cases where individuals held office 'at pleasure', such as Crown servants. Such persons had no right to be heard before being dismissed (but note internal Civil Service safeguards). Third, there were cases, like that of Charles Ridge, where an individual was being stripped of some office or status. Lord Reid stated that there was, in his view, an unbroken line of authority to the effect that a man could not be denied an office, without first being told what it was that was being alleged against him, and being given an opportunity of putting his defence or providing an explanation.

Of the judicial/administrative dichotomy, Lord Reid explained that previous cases may have been wrongly decided by courts assuming that certiorari was only available to quash a decision, arrived at following a procedure that had breached natural justice, where the decision-making body was acting 'judicially'. He suggested that the 'judicial' element should be deduced from the nature of the power being exercised. In short, the applicability of the rules of natural justice should not depend so much on a sterile academic classification of powers as administrative or judicial, but on the importance of what was at stake for the individual whose rights were affected by the decision.

Application of the rules to administrative procedures

Another key development in the application of the principles of natural justice to executive actions has been the recognition that it is not just traditional property rights that attract the protection of the rules. In *R* v *Deputy Governor of Parkhurst Prison, ex parte Leech* [1988] 1 All ER 485 the applicants sought judicial review of the decisions of a prison governor in relation to his imposition of punishments for breach of prison rules, alleging that he had acted in breach of natural justice. The

House of Lords held that in exercising his statutory powers to discipline prisoners, a prison governor was amenable to judicial review, because he was exercising a power which affected the legitimate expectations or rights of citizens, and such a power had to be exercised in accordance with the rules of natural justice. In the course of his speech, Lord Bridge stressed the significance of the rights affected as the key to the application of natural justice:

> 'Can it then be right for the court to refuse jurisdiction to afford what seems prima facie to be both the appropriate and the necessary remedy on the ground of "public policy"? My Lords ... It may be a virtual certainty that a number of trouble makers will take every opportunity to exploit and abuse the jurisdiction. But that is only one side of the coin. On the other side it can hardly be doubted that governors and deputy governors dealing with the offences against discipline may occasionally fall short of the standards of fairness which are called for in the performance of any judicial function. Nothing, I believe, is so likely to generate unrest among ordinary prisoners as a sense that they have been treated unfairly and have no effective means of redress. If a prisoner has a genuine grievance arising from disciplinary proceedings unfairly conducted, his right to petition a faceless authority in Whitehall for a remedy will not be of much comfort to him. Thus, I believe, it is at least possible that any damage to prison discipline that may result from frivolous and vexatious applications for judicial review may be substantially offset by the advantages which access to the court will provide for the proper ventilation of genuine grievances and perhaps also that the availability of the court's supervisory role may have the effect on the conduct of judicial proceedings by governors which it appears to have had in the case of boards of visitors of enhancing the standards of fairness observed ... I am firmly of the opinion that, if the social consequences of the availability of judicial review to supervise governors' disciplinary awards are ... detrimental to the proper functioning of the prison system ... it lies in the province of the legislature, not of the judiciary, to exclude the court's jurisdiction.'

It may well be the case that the application of the rules of natural justice is in some way gradual, in the sense that the more a decision or process is seen as being 'administrative' as opposed to 'judicial' the less proscriptive the courts will be in terms of reading in requirements of procedural fairness. The same applies where a litigant is seen as applying to a tribunal for a 'privilege' as opposed to situations where he is acting to protect a more substantive right. Hence in *R* v *Gaming Board for Great Britain, ex parte Benaim and Khaida* [1970] 2 QB 417 the decision of the Board refusing the applicants a gaming licence was upheld even though they had not been given reasons for the refusal or notified of the case they had to answer. As Lord Denning subsequently explained in *Breen* v *AEU* [1971] 1 All ER 1148:

> 'If a man seeks a privilege to which he has no particular claim ... then he can be turned away without a word. He need not be heard. No explanation need be given ...'

In *McInnes* v *Onslow-Fane* [1978] 1 WLR 1520 Megarry V-C expressed the view that the Board dealing with an application for a boxing manager's licence was under a duty to act fairly, but that did not necessitate granting an oral hearing, or informing the applicant of the case against him. It merely required the body making the decision to do so honestly, without bias and caprice. See further *Central Council for Education and Training in Social Work* v *Edwards* (1978) The Times 5 May (an applicant for a place on a polytechnic course held to have no right to a hearing, or to be given the reasons for being denied a place).

The concept of legitimate expectation

The factors adverted to above, such as the 'administrative' nature of the process impugned, the rights and privileges dichotomy, have led the courts towards the development of a doctrine of a concept of 'legitimate expectation' as a basis for determining whether or not intervention the grounds of breach of natural justice can be justified.

Four different bases for legitimate expectation can be identified. The first involves those cases where the litigant asserts a substantive right, in the form of an entitlement that should not be denied him. In *R* v *Secretary of State for the Home Department, ex parte Khan* [1985] 1 All ER 40 the Home Office published a circular indicating the criteria that would be applied when persons in the United Kingdom wished to adopt a child from abroad. The applicant, who sought to adopt the child of a relative who lived in Pakistan, applied for an entry clearance certificate for the child, but his request was refused by the Secretary of State who applied criteria other than those set out in the circular. The applicant applied for judicial review of the Secretary of State's refusal, contending that he had a 'legitimate expectation', arising out of the circular, that the procedure set out therein would be followed. The Secretary of State claimed that his discretion in such matters was unfettered. The court held that, provided the circular did not conflict with the Minister's statutory duty, he was under a duty to apply the criteria and could only resile from the provisions of the circular if there was: (i) an overriding public interest that he should do so; and (ii) interested persons were first afforded a hearing. In the circumstances the court felt that the Secretary of State had acted unfairly and unreasonably in deciding the applicant's case after applying criteria different from those set out in the circular. This first category appears, therefore, to involve cases where the litigant can say that because of an existing published policy he has an identifiable substantive right – not just as to the procedure to be followed, but as to a decision being made in his favour provided established criteria are met.

A second category arises where the applicant's interest lies in some ultimate benefit that he hopes to attain or, possibly, retain. This classification can be traced back to decisions such as *Schmidt* v *Secretary of State for Home Affairs* [1969] 2 Ch 149, where two Scientology students, who were refused an extension of their permission to remain in the United Kingdom when their right to remain had expired, complained that they had not been granted a hearing. The Court of Appeal held that there had been no breach of natural justice, Lord Denning stating that as they had no right to remain in the country, they had no legitimate expectation of being granted a hearing. Significantly, however, he was willing to accept that the situation might have been different if their right to stay had been revoked before its expiry, ie they had had an expectation that their right to remain would not be revoked prior to its expiry.

The third category arises where the concept of legitimate expectation is used to refer to the fair procedure itself, ie the applicant claims to have a legitimate expectation that the public body will act fairly towards him. The fourth category involves those cases where a particular procedure, not otherwise required by law, has to be followed as a result of a previous promise or course of dealing. For example, in *Attorney-General of Hong Kong* v *Ng Yuen Shiu* [1983] 2 All ER 346 the Hong Kong government had made public its changed policy towards illegal immigrants, stating that each one, if he or she came forward, would be interviewed and, although no guarantee would be given that they would not subsequently be removed, each case would be treated on its merits. The respondent, who had entered Hong Kong illegally in 1976, was interviewed by an immigration officer and subsequently detained pending the making of a removal order. His appeal to the immigration authorities was dismissed without a hearing, but the Court of Appeal of Hong Kong granted the respondent an order of prohibition preventing his removal, pending a proper hearing of his case, a decision in respect of which the Attorney-General of Hong Kong appealed to the Privy Council. Quashing the order of prohibition, the Privy Council held that, assuming there was no general right in an alien to have a hearing in accordance with the rules of natural justice before the making of a removal order against him, a person was nevertheless entitled to a fair hearing before a decision adversely affecting his interests was made by a public official or body if he had a legitimate or reasonable expectation of being accorded such a hearing. Such an expectation might be based on some statement or undertaking by, or on behalf of, the public authority which had the duty of making the decision if the authority had, through its officers, acted in a way which would make it unfair or inconsistent with good administration to deny the person affected an inquiry into his case. That principle was as much applicable where the person affected was an alien as where he was a British subject, because a public authority was bound by its undertaking as to the procedure it would follow, provided those undertakings did not conflict with its statutory duty. It followed that the government undertaking that each case would be treated on its merits had not been implemented since the respondent had been given no opportunity to explain the humanitarian grounds on which he might have been allowed to remain in Hong Kong, in particular that he was a partner in a business which employed a large number of workers.

The impact of the Human Rights Act 1998

As is explained more fully in Chapter 9, the Human Rights Act 1998 places every public body under a duty to abide by certain articles of the European Convention on Human Rights. Of particular significance here is art 6 of the Convention, which provides that a citizen has the right to a 'fair and public hearing within a reasonable time by an independent and impartial tribunal' where his civil rights and obligations are to be determined. In *R v Secretary of State for the Environment, Transport and the Regions, ex parte Holding and Barnes plc; R v Same, ex parte Alconbury Developments Ltd and Others; Secretary of State for the Environment, Transport and the Regions* v *Legal and General Assurance Society Ltd* [2001] 2 All ER 929 Lord Clyde regarded it as clear that art 6 rights were engaged where what was impugned was administrative action, ie an exercise of discretionary power, provided the action directly affected an applicant's civil rights and obligations, was of a genuine and serious nature. Hence the rules of natural justice at common law are not strengthened by the jurisprudence of Strasbourg in appropriate cases.

In assessing whether or not a decision-making process is fair the courts will consider the process as a whole, not just the first instance hearing. As Simon Brown LJ observed in *R (On the Application of Adlard)* v *Secretary of State for the Environment* [2002] EWCA Civ 735:

> '... I can find no warrant, whether in domestic or in Strasbourg jurisprudence, for concluding that where ... the administrative decisions taken at first instance are generally likely to turn on questions of judgment and discretion rather than on findings of fact, the statutory scheme must provide for an oral hearing at that initial stage ... The remedy of judicial review in my judgment amply enables the court to correct any injustice it perceives in an individual case. If, in short, the court were satisfied that exceptionally, on the facts of a particular case, [that a decision maker had] acted unfairly or unreasonably in denying an objector any or any sufficient oral hearing, the court would quash the decision and require such a hearing to be given.'

8.4 Aspects of a fair procedure

Express statutory requirements

Where Parliament lays down the procedure to be followed by an executive body in exercising its discretion the provisions of the statute will displace any common law requirements relating fair procedure. Where a body fails to comply with an express requirement relating to procedural matters such as time limits, the giving of notice of hearings, or the need to have evidence recorded in writing, the task of the court will be to determine whether or not the non-compliance is fatal to the legality of the decision-making body's determination. For these purposes procedural requirements can be allocated to one of two broad categories. Either the requirement will be seen as mandatory, where failure to observe the requirement will normally render any subsequent action void, or the requirement will be seen as directory, where failure to observe will not normally be fatal to the validity of the ensuing determination.

As regards making that distinction, Lord Penzance in *Howard* v *Boddington* (1877) 2 PD 203 offered the following advice:

> 'You cannot safely go further than that in each case you must look to the subject matter;

consider the importance of the provision that has been disregarded and the relation of that provision to the general object intended to be secured by the Act.'

Even when the distinction appears to have been made, and one has decided that a requirement must be mandatory because of its significance, one still has to bear in mind the doctrine of substantial compliance. This operates with the effect that, even though a requirement is generally mandatory, an inferior body's actions will not be invalidated because it has failed to comply with it in some minor way: see *Coney* v *Choice* [1975] 1 All ER 979.

Procedural requirements likely to be regarded as mandatory include:

1. A statutory requirement that a body should consult prior to using its powers is almost invariably regarded as mandatory by the courts: see *Agricultural, Horticultural and Forestry Industry Training Board* v *Aylesbury Mushrooms Ltd* [1972] 1 All ER 280 and *Grunwick Processing Laboratories* v *ACAS* [1978] AC 655.
2. The requirement that prior notice be given of a decision: see *R* v *Swansea City Council, ex parte Quietlynn* (1983) The Times 19 October.
3. The requirement that certain matters to be put in writing: see *Epping Forest District Council* v *Essex Rendering Ltd* [1983] 1 WLR 158.
4. A statutory requirement that notice of the right to appeal be given: see *London and Clydeside Estates Ltd* v *Aberdeen District Council* [1979] 3 All ER 876.

Procedural fairness at common law

A basic requirement of a fair administrative process is that those likely to be affected by decisions are given adequate notice that they are going to be made. Adequate notice allows an individual to prepare his case properly and conduct his affairs accordingly. The case law illustrates situations where the courts will intervene. In *Willis* v *Childe* (1851) 13 Beav 117 it was held that a school master, who was informed, a few hours before a meeting of the trustees was due to take place, that they would be considering representations from him on their decision to dismiss him, had been given inadequate notice of the meeting and its subsequent proceedings were of no effect. Similarly, in *Glynn* v *Keele University* [1971] 1 WLR 487, a breach of natural justice was held to have occurred where a student was fined by the University without first being told the reasons why or being granted a hearing, although relief was denied on other grounds.

Where natural justice requires some notice to be given of an impending decision, it also requires the decision-making body to provide some information as to the nature of the hearing, what is being determined etc. If this were otherwise, giving notice of the decision being taken would be pointless, as the individual would not be able to prepare his case properly. The logical extension of this line of reasoning is that if a decision-making body informs an individual that a hearing is to be held to consider 'X' and once at the hearing, the individual finds that the decision-making body has decided to deal with 'Y', there will have been a breach of natural justice because the decision-making body will not have kept to the terms of the notice given: see *Andrews* v *Mitchell* [1905] AC 78.

It is frequently assumed that, if natural justice or a duty to act fairly applies to a procedure, then an individual automatically has a right to be heard. This is not necessarily the case. Where a person's livelihood is at stake, or allegations have been made which amount to an attack on an individual's integrity, then representations will almost certainly have to be allowed. Where a privilege is being sought a hearing might not be justified. If an applicant is to be permitted to make any representations, compliance with a fair procedure should require that he is informed of the case against him, to the extent that there is one, so that he can tailor his submissions accordingly and, where appropriate, refute some of the allegations, correct mistakes, or explain away otherwise damaging evidence: see *Re Pergamon Press Ltd* [1971] Ch 388. The principal argument against disclosure will usually be the need to maintain confidentiality but, as the court held in *R* v *Department of Education and Science, ex parte Kumar* (1982) The Times 18 November, such objections can be overcome to some extent by the applicant being given an opportunity to comment on the gist of the allegations. In addressing the issue as to what might constitute the 'gist' of the evidence in any given case Lightman J observed in *R* v *Secretary of State for the Home Department, ex parte Harry* [1998] 3 All ER 360 (at p370g):

> '... what is sufficient to constitute the gist for one purpose may not be sufficient for another. When a fundamental right is in issue, a more expansive and informative summary may be called for. The detail required must depend on what ... fairness requires to enable the making of meaningful and focused representations ... Good administrative practice may call for the production of a document where this is necessary to avoid the risk of a legitimate sense of concern or grievance and there is no countervailing consideration of any weight and no legitimate reason for wishing to withhold it.'

Clearly the more that is at stake for the applicant, the greater the obligation to give notice of the case to be met. Hence in *R* v *Secretary of State for the Home Department, ex parte Mohammed Al Fayed* [1997] 1 All ER 228 the Court of Appeal (Kennedy LJ dissenting) held that the applicants ought to have been given an outline of the concerns harboured by the Home Secretary that caused him to believe that they were not of sufficiently good character to warrant having British citizenship bestowed upon them. Not only did the refusal amount to a slur upon their characters, but also it deprived them of the benefits of British and European Union citizenship.

It is again sometimes wrongly assumed that if natural justice requires a person to be allowed to make representations, they must take the form of an oral hearing. In fact, an oral hearing is the exception, not the rule. In many cases an individual can put all necessary evidence before a decision making body in the form of written representations. A leading authority on this issue is the decision of the House of Lords in *Lloyd and Others* v *McMahon* [1987] 2 WLR 821, a case concerning the surcharging of councillors who refused to set a lawful rate within the required time limit, causing consequent financial loss to the authority of which they were members. The House of Lords held that there was clear evidence of wilful misconduct by the councillors, and that the district auditor had not acted unfairly in refusing to allow them an oral hearing prior to his issuing of the certificate under the Local Government Finance Act 1982. As Lord Keith stated (at p872):

'It is easy to envisage cases where an oral hearing would clearly be essential in the interests of fairness, for example where an objector states that he has personal knowledge of some facts indicative of wilful misconduct on the part of a councillor. In that situation justice would demand that the councillor be given an opportunity to depone to his own version of the facts. In the present case the district auditor had arrived at his provisional view upon the basis of the contents of documents, minutes of meetings and reports submitted to the council from the auditor's department and their own officers. ... No facts contradictory of or supplementary to the contents of the documents were or are relied on by either side. If the appellants had attended an oral hearing they would no doubt have reiterated the sincerity of their motives from the point of view of advancing the interests of the inhabitants of Liverpool. It seems unlikely, having regard to the position adopted by their counsel on this matter before the Divisional Court, that they would have been willing to reveal or answer questions about the proceedings of their political caucus. The sincerity of the appellants' motives is not something capable of justifying or excusing failure to carry out a statutory duty, or of making reasonable what is otherwise an unreasonable delay in carrying out such a duty. In all the circumstances I am of opinion that the district auditor did not act unfairly, and that the procedure which he followed did not involve any prejudice to the appellants.'

As Lord Mustill later observed in *R* v *Secretary of State for the Home Department, ex parte Doody and Others* [1993] 3 WLR 154, in relation to whether or not a prisoner sentenced to mandatory life imprisonment should be given the opportunity to make representations prior to the Home Secretary's determination of the minimum period to be served:

'What does fairness require in the present case? My Lords I think it unnecessary to refer by name or to quote from, any of the oft-cited authorities in which the courts have explained what is essentially an intuitive judgment. They are far too well known. From them, I derive the following. (1) Where an Act of Parliament confers an administrative power there is a presumption that it will be exercised in a manner which is fair in all the circumstances. (2) The standards of fairness are not immutable. They may change with the passage of time, both in the general and in their application to decisions of a particular type. (3) The principles of fairness are not to be applied identically by rote in every situation. What fairness demands depends on the context of the decision, and this is to be taken into account in all its aspects. (4) An essential feature of the context is the statute which creates the discretion, as regards both its language and the shape of the legal and administrative system within which the decision is taken. (5) Fairness will very often require that a person who may be adversely affected by the decision will have an opportunity to make representations on his own behalf either before the decision is taken with a view to producing a favourable result, or after it is taken, with a view to procuring its modification, or both. (6) Since the person affected cannot usually make worthwhile representations without knowing what factors may weigh against his interests fairness will very often require that he is informed of the gist of the case that he has to answer.'

In *R* v *Army Board of the Defence Council, ex parte Anderson* [1991] 3 All ER 375, Taylor LJ summarised what he regarded as the correct approach to ensure fairness in hearings where the tribunal was exercising a disciplinary function, not merely making an administrative decision. He observed that an oral hearing was not essential to fairness but was probably required where there were substantial differences on issues of fact that could not be resolved on the papers. It was clear in that particular case that the respondents were not entitled to adopt, as an inflexible policy, the approach that oral hearings would never be permitted. The question of whether evidence should be tested by cross-examination stood or fell with the question of whether or not an oral hearing should be granted. Further, even if an oral hearing was not granted, a complainant should be given the opportunity to respond to the respondent body's findings of fact following its investigations, subject to public interest immunity.

As a rule, if an individual is afforded the right to make oral representations he will normally be allowed the right to cross-examine those giving evidence against him. The purpose of cross-examination, it should be remembered, is to test the veracity of evidence. In *University of Ceylon* v *Fernando* [1960] 1 All ER 631 the Privy Council held it was not a breach of natural justice for an inquiry into allegations of misconduct at examinations not to inform the plaintiff of his right to cross-examine a witness, but it may have been if the plaintiff had been denied permission to cross-examine the witness.

Whether or not a fair procedure at common law requires that a party should be permitted legal representation if he requests it will depend on what is at stake for the individual concerned as a result of the tribunal's decision. Where an individual's reputation or livelihood is at stake there may be a much stronger argument in favour of legal representation: see *Pett* v *Greyhound Racing Association* [1969] 1 QB 125. The same applies where the proceedings are disciplinary in character. In *R* v *Secretary of State for the Home Department, ex parte Tarrant* [1984] 1 All ER 799 it was held that, although a prisoner appearing before a board of visitors on a disciplinary charge did not have an automatic right to legal representation, the board did have a discretion to permit it. In that case it had been a breach of natural justice to deny the prisoner legal representation, given the grave nature of the charge and the consequences for the prisoner of his being found guilty.

Whether or not a hearing has been held prior to a decision being taken those affected will often want to have the reasons for the decision. Sometimes this may be out of natural interest and curiosity, sometimes because it is hoped that the reasons might reveal some illegality on the part of the decision-maker, opening the decision up to judicial review. The trend now is towards greater openness in decision-making, the courts approaching the issue on the basis of requiring reasons unless there are some compelling public policy reasons for their not being provided. A key development in the trend towards more open decision making was the House of Lords' decision in *R v Secretary of State for the Home Department, ex parte Doody and Others* (above). The Secretary of State, acting under s61 of the Criminal Justice Act 1967, had the power to determine the first date upon which prisoners who had received mandatory life sentences for murder might be considered for release (ie the point at which the 'penal element' of the sentence would expire). The procedure adopted involved the Secretary of State obtaining the views of the trial judge and the Lord Chief Justice prior to informing a prisoner of the first date for review of his continued detention. The effect was that a prisoner would then be aware of his minimum period of imprisonment. The applicants, each of whom was a prisoner serving a life sentence following conviction for murder, sought to challenge the decision of the Secretary of State in respect of the date set for review as regards their own cases. Inter alia they each sought a declaration to the effect that the Secretary of State should inform a prisoner of his reasons for departing from the judicial recommendation if this was what he intended to do. The House of Lords held that the Secretary of State was obliged to give reasons for departing from the period recommended by the judiciary as regards the 'penal element' of the sentence.

Lord Mustill, whilst confirming that there was no general legal duty to give reasons for an administrative decision, went on to observe that it was important that there should be 'an effective means of detecting the kind of error which would entitle the court to intervene' should a decision as to sentencing be wrong in law. In his Lordship's view, a requirement that reasons be given for departing from a judicial recommendation as to the minimum term could provide evidence of any such errors. Lord Mustill regarded *Payne v Lord Harris of Greenwich* [1981] 1 WLR 754 as reflecting an outmoded view of the duty to give reasons. In particular he felt that in the 13 years since that decision the perception of society's obligation towards persons serving prison sentences had changed noticeably, and that the trend in administrative law was now firmly towards openness in decision-making. He observed:

'There is no true tariff, or at least no tariff exposed to the public view which might give the prisoner an idea of what to expect. The announcement of his first review date arrives out of thin air, wholly without explanation. The distant oracle has spoken and that is that ... I doubt whether in the modern climate of administrative law such an entirely secret process could be justified.'

A useful summary of the current law was provided by Sedley J in *R v Higher Education Funding Council, ex parte Institute of Dental Surgery* [1994] 1 All ER 651, where he observed:

'1. There is no general duty to give reasons for a decision, but there are classes of case where there is such a duty.
2. One such class is where the subject matter is an interest so highly regarded by the law – for example personal liberty – that fairness requires that reasons, at least for particular decisions, be given as of right.

3. (a) Another such class is where the decision appears aberrant. Here fairness may require reasons so that the recipient may know whether the aberration is in the legal sense real (and so challengeable) or apparent.

(b) It follows that this class does not include decisions which are in themselves challengeable by reference only to the reasons for them. A pure exercise of academic judgment is such a decision.

(c) Procedurally, the grant of leave in such cases will depend upon prima facie evidence that something has gone wrong. The respondent may then seek to demonstrate that it is not so and that the decision is an unalloyed exercise of an intrinsically unchallengeable judgment. If the respondent succeeds, the application fails. If the respondent fails, relief may take the form of an order of mandamus to give reasons, or (if a justiciable flaw has been established) other appropriate relief.'

8.5 The rule against bias

The rule against bias is a common law doctrine that provides that no man should be a judge in his own cause. Where an applicant can provide the court with evidence of actual bias, the court should be willing to quash the decision in question, subject to any statutory considerations. In practice actual bias is rare, either because it is easily avoided by decision-makers disqualifying themselves, or because it is difficult to prove. Most cases of bias come within the categories of pecuniary interest or through interest or connection.

Automatic bias: pecuniary interest

In the majority of cases, pecuniary interest by a decision-maker in a matter subject to his influence is sufficient to invalidate any resulting determination. The leading case is *Dimes* v *Grand Junction Canal Proprietors* (1852) 3 HL Cas 759, where Lord Cottenham LC had affirmed decrees made by the Vice-Chancellor in litigation between Dimes and the canal proprietors. Dimes discovered that, despite the fact that the Lord Chancellor had for a long period held shares in the canal company in his own right and as trustee, he had continued to hear matters arising out of the litigation relying on the advice of the Master of the Rolls who sat with him. Dimes appealed to the House of Lords against all the decrees made by the Lord Chancellor on the ground that he was disqualified by interest. The House of Lords set aside the decrees issued by the Lord Chancellor on the ground of pecuniary interest. In the course of his speech Lord Campbell stated:

'No one can suppose that Lord Cottenham could be, in the remotest degree, influenced by the interest that he had in this concern; but, my Lords, it is of the last importance that the maxim that no man is to be a judge in his own cause should be held sacred. And that is not to be confined to a cause in which he has an interest. Since I have had the honour to be Chief Justice of the Court of Queen's Bench, we have again and again set aside proceedings in inferior tribunals because an individual, who had an interest in a cause, took a part in the decision. And it will have a most salutary influence on these tribunals when it is known that this High Court of last resort, in a case in which the Lord Chancellor of England had an interest, considered that his decree was on that account a decree not according to law, and was set aside. This will be a lesson to all inferior tribunals to take care not only that in their decrees they are not influenced by their personal interest, but to avoid the appearance of labouring under such an influence.'

The rule against pecuniary interest is subject to a number of qualifications. First, it is subject to a remoteness principle, to the effect that where the pecuniary interest is so minimal or indirect as to be of negligible significance, it will not be used as justification for invalidating a decision. Second, the operation of the rule against pecuniary interest may be affected by statute: see *R v Barnsley County Borough Licensing Justices, ex parte Barnsley and District Licensed Victuallers Association* [1960] 2 QB 167.

Automatic bias: connection with the parties or espousal of the cause in issue

In *R v Sussex Justices, ex parte McCarthy* [1924] 1 KB 256 a solicitor who was representing a client against McCarthy in a motoring accident also worked as a clerk to the Sussex justices who were trying McCarthy on a criminal charge arising out of the same motoring incident. When the justices retired to consider their verdict, the clerk retired with them and they convicted the defendant of dangerous driving. Quashing the conviction on the ground that the appearance of bias was fatal, Lord Hewart CJ uttered his famous dictum to the effect that justice not only had to be done, but had to be seen to be done. The point he was making was that, given the connection between the solicitor and the plaintiff, there could be no confidence in the impartiality of the proceedings. A modern parallel of this is provided by *R v Bow Street Metropolitan Stipendiary Magistrate, ex parte Pinochet Ugarte (No 2)* [1999] 1 All ER 577, where the House of Lords confirmed that automatic disqualification of a decision-maker on grounds of bias was not limited to cases of pecuniary interest alone. The rule also applied where the adjudicator was a supporter of, or was connected with, a cause or interest group involved in the case before him. In the *Pinochet* case Lord Hoffmann was held to have been automatically disqualified from sitting on the appeal arising out of the extradition hearings because he was a director of a charity linked to, and sharing the same aims as, Amnesty International, one of the parties to the litigation. Lord Browne-Wilkinson expressed the view that even though the matter at issue did not relate to money or economic advantage the rationale disqualifying a judge still applied.

In the light of Lord Browne-Wilkinson's comments it is submitted that cases such as *R v Sussex Justices, ex parte McCarthy* (above) might now be regarded as 'automatic disqualification' cases.

There is no reason to suppose that the extension of the automatic disqualification concept should not encompass quasi-judicial bodies such as tribunals. In

Metropolitan Properties Co v *Lannon* [1968] 3 All ER 304 a number of tenants applied to the rent officer to fix a fair rent for their flats. The landlord objected to the rent officer's decision and appealed to the rent assessment committee, the chairman of which was a solicitor who lived with his father, who was himself a tenant of the company that was associated with the landlords in the present case. The chairman's firm had from time to time acted for his father's fellow tenants against the associated company on matters similar to the ones in issue here; the chairman himself had assisted his father in writing to the rent officer. The committee fixed rents for the flats below that assessed by the experts and below that asked for by the tenants themselves. The Court of Appeal held that the committee's decision was vitiated by bias. It seems likely that if such facts were to come before the courts again this would be seen as a case warranting automatic disqualification.

Non-automatic disqualification: where the appearance of bias may lead to disqualification

In *Locabail (UK) Ltd* v *Bayfield Properties Ltd; Locabail (UK) Ltd* v *Waldorf Investment Corporation; Timmins* v *Gormley; Williams* v *Inspector of Taxes; R* v *Bristol Betting and Gaming Licensing Committee, ex parte O'Callaghan* [2000] 1 All ER 65 the court sought to offer some general guidance on factors that might or might not lead to a finding of bias in those cases where disqualification was not otherwise automatic. It was thought that no sensible objection could ever be based on factors such as religious persuasion, ethnic origin, gender, age, class, means or sexual orientation. The court doubted whether a challenge could ever succeed on the basis that the adjudicator had a particular social or educational background, employment history, political associations, was a member of any social, sporting or charitable bodies, or had Masonic associations. Also regarded as unimportant were: previous judicial decisions; extracurricular utterances; and membership of the same Inn, circuit or local Law Society. By contrast it was felt that a real danger of bias might arise where there was a friendship or personal animosity between the judge and a member of the public involved in a case, or if the judge had doubted the credibility of a party in previous proceedings in outspoken terms suggesting that he was unable to approach a party's evidence with an open mind, or if for any other reason there were real ground for doubting the judge's ability to ignore extraneous considerations and bring an objective judgment to bear on the issues before him.

Apparent bias can also arise where a decision-maker is involved at more than one stage in the decision-making process, for example at first instance and on appeal, or as investigator and judge: see *Hannam* v *Bradford Corporation* [1970] 1 WLR 937 and *R* v *Kent Police Authority, ex parte Godden* [1971] 2 QB 662. In *R* v *Barnsley Metropolitan Borough Council, ex parte Hook* [1976] 1 WLR 1052 the applicant, a market trader licensed by the local authority, was seen urinating in the street by two council workmen. The applicant had done this because the council lavatories were shut. Heated words were exchanged, and the incident was reported to the market manager, who wrote to the applicant revoking his licence. The applicant appealed unsuccessfully to two council committees, the market manager having been present whilst these committees had deliberated on the outcome of these appeals. The Divisional Court refused to grant certiorari on the ground that the revocation was merely an administrative act. The Court of Appeal held that the relief sought would be granted, on the basis that in revoking a trader's licence the council was under a duty to act judicially, the duty being inferred from the fact that the decision was one affecting the applicant's livelihood. The decision had been vitiated by the market manager's presence throughout the committees' proceedings, as this amounted to the prosecutor being present, in the absence of the accused, when the adjudicators were making their decisions.

There may be situations where those exercising discretion in respect of an applicant's rights have prior knowledge of the applicant or have otherwise been involved at an earlier stage in the decision-making process. In *R* v *Board of Visitors of Frankland Prison, ex parte Lewis* [1986] 1 All ER 272 the applicant, a prisoner who had been found guilty of an offence against prison discipline by the prison's board of visitors, subsequently discovered that the chairman of the board had also been involved in a consideration of his application to the parole board, and hence had knowledge of his background, in particular his previous convictions. Considering his application for judicial review of the board's finding of guilt on the basis that it was vitiated by bias, the court held that although prison boards of visitors were under a duty to act judicially when considering disciplinary hearings, a member was not disqualified from acting simply because he had acquired information about the prisoner in a different administrative capacity. Woolf J felt that it was inevitable that members of boards of visitors would know more about those appearing before them than, for example, magistrates, because of the administrative duties they frequently performed, such as considering the suitability of prisoners for release on parole. A board of visitors always had a discretion not to proceed with a hearing if it was of the opinion that, as presently constituted, it would be improper for it to proceed. He regarded it as significant that Parliament had constituted these bodies to act on the basis of their special knowledge of the prison system, thus their members should not be too ready to regard a general background knowledge of the prisoner as a ground for not adjudicating. In this case his Lordship felt that a reasonable and fair-minded person would not have regarded the chairman as disqualified.

The extent to which these decision have to be reconsidered following the incorporation of the European Convention on Human Rights by means of the Human Rights Act 1998 was considered in *Kingsley* v *United Kingdom* (2001) The Times 9 January. Whilst the Court of European Human Rights noted that the procedures adopted by the Gaming Board (who had revoked the applicant's licence) lacked the required appearance of impartiality, and thus caused a violation of the applicant's rights under art 6, those failings could have been cured if there had been sufficient judicial safeguards. That begged the question of whether judicial review provided a sufficient judicial safeguard in the circumstances. The Court observed that, although the Gaming Board had conceded the appearance of bias at the judicial review hearings, Jowitt J had taken the view at first instance that the test for bias was not satisfied and that, in any event, Parliament had not provided for any other body to make the decision in question – thus it was a case of inevitable bias. The Court of Appeal also recognised the appearance of bias but refused to quash the decision because the Gaming Board was not empowered to delegate the revocation decision to an independent panel. Hence the allegation of bias could not be cured be remitting the decision to the Gaming Board to be made again. On this basis the European Court of Human Rights concluded that there had been a violation of art 6(1) because the High Court and the Court of Appeal did not have full jurisdiction within the meaning of the case law on art 6 when they reviewed the panel's decision.

The key issue, therefore is the extent to which appeal or review processes can 'cure' any failure to comply with the requirements of art 6. In *Adan* v *Newham London Borough Council* [2001] 1 All ER 930 the Court of Appeal considered statutory provisions that empowered a local housing authority to determine applications for assistance under the Housing Act 1996. Applications were determined by a housing officer with a right of appeal to an appeal officer. A right to appeal on a point of law could be pursued further in the county court. Although it was accepted that the appeal officer did not possess the degree of impartiality required by art 6, the Court held that, viewing the process as a whole, the existence of a right of appeal to the county court ensured that the procedure was Convention compliant.

The test for bias

In cases of apparent bias that do not lead to automatic disqualification the test to be applied by the courts in order to determine whether or not proceedings are to be regarded as having been vitiated by bias has been developed through decisions such as *Director General of Fair Trading* v *The Proprietary Association of Great Britain (In Re Medicaments and Related Classes of Goods)* (2001) The Times 2 February. It was noted that the approach of the European Court of Human Rights was to decide whether, on an objective appraisal, the material facts gave rise to a legitimate fear that the judge might not have been impartial. For these purposes the material facts were not limited to those that were apparent to the applicant, but included those ascertained upon investigation by the court. This approached was approved by the House of Lords in *Porter* v *Magill; Weeks* v *Magill* [2002] 1 All ER 465, where the correct test to be applied by a court to determine whether or not there was a reasonable apprehension of bias (having first ascertained all the relevant circumstances) was confirmed as whether those circumstances would lead a fair-minded and informed observer to conclude that there was a real possibility that the tribunal was biased.

Strictly speaking this decision only alters the test for bias in those cases where Convention rights are at stake, but it is hard to imagine a case where an applicant would be alleging bias that would not involve a determination of his civil rights. In any event, to have two different tests, one for domestic purposes and one for Convention cases, would be hard to defend.

Even with a single, tolerably clear test for apparent bias the question of whether or not such bias had been established will depend on the facts of each case, regard being had to the proximity of the interest to the issue being decided. Where an apparent conflict of interest arises because a member of a decision-making body has an interest in the subject matter of the decision, or has a relevant pecuniary interest, the wise course of action for that member would be not only to abstain from partaking in the discussion and any voting, but also to withdraw whilst remaining members of the decision-making body concluded their deliberations.

8.6 Reasonableness and proportionality

Just as the ultra vires doctrine is built upon the assumption that no executive body is empowered by Parliament to act unfairly, so too is it built on the assumption that executive discretion is not to be exercised unreasonably. It is common to see these two elements, fairness and reasonableness, as alternative grounds for judicial review, but in truth they are very much interrelated. A decision can be attacked on grounds of unreasonableness because the decision-maker has taken into account irrelevant considerations, or has failed to take relevant considerations into account. Whilst this might result in an unreasonable decision, it can also be seen that the procedure leading up to the decision must have been defective, because the decision-maker did not review the evidence properly. The divisions are thus, to some extent, artificial and far from watertight, and many major decisions can as easily be placed under one heading as another.

The difficulty with unreasonableness as a basis for judicial review is that it is such a subjective concept. Opinions can obviously vary widely on whether a particular decision is reasonable or not. Judicial review is supposed to be concerned with the legality of a decision not its merits. Thus a public body can make a 'bad' decision with which people may disagree, but that does not necessarily mean it is an ultra vires decision. Determining the reasonableness of a decision, however, invariably involves questioning its merits, thus when one introduces unreasonableness as a ground of review, one is immediately asking judges to make value judgments about the quality of the decisions made by inferior bodies.

The Wednesbury *test*

For many years the basis for the test for reasonableness in English administrative law has been that derived from the Court of Appeal's decision in *Associated Provincial Picture Houses Ltd* v *Wednesbury Corporation Ltd* [1948] 1 KB 223. The local authority had the power to grant permission for the opening of cinemas, subject to such conditions as they saw fit to impose. The plaintiff sought a declaration that a condition imposed on a grant of permission to open one of their cinemas, namely that no child under the age of 15 was to be allowed in without an adult, was ultra vires. Lord Greene MR outlined the principles upon which the authority's decision might be open to attack. These were: not directing itself properly in law; not taking into account relevant considerations, or conversely taking into account irrelevant consideration; acting unreasonably; acting in bad faith; or acting in disregard of public policy. As regards the condition imposed by the defendant authority, Lord Greene thought it was important to bear in mind that Parliament had entrusted the local authority with the discretion to impose conditions because of its knowledge of the area's needs, and (impliedly) because having been elected it reflected the views of the area's inhabitants. He felt that courts should therefore be slow to intervene to quash a condition imposed by such a body, but should do so where a condition was seen to be unreasonable. This meant that the condition would have to be one that was so unreasonable, no reasonable authority would have imposed it, and to prove a case of that kind would require compelling evidence. He explained the concept in these terms:

'... discretion must be exercised reasonably. Now what does that mean? ... It appears to me quite clear that the matter dealt with by this condition was a matter which a reasonable authority would be justified in considering when they were making up their mind what condition should be attached to the grant of this licence. Nobody, at this time of day, could say that the well-being and the physical and moral health of children is not a matter which a local authority, in exercising their powers, can properly have in mind when those questions are germane to what they have to conside. ... It is clear that the local authority are entrusted by Parliament with the decision on a matter which the knowledge and experience of that authority can best be trusted to deal with. The subject matter with which the condition deals is one relevant for its consideration. They have considered it and come to a decision upon it. It is true to say that, if a decision on a competent matter is so unreasonable that no reasonable authority could ever have come to it. ... It is not what the court considers unreasonable, a different thing altogether. If it is what the court considers unreasonable, the court may very well have different views to that of a local authority on matters of high public policy of this kind. Some courts might think that no children ought to be admitted on Sundays at all, some courts might think the reverse, and all over the country I have no doubt on a thing of that sort honest and sincere people hold different views. The effect of the legislation is not to set up the court as an arbiter of the correctness of one view over another. It is the local authority that are set in that position and, provided they act, as they have acted, within the four corners of their jurisdiction, this court, in my opinion, cannot interfere ...'

Any applicant for judicial review seeking to establish unreasonableness on the part of a public body bears a heavy evidential burden. As Lord Greene observed in *Wednesbury*, 'to prove a case of that kind would require something overwhelming, and, in this case, the facts do not come anywhere near anything of that kind.' Some extreme cases present no difficulty. In *Short* v *Poole Corporation* [1926] Ch 66 the example was given of taking a decision to dismiss a teacher because she had red hair;

in *Williams* v *Giddy* [1911] AC 381, the Public Service Board of New South Wales awarded a retiring civil servant a gratuity of one penny per year of service; in *Backhouse* v *Lambeth London Borough Council* (1972) 116 SJ 802 the local authority increased the rent payable on a council property to £18,000 per week (this was part of a campaign against the Conservative government's 'Fair Rents' legislation). In other cases it will be far more difficult. In *Re Walker's Application* (1987) The Times 26 November the applicant for review was a mother whose child urgently needed a heart operation. The health authorities in Birmingham had already postponed the operation five times due to a shortage of trained nursing staff. The basis of the application was the alleged failure of the authority to provide an adequate service. The Court of Appeal held, in rejecting the application, that whilst the health authorities were clearly public bodies amenable to review, the rationing of resources was a matter for them and not the courts. Only if it could be shown that the allocation of funds by the authority was unreasonable in the *Wednesbury* sense, or if there were breaches of public law duties, would the courts be prepared to intervene. The decision perhaps begs the question as to how bad the provision of a public service has to become before the courts would be willing to label an allocation of resources as perverse: see further *R* v *Camden London Borough Council, ex parte Gillan* (1988) 21 HLR 114 and *R* v *Cambridge District Health Authority, ex parte B* [1995] 1 WLR 898.

The decision in *Associated Provincial Picture Houses* v *Wednesbury Corporation* is still good law, but it is significant that Lord Diplock, in the course of his speech in *Council of Civil Service Unions* v *Minister for the Civil Service* [1984] 3 All ER 935, preferred to use the term 'irrationality' to describe what had hitherto traditionally been regarded as *Wednesbury* unreasonableness. He stated (at p951):

'By "irrationality" I mean what can by now be succinctly referred to as "*Wednesbury* unreasonableness". ... It applies to a decision which is so outrageous in its defiance of logic or of accepted moral standards that no sensible person who had applied his mind to the question to be decided could have arrived at it. Whether a decision falls within this category is a question that judges by their training and experience should be well equipped to answer, or else there would be something badly wrong without judicial system ... "Irrationality" by now can stand on its own feet as an accepted ground on which a decision may be attacked by judicial review.'

It could be argued that irrationality might be more difficult to establish than unreasonableness, given the words used by Lord Diplock, but that distinction is not necessarily borne out in the decisions that followed the GCHQ case: see *R* v *Secretary of State for the Home Department, ex parte Handscomb* (1988) 86 Cr App R 59.

Cases such as *R* v *Secretary of State for the Environment, ex parte Hammersmith and Fulham London Borough Council* [1991] 1 AC 521 and *R* v *Secretary of State for the Environment, ex parte Nottinghamshire County Council* [1986] AC 240 suggest that the courts are less likely to apply the standard *Wednesbury* test to an exercise of ministerial discretion that has been expressly approved by the House of Commons, in the sense that such action will only be declared ultra vires if it is manifestly absurd, motivated by bad faith or based on other improper motives. It is submitted, however, that there is little or no constitutional basis for such judicial reticence. A vote in the House of Commons as such has no legal significance in terms of validating administrative action, or making it proof against judicial review. Perhaps a better explanation for the courts' adoption of what might be described as a 'super-*Wednesbury*' test in such cases is that they involve questions of national policy best determined by politicians in the appropriate political forum. For the courts to declare such policy decisions to be unreasonable in the *Wednesbury* sense might raise the possibility of the judges being dragged into what are essentially party political debates.

The impact of the Human Rights Act 1998 and the importation of proportionality

Proportionality has long been a feature of the jurisprudence of the European Court of Human Rights and some English judges have been willing to reflect this in their judgments: see *R v Brent London Borough Council, ex parte Assegai* (1987) 151 LG Rev 891 and *R v Secretary of State for ex the Home Department, ex parte Simms; R v Governor of Whitemoor Prison, ex parte Main* [1998] 2 All ER 491. The enactment of the Human Rights Act 1998, and the consequent incorporation of most significant rights under the Convention, means that the doctrine of proportionality, as developed in the jurisprudence of the European Court of Human Rights, will in future have to be applied by domestic courts considering applications for judicial review.

In *R (Daly) v Secretary of State for the Home Department* [2001] 3 All ER 433 the House of Lords considered the legality of certain prison procedures relating to the searching of cells and the examination of prisoners' correspondence. One issue was the test to be applied to the legality of these administrative procedures. Under the *Wednesbury* test they could only be declared ultra vires if they were so unreasonable that no reasonable authority would have adopted them. If Convention rights were engaged the test would essentially be whether or not the interference with the applicant's Convention rights was a proportionate response to the problem that was being dealt with. In Lord Steyn's view there was an overlap between *Wednesbury* and proportionality, but the intensity of review would be greater under the proportionality approach. He went on to identify a number of 'concrete differences' between the two approaches:

1. the doctrine of proportionality might require a reviewing court to assess the balance which the decision-maker has struck, 'not merely whether it is within the range of rational or reasonable decisions';
2. proportionality might go further than the traditional grounds of review 'inasmuch as it may require attention to be directed to the relative weight accorded to interests and considerations'.

This ruling begs the question of whether or not the incorporation of the European Convention on Human Rights has brought about a major change in judicial review cases where Convention rights are engaged – a shift from review based on legality (ie intra vires or ultra vires) to review based on merits (ie good decision or bad decision).

Where Convention rights are engaged the reviewing court will first ask whether the interference was necessary – ie could the public body have achieved its legitimate aims adopting means that caused less interference with the applicant's rights. If a policy, such as intercepting prisoners' correspondence, is shown to be necessary the court will go on to consider the question of proportionality – did the interference go further than was necessary to achieve the legitimate aims of the public body? In considering this second question the court will be considering whether the public body has struck a fair balance between the legitimate aims on the one hand and the affected person's Convention rights on the other. Allowing the public body an appropriate margin of appreciation, the court will intervene if the weight accorded to the legitimate aims is unfair and unreasonable. As indicated above, such an approach inevitably leads the court into a closer examination of the factual basis for the actions of a public body, and hence the merits of the decision – although in a sense they will be doing what they have always done, ie looking to see whether the decision-maker has given sufficient weight to relevant factors, or too much weight to irrelevant factors. The role of the court in judicial review proceedings has not become one of substituting its view for that of the primary decision-maker, but it does have an enhanced role in assessing the legality of the decisions of public bodies where Convention rights are in issue.

8.7 Relevant and irrelevant factors

As Lord Esher MR observed in *R* v *St Pancras Vestry* (1890) 24 QBD 371 at 375, a decision-making body must fairly consider the case before it and not take into account any reason for the decision which is not a legal one. Similarly, the decision-maker must take into account relevant considerations. Determining what are, and what are not, relevant considerations will involve the decision-maker in a balancing act – in short an application for judicial review should not be granted unless there is evidence that the decision-making body has carried out the 'balancing act' unreasonably.

A classic illustration of how taking irrelevant factors into account can invalidate executive action is provided by the House of Lords' decision in *Padfield* v *Minister of Agriculture* [1968] AC 997, where the Minister was empowered to order an investigation into complaints relating to the administration of the Milk Marketing Scheme 'as he thought fit'. The litigation arose out of the Minister's refusal to refer the plaintiff's complaint to a committee of inquiry, and the evidence indicated that the Minister had been motivated by a fear that an inquiry might prove politically embarrassing. The House of Lords, by a majority, held that the Minister, in refusing an inquiry, was abusing his discretion so as to frustrate the aims and objects of the parent Act, the Agricultural Marketing Act 1958. The Minister had been granted subjectively worded powers, but the House of Lords made clear that these were not to be used to thwart the policy behind the legislation. The decision, in its time, was of great constitutional significance, confirming as it did the power of the judiciary to control the exercise of executive discretion at the highest level.

Since *Padfield*, judicial intervention to quash ministerial decision-making has become the norm. Any minister, or other executive body, purporting to exercise a statutory power in a manner that contradicts any of the general assumptions regarding Parliament's legislative intent is likely to have its actions declared ultra vires. Hence in *R* v *Secretary of State for the Home Department, ex parte Pierson* [1997] 3 All ER 577, where the House of Lords held (Lords Browne-Wilkinson and Lloyd dissenting) that the Home Secretary was acting unlawfully in purporting to revise upwards the penal element of the tariff set for a life sentence that had been imposed at a time when a different policy (ie of not altering the tariff once fixed at the outset of a life sentence) applied, Lord Steyn observed:

> 'Parliament does not legislate in a vacuum. Parliament legislates for a European liberal democracy founded on the principles and traditions of the common law. And the courts may approach legislation on this initial assumption.'

Similarly, in *R* v *Secretary of State for the Home Department, ex parte Venables and Thompson* [1997] 3 All ER 97, the House of Lords held (Lord Lloyd dissenting), that the Home Secretary had acted unlawfully in taking public opinion (expressed in petitions and tabloid newspaper campaigns) into account in determining the minimum period of imprisonment to be served by the children convicted of murdering James Bulger.

Following the enactment of s2(1) of the European Communities Act 1972 domestic courts are obliged to give effect to EC law regardless of whether conflicting domestic law was enacted before or after the 1972 Act came into effect. A public body must, therefore, have regard to the demands of EC law when exercising its discretion: see *R* v *Chief Constable of Sussex, ex parte International Trader's Ferry Ltd* (above). Similarly, the incorporation of the European Convention on Human Rights, as effected by the Human Rights Act 1998, means that it becomes unlawful for any public authority to act in a way which is incompatible with a Convention right: s6(1). Hence a public body, exercising its discretion, will now have to have regard to whether or not its decision is compatible with the Convention rights protected by the Act.

Ulterior motives

Where a decision-maker clearly has some ulterior motive in mind in exercising discretion, the courts will have the discretion to declare the action ultra vires if they deem it appropriate to do so. For example in *Sydney Municipal Council* v *Campbell* [1925] AC 388, the Privy Council held that compulsory purchase powers, vested in a local authority, were not to be used for speculating in property, even if the profit made was used to offset the rates. In *R* v *Hillingdon London Borough Council, ex parte Royco Homes Ltd* [1974] QB 720 the imposition of planning conditions on a grant of planning permission was held to be ultra vires where the conditions were not for a planning purpose but to help relieve the council of a significant part of its burden as housing authority to provide houses for the homeless. In determining whether or not there is illegality the courts will look at the 'dominant' purpose of the decision-maker: see *Westminster Corporation* v *London and North Western Railway Co* [1905] AC 426.

It is an important constitutional issue that an authority cannot levy a tax or otherwise raise revenue without there being an express statutory power for the purpose. The courts will thus invalidate the exercise of discretion, even where the raising of revenue is merely a side effect of the decision. *Congreve* v *Home Office* [1976] QB 629 concerned the Secretary of State's announcement that the cost of a colour television licence was to be increased from £12 to £18, the increase taking effect on 1 April 1975. Congreve, along with another 20,000 licence holders, applied for a new licence shortly before the date set for the increase, even though his own licence had not expired, because he would still make an overall saving. Contemplating a substantial loss of revenue if this practice was allowed, the Secretary of State adopted a policy of revoking any new 'overlapping' licences after eight months if the extra £6 was not paid by the holder. The minister purported to act under s1(2) of the Wireless Telegraphy Act 1949, which states that a licence may be revoked by a notice in writing served on the holder. In an action seeking a declaration that the minister's action was unlawful the Court of Appeal held that the Secretary of State had acted ultra vires in using his statutory power of revocation for a purpose for which it was never intended, namely, the raising of revenue. Citing *Padfield* as authority, Lord Denning MR spoke of the courts having a duty to correct a misuse of power where a minister exercised discretion for reasons that were bad in law. The Master of the Rolls also adverted to the issue of taxation:

> 'There is yet another reason for holding that the demands for £6 to be unlawful. They were made contrary to the Bill of Rights. They were an attempt to levy money for the use of the Crown without the authority of Parliament: and that is quite enough to damn them: see *Attorney-General* v *Wilts United Dairies Ltd* (1921) 37 TLR 884.'

The exercise of discretion by local authorities

In *R* v *Board of Education* [1910] KB 165 Farwell LJ took the view that allowing political considerations to influence decision-making would necessarily invalidate the process. They were, to his mind, 'pre-eminently extraneous'. Today such a view seems to be untenable. Local government is always dominated by party politics, and to that extent resolutions passed by majority groupings are bound to be motivated by adherence to one political viewpoint or another: see *Secretary of State for Education* v *Tameside Metropolitan Borough Council* [1977] AC 1014 and *Cardiff Corporation* v *Secretary of State for Wales* (1971) 22 P & CR 718.

Where a local authority is likely to fall into error is where its decisions seek to pursue some political goal that is extraneous to its powers and duties as a public authority. Hence, in *R* v *Ealing London Borough Council and Others, ex parte Times Newspapers Ltd* (1986) 85 LGR 316, the court held that the local authority acted unlawfully in resolving that the libraries under its control should not stock publications produced by Times Newspapers and others whilst the publishers were in dispute with sacked employees of the newspapers. The purpose of the ban was to show solidarity with the dismissed workers. The authority had a discretion as to how it carried out its duties under the Public Libraries and Museums Act 1964, but the court was of the view that the ban imposed by the authority was clearly related to an ulterior purpose, ie to show solidarity towards the print workers involved in an industrial dispute. No rational authority could have thought that this was a proper way of discharging its duties under the 1964 Act.

In *R* v *Somerset County Council, ex parte Fewings* [1995] 3 All ER 20 the Court of Appeal held (by a majority) that a resolution passed by the respondent authority prohibiting stag hunting on certain land within its ownership was unlawful. Sir Thomas Bingham MR, whilst rejecting the view of Laws J in the court below, to the effect that the ethical arguments based on assertions that hunting was inherently cruel were necessarily extraneous to the local authority's exercise of its discretion, explained that the authority's councillors may have given undue weight to the moral question concerning the desirability of hunting, at the expense of the statutory requirement to manage the land for the benefit of the authority's area. In adopting a ban, the local authority would, in his view, have to demonstrate how its decision was conducive to this statutory objective. Evidence of the documentation circulated prior to the meeting at which the authority had arrived at its decision indicated that councillors might have underestimated the statutory constraints imposed upon a public landowner. Swinton Thomas LJ went further in expressing the view that the morality or otherwise of hunting was not a matter for public landowners, but a matter for Parliament to resolve by way of legislation if necessary. Note that Simon Brown LJ (dissenting) felt that, all other factors being properly considered, the councillors had been right to regard the ethical issue as decisive and he would have been prepared to uphold the legality of the authority's resolution on that basis. In the light of this case it might be tempting to advise local authorities that want to ban hunting on their land not to advert to any moral issues in justifying their actions, but merely to advance their cases on issues related to husbandry and land management. Arguably, only if an objector could show that a ban was irrational, or based on no evidence, could the courts intervene.

Decisions on expenditure by local authorities must also be made on a proper basis, and for a proper purpose. A classic illustration of the competing interests at work when such spending decisions are made is provided by the House of Lords' ruling in *Roberts* v *Hopwood* [1925] AC 578. Poplar Borough Council, acting under statutory powers to pay its workers such wages as it thought fit, resolved to pay its male and female workers a wage of £4 per week. The payments made in pursuance of this resolution were challenged by the District Auditor as being contrary to law, and this contention was eventually approved by the House of Lords. The local authority was held to have taken into account irrelevant considerations in wishing to set an example as a 'model employer'; further it had been motivated, wrongly, by considerations of 'socialist philanthropy, and feminist ambition'. The authority was also found to have failed to take into account the fact that during this period the cost of living was actually falling and therefore wages should have been reduced, not increased. The authority was also found to have failed to give sufficient regard to the interests of its ratepayers, who would in part have to finance the increases. In this regard the House of Lords took the view that the authority was under a fiduciary duty to spend ratepayers' money wisely.

In more recent times the problems have not been so much about excessive expenditure by local authorities, but rather the refusal of authorities to incur expenditure in the face of tighter budgetary controls. Whether the refusal to incur expenditure is lawful or not will depend largely on the statutory context. Where the statute is drawn in wider, more generalised, terms the courts may be able to grant an authority some flexibility: see *R* v *Gloucestershire County Council, ex parte Barry* [1997] 2 All ER 1, where the House of Lords ruled (Lords Lloyd and Steyn dissenting) that, in determining whether or not a person had 'needs' that had to be met under s2(1) of the Chronically Sick and Disabled Persons Act 1970, a local authority was entitled to take into account its financial resources. By contrast, in *R* v *East Sussex County Council, ex parte Tandy* [1998] 2 All ER 769, the respondent authority was held to have acted unlawfully in taking into account its available resources in determining what was a 'suitable education' for an individual pupil.

Taking the European Convention on Human Rights into account when exercising power

As indicated above, the incorporation of the European Convention on Human Rights, as effected by the Human Rights Act 1998, has the effect that it becomes unlawful for any public authority to act in a way which is incompatible with a Convention right: s6(1). This duty is subject to the proviso that no unlawfulness will be held to have occurred if the public body was unable to avoid the incompatibility because of one or more provisions of primary or subordinate legislation. Hence a public body, exercising its discretion, will now have to have regard to whether or not its decision is compatible with the Convention rights protected by the Act. Similarly, a court exercising its reviewing function will have to have such factors in mind, as it too is a public authority for these purposes and will act unlawfully if it fails to uphold the Convention rights. The impact of this likely to be felt most strongly in decisions relating to individual welfare such as housing and child care issues that have a direct bearing on art 8 rights.

8.8 Is an application for judicial review appropriate?

The procedure for making an application for judicial review is governed by s31 of the Supreme Court Act 1981, which provides that:

'(1) An application to the High Court for one or more of the following forms of relief, namely –
(a) an order of mandamus, prohibition or certiorari;
(b) a declaration or injunction under subsection (2); ...
shall be made in accordance with rules of court by a procedure to be known as an application for judicial review.
(2) A declaration may be made or an injunction granted under this subsection in any case where an application for judicial review, seeking that relief, has been made and the High Court considers that, having regard to –
(a) the nature of the matters in respect of which relief may be granted by orders of mandamus, prohibition or certiorari;
(b) the nature of the persons and bodies against whom relief may be granted by such orders; and
(c) all the circumstances of the case,
it would be just and convenient for the declaration to be made or the injunction to be granted, as the case may be.'

These provisions make it clear that where one of the prerogative orders is sought judicial review must be used. Where one of the private law remedies of injunction or declaration is sought, judicial review may be used. The relevant procedural rules were to be found in the Rules of the Supreme Court O.53 (RSC O.53); they are now to be found in the Civil Procedure Rules (CPR) Part 54, introduced in 1998.

The O'Reilly *v* Mackman *public/private dichotomy*

Between 1977 (when a reformed procedure for judicial review was introduced) and 1998 (when the CPR started to come into effect), there was a considerable amount of legislation concerning when judicial review should or could be used, when it would be an abuse of process not to use judicial review, how decision-makers might be classified as public law bodies, and whether or not a given issue gave rise to issues of public law. As will be seen much of this debate is now redundant, the CPR giving the courts power to transfer cases according to the most appropriate procedure given the subject matter involved, but it is necessary to have a grasp of the background issues to fully understand the significance of the more flexible procedures that exist today.

O'Reilly v *Mackman* [1983] 2 AC 237 concerned a number of prisoners serving long sentences of imprisonment who issued writs and originating summonses against members of the Board of Visitors of Hull Prison, seeking declarations that the disciplinary awards of forfeiture of remission made by the Board were null and void on the ground of breach of natural justice. The House of Lords held that the appellants had no private law rights as regards the Board, only a public law right to be given a fair hearing. Further, as the Board was a public law body, deriving its status and powers from statute, it would be an abuse of the court's processes to allow the prisoners to proceed by way of action to challenge the Board's determinations. Hence the appellants should have applied for judicial review, although the time limit for applying for review had expired by the time the House of Lords handed down its decision

Lord Diplock insisted that judicial review was the only procedure open to the prisoners because of the procedural provided safeguards it provided to public bodies. Applications for judicial review had to be made without delay, usually within three months of the action complained of, as it was important that a public body should know quickly of any significant challenge to the legality of its actions in public law so that third party interests were not adversely affected. The requirement that those seeking review should have 'sufficient interest' in the matter to which their application related, and should have to obtain leave to apply for review, provided an important 'filter' of cases against public bodies. By the very nature of their activities such bodies were likely to attract the attention of 'cranks and busybodies'. If such persons were allowed to proceed by way of action the defendant public body would be put to the expense of instructing lawyers to put in a defence, no matter how worthless the allegation. The requirement of leave ensured that no participation from the respondent body was required until a prima facie case for review had been made out by the applicant.

Lord Diplock was willing to accept that there might be exceptions to this rule, notably where the invalidity of a decision arose as a collateral issue in a claim for infringement of a right of the plaintiff arising under private law.

Extending the scope of judicial review: the concept of the public body

Bodies such as ministers and local authorities are clearly 'public bodies'. We recognise them as such because they are either creatures of statute or exercise statutory power. Partly as a result of moves towards deregulation, privatisation, and the promotion of self-regulation, the courts recognised that important powers were wielded by bodies that were not statutory in origin. Some derived their powers from private contracts, some merely exercised de facto power only. The challenge for the courts was to determine whether or not the concept of the public law body could be developed to encompass such decision-makers.

In this respect, the Court of Appeal's decision in *R v Panel on Take-overs and Mergers, ex parte Datafin plc* [1987] 2 WLR 699 is of crucial significance. It was held that the Panel was a body subject to review, even though it exercised no statutory or prerogative powers, and was not even based on a private contract or constitution. As the Master of the Rolls observed, it possessed no visible means of legal support. The court held that the panel's functions were amenable to review, however, on the basis of the enormous de facto power it possessed to take decisions affecting the public and, significantly, the fact that there was no other means by which those affected by the decisions of the Panel could have challenged them in the courts.

The overriding issue here is one of control, ie the scope of the court's supervisory jurisdiction by way of judicial review. Once the court determines that the decision-making body should be brought within the scope of judicial review because, for example, of the inadequacy of other means of control, or the effect of its decisions, it follows that the decision-making body has to be classified as a public law body, as these are the only decision-makers that are amenable to judicial review. This emphasis on what a body does, rather than the source of its power, is sometimes referred to as the 'functionalist' approach.

It should also be noted that s6 of the Human Rights Act 1998 embraces the concept of public body in describing those bodies under a duty to uphold Convention rights: see further Chapter 9. In *R (On the Application of Heather and Another)* v *Leonard Cheshire Foundation* [2002] 2 All ER 936 Lord Woolf CJ expressed the view that the concept of 'public body' for the purposes of a HRA 1998 claim was not necessarily co-terminus with the concept as developed for the purposes of judicial review in domestic law. Much will depend on the extent to which the respondent body is carrying out functions on behalf of a public body, and the nature of the statutory underpinning, if any.

Public law issue or private law issue?

Assuming the respondent is a public law body for the purposes of judicial review, there might still be objection to the procedure adopted. Where the claimant proceeds by way of action the respondent public body might maintain that he should have applied for judicial review because the issue falls within the sphere of public law; conversely, where judicial review is used, the respondent might contend that it is inappropriate because the issue is one raising only private law considerations.

For example, in *O'Rourke* v *Camden London Borough Council* [1997] 3 All ER 23 the plaintiff's action for damages for breach of the statutory duty created by s63(1) of the Housing Act 1985 (which requires a local authority to provide accommodation for those in priority need) was struck out by the county court on the basis that it could only be pursued by way of an application for judicial review, a ruling subsequently upheld by the House of Lords. In determining that s63 was not to be construed as if it created a private law right to damages by way of an action for breach of statutory duty, Lord Hoffmann identified three key factors:

1. the Act created a scheme of social welfare (ie having no equivalence in the sphere of private law);
2. the Act conferred benefits on applicants at the public expense for the benefit of the applicants and society at large;

3. the provision of housing and the assessment of applicants' needs necessarily involved the exercise of discretion by a public body such as a Housing Authority, hence the appropriate way in which to assess the legality of such decisions was by way of reference to the principles of public law.

It would appear to be the case that an assessment of whether a claimant comes within a general statutory function is a public law matter, private law rights only arising when promises are made to the claimant, which creates something akin to a contractual relationship between the authority and that particular claimant.

Commercial or contractual disputes and those arising out of a voluntary submission to self-regulation will normally be regarded as falling within the sphere of private law: see for example *Mercury Energy Ltd* v *Electricity Corporation of New Zealand Ltd* [1994] 1 WLR 521. Disputes concerning contracts of employment will also be regarded as giving rise to private law issues, even where the employer is a public body, provided private law provides some scope for the provision of remedies. Hence, in *R* v *East Berkshire Health Authority, ex parte Walsh* [1984] 3 WLR 818 the Court of Appeal held that it would be inappropriate for a senior nursing officer, employed under the National Health Service, to challenge his dismissal by way of judicial review. Conversely, in *R* v *Secretary of State for the Home Department, ex parte Benwell* [1985] QB 554 it was held that the applicant prison officer who sought to challenge the validity of his dismissal from the Prison Service by way of judicial review had not opted for an inappropriate procedure, the distinguishing factor being that the applicant was subject to a statutory code of discipline which denied him any private law right to challenge the validity of his dismissal.

Other exceptions to the rule in O'Reilly v Mackman

It is possible to identify three other situations where the courts have been prepared to allow a defendant to challenge a public law decision other than by way of an application for judicial review:

1. Cases where the public law issue is merely collateral to the private law matter. See for example *Davy* v *Spelthorne Borough Council* [1984] AC 262, where an action for negligence raised the issue of whether or not a planning decision was valid, or *Roy* v *Kensington and Chelsea and Westminster Family Practitioner Committee* [1992] 1 All ER 705 where the plaintiff, a general practitioner, sought payment from the defendant committee of part of his basic practice allowance that the committee had decided to withhold, having concluded that the plaintiff had failed to devote a substantial amount of his time to general practice. The committee, which derived its jurisdiction in this matter from the National Health Service (General Medical and Pharmaceutical) Regulations 1974, and the Statement of Fees and Allowances published thereunder, applied unsuccessfully

to have the plaintiff's claim struck out as an abuse of process on the basis that he was seeking to challenge a public law decision.

2. Where the public law issue arises by way of a defence to civil proceedings. See for example *Wandsworth London Borough Council* v *Winder* [1984] 3 All ER 976, where the House of Lords held that a tenant was entitled to resist a possession action brought by the local authority on the basis that its claim for rent was unlawful, the decision to raise rents having been ultra vires.

3. Where the public law issue is raised as a defence to criminal proceedings. In *Boddington* v *British Transport Police* [1998] 2 All ER 203 the House of Lords held that it was acceptable to permit a public law issue to be raised by way of defence in such proceedings.

The impact of the Civil Procedure Rules

Claims for judicial review are dealt with in the Administrative Court of the High Court.

CPR Part 54.1 defines a 'claim for judicial review' as a claim to review 'the lawfulness of an enactment; or a decision, action or failure to act in relation to the exercise of a public function.' The procedure must be used in a claim for judicial review where the claimant is seeking a mandatory order, a prohibiting order or a quashing order. The procedure may be used where the claimant is seeking a declaration or an injunction

Under CPR Part 54.20 the court may order a claim to continue as if it had not been started by way of an application for judicial review and, where it does so, it may give directions about the future management of the claim: see CPR Part 30 regarding transfers to and from the Administrative Court. Clearly this means that the court has a discretion to treat an application for judicial review as a private law claim if this is more appropriate. Alternatively, private law actions can be transferred to the Administrative Court if the judicial review procedure is more appropriate.

In *Clark* v *University of Lincolnshire and Humberside* [2000] 3 All ER 752 Lord Woolf MR explained the flexibility that the CPR now offered. The claimant (C), a humanities student at the respondent university, was awarded 0 per cent in a final year paper. Initially it was alleged that she had been guilty of plagiarism but this allegation was subsequently dropped. C sued for breach of contract and the claim was struck out on the grounds that breaches of contract by universities were not justiciable in the courts. C appealed, having amended her statement of claim to include allegations that the respondent had breached its own student regulations. The respondent contended that C's action was an abuse of process, and that she should have proceeded by way of an application for judicial review – the time limit for which had long since passed. Allowing her appeal Lord Woolf MR went on to explain that under the CPR:

'... if proceedings involving public law issues are commenced by an ordinary action under Pt 7 or Pt 8 [of the CPR] they are now subject to Pt 24. Part 24 is important because it enables the court, either on its own motion or on the application of a party, if it considers that a claimant has no real prospect of succeeding on a claim or an issue, to give summary judgment on the claim or issue. This is a markedly different position from that which existed when *O'Reilly* v *Mackman* was decided. if a defendant public body or an interested person considers that a claim has no real prospect of success an application can now be made under Pt 24. This restricts the inconvenience to third parties and the administration of public bodies caused by a hopeless claim to which Lord Diplock referred. ... The distinction between proceedings under O.53 and an ordinary claim are now limited. Under O.53 the claimant has to obtain permission to bring the proceedings so that the onus is upon him to establish he has a real prospect of success. In the case of ordinary proceedings the defendant has to establish that the proceedings do not have a real prospect of success.'

See further *R (On the Application of Heather and Another)* v *Leonard Cheshire Foundation* (above), where Lord Woolf CJ observed;

'... CPR 54.1 has changed the focus of the test so that it is also partly functions based. ... These changes have not been reflected in any complementary change to s31 of the Supreme Court Act 1981, which still is in virtually the same language as RSC O.53. None the less, there was ... reflected in the decision of the court below ... with its reference to "A gap in judicial review", an idea that if the Leonard Cheshire Foundation [LCF] was not forming a public function, proceedings by way of judicial review were wrong. This is an echo of the old demarcation disputes as to when judicial review was or was not appropriate under RSC O.53. CPR Pt 54 is intended to avoid any such disputes which are wholly unproductive. In a case such as the present where a bona fide contention is being advanced (although incorrect) that LCF was performing a public function, that is an appropriate issue to be brought to the court by way of judicial review. Because LCF is a charity further procedural requirements may be involved. ... We wish to make clear that the CPR provide a framework which is sufficiently flexible to enable all the issues between the parties to be determined.'

8.9 How to apply for judicial review

The procedural rules governing applications for judicial review are to be found in s31 Supreme Court Act 1981 and CPR Part 54. As indicated above an application for judicial review must be made if a claimant is seeking a mandatory order, a prohibiting order or a quashing order. It may be used if a declaration or injunction is sought. Whether or not judicial review is the appropriate procedure has been considered above. Assuming it is the appropriate procedure, there are a number of procedural considerations that have to be borne in mind by the claimant.

Permission

The claimant must obtain permission to apply for judicial review. Section 31(3) of the Supreme Court Act 1981 provides that: 'No application for judicial review shall be made unless the leave of the High Court has been obtained'. CPR Part 54.4

similarly provides that the 'court's permission to proceed is required in a claim for judicial review whether started under this Part or transferred to the Administrative Court.' The permission stage offers protection to public bodies in that the court will have an opportunity to 'weed out' unmeritorious cases at an early stage. The application is made ex parte to a judge who will generally determine the application without a hearing.

Locus standi

The right to challenge the decisions of public bodies by way of judicial review is restricted to those who have some connection with the decision being impugned. Under s31(3) of the Supreme Court Act 1981 a court will not grant leave to make an application unless it considers that the applicant has a sufficient interest in the matter to which the application relates. The leading authority on locus standi is the decision of the House of Lords in *Inland Revenue Commissioners* v *National Federation of Self-Employed and Small Businesses* [1982] AC 617. In an effort to prevent large-scale tax evasion by casual workers in Fleet Street, the Revenue came to an understanding with the relevant trade unions, whereby it would agree to an amnesty as regards the investigation of unpaid tax in previous years, in return for the casual workers now providing accurate information when they registered for work so that tax could be collected. The Federation, which felt that its members were often unfairly harassed by the Revenue with regard to the collection of tax, sought a declaration that the amnesty was ultra vires the Revenue, and an order of mandamus to compel it to recover the tax due. In concluding that the Federation did not have locus standi to challenge the tax amnesty Lord Wilberforce sought to outline how the matter should be addressed. He explained that the issue of sufficient interest was to be regarded as a mixed decision of fact and law for the courts to decide on legal principles, ie it was not simply a matter of judicial discretion. Further, that it should not be assumed that because one generic phrase was used as the test for standing it would necessarily be applied in the same way regardless of the remedy sought. As regards mandamus (now a mandatory order), for example, he agreed with the views expressed by the Lord Advocate to the effect that the courts should be guided by the definition of the duty, and should inquire whether expressly, or by implication, the definition indicates that the complaining applicant is within the scope or ambit of the duty.

His Lordship was at pains to emphasise that standing should not be viewed as a preliminary or threshold issue. As he observed:

> 'There may be simple cases in which it can be seen at the earliest stage that the person applying for judicial review has not interest at all, or no sufficient interest to support the application: then it would be quite correct at the threshold to refuse him leave to apply. The right to do so is an important safeguard against the courts being flooded and public bodies harassed by irresponsible applications. But in other cases this will not be so. In these it will be necessary to consider the powers or the duties in law of those against

whom the relief is asked, the position of the applicant in relation to those powers or duties, and to the breach of those said to have been committed. In other words, the question of sufficient interest cannot, in such case, be considered in the abstract, or as an isolated point: it must be taken together with the legal and factual context.'

What was seen as fatal to the success of the Federation's application was not only its failure to establish any illegality on the part of the Revenue, but also the confidential nature of the relationship between the Revenue and any individual taxpayer. As Lord Wilberforce observed:

'As a matter of general principle I would hold that one taxpayer has no sufficient interest in asking the court to investigate the tax affairs of another taxpayer or to complain that the latter has been under-assessed or over-assessed: indeed, there is a strong public interest that he should not. And this principle applies equally to groups of taxpayers: an aggregate of individuals each of whom has no interest cannot of itself have an interest ...'

Lord Diplock sought to explain the rationale for the two-stage approach to the application for judicial review, and the way in which the assessment of standing might alter from one stage to another. He regarded the application for leave stage as involving the court in determining whether or not the case disclosed 'what might on further consideration turn out to be an arguable case in favour of granting to the applicant the relief claimed'. This was to be contrasted with the consideration of standing when the application for review was considered, with all the evidence in, and full argument delivered. Hence it would be perfectly possible for a claimant to be regarded as having standing for the purposes of the application for leave, but not for the full application for review.

The fact that an applicant has been involved in a decision-making process as an interested party, and possibly consulted during that process, does not necessarily give that party sufficient interest to for the purposes of review, especially where there are other parties better placed to contribute to the decision-making process. Hence, in *R v Secretary of State for the Home Department, ex parte Bulger* [2001] 3 All ER 449, the Divisional Court rejected the contention that the father of James Bulger, the two-year-old child murder by Thompson and Venables, had sufficient interest to intervene to challenge the decision of the Lord Chief Justice regarding the defendants' eligibility for parole. The court held that, in criminal cases, the two parties with an interest were the Crown and the defendant. The rule of law could be maintained through those two parties. There was, therefore, no need for a third party to intervene. As Rose LJ observed

'It is true ... that the threshold for standing in judicial review has generally been set by the courts at a low level. This, as it seems to me, is because of the importance in public law that someone should be able to call decision-makers to account, lest the rule of law break down and private rights be denied by public bodies. ... But in the present matter the traditional and invariable parties to criminal proceedings, namely the Crown and the defendant, are both able to, and do, challenge those judicial decisions which are susceptible to judicial review as ... It follows that in criminal cases there is no need for a third party to seek to intervene to uphold the rule of law. Nor, in my judgment, would such intervention generally be desirable. If the family of a victim could challenge the sentencing process, why not the family of the defendant? Should the Official Solicitor be permitted to represent the interests of children adversely affected by the imprisonment of their mother? Should organisations representing victims or offenders be permitted to intervene? In my judgment, the answer in all these cases is that the Crown and the defendant are the only proper parties to criminal proceedings. A proper discharge of judicial functions in relation to sentencing requires that the judge take into account … the impact of the offence and the sentence on the public generally, and on individuals, including the victim and the victim's family and the defendant and the defendant's family. The nature of that impact is properly channelled through prosecution or defence.'

As the *Federation* case itself shows, the interpretation of the phrase 'sufficient interest' is of especial significance to campaigning pressure groups who, by their very nature, may not be directly affected by the decision being challenged, but will represent those who have a concern about the issues involved. It is perhaps not unfair to describe the development of the law on this issue as a case of 'two steps forwards, one step back'. Decisions such as that in *R v Secretary of State for Social Services, ex parte Child Poverty Action Group; Same, ex parte Greater London Council* (1985) The Times 8 August displayed a broadly rational approach, and suggest that if there is a sufficient nexus between the pressure group and those affected by the decision, the courts will normally find the locus standi requirement satisfied. Against this, there was what might be regarded as the somewhat aberrant decision of Schiemann J in *R v Secretary of State for the Environment, ex parte Rose Theatre Trust Company* [1990] 1 All ER 754, where he refused to accept that a pressure group, which had formed itself into a company solely for the purpose of challenging the minister's failure to grant the site of the Rose Theatre protected status, had locus standi to challenge the minister's decision. It was his view that merely because an applicant asserted that he or she had an interest did not of itself create such an interest; that a company would not necessarily have sufficient interest simply because it was formed by persons sharing a common view, even if the company's memorandum empowered it to campaign on a particular issue; that the company could have no greater claim to standing than that possessed by individual members of the campaign prior to its incorporation; that the minister's decision was not one in respect of which the ordinary citizen had sufficient interest so as to entitle him to apply for judicial review. In his Lordship's view, the law was not there for every individual who wished to challenge the legality of an administrative decision, and on the facts 'no individual [had] the standing to apply for judicial review'.

The useful role played by pressure groups in public interest litigation is illustrated by *R v Secretary of State for Foreign and Commonwealth Affairs, ex parte World Development Movement Ltd* [1995] 1 WLR 386, wherein it was held that the applicants had sufficient interest to challenge the provision of grants to the Malaysian government for the building of the Pergau Dam. Rose LJ recognised that, whilst the dominant factor was the merit of the application itself, other significant matters included the need to uphold the rule of law, the fact that no other organisation was likely to launch such a challenge, and the key role played by the applicants in giving advice, guidance and assistance regarding aid. In particular it was felt that if the applicant in *R v Secretary of State for Foreign and Commonwealth Affairs, ex parte Rees-Mogg* [1994] 2 WLR 115 was properly regarded as having had locus standi on the basis of his 'sincere concerns for constitutional issues', then a fortiori the applicants in the present case should have standing, given their track record in promoting aid for under-developed nations.

Note that where an application for review is based on a failure to comply with the Human Rights Act 1998, s7(3) provides that the applicant will only be regarded as having sufficient interest in relation to the unlawful act if he is, or would be, a victim of that act.

Delay in applying for relief

Broadly stated, the time limit for applying for judicial review is three months. The rationale for such a short time limit for challenging executive decisions in public law is that both decision-makers and those acting in reliance on the decisions of public bodies need to know that after a given time period the decision will not be quashed as a result of any legal challenge. CPR Part 54.5 provides that the claim form must be filed 'promptly; and in any event not later than three months after the grounds to make the claim first arose'. It further specifies that the time limit may not be extended by agreement between the parties, and that it does not apply when any other enactment specifies a shorter time limit for making the claim for judicial review. The Practice Direction that accompanies CPR Part 54 provides that: 'Where the claim is for a quashing order in respect of a judgment, order or conviction, the date when the grounds to make the claim first arose, for the purposes of rule 54.5 is the date of that judgment, order or conviction.' See further *R (On the Application of Burkett)* v *Hammersmith and Fulham London Borough Council* [2002] 3 All ER 97. Where permission has been granted it is not open to a judge hearing a substantive application for judicial review to dismiss the application solely on the ground that there had been undue delay in applying for leave. Assuming an applicant establishes a claim regarding the illegality of the administrative action, delay in applying for review can only come back into play as a factor if there is evidence that granting the relief sought would be likely to cause hardship, prejudice or detriment to others. If such is the case the court will then be engaged in a balancing act determining whether the applicant should have to suffer the consequences of the impugned decision, or whether the respondent and others should have to deal with the consequences of the decision being quashed. The relevant factors would be the length of the delay, whether the delay had been caused by the applicant, the extent of the hardship caused to others by allowing the application to succeed, and whether the applicant has misled the court at the permission stage: see *R v Criminal Injuries Compensation Board, ex parte A* [1997] 3 WLR 776.

9

The European Convention on Human Rights

9.1 Introduction: the political background

9.2 The place of the ECHR in English law

9.3 The Human Rights Act 1998: the rights protected

9.4 Pursuing a Human Rights Act claim before the domestic courts

9.5 Taking a case to Strasbourg

9.6 The European Convention on Human Rights and EC law

9.1 Introduction: the political background

Although the Bill of Rights 1689 has been a feature of the British constitutional landscape for over 300 years, it would be quite inappropriate to contend that it provides anything like the comprehensive protection for basic individual rights and freedoms that one normally associates with a modern Bill of Rights. The British constitution has traditionally looked to the common law to ensure that individual rights are recognised and upheld, but this has operated in an essentially negative fashion. Hence citizens have been entitled to do as they please, subject to the restrictions imposed by common law and statute, rather than being able to point to positive legal rights to such things as freedom of expression, association, or privacy.

While the protection of fundamental rights and freedoms on the international plane has proved a slow and difficult process (witness the implementation of the Universal Declaration of Human Rights since 1948), the protection of human rights on the regional level among groups of states sharing common ideals and standards has been more effective. One of the most highly regarded of the regional conventions for the protection of human rights is the European Convention on Human Rights (hereinafter the ECHR). The ECHR is very much a product of the determination amongst the Allies in the immediate post-war years to ensure that the wide spread atrocities, witnessed during the Second World War, and the concomitant violations of human rights should not be repeated in mainland Europe. There was a realisation that the way in which individual states treated their citizens was no longer a purely domestic matter. The evidence was all too clear that any state that started out by denying the basic rights of its own citizens would, in all likelihood, be only too willing to treat inhabitants of neighbouring states in a like fashion if the opportunity arose. The essential concept underpinning the ECHR is that signatory states should police each other and, where applicable, the nationals of signatory states should be able to draw attention to violations.

The United Kingdom was one of the original signatories of the ECHR, on 4 November 1950 and of its First Protocol on 8 March 1952. The instruments of ratification of the ECHR and its First Protocol were deposited with the Secretary-General of the Council of Europe on 8 March 1951 and 3 November 1952, respectively. The ECHR entered into force on 3 September 1953. On 23 October 1953 a declaration was made under art 63(1) extending the ECHR's force to certain territories for whose international relations the United Kingdom was responsible. On 14 January 1966, the United Kingdom recognised the competence of the European Commission on Human Rights (hereinafter 'the Commission') to receive individual applications, and recognised the compulsory jurisdiction of the European Court of Human Rights. With the enactment of the Human Rights Act 1998 those rights have now been 'brought home' with the effect that, from 2 October 2000, certain Convention provisions have direct effect as part of the domestic law of the United Kingdom (see section 9.4 below).

9.2 The place of the ECHR in English law

Historically the approach of United Kingdom governments and courts has, to a large extent, been that incorporation of the ECHR was unnecessary, given the track record of the United Kingdom in respecting human rights, and the ability of the common law to respond to changing circumstances. As indicated above, the Human Rights Act 1998 marks a significant departure from this approach by placing positively expressed rights firmly in the context of domestic law of the United Kingdom. The enactment of the 1998 Act was necessary because the United Kingdom legal system is dualist in nature. Whilst the Crown has power to enter into treaty obligations on the international plane, such treaties can only resound in domestic law if incorporated by Act of Parliament. Hence although the ECHR and its First Protocol have (subject to derogations and reservations) been signed and ratified by United Kingdom governments they could not become part of domestic law without first being enacted in an Act of Parliament. This mirrors the position regarding the Treaty of Rome (as it was then known) and the European Communities Act 1972. By contrast, many other signatory states have monist legal systems, whereby the ECHR became part of their domestic law once ratified.

Whilst the incorporation of the ECHR is doubtless of huge totemic significance, one should not lose sight of the basic fact that the Human Rights Act 1998 does not create any new substantive rights. The real change effected by the 1998 Act is procedural – litigants being allowed to take ECHR points in argument before domestic courts, rather than having to opt for the rather daunting prospect of taking a case to Strasbourg: see further section 9.5.

The pre-incorporation era

To understand the impact of the Human Rights Act 1998 on the United Kingdom constitution it is instructive to review the position as it was in the pre-incorporation era, not least because it may prove to be the case that the courts are not as willing to accede to arguments based on the ECHR as might be assumed. The courts were always been willing to use the ECHR to resolve ambiguities in domestic legislation, on the basis that it was presumed that Parliament would not have legislated in contravention of those obligations without clearly flagging that fact. What the United Kingdom courts refused to do was to recognise rights created by the ECHR where no such corresponding right existed in domestic law.

For example, in *Uppal* v *Home Office* (1980) 3 EHRR 391, the applicants, illegal immigrants, applied for declarations that they should not be deported from the United Kingdom until the European Commission on Human Rights had determined whether deportation would contravene their right to respect for family life under art 8 of the ECHR, and argued that deportation would hinder the effective exercise of the right of individual petition. In his judgment, Sir Robert Megarry doubted the validity of this argument; but in any event held that obligations in international law which were not enforceable as part of English law could not be the subject of declaratory judgments or orders. Subsequently, when considering the legality of telephone tapping in *Malone* v *Metropolitan Police Commissioner* [1979] Ch 344, he reaffirmed his decision in *Uppal* after full argument on the point.

Whilst Lord Denning MR in *R* v *Home Secretary, ex parte Bhajan Singh* [1976] QB 198, observed that the executive should have regard to the ECHR in exercising its discretion because it was, in his view, only a statement of the principles of fair dealing, the House of Lords made it clear in *R* v *Secretary of State for the Home Department, ex parte Brind* [1991] 2 WLR 588, that public bodies exercising discretion were not bound to take into account the terms of the ECHR as a precondition of acting intra vires. The House of Lords recognised that to have accepted such a contention would have amounted to the incorporation of the ECHR via the 'back door'. This was true whether the power in question was one derived from statute, or the prerogative: see *R* v *Secretary of State for the Home Department, ex parte Ahmed and Others* [1998] INLR 570.

Elsewhere the courts tended to adopt the view that the common law and the ECHR provided, in any event, the same rights and freedoms. For example, in holding that a local authority could not use the law of defamation against a newspaper that had been critical of its conduct in certain financial matters, the House of Lords appeared to regard any argument based on art 10 of the ECHR as redundant. Whilst Balcombe LJ, in the Court of Appeal, had felt that domestic law was uncertain on the point and observed that 'where the law is uncertain, it must be right for the court to approach the issue before it with a predilection to ensure that our law should not involve a breach of art 10', Lord Keith expressed the view that he had reached his conclusion based on the common law of England, adding only that it was 'consistent with obligations assumed by the Crown under the Treaty in this particular field': see *Derbyshire County Council* v *Times Newspapers Ltd and Others* [1993] 2 WLR 449.

A more positive approach to reliance on the ECHR was expressed in *Rantzen* v *Mirror Group Newspapers (1986) Ltd* [1993] 3 WLR 953, where the Court of Appeal held that to allow juries to award unlimited amounts of damages to successful plaintiffs in defamation actions could amount to a breach of art 10, in the sense that as a restriction on free speech the threatened sanction of a large award of damages had to be shown to be necessary in a democratic society, and 'prescribed by law'. Like the House of Lords in the *Derbyshire County Council* case the court expressed the view that art 10 reflected the rules of the common law in relation to freedom of expression.

The Human Rights Act 1998: the debate over incorporation

The 20-year period prior to the enactment of the Human Rights Act 1998 saw growing support for the notion that the United Kingdom should 'bring human rights home' by incorporating the ECHR into domestic law. Significantly the Labour Party, which won the May 1997 general election with a huge majority, included a commitment to incorporating the ECHR at the earliest opportunity as part of its manifesto.

In observance of this promise, the Human Rights Bill was duly introduced into the House of Lords in November 1997, at the same time as the publication of the White Paper *Rights Brought Home: The Human Rights Bill* (Cmnd 3782).

Various arguments were advanced in favour of incorporation. Essentially they stressed the following; that it was better for the United Kingdom's reputation (as a nation that taking human rights seriously) for human rights issues to be determined by domestic courts; that the provision of domestic remedies would provide litigants with cheaper and speedier legal redress; and that it was illogical for the United Kingdom to agree to protect various rights in an international treaty but not extend that protection by incorporation into its domestic law. As the White Paper stated:

'It is plainly unsatisfactory that someone should be the victim of a breach of the Convention standards by the State yet [be unable to] bring any case at all in the British courts, simply because British law does not recognise the right in the same terms as one contained in the Convention.' (para 1.16)

Further there was the view, expressed by Lord Irvine LC, introducing the Human Rights Bill in the House of Lords, that an unwritten constitution could not provide the citizen with adequate protection from abuses of state power that infringe human rights.

The proposals for incorporation were, at least superficially, seductive, particularly to those who equating the provision of rights with some form of political empowerment. They marked a shift from rights being associated with freedoms, towards rights being seen as entitlements given by the state. On the other hand, traditionalists, such as Lord Donaldson, argued that incorporation was 'constitutionally unacceptable' and that Parliament's right to govern should not be curtailed by Strasbourg. Other objections raised were that: the ECHR was out of keeping with the traditional style of domestic legislation; it represented an imported written constitution, whereas it would be preferable for the United Kingdom to be devising its own; it was undemocratic, because it sought to transfer power from the elected legislature to the courts; and that if enacted as domestic law, it could cause an unnecessary increase in litigation. Lord Mackay, speaking during a two-day debate on the constitution in the House of Lords in July 1996 expressed the view that the common law offered sufficient protection, and warned of judges being dragged into political controversy. The point has been made by many commentators that judges declaring domestic legislation to be incompatible with the ECHR (see further section 9.4) would effectively be ordering the legislature to act, a complete reversal of the doctrines of the separation of powers and parliamentary sovereignty.

The statistics concerning cases brought against the United Kingdom were frequently relied upon to support the contention that the human rights of United Kingdom citizens were not sufficiently safeguarded by United Kingdom law, and that justice could only be obtained by resort to Strasbourg, or by incorporation of the ECHR into domestic law. It is true that, in the period from 1990–1995 the United Kingdom was the subject of over 3,000 claims lodged by individuals with the Commission, of which approximately 600 were declared admissible, and that the United Kingdom has lost over 50 cases at Strasbourg. Few signatory states, other than Turkey and Italy, have suffered a higher rate of successful challenge. Against this some argued that many of the cases involved what some might regard as peripheral human rights issues, as opposed to dealing with matters of life and death, and many cases turned upon issues in relation to which perfectly reasonable persons could agree to differ without either forfeiting the right to be described as reasonable. Furthermore, the frequency with which a signatory state was cited as a respondent before the court at Strasbourg did not necessarily have any correlation with its having incorporated the ECHR, as the track records of Turkey and Italy indicated.

9.3 The Human Rights Act 1998: the rights protected

The Human Rights Act 1998 received the Royal Assent in early November 1998. Sections 18, 20 and 21(5) coming into effect on enactment, the remaining sections coming into effect on 2 October 2000. The Act seeks to give effect to the European Convention on Human Rights in the domestic law of the United Kingdom, but the actual Convention rights to be incorporated are stated in s1 as being arts 2–12 and

14 of the Convention, arts 1–3 of the First Protocol, and arts 1 and 2 of the Sixth Protocol, as read with arts 16–18 of the Convention. This restricted definition of Convention rights must also be read in the light of the derogations and reservations claimed by the United Kingdom in respect of art 5(3) and art 2 of the First Protocol.

The rights protected under the ECHR

A detailed examination of the working of the ECHR and its jurisprudence is beyond the scope of a text of this nature, but what follows is a summary of the main provisions of the ECHR with illustrative case law reflecting the impact of the ECHR on domestic law. Note that the issue of public order (see art 11) is considered at greater length in Chapter 13; freedom of the individual and police powers (arts 5 and 6) is considered at greater length in Chapter 10; and freedom of expression, religious beliefs and privacy (arts 8, 9 and 10 respectively) are considered in more depth in Chapters 11 and 12.

Article 2: right to life

Article 2 provides as follows:

'(1) Everyone's right to life shall be protected by law. No one shall be deprived of his life intentionally save in the execution of a sentence of a court following his conviction of a crime for which this penalty is provided by law.
(2) Deprivation of life shall not be regarded as inflicted in contravention of this Article when it results from the use of force which is no more than absolutely necessary:
(a) in defence of any person from unlawful violence;
(b) in order to effect a lawful arrest or to prevent the escape of a person lawfully detained;
(c) in action lawfully taken for the purpose of quelling a riot or insurrection.'

The scope of this article was considered in *McCann and Others* v *United Kingdom* Case No 17/1994/464/545 (1995) 21 EHRR 97. The applicants were parents of IRA terrorists who had been killed by members of the SAS in Gibraltar in March 1988. The soldiers carrying out the killings did so in the belief that such action was necessary to prevent the suspects from remotely detonating a car bomb, with subsequent loss of life on a large scale. The applicants alleged that the killings amounted to a violation of art 2. The Commission ruled, by 11 votes to six, that the United Kingdom had not breached the ECHR but the European Court of Human Rights viewed the matter differently. Whilst holding, by ten votes to nine, that the actions of the SAS soldiers, given the information on which they acted, did not in themselves amount to a violation of art 2, the Court held that the lack of care on the part of the authorities regarding the execution of the control operation led to the conclusion that the force used had been in excess of what was absolutely necessary in order to defend others from unlawful violence. In particular, the majority of the Court took the view that the suspects could have been detained upon entering

Gibraltar, and that the authorities unjustifiably assumed that the intelligence available was correct. Hence the conditions set forth in art 2(2) were not met. Despite its finding against the United Kingdom, the Court declined to award any monetary compensation.

One area where art 2 may become significant is in relation to NHS treatment of patients with life-threatening conditions, especially where health authorities make questionable decisions regarding the allocation of resources, such as the rationing of health care by reference to age, life-style or even postcode. The applicant may be able to contend that the denial of treatment is inconsistent with the right to life: see further *D* v *United Kingdom* (1997) 24 EHRR 423.

The right to life has also been held to carry with it the duty upon signatory states to provide some form of effective official investigation when individuals are killed as a result of the use of state force: see *Jordan and Others* v *United Kingdom* Application No 24746/94 (2001) The Times 18 May.

The right to life does not carry with it an implied right to die. In *R (Pretty)* v *DPP* [2002] 1 All ER 1 the applicant suffered from motor neurone disease and faced the prospect of death in the near future. She was fully sentient however, and expressed the view that if she could she would take her own life. Because of her condition she was incapable of doing so, hence she unsuccessfully sought from the Director of Public Prosecutions (DPP) an undertaking that, if her husband assisted her in the act of committing suicide, he would not be prosecuted under s2(1) of the Suicide Act 1961. The House of Lords, unanimously dismissing her appeal, held that the right to life guaranteed under art 2 could not be interpreted as conferring a right to die or to enlist the aid of another in bringing about one's own death. Also unsuccessful was the contention that the refusal to allow her husband to put her out of her suffering amounted to torture contrary to art 3. As Lord Bingham observed, a state might be justified in inflicting treatment that would otherwise be in breach of art 3 in order to ensure the protection of rights under art 2. Arguments based on arts 8 and 9 were also rejected. Note that the DPP prayed in aid the argument that he had no power, under the constitution, in particular the Bill of Rights 1689, to suspend the law as enacted by Parliament. The stance adopted by the House of Lords was subsequently vindicated by the European Court of Human Rights when it considered the applicant's submissions: see *Pretty* v *United Kingdom* [2002] All ER (D) 286. Although some Convention rights have been interpreted as being applicable in a negative sense, such as the right not to join an association under art 11, art 2 did not provide for any right to die. Any interference with the applicant's art 8 rights arising from the DPP's refusal to give the undertaking sought would have to be seen as a proportionate response by the executive.

A decision by medical practitioners not to continue providing life support treatment to a patient in a persistent vegetative state was held not to amount to a violation of art 2 in the absence of any circumstances imposing a positive legal duty to prolong a patient's life: see *NHS Trust A* v *M* (2000) The Times 29 November.

Article 3: prohibition of torture

Article 3 provides that 'No one shall be subjected to torture or to inhuman or degrading treatment or punishment.'

It is understandably rare for this provision to be breached as a result of the deliberate executive action, although a landmark decision in this regard is *Ireland* v *United Kingdom* (1978) 2 EHRR 25 concerning the interrogation techniques employed by security forces operating in Northern Ireland. The European Court of Human Rights found that individuals had been subjected to inhuman treatment by members of the armed forces. It was also successfully invoked against the United Kingdom so as to prevent deportation, following refusal of a request for political asylum, in *Chahal* v *United Kingdom* (1996) 23 EHRR 413. The European Court of Human Rights emphasised that the prohibition of torture under art 3 of the Convention was absolute. Given that there was compelling evidence that, if deported, the applicant would be mistreated by certain elements in the Indian security forces, the refusal of asylum would amount to a breach of art 3, notwithstanding the national security issues put forward by the United Kingdom.

In most cases the alleged violation of art 3 rights is a collateral aspect of executive action (ie an unintended consequence). Hence, in *D* v *United Kingdom* (1997) 24 EHRR 423 the applicant, a native of St. Kitts, was a drugs courier who had been detained whilst trying to enter the United Kingdom in possession of £120,000 worth of cocaine. He was subsequently convicted of drugs offences and imprisoned for six years. One year into his sentence the applicant was diagnosed as being HIV positive and began a course of treatment on the NHS. His condition continued to deteriorate and a few days before he was due to be released on licence the immigration authorities ordered his removal to St Kitts. The applicant unsuccessfully sought judicial review of this decision. The Court of Appeal noted that, as the applicant's case was, technically, one of seeking leave to enter, rather than remain in, the United Kingdom, the immigration authorities were not bound to take into account the government guidelines on the treatment of applicant suffering from AIDS. The Commission found that his removal to St Kitts would amount to inhuman and degrading treatment contrary to art 3 of the ECHR, a decision upheld on referral to the Court. The protection offered by art 3 applied notwithstanding that the applicant had been convicted of a serious criminal offence which itself created grave social dangers. Whether or not a violation of art 3 would occur was not to be decided merely by reference to the actions of a third party (ie the actions of those who might provide some help and support in St Kitts). The court looked at the effect of the applicant's removal from the United Kingdom. There was no way in which the care available in St Kitts could match that being provided to the applicant in the United Kingdom. The applicant had reached a stage in his illness where the removal of care would have catastrophic personal consequences for him, and the real possibility of his dying in the most distressing circumstances created the risk of inhuman and degrading treatment that art 3 was designed to prohibit.

Similarly, in *Price* v *United Kingdom* (2001) The Times 13 August the failure to provide suitable accommodation for a severely disabled person who was being held in detention at a police station following arrest was held to amount to a violation of art 3 rights.

Physical chastisement of children by parents and guardians was also declared to be a violation of art 3 in *A* v *United Kingdom* Case 100/1997/884/1096 (1998) The Times 1 October. The applicant's stepfather, who regularly beat him with a stick, had been acquitted on charges of causing actual bodily harm after raising the common law defence of lawful chastisement. The European Court of Human Rights in (unanimously) holding that there had been a violation of art 3, concluded that the ill treatment attained the minimum level of severity required for it to fall within art 3. In doing so it had regard to the circumstances of the case, including the nature of the punishment, its duration, the age and health of the victim and its effect on the mental health of the victim. Although the ECHR created obligations for member states, not private individuals, the court reiterated its view that the state was required to ensure that all those within its jurisdiction enjoyed the rights protected by the ECHR. In particular the state was required to ensure that these rights were secured for vulnerable groups such as children. The existing state of English criminal law, which permitted a defence of law reasonable chastisement, did not provide adequate protection for children.

Article 4: prohibition of slavery and forced labour

Article 4 provides that 'No one shall be held in slavery or servitude' and that 'No one shall be required to perform forced or compulsory labour.' For these purposes the term 'forced or compulsory labour' does not include: '(a) any work required to be done in the ordinary course of detention imposed according to the provisions of art 5 of this Convention or during conditional release from such detention; (b) any service of a military character or, in case of conscientious objectors in countries where they are recognised, service exacted instead of compulsory military service; (c) any service exacted in case of an emergency or calamity threatening the life or well-being of the community; (d) any work or service which forms part of normal civic obligations.'

Article 5: right to liberty and security

Article 5 seeks to ensure that deprivation of liberty should only occur where sanctioned by law and following the correct procedure.

It is considered in the context of police powers in Chapter 10.

Article 6: right to a fair trial

Article 6 is effectively a 'due process' clause designed to ensure that both civil and criminal proceedings provide adequate protection for the parties involved. Article 6(1) provides:

'In the determination of his civil rights and obligations or of any criminal charge against him, everyone is entitled to a fair and public hearing within a reasonable time by an independent and impartial tribunal established by law. Judgment shall be pronounced publicly but the press and public may be excluded from all or part of the trial in the interest of morals, public order or national security in a democratic society, where the interests of juveniles or the protection of the private life of the parties so require, or to the extent strictly necessary in the opinion of the court in special circumstances where publicity would prejudice the interests of justice.'

In assessing the fairness of any proceedings the court should look at the whole decision-making process, in particular the extent to which any appeal or review stage can be said to have cured apparent unfairness at first instance.

As Simon Brown LJ explained in *R (On the Application of Adlard)* v *Secretary of State for the Environment* [2002] EWCA Civ 735:

'The question whether or not art 6 is satisfied ... falls to be considered by reference not merely to the initial decision-making process but also in the light of the High Court's review jurisdiction ... The remedy of judicial review in my judgment amply enables the court to correct any injustice it perceives in an individual case. If, in short, the court were satisfied that exceptionally, on the facts of a particular case, [a public body exercising a decision making discretion] had acted unfairly or unreasonably ... the court would quash the decision and require such a [fair] hearing to be given.'

See further on the extent to which administrative procedures can be cured by the availability of judicial review: *Adan* v *Newham London Borough Council* [2001] 1 All ER 930 and *R (On the Application of McLellan)* v *Bracknell Forest Borough Council* [2002] 1 All ER 899. In *R (On the Application of Beeson)* v *Dorset County Council* (2002) The Times 21 December the Divisional Court held that a local authority review panel, making decisions as to whether or not an applicant was required to contribute to the cost of residential care, was not sufficiently independent of the council as a majority of its members were council members. This unfairness could not be remedied by judicial review as the review panel was required to determine findings of fact – such as the assessing the credibility of claimants. It was impossible for a court hearing a judicial review case to determine whether or not the review panel's findings would have been affected by its connection with one of the parties. A reviewing court could not become an appeal body in relation to the panel's decisions.

Procedures adopted by United Kingdom tribunals have, nevertheless, been found wanting on a number of occasions. In *T* v *United Kingdom; V* v *United Kingdom* (1999) The Times 17 December the applicants had been convicted of murder in November 1993. At the time they were aged ten and 11. The trial took place in public in the Crown Court. The European Court of Human Rights, holding that the applicants had been denied a fair trial, expressed the view that proceedings involving children that were likely to invoke a high level of media interest should be conducted in private with only those strictly required in attendance. Whilst the Court noted that special measures were taken in respect of the applicants, such as providing them with explanations of the procedure, allowing them to see the courtroom in advance, and reducing the length of hearings so as to avoid tiredness, some other measures had actually been counter-productive, such as raising the dock so as to provide the applicants with a better view of the proceedings. The Court felt that this simply emphasised the level of scrutiny felt by the applicants. Although the applicants had been represented by skilled and experienced lawyers seated in court within 'whispering distance' of the applicants, the court felt that they had been so intimidated and traumatised by the proceedings that they were not able to communicate effectively with their lawyers or give information for the purposes of the defence.

In *Findlay* v *United Kingdom* Case 110/1995/616/706 (1997) 24 EHRR 221 the European Court of Human Rights ruled, unanimously, that the procedures for court martials, laid down by the Army Act 1955, whereby the convening officer was responsible for appointing the prosecutor and members of the court, amounted to a violation of art 6: see also *Coyne* v *United Kingdom* Case 124/1996/743/942 (1997) The Times 24 October; *Hood* v *United Kingdom* (2000) 29 EHRR 365; *Cable and Others* v *United Kingdom* (1999) The Times 11 March; and *Jordan* v *United Kingdom* (2000) The Times 17 March.

As regards the right to a hearing before a court or tribunal for the determination of civil rights, the European Court of Human Rights has held, in *Stubbings* v *United Kingdom* (1996) 23 EHRR 213, that the limitation periods for actions in tort, laid down by the Limitation Act 1980, did not amount to a denial of access contrary to art 6(1). The Court expressed the view that limitation periods served legitimate aims of ensuring that stale claims were not pursued to the prejudice of third parties, and prevented injustice from occurring, as might be the case where a court proceeded on the basis of evidence that had become unreliable with the passing of time. The failure to determine liability to costs within a reasonable time (due to the incompetence of public officials) was found to be a breach of art 6(1) in *Robins* v *United Kingdom* Case 118/1996/737/936 (1997) The Times 24 October. Other measures that restrict or effectively deny access to a court or tribunal for the determination of rights may fall foul of art 6 if they go further than is necessary to secure some other legitimate aim. Hence, in *Tinnelly and Sons Ltd and Others* v *United Kingdom*; *McElduff and Others* v *United Kingdom* (1998) 4 BHRC 343, the European Court of Human Rights held that certificates issued by the Secretary of State for Northern Ireland, under s42 of the Fair Employment Act (Northern Ireland) 1976, to the effect that the decision not to award the applicants a contract for work on electricity stations was an act done 'or the purpose of safeguarding national security or the protection of public safety or order' amounted to a violation of art 6(1). Section 42(2) of the 1976 Act provided that such a certificate was conclusive proof that the act in question was carried out for the purposes stated, and in judicial review proceedings to challenge the legality of the certificate the Court had upheld ministerial claims that relevant documents were protected from disclosure by public interest immunity. The European Court of Human Rights accepted the need for vigilance as regards ensuring the security of essentials such as electricity, and the threat posed by terrorist organisations having access to sensitive information. It was felt, however, that the total ban imposed by the s42 certificates had a disproportionate effect on the applicants' rights of access to the courts. The Court was also concerned that rights guaranteed by art 6 could be overridden by the ipse dixit of a member of the executive. Overall the United Kingdom government had failed to demonstrate why some compromise arrangement could not have been arrived at that would have provided the applicants with more information whilst at the same time ensuring security matters were adequately safeguarded: see *Devenney* v *United Kingdom* (2002) The Times 11 April.

Under art 6(2) everyone charged with a criminal offence shall be presumed innocent until proved guilty according to law. The extent which the removal of the right to silence pursuant to the introduction of the Criminal Evidence (Northern Ireland) Order (SI 1988/1987 (NI 20)) amounted to a violation of art 6 was contested in *Murray* v *United Kingdom* (1996) 22 EHRR 29, the Court holding (by 14 votes to five) that although the right to remain silent under questioning and the privilege against self-incrimination were generally recognised international standards which lay at the heart of the notion of a fair procedure under art 6, they were not absolute rights. The matter had to be viewed in the light of the sufficiency of the procedural safeguards designed to prevent oppression, such as regular cautioning and access to legal advice, and the amount of evidence against the accused that was regarded as justifying the drawing of adverse inference in the event of his failing to refute it. The Court was satisfied that sufficient safeguards were in place to ensure that the objectives of art 6 could still be achieved, and that the drawing of reasonable inferences from the applicant's behaviour did not have the effect of shifting the burden of proof contrary to art 6(2).

Note however, that the tribunal of fact in *Murray* was an experienced judge (sitting in a 'Diplock' court). Much more care may be needed when directing a jury as to the drawing of adverse inferences from silence, and a failure to do so adequately will amount to a violation of art 6, notwithstanding provisions of domestic law that appear to permit such inferences: see further *Condron* v *United Kingdom* (2000) The Times 9 May.

Article 6 has also raised questions as to the legality of provisions of domestic law that place an individual under some compulsion to provide information to the authorities, under threat of prosecution if the information is withheld. In *Saunders* v *United Kingdom* (1996) 23 EHRR 313, the use by the prosecution, during the applicant's trial for fraud, of statements made by him during investigations conducted by Department of Trade and Industry, was found to be a violation of art 6(1) because the applicant had faced the possibility of imprisonment for contempt of court if he refused to answer. By contrast, in *Stott (Procurator Fiscal, Dunfermline)* v *Brown* (2000) The Times 6 December the Privy Council held that a reply given to a police office by a motorist, confirming that she had been the driver of a car, could be lead in evidence by the prosecutor in a drink-driving case, notwithstanding the fact that the motorist had faced the prospect of a conviction under s172 of the Road Traffic Act 1988 if she had refused to provide the information to the police officer. Lord Bingham explained that the ECHR did not expressly provide any guarantee of the privilege against self-incrimination. In determining whether any given statutory provision compromised the overall fairness of a trial there were a number of factors the court had to take into account, in particular the need to strike the right balance between the interests of the individual and the general interest of the community as a whole. Given the high incidence of death and injury caused by the misuse of motor vehicles there was a clear public interest in the effective enforcement of road traffic legislation. Whilst the operation of s172 could result in a suspect being coerced (under pain of prosecution for not providing evidence) into making a statement that could result in his or her being convicted of a criminal offence, it did not represent a disproportionate response to the problem created by the need to identify vehicles and their drivers. Further, reliance on the evidence so obtained had not undermined the defendant's right to a fair trial. His Lordship distinguished the instant case from that of *Saunders* v *United Kingdom* on the basis that under s172 the questioning was limited to a simple query, there was no prolonged interrogation, and the penalties for refusing to supply information were moderate and non-custodial. The court accepted the prosecutor's argument that it was illogical to allow the use in evidence of body samples taken by force, but to prohibit reliance on the use of statements provided under threat of prosecution. More generally the court thought it significant that those who chose to drive cars knowingly subjected themselves to a regulatory regime, which did not apply to the public as a whole. That regime was imposed because of the potential for serious harm to be caused by the misuse of motor vehicles.

Article 6(3) lists the minimum rights of an individual charged with a criminal offence as being:

'(a) to be informed promptly, in a language which he understands and in detail, of the nature and cause of the accusation against him;
(b) to have adequate time and facilities for the preparation of his defence;
(c) to defend himself in person or through legal assistance of his own choosing or, if he has not sufficient means to pay for legal assistance, to be given it free when the interests of justice so require;
(d) to examine or have examined witnesses against him and to obtain the attendance and examination of witnesses on his behalf under the same conditions as witnesses against him;
(e) to have the free assistance of an interpreter if he cannot understand or speak the language used in court.'

In a series of cases the European Court of Human Rights has confirmed that compliance with art 6 requires the provision of legal representation in any proceedings that could be regarded as punitive, for example proceedings for tax enforcement or proceedings that could result in the loss of liberty: see further

Benham v *United Kingdom* (1995) The Independent 8 February and *Wynne* v *United Kingdom* Case 26/1993/421/500 (1994) 19 EHRR 333. In *Bonner* v *United Kingdom; Maxwell* v *United Kingdom* (1994) The Times 1 November the Court held that the rights guaranteed by art 6 extended to the provision of legal aid to everyone charged with a criminal offence where the interests of justice so required, in light of the importance of the hearing (as regards the sentences imposed on the applicants), the limited scope for the unrepresented applicant to present his case competently, the nature of the proceedings, and clear evidence that the applicants lacked the financial resources to pay for their own lawyers. Similarly, the denial of access to a solicitor during the first 48 hours of police questioning has been held to be a violation of art 6(3)(c): see *Murray* v *United Kingdom* (1996) 22 EHRR 29. *Brennan* v *United Kingdom* (2001) The Times 22 October confirms that art 6(3)(c) includes the right to consult privately with a solicitor.

The concept of 'equality of arms' underpins much of art 6(3), hence any action, or failure to act, on the part of the prosecution that has the result of undermining the ability of the defendant to represent his case adequately may amount to a violation of the provision. Hence in *Rowe and Others* v *United Kingdom* (2000) The Times 1 March the ECHR ruled that the prosecution's failure to provide a trial judge with the opportunity of ruling upon whether evidence, to be relied on by the prosecution in the course of the trial, should be disclosed to the defence or withheld on the grounds of public interest immunity, resulted in the applicants being denied a fair trial. (Note that the domestic law relating to pre-trial disclosure was changed after the domestic trials giving rise to the application but before the applications were considered by the ECHR.)

The 'equality of arms' principle was also invoked in *R* v *Secretary of State for the Home Department, ex parte Quaquah* (2000) The Times 21 January, where the Divisional Court quashed a direction ordering the removal of the applicant, an unsuccessful asylum seeker, from the jurisdiction. Prior to the direction being given the applicant had commenced an action against the Secretary of State for malicious prosecution arising out of alleged involvement in disturbances whilst the applicant was being held at a detention centre. The court could find no compelling argument to justify the interference with the applicant's right to a fair trial of his action, and also found no evidence that his need to remain in the jurisdiction to properly conduct the litigation had been taken into account. On police powers and procedures generally: see Chapter 10.

Article 7: no punishment without law

Article 7 provides for a prohibition on retrospective legislation creating any criminal offence or increasing the penalty for an offence, by providing that: 'No one shall be held guilty of any criminal offence on account of any act or omission which did not constitute a criminal offence under national or international law at the time when it was committed. Nor shall a heavier penalty be imposed than the one that was applicable at the time the criminal offence was committed.'

This prohibition is modified by art 7(2) to the extent that it should apply without prejudice to the possibility of a person being tried and punished for any act or omission which, at the time when it was committed, was criminal according to the general principles of law recognised by civilised nations.

This provision was successfully invoked by the applicant in *Welch* v *United Kingdom* (1995) 20 EHRR 247, who had been convicted of drug related offences and sentenced to a long term of imprisonment. An order was made under the Drug Trafficking Offences Act 1986 (now the 1994 Act) which resulted in the confiscation of certain of the applicant's assets that could be regarded as the proceeds of drug dealing, even though the offences in question had been committed prior to the commencement of the Act. The applicant complained that the operation of the 1986 Act was a violation of art 7(1) of the ECHR as it involved the imposition of a heavier penalty than could lawfully have been imposed at the time the offence was committed. Granting the application, the court held that the measure was clearly penal in nature, and did violate art 7(1) by providing for a more severe penalty than could have been imposed when the drug dealing offences were carried out.

More generally, the way in which judges develop the principles of the common law within the English legal system has lead to questions as to whether defendants are victims of retrospective law-making. In *SW* v *United Kingdom* Case 47/1994/576; *CR* v *United Kingdom* Case 48/1994/577 (1996) The Times 3 December both applicants, who had been convicted of rape and attempted rape of their wives, claimed that there had been a violation of art 7 of the ECHR since, at the time the incidents giving rise to the convictions had occurred, there was, at common law, a rule that a husband could not be guilty of raping his wife. In rejecting the applicants' contention that the decision of the English court (see *R* v *R* [1991] 3 WLR 767) to disregard the common law rule and uphold the convictions amounted to the imposition of retrospective criminal liability, as their actions had not been contrary to the common law at the time they were committed, the Court held that art 7 did not prohibit the gradual clarification of the principles of criminal liability on a case-by-case basis provided the development could be reasonably foreseen. The gradual evolution of restrictions upon the husband's immunity from liability for marital rape, and the mounting criticism of the immunity, made the judicial development in the instant case reasonably foreseeable.

Article 8: right to respect for private and family life

This right is considered in more depth in Chapter 11.

Article 9: freedom of thought, conscience and religion

This right is considered in more depth in Chapter 12 in the context of freedom of expression and blasphemy.

Article 10: freedom of expression

See Chapter 12.

Article 11: freedom of assembly and association

See Chapter 13.

Article 12: right to marry

See Chapter 11.

Article 14: prohibition of discrimination

The enjoyment of the rights and freedoms set forth in the Convention are to be secured by the contracting states without discrimination on any ground such as sex, race, colour, language, religion, political or other opinion, national or social origin, association with a national minority, property, birth or other status.

Article 16: restrictions on political activity of aliens

Nothing in arts 10, 11 and 14 should be regarded as preventing the contracting states from imposing restrictions on the political activity of aliens.

Article 17: prohibition of abuse of rights

Nothing in the Convention may be interpreted as implying for any state, group or person any right to engage in any activity or perform any act aimed at the destruction of any of the rights and freedoms set forth in the Convention or at their limitation to a greater extent than is provided for in the Convention.

The First Protocol

There are a number of protocols to the ECHR that states can sign up to as they see fit. In effect they are 'optional extras' on the human rights menu. The First Protocol, to which the United Kingdom is a signatory, provides (under art 1) that:

> 'Every natural or legal person is entitled to the peaceful enjoyment of his possessions. No one shall be deprived of his possessions except in the public interest and subject to the conditions provided for by law and by the general principles of international law.
>
> The preceding provisions shall not, however, in any way impair the right of a state to enforce such laws as it deems necessary to control the use of property in accordance with the general interest or to secure the payment of taxes or other contributions or penalties.'

See further *National and Provincial Building Society and Others* v *United Kingdom* (1997) 25 EHRR 127.

Article 2 details a right to education:

> 'No person shall be denied the right to education. In the exercise of any functions which it assumes in relation to education and to teaching, the state shall respect the right of parents to ensure such education and teaching in conformity with their own religious and philosophical convictions.'

Note that the United Kingdom has filed a reservation in respect of art 2 to the First Protocol to the effect that the principle affirmed in the second sentence of art 2 is accepted 'only so far as it is compatible with the provision of efficient instruction and training, and the avoidance of unreasonable public expenditure' (reservation dated 20 March 1952).

As the White Paper *Rights Brought Home: The Human Rights Bill* (Cmnd 3782) indicates:

> 'The reservation reflects the fundamental principle originally enacted in the Education Act 1944, and now contained in s9 of the Education Act 1996, "that pupils are to be educated in accordance with the wishes of their parents so far as that is compatible with the provision of efficient instruction and training and the avoidance of unreasonable public expenditure". There is similar provision in Scottish legislation. The reservation does not affect the right to education in art 2. Nor does it deny parents the right to have account taken of their religious or philosophical convictions. Its purpose is to recognise that in the provision of state-funded education a balance must be struck in some cases between the convictions of parents and what is educationally sound and affordable.' (para 4.5)

Article 3 provides for a right to free elections:

> 'The High Contracting Parties undertake to hold free elections at reasonable intervals by secret ballot, under conditions which will ensure the free expression of the opinion of the people in the choice of the legislature.'

See further *Matthews* v *United Kingdom* (1999) 28 EHRR 361, considered at Chapter 5, section 5.4.

Other Protocols

Protocol Four prohibits deprivation of liberty on grounds of inability to fulfil contractual obligations; provides a right to liberty of movement; a right to non-expulsion from the home state; a right of entry to the state of which a person is a national; and a prohibition on the collective expulsion of aliens. The United Kingdom signed Protocol Four in 1963 but has not subsequently ratified it because of concerns regarding the compatibility of domestic law. Protocol Six prohibits the death penalty. Again this has not been ratified on the basis that the issue of whether or not to retain the death penalty has always been regarded as one best determined by individual MPs as a matter of conscience. Protocol Seven prohibits the expulsion of aliens without a decision in accordance with the law or opportunities for review; a right to a review of conviction or sentence after criminal conviction; a right to compensation following a miscarriage of justice; a prohibition on double jeopardy in criminal cases; and a right to equality between spouses. The present government intends to ratify Protocol Seven once certain aspects of domestic law have been rationalised. Protocol Twelve, which deals with discrimination on the grounds of sex, race or religion, opened for signature in November 2000.

Limitations, restrictions and derogations

A number of articles contain express exemption provisions. For example, arts 11(2), 8(2), 9(2) and 10(2). As regards derogation in time of war or public emergency Article 15 provides:

'(1) In time of war or other public emergency threatening the life of the nation any High Contracting Party may take measures derogating from its obligations under this Convention to the extent strictly required by the exigencies of the situation, provided that such measures are not inconsistent with its other obligations under international law. But: (2) No derogation from art 2, except in respect of deaths resulting from lawful acts of war, or from arts 3, 4(1) and 7 shall be made under this provision.'

Following *Brogan* v *United Kingdom* (1989) 11 EHRR 117 the United Kingdom applied for a derogation in respect of art 5(3) in the light of that fact that:

'There have been in the United Kingdom in recent years campaigns of organised terrorism connected with the affairs of Northern Ireland which have manifested themselves in activities which have included repeated murder, attempted murder, maiming, intimidation and violent civil disturbance and in bombing and fire raising which have resulted in death, injury and widespread destruction of property. As a result, a public emergency within the meaning of Article 15(1) of the Convention exists in the United Kingdom.' (Derogation notification of 23 December 1988).

In *Brannigan and McBride* v *United Kingdom* (1994) 17 EHRR 539 the European Court of Human Rights accepted the contention of the United Kingdom that the situation in Northern Ireland justified a derogation under art 15 in respect of the provisions of the ECHR relating to detention without charge. Hence the detention of the applicants under the Prevention of Terrorism (Temporary Provisions) Act 1984 (see now s14 and para 6 of Sch 5 to the Prevention of Terrorism (Temporary Provisions) Act 1989, which make comparable provision) did not amount to a violation of the ECHR, vindicating, to some extent, the refusal of the United Kingdom government to alter the law relating to the detention of suspected terrorists following the ruling in *Brogan* v *United Kingdom* (above).

The certification and detention powers (detention without trial) given to the Home Secretary under s21 of the Anti-terrorism, Crime and Security Act 2001, in the wake of the 11 September 2001 terrorist attacks, are clearly at odds with the rights provided for under art 5(1) of the European Convention on Human Rights, hence the United Kingdom government had to apply for a derogation, pleading the threat caused by international terrorism as the reason: see further s30 of the 2001 Act.

9.4 Pursuing a Human Rights Act claim before the domestic courts

Procedure for enforcement

The Human Rights Act 1998 Act does not expressly create a new procedure for raising alleged violations of Convention rights. Section 7(1) envisages that individuals will be able to bring proceedings (or a counterclaim) against a public body in the appropriate court or tribunal 'as may be determined in accordance with rules': s7(2). Section 7(9) provides that these rules are to be made by the Lord Chancellor. Alternatively, litigants will be allowed to 'rely on the Convention right or rights concerned in any legal proceedings' (s7(1)(b)), legal proceedings including, for these purposes 'proceedings brought by or at the instigation of a public authority; and ... an appeal against the decision of a court or tribunal': s7(6)(a) and (b). Section 22(4) provides that proceedings can only be brought against a public body by an individual under s7(1)(b) in respect of acts taking place after the Act came into force; however, an individual seeking to rely on Convention rights in proceedings brought by or at the instigation of a public body is able to do so after October 2000 regardless of when the impugned action of the public body took place: see *R* v *Director of Public Prosecutions, ex parte Kebilene; Same, ex parte Rechachi* [1999] 3 WLR 175.

Only the 'victim' of the alleged unlawful act is permitted to bring proceedings or rely on the Convention in legal proceedings: s7(1). The 'victim' in this context can be a limited company: see *County Properties Ltd* v *The Scottish Ministers* 2000 SLT 965.

It is clear that many of the cases involving reliance on Convention rights will take the form of applications for judicial review – given that the Act is of direct application to public bodies (see below). The result is that a narrower test for locus standi will be applied in applications alleging a breach of Convention rights, as compared to applications for review generally. As s7(3) makes clear: 'If the proceedings are brought on an application for judicial review, the applicant is to be taken to have a sufficient interest in relation to the unlawful act only if he is, or would be, a victim of that act.' 'Victim' for the purposes of s7 is defined as 'a victim for the purposes of art 34 of the Convention if proceedings were brought in the European Court of Human Rights': s7(7). In particular, whereas pressure groups are increasingly seen as having 'sufficient interest' for the purposes of applying for judicial review, it will be difficult for them to satisfy the 'victim' test adopted by the Act.

The curious possibility thus arises that a pressure group might be regarded as having sufficient interest to challenge a decision affecting Community law rights by way of judicial review, but might lack locus standi – not being the victim – to assert Convention rights by way of judicial review.

An applicant can only be a 'victim' for the purposes of a challenge by way of judicial review if there has been a decision, action, or failure to act in relation to the exercise of a public function. As a result there would be no basis for a 'free-standing' application for judicial review of a statute simply because an individual was of the opinion that it was incompatible with the rights protected by the 1998 Act. The applicant would have to have his Convention rights adversely affected by action taken under the impugned statute. In *Rushbridger* v *Attorney-General* [2001] EWHC Admin 529 the applicant (the editor of *The Guardian* newspaper) sought assurances from the Attorney-General that he would not be prosecuted under s3 of the Treason Felony Act 1848 in respect of articles he intended to publish espousing the non-violent removal of the monarchy and the establishing of a republic in the United Kingdom. The applicant contended that if a prosecution did follow the publication of the articles the trial court would be required to 'read down' s3 of the 1848 Act, or grant a declaration of incompatibility on the basis that s3 was incompatible with the right to free expression guaranteed by art 10 of the European Convention on Human Rights, as incorporated into domestic law by the Human Rights Act 1998. The Attorney-General declined to give the undertaking sought. Refusing leave to apply for judicial review of the Attorney-General's refusal, the court endorsed the view that the application could not succeed because there was no 'decision' of the Attorney-General to challenge. He had merely expressed his view that it was not his function to give assurances that criminal proceedings would not be instituted in certain situations. As a result the applicant could not be accorded the 'victim' status necessary for him to bring proceedings under s7 of the 1998 Act. It was not possible for him to obtain a declaration from the court that the 1848 Act was incompatible with art 10 of the European Convention on Human Rights simply because he was a journalist who might be prosecuted if he published articles calling for the peaceful demise of the monarchy.

Section 7(5) provides for a time limit of 12 months for the bringing of proceedings where it is claimed that a public authority has acted in breach of Convention rights, time running from the date on which the act complained of took place. Beyond this a court or tribunal will have a discretion to allow proceedings outside this time limit if it considers it equitable to do so having regard to all the circumstances. This time limit would apply subject to any rule imposing a stricter time limit, hence the three-month rule in relation to applications for judicial review would still apply.

Significantly the Act makes no provision for a Human Rights Commission to oversee compliance with the Act and bring proceedings in respect of non-compliance. This omission has drawn criticism from some quarters, particularly where comparisons have been drawn with the work of the Equal Opportunities Commission and Commission for Racial Equality in overseeing legislation dealing with discrimination on the grounds of gender and ethnicity. Northern Ireland does have a Human Rights Commission, but not one instituted as a result of the Human Rights Act 1998. A Parliamentary Joint Committee on Human rights was appointed in January 2001.

Who can be the subject of these proceedings?

By virtue of s6(1) it becomes unlawful for a public authority to act (or fail to act: see s6(6)) in a way that is incompatible with a Convention right. A public body for these purposes includes a court or tribunal, and 'any person certain of whose functions are functions of a public nature, but does not include either House of the [United Kingdom] Parliament or a person exercising functions in connection with proceedings in the [United Kingdom] Parliament': s6(3). The term 'Parliament' as used in s6(3) does not include the House of Lords in its judicial capacity. By contrast the Scottish Parliament and the Welsh Assembly, as subordinate legislatures, are bound by the 1998 Act. Section 29(2)(d) of the Scotland Act 1998 provides that the Scottish Parliament does not have legislative competence to enact legislation that is incompatible with Convention rights, and Sch 4 to the 1998 Act further provides that no Act of the Scottish Parliament can modify the Human Rights Act 1998. Section 107 of the Government of Wales Act 1998 imposes similar restraints on the Welsh Assembly, subject to the fact that the Assembly is not, in any event, empowered to enact primary legislation.

Under s6(1) a public body such as a tribunal or local authority will be bound to observe the ECHR whether it is engaged in a public law or private law activity. Other bodies may be regarded as public bodies if certain of their functions are of a public nature (see s6(3)(b)), but the 1998 Act will only apply to acts of such bodies that are of a public nature. In determining whether or not a body has public law functions it seems likely that the courts will be influenced by the jurisprudence built up in relation to applications for judicial review where the issue has been whether a non-statutory body can be regarded as a public authority: see for example *R* v *Panel on Take-overs and Mergers, ex parte Datafin plc* [1987] 2 WLR 699; *R* v *Disciplinary Committee of the Jockey Club, ex parte The Aga Khan* [1993] 1 WLR 909; and *R* v *Insurance Ombudsman Bureau and the Insurance Ombudsman, ex parte Aegon Life* [1994] COD 426.

Potentially within the scope of the public bodies subject to the 1998 Act are organisations such as the BBC, the Church of England and other religious bodies, universities, the governing bodies of various sports, self-regulatory bodies and any organisation that has taken over what was previously a public law function, such as running prisons.

The courts are developing the concept of public body for the purposes of s6 on a case-by-case basis, but useful guidance can be obtained from the judgment of Lord Woolf CJ in *Poplar Housing and Regeneration Community Association Ltd* v *Donoghue* [2001] 4 All ER 604, where one of the issues was the extent to which the respondent housing association was governed by the Human Rights Act 1998. Lord Woolf CJ observed:

> 'The purpose of s6(3)(b) is to deal with hybrid bodies which have both public and private functions. It is not to make a body, which does not have responsibilities to the public, a public body merely because it performs acts on behalf of a public body which would constitute public functions were such acts to be performed by the public body itself. ... In coming to our conclusion as to whether Poplar is a public authority within the 1998 Act meaning of that term, we regard it of particular importance in this case that ... Tower Hamlets, in transferring its housing stock to Poplar, does not transfer its primary public duties to Poplar. Poplar is no more than the means by which it seeks to perform those duties ... the fact that a body is a charity or is conducted not for profit means that it is likely to be motivated in performing its activities by what it perceives to be the public interest. However, this does not point to the body being a public authority. In addition, even if such a body performs functions that would be considered to be of a public nature if performed by a public body, nevertheless such acts may remain of a private nature for the purpose of s6(3)(b) and (5). ... What can make an act, which would otherwise be private, public, is a feature or a combination of features which impose a public character or stamp on the act. Statutory authority for what is done can at least help to mark the act as being public; so can the extent of control over the function exercised by another body which is a public authority. The more closely the acts that could be of a private nature are enmeshed in the activities of a public body, the more likely they are to be public. However, the fact that the acts are supervised by a public regulatory body does not necessarily indicate that they are of a public nature ... there is no clear demarcation line which can be drawn between public and private bodies and functions In a borderline case, such as this, the decision is very much one of fact and degree.'

See further *R (On the Application of Heather and Another)* v *Leonard Cheshire Foundation* [2002] 2 All ER 936 where Lord Woolf CJ emphasised again that the concept of 'public body' for the purposes of a HRA 1998 claim was not necessarily co-terminus with the concept as developed for the purposes of judicial review in domestic law.

Where the claim of unlawfulness under s6 is based upon a judicial act, proceedings under s7(1)(a) may only be brought by exercising a right of appeal, making an application for judicial review, or by following such procedure as may be laid down in rules made from time to time: s9(1). So-called 'ouster' clauses that seek to remove rights of appeal or exclude judicial review would not be affected by this requirement: see s9(2).

Section 6(1) effectively creates a new 'head' of ultra vires as regards applications for judicial review of public bodies. If a public body fails to pay due regard to the terms of the Convention, or the jurisprudence of the European Court of Human Rights, in exercising its discretion or discharging a statutory duty, prima facie grounds for review will exist. In particular the notion of proportionality as developed by the European Court of Human Rights (ie comparing what was needed to deal with a situation with the extent of the power actually used) becomes a facet of domestic law to which reviewing courts will now be obliged to have regard.

Section 6(2) restricts the scope of s6(1) by providing that the latter does not apply if, as the result of one or more provisions of primary legislation, or because of the way in which subordinate legislation has to be applied in the light of primary legislation, the public body alleged to have acted unlawfully could not have acted differently. If such a situation arises the court may still be willing to make a declaration of incompatibility, as to which, see below.

It remains to be seen to what extent the courts are willing to allow the concept a 'constitutional tort' to develop under s6 whereby claimants seek damages for the failure on the part of a public body to observe its duty under s6 not to act in a manner incompatible with the rights set forth in the ECHR (see judicial remedies, below).

Further, no action will lie against a minister for not laying a proposal for legislation before Parliament or for not making any primary legislation or remedial order: see s6(6)(a) and (b), and below.

Given that it includes the courts and tribunals, the definition of public authority in s6 creates the possibility of the Convention having indirect 'horizontal' effect. Although the 1998 Act does not expressly create any obligation on the part of private individuals to abide by the terms of the Convention, proceedings could be brought against a court that failed to uphold a Convention right in proceedings between private individuals. An example might be an allegation that a newspaper had invaded the privacy of an individual. There is no common law right to privacy as such. Article 8 of the Convention is now part of domestic law, but appears only to apply to public authorities, not newspapers. If a court were to strike out proceedings brought by a private individual against a newspaper alleging invasion of privacy as disclosing no cause of action, the court might itself then become the focus of an action for not upholding Convention rights.

It might be further argued that whether or not there has been a violation of an individual's human rights should be judged by looking at the effect of the actions on the victim, rather than concentrating on the legal niceties of the status of the perpetrator. Suppose a group of anti-abortionists terrorised doctors willing to carry out abortions to the point where the doctors were too frightened to express their views publicly. Could the doctors claim that their right to free speech had been violated on the basis that the state had not provided adequate protection in respect of the actions of other private individuals?

Thus far the courts have stopped short of developing a concept of horizontal effect, but a form of 'indirect horizontal effect' is detectable. In *Douglas* v *Hello! Ltd* [2001] IP & T 391 the Court of Appeal agreed to extend the concept of breach of confidence so that private parties would be bound, in certain circumstances, to act in conformity with Convention rights, such as the right to privacy: see further the application in *A* v *B plc and Another* (2001) The Times 2 November.

What is required of a court considering a case involving an allegation that a Convention right has been violated?

Section 2(1) of the 1998 Act makes it clear that any court or tribunal determining a question arising in connection with a Convention right must take into account: any judgment, decision, declaration or advisory opinion of the European Court of Human Rights; any opinion of the Commission given in a report adopted under art 31 of the Convention; any decision of the Commission in connection with art 26 or 27(2) of the Convention, or any decision of the Committee of Ministers taken under art 46 of the Convention, 'whenever made or given, so far as, in the opinion of the court or tribunal, it is relevant to the proceedings in which that question has arisen.'

This is a relatively weak obligation as a court may take into account the jurisprudence of the ECHR, such as the doctrine of the 'margin of appreciation' and the role of proportionality in justifying interference with rights, but then decide not to give it full effect when considering the compatibility of domestic law.

It may also be the case that the courts take into account rulings of the Privy Council in appeals concerning constitutional rights for those countries having written constitutions incorporating terms similar to those found in the ECHR: see for example *DPP* v *Tokai* [1996] AC 856 and *Robinson* v *The Queen* [1985] AC 956. In *R* v *Director of Public Prosecutions, ex parte Kebilene; Same, ex parte Rechachi* (see above), Lord Hope, referring to the likely impact of the 1998 Act once in force, observed:

> '... the vigorous public debate which [has accompanied the passage through Parliament of the Human Rights Act 1998] has already had a profound influence on thinking about issues of human rights. It is now plain that the incorporation of the European Convention on Human Rights into our domestic law will subject the entire legal system to a fundamental process of review and, where necessary, reform by the judiciary ... Lord Wilberforce ... in *Minister of Home Affairs* v *Fisher* [1980] AC 319, 328 [observed] that instruments of this nature call for a generous interpretation suitable to give to individuals the full measure of the fundamental rights and freedoms referred to, and Lord Diplock's comment in *Attorney-General of The Gambia* v *Momodou Jobe* [1984] AC 689, 700 that a generous and purposive construction is to be given to that part of a constitution which protects and entrenches fundamental rights and freedoms to which all persons in the state are to be entitled. The same approach will now have to be applied in this country when issues are raised under the 1998 Act about the compatibility of domestic legislation and of acts of public authorities with the fundamental rights and freedoms which are enshrined in the Convention.'

See also comments of Lord Woolf in *Attorney-General of Hong Kong* v *Lee Kwong-Kut* [1993] AC 951 at 975, where he referred to the need (as regards the Hong Kong Bill of Rights) to ensure that disputes did not get out of hand, to ensure that the Bill was approached with realism and a sense of proportion so that it did not become a 'source of injustice' and thereby 'debased in the eyes of the public'. If the Scottish experience is any guidance the courts will be robust in their treatment of vexatious or outlandish claims: see observations of Lord President, Lord Rodger of Earlsferry, in *Anderson* v *The Scottish Ministers and Another* (2000) The Times 21 June.

The more striking duty is that created by s3(1) of the 1998 Act which provides that a court or tribunal called upon to do so must interpret primary legislation and subordinate legislation 'in a way which is compatible with the Convention rights.' In effect it means that a court will try to ensure it arrives at an interpretation of domestic law that is consistent with the ECHR even if this means resorting to creative or dynamic methods of statutory interpretation. Bearing in mind that this applies to legislation enacted both before and after the Human Rights Act 1998 came into force it means that the doctrine of implied repeal does not operate fully in respect of the 1998 Act. Normally the 1998 Act would prevail over any inconsistent provision in earlier legislation. The effect of s3, however, is that earlier inconsistent legislation might still prevail over the 1998 Act if the courts cannot arrive at an interpretation of the earlier legislation that is consistent with the terms of the ECHR (see judicial remedies, below, for consideration of declarations of incompatibility).

It seems inevitable that the courts will adopt a new approach to statutory interpretation where Convention rights are concerned, rather than stick rigidly to the traditional 'rules' of interpretation. The tradition of the European Court of Human Rights is to be more flexible and evaluative in its exercise of its interpretative functions. Thus domestic judges will have a more explicit role in assessing the merits of executive decision making (ie its legitimacy within the context of the ECHR), whereas their role to date, at least in theory, has been limited to scrutinising the legality of executive action by means of judicial review. As Lord Irvine LC observed:

> '[Once the ECHR is incorporated in domestic law] The courts' decisions will be based on a more overtly principled, indeed moral, basis. The court will look at the positive right. It will only accept an interference with that right where a justification, allowed under the Convention, is made out. The scrutiny will not be limited to seeing if the words of an exception can be satisfied. The court will need to be satisfied that the spirit of this exception is made out. It will need to be satisfied that the interference with the protected right is justified in the public interests in a free democratic society. Moreover, the courts will in this area have to apply the Convention principle of proportionality. This means the court will be looking substantively at that question. It will not be limited to a secondary review of the decision making process but at the primary question of the merits of the decision itself.
>
> In reaching its judgment, therefore, the court will need to expand and explain its own view of whether the conduct is legitimate. It will produce in short a decision on the morality of the conduct and not simply its compliance with the bare letter of the law.'
> (Tom Sargant Memorial Lecture, December 1997)

The current debate is as to whether the courts should adopt a 'narrow' interpretive approach – with the result that limited powers of interpretation may leave the court with no option but to conclude that a statue is incompatible with the Convention and grant a declaration accordingly – or a 'broad' interpretative approach whereby the need to issue declarations of incompatibility is avoided by a radical and dynamic reading of a statute that ensures compliance with the Convention, even though the meaning given to the statutory provision is the precise opposite of what Parliament appears to have enacted.

Strong support for the broad approach is to be found in the speech of Lord Steyn in *R* v *A* [2001] 3 All ER 1. The defendant had been charged with rape and sought to adduce evidence concerning his previous sexual history with the complainant. At a preparatory hearing prior to the defendant's trial the judge had ruled that such questioning was prohibited by the operation of s41(3)(c) of the Youth Justice and Criminal Evidence Act 1999. The Court of Appeal ruled in the defendant's favour, and the Director of Public Prosecutions (DPP) appealed further to the House of Lords. The defendant contended that to prohibit questioning of a complainant, regarding her previous sexual history with the defendant, prevented the defendant from having a fair trial as required by art 6 of the European Convention on Human Rights. Dismissing the DPP's appeal, Lord Steyn observed that the provisions of the 1999 Act could be and had to be interpreted so as to ensure that a defendant had a fair trial. Hence the provisions had to be read so as to provide the trial judge with the discretion to permit questioning regarding the complainant's previous sexual history with the defendant if in his view such questioning was a precondition of a fair trial process.

Regarding the approach of the courts to provisions in primary legislation apparently at odds with the requirements of the European Convention on Human Rights, Lord Steyn noted that the first stage was for the court to determine whether or not the legislation did interfere with a right protected under the Convention. If it did, it was for the Crown to justify the interference, an argument that would involve an examination of the purpose of the impugned legislation. In this case the provisions of the 1999 Act had the purpose of preventing the humiliation of complainants in rape cases by their being subjected to unnecessary and irrelevant questioning regarding their past sexual liaisons. The question then arose as to whether or not these provisions were a proportionate response, given the inroads that the prohibitions of ss41–43 of the 1999 Act made on the defendant's right to a fair trial. In assessing proportionality a court would have regard to whether: (i) the legislative objective was sufficiently important to justify limiting a fundamental right; (ii) the measures designed to meet that objective were rationally connected to it; and (iii) the means used to impair the right or freedom were no more than necessary to accomplish the objective.

Having considered the relevant provisions of the 1999 Act, Lord Steyn concluded that that they could not be interpreted so as ensure a fair trial for the defendant by recourse to ordinary methods of purposive construction. Although the provisions pursued desirable goals, the blanket ban on questioning about past sexual history (save for some 'similar fact' type exceptions) amounted to 'legislative overkill'.

As he explained, however, s3 of the Human Rights Act 1998 placed the courts under a strong interpretative obligation to ensure the conformity of primary legislation with the Convention even if there was no ambiguity in the language of the statute in the sense that it was capable of two different meanings. Whilst the courts had always been free to depart from the language of a statute to avoid absurd consequences, s3 of the 1998 Act required a court to go even further – even adopting an interpretation that, linguistically, might appear strained. Hence s3 of the 1998 Act required the court to subordinate the niceties of the language of s41(3)(c) of the 1999 Act to broader considerations of relevance judged by logical and common sense criteria of time and circumstances. The basis for thus interpreting the provisions of the 1999 Act so as permit questioning about past sexual history was the view that Parliament, if aware of the problem, would not have wanted to deny the right to an accused to put forward a full and complete defence by advancing truly probative material required to ensure a fair trial under art 6. See further observations in *R* v *Lambert* [2001] 3 All ER 577.

Compare this with the approach of Lord Woolf CJ in *Poplar Housing and Regeneration Community Association Ltd* v *Donoghue* (above), where he observed:

'It is difficult to overestimate the importance of s3 [of the Human Rights Act 1998] it applies to legislation passed both before and after the 1998 Act came into force. Subject to the section not requiring the court to go beyond that which is possible, it is mandatory in its terms. In the case of legislation predating the 1998 Act where the legislation would otherwise conflict with the convention, s3 requires the court to now interpret legislation in a manner which it would not have done before the 1998 Act came into force. When the court interprets legislation usually its primary task is to identify the intention of Parliament. Now, when s3 applies, the courts have to adjust their traditional role in relation to interpretation so as to give effect to the direction contained in s3. It is as though legislation that predates the 1998 Act and conflicts with the convention has to be treated as being subsequently amended to incorporate the language of s3. However, the following points, which are probably self-evident, should be noted: (a) unless the legislation would otherwise be in breach of the Convention s3 can be ignored (so courts should always first ascertain whether, absent s3, there would be any breach of the convention); (b) if the court has to rely on s3 it should limit the extent of the modified meaning to that which is necessary to achieve compatibility; (c) s3 does not entitle the court to legislate (its task is still one of interpretation, but interpretation in accordance with the direction contained in s3); (d) the views of the parties and of the Crown as to whether a 'constructive' interpretation should be adopted cannot modify the task of the court (if s3 applies the court is required to adopt the s3 approach to interpretation); and (e) where despite the strong language of s3, it is not possible to achieve a result which is compatible with the Convention, the court is not required to grant a declaration and presumably in exercising its discretion as to whether to grant a declaration or not it will be influenced by the usual considerations which apply to the grant of declarations.

The most difficult task that courts face is distinguishing between legislation and interpretation. Here practical experience of seeking to apply s3 will provide the best guide. However, if it is necessary in order to obtain compliance to radically alter the effect of the legislation this will be an indication that more than interpretation is involved.'

If great uncertainty, and a great deal of speculative litigation, is to be avoided the courts are going to have to develop a clearer line on the approach to the judicial role under s3. There are dangers that the courts might be seen as subverting the rule of law and the democratic will if there is an over-readiness to ride roughshod over the 'niceties' of the legislation to achieve a reading compatible with the Convention's demands.

Margin of appreciation

The extent to which the courts will be prepared to intervene to quash an executive decision on the grounds that it is incompatible with Convention rights will vary according to the type of right in question. As is so often the case in public law context is everything. Where 'absolute rights' are involved, such as art 3 (freedom from torture) or art 7 (non-retrospective criminal law), there is little scope for allowing a public body any 'margin of appreciation'. Where rights subject to specified narrow limitations are involved, such as art 2 (the right to life) or art 5 (liberty of the person), the court must investigate whether or not the conditions for satisfying the exception have been made out. Finally, there are those rights that are provided subject to general exceptions, typically the rights to privacy, freedom of expression, freedom of religion and freedom of assembly. Where these rights are concerned the court, in addition to considering whether the preconditions for any exception are met, will also have to apply a broad test of proportionality, for example questioning whether the restrictions imposed on the enjoyment of a particular right are necessary in a democratic society, or are necessary to maintain public order. This inquiry also involves consideration of whether or not the restrictions went further than was required. It is in relation to this last group of rights that the doctrine of 'margin of appreciation' is most significant. Under the Strasbourg jurisprudence it is accepted that national judges are best placed to conduct the sort of 'balancing of rights' that arises under arts 8–11: see *Handyside* v *United Kingdom* (1976) 1 EHRR 737. The less uniformity there is between member states in their approach to a particular issue (for example the age of criminal responsibility), the greater the margin of appreciation allowed. Compare this to the very narrow margin of appreciation allowed where commonly agreed standards are involved, such as the desirability of democracy. For example, see *R* v *Secretary of State for Health, ex parte Lally* (2000) The Times 26 October, where the Divisional Court upheld the validity of a Health Service circular prohibiting visits by children to certain categories of patients in prison hospitals. The applicant (a patient at a secure hospital) had argued that the circular, in its operation, amounted to a violation to his right to a family life under art 8. Scott Baker J confirmed that where there were conflicting rights under art 8 a member state, and hence the Secretary of State for Health, was entitled to a wider margin of appreciation. He went on to confirm that the directions contained in the circular were not disproportionate to the aim they sought to achieve, ie the protection of children.

In *R (On the Application of International Transport Roth GmbH)* v *Secretary of*

State for the Home Department (2002) The Times 26 February Laws LJ sought to identify four principles that could be applied to determine the degree to which a decision-maker might be allowed a margin of appreciation by a domestic court where Convention rights were in play. The first was that greater deference would be paid to an Act of Parliament than to a decision of the executive or a subordinate measure. He explained:

> 'Where the decision-maker is not Parliament, but a minister or other public or governmental authority exercising power conferred by Parliament, a degree of deference will be due on democratic grounds – the decision-maker is Parliament's delegate – within the principles accorded by the cases. But where the decision-maker is Parliament itself, speaking through main legislation, the tension of which I have spoken is at its most acute. In our intermediate constitution the legislature is not subordinate to a sovereign text, as are the legislatures in "constitutional" systems. Parliament remains the sovereign legislator. It, and not a written constitution, bears the ultimate mantle of democracy in the state.'

The second principle was that there was more scope for deference where Convention rights were expressed in terms of the executive having to strike a balance between competing interests, rather than where a Convention right was expressed in unqualified terms. Explaining this in the context of the case before the court, he observed:

> 'In the present case we are principally concerned with art 6, which does not on its face require any balance to be struck: it contains no analogue of para 2 in arts 9–11, dealing with political rights. It is thus a context that militates against deference. But even here, there is no sharp edge. The right to a fair trial under ECHR art 6(1) is certainly unqualified and cannot be abrogated. So also is the presumption of innocence (in a criminal case) arising under art 6(2). But what is required for fairness, what is required to satisfy the presumption of innocence, may vary according to context ... I think it misleading to describe art 6 rights as "absolute", an adjective which tends to suggest that the nature of such rights is uniform, the same for every class of case (bar the distinction between civil and criminal). That is not right. The requirements of independence and impartiality are perhaps as close as one can get to uniform requirements. But even there, there may be scope for reasonable differences of view as to the conditions which have to be met.'

The third principle was that greater deference would be awarded to democratic powers where the subject matter was something peculiarly within the decision-maker's constitutional responsibility. Less deference would be afforded where the issue was something more appropriately within the constitutional responsibility of the courts. Laws LJ gave the following example:

> 'The first duty of government is the defence of the realm. It is well settled that executive decisions dealing directly with matters of defence, while not immune from judicial review (that would be repugnant to the rule of law), cannot sensibly be scrutinised by the courts on grounds relating to their factual merits. ... The first duty of the courts is the maintenance of the rule of law. That is exemplified in many ways, not least by the extremely restrictive construction always placed on no certiorari clauses.

Now this is not a case, of course, in which the courts are intruding in defence policy, or the democratic powers in the rule of law. There are no tanks on the wrong lawns. But ... the constitutional responsibility of the democratic powers particularly includes the security of the state's borders, thus including immigration control, and that of the courts particularly includes the doing of criminal justice. If the scheme of the 1999 Act is essentially to be treated as an administrative scheme for the betterment of immigration control in a context – clandestine entrants in vehicles – acknowledged to be especially acute, the courts will accord a much greater deference to Parliament in deciding whether there is any violation of Convention rights than if it is to be regarded as a criminal statute. In the latter case, the courts are of course obliged to apply art 6(2) and (3) as well as (1). They would do so rigorously, with much less deference to the legislature, not only in fulfilment of their duty under the HRA but also because their own constitutional responsibility makes the task a necessarily congenial one.'

The fourth principle identified by Laws LJ was that greater or lesser deference would be permitted depending upon the extent to which the subject matter fell within the actual or potential expertise of the democratic powers or the courts. By way of example he indicated that, in his view, decisions in the area of macro-economic policy would be remote from judicial control. He added:

'I have no doubt that the social consequences which flow from the entry into the United Kingdom of clandestine illegal immigrants in significant numbers are far-reaching and in some respects complex. While the evidence before us gives more than a flavour of the problems, the assessment of these matters (and therefore of the pressing nature of the need for effective controls) is in my judgment obviously far more within the competence of government than the courts.'

See further on this *R (On the Application of ProLife Alliance) v BBC* [2002] 2 All ER 756, where the Court of Appeal drew a distinction between the margin of appreciation that might be afforded to signatory states by the European Court of Human Rights in Strasbourg and the margin of deference or discretion that might be afforded by domestic courts to a statutory decision-maker such as a national broadcaster. The clear implication is that domestic decision-makers would be given less latitude, especially where sensitive issues such as the expression of political views were involved.

Judicial remedies

A court dealing with an application for judicial review of subordinate legislation would be able to declare it to be ultra vires if it was found to incompatible with the Convention rights. The courts have no such power in relation to primary legislation, however. Indeed s3(2)(b) expressly provides that the section 'does not affect the validity, continuing operation or enforcement of any incompatible primary legislation'. Further the section cannot be relied upon to invalidate incompatible subordinate legislation if '(disregarding any possibility of revocation) primary legislation prevents removal of the incompatibility': s3(2)(c).

Where an irreconcilable issue of compatibility arises before the House of Lords, the Judicial Committee of the Privy Council, the Courts-Martial Appeal Court, the High Court or the Court of Appeal, that court is empowered to grant a declaration of incompatibility. The House of Lords has indicated, in *R* v *A* (above), that the granting of declarations of incompatibility should be regarded as the last resort, where creative interpretation to achieve conformity is simply impossible. A number of such declarations have been made, however. In *H* v *Mental Health Review Tribunal* [2001] 3 WLR 553 the court was unable to construe the burden of proof provisions relating to applications to the Tribunal in a manner consistent with art 5. See also *Wilson* v *First County Trust (No 2)* [2001] 3 WLR 42 (declaration of incompatibility granted in respect of s127 of the Consumer Credit act 1974).

In relation to subordinate legislation the power to make such declarations will arise provided (disregarding any possibility of revocation) the primary legislation concerned prevents removal of the incompatibility. Where such a declaration is made it does not 'affect the validity, continuing operation or enforcement of the provision in respect of which it is given; and ... is not binding on the parties to the proceedings in which it is made': s4(6). The Crown can be joined as a party to the proceedings if a court is considering whether to make a declaration of incompatibility: s5(1). Where legislation of the Scottish Parliament is concerned the court does have the power to declare it to be ultra vires on the basis of non-compliance with the ECHR as the legislation is the product of a body of limited jurisdiction, unlike the United Kingdom Parliament at Westminster.

It could be argued that the 1998 Act is further evidence of the steady erosion parliamentary sovereignty. Although a declaration of incompatibility does place a minister under a duty to take remedial action (see below), the political pressure to do so will be intense. It suggests more clearly than ever before that it is the judiciary that are to be the protectors of minority groups, not a legislature that represents, by definition, the interests of majority groups.

Whilst the 1998 Act does not provide for any new judicial remedies (other than the declaration of incompatibility), a court finding that a public authority has acted unlawfully within the terms of s6 'may grant such relief or remedy, or make such order, within its powers as it considers just and appropriate': s8(1). In particular there is no new power to award damages simply because Convention rights have been violated: see s8(2). Where damages are awarded, however, they should not be minimal and should reflect the policy of the 1998 Act: see *R (Bernard and Another)* v *Enfield Borough Council* (2002) The Times 8 November. Referring to the Law Commission publication *Damages under the Human Rights Act 1998* (Law Com No 266), the court noted the guidance that damages should be moderate, rather than exemplary or aggravated, but rejected the notion that they should be 'on the low side by comparison with tortious awards'. Its preference was for awards analogous to those recommended by local government ombudsmen for delay and distress in cases of maladministration. In any event the power to award should only be exercised if, having taken into account all the circumstances of the case, including 'any other relief or remedy granted, or order made, in relation to the act in question (by that or any other court), and ... the consequences of any decision (of that or any other court) in respect of that act, the court is satisfied that the award is necessary to afford just satisfaction to the person in whose favour it is made': s8(3). A court should also have regard to 'the principles applied by the European Court of Human Rights in relation to the award of compensation under art 41 of the Convention' in determining whether to make an award and in determining quantum. The aim of any award of damages should be to put the claimant into the position he enjoyed before the violation occurred.

Remedial action by ministers

Where a declaration of incompatibility has been made and rights of appeal have been exhausted, abandoned or become time barred, or it appears to a minister that (in the light of a finding of the European Court of Human Rights) a provision of legislation is incompatible with obligations under the Convention, a minister may, if he considers that there are compelling reasons for so doing, make orders to amend the relevant legislation to the extent that considers necessary to remove the incompatibility: see s10(1) and (2).

Note the far-reaching effect of these provisions. A minister will be able to amend primary legislation by means of a statutory instrument: s20(1). Amendments can be retrospective in effect (but not so as to create criminal liability): see Sch 2 paras 1(1)(b) and 1(4). Schedule 2 provides for two types of procedure for the making of remedial orders, depending upon the urgency of the situation. In most cases a minister will prepare a 'document' comprising the draft order and other details required by Sch 2 para 5 (ie details of the incompatibility to be removed and the reasons for proceeding under s10). There then follows a 60-day consultation period during which representations can be made both inside and outside Parliament. Following this period of consultation the minister lays before Parliament the draft remedial order together with a summary of the representations made and details of any revisions made to the order in the light of those representations. To come into effect the draft order must have been laid before Parliament for 60 days and must then be approved by Parliament. In urgent cases a minister will be able to bring an order into effect without parliamentary approval. The safeguards take the form of requirements that the minister should then lay the 'made' order before Parliament with the details required by Sch 2 para 5. Once 60 days have passed the minister must lay before Parliament a summary of the representations made and details (if any) of revisions made to the order in the light of those representations. At the end of a period of 120 days from the date when the order was first laid before Parliament it will cease to have effect unless approved by both Houses of Parliament. The failure by Parliament to affirm such an order does not affect the validity of actions taken pursuant to that order within the 120-day period.

For example, as a consequence of the decision in *H* v *Mental Health Review*

Tribunal (above), Parliament approved the Mental Health Act 1983 (Remedial) Order 2001 (SI 2001/3712).

Pre-enactment procedures

Section 19 places the relevant minister in charge of a Bill under a duty to 'make a statement to the effect that in his view the provisions of the Bill are compatible with the Convention rights' or to make a statement to the effect that 'although he is unable to make a statement of compatibility the government nevertheless wishes the House to proceed with the Bill.' Such statements must be made before the Second Reading of a Bill, must be in writing and should be published in such manner as the minister considers appropriate. A statement of non-compliance is normally only made where the government intends to secure derogations or reservations in respect of certain Convention provisions. Were it otherwise Parliament would be being invited to enact legislation acknowledged to be in breach of the Convention. If such legislation were to be enacted the courts would then be in a position to grant declarations of incompatibility to litigants alleging that action taken on the basis of the non-compliant legislation was unlawful. If no remedial order was forthcoming, the litigant would presumably take his case to the European Court of Human Rights and have the United Kingdom found to be in breach of its obligations.

For an example of this process in action: see the Human Rights Act 1998 (Designated Derogation) Order 2001 (SI 2001/3644), and the Human Rights Act 1998 (Amendment No 2) Order 2001 (SI 2001/4032) which derogates from art 5 of the ECHR so as to permit the interferences with individual liberty resultant upon the provisions of the Anti-terrorism, Crime and Security Act 2001.

9.5 Taking a case to Strasbourg

Article 1 of the ECHR provides that the High Contracting Parties shall secure to everyone within their jurisdiction the rights and freedoms defined in the ECHR. To help achieve compliance with this objective the ECHR established a procedure for enforcement (arts 19–56). As originally enacted this enforcement process comprised a Commission on Human Rights, a Committee of Ministers and a Court of Human Rights. The Commission itself comprised a number of members equal to that of the High Contracting Parties, with members elected by the Committee of Ministers of the Council of Europe for a period of six years. Inter-state applications could be received by the Commission, and individual applications were accepted where a signatory state accepted the right of individual petition. Approximately 90 per cent of the petitions submitted by individuals under art 25 were declared inadmissible by the Commission at this stage, which suggests that there was still widespread misunderstanding of the scope and purpose of the ECHR.

The Commission, on accepting a petition referred to it, would then ascertain the facts and try to secure a friendly settlement of the matter on the basis of respect for human rights as defined in the ECHR. If a solution was not reached the Commission would draw up a report on the facts and state its opinion as to whether the facts found disclosed a breach by the state concerned of its obligations under the ECHR. The report was forwarded to the Committee of Ministers together with such proposals as the Commission thought fit. Absenting any settlement, the case would have been referred, in due course, to the European Court of Human Rights.

With an increasing number of states accepting the right of individual petition it became evident that the effective protection offered by the Commission and the Court was in danger of being undermined by its inability to deal with the ever-growing caseload. Between 5,000 and 6,000 applications were received each year, of which approximately 1,600 were registered, and approximately 200 declared admissible. Between 1959 and 1973 only 11 cases where referred to the European Court of Human Rights. In 1991 alone 93 cases were referred. The backlog of unconsidered cases as a whole reached over 1,500. The average time taken for an application to reach the European Court of Human Rights had stretched to five years. With Eastern European countries applying to join the Council of Europe the prospect emerged of some 800 million citizens having the right to have recourse to the European Court of Human Rights.

The procedure under Protocol 11

In response to the pressures outlined above the text of what is now known as Protocol Eleven was opened for signature in April 1994. The purpose of the Protocol was to completely overhaul the procedure for dealing with applications under the Convention. Because the Protocol altered the provisions of the Convention itself it could not come into force until all states had signed – a process that was completed in time for it to come into effect in November 1998.

The changes introduced by Protocol Eleven had been trailed by limited reforms introduced in 1990, with Committees being used to rule on admissibility, and Chambers determining routine cases. There was a resultant improvement in processing rates, but concerns about the system being overwhelmed continued.

As a result of Protocol Eleven there is a new permanent European Court of Human Rights, replacing the previous structure of Commission and Court. The new Court comprises 40 judges (one from each member state) allocated to Committees (three judges to each Committee), Chambers (comprising seven judges) and a Grand Chamber of 17 judges. The Court is assisted by a single Registry comprising the Commission secretariat and the Court secretariat (around 100 lawyers in total). The newly constituted Court of Human Rights heard its first case under the new procedure in November 1998 and delivered its first judgment in January 1999.

The right of individual petition to the new court becomes mandatory upon Member States. The ECHR is itself restructured so that Section I deals with the rights protected; Section II with the machinery for enforcement; and Section III with miscellaneous matters.

The revised procedure involves an applicant filing his application with the Court's registry, which assigns it to a Chamber and a judge rapporteur who has responsibility for overseeing the progress of the application. A Committee, or tribunal, of judges considers the admissibility of the application and, provided at least one of the three considers it to be admissible, the ruling is communicated to the member state against whom the application has been made. If a friendly settlement cannot be reached the Chamber (seven judges) will give its judgment. The procedure also applies to applications between states. The authors of these reforms envisage that an application will only need to be referred to the Grand Chamber in exceptional cases, and a panel of five Grand Chamber judges will decide whether there are grounds for re-examination, unless the case is one where the Chamber itself has relinquished jurisdiction. Early indications are that there are still major problems in terms of a backlog of applications. A year after the new system came into operation there were 12,500 applications waiting to be considered.

The Committee of Ministers becomes responsible for overseeing the enforcement of the Court's rulings and can check on the steps taken by signatory states to comply with rulings of the court. The Committee can also request Member States to address specific issues of general concerns, such as the treatment of asylum seekers.

Alternative mechanisms for entrenching rights

The Human Rights Act 1998 is a cleverly worded compromise between the demands of those who wished to see the courts being given the power to invalidate primary legislation found to be incompatible with Convention rights, and those who feared that the Act would, almost by default, mark a serious erosion of parliamentary sovereignty. It is nevertheless instructive to examine briefly the alternative strategies that could have been adopted to ensure that the courts accord special status to human rights provisions. First, the Act could have avoided any reference to incompatibility altogether, and simply allowed existing constitutional principles to apply. This would clearly have been unsatisfactory for a government wanting to be seen to take the incorporation of the Convention seriously. The resulting Act would have taken precedence over previous incompatible legislation by virtue of implied repeal, but would have been a the mercy of any subsequent legislation: see further the Hong Kong Bill of Rights Ordinance 1991. Second, at the other extreme, the model provided by the Canadian Charter of Rights and Freedoms could have been adopted, whereby the Canadian courts have been given the power to disapply incompatible legislation, unless the legislation in question expressly states that it is to apply notwithstanding any such incompatibility. In practice this means that the Canadian courts 'read in' the missing rights, or make it clear that, for certain purposes, a statute no longer applies. The Canadian Parliament remains at liberty to amend legislation as it sees fit following such a ruling. Third, the government could have copied the approach taken following the incorporation of the Treaty of Rome (as it then was), whereby the European Communities Act 1972 operates to make certain aspects of EU directly part of domestic law: see Chapter 2. This latter proposal was rejected, however, on the basis that it is a prerequisite of EU membership that Member States give priority to EC law, whilst becoming a signatory to the Convention creates no such obligations.

The approach adopted for the incorporation of the ECHR in the United Kingdom bears close similarity to the New Zealand Bill of Rights Act 1990, which adopts what is known as an 'interpretative' approach, requiring courts to strive for an interpretation which gives effect to the human rights legislation, but leaving intact legislation that cannot be complied with in a manner consistent with those rights. Defending the adoption of this method the White Paper states:

> 'The government has reached the conclusion that courts should not have the power to set aside primary legislation, past or future, on the ground of incompatibility with the Convention. This conclusion arises from the importance that the Government attaches to parliamentary sovereignty. In this context, parliamentary sovereignty means that Parliament is competent to make any law on any matter of its choosing and no court may question the validity of any Act that it passes. In enacting legislation, Parliament is making decisions about important matters of public policy. The authority to make those decisions derives from a democratic mandate. Members of Parliament in the House of Commons possess such a mandate because they are elected, accountable and representative. To make provision in the Bill for the courts to set aside Acts of Parliament would confer on the judiciary a general power over the decisions of Parliament which under our present constitutional arrangements they do not possess, and would be likely on occasions to draw the judiciary into serious conflict with Parliament. There is no evidence to suggest that they desire this power, nor that the public wishes them to have it. Certainly, this government has no mandate for any such change.' (para 2.13).

9.6 The European Convention on Human Rights and EC law

The ECHR does not form part of EC law in the strict sense, but it is accepted that respect for fundamental human rights is a precondition for the lawfulness of Community acts: see comments in *Opinion No 2/94* [1996] ECR 1–1759. The preamble to the Single European Act 1986 also makes express reference to the need to respect such fundamental rights, and similar commitments to respect fundamental human rights are to be found in the TEU 1992. In *Opinion No 2/94*, the opinion of the European Court of Justice was sought on the question of whether the accession of the European Community to the ECHR would be compatible with the EC Treaty. Whilst the Court declined to answer the question as posed, it held that, as EC law presently stood, the Community had no competence to accede to the ECHR. Notwithstanding the provisions of the EC Treaty empowering the Council to take appropriate measures to ensure that the Community was empowered to achieve its objectives, there was no specific Treaty power that enabled the Community institutions to enact rules relating to human rights or to become a party to international conventions on human rights. In the Court's view, accession to the ECHR would effectively make its provisions part of Community law, with profound consequences for the institutions of the Community and for Member States, and would hence involve changes of such constitutional significance that it could only be brought about by amendment of the EC Treaty.

An individual asserting that the domestic legislation of a Member State is in breach of the ECHR, and thus EC law, will not succeed before the ECJ where the domestic legislation does not deal with a matter falling within the field of application of Community law, and has not been enacted by a Member State so as to ensure compliance with Community law: see further *Kremzow* v *Republik Osterreich* [1997] ECR 1–2629. There remains the possibility of the ECHR being indirectly invoked where the application of EC law having direct effect is held, by the European Court of Justice, to require reference to, and conformity with, provisions of the ECHR: see for example *R* v *Kirk* [1984] CMLR 522.

The European Charter of Fundamental Rights

In the future lies the possibility of a European Charter of Fundamental Rights agreed by members of the European Community and forming part of directly applicable Community law. Unlike the ECHR the Charter, as currently proposed, comprises some 50 articles that would introduce many significant social and economic rights such as the right to vote, right to strike, biotechnical, environmental and gender issues as well as data protection. The motivation behind the Charter is to make the fundamental rights and freedoms that are part of the common currency of EC Member States more relevant and visible. What proponents have in mind is that EU enlargement may lead to the admission of a number of eastern European states with little recent history of liberal democracy. The view expressed by supporters of the Charter is that enlargement can only take place if these newly admitted countries sign up to measures that will give effective protection to minority groups, social rights and labour rights. The House of Lords Select Committee on the European Union reported in May 2000 that the Charter was a major opportunity to give effective protection to individuals in dealing with EU institutions (note the EU is not a signatory to the ECHR).

The Charter is also strongly supported by the European Commission, but many opponents are concerned that it could form the basis of a constitution for the EU. Clearly if the Charter were to be agreed and ratified by the United Kingdom it would have far greater legal force in the domestic courts than the ECHR, and would place even more power in the hands of the European Court of Justice. Given the 'democratic deficit' besetting Community institutions there are bound to be concerns regarding the gap that might open up between the law-makers in the ECJ and the governed, although the European Parliament will have a right of veto over the Charter.

Thought would also have to be given to the relationship between the Charter and the ECHR. The Charter could subsume the ECHR, or alternatively the EU could simply become a signatory to the ECHR. The middle way could be chaotic – to have two human rights treaties that overlap and contradict each other, with two separate systems for adjudication – again raising the spectre of conflicting decisions.

10

Police Powers

10.1 Introduction: the human rights framework

A police force is a public body. As such its members are under a positive legal duty to uphold the rights enshrined in the ECHR as enacted in the HRA 1998. This Chapter examines the balance that the law tries to strike between the right of freedom of the person and the public interest in ensuring that police officers have sufficient powers to prevent and detect criminal activity. The framework for this examination is provided by art 5 of the ECHR, which seeks to ensure that deprivation of liberty should only occur where sanctioned by law and in accordance with correct procedures. It provides thus:

'(1) Everyone has the right to liberty and security of person. No one shall be deprived of his liberty save in the following cases and in accordance with a procedure prescribed by law:
(a) the lawful detention of a person after conviction by a competent court;
(b) the lawful arrest or detention of a person for non-compliance with the lawful order of a court or in order to secure the fulfilment of any obligation prescribed by law;
(c) the lawful arrest or detention of a person effected for the purpose of bringing him before the competent legal authority on reasonable suspicion of having committed an offence or when it is reasonably considered necessary to prevent his committing an offence or fleeing after having done so;
(d) the detention of a minor by lawful order for the purpose of educational supervision or his lawful detention for the purpose of bringing him before the competent legal authority;
(e) the lawful detention of persons for the prevention of the spreading of infectious diseases, of persons of unsound mind, alcoholics or drug addicts or vagrants;
(f) the lawful arrest or detention of a person to prevent his effecting an unauthorised entry into the country or of a person against whom action is being taken with a view to deportation or extradition.'

In essence any detention of an individual by the executive has to be referable to a legal power. Where the grounds for that detention cease to exist, or the conditions of the detention breach certain minimum requirements, the detention becomes unlawful. For example, in *Johnson* v *United Kingdom* Case 19/1996/738/937 (1997) The Times 4 December the absence of safeguards, to ensure that the continued detention of a patient at a mental hospital was still required, was held to be a violation of art 5(1) where it resulted in the applicant's release being unnecessarily delayed. Further, in *Benham* v *United Kingdom* (1995) The Independent 8 February, the applicant, who had been summonsed in respect of his failure to pay his community charge, was found guilty and ordered to serve 30 days in prison, even though he had no means to pay, had no assets, and was not entitled to receive income support. The European Court of Human Rights held that the failure by the justices to conduct an adequate inquiry as to why the applicant had not paid his community charge prior to ordering his detention amounted to a denial of the right to liberty contrary to art 5. In *R (Saadi)* v *Secretary of State for the Home Department* (2001) The Times 22 October the Court of Appeal confirmed that the detention of asylum seekers for up to ten days to permit the speedier processing of applications for asylum was permissible within the terms of art 5. The interference with the right to liberty was proportionate to the aim of preventing unlawful entry.

The wording of art 5 suggests that obscurely or vaguely worded criminal provisions will be in breach of the ECHR because they do not satisfy the requirement that the deprivation of liberty should be 'prescribed by law'. This contention was tested in *Steel and Others* v *United Kingdom* (1998) 5 BHRC 339 in respect of the common law power of police constable to arrest and detain in respect of alleged breaches of the peace (breach of the peace being treated as an offence for these purposes). The European Court of Human Rights held that where a defendant's actions clearly gave rise to a breach of the peace, or created an obvious possibility that a breach of the peace might occur, the common law was sufficiently clear so as not to amount to a breach of art 5. Where, however, powers to arrest for breach of the peace were used against peaceful demonstrators a violation of art 5 would occur, there being no grounds to justify the use of the power.

Further safeguards provided under art 5 are that: 'Everyone who is arrested shall be informed promptly, in a language which he understands, of the reasons for his arrest and of any charge against him (art 5(2)); 'Everyone arrested or detained in accordance with the provisions of paragraph [art 5(1)(c)] of this article shall be brought promptly before a judge or other officer authorised by law to exercise judicial power and shall be entitled to trial within a reasonable time or to release pending trial. Release may be conditioned by guarantees to appear for trial': art 5(3). In *Brogan* v *United Kingdom* (1989) 11 EHRR 117 it was held that detention of terrorist suspects without charge for more than four days was in breach of art 5(3), but see the discussion of derogations, below.

Predictably, the provisions of s25 of the Criminal Justice and Public Order Act 1994, which sought to automatically prohibit the granting of bail to certain categories of accused persons, such as those charged with rape or murder, were found to be in breach of art 5(3) by the European Court of Human rights in *Caballero* v *United Kingdom* (2000) The Times 29 February.

The right of anyone who is deprived of his liberty by arrest or detention to 'take proceedings by which the lawfulness of his detention shall be decided speedily by a court and his release ordered if the detention is not lawful' (art 5(4)), was found to have been violated by the United Kingdom in *T* v *United Kingdom; V* v *United Kingdom* (1999) The Times 17 December. The Home Secretary had determined the original tariff period (ie the length of time the applicants would have to be imprisoned to satisfy the requirements of punishment and retribution) and, when the period imposed by him was declared unlawful by the House of Lords, he had failed to impose a substitute tariff. The Parole Board would only be able to review the continued detention of the applicants after the expiry of a tariff period. Hence not only had a member of the executive performed a judicial function (thus violating the requirement of an independent tribunal for sentencing), the Parole Board had been prevented from supervising the continued detention (thus violating the requirement that there should be an independent judicial supervision of detention): see further

Hussain v *United Kingdom* (1996) 22 EHRR 1. Similarly, in *Chahal* v *United Kingdom* (above), the determination of appeals against deportation orders by an advisory panel, where issues of national security were involved, was deemed to be a violation of art 5(4), because the panel did not provide sufficient procedural safeguards to amount to a 'court' as that term was used in the Convention.

Under art 5(5), everyone who has been the victim of arrest or detention in contravention of art 5 should have an enforceable right to compensation.

10.2 Police powers: the legal framework

In the majority of criminal cases, the defendant's first involvement in the criminal process will be his contact with the police. It is with these first stages of the criminal process that this chapter is primarily concerned.

Police powers to stop, search, detain and arrest persons were developed piecemeal across many decades. There were wide variations between rural and metropolitan areas, and many anomalies, for example inconsistencies in the scope of powers to enter, search premises and seize evidence: see *Ghani* v *Jones* [1970] 1 QB 693. Rights to stop and search were often conferred in wide and uncertain terms, such as the much-criticised and now repealed 'sus' laws, and different conditions attached to the exercise of those rights according to the particular statutes creating them. Much has now been placed upon a more consistent footing with the introduction of the Police and Criminal Evidence Act 1984 (PACE) and the Codes of Practice issued thereunder.

The Codes of Practice, issued by the Home Secretary, aim to provide guidelines as to how the discretion given to police officers under PACE should be exercised. Unlike the statute, the Codes are written in a non-technical style that should be readily comprehensible by police constables, if not the averagely educated lay person. Four Codes (A–D) were initially introduced in January 1986, supplemented by Code E in 1988. A revised version of Codes A–D was introduced in April 1991, and the current versions, amended to incorporate the recommendations of the Royal Commission on Criminal Justice, and the changes in the law consequent upon the enactment of the Criminal Justice and Public Order Act 1994, came into effect on 10 April 1995. Code A was further revised in May 1997 and March 1999. The Codes now cover the following:

Code A: The exercise by police officers of statutory powers of stop and search.

Code B: The searching of premises by police officers and the seizure of property found by police officers on persons or premises.

Code C: The detention, treatment and questioning of persons by police officers.

Code D: The identification of persons by police officers.

Code E: The tape recording of interviews by police officers at police stations with suspected persons.

Under s67(8) of PACE, as originally enacted, a police officer was liable to disciplinary proceedings for a failure to comply with any provision of the Codes. This provision has, however, been repealed by s37(a) of the Criminal Justice and Public Order Act 1994, so that police forces have more discretion as to how they deal with officers who fail to follow guidelines on best practice. It is assumed that flagrant breaches of the Codes would still render an officer liable to disciplinary proceedings. Whilst a breach of the Codes may not, as such, affect the legality of an officer's action, and may not, of itself, render him liable to any criminal or civil proceedings, the Codes are admissible in evidence in civil and criminal and must be taken into account where relevant.

Although the Codes are not law in the strict sense, a trial judge can recognise non-compliance on the part of the police by excluding evidence obtained in breach of the Codes. Thus in *R v Saunders* [1988] Crim LR 521, where D was not shown a record of her statements made so that she could attest to their accuracy, and was not cautioned in terms that made clear her right to remain silent, the trial judge ruled the evidence inadmissible under s78. Note, however, the obiter statements of Lord Lane CJ in *R v Delaney* [1989] Crim LR 39, to the effect that the courts should not punish police officers for non-compliance by excluding evidence obtained in breach of the Codes. His view was that judges should only exclude evidence where it has been obtained after substantial and significant breaches that make it good sense to exclude evidence. Useful guidance is provided by the Court of Appeal in *R v Keenan* [1989] 3 All ER 598. D was charged with possession of an offensive weapon. Shortly before his trial defence counsel were served with copies of statements allegedly made by D to police officers in which he admitted knowledge that the weapon was in his car. D, who denied ever having made the statement, had not been invited to read and sign the statement. On appeal following conviction, the Court of Appeal held that the evidence of the statement should not have been admitted. The test to be adopted was, if the other evidence was compelling, the police would still secure a conviction, despite the exclusion of evidence obtained in breach of the Code. If the other evidence was weak, then it was right that the 'vital' evidence obtained in breach of the Code should be excluded since the safeguards designed to ensure its reliability had not been complied with.

In exercising the powers of stop, search, entry, seizure and arrest considered below, s117 of PACE makes it clear that, provided the power is not one that can only be exercised with the consent of some person, other than a police officer, the officer may use reasonable force, if necessary, in the exercise of the power.

10.3 Police powers to stop and search

Traditionally police officers have not possessed a common law power to detain suspects for questioning, short of first exercising a power of arrest. Whilst cases such as *Donnelly* v *Jackman* [1970] 1 All ER 987 confirm that a constable can commit a trivial interference with an individual's liberty, for example tapping him on the shoulder to attract his attention, without exceeding the scope of his duty, *Rice* v *Connolly* [1966] 2 QB 414 is still authority for the proposition that a citizen is not required to stop and answer police enquiries per se. In that case D refused to answer a constable's questions concerning his activities and refused to provide him with his address. D's conviction for obstructing a police officer in the execution of his duty, contrary to s51(3) of the Police Act 1964, was allowed on the ground that D had been under no legal duty to provide the police with information. (Note that to provide deliberately misleading information could give rise to liability.) Similarly in *Kenlin* v *Gardner* [1967] 2 QB 510, where the defendants, two schoolboys going from house to house to remind fellow members of their rugby team of a fixture, were stopped by a constable who produced a warrant card in order to hold the boys for questioning. The defendants struggled and assaulted the officer. The question arose as to the availability of the defence of self-defence on a charge under s51(1) of the Police act 1964 – assaulting an officer in the execution of his duty. The court held that the defence was available, as the constable had no power short of arrest to physically detain the boys for questioning.

In theory the 1984 Act does not invalidate any of these decisions but, as indicated below, a constable can now detain a suspect in order to conduct a search under s1, and failure to provide personal details may give rise to a power to arrest without a warrant under s25.

Part I of PACE confers general powers of stop and search, not restricted to metropolitan areas, and provides for the keeping of records of searches. Section 1(2) creates a general power in constables to search a person or a vehicle or anything that is in or on a vehicle, and to detain the person or vehicle for the search. The power may only be exercised if the police constable has reasonable grounds for suspecting that he will find stolen or prohibited articles as a result of the search: s1(3). In addition, the search may only be carried out if the person or vehicle is in any place to which at the time when the constable proposes to exercise the power the public or any section of the public has access, on payment or otherwise, as of right or by virtue of express or implied permission; or in any other place to which people have a ready access at the time when the constable proposes to exercise the power but which is not a dwelling: see s1(1).

So far as concerns searches of persons or vehicles on land adjacent to a dwelling-house, the Act provides by s1(4) and (5):

'(4) If a person is in a garden or yard occupied with and used for the purposes of a dwelling or on other land so occupied and used, a constable may not search him in the exercise of the power conferred by this section unless the constable has reasonable grounds for believing –

(a) that he does not reside in the dwelling; and

(b) that he is not in the place in question with the express or implied permission of a person who resides in the dwelling.

(5) If a vehicle is in a garden or yard occupied with and used for the purposes of a dwelling or on other land so occupied and used, a constable may not search the vehicle or anything in or on it in the exercise of the power conferred by this section unless he has reasonable grounds for believing

(a) that the person in charge of the vehicle does not reside in the dwelling;

(b) that the vehicle is not in the place in question with the express or implied permission of a person who resides in the dwelling.'

The purpose of the search is to locate stolen goods or 'prohibited articles'. The definition of the former may be analogous to s24(2) of the Theft Act 1968, so that goods are 'stolen goods' if they are goods originally stolen, or which directly or indirectly represent or have at any time represented stolen goods, or are the proceeds of any disposal or realisation of stolen goods, or are goods obtained by blackmail or by deception. As regards 'prohibited articles', the Act provides by s1(7), (8) and (9) that an article is prohibited for the purposes of this part of PACE if it is an offensive weapon (defined as an article made or adapted for use for causing injury to persons, or intended by the person having it with him for such use by him or by some other person) or an article made or adapted for use in the course of or in connection with any one of a number of offences (burglary; theft; taking a conveyance, and obtaining by deception) or is intended by the person having it with him for such use by him or by some other person. Section 140 of the Criminal Justice Act 1988 extends the meaning of offensive weapon to include any article with a blade or point carried in a public place, except a folding pocket-knife.

If a search results in the discovery of what the constable has reasonable grounds to believe are stolen or prohibited arts, s1(6) of PACE confers upon him the power to seize such items. Further, by virtue of s51 of the Criminal Justice and Police Act 2001, a constable can also seize property that is inextricably linked to the property sought, or property that constitutes a collection to which the property sought belongs and cannot conveniently be removed. Hence, a constable may seize and retain a handheld computer believed to contain information that he has the power to retain.

The exercise of many of the powers granted to the police under PACE are subject to the precondition that there must be 'reasonable suspicion' or 'reasonable grounds to suspect' that a given state of affairs exists. This is particularly so in relation to the exercise of stop and search powers under s1 and also summary arrest under ss24 and 25: see further sections 10.12 and 10.13 below. Code A (as amended) gives some further guidance as to the interpretation of the phrase 'reasonable suspicion' in the context of stop and search powers. The Code provides:

'1.6 Whether a reasonable ground for suspicion exists will depend on the circumstances of each case, but there must be some objective basis for it. An officer will need to consider the nature of the article suspected of being carried in the context of other factors such as the time and the place, and the behaviour of the person concerned or those with him. Reasonable suspicion may exist, for example, where information has been received such as a description of an article being carried or of a suspected offender; a person is seen acting covertly or warily or attempting to hide something; or a person is carrying a certain type of article at an unusual time or in a place where a number of burglaries or thefts are known to have taken place recently. But the decision to stop and search must be based on all the facts which bear on the likelihood that an article of a certain kind will be found.

1.7 Reasonable suspicion can never be supported on the basis of personal factors alone. For example, a person's colour, age, hairstyle or manner of dress, or the fact that he is known to have a previous conviction for possession of an unlawful article, cannot be used alone or in combination with each other as the sole basis on which to search that person. Nor may it be founded on the basis of stereotyped images of certain persons or groups as more likely to be committing offences.

1.7A Where a police officer has reasonable grounds to suspect that a person is in innocent possession of a stolen or prohibited article or other item for which he is empowered to search, the power of stop and search exists notwithstanding that there would be no power of arrest. However every effort should be made to secure the person's co-operation in the production of the article before resorting to the use of force.'

10.4 Conduct of searches under s1 of the 1984 Act

Once satisfied that the conditions of s1 are met, and that there are the required 'reasonable grounds' for exercising the stop and search power, a constable must, in carrying out the search, follow the procedure laid down by s2 and must usually make a record of it in accordance with s3. If, having stopped a person or vehicle for the purpose of search, the constable thinks it unnecessary actually to make the search, he need not do so (s2(1)), but that decision does not affect the lawfulness of his initial act in detaining that person or vehicle. If the constable wishes to search a person, or a vehicle which is 'attended' (which presumably means that there is a person in it or appearing to be in charge of it nearby), s2(2) and (3) ensure that the intended object of the search is made aware of the identity of the searcher and the reasons for the search.

PACE does not state what is to be done when the constable is unable to determine which of several persons is 'in charge' of a vehicle: presumably all should be told the matters in s2(3). The requirement laid down by s2(3)(a) of PACE, to the effect that a police constable about to conduct a search must provide details of his identity and of the police station to which he is attached, is mandatory. Failure to comply will render any subsequent search unlawful, even if the identity of the officer can be ascertained in broad daylight from his badge: see *Osman* v *DPP* (1999) The Times 28 September. The detainee will, presumably, be entitled to use reasonable force to resist any such search. Sedley LJ, in *Osman*, observed that a police officer could comply with the duty to inform by handing out a slip of paper detailing his name and station to a person about to be searched.

The extent of the search is governed by s2(9), which provides that neither the power conferred by s1 nor any other power to detain and search a person without first arresting him or to detain and search a vehicle without making an arrest is to be construed as authorising a constable to require a person to remove any of his clothing in public other than an outer coat, jacket or gloves; or as authorising a constable not in uniform to stop a vehicle.

The ambiguous wording of s2(9) could be taken to mean that a constable can require a person to remove other articles of clothing provided such removal is not made 'in public'. Thus if the constable asked the subject of the search to remove his trousers, and offered to allow him to do so in the privacy of a closed police van, or inside a nearby house, it may well be that the power exists to compel the subject to comply. Code A para 3.5 clearly contemplates that such power is implied into s2(9) in that it states:

> 'Where on reasonable grounds it is considered necessary to conduct a more thorough search (eg by requiring someone to take off a T-shirt or headgear), this shall be done out of public view for example, in a police van or police station if there is one nearby.'

Note that such searches may only be conducted by an officer of the same sex as the person searched and may not be made in the presence of anyone of the opposite sex unless the person being search consents to their presence.

Provided the conditions in s1 are met, vehicles that are not 'attended' may be searched even though there is no person during the search who is in charge of the vehicle or otherwise responsible for it. In such a case, s2(6) and (7) provide that the fact that a search has taken place be brought to the attention of the vehicle's owner, driver or other person responsible for it. The note should specify the name of the constable conducting the search, and should inform the owner that an application for compensation for any damage caused by the search may be made. The note should be left inside the vehicle unless it is not reasonably practicable to do so without damaging the vehicle.

So as to avoid excessive delay in the carrying out of a search of persons or vehicles, s2(8) imposes a statutory (if rather vague) duty upon the police where it states that: 'The time for which a person or vehicle may be detained for the purposes of such a search is such time as is reasonably required to permit a search to be carried out either at the place where the person or vehicle was first detained or nearby.'

How much time is 'reasonably required' must of course depend upon the facts of each case, but it is to be hoped that the subsection will encourage the police to make the search quickly, rather than risking a civil action for unlawful detention for a period beyond what a court could later find to have been adequate.

10.5 Other powers to stop and search

The 1984 Act significantly tidies up a confused morass of varying general and local powers. Nonetheless, several powers peculiar to particular offences, places or persons survive the Act, and some have been added since. The most notable are:

1. To stop and search for prohibited drugs. The conditions for search remain those stated in s23 of the Misuse of Drugs Act 1971.
2. To search persons in public places for unlicensed firearms, or for firearms used or suspected of being intended for use in the course of crime. This power is still governed by s47 of the Firearms Act 1968.
3. To stop and search persons suspected of terrorist offences: see the Terrorism Act 2000 and the Criminal Justice and Police Act 2001.
4. Under s60 of the Criminal Justice and Public Order Act 1994, a police officer of or above the rank of superintendent may, if he reasonably believes that incidents involving serious violence may take place in any locality in his area, and it is expedient to prevent their occurrence, authorise the use of stop and search powers in the area for which he is responsible for a period of up to 24 hours. The period may be extended by a further six hours where it appears to the officer who gave the initial authorisation that it is expedient to do so. The stop and search powers conferred by this section extend to stopping any pedestrian, or vehicle and searching him or the occupants of any such vehicle, or the vehicle itself, for offensive weapons or dangerous instruments (ie bladed or pointed), whether or not a constable has any grounds for suspecting that he might find such articles. If any such articles are found they may be seized by a constable.

    These powers have been further extended by s25 of the Crime and Disorder Act 1988, which inserts a new subs (4A) into s60. Under this provision a police officer may require a person to remove any item that the police officer reasonably believes he is wearing wholly or mainly for the purpose of concealing his identity, such as a mask, hood or other garment. Items worn for these purposes can be seized and retained by a police officer.
5. Section 81 of the Criminal Justice and Public Order Act 1994 Act provides additional powers of stop and search in relation to terrorism by adding a s13A to the Prevention of Terrorism (Temporary Provisions) Act 1989: see further Chapter 13, section 13.7.

Constables employed by certain statutory undertakers are also given a power of stop and search wider than that conferred on the police in general, and by s6 of the 1984 Act they may stop, detain and search any vehicle before it leaves a 'goods area' included in the premises of their employers. There is no need in such cases for the holding of 'reasonable grounds' for any suspicion of carriage by the vehicle of stolen or prohibited articles – the power is almost unlimited, though it applies only to searches of vehicles and not to searches of persons, so that any search of a person may be carried out only if the conditions mentioned in s1 of the Act are met. 'Goods area' is defined by s6(2) as 'any area used wholly or mainly for the storage or handling of goods'. The principal beneficiaries of the s6 power will be railway, dock, canal and other transport police forces, which are in theory not a part of the police force of the county in which they operate.

10.6 Road checks

Where a serious crime has been committed, it is of great assistance to the police to be able to establish roadside stations through which motor vehicles must pass and be checked to see whether they are carrying the suspect criminal or someone who may be a witness to the offence. The example of an armed raid upon an armoured security van springs first to mind; the police must act quickly if the villains are to be identified and caught before their trail becomes cold. To help in this case, and in a wide variety of others, s4 of the 1984 Act provides for short-term local powers of stop and search of vehicles. An officer may only authorise a road check under s4(3) if he has reasonable grounds for believing that a 'serious arrestable offence' has been committed; and has reasonable grounds to suspect that persons sought in connection with the offence are, or will be, in the locality in which vehicles would be stopped if the road check were authorised. Normally the authorisation to set up roadblocks must be given in writing by an officer of at least the rank of superintendent. An officer below that rank may authorise such a road check only if it appears to him that it is required as a matter of urgency.

The authorisation must specify the locality in which vehicles are to be stopped and the length of time for which the order remains in operation (normally not exceeding seven days). If a road block authorisation is granted, officers may conduct road checks for the purpose of ascertaining whether a vehicle is carrying a person who has committed an offence other than a road traffic offence or a vehicle excise offence; a person who is a witness to such an offence; a person intending to commit such an offence; or a person who is unlawfully at large. Where a vehicle is stopped in a road check, the person in charge of the vehicle at the time when it is stopped is entitled to obtain a written statement of the purpose of the road check if he applies for such a statement not later than the end of the period of 12 months from the day on which the vehicle was stopped. In practice this power will not be used to permit a full search of vehicles, but to allow for a rather cursory inspection and interrogation to determine whether any of the persons sought is driving or being carried in the vehicle.

The phrase 'serious arrestable offence', which occurs elsewhere in PACE, is defined by s116. It provides that the following arrestable offences are always serious:

1. an offence (whether at common law or under any enactment) specified in Part I of Sch 5 of PACE (see below);

2. any of the offences mentioned in paras (a)–(dd) of the definition of 'drug trafficking offences' in s38(1) of the Drug Trafficking Offences Act 1986;
3. Any other arrestable offence is serious only if its commission has led to, or is intended or is likely to lead to: serious harm to the security of the state or to public order; serious interference with the administration of justice or with the investigation of offences or of a particular offence; the death of any person; serious injury to any person; substantial financial gain to any person; and serious financial loss to any person. Loss is serious for these purposes if, having regard to all the circumstances, it is serious for the person who suffers it. 'Injury' includes any disease and any impairment of a person's physical or mental condition.

Part I of Sch 5 lists those offences conclusively regarded as serious arrestable offences. These include murder, rape, buggery, treason, manslaughter, kidnapping, incest with a girl under the age of 13 and so on. Part II provides details of other specific offences to be treated as serious arrestable offences, and is subject to amendment as new offences are created: see for example the offences added to Part II by s85 of the Criminal Justice and Public Order Act 1994. Other offences will fall within the definition only if they are 'arrestable' in the meaning given by s24 of PACE, but have also caused or were intended to cause harm classified as 'serious' by s116(6). For example, theft contrary to s1 of the Theft Act 1968 is an 'arrestable' offence, but can qualify as a 'serious arrestable offence' only if it has caused or was intended to cause one of the s116(6) consequences, notably 'substantial financial gain to any person or serious financial loss to any person'. These phrases necessarily lack precision and whether or not the definitions are satisfied will be a question of fact in each case. In *R* v *Neil McIvor* [1987] Crim LR 409 (a Crown Court decision) the trial judge ruled that access to a solicitor under s58 should not have been denied as the theft alleged, 28 hunt dogs valued at £800, was not a serious arrestable offence as it did not involve a substantial loss to the victim. Similarly, in *R* v *Eric Smith* [1987] Crim LR 579 the theft of two video recorders from Woolworths plc was not regarded as involving substantial loss.

As will be seen further in this chapter the concept of 'serious arrestable offence' also has a key part to play in determining the extent of police powers to detain, isolate and interrogate arrested persons.

10.7 Powers of entry, search and seizure on premises

The powers of stop, search and seizure thus far discussed have all related to persons or vehicles in public places, whether those places be roads, pavements, or the gardens and yards provided for by s1(4) and (5). What of the police powers to enter buildings and other premises for the purpose of search or seizure? In the same way that Part I of PACE has clarified and consolidated rights to stop and search in public places, so Part II substantially amends the powers of entry and search of premises, and several anomalous lacunae have been closed in the process.

The police are now authorised to enter and search premises on the authority of a warrant issued by a Justice of the Peace if they suspect the commission of a 'serious arrestable offence' and the presence on those premises of evidence relevant to that suspected offence. For the purposes of the 1984 Act 'premises' includes any vehicle, vessel, aircraft, and any tent or movable structure: see s23.

Specifically, s8 provides:

'(1) If on an application made by a constable a Justice of the Peace is satisfied that there are reasonable grounds for believing –
(a) that a serious arrestable offence has been committed; and
(b) that there is material on premises specified in the application which is likely to be of substantial value (whether by itself or together with other material) to the investigation of the offence; and
(c) that the material is likely to be relevant evidence; and
(d) that it does not consist of or include items subject to legal privilege, excluded material or special procedure material; and
(e) that any of the conditions specified in subsection (3) below [considered below] applies, he may issue a warrant authorising a constable to enter and search the premises.'

The references to items 'subject to legal privilege', 'excluded material' and 'special procedure material' mean that no warrant may be issued by a magistrate which gives authority to enter and search for any of the following classes of evidence:

1. Documents subject to legal professional privilege according to the principles of the law of evidence and s10 of the Act. Such items are excluded from the right to search so as to preserve the defendant's right not to be compelled to incriminate himself by disclosure of anything he may have told to, or been told by, his legal advisers in connection with some legal matter, even though it is not the matter raised in the warrant.
2. Excluded material includes personal records of any person's physical or mental health or personal welfare acquired or created in confidence, and any human tissue or tissue fluid taken for the purposes of diagnosis or medical treatment and held in confidence, and also journalistic material held in confidence. The precise definitions of this phrase appear in s11, and a right of access to excluded material arises only on the order of a circuit judge made in an application by the police under Sch 1 of the Act. Thus, there is a safeguard against unjustified invasion of privacy.
3. Special procedure material includes certain journalistic material other than that in the definition of 'excluded material', together with certain business records held in confidence or subject to an obligation by statute not to disclose them. Such material can once again only be made the lawful object of police search and seizure on the authority of a circuit judge: s14.

Provided, therefore, that none of the evidence sought falls into the categories of 'legal privilege', 'excluded' or 'special procedure' material, a justice's warrant may issue to authorise the entry and search of premises. As s8(1)(e) provides, however, a warrant will not be issued unless one of the conditions in s8(3) applies. These conditions are designed to ensure that the draconian weapon of warrant operates only where it is impracticable or undesirable to gain access to evidence by request to the person who holds the right to grant access to it, perhaps because the evidence might be destroyed if the police are compelled to await an occupier's permission to enter, or cannot find out who has the right to allow them entry. The subsection provides:

'(3) The conditions mentioned in subsection (1)(e) above are –
(a) that it is not practicable to communicate with any person entitled to grant entry to the premises;
(b) that it is practicable to communicate with a person entitled to grant entry to the premises but it is not practicable to communicate with any person entitled to grant access to the evidence;
(c) that entry to the premises will not be granted unless a warrant is produced;
(d) that the purpose of a search may be frustrated or seriously prejudiced unless a constable arriving at the premises can secure immediate entry to them.'

The application to a Justice of the Peace for issue of the warrant must be made in the form prescribed by s15, which is intended to ensure that there is good reason for its grant, and that it clearly specifies the suspected offence and, so far as is possible, the evidence sought. The constable applying for the warrant must: state the ground on which he makes the application; state the enactment under which the warrant would be issued; specify the premises which it is desired to enter and search; to identify, so far as is practicable, the articles or persons to be sought

Each warrant authorises entry on one occasion only: s15(5). If granted the warrant must specify: the name of the person who applies for it; the date on which it is issued; the enactment under which it is issued; the premises to be searched; and, so far as is practicable, the articles or persons to be sought: s15(6).

Once issued, the search warrant remains in force for only one month, and if it has not been executed within that period it lapses and must be returned to the court office from which it issued: s16(3) and (10). It must be executed at a 'reasonable hour' unless it appears to the constable executing it that the purpose of a search may be frustrated on an entry at a reasonable hour: s16(4). This test seems to be wholly subjective, so that the constable's honest even though unreasonable belief will be conclusive. The occupier or apparent occupier of the premises to be searched must be shown the warrant, provided with a copy of it, and given documentary evidence that the person seeking to execute it is a constable: s16(5).

Thus far, the courts appear to be taking a hard line in requiring compliance by the police with the search warrant safeguards. In *R v South Western Magistrates' Court, ex parte Cofie* [1997] 1 WLR 885 the court granted a declaration that a search warrant was unlawful on the ground that the officer applying for it had specified the building to be searched was '78, Oxford Gardens, W10', when in fact he knew that the building was divided into flats and that only the common parts of the building, and flat 78F in particular, needed to be searched. Beldam LJ confirmed that s15(6) of PACE was to be construed strictly, and that the officer had failed to specify the premises to be searched with sufficient particularity.

In *R* v *Chief Constable of Lancashire, ex parte Parker* [1993] 2 WLR 428 the applicants' premises were entered by police offices purporting to act under search warrants and items were seized. The officers carrying out the searches provided the occupiers with warrants comprising photocopies of the authorisations unaccompanied by the schedules that would have detailed the articles sought. The applicants sought judicial review seeking orders of certiorari to quash the warrants and a declaration to the effect that the entries and searches had been unlawful. The Divisional Court, granting the declarations sought, held that a search warrant comprised two documents, the authorisation and the schedule of articles to be seized. Subsections 15(7) and (8) of the Police and Criminal Evidence Act 1984 required that two certified copies should be made of any warrant, so that one might be given to the occupier, or left at the premises. The certification was required so that the occupier did not have to rely on the word of the police as to the warrant's validity. Showing the occupier a copy of the warrant would not suffice. As Nolan LJ observed:

> 'It seems to us clear beyond argument that when the Act refers to a warrant issued by a judge it means the whole of the original document seen and approved and put forth by him. It would be wholly contrary to the purpose of the legislation if a judge could authorise the police to replace the whole or a part of the original warrant, for the purposes of its execution, by an uncertified photocopy which he has not seen.'

Hence the original warrant had been valid, and certiorari would not be granted to quash it, but the subsequent searches were unlawful given the failure to comply with the statutory requirements concerning authentification an completeness of copies.

Provided the documents are in order, *R* v *Longman* [1988] Crim LR 534 suggests that the police can gain entry to premises before informing the occupants as to who they are. In that case a female officer, posing as an 'Interflora' delivery woman, gained entry and then produced her warrant card. The court declared such a procedure lawful, provided the police could show that providing information prior to entry would render the subsequent search nugatory.

If the constable finds the evidence connected with the suspected offence for which the warrant issued, he may seize it: s8(2) of PACE.

In *R* v *Chesterfield Justices and Chief Constable of Derbyshire, ex parte Bramley* [2000] 1 All ER 411 it was held that the provisions of PACE did not entitle the police to seize material for the purposes of sifting it elsewhere. This presented significant problems where the material sought was part of a large collection of material that could not be investigated by police officers in situ, or where the material sought was inextricably linked to other material, as for example where data was held on a computer. Sections 50–70 of the Criminal Justice and Police Act 2001 address this problem by enabling police officers and other law enforcement agents to seize and sift property for specific items, provided a pre-existing power to retain property can be established. It means in practice that a pre-existing power of search and seizure extends to property inextricably linked to the property sought, and to collections of items of which the property sought forms a part. Sections 52 and 53 provide for safeguards regarding notification of seizure, the giving of information on the grounds for the seizure, and the extent of the examination of any retained property.

If, when sifting through material that has been seized, the police encounter any material protected by legal professional privilege (as defined by s65 of the Act), or any other protected material as that term is understood under PACE, it must be returned to the owner unless s56 applies. Under s56 a police officer may seize and retain any item if there are reasonable grounds for believing that it is property obtained in consequence of the commission of an offence, and that it is necessary for it to be retained in order to prevent its being concealed, lost, damaged, altered or destroyed. Items may also be seized under s56 if there are reasonable grounds for believing that they are evidence in relation to any offence, and it is necessary for them to be retained in order to prevent them being concealed, lost, altered or destroyed.

A person with a relevant interest in any property that has been seized and retained can apply to an appropriate judicial authority (normally a Crown Court judge: see s69) for an order that retained property should be returned to the applicant. The grounds for making such an order are specified in s59(3) as being that: there was no power to make the seizure; and the seized property is or contains an item subject to legal privilege or special procedure material, the retention of which is not otherwise authorised under the 2001 Act.

10.8 Entry, search and seizure without warrant

The powers to enter and search premises thus far discussed have concerned the grant of a justices' warrant (or, if the search is for 'excluded' or 'special procedure' material, on the authority of a circuit judge), without the arrest of any suspect. It is now necessary to consider the police powers of entry and search of premises without such a warrant. These are contained in general terms in s17 and s18. They are in addition to any other statutory powers of entry and search, and to the sole remaining such power at common law, that of entry to deal with or prevent a breach of the peace: s17(6). Under s17 a constable may enter and search any premises for the purpose of: executing a warrant of arrest issued in connection with or arising out of criminal proceedings; arresting a person for an arrestable offence; arresting a person for an offence under s1 of the Public Order Act 1936 (prohibition of uniforms in connection with political objects), any enactment contained in ss6–8 or 10 of the Criminal Law Act 1977 (offences relating to entering and remaining on property) or s4 of the Public Order Act 1986. A constable may also enter and search any premises for the purpose of: recapturing a person who is unlawfully at large and whom he is pursuing; saving life or limb; or preventing serious damage to property.

With the exception of entry in order to save life and limb, a constable can only exercise the power of entry under s17 if he has reasonable grounds for believing that the person whom he is seeking is on the premises. In relation to premises consisting of two or more separate dwellings, the power to enter and search is limited to any parts of the premises which the occupiers of any dwelling comprised in the premises use in common with the occupiers of any other such dwelling; and any such dwelling in which the constable has reasonable grounds for believing that the person whom he is seeking may be.

The power to search provided by s17 is limited in the sense that it a power to search to the extent that is reasonably required for the purpose for which the power of entry is exercised.

The power to enter under s17(1)(b) (to arrest a person for an arrestable offence) is only exercisable by a constable who has reasonable grounds to suspect that an arrestable offence has been committed and who believes that the suspect is in the premises to be entered. It does not permit, for example, entry in order to question a suspect (unless it could be shown that this was for a purpose closely linked to those listed in s17(1)(e)). Where the power to enter under s17(1) is exercised, the occupant must be informed of the reasons for the entry if at all possible: see further *O'Loughlin* v *Chief Constable of Essex* (1997) The Times 12 December.

The need for an arrestable offence to have been committed was considered in *Chapman* v *DPP* (1989) 89 Cr App R 190. A constable Sneller was called to assist an officer who was being assaulted by a number of youths. Sneller saw a youth he suspected of being involved in the attack run into the flat occupied by his father, the defendant. Sneller sought entry to the defendant's premises, but the defendant resisted, and was arrested for obstructing a constable in the execution of his duty. Sneller purported to be exercising his power of arrest under s24(6) of the Police and Criminal Evidence Act 1984, in relation to the defendant's son. The defendant's submission of no case to answer, in relation to the obstruction charge, was rejected by the justices, and he appealed by way of case stated, the question for the court being 'whether the justices were right to conclude that [Sneller] at the time of the assault was exercising a statutory power of entry and so was a constable acting in the execution of his duty.' The court felt compelled to allow the appeal on the ground that the common assault on a fellow officer was not an arrestable offence, hence now power of arrest existed under s24(6), and in turn no power to enter under s17(1)(b). As Bingham LJ commented:

'What is ... inescapable and fatal to this conviction is that the justices have not found as a fact that Constable Sneller reasonably suspected .any .arrestable offence, to have been committed, or any facts amounting to an arrestable offence to have occurred. Such a reasonable suspicion is the source from which all a police constable's powers of summary arrest flow and the justices have felt unable to make the crucial finding which the prosecutor required. This was plainly not the result of oversight or inadvertence. Had the justices found that Constable Sneller reasonably suspected an arrestable offence to have been committed, it would have been incumbent on them to identify, at least in general terms, the arrestable offence which the police constable suspected and this, it is plain, the evidence adduced did not enable them to do. It is not of course to be expected that a police constable in the heat of an emergency, or while in hot pursuit of a suspected criminal, should always have in mind specific statutory provisions, or that he should mentally identify specific offences with technicality or precision. He must, in my judgment, reasonably suspect the existence of facts amounting to an arrestable offence of a kind which he has in mind. Unless he can do that he cannot comply with s28(3) of the Act by informing the suspect of grounds which justify the arrest.'

It seems clear, following the House of Lords' decision in *D'Souza* v *DPP* [1992] 1 WLR 1073, that the power to enter without a warrant under s17(1)(d) (to recapture a person unlawfully at large) is only to be used in cases of 'hot pursuit'. In that case the appellant's mother had left a hospital where she was being detained for psychiatric assessment without leave being granted as required under s17 of the Mental Health Act 1983. Several hours later, uniformed officers arrived at the house where the appellant lived with her parents in order to take her mother back to the hospital. The appellant and her father refused the police officers entry as they did not have a warrant to enter the premises, but the officers nevertheless exercised a forced entry and were attacked by the appellant and her father, who were subsequently convicted of assaulting police officers in the execution of their duty contrary to s51(1) of the Police Act 1964. Allowing their appeals against conviction, the House of Lords held that s17(1)(d) of the 1984 Act could only be used by officers seeking to enter premises where they sought to apprehend a person who was unlawfully at large, and at the time of entering the premises the police officers were in 'hot pursuit' of the said person. Whilst a person absconding from a hospital in breach of the Mental Health Act would be a person unlawfully at large, in the present case there was no evidence that the police had entered the dwelling in question whilst in hot pursuit of the appellant's mother. It would appear from this ruling that if the officers had spotted the appellant's mother entering her house and had chased after her, they would have had the power of entry without warrant provided for by s17(1)(d). As a consequence of this decision it must be the case that the subsection cannot be relied upon by a constable who, acting upon information received that a person unlawfully at large is at a particular dwelling, then proceeds to visit and enter the premises to effect the recapture of such a person. Whether a constable is in 'hot pursuit' will inevitably be a question of fact to be determined in each case.

Further powers of entry and search are also conferred by s18, which permits a search of premises following the arrest of a suspect for an 'arrestable' offence, if the suspect arrested occupies or controls the premises to be searched. A constable may enter and search any premises occupied or controlled by a person who is under arrest for an arrestable offence, if he has reasonable grounds for suspecting that there is on the premises evidence, other than items subject to legal privilege, that relates to that offence or to some other arrestable offence which is connected with or similar to that offence.

A search under s18 must normally be authorised in advance, in writing, by an officer of the rank of inspector or above. Under s18(5) however, a constable may conduct a search under s18(1) before taking the suspect to a police station, and without obtaining the usual authorisation if the presence of the suspect at a place other than a police station is necessary for the effective investigation of the offence

There is no residual power to search an enter premises controlled or occupied by an arrested person other than that provided for by s18 – hence there is no common law power to enter an search premises of a defendant arrested to facilitate extradition: see *R (Rottman)* v *Commissioner of Police of the Metropolis and Another* (2001) The Times 26 October.

10.9 Powers of seizure

Certain powers to seize evidence have already been examined, for instance that permitting seizure of evidence specified in a search warrant under s8(2). A general power of seizure is conferred upon constables who are 'lawfully on any premises' by s19. The term 'lawfully on premises' encompasses not only lawful presence following entry to effect an arrest, or following arrest of a suspect, or on the authority of a search warrant, but also cases where the constable has been allowed into the premises by a person with the power to give him permission to enter, even though he is not there pursuant to any statutory or common law right of entry. For example, where the constable visits a suspect to question him, and the suspect invites the constable into his house. Under s19 a constable may seize anything which is on the premises if he has reasonable grounds for believing: that it has been obtained in consequence of the commission of an offence and that it is necessary to seize it in order to prevent it being concealed, lost, damaged, altered or destroyed; that it is evidence in relation to an offence which he is investigating or any other offence and that it is necessary to seize it in order to prevent the evidence being concealed, lost, altered or destroyed. Subsection 19(4) empowers a constable to require any information which is contained in a computer and is accessible from the premises to be produced in a form in which it can be taken away and in which it is visible and legible if he has reasonable grounds for believing that it is evidence in relation to an offence which he is investigating or any other offence, or it has been obtained in consequence of the commission of an offence, and that it is necessary to do so in order to prevent it being concealed, lost, tampered with or destroyed. Subsection 19(6) makes it clear that no power of seizure conferred on a constable under any enactment (including an enactment contained in an Act passed after PACE) is to be taken to authorise the seizure of an item which the constable exercising the power has reasonable grounds for believing to be subject to legal privilege.

Although the powers under ss18 and 19 are clearly intended to empower police officers to remove items from premises, it may be possible for police officers to seize and remove the premises itself, where they take a form that makes seizure and remove practicable: see *Cowan* v *Commissioner of Police of the Metropolis* [2000] 1 WLR 254. Hence, where the police believe that a car, boat or caravan has within it evidence of offences that can only be properly ascertained by, for example, subjecting it to examination in a forensic laboratory, it can be seized under these provisions. The only limitation seems to be whether it is physically possible for the police to remove the premises.

Where the s19 power is invoked, and articles seized, those articles may be retained 'so long as is necessary in all the circumstances', for instance for use at the trial of an accused, or to allow a forensic examination of them or to find out who is their lawful owner, but must be released to the person from whom they were seized – unless there is reason to believe that they have been obtained in consequence of the commission of an offence – if a photograph or copy of them would be sufficient for the purpose for which retention is desired. These matters are governed by s22.

As indicated above, the power to seize and retain property has been augmented by the provisions found in ss50–70 of the Criminal Justice and Police Act 2001, whereby police officers and other law enforcement agents are permitted to seize and sift property for specific items, provided a pre-existing power to retain property can be established.

10.10 Powers of arrest

Where time permits, the arrest of a suspect will often be made on the authority of a warrant issued by a justice of the peace under s1 of the Magistrates' Courts Act 1980. Such a warrant may issue in respect of any offence known to law, and is obtained by deposing to the facts of the alleged offence on oath. In addition to its use as a means of taking a suspect into custody before any charge has been made, the warrant procedure also aids in detaining those who have absconded while on bail awaiting trial, or who have failed to appear at court to answer to a summons.

In many cases, however, there is not sufficient time to apply for a warrant, and the statutory powers to arrest without it will now be considered. The 1984 Act significantly simplifies the law in this area, though several powers of arrest without warrant remain in other legislation, for example s7(3) of the Public Order Act 1936 and s28(2) of the Children and Young Persons Act 1969. These preserved additional powers of arrest are listed in Sch 2 of the 1984 Act. The Act draws a distinction between 'arrestable offences', for which a power of arrest without warrant exists in every case, subject to certain conditions, regardless of the seriousness of the harm or damage done in the actual offence, and other offences which become arrestable without warrant only if the gravity of the harm, or risk of further harm, or of the suspect's absconding without having given a true name and address, call for immediate detention.

It should be borne in mind that, notwithstanding the statutory provisions considered below, there is still a common law power to arrest for breach of the peace. As the court in *Foulkes* v *Chief Constable of Merseyside Police* [1998] 3 All ER 705 confirmed, the power can be exercised even if a breach of the peace has not yet occurred, provided the person exercising the power reasonably believes that a breach of the peace might be about to occur. There must be a sufficiently real and present threat to the peace to justify depriving a citizen of his liberty at a time when he is not actually acting unlawfully.

10.11 Arrestable offences

By virtue of s24, a power to arrest without warrant exists where an offence of the following kinds is suspected: the offences is one for which the sentence is fixed by law (eg murder); the offences is one for which a person of 21 years of age or over (not previously convicted) may be sentenced to imprisonment for a term of five years (or might be so sentenced but for the restrictions imposed by s33 of the Magistrates' Courts Act 1980) – this would include serious assaults, theft, robbery and some burglaries; or the offence is one specifically stated as coming within the scope of the s24 powers.

These offences include any offences: for which a person may be arrested under the Customs and Excise Acts, as defined in s1(1) of the Customs and Excise Management Act 1979; under the Official Secrets Act 1920 that are not arrestable offences by virtue of the term of imprisonment for which a person may be sentenced in respect of them; offences under any provision of the Official Secrets Act 1989 except s8(1), (4) or (5); under ss14 (indecent assault on a woman), 22 (causing prostitution of women) or 23 (procuration of girl under 21) of the Sexual Offences Act 1956; under s12(1) (taking motor vehicle or other conveyance without authority etc) or 25(1) (going equipped for stealing etc) of the Theft Act 1968; under the Football (Offences) Act 1991; under s2 of the Obscene Publications Act 1959 (publication of obscene matter); under s1 of the Protection of Children Act 1978 (indecent photographs and pseudo-photographs of children); under s166 of the Criminal Justice and Public Order Act 1994 (sale of tickets by unauthorised persons); under s19 of the Public Order Act 1986 (publishing etc material intended or likely to stir up racial hatred); under s167 of the Criminal Justice and Public Order Act 1994 (touting for car hire services); or s60(8)(b) of the Criminal Justice and Public Order Act 1994 (failing to comply with requirement to remove a mask etc).

Under s46 of the Criminal Justice and Police Act 2001 the offence of placing of advertisements relating to prostitution on, or in the immediate vicinity of, a public telephone with the intention that the advertisement should come to the attention of any other person or persons becomes an arrestable offence, as do, by virtue of s71, the offences under s1 of the Sexual Offences Act 1985 (kerb-crawling) and s170(4) of the Road Traffic Act 1988 (failure to stop and report an accident causing personal injury).

The Police Reform Act 2002 further amends s24 of PACE by providing a new Sch 1A to the 1984 Act listing arrestable offences, and adding three further offences: making off without payment contrary to s3 of the Theft Act 1978; driving while disqualified contrary to s103(1)(b) of the Road Traffic Act 1988; and assaulting a police officer in the execution of his duty or a person assisting such an officer contrary to s89(1) of the Police Act Act 1996.

Without prejudice to s2 of the Criminal Attempts Act 1981, the powers of summary arrest conferred by s24 also apply to the offences of: conspiring to commit any of the offences mentioned in subs24(2); attempting to commit any such offence (provided it is not a summary offence: see s48 of the Police Reform Act 2002); and inciting, aiding, abetting, counselling or procuring the commission of any such offence.

Section 26 of PACE provides that, subject to specifically provided for or preserved statutory powers of arrest without warrant (and those under s25 considered below) any power vested in a constable to arrest without a warrant shall cease to have effect. Care needs to be taken, however, in assessing the ambit of this provision. As the Court of Appeal held on *Gapper* v *Chief Constable of Avon and Somerset Constabulary* [1998] 4 All ER 248, s26 has no effect on those statutory powers of arrest vested in both police constables and private citizens not expressly repealed by PACE. The plaintiff therefore failed in his action for wrongful arrest where he contended that a police constable had no power to arrest without a warrant under s6 of the Vagrancy Act 1824, on the basis that the power had not been expressly preserved by s24 and Sch 2 of PACE. The Court of Appeal confirmed that s26 only abolished those statutory powers of arrest where the power was given to a police constable only (the power to arrest under s6 could be exercised by anyone); further, if the plaintiff's contention was correct it would have resulted in the manifest absurdity that a police constable's power to arrest under s6 had been abolished, whilst the citizen's power to arrest under s6 remained undiminished.

10.12 Power to arrest for arrestable offences

Given that the offence suspected falls within s24, to whom is a power of arrest is allowed, and in what circumstances? There are differences between the powers of constables and those of private citizens. Section 24(4) and (5) detail the powers available to both:

'(4) Any person may arrest without a warrant –
(a) anyone who is in the act of committing an arrestable offence;
(b) anyone whom he has reasonable grounds for suspecting to be committing such an offence.

(5) Where an arrestable offence has been committed, any person may arrest without a warrant –

(a) anyone who is guilty of the offence;

(b) anyone whom he has reasonable grounds for suspecting to be guilty of it.'

It can be seen that a power to arrest arises against anyone who is in the act of committing an arrestable offence, or who is suspected on reasonable grounds to be committing such an offence, that is, someone who is still committing and has not yet completed the suspected crime, by s24(4). The power to arrest after the event given by s24(5) requires that an arrestable offence has been committed. If a private citizen arrests someone he suspected of having committed an arrestable offence, but it emerges that no arrestable offence was committed, the private citizen is liable in damages for false arrest. Such was the law prior to 1968, as enshrined in decisions such as *Walters* v *WH Smith* [1914] 1 KB 595, and it has since been confirmed in relation to s24(5) by the Court of Appeal in *R* v *Self* [1992] 1 WLR 476. The appellant, who was believed to have stolen a bar of chocolate, was arrested by a store detective and another member of the public. During the course of the arrest the appellant assaulted those trying to apprehend him. The appellant, who was ultimately acquitted of theft, but convicted of assault with intent to resist or prevent lawful apprehension, contrary to s38 of the Offences Against the Person Act 1861, contended that as he had been acquitted on the theft charge, neither the store detective nor any other member of the public could have been empowered to arrest him under s24(5) of the 1984 Act, since this required proof that an arrestable offence had been committed. It followed, therefore, that the detention had not been lawful, and thus he should not have been convicted under s38. Allowing the appeal, the Court confirmed that a condition precedent to the exercise of the citizen's power of arrest under s24(5) was that an arrestable offence had already been committed, and hence the contention in relation to s38 had to succeed. As Garland J observed:

'Subsection (5) makes it abundantly clear that the powers of arrest without a warrant where an arrestable offence has been committed require as a condition precedent an offence committed. If subsequently there is an acquittal of the alleged offence no offence has been committed. The power to arrest is confined to the person guilty of the offence or anyone who the person making the arrest has reasonable grounds for suspecting to be guilty of it ... if it is necessary to go further, one contrasts the words of subsection (5) with subsection (6), the very much wider powers given to a constable who has reasonable grounds for suspecting that an arrestable offence has been committed.'

Powers of arrest in wider terms are conferred on constables, in addition to those they possess in their capacity as citizens, by s24(4) and (5). These allow arrest even where no arrestable offence has in fact been committed. Under s24(6) if a constable has reasonable grounds for suspecting that an arrestable offence has been committed, he may arrest without a warrant anyone whom he has reasonable grounds for suspecting to be guilty of the offence. Under s24(7) a constable may arrest without a warrant anyone who is about to commit an arrestable offence and anyone whom he has reasonable grounds for suspecting to be about to commit an arrestable offence.

The 1984 Act does not contain a definition of what constitutes an arrest. However, in *R* v *Brosch* [1988] Crim LR 743 the court held, following *Alderson* v *Booth* [1969] 2 All ER 271, that an arrest might be effected by any action or words indicating to D that he is under a compulsion and is no longer at liberty.

Reasonable suspicion

The provisions of the 1984 Act conferring powers of arrest provided a constable has reasonable suspicion that certain preconditions exist must be read on the basis that the officer himself must have the suspicion, ie it must be based upon matters present in the mind of the constable. The rationale for this approach is that Parliament has proceeded on the basis that police constables are independent executive officers, accountable in law for the way in which they exercise their powers. As Lawton LJ observed in *R* v *Chief Constable of Devon and Cornwall, ex parte Central Electricity Generating Board* [1982] QB 458 (at p474):

> '... [chief constables] cannot give an officer under command an order to do acts which can only lawfully be done if the officer himself with reasonable cause suspects that a breach of the peace has occurred or is imminently likely to occur or an arrestable offence has been committed.'

Hence, a constable cannot be regarded as having a reasonable suspicion that a suspect has committed an offence simply because a superior officer orders him to effect an arrest of that suspect. The position was usefully summarised by Lord Steyn, in *O'Hara* v *Chief Constable of the Royal Ulster Constabulary* [1997] 2 WLR 1, as follows:

> '(1) In order to have a reasonable suspicion the constable need not have evidence amounting to a prima facie case. Ex hypothesi one is considering a preliminary stage of the investigation and information from an informer or a tip-off from a member of the public may be enough: *Hussien* v *Chong Fook Kam* [1970] AC 942, 949. (2) Hearsay information may therefore afford a constable reasonable grounds to arrest. Such information may come from other officers: *Hussien*'s case, ibid. (3) The information which causes the constable to be suspicious of the individual must be in existence to the knowledge of the police officer at the time he makes the arrest. (4) The executive "discretion" to arrest or not as Lord Diplock described it in *Mohammed-Holgate* v *Duke* [1984] AC 437, 446, vests in the constable, who is engaged on the decision to arrest or not, and not in his superior officers.'

The test to be applied, therefore, is (assuming the arresting officer does suspect that circumstances justifying the exercise of the power to arrest exist) whether or not a reasonable person would have shared the officer's opinion, given the information that was in the mind of the arresting officer.

Hence, in *Hough* v *Chief Constable of Staffordshire Police* (2001) The Times 14 February, the court held that a constable could have reasonable grounds for exercising power of arrest where he had received information from a police computer check indicating that an individual might be carrying a firearm. As the court noted, if information from an informer or member of the public could properly found suspicion for an arrest, common sense suggested that an appropriate entry in a police database should also be sufficient: see further *Castorina* v *Chief Constable of Surrey* (1988) 138 NLJ 180. The approach in *O'Hara* was subsequently upheld by the European Court of Human Rights in *O'Hara* v *United Kingdom* Application No 37555/97 (2001) The Times 13 November.

In applying the test for reasonable suspicion the courts appear to be willing to grant the arresting officer a margin of appreciation, given that he may have been acting in the heat of the moment: see *G* v *Superintendent of Police, Stroud* (1985) The Times 29 November.

As a police constable is a public officer (ie an officer of the executive) the legality of his actions can be tested by the application of the so-called *Wednesbury* test: see *Associated Provincial Picture Houses Ltd* v *Wednesbury Corporation* [1948] 1 KB 223. Hence he should exercise his discretion as would a reasonable police officer, not taking into account irrelevant considerations, and not failing to take into account relevant considerations. Ultimately it will be for the court to decide whether the test has been satisfied. Hence in *Lyons* v *Chief Constable of West Yorkshire* (1997) (CCRTF 96/1379/C), it was held that a police officer had not acted unreasonably in exercising his power of arrest in relation to a L, notwithstanding that he had been previously informed (by a friend of L) that L had an alibi and hence could not have committed the crime under investigation. In *R* v *Chalkley* [1998] 2 All ER 155 police officers suspected the defendant of involvement in a robbery. Having obtained the necessary authorisation they decided to place a listening device in his home. In order to do so they arrested the defendant on suspicion of involvement in a number of credit card frauds so that he would be out of the house. On the basis of the evidence obtained the defendant was convicted of conspiracy to rob and appealed. One of the issues raised at the appeal was as to the legality of the arrest in relation to the credit card fraud. The Court of Appeal held that the arrest had been lawful. The Court felt that, provided the police officers had reasonable grounds to suspect that the defendant was involved in the credit card frauds, his arrest was lawful notwithstanding that his absence from his house provided the police with the opportunity to place the listening devices. Counsel for the defendant relied upon the proposition of Viscount Simon from *Christie* v *Leachinsky* [1947] 1 All ER 567 at 572, where he observed that:

'1. If a policeman arrests without warrant on reasonable suspicion of felony, or of other crime of a sort which does not require a warrant, he must in ordinary circumstances inform the person arrested of the true ground of arrest. He is not entitled to keep the reason to himself or to give a reason which is not the true reason. In other words, a citizen is entitled to know on what charge or on suspicion of what crime he is seized.
2. If the citizen is not so informed, but is nevertheless seized, the policeman, apart from certain exceptions, is liable for false imprisonment.'

The Court, however, rejected the notion that an ulterior motive would necessarily render an arrest unlawful. As Auld LJ observed (pp176j–177g):

'In our view, the judge correctly held that the arrests were lawful. We acknowledge the importance of the liberty of the subject. It is a fundamental right of which he may only be deprived by the due process of law, which process includes an entitlement to be told why he is being deprived of it. However, a collateral motive for an arrest on otherwise good and stated grounds does not necessarily make it unlawful. It depends on the motive. That is clear from the materially different facts of *Christie* v *Leachinsky* and the qualified manner in which the members of the judicial committee expressed the important principle for which the case is famous.

First, as to the facts, there, the police informed Leachinsky of a ground of arrest which was not a valid ground for it; here the suspected credit card fraud was a valid ground for the arrests. There, there was an alternative and valid ground for arrest of which the officers had not informed him; here there was no alternative ground or reason, valid or invalid, for arrest as distinct from the object of removing [the defendant from his house] for a while to enable the installation of the device.

Second, Viscount Simon, Lord Simonds and Lord du Parcq (with whom Lord Thankerton and Lord Macmillan agreed) were all of the view that there were qualifications and possible exceptions to the general principle that the police, in making an arrest, should be motivated only by matters relevant to the suspected offence and should tell the subject the true reason for it. Viscount Simon said ([1947] 1 All ER 567 at 573, [1947] AC 573 at 588): "There may well be other exceptions to the general rule in addition to those I have indicated, and the above propositions are not intended to constitute a formal or complete code, but to indicate the general principles of our law on a very important matter."

Lord Simonds and Lord du Parcq ([1947] 1 All ER 567 at 575 and 581–582, [1947] AC 573 at 592 and 603–604) allowed for the legality of arrest and detention by the police of a man on one charge on which they have reasonable grounds for suspecting his guilt, but with the real or main purpose of enabling them to investigate another, possibly more serious, offence of which they have as yet no such grounds and with a view to preventing his escape from justice. As Lord Simonds observed ([1947] 1 All ER 567 at 575, [1947] AC 573 at 593): "In all such matters a wide measure of discretion must be left to those whose duty it is to preserve the peace and bring criminals to justice." The reasoning for that well-known and respectable aid to justice, "a holding charge", seems to us equally appropriate to circumstances where, as here, the police have, and have so informed the subject(s) when arresting them, reasonable grounds for doing so, but were motivated by a desire to investigate and put a stop to further, far more serious, crime. Accordingly, we agree with the judge's ruling that the arrests were lawful.'

Note that the requirement of reasonable suspicion accords with art 5(3) of the European Convention on Human Rights which requires that a person should not be deprived of his liberty except, inter alia, where he is lawfully arrested or detained for the purpose of bringing him before the competent legal authority on reasonable suspicion of having committed an offence or when it is reasonably considered necessary to prevent his committing an offence or fleeing after having done so.

10.13 Power to arrest for offences that are not arrestable

Where the suspected offence does not fall within the definition of arrestable given by s24, a power to arrest without warrant is conferred upon constables – but not upon private citizens – where it is thought undesirable to follow the normal procedure of leaving the suspected offender at large and proceeding against him by simple summons to appear at court later. The general purpose of this power is to prevent the suspect's avoiding prosecution by giving false particulars, or by refusing to give any particulars at all, or to remove the risk of further harm to the suspect himself or to the public or to property. Section 25 provides that, provided a constable has reasonable grounds for suspecting that any offence which is not an arrestable offence has been committed or attempted, or is being committed or attempted, he may arrest the 'relevant person' if it appears to him that service of a summons is impracticable or inappropriate because any of the general arrest conditions are satisfied. For these purposes 'relevant person' is defined by s25(2) as any person the constable has reasonable grounds to suspect of having committed, having attempted to commit, being in the course of committing or attempting to commit the offence.

The general arrest conditions referred to in s25(3) are: that the name of the relevant person is unknown to, and cannot be readily ascertained by, the constable; that the constable has reasonable grounds for doubting whether a name furnished by the relevant person as his name is his real name; that the relevant person has failed to furnish a satisfactory address for service, or the constable has reasonable grounds for doubting whether an address furnished by the relevant person is a satisfactory address for service; that the constable has reasonable grounds for believing that arrest is necessary to prevent the relevant person causing physical injury to himself or any other person, suffering physical injury, causing loss of or damage to property, committing an offence against public decency, or causing an unlawful obstruction of the highway; that the constable has reasonable grounds for believing that arrest is necessary to protect a child or other vulnerable person from the relevant person.

Under s25, an address is a 'satisfactory address' for service if it appears to the constable that the relevant person will be at it for a sufficiently long period for it to be possible to serve him with a summons; or that some other person specified by the relevant person will accept service of a summons for the relevant person at it. A constable is not authorised to arrest under s25(3)(d)(iv) (constable has reasonable grounds for believing arrest is necessary to prevent the relevant person committing an offence against public decency) unless members of the public going about their normal business cannot reasonably be expected to avoid the person to be arrested.

In *Edwards and Others* v *DPP* (1993) 97 Cr App R 301 two men, Fox and Sumner, were observed by police officers who believed them to be using cannabis. When challenged, the men appeared to try to dispose of certain substances. They were informed that they were being arrested for obstructing the officers in the execution of their duties under the Misuse of Drugs Act 1971. A woman named

Prendergast intervened to prevent the arrest of Fox and was arrested for obstruction contrary to s51(3) Police Act 1964. Edwards intervened to prevent the arrest of Prendergast and was similarly arrested for obstruction contrary to s51(3). The defendants submitted that there was no case to answer since there was no power to arrest without warrant for obstruction under the Misuse of Drugs Act 1971. The magistrates found that in the circumstances there was a power to arrest under s25 of the 1984 Act as, on the facts now known, the arresting officer would have every reason to doubt the truth of any name he was given by the suspect, hence the arrests were lawful. On appeal by way of case stated, the Divisional Court considering the question of whether or not the arresting officer, in the circumstances of the case, had had the power to arrest Fox under s25(3)(a) and (b) and/or s25(3)(d)(i) of the 1984 Act, held that, as the power to arrest without warrant for obstruction of a police officer in the execution of his duty contrary to the Misuse of Drugs Act 1971 had been abolished by s26 of the Police and Criminal Evidence Act 1984, the only power to arrest for such obstruction would be that now arising under s25 of the 1984 Act, ie the power of summary arrest in relation to a non-arrestable offence. By simply telling Fox that he was 'nicked for obstruction', the officer had failed to give s25(1) of the 1984 Act or any of the general arrest conditions detailed in s25(3) as justification. The court confirmed that, by virtue of s28(5) of the 1984 Act, an arrest was not lawful unless the arrestee was informed of the grounds of arrest. In the instant case the court felt that there were no circumstances that precluded the giving of that information; it had obviously practicable for the officer to give reasons for the arrest, because that was precisely what he had done, although they were invalid. The arrest might have been valid if the general arrest conditions under s25 had been given as the reason for arrest, but the arrest could not be retrospectively validated. As Evans LJ observed:

> 'It may seem unrealistic that the court should be concerned after the event with the precise words that were used ... Nevertheless, it has to be borne in mind that giving correct information as to the reasons for an arrest is a matter of the utmost constitutional significance in a case where a reason can be and is given at the time.'

10.14 Information on arrest

Section 28 of the 1984 Act codifies certain established principles of common law relating to the duty of the police to inform an arrested person of the fact of and reason for his arrest. Under s28(1) where a person is arrested, otherwise than by being informed that he is under arrest, the arrest is not lawful unless the person arrested is informed that he is under arrest as soon as is practicable after his arrest. Where a person is arrested by a constable this requirement applies regardless of whether the fact of the arrest is obvious. This information does not necessarily have to be supplied by the officer who actually exercises the power of arrest: see *Dhesi* v *Chief Constable of West Midlands Police* (2000) The Times 9 May.

Some latitude is allowed to arresting officers by s28(5) which provides that there is no duty to inform a person that he is under arrest, or of the ground for the arrest, if it is not reasonably practicable at that time for him to be so informed by reason of his having escaped from arrest before the information could be given. Note that s28 accords with the requirements of art 5(2) of the European Convention of Human Rights which provides that everyone who is arrested should be informed promptly of the reasons for the arrest.

It would appear that even though reasons for an arrest are not given at the time of the arrest, the arrest can become lawful once those reasons are supplied. In *Lewis* v *Chief Constable of the South Wales Constabulary* [1991] 1 All ER 206, the plaintiffs had been arrested on suspicion of burglary and taken to a police station. One had been told the reason for the arrest 10 minutes after it had occurred, the other some 23 minutes after arrest. They were detained for about five hours and then released. In an action for false arrest and wrongful imprisonment, they were awarded damages for unlawful detention of only ten and 23 minutes respectively. On appeal, Balcombe LJ rejected the contention of counsel for the plaintiffs to the effect that, if at the moment of initial apprehension the arrest was unlawful, the act was a nullity. His Lordship expressed the view that arrest was a situation; a matter of fact, citing *Spicer* v *Holt* [1976] 3 All ER 71. Whether a person has been arrested depended not on the legality of his arrest but on whether he has been deprived of his liberty to go where he pleased. There was no doubt that, on the facts of this case, the plaintiffs had been deprived of their liberty at the moment that they were arrested, and that that act was not a nullity. Arrest was a continuing act, and in his Lordship's view there was nothing inconsistent with the wording of s28(3) to say that from that moment when reasons were given the arrest became lawful, or the continued deprivation of liberty became lawful, or the continued custody became lawful. Hence the trial judge had been correct in the ruling that the period in respect of which the plaintiffs were entitled to damages was that between the arrest and the giving of reasons. The decision confirms the earlier case of *DPP* v *Hawkins* [1988] 1 WLR 1166.

Decisions such as *Abbassy* v *MPC* [1990] 1 WLR 385, confirm that a constable exercising his powers of arrest need not use technical language to indicate the offence for which D is being arrested. It is sufficient that the type of offence is identified, so that D may volunteer information that would render the arrest unnecessary. Where the arrest is made pursuant to s25, *DPP* v *Nicholas* [1987] Crim LR 474 suggests that a constable telling D that he is being arrested because of his failure to provide a name and address is enough.

10.15 Procedure following arrest

At common law the status of someone who was 'helping the police with their inquiries', but without having been formally arrested, was never very clear. It was repeatedly stated that a person was either under arrest or at liberty to leave the police station, and that the law did not recognise any form of detention as legal unless it was a lawful arrest. For the avoidance of doubt, and following the recommendations of the 1981 Royal Commission on Criminal Procedure, s29 of the 1984 Act now provides:

> 'Where for the purposes of assisting with an investigation a person attends voluntarily at a police station or at any other place where a constable is present or accompanies a constable to a police station or any such other place without having been arrested –
> (a) he shall be entitled to leave at will unless he is placed under arrest;
> (b) he shall be informed at once that he is under arrest if a decision is taken by a constable to prevent him from leaving at will.'

Once a suspect has been arrested, whether with or without a warrant, he must be taken to a police station as soon as is practicable after his arrest, unless the arrest was made at such a station: s30(1). Provision is made by that section for conveying the suspect to a 'designated police station', defined by s35 as being one specified by the Chief Officer of Police for the detention of arrested persons, unless it is impracticable to do so in the short term. The suspect may be searched at the time of his arrest if there is reason to believe that he may present a danger to himself or to others, or may have upon him anything which he might use to escape from lawful custody, or which might be evidence relating to an offence: s32(1) and (2). These latter words are wide enough to allow a search for evidence of an offence other than that for which the arrest has been made. The search may also extend to premises in which the suspect was arrested, or in which he was present, immediately before his arrest, in order to discover evidence relating to the offence for which the arrest was made, if the arresting constable has reasonable grounds for believing that such evidence exists: s32(2) and (6), and see *R* v *Badham* [1987] Crim LR 202.

On arrival at a designated police station, the suspect will come under the supervision of a custody officer of at least the rank of sergeant, whose duties are prescribed by Part IV of the 1984 Act: see also *Vince* v *Chief Constable of Dorset Police* [1993] 1 WLR 415. In brief, an arrested person should not be kept in detention, but should be released either without charge or on bail, at the earliest reasonable opportunity. The custody officer must first decide, if the arrest has been without warrant, whether there is sufficient evidence to justify a charge against the suspect: s37(1). If insufficient evidence exists, the suspect must be released, either on bail or not, unless the officer has reasonable grounds for believing that continued detention is necessary to secure or preserve evidence relating to an offence, or to obtain evidence by questioning the suspect: s37(2). Records must be kept throughout the suspect's detention, detailing the decisions and reasons of the custody officer. If there is sufficient evidence to justify a formal charge, the suspect must be charged or released with or without bail: s37(7). Suspects who are not in a fit state to allow the custody officer to make a charge under subs(7) or to be released under that subsection, for example, through drunkenness or the influence of drugs, may be detained until they are fit: s37(9).

Once a charge has been made against the suspect and entered in the charge book, there is a presumption that the suspect will be released. He may be detained further only if he is an adult, his name or address cannot be ascertained or is reasonably suspected by the custody officer to be false, the custody officer has reasonable grounds for believing that the person arrested will fail to appear in court to answer to bail; in the case of a person arrested for an imprisonable offence the custody officer has reasonable grounds for believing that the detention of the arrested person is necessary to prevent him from committing an offence; in the case of case of a person arrested for a non-imprisonable offence the custody officer has reasonable grounds for believing that the detention of the arrested person is necessary to prevent him from causing physical injury to any other person or from causing loss of or damage to property; the custody officer has reasonable grounds for believing that the detention of the arrested person is necessary to prevent him interfering with the administration of justice or with the investigation of offences; or the custody officer has reasonable grounds for believing that continued detention is necessary for the protection of the suspect: s38(1) as amended by s28 of the Criminal Justice and Public Order Act 1994.

Whether or not a charge has been made, the continued detention of every suspect depends upon a review made at intervals by the custody officer or, in the case of a suspect not yet charged, an officer of at least the rank of inspector who has not been directly involved in the investigation of the offence for which the arrest was made: s40(1). The first review must be made not later than six hours after detention was first authorised under s37 or s38, the second review not later than nine hours after the first, and subsequent reviews at intervals of not more than nine hours: s40(3). There is power to postpone a review if it is 'not practicable' to carry it out by the stated time, for instance if the review would interrupt a period of interrogation and the review officer is satisfied it would prejudice the investigation subject of the interrogation, or if no review officer is available at the stated time: s40(4). In such a case, the review must take place as soon as is practicable: s40(5).

The purpose of the review is to decide whether the reason for which detention was first authorised still holds good, for example, that the suspect was a source of harm to himself or others, or that evidence for use against him might be destroyed if he were to be released. If it does not, the suspect must be released. In deciding whether detention remains justified, s40(12) requires the officer to consider any representations made by the suspect himself or by any solicitor acting for him and available at the time of the review, though he need not consider what the suspect may have to say if the latter is asleep, or unfit to make representations by reason of his condition or behaviour: s40(14).

Sections 73–76 of the Criminal Justice and Police Act 2001 have introduced amendments to s40 so at to permit, in certain situations, the use of video links and telephone links for the making of decisions about detention and for the discharge of duties relating to the review of detention. Judicial extensions of detention under para

33 of Sch 8 to the Terrorism Act 2000 can also now, by virtue of s75 of the 2001 Act, be made by means of video link.

Where the suspect has been arrested and is being detained without charge, s41 imposes a maximum period for which he can be detained in police custody without being brought before a court. The general maximum is 24 hours, calculated from the time of his arrival at the first police station to which he is taken after his arrest: s41(1) and (2)(d). The period is calculated from the time of arrest if he voluntarily attended at a police station and was subsequently arrested there or if he is arrested in a police area other than that in which he has been sought for instance, the suspect who is wanted by the Metropolitan Police but who is arrested by a different police force and has not been questioned by the arresting police force with a view to discovering evidence of the offence. Other special provisions for calculating the 24-hour period are made in the cases of suspects who are removed from police detention for medical treatment in hospital, or who are arrested outside England and Wales.

Where the 24-hour period has expired and no charge has been made, the suspect must be released, with or without bail, unless detention beyond the 24 hours has been authorised by a superintendent under s42 or has been allowed by a magistrate's warrant of further detention under s43. Section 42 allows detention up to a total of 36 hours without charge on reasonable grounds for belief that it is necessary to secure or preserve evidence, and that the offence for which the investigation is continuing is a 'serious arrestable offence' and that the investigation is being conducted diligently and expeditiously. A warrant under s43 is issued on very similar grounds to the superintendent's authority under s42, and permits detention in police custody and without charge beyond 36 hours and up to a maximum total of 96 hours, in periods of not more than 36 hours at a time before further application to the court is necessary: see further ss42–44 for details of the procedure at the hearing and the grounds for warrants of further detention.

The courts will construe the requirements relating to extension of detention as mandatory, unless the Act expressly provides for some discretion. Hence in *R v Slough Justices, ex parte Stirling* [1987] Crim LR 576, where the police arrived after 38 hours with an application to extend detention, the application was refused, on the basis that, under s43(7), it would have been reasonable for the police to apply in good time for an extension. Similarly in *In the matter of an application for a warrant of further detention* [1988] Crim LR 296, where detainees were not given the opportunity to make representations via a solicitor before a superintendent extended detention from 24 to 36 hours, and a brief note was placed on custody record to the effect that the superintendent considered detention necessary because the detainee's might impede the course of justice if released, the justices accepted the detainees' contentions that the police had failed to comply with the mandatory requirements under s42. Detention beyond 24 hours had, therefore, been unlawful. Either the justices therefore had no jurisdiction to consider an application for further detention, or if they did they would decline to exercise it.

Where a suspect is detained without the review safeguards having been observed the police may be liable in damages for the tort of unlawful imprisonment: see *Roberts* v *Chief Constable of the Cheshire Constabulary* [1999] 2 All ER 326. It makes no difference that, had the review been conducted as required, continued detention would have been authorised.

Note that under s14 of the Prevention of Terrorism (Temporary Provisions) Act 1989 a person suspected of involvement in terrorist activities can be detained for up to five days without charge: see further *Brannigan and McBride* v *United Kingdom* (1993) 17 EHHR 539. Detention without charge for such a long period of time is per se a breach of art 5(3) of the European Convention on Human Rights, but the United Kingdom has entered a derogation in respect of terrorist suspects: see Chapter 9.

An arrested person who has been charged but who, pursuant to ss38–40 of the 1984 Act, has been detained in police custody, must be brought before a magistrates' court as soon as is practicable after charge, and not later than the first sitting of the court after he has been charged with the offence: s46(2). This will usually be on the day of the charge or the day after, but in cases where no court sitting is to be held for either of those days, detention in police custody is permitted until the next sitting, provided the clerk to the justices is informed of the fact that the suspect is in custody and awaiting appearance at the next sitting. It is then the duty of the clerk to arrange for a hearing not later than the day on which the charge was made, or, if a public holiday or weekend intervenes, the day after that holiday or weekend: s46(3)–(9). The obligation to bring the suspect before the court does not apply if he is not well enough: s46(9).

10.16 Interrogation of suspects and the right to legal advice

Whilst the common law recognised a general right in an accused person to communicate and consult privately with his solicitor outside the interview room (see the *Judges' Rules*), there was no common law right entitling an accused person to have a solicitor present during police interviews: see further the speech of Lord Browne-Wilkinson in *R* v *Chief Constable of the Royal Ulster Constabulary, ex parte Begley; R* v *McWilliams* [1997] 4 All ER 833. Under PACE, however, persons arrested, whether by warrant or not, and held at a police station, are given by rights to have someone named by them informed of the fact and place of their detention, and are to be allowed access to legal advice from a solicitor. Although these rights are not absolute, and can be denied for a period of time in certain circumstances, the intent of PACE is clearly that they should be respected and granted in all but the clearest cases calling for their denial.

So far as concerns notification to an outside person of the fact and place of arrest, s56 provides that when a person has been arrested and is being held in custody in a police station or other premises, he shall be entitled, if he so requests, to have one friend or relative or other person who is known to him or who is likely to take an interest in his welfare told, as soon as is practicable except to the extent that delay is permitted by other provisions in s56, that he has been arrested and is being detained there.

Delay will be permitted if the detainee is being held in connection with a serious arrestable offence, and an officer of at least the rank of inspector (see s74 Criminal Justice and Police Act 2001) has authorised it in writing. The basis for delaying access must be that the authorising officer has reasonable grounds for believing that telling the named person of the arrest will lead to interference with or harm to evidence connected with a serious arrestable offence or interference with or physical injury to other persons, or will lead to the alerting of other persons suspected of having committed such an offence but not yet arrested for it, or will hinder the recovery of any property obtained as a result of such an offence. Under s56(5A) an officer may also authorise delay where the serious arrestable offence is a drug-trafficking offence. In any event access can only be delayed for 36 hours.

If a delay in granting access is authorised the detained person shall be told the reason for it and the reason for the delay must be noted on his custody record. These conditions must be complied with as soon as is practicable.

The provision governing access to legal advice by a person detained following arrest is s58. In its terms it is very similar to s56. A person arrested and held in custody in a police station or other premises is entitled, if he so requests, to consult a solicitor privately at any time. 'Privately' means in a setting that cannot be overheard by police officers: see *Brennan* v *United Kingdom* (2001) The Times 22 October. Access to a solicitor can only be delayed if the person who is in police detention is being held in connection with serious arrestable offence and the delay is authorised by an officer of at least the rank of superintendent. The grounds for delaying access are set out in s58(8) – the officer authorising delay must have reasonable grounds for believing that the exercise of the right to consult privately with a solicitor will lead to interference with or harm to evidence connected with a serious arrestable offence or interference with or physical injury to other persons; will lead to the alerting of other persons suspected of having committed such an offence but not yet arrested for it; or will hinder the recovery of any property obtained as a result of such an offence. Generally access to a solicitor may only be delayed for 36 hours (see s58(5)), although other provisions permit longer periods in certain specified circumstances. For example, the Criminal Justice Act 1988 extends the power to delay access where serious drug-trafficking offences are involved, as do various provisions relating to suspected terrorist activity.

Thus, in general terms, a person held in custody at a police station will be entitled to consult a solicitor at any time, if he so requests. The detainee may consult a solicitor of his own choice, but if he knows of none he should be informed by the police of the availability of the duty solicitor.

Simply because a detainee has a right to a solicitor, it does not follow that a solicitor had a right to enter a police station to see a detainee. The right of access to a solicitor is vested in the detainee. If it is denied the detainee can pursue an appropriate remedy in public law or raise the issue to challenge the admission of evidence at any subsequent trial. Hence no action will lie in negligence or misfeasance in public office against the police, initiated on behalf of a solicitor denied access to a client, where that solicitor has been prevented by the police from attending upon a client being held in detention at a police station: see *Rixon* v *Chief Constable of Kent* (2000) The Times 11 April.

Much depends on the nature of the prohibition and the grounds for it. A blanket ban on a former police constable acting as a solicitor's representative because he was involved in an ongoing dispute with the police force in question was held to be an inappropriate reason for denying access in *R (On the Application of Thompson)* v *Chief Constable of Northumbria Constabulary* [2001] 4 All ER 354. A decision to exclude must be taken on a case-by-case basis in the context of the investigation concerned.

In what circumstances, if any, will the courts permit the police to rely on evidence obtained during interrogations at a police station, where D has not been permitted to exercise his right to consult with a solicitor? In *R* v *Samuel* [1988] 2 WLR 920 the appellant was interviewed by the police on four occasions about a robbery and two burglaries. The appellant denied any involvement. During the second interview he asked for access to a solicitor, but his request was refused on the basis that there was a likelihood of other suspects involved in the robbery being inadvertently warned. At the fourth interview the appellant confessed to the two burglaries and he was charged with those offences at 4.30pm. At 4.45pm. a solicitor was informed of the charges, but denied access. Shortly afterwards the appellant confessed to the robbery and the solicitor was allowed to see him one hour later. At the trial, the appellant contended that evidence of the latter confession should be excluded, but it was admitted and he was convicted of robbery. On appeal the Court of Appeal held that the conviction should be quashed as, in the circumstances, the refusal of access to a solicitor had been unjustified and the interview in question should not have taken place. The court held that the crucial aspect of an interrogating officer's decision to exclude access to a solicitor under s58 was that, at the time of exclusion he has reasonable grounds to believe that access will lead to or hinder one or more of the things set out in paras (a)–(c) of s58(8). As Hodson J observed:

> 'The use of the word "will" is clearly of great importance. There were available to the draftsman many words or phrases by which he could have described differing nuances as to the officer's state of mind, for example "might", "could", "there was a risk", "there was a substantial risk" etc. The choice of "will" must have been deliberately restrictive. Of course, anyone who says that he believes that something will happen, unless he is speaking of one of the immutable laws of nature, accepts the possibility that it will not happen, but the use of the word "will" in conjunction with belief implies in the believer a belief that it will very probably happen. ... What is it that the officer has to satisfy the court he believed? The right denied is a right "to consult a solicitor privately". The

person denied that right is in police detention. In practice, the only way that the person can make any of the matters set out in paras (a) to (c) happen is by some communication from him to the solicitor. For the matters set out in paras (a) to (c) to be made to happen the solicitor must do something. If he does something knowing that it will result in anything in paras (a) to (c) happening he will, almost inevitably, commit a serious criminal offence. Therefore, inadvertent or unwitting conduct apart, the officer must believe that a solicitor will, if allowed to consult with a detained person, thereafter commit a criminal offence. Solicitors are officers of the court. We think that the number of times that a police officer could genuinely be in that state of belief will be rare. Moreover it is our view that, to sustain such a basis for refusal, the grounds put forward would have to have reference to a specific solicitor. We do not think they could ever be successfully advanced in relation to solicitors generally.'

It is submitted that to deny access to a specified solicitor may be tantamount to defamation, unless the police can produce evidence justifying the decision. As the above extract indicates, this will have to be evidence that the solicitor is likely to be duped by the suspect, or will help him pervert the course of justice. The former is perhaps possible. In *Re Walters* [1987] Crim LR 577 the Court accepted that access to a solicitor could be denied where there was evidence that the suspects had been using 'Delphic phrases' to communicate with each other. A solicitor could be used in such a case to convey an apparently innocent message that could alert other gang members. To suggest that a solicitor would knowingly engage in such activities would obviously be a very grave allegation indeed. *Samuel* was followed in *R* v *Alladice* (1988) 87 Cr App R 380.

Where the interrogating officers fail to inform D of his right to consult with a solicitor, or fail to act upon his request for such consultation, the trial judge will have to assess the extent to which the failure to follow the provisions of the Act and the Codes vitiates any subsequent interrogations.

In *R* v *Dunford* (1990) 91 Cr App R 150, where the Court of Appeal upheld the trial judge's decision to admit D's statement made in the absence of a solicitor on the basis that a solicitor's advice would not have added anything to the appellant's knowledge of his rights, Neill LJ expressly approved of the approach taken in *R* v *Walsh* (1990) 91 Cr App R 161, where it was stated that, whilst a breach of s58 would prima facie have an adverse effect on the fairness of proceedings:

'This does not mean, of course, in every case of a significant or substantial breach of s58 or the Code of practice the evidence concerned will automatically be excluded. The task of the court is not merely to consider whether there would be an adverse effect on the fairness of the proceedings, but such an adverse effect that justice requires the evidence to be excluded. ... Breaches which are in themselves significant and substantial are not rendered otherwise by the good faith of the officers concerned.'

This decision, and others, suggests that the courts are willing to adopt a causation based approach, assessing what difference access to legal advice might have had on D's conduct. Thus in *R* v *Absolam* (1989) 88 Cr App R 322, the Court of Appeal allowed D's appeal against conviction where the trial judge had allowed in evidence statements made before access to a solicitor was submitted. Bingham LJ noted that the interrogating officers should have informed D of his right to consult a solicitor when it became apparent to them that an offence had been committed, even though the series of questions and answers taking place between the officers and D was not in any formal sense a conventional interview. He continued:

> '... it seems to us that if the learned judge had been persuaded that there were here significant and substantial breaches of the Code he would, in all probability, have excluded the answers given by the appellant ... he would, we think, had he taken the same view of the Code as we have, have formed the opinion that this was a case in which, as a result of a line of questioning initiated in remarkable circumstances but with no warning to the appellant of his right, the appellant would not have given the answers that he did, and that the prosecution would not have been in receipt of these admissions if the appropriate procedures had been followed.'

Complications can arise in cases such as *R* v *Anderson* [1993] Crim LR 448, where D does not request access to a solicitor, later changes his mind, but due to a breakdown in communications, the interviewing officer is unaware that D has made such a request. In that case the Court of Appeal upheld the trial judge's decision to permit in evidence D's confession, under s78, on the basis that there was insufficient evidence that 'but for' the failure to provide legal advice D would not have made the statement, and further because there was no evidence to suggest the police had acted in any way to make the statement unreliable. See further *R* v *Parris* (1989) 89 Cr App R 68 and *R* v *Silcott* (1991) The Times 9 December.

Note that in *R* v *Chief Constable of South Wales, ex parte Merrick* [1994] 1 WLR 663 the Divisional Court ruled that whilst the statutory right to consult privately with a solicitor created by s58(1) did not extend to a prisoner held in custody at a court following a refusal of bail, such a prisoner did have a common law right to consult with a legal adviser as soon as was reasonably practicable, bearing in mind the other demands on police officers responsible for the custody of prisoners being held at the court. On this basis the policy adopted at Cardiff Magistrates' Court (of not permitting interviews between prisoners and solicitors after 10.00am, unless there were good reasons for the interview not having taken place earlier) was declared to be unlawful.

The incorporation of the European Convention on Human Rights has inevitably refocused attention on this aspect of the criminal process. Article 6(3) provides that everyone charged with a criminal offence has the right to 'defend himself ... through legal assistance'.

This does not specifically refer to access to a solicitor whilst in detention, but increasingly the European Court of Human Rights is coming to recognise what the Americans might refer to as a 'right to counsel' in so far as denial of access to a solicitor during detention might be seen as vitiating the fairness of any subsequent trial. In *Averill* v *United Kingdom* Application No 36408/97 (2000) The Times 20 June adverse inferences where drawn from applicant's failure to answer questions during detention. Being detained under s14(1)(b) of the Prevention of Terrorism (Temporary Provisions) Act 1989, he was denied access to a lawyer for the first 24 hours of his detention. The European Court of Human Rights ruled that the concept of fairness underpinning art 6 required that the accused should have the benefit of assistance from a lawyer when faced with such the dilemma of whether or not to respond to questions during police interrogations. Similarly in *Magee* v *United Kingdom* Application No 28135/95 (2000) The Times 20 June the applicant was denied access to a solicitor for approximately the first 54 hours of detention, during which time he was subjected to intense questioning, eventually admitting his involvement in terrorist offences after approximately 48 hours of questioning. The Court held that denial of access to a solicitor would amount to a violation of arts 6(1) and 6(3) if it could be shown that the denial occurred in circumstances where the rights of the defendant were irretrievably prejudiced so that the fairness of any subsequent trial was irretrievably vitiated. The Court went on to express the view that procedural fairness required that the applicant should have been granted access to a solicitor as a counterweight to the intimidating atmosphere specifically devised to sap his will and make him confide in his interrogators.

Under Code C accurate records must be made of each interview and interrogation, and in some circumstances tape recordings and video recordings of interviews will be permitted under s60, as amended by s76 of the Criminal Justice and Police Act 2001. The suspect must be cautioned, and that caution must be administered as soon as the constable has grounds for believing that he has committed an offence. A further caution must be given before the arrested person is interviewed and, if the interview is interrupted for more than one hour, yet another caution is to be given before it is continued. Interviews of arrested persons can be carried out only with the agreement of the custody officer responsible for them and they must be allowed at least eight hours' continuous rest in any period of 24 hours. No form of oppressive conduct is to be used in questioning, and the suspect may make a written statement if he wishes. Code C also details the records to be kept, and provides for the conduct of identification parades and interrogation of those who are physically or mentally ill or who are under the age of 17, and provides that detainees must be informed of their right to free legal advice, and must be reminded of this right before any interview takes place.

A frequently voiced criticism of PACE and the original Code on interrogation was the absence of any explicit prohibition on interviews with suspects prior to their arrival at the police station. The revised Code C goes some way to meeting these objections by providing that interviews can only be held outside a police station in certain specified circumstances. Under paragraph 11.1 exceptions can only be made where no decision to arrest the interviewee has been taken; or, the interchanges do not amount to the questioning of a person regarding his involvement or suspected involvement in criminal activity; or, delaying the interview would be likely to lead to endangering others or enabling other suspects to flee or hinder the return of any property. In *R* v *Khan* [1993] Crim LR 54 the Court of Appeal upheld the decision of the trial judge not to exclude, under s78 of PACE, evidence obtained by police asking D questions whilst they were searching his dwelling. The Court confirmed that the proper venue for any interrogation was the police station, where the safeguards provided by s58 and the Codes would apply, but was satisfied that, on the facts, the main thrust of the police questioning had related to the whereabouts of property.

10.17 Searches and fingerprinting following arrest

The general power to search an arrested person at the time of arrest has already been considered. Once at the police station, a search may be conducted on the authority of the custody officer, and what is found may be seized in the circumstances provided for by s54(3) and (4). Under s54(4) clothes and personal effects may only be seized if the custody officer believes that the person from whom they are seized may use them to cause physical injury to himself or any other person; to damage property; to interfere with evidence; or to assist him to escape; or if the custody officer has reasonable grounds for believing that the items may evidence relating to an offence. Additional powers are granted under s90 of the Anti-terrorism, Crime and Security Act 2001, which adds s54A.

In certain situations it will be necessary for the search carried out upon an arrested person to go beyond a simple inspection of his outer clothing and personal effects. As originally enacted, PACE provided the power to conduct an intimate search of a detainee, defining such a search as one that involved examination of the bodily orifices. This definition proved problematic in drugs cases where frequently a suspect was believed to be concealing prohibited substances in his mouth. Police officers had no right to carry out the necessary search without invoking the procedure required for intimate searches (see below). A possible loophole was identified by the court in *R v Hughes* [1995] Crim LR 407, where a constable conducting a search in public held D's nose and jaw causing D to expel the drugs he had been concealing in his mouth. D was subsequently convicted of possession of cannabis. The Court of Appeal, being asked to rule on whether: (a) there had been a search; (b) it had been an intimate search; and (c) whether the evidence so obtained should have been excluded because the constable had failed to inform the defendant of the purpose of the search and had failed to make a formal record of it, dismissed the appeal, holding that the conduct of the police officer amounted to a search and there had, therefore, been breaches of the Codes of Practice, although they were not such as to render the evidence inadmissible on the grounds of unfairness. The search itself could not be classified as intimate as there had been no intrusion into the bodily orifices.

The problem has now been addressed by s59 of the Criminal Justice and Public Order Act 1994, which amends PACE so as to exclude searches of the mouth from the scope of intimate searches. The future relevance of *Hughes*, therefore will be as regards instances where concealed items are retrieved from a suspect's vagina or rectum without a physical examination having been carried out, although quite how this might be achieved poses an interesting anatomical question.

Section 55 of PACE provides for the carrying out of an intimate search where an officer of at least the rank of inspector (see s80 Criminal Justice and Police Act 2001) has reasonable grounds to believe that a person who has been arrested and is in police detention may have concealed on him anything which he could use to cause physical injury to himself or others, or that he might so use, while he is in police detention or in the custody of a court. Alternatively, the power can be based upon reasonable belief that such a person may have a Class A controlled drug concealed on him and was in possession of it with the appropriate criminal intent before his arrest.

An intimate search may only be carried out at a police station, hospital, doctor's surgery or other place used for medical purposes (see s55(8)), and may not be made by a person of the sex opposite to the person searched. Intimate searches for evidence of drugs offences may not be made at a police station: see s55(9). Non-intimate samples, such as hair (other than pubic hair), from a nail or under a nail, from body swabs (including mouth swabs but excluding other bodily orifices), saliva and footprints or similar impressions of the body other than a part of the hand, may be taken from an arrested person without his consent under conditions very similar to those allowing intimate searches: see s63.

Note that the power to take intimate and non-intimate sample extends to all recordable offences, and not merely serious arrestable offences. Following amendments introduced by the Criminal Evidence (Amendment) Act 1997, the range of persons from whom a non-intimate sample can be taken, notwithstanding that the appropriate consent has not been given, has been extended to include persons convicted of an offence listed in Sch 1 to the 1997 Act (notably sexual offences and offences of violence) before 10 April 1985 who are still in custody for that offence, or detained under the Mental Health Act 1983. The 1997 Act also extends the power to take non-intimate samples without consent from those detained following an acquittal on grounds of insanity or a finding of unfitness to plead.

Intimate samples, meaning a sample of blood, semen or other body tissue, fluid, urine, pubic hair, dental impression, or a swab from a body orifice other than the mouth, may not be taken against the arrested person's will. An intimate sample, other than one of urine or a dental impression, may be taken only by a registered nurse, and a dental impression may only be taken by a registered dentist. A court may draw such inferences as seem justified from a person's refusal to consent to the taking of an intimate sample.

Once samples are taken, they can be used by the police to investigate offences other than that for which the suspect has been detained. Hence, in *R* v *Kelt* [1994] 2 All ER 780 the Court of Appeal held that it was permissible for the police to use a blood sample lawfully obtained from D in connection with a murder enquiry, in order to compare it with blood samples found on evidence relating to a separate incident of robbery. Express provision is now made for such cross-referencing of evidence by s65 of PACE, as amended.

A significant new power, resulting from the amendment to s62 of PACE by s54 of the Criminal Justice and Public Order Act 1994, will permit the taking of intimate samples from persons not in police detention, provided such action is authorised by an officer of at least the rank of inspector and the consent of the person is given (although adverse inferences can be drawn from a failure to grant such consent). The criteria to be satisfied are that two or more non-intimate samples must have been provided by the person in question, in the course of the investigation into an offence, which have proved insufficient (for the purposes of DNA analysis). Alternatively, non-intimate samples can be taken from a person not in detention regardless of his consent if he has been charged with a recordable offence or informed that he will be reported for such an offence and either he has not had a non-intimate sample taken from him in the course of the investigation of that offence, or if he has, it has not proved suitable for analysis.

Under s63B, added to the Police and Criminal Evidence Act 1984 by s57 of the Criminal Justice and Courts Act 2000, a sample of urine or a non-intimate sample may be taken from a person in police detention for the purpose of ascertaining whether he has any specified Class A drug in his body if a number of conditions are met. These are that the detainee has been charged with a 'trigger' offence; or has been charged with an offence and a police officer of at least the rank of inspector, who has reasonable grounds for suspecting that the misuse by that person of any specified Class A drug caused or contributed to the offence, has authorised the sample to be taken. Further conditions are that the detainee is over 18, and that a police officer has requested that the detainee give the sample. Under s57(8) it becomes a summary offence for a person to fail, without good cause, to give any sample that may be taken from him under s57.

Fingerprints may normally be taken from an arrested person only with his consent, but s61 provides for them to be taken without consent, on the authority of an officer of at least the rank of inspector if he has reasonable grounds for suspecting the involvement of the person whose fingerprints are to be taken in a criminal offence; and for believing that his fingerprints will tend to confirm or disprove his involvement. Further to amendments introduced by the Criminal Justice and Police Act 2001 fingerprints of a convicted or charged person can be retaken where the originals are of poor quality or where there are problems in recording the data, and the individuals cautioned under s65 of the Crime and Disorder Act 1998 will now routinely be fingerprinted. Section 64 of PACE, dealing with the restrictions on the use of, and requirements for the destruction of, fingerprints and samples, is amended by s82 of the Criminal Justice and Police Act 2001 so as to permit the retention of such evidence for specified purposes even where the person from whom the evidence was obtained has been acquitted. Section 92 of the Anti-terrorism, Crime and Security Act 2001 adds a further s64A providing further powers in relation to the photographing of suspects detained at police stations. Evidence given voluntarily by a person who was not a suspect cannot be retained without that person's consent.

10.18 Confessions: general

Confessions are an important form of evidence in that they will presumably tend to produce a plea of guilty at trial, and hence are the best evidence that the accused has actually committed the offence with which he is charged. A defendant may, however, make a confession for a number of reasons other than guilt. For example, he may be attempting to shield the truly guilty party; he may be one of those whose psychological condition or state of mind makes him a compulsive confessor (police investigations are beset with those who invent confessions to prominent crimes which they could not possibly have committed); he may confess because he is intimidated or induced to make a statement by promises; he may feel that, if the offence is not serious, a confession and even a guilty plea is preferable just to 'get things over'.

In such circumstances it is clear that confessions should be treated with care and not admitted in evidence, as they are unreliable as evidence of the truth. The police may wish to obtain evidence by questioning a suspect and they are allowed to do so by virtue of the notes for guidance issued in relation to Code C, which provide:

> '1B This Code does not affect the principle that all citizens have a duty to help police officers to prevent crime and discover offenders. This is a civic rather than a legal duty; but when a police officer is trying to discover whether, or by whom, an offence has been committed he is entitled to question any person from whom he thinks useful information can be obtained, subject to restrictions imposed by this Code. A person's declaration that he is unwilling to reply does not alter this requirement.'

This means that the police can ask anyone questions despite that person's unwillingness to answer them. It is possible that those questions may lead to a confession. Leaving aside the special requirements regarding juveniles and the mentally ill or handicapped, Code C states:

> '11.3 No police officer may try to obtain answers to questions or to elicit a statement by the use of oppression. Except as provided for in paragraph 10.5C, no police officer shall indicate, except in answer to a direct question, what action will be taken on the part of the police if the person being interviewed answers questions, makes a statement or refuses to do either. If the person asks the officer directly what action will be taken in the event of his answering questions, making a statement or refusing to do either, then the officer may inform the person what action the police propose to take in that event provided that that action is itself proper and warranted.
> 11.4 As soon as a police officer who is making inquiries of any person about an offence believes that a prosecution should be brought against him and that there is sufficient evidence to succeed, he shall ask the person if he has anything further to say. If the person indicates that he has nothing more to say the officer shall without delay cease to question him about that offence.'

The first part of this leads back to s76 of PACE. The second shows it is not intended that, where the police have decided there is sufficient evidence to succeed in a prosecution, they should press on to secure a confession. It is perhaps unfortunate that in a number of cases a confession is the only substantial piece of evidence the police have. The confession will, after all, be a valuable constituent towards the element of the defendant's mens rea. In theory, the defendant wants to confess in order to clear his conscience and to unburden himself of guilt. Arguably, this is a very powerful compulsion. The problem in the courts is that some defendants recant and seek to withdraw their confessions. In this situation it is up to the judge to decide in the absence of the jury whether or not the confession should be admitted in evidence; this is known as a 'voir dire' or a 'trial within a trial'.

10.19 The use of the caution and the right to silence

The position at common law

Historically, the position at common law has long been that a defendant is innocent until proven guilty, and that it is the task of the prosecution to convince the court of the defendant's guilt, principles reflected in the criminal process by the existence of the so-called right to silence. The phrase 'right to silence' is something of a misnomer in that every defendant can chose to remain silent if he so wishes – there is never any possibility of a suspect being physically compelled to respond to questioning by law. What the phrase actually relates to is the proposition that the courts were not permitted to draw any adverse inferences from the defendant's failure to provide an exculpatory answer when taxed with the details of the offence he is alleged to have committed. The rationale for the common law right to silence was that the suspect and interrogator would not have been on equal terms, given that the interrogator would inevitably be a police officer. Exceptions were recognised where the defendant could be regarded as being on equal terms with his accuser, for example in *Parkes* v *R* [1976] 64 Cr App Rep 25, where the defendant was accused by his landlady of murdering her daughter.

The right to silence was reflected in the old form of the caution to be administered by a police officer conducting an investigation into alleged offences, ie: 'You do not have to say anything unless you wish to do so, but what you say may be given in evidence.' Minor deviations were permitted provided the sense of the caution was preserved.

The pressure for change

The view expressed in some quarters was that the right to silence was open to abuse by more sophisticated and experienced criminals and was partly responsible for some allegedly guilty defendants escaping conviction. The criticisms of the right to silence rest to a large extent on the assertion that any innocent person would seek to exculpate himself at the earliest possible moment if he had nothing to hide. Such research as has been conducted suggests that relatively few suspects choose to remain silent when interrogated by the police, although the percentage exercising this right has substantially increased since the enactment of PACE.

Given the right of a detained person to consult privately with a solicitor under s58 of PACE, questions have been raised as to the extent to which it remains true to say that detainee and interrogator are not on equal terms. Lawton LJ, in *R v Chandler* [1976] 1 WLR 585, suggested that this might be the case, but went on to observe that, once a detainee had been cautioned, no adverse inferences were to be drawn from his silence. Curiously, the effect of this view suggests that the police would be better off allowing a detainee to have access to a solicitor but not to caution him, although such a practice would undoubtedly involve a breach of the Codes. Some, such as Lord Lane CJ, commenting in *R v Alladice* (above), have called for a re-assessment of the position. He stated:

> 'Paragraph 6.3 of the code provides that a person who asks for legal advice may not be interviewed or continue to be interviewed until he has received it unless delay has been lawfully authorised. … The result is that in many cases a detainee who would otherwise have answered proper questioning by the police will be advised to remain silent. Weeks later at his trial such a person not infrequently produces an explanation of, or a defence to the charge the truthfulness of which the police have had no chance to check. Despite the fact that the explanation or defence could, if true, have been disclosed at the outset and despite the advantage which the defendant has gained by these tactics, no comment may be made to the jury. The jury may in some cases put two and two together, but it seems to us that the effect of s58 is such that the balance of fairness between prosecution and defence cannot be maintained unless proper comment is permitted on the defendant's silence in such circumstances. It is high time that such comment should be permitted together with the necessary alteration to the words of the caution.'

In July 1993 the Royal Commission on Criminal Justice, chaired by Lord Runciman, produced its report. A majority of its members proposed no change to the common law position on the 'right to silence' at a police station, but recommended that once the prosecution case was fully disclosed, it should be possible to draw adverse inferences from the introduction of any new defence or departure from any previously disclosed defence.

As a prelude to reform of the law in England and Wales, the law in Northern Ireland was amended, by virtue of the Criminal Evidence (Northern Ireland) Order 1988, to permit the trial judge to direct the jury (or himself where the case involved a 'Diplock' court) that adverse inferences could be drawn from the defendant's failure to give evidence.

Such inferences are permitted if D is silent and offers an explanation for his conduct for the first time at his trial which he could reasonably have been expected to produce when being questioned; the prosecution satisfies the court that there is a case to answer and D declines to give evidence; he gives no explanation in relation to certain facts such as substances found, or marks on clothing; he gives no explanation for his presence in a particular place.

The changes introduced by the Criminal Justice and Public Order Act 1994

Section 34 of the 1994 Act introduces a major change in the law by providing that, if a suspect fails to mention any fact relied on in his defence (being something that he could reasonably be expected to have mentioned) either when being questioned after cautioning by a constable, or after having been charged with an offence or officially informed that he might be prosecuted, the court or jury may draw such inferences from the failure as appear proper. Section 36 provides similarly in relation to an arrested person's failure to account for any object in his possession, or any substance or mark on his person, clothing or article in his possession when required to do so by a constable investigating an offence, and s37 applies similarly to an arrested person's failure to account for his presence at a particular location.

A consequence of this change in the law is the amendment to the police caution that has been in use for over 30 years. In place of the previous wording (see above) para 10.4 of Code C now requires the following wording:

> 'You do not have to say anything. But it may harm your defence if you do not mention when questioned something which you later rely on in court. Anything you do say may be given in evidence.'

Under the guidelines contained in Code C a caution must be given before any questions are put to a suspect for the purpose of obtaining evidence that may be given in a court in a prosecution. The defendant, therefore, need not be cautioned if questions are put for other purposes, for example, to establish his identity, his ownership of, or responsibility for, any vehicle or the need to search him in the exercise of powers of stop and search. A person must be cautioned upon arrest for an offence unless it is impracticable to do so by reason of his condition or behaviour at the time; or he has already been cautioned immediately prior to his arrest. When there is a break in questioning under caution the interviewing officer must ensure that the person being questioned is aware that he remains under caution. If there is any doubt on this matter the caution should be given again in full when the interview resumes.

In relation to the Criminal Evidence (Northern Ireland) Order 1988, the House of Lords has confirmed, in *R* v *Murray* [1994] 1 WLR 1, that it has had the effect of changing the law and practice relating to the defendant who fails to give evidence, thus permitting the jury to infer guilt from his silence where the prosecution had established a prima facie case against him. The European Court of Human Rights has in turn considered the extent to which the Order was at odds with the requirements of art 6 of the European Convention on Human Rights and, in *Murray* v *United Kingdom* (1996) 22 EHRR 29, confirmed (by 14 votes to five) that, given the sufficiency of the procedural safeguards designed to prevent oppression, the objectives of art 6 could still be achieved, in particular the drawing of reasonable inferences from the applicant's behaviour did not have the effect of shifting the burden of proof contrary to art 6(2). It should be noted, however, that whilst this ruling clarifies the position as regards the law in the Province, some questions may still remain in respect of ss34 and 35 of the 1994 Act. The European Court of Human Rights was willing to accept the restriction imposed by the Northern Ireland Order partly because, in the Diplock courts operating in Northern Ireland, reasons will be given by the trial judge for drawing adverse inferences if any, thus there will be evidence of the weight given to the accused's decision to remain silent. In England and Wales juries will not be required to embroider their verdicts with such explanations.

10.20 Challenging the admissibility of evidence

A confession made by an accused person may be given in evidence against him at the trial provided it is relevant and has not been excluded by the court in pursuance of s76. This initial requirement is laid down because a confession is essentially an out-of-court statement and would normally be excluded by the rule against hearsay, that only testimony given under oath by a witness as to what he directly heard or otherwise experienced is to be regarded as good evidence. A confession is admitted as an exception to the hearsay rule and is tendered by the prosecution as evidence of the truth of its contents because it is thought that a person would not make a statement against himself unless it were true. According to s82 the term 'confession' includes any statement wholly or partly adverse to the person who made it, whether made to a person in authority or not and whether made in words or otherwise.

A statement made by the accused that serves to exculpate him may be excluded as a self-serving statement. It may, of course, be that a statement contains material of both an inculpatory and an exculpatory nature. Both elements would then have to be put before the court.

Section 76(2) contains the vital provision with regard to the exclusion of confessions. This states that:

> 'If, in any proceedings where the prosecution proposes to give in evidence a confession made by an accused person, it is represented to the court that the confession was or may have been obtained –
> (a) by oppression of the person who made it; or
> (b) in consequence of anything said or done which was likely, in the circumstances existing at the time, to render unreliable any confession which might be made by him in consequence thereof,
> the court shall not allow the confession to be given in evidence against him except in so far as the prosecution proves to the court beyond reasonable doubt that the confession (notwithstanding that it may be true) was not obtained as aforesaid.'

Thus where D alleges that the confession has been improperly obtained it is for the prosecution to prove beyond all reasonable doubt that this is not the case. Section 76(3) provides that, in any event, the court may require of its own motion that the prosecution should prove that the confession was not obtained as mentioned in s76(2). One effect of the subsection is that if there has been oppression the resulting confession so obtained can be excluded even though it is true, presumably to deter the police from using oppression. In this sense police impropriety is to be deprecated more than the obtaining of what may be a true confession. 'Oppression' is defined by s76(8) as including 'torture, inhuman or degrading treatment, and the use or threat of violence (whether or not amounting to torture)'. In *R* v *Fulling* [1987] 2 WLR 923, Lord Lane CJ commented:

> '..."oppression" in s76(2)(a) should be given its ordinary dictionary meaning. The Oxford English Dictionary as its third definition of the word runs as follows: "Exercise of authority or power in a burdensome, harsh, or wrongful manner; unjust or cruel treatment of subjects, inferiors, etc; the imposition of unreasonable or unjust burdens." One of the quotations given under that paragraph runs as follows: "There is not a word in our language which expresses more detestable wickedness than oppression." We find it hard to envisage any circumstances in which such oppression would not entail some impropriety on the part of the interrogator.'

Fulling was applied in *R* v *Paris; R* v *Abdullahi; R* v *Miller* (1993) 97 Cr App R 99 (the 'Cardiff Three' case), where convictions were set aside on the basis that confessions had been obtained by means of oppression, following evidence that interrogating officers had continued to shout at one of the appellants the words they wanted him to say over 300 times, despite his denials of guilt. The court commented upon the importance of officers complying with the letter and spirit of the Codes of Practice.

Prior to the 1984 Act a confession would only be admitted if it were voluntary. This meant that it should not have been induced 'by fear of prejudice or hope of advantage exercised or held out by a person in authority'. This seems to be the general purport of s76(2)(b) although it is of wider application than the previous rule. It remains for the defendant to raise the question of the confession having been made in consequence of something said or done, and for the saying or doing to render unreliable the confession obtained in consequence. Presumably the repetition of 'in consequence' is not merely pleonastic or intended for emphasis but requires that the confession is made as a consequence as well as the unreliability being consequential.

A confession which has been excluded may not affect the admissibility in evidence of facts discovered as a result of the confession – although the facts should not be related to the confession itself – or of showing that the accused speaks, writes or expresses himself in a particular way.

At common law, following the decision in *R* v *Sang* [1980] AC 402, the judge's discretion to exclude evidence which had been improperly obtained was to be exercised on the basis that evidence should be admitted provided that its effect was not more prejudicial than probative. Pre-PACE authorities reveal a relaxed approach. Thus, in *R* v *Leatham* (1861) 8 Cox CC 489, Crompton J expressed the view that 'It matters not how you get it; if you steal it even, it would be admissible in evidence.' Similarly, in *Kuruma, Son of Kania* v *R* [1955] 1 All ER 236, Lord Goddard CJ expressed the view that if evidence was admissible the court would not be overly concerned with how it had been obtained. Lord Widgery CJ said much the same thing in *Jeffrey* v *Black* [1978] 1 All ER 555, where an unlawful search of the defendant's premises was undertaken and cannabis discovered there after he had been arrested for stealing a sandwich. He commented:

'I have not the least doubt that an irregularity in obtaining evidence does not render the evidence inadmissible. Whether or not the evidence is admissible depends on whether or not it is relevant to the issues in respect of which it is called.'

In Australia, Barwick CJ put the problem succinctly in *R* v *Ireland* (1970) 126 CLR 321:

'On the one hand there is the public need to bring to conviction those who commit criminal offences. On the other hand there is the public interest in the protection of the individual from unlawful and unfair treatment. Convictions obtained with the aid of unlawful and unfair treatment may be obtained at too high a price.'

In *R* v *Maqsud Ali, R* v *Ashiq Hussain* [1965] 2 All ER 464 murder suspects went voluntarily with police officers to a room where they were left alone. In their conversation incriminating remarks were made and tape-recorded by a hidden microphone. In the Court of Appeal the view was expressed that: 'The criminal does not act according to the "Queensbury rules" hence the method of the informer and of the eavesdropper is commonly used in the detection of crime.'

In *R* v *Murphy* [1965] NI 138 (Courts-Martial Appeal Court) the accused had been convicted having made disclosures of information useful to an enemy to police officers posing as subversives. Lord Macdermott CJ observed:

'Detection by deception is a form of police procedure to be directed and used sparingly and with circumspection: but as a method it is as old as the constable in plain clothes and, regrettable as the fact may be, the day has not yet come when it would be safe to say that law and order could always be enforced and the public safety protected without occasional resort to it.'

Section 78 of the 1984 Act now provides a statutory basis for the trial judge's discretion. It states:

'(1) In any proceedings the court may refuse to allow evidence on which the prosecution proposes to rely to be given if it appears to the court that, having regard to all the circumstances in which the evidence was obtained, the admission of the evidence would have such an adverse effect on the fairness of the proceedings that the court ought not to admit it.
(2) Nothing in this section shall prejudice any rule of law requiring a court to exclude evidence.'

This section curiously refers to the 'fairness of the proceedings', although it also speaks of the circumstances in which the evidence was obtained. It must be assumed that it is referring to the general fairness of the obtaining of the evidence, rather than the fairness of the proceedings as such.

In *R* v *Mason* [1988] 1 WLR 139 the Court of Appeal held that 'evidence' for the purposes of s78 included a confession notwithstanding that confessions were expressly dealt with by s76. Thus a confession that was admissible through not falling foul of s76(2) could nevertheless still be excluded on the grounds of its unfairness. Mason, who had been arrested in connection with an arson offence, was told by the police that they had glass fragments of the petrol-filled bottle used to perpetrate the offence on which they had Mason's fingerprints. In reality this was simply a trick, and the police thought it would be fair, even if deceitful, in that Mason would not have confessed if he knew that he had nothing to do with the bottle. Watkins LJ was highly critical of the tactics practised by the police, and in quashing the conviction, was clearly at pains not to be seen to be encouraging the use of such tactics.

Difficulties still exist where evidence has been obtained through the use of officers working 'under cover'. *R* v *Smurthwaite* [1994] Crim LR 53 suggests that if an officer is in the role of an agent provocateur, the courts are likely to exclude evidence thus obtained, but not where it is clearly D who initiates the criminal activity (eg soliciting a plain clothes policeman to carry out a contract killing). The problem for the court lies in making the distinction. The courts have confirmed that there is no defence in English law of entrapment. Hence convictions have been upheld where police officers have used children to purchase '18' category films (see *London Borough of Ealing* v *Woolworths plc* [1995] Crim LR 58); where plain clothes officers have made test purchases of alcohol being sold in breach of liquor licence conditions (*DPP* v *Marshall* [1988] 3 All ER 683); and where police officers have posed as proprietors of a second-hand 'shop' to catch handlers selling off stolen goods: *R* v *Christou* [1992] 3 WLR 228.

What the courts will be wary of are procedures adopted by the police (eg activity that amounts to interrogation) that are not conducted in accordance with the Codes of Practice, thus undermining the reliability of evidence obtained. This problem was starkly illustrated by the decision of Ognall J to throw out the case against Colin Stagg, who had been charged with the murder of Rachel Nickell, because his 'confession' had been induced by repeated and persistent questioning by a WPC posing as Stagg's girlfriend: see *R* v *Stagg* (1994) The Times 15 September.

Where there is a reliable and permanent record of the evidence, the courts may lean more in favour admitting it. In *R* v *Cadette* (1995) Crim LR 229 the appellant had been involved in a plan to unlawfully import controlled drugs. Her telephone number had been found on a courier who had been intercepted at Heathrow Airport. The courier had planned to telephone the appellant upon arrival, and following her arrest, agreed to make the telephone call as planned in order to try to persuade the appellant to come to the airport. The courier gave the appellant no indication that she had been intercepted by the authorities. The telephone conversation was taped by the police and used in evidence against the appellant at her trial. On appeal she contended, unsuccessfully, that the evidence contained in the recording should have been excluded under s78 of PACE on the ground of unfairness. The court accepted that police officers, seeking to combat those involved in the commission of drugs trafficking, might have to resort to subterfuge. The court would examine the circumstances to see if police officers were resorting to subterfuge in order to circumvent the protections provided by the PACE and the relevant Codes. Unacceptable tactics would include a police officer obtaining statements by disguising his or her identity, participating in the commission of the criminal offence, or inciting the commission of the offence. In the instant case the evidence was admissible because the officers had simply given the appellant an opportunity to involve herself in the offence by allowing a pre-planned telephone conversation to take place. There was no question of the telephone conversation amounting to an 'interview'. The court was also persuaded by the reliability of the evidence (ie the fact that it was tape-recorded) and the fact that the administering of a caution at the outset of the conversation would have rendered the operation otiose.

Similarly, in *R* v *Khan (Sultan)* [1996] 3 WLR 162, the House of Lords rejected the appellant's assertions that evidence obtained by means of listening devices attached to private premises without the owner's consent should be excluded on the basis that the evidence had been obtained in breach of any right to privacy. Lord Nolan held that a trial judge had a residual discretion, under s78 of PACE, to exclude evidence if its admission would render the trial unfair, and in assessing this issue art 8 of the European Convention on Human Rights was relevant, but not decisive, of the matter. As he went on to observe:

> 'If evidence obtained by way of entrapment is admissible, then a fortiori there can hardly be a fundamental objection to the admission of evidence obtained in breach of privacy. In *R* v *Sang* itself, Lord Diplock noted that if evidence obtained by entrapment were inadmissible, this would have the effect of establishing entrapment as a defence to a criminal charge. ... By parity of reasoning, if evidence obtained by a breach of privacy were inadmissible, then privacy too would become a defence to a criminal charge where the substance of the charge consisted of acts done or words spoken in private. Such a proposition does not bear serious examination.'

10.21 Complaints against the police

Prior to the enactment of the Police and Criminal Evidence Act 1984, complaints against the police were dealt with by the Police Complaints Board, a system subject to heavy criticism in light of the extent to which it empowered the police to adjudicate upon the merits of complaints made against them: see further comments made by Sir Robert Mark, former Commissioner of Police for the Metropolis, in his autobiography *In the Office of Constable*, pp214–215.

Under the regime introduced by PACE the role previously undertaken by the Police Complaints Board was vested in the Police Complaints Authority (PCA). The relevant provisions of PACE dealing with complaints and the role of the PCA were subsequently re-enacted as ss65–88 of the Police Act 1996. The PCA was essentially a supervisory body, in that it oversaw the investigation of complaints by police officers unconnected with the complaint. Following criticism of the police complaints system on the grounds that there was insufficient independence in the investigation of the police (ie it essentially involved police officers investigating complaints against police officers), an entirely new scheme has been introduced by the Police Reform Act 2002.

The PCA is replaced by a body to be known as the Independent Police Complaints Commission (IPCC). The aim of these reforms is to increase public confidence in the police complaints machinery by providing a more independent and transparent process.

The key roles assigned to the IPCC are those set out in s10 of the 2002 Act, which provides that the IPCC functions are (inter alia): to secure public confidence in the complaints procedures; to handle complaints made about the conduct of persons serving with the police; and to record matters from which it appears that there may have been conduct by such persons which constitutes or involves the commission of a criminal offence or behaviour justifying disciplinary proceedings. Section 10(8) expressly excludes the IPCC from dealing with complaints where the subject matter relates to the direction and control of a police force by the chief officer of police of that force or a person for the time being carrying out the functions of the chief constable.

What constitutes a complaint is set out in s12 which provides that it can encompass any 'complaint about the conduct of a person serving with the police which is made' (a) by a member of the public who claims to be the person in relation to whom the conduct took place; (b) by a member of the public not falling within (a) who claims to have been adversely affected by the conduct; (c) by a member of the public who claims to have witnessed the conduct; and (d) by a person acting on behalf of a person falling within (a), (b) or (c). Section 12(7) extends the range of those against whom complaints can be made to include employees of police authorities acting under the direction and control of a chief officer and special constables. Hence the right to make a complaint will no longer be limited to the victim of the police action and complaints can be pursued by independent organisations.

All serious cases will be referred to the IPCC regardless of whether or not a complaint has been made. It will also have its own powers of investigation exercised by a body of independent investigators. Where it carries out an investigation a chief officer of police will be required to co-operate with the IPCC and will be under a legal obligation to provide investigators with access to documentation or other material. As appropriate it will also have the power to manage or to supervise police investigations of complaints. If necessary the IPCC will be able to call in any case being investigated by the police. Section 19 provides that, if necessary, the Secretary of State may authorise the use of directed and intrusive surveillance, and the conduct and use of covert human intelligence sources, for the purposes of carrying out of the Commission's functions.

Civil remedies

Section 88 of the Police Act 1996 provides that the chief constable shall, in certain circumstances, be vicariously liable for the acts of police constables under his direction and control. It is now largely commonplace for lawyers to advice those with serious complaints in respect of the conduct of individual police officers to consider pursuing actions for assault, false imprisonment or trespass, not least because of the prospect of an award of damages if the action succeeds.

Negligence

Actions for negligence are viewed somewhat differently by the courts, however, in that it cannot be assumed that all aspects of police activity will necessarily be regarded as giving rise to a private law duty of care. The courts will consider the issue of tortious liability with reference to the intention of Parliament, where the allegation relates to the negligent exercise of statutory powers, and issues such as loss distribution and how best to promote the efficient functioning of public services. The result is that a duty of care will not be imposed if there is some other more suitable way of obtaining a remedy; there is insufficient proximity between the plaintiff and the action complained of; the loss should lay where it falls; or it would be otherwise contrary to public policy to impose such a duty.

In *Hill* v *Chief Constable of West Yorkshire* [1989] AC 53 a claim in negligence brought against the defendant in respect of his force's failure to apprehend Peter Sutcliffe (alias 'the Yorkshire Ripper') before he murdered the plaintiff's daughter, was rejected on a number of grounds. First, it was held that no general duty of care was owed in respect of the policy adopted regarding the investigation of crime, as this was largely a matter within the discretion of police officers that the courts were not well versed to comment upon. Second, because there was insufficient proximity between the plaintiff and the defendant's action; in hunting for Sutcliffe the police were seeking to protect the public at large, not the plaintiff's daughter in particular. Third, because it was not in the public interest to subject the police to a duty of care in such circumstances. There was no evidence that it would be an effective mechanism for improving detection rates or preventing crime. As Lord Keith observed:

> '... if there is no general duty of care owed to the public to prevent the escape of a known criminal there cannot reasonably be imposed upon any police force a duty of care similarly owed to identify and apprehend an unknown one.'

He went on to express the view that, regardless of the issue of liability in negligence as an issue of private law, it was contrary to public policy to impose such liability in relation to the conduct of investigations, since it was to be assumed that police officers used their best endeavours to prevent crime in any event, and it would be undesirable for the courts to be placed in a situation of having to judge whether or not a particular line of enquiry ought to have been pursued by the police during an investigation. Similar thinking can be identified in the attitude taken by the courts in respect of the liability of fire authorities: see *John Munroe (Acrylics) Ltd* v *London Fire and Civil Defence Authority and Others* [1996] 4 All ER 318.

Even if the imposition of a duty of care is not contrary to public policy the plaintiff will still fail if the court takes the view that there is insufficient proximity, ie that the plaintiff was too remote from the exercise of discretion or discharge of duty to be owed a duty of care. Where a policing decision is characterised as one falling within the sphere of policy-making it is likely that any claim in negligence based on losses alleged to flow from that decision would be regarded as too remote. By contrast, if the negligence falls within the operational sphere, the plaintiff is more likely to be able to establish sufficient proximity: see further the speech of Lord Diplock in *Home Office* v *Dorset Yacht* [1970] AC 1004. The point is usefully illustrated in *Rigby* v *Chief Constable of Northamptonshire* [1985] 1 WLR 1242, where the plaintiff's gun shop had been broken into by a psychopath who had armed himself and refused to leave. The police laid siege to the shop, eventually firing a canister of CS gas to smoke out the intruder, the canister setting the shop ablaze. The plaintiff sought damages for negligence on the grounds that the police had used CS gas canisters known to have a propensity to burst into flames, without having on hand the necessary fire-fighting equipment. There was evidence that the police had not been equipped with the less dangerous 'Ferret' CS gas canisters. Although the court held that the decision not to provide the local police force with the 'Ferret' CS gas equipment was one falling into the category of policy, and thus could not be attacked on the ground of negligence, and that, in any event, it would not have been negligent to decide not to equip the local police force with such equipment, the court did find the police to have been negligent in firing the CS gas cylinders in the absence of adequate fire-fighting equipment.

In determining whether or not an action against in negligence against the police will succeed, a key factor is whether or not any special relationship can be identified as arising between the police and the plaintiff. Thus, in *Ancell* v *McDermott* [1993] 4 All ER 355, the court, following *Hill*, refused to accept the contention that police officers, who had reported a spillage of diesel oil on the highway, were under a duty to remain at the scene and warn other road users of the hazard, there being no duty of care to the motoring public at large: see further *Hughes* v *National Union of Mineworkers* [1991] 4 All ER 278. By contrast, in *Swinney* v *Chief Constable of Northumbria Police* [1996] 3 All ER 449, it was held that the defendants were liable in negligence for failing to take proper care of information supplied by the plaintiffs which lead to their being terrorised by the suspect they had identified. The Court of Appeal held that the nature of the information contained in the plaintiffs' statement, and the known danger presented by the named suspect, suggested that a special relationship did exist between the defendants and the plaintiffs such as to render the plaintiffs distinguishable from the general public in terms of their being owed a specific duty of care by the defendants. Notwithstanding the decision of the House of Lords in *Hill*, the Court felt that the police did not enjoy a blanket immunity from actions in negligence in respect of the conduct of investigations.

The ruling was endorsed at the subsequent trial of the action (see *Swinney* v *Chief Constable of Northumbria Police (No 2)* (1999) The Times 25 May), although the court found that the police had not failed to take reasonable care. Other public policy considerations, such as the need to protect informants, also had to be given due weight, along with the fact that this was a situation where the police had voluntarily accepted responsibility for ensuring confidentiality: see also *Alexandrou* v *Oxford* [1993] 4 All ER 328.

Breach of statutory duty

A police force could, in theory, incur liability for breach of statutory duty, but much depends on the wording of the duty in question and whether or not it was the intention of Parliament that a breach should result in compensation by way of damages: see further *Hague* v *Deputy Governor of Parkhurst Prison* [1991] 3 All ER 733; *Cutler* v *Wandsworth Stadium Ltd* [1949] AC 398; and *West Wiltshire District Council* v *Garland & Others* [1995] 2 All ER 17. In *X (Minors)* v *Bedfordshire County Council* [1995] 3 WLR 152 Lord Browne-Wilkinson observed that an action for breach of statutory duty might be permissable, first where there was no other means of enforcing the performance of the duty, and, second, where Parliament intended to protect an ascertainable class – otherwise the statute could not provide the protection it intended to confer. As he explained:

> 'Although regulatory or welfare legislation affecting a particular area of activity does in fact provide protection to those individuals particularly affected by that activity, the legislation is not to be treated as being passed for the benefit of those individuals but for the benefit of society in general. The cases where a private right of action for breach of statutory duty have been held to arise are all cases in which the statutory duty has been very limited and specific as opposed to general administrative functions imposed on public bodies and involving the exercise of administrative discretions.'

Misfeasance

Where loss is suffered as a result of a public officer, such as a police officer, knowingly acting ultra vires, a party suffering loss may be able to succeed with an action for the tort of misfeasance: see for example *Roncarelli* v *Duplessis* (1959) 16 DLR (2d) 689. Whilst proof of actual ill-will aimed at the plaintiff by a public officer will substantiate a claim for misfeasance, malice as such is not a precondition for a successful claim: see *Bourgoin SA and Others* v *Minister of Agriculture, Fisheries and Food* [1985] 3 All ER 585 and *Three Rivers District Council* v *Bank of England* [2000] 3 All ER 1. In the latter case Clarke J observed that the tort of misfeasance in public office was primarily concerned with public officers who deliberately and dishonestly abused their powers. Proof of malfeasance could, therefore, be based upon evidence that a public officer had, by an act or omission: (a) intended to injure another, or a person in a class to which that other belonged, by abusing his powers; or (b) known that he did not have the power to act as he did. Malice, in the sense of an intent to injure, and knowledge that a certain activity would be ultra vires, were alternative, not cumulative, bases for an allegation of misfeasance. In cases falling within (b) it was sufficient to show that the officer knew that his acts would be ultra vires or, in cases where he suspected or believed such to be the case, that he had not taken the steps that would have be taken by an honest and reasonable person to ascertain the true position. As regards the requirement that the public officer must have known that his act would probably damage the plaintiff, in cases where he suspected or believed that damage would probably result, it was sufficient for the plaintiff to prove that the public officer failed to make inquiries into the possibility of such damage as an honest and reasonable person would.

The courts have confirmed that there are no public policy reasons for providing the police with immunity as regards liability for misfeasance: see *Bennett* v *Commissioner of Police of the Metropolis* (1997) The Times 24 October.

In *Elliott* v *Chief Constable of Wiltshire* (1996) The Times 5 December the court ruled that the plaintiff should be allowed to proceed with an action in misfeasance against a chief constable alleged to have used the Police National Computer to gain evidence of the plaintiff's previous convictions, and to have sent them to the plaintiff's employer resulting in the plaintiff's dismissal. Sir Richard Scott V-C was persuaded by the fact that the defendant had acquired and disseminated the information in his capacity as a police officer.

11

The Right to Privacy and Family Life: Article 8 of the European Convention on Human Rights

11.1 A right to privacy?

In the legal context privacy is a concept with two distinctive features: the right to be left alone, in the sense of not being spied on or overheard; and the right to confidentiality in respect of personal information. Hence on the one hand an invasion of privacy can involve attention being drawn to the victim so that he becomes the subject of speculation and comment amongst the press and public, and may as a result be unable to go freely about his business or enjoy the unfettered use of his property. Alternatively, an invasion of privacy can arise from an unauthorised disclosure of information, raising the issue of when, if ever, an individual has the right in law to have sensitive information suppressed.

As with free speech, historically there has been no specific right to privacy in English law. It has not been one of the recognised torts to invade the privacy of another. In *Secretary of State for the Home Department* v *Wainwright and Another* (2002) The Times 4 January the Court of Appeal confirmed that (pre–October 2000) there was no common law basis upon which a citizen could claim that his privacy had been invaded by the state – hence a strip search by prison officers might attract an award of damages for battery if it exceeded what was required, but not aggravated damages in respect of any invasion of privacy occasioned by such a search.

An individual seeking legal redress for a perceived invasion of privacy has, historically, had to have to resort to some collateral legal remedy in tort, an action for breach of confidence, or has had to seek a remedy before the European Commission, or Court, of Human Rights. Certain of the Convention rights have, of course, now been incorporated into domestic law with the enactment of the Human Rights Act 1998, including the right to privacy under art 8, which provides:

> '(1) Everyone has the right to respect for his private and family life, his home and his correspondence.
> (2) There shall be no interference by a public authority with the exercise of this right except such as is in accordance with the law and is necessary in a democratic society in the interests of national security, public safety or the economic well-being of the country, for the prevention of disorder or crime, for the protection of health or morals, or for the protection of the rights and freedoms of others.'

Article 8 has been successfully invoked against the United Kingdom in cases such as *Malone* v *United Kingdom* (1985) 7 EHRR 14; *Halford* v *United Kingdom* (1997) 24 EHRR 523 (interception of telephone calls); and *Dudgeon* v *United Kingdom* (1981) 4 EHRR 149 (criminalisation of homosexuality). In *Winer* v *United Kingdom* Case 10871/84 (1986) 48 DR 154 the European Commission of Human Rights declared that the failure of the United Kingdom to develop a right to privacy (prior to the enactment of the 1998 Act) did not amount to a violation of art 8, given the other remedies available, such as the right to sue for defamation. Where the information disclosed is true, however, the individual who feels that his privacy has been interfered with by the disclosure has no legal remedy, other than an action for breach of confidence in certain situations. The Commission did not interpret art 8 as placing any duty upon a signatory state to provide further remedies in such cases, noting in particular that the right to privacy under art 8 had to be balanced against the right to free speech under art 10.

When the Bill that became the Human Rights Act 1998 was first published, Lord Irvine LC ventured the view that incorporation of the Convention would result in judges developing a law of privacy. As will be seen this has, to some extent, occurred, but not necessarily as some would have foreseen.

The 1998 Act places public bodies under a duty to comply with the Convention rights. Hence the BBC and other broadcasting bodies have to abide by the Convention whilst it does not apply, for example, to newspapers. If a complaint concerning intrusive journalism was made to, and rejected by, the Press Complaints Commission (considered below) an indirect method of getting the press to respect art 8 rights would be for the courts to permit actions to be brought against the Commission on the basis that it was a public authority, and that in refusing a valid complaint it has failed to uphold one of the Convention rights.

For the moment the courts seem more prepared to invoke the provisions of art 8 in developing the common law, notably breach of confidence, in providing individuals with some protection for their privacy against sections of the press: see *Douglas v Hello! Ltd* [2001] IP & T 391, considered below.

To the extent that there is likely to be a conflict between those seeking to exercise the right to free speech under art 10 and those seeking to assert a right to privacy under art 8, s12(4) the 1998 Act provides that the courts must have particular regard to the importance of the Convention right to freedom of expression. It requires the court, in those cases where the proceedings relate to material claimed to be journalistic, literary or artistic in nature, to have regard to factors such as the likelihood of it becoming publicly available, the public interest in the material being published, and any relevant privacy code. Whether this provision will have any genuine effect remains to be seen. It was enacted effectively as a sop to the popular press concerned about the extent to which the incorporation of art 8 might curtail their activities.

11.2 Protecting privacy by invoking the law of torts

Protecting privacy by reliance on the tort of trespass

If a person enters upon the private property of another without permission, he commits the tort of trespass and can be removed, prevented from committing further trespass by way of injunction, and sued for damages in respect of any harm caused to the property. Thus, in theory, privacy could be protected where someone enters the grounds of a house to spy upon its occupants, by invoking the tort of trespass. Arguably the same rules apply if this surveillance is conducted from the public highway, as it is dedicated for users to pass and repass, not to watch and beset neighbouring properties: see *Hickman v Maisey* [1990] 1 QB 752. This case concerned the defendant loitering on a road owned by the plaintiff in order to watch the plaintiff's racehorses at the gallops. A highway authority may not necessarily be as eager to help the victim of a voyeur stationed on a public road. In any event, once information has been obtained as a result of a trespass, the law of trespass itself cannot be used to prevent publication. In *Baron Bernstein of Leigh v Skyviews and General Ltd* [1978] QB 479 the court rejected the plaintiff's claim for trespass to his property arising out of the defendant's flying over the property and taking aerial photographs. As Griffiths J observed: 'the mere taking of a photograph cannot turn an act which is not a trespass into ... a trespass.'

As the law stands, therefore, a journalist would not commit any criminal offence by gaining unauthorised access (assuming no damage is caused to property) to the house of a well known actress, entering her bathroom and photographing her bathing. It would be too late to restrain the trespass and, subject to the courts recognising a duty of confidence (as to which see below), the photographs could be published provided they did not constitute a libel (see also the comments of Laws J in *Hellewell* v *Chief Constable of Derbyshire*, considered below).

In *Morris* v *Beardmore* [1980] 3 WLR 283, a case in which the House of Lords held that a defendant's refusal to provide a specimen in relation to alleged drink-driving offence could not be used as the basis for a prosecution where the request had been made by officers who were trespassing in his home, Lord Scarman observed:

> 'I have described the right to privacy as "fundamental". I do so for two reasons. First, it is apt to describe the importance attached by the common law to the privacy of the home ... [S]econd, the right enjoys the protection of the European Convention on Human Rights ... [T]he present appeal ... turns on the respect which Parliament must be understood ... to pay to the fundamental right to privacy in one's own home which has for centuries been recognised by the common law.'

Where, by contrast, the person gathering information surreptitiously is present with the consent of the occupier, or has a legal right to be present (eg a police officer), the complainant will be in a much weaker position. In *Mrs R* v *Central Independent Television plc* [1994] 3 WLR 20 the Court of Appeal declined to prevent the broadcasting of film that had been secretly recorded by police officers (for use in a 'fly on the wall' documentary) present at the complainant's house for the lawful purpose of arresting her husband, notwithstanding that the programme would identify him as a convicted child molester, a fact that she had sought to withhold from their infant daughter.

Protecting privacy by reliance on the tort of assault

If a person is physically manhandled by others, notably reporters and photographers, the possibility of a civil action for assault and battery or trespass to the person might be sustainable, although the damages are likely to be small. In *Kaye* v *Robertson* [1991] FSR 92 the court rejected a claim that to take flash photographs at close range without the consent of the subject could constitute a trespass to the person, although to deliberately cause harm to another's eyesight, albeit temporarily, might constitute a battery.

Protecting privacy by reliance on the tort of nuisance

The tort of nuisance could be invoked in extreme cases, but only where the plaintiff can show that the defendant's activities are interfering with the normal use of his property. Cases of surreptitious surveillance, such as the neighbour who observes the complainant from behind net curtains, or constantly watches him in the garden from an upstairs window, would be likely to fall outside the scope of nuisance.

Protecting privacy by reliance on the tort of defamation

To use a photograph or image of a person, without their consent, in order to advertise a product or promote some cause, or indeed to boost the circulation of a newspaper, may amount to defamation if the inference that the person had endorsed the use of their name or image would have the effect of lowering the reputation of that person in the minds of right thinking people. In *Tolley* v *Fry* [1931] AC 333 the defendants had, without obtaining his consent, published an advertisement showing the plaintiff, an amateur golfer, sporting a bar of their chocolate in his back pocket. The plaintiff was successful in recovering damages for defamation on the basis that the advertisement created an innuendo that he had forfeited his amateur status by agreeing to be featured for reward. Greer LJ was, however, at pains to point out that in such cases, no remedy will be available unless the plaintiff can establish that the association is defamatory. Hence if Tolley had been a professional golfer he may not have succeeded. Similarly, in *Charleston and Another* v *News Group Newspapers Ltd* [1995] 2 WLR 450, the defendants published the faces of the plaintiffs (who were both actors appearing in the television serial *Neighbours*), superimposed onto the naked bodies of models engaged in pornographic activities. The article accompanying the photographs claimed that they were evidence of a type of computer pornography that was, unknown to the plaintiffs, available to children. The plaintiffs sought damages alleging that the publication of the photograph was defamatory. The Court of Appeal held that the publication was not capable of having the defamatory meaning for which the plaintiffs contended, as the publication had to be considered in its totality. As the law stood it could offer no protection to the plaintiffs. The Court remained unpersuaded by arguments, drawing attention to the nature of tabloid journalism and the likely reaction of tabloid newspaper readers, ie that they were likely to concentrate on the photographs rather than note the contents of the accompanying article. The decision was upheld by the House of Lords: see further *Sim* v *Heinz* [1959] 1 WLR 313.

Even if defamation is established, the remedy is likely to lie in damages. A plaintiff seeking to prevent publication will only be granted an interlocutory injunction in a very clear case where any properly directed jury would conclude that the matter complained of was libellous: see *Bonnard* v *Perryman* [1891] 2 Ch 269 and *Francombe* v *Mirror Newspapers* [1984] 2 All ER 408. See further *Corelli* v *Wall* (1906) 22 TLR 532 and *Dockerell* v *Dougall* (1899) 80 LT 556.

In *Kaye* v *Robertson* [1991] FSR 62 the plaintiff, a leading actor in a popular television comedy series, had been hospitalised following an accident necessitating brain surgery. Photographers and a journalist from the *Sunday Sport* newspaper entered his hospital room without permission, photographed the plaintiff, and purported to interview him. At first instance the plaintiff obtained an injunction preventing publication on the basis that such publication would constitute a libel. On appeal, however, the Court narrowed the injunction, holding that it could not be granted on the basis of libel, as it was not 'inevitable' that the plaintiff would be defamed by the publication. The Court did agree to the maintenance of an injunction to prevent publication on the basis that, if permitted, the publication could be a malicious falsehood, as the journalists concerned knew that to claim that the plaintiff had consented to the interview would be a deliberately false claim. The result was something of a pyrrhic victory for the plaintiff as the revised injunction allowed the newspaper to publish some of the photographs, provided it did not claim that the plaintiff had in any way consented to the publication. Note that the hospital, unlike the plaintiff, could have proceeded against the journalists for trespass.

Where the copyright in photographs or film is owned by the person featured, he or she can invoke the laws relating to copyright in order to prevent unauthorised publication, although these rights may be waived by contract: see further Copyright, Designs and Patents Act 1988, ss85 and 87: *Williams* v *Settle* [1960] 1 WLR 1072. It may be possible for celebrities, particularly pop stars, to argue that they have copyright in their image if, for example, it forms part of some distinctive logo. In the United States the law has been developed to protect the so-called right of publicity, which perhaps should be renamed as the right to self-publicity: see *Carson* v *Here's Johnny Portable Toilets Inc* 698 F 2d 831 (1983). The American courts have recognised that the celebrity status has commercial value from a marketing perspective, and that the celebrity concerned should be able to control the use of his name and image, even where the associations are not defamatory or such as to amount to malicious falsehood.

Protecting privacy by reliance on the criminal law

The courts have, in the past, had to resort to creative use of statutory provisions or equitable doctrines to deal with what are in effect invasions of privacy. Hence in *Vigon* v *DPP* [1998] Crim LR 289 the appellant, who owned a business selling women's swimwear, was convicted of disorderly and insulting behaviour within sight of a person likely to be caused harassment, alarm or distress contrary to s5 of the Public Order Act 1986, when he was found to have fitted one of the changing rooms used by customers with a concealed video camera and taped them undressing.

11.3 Breach of confidence as a violation of privacy by public bodies

Although there are pre-October 2000 cases (considered below) where the courts have discussed the possibility of imposing a duty of confidence on public bodies not to divulge information, as the law currently stands where a public body discloses information it must act reasonably in doing so (ie within its powers), and the question of whether or not it has acted within its powers will entail an examination of the extent to which it has had due regard to an individual's rights under art 8 of the European Convention on Human Rights. As outlined above, under art 8 the right to privacy can be interfered with if it is necessary to do so in order, for example, to prevent crime or disorder.

In *R* v *Chief Constable of North Wales Police, ex parte AB* [1998] 3 All ER 310 the Court of Appeal upheld the legality of a policy adopted by a local police force whereby it divulged information to local people (on a 'need to know' basis) about convicted sex offenders moving into its area following release from prison. On the facts that court was satisfied that the public interest warranted such disclosure. Although the applicants had not sustained their arguments based on breach of confidence before the Court of Appeal, the observations of Lord Bingham CJ at first instance ([1997] 4 All ER 691 at p698h–j), regarding the wider issue of disclosure of information by public bodies, are instructive. As he observed:

> 'When in the course of performing its public duties, a public body … comes into possession of information relating to a member of the public, being information not generally available and potentially damaging to that member of the public if disclosed, the body ought not to disclose such information save for the purpose of and to the extent necessary for the performance of its public duty. This principle would not prevent the police making factual statements concerning police operations, even if such statements involved a report that an individual had been arrested or charged, but it would prevent the disclosure of damaging information about individuals acquired by the police in the course of their operations unless there was a specific public justification for such disclosure. This principle does not in my view rest on the existence of a duty of confidence owed by the public body to the member of the public, although it might well be that such a duty of confidence might in certain circumstances arise. The principle, as I think, rests on a fundamental rule of good public administration, which the law must recognise and if necessary enforce.'

Hence in *Woolgar* v *Chief Constable of Sussex Police* [2000] 1 WLR 25 the Court of Appeal held that it was permissible for the police to pass on information gained in interviews with W to the United Kingdom Central Council for Nursing Midwifery and Health Visiting (UKCC). W had been interviewed by the police. The interviews had been conducted during the course of investigations into the death of a patient at the nursing home where W worked. The police were particularly concerned about evidence suggesting that there had been an over-administration of diamorphine to the deceased. As the evidence obtained did not warrant a criminal prosecution, no further proceedings were taken against the plaintiff, but the matter was referred to UKCC, a disciplinary body empowered to remove nurses from the register if this was felt to be necessary in order to protect patients. Confirming the right of the police to pass on such information, the court observed that statements made under caution during police interviews were confidential, unless the maker of the statement waived confidentiality: see *Taylor* v *Serious Fraud Office* [1997] 4 All ER 801.

Exceptions would be recognised, however, where they could be shown to be in the public interest. Kennedy LJ went on to express the view that where a regulatory body such as the UKCC sought information contained in police interviews, the material would remain confidential save to the extent that it was used by the regulatory body for the purposes of its inquiry. Furthermore, art 8 of the European Convention on Human Rights, whilst providing for a right to privacy, also provided that disclosure could be permitted where it was in the interests of the public, particularly to safeguard health. On this basis the police would have been justified in passing the information on to the UKCC even if it had not requested it. Conversely, had the police refused a request from UKCC to disclose the information, a court order could have been applied for to obtain it. Ultimately the primary decision as to disclosure of the content of interviews will rest with the police and not the court, but where the police are minded to disclose they ought to advise the interviewee that it is their intention to do so.

See further *R* v *Brentwood Borough Council, ex parte Peck* [1998] EMLR 697 where the court upheld the right of a local authority to pass on tapes from its town centre CCTV cameras to the media for broadcast, even though the recordings had been made without the subject's consent.

In *Hellewell* v *Chief Constable of Derbyshire* [1995] 1 WLR 804 (obviously decided before the Human Rights Act came into force) the court adopted the view that the unauthorised publication of photographs by a public body could be challenged on the grounds of breach of confidence. The plaintiff, whilst being detained at a police station following his arrest in connection with theft offences, was photographed and had his fingerprints taken in accordance with the provisions of the Police and Criminal Evidence Act 1984. In due course he was charged with, and convicted of, the theft offences. Local shopkeepers, concerned about the prevalence of shoplifting, sought the assistance of the police who agreed to supply photographs of known local offenders. The photographs were to used by the shopkeepers so that their staff could be made aware of potential offenders and take precautions accordingly. On learning that his was one of the photographs being circulated, the plaintiff, who had 19 previous convictions for theft, commenced proceedings by way of writ seeking: a declaration that the disclosure of his photograph was unlawful; an injunction to prevent disclosure; and damages. Although the court struck out the claim as disclosing no reasonable cause of action, it should be noted that it did so on the basis that the police had acted reasonably and in good faith to prevent the commission of crimes, to assist in the investigation of offences, and to assist in the apprehension of offenders. More generally Laws J was of the opinion that breach of confidence could be used to prevent the publication of photographs, the duty of confidence arising simply out of the relationship between the parties without, as Laws J put it, 'any express notice from confider to confidant'. On the issue of privacy, he continued:

> 'If someone with a telephoto lens were to take from a distance and with no authority a picture of another engaged in some private act, his subsequent disclosure of the photograph would, in my judgment, as surely amount to a breach of confidence as if he had found or stolen a letter or diary in which the act was recounted and proceeded to

publish it. In such a case, the law would protect what might reasonably be called a right of privacy, although the name accorded to the action would be breach of confidence.'

See further *Bunn* v *BBC* [1998] 3 All ER 552.

11.4 Breach of confidence as a violation of privacy by individuals

An action for breach of confidence has, for many years, been recognised as a way of enforcing a duty of confidentiality upon a party to whom sensitive information has been confided. The incorporation of the European Convention on Human Rights by virtue of the Human Rights Act 1998 has given this form of action a new lease of life. As noted above, the 1998 Act requires public bodies to recognise that individuals have a right to privacy, but the courts have gone further and have opted to develop the action for breach of confidence as a way of upholding what is effectively a right to privacy between private parties.

When does a duty of confidentiality arise?

In *Campbell* v *MGN Ltd* (2002) The Times 29 March Morland J explained that three factors had to be established to support a successful claim for breach of confidence:

1. the material divulged had to have the 'necessary quality of confidence' about it;
2. the details must have been imparted in confidence; and
3. the publication of the details must have been to the claimant's detriment.

That case concerned the publication in the *Daily Mirror* newspaper of articles detailing the claimant's attendance at a drug rehabilitation centre. As regards (1) he was satisfied that details of the claimant's attendance at Narcotics Anonymous did have the necessary quality of confidence. It was easily identifiable as private and disclosure of such information would be highly offensive to a reasonable person of ordinary sensibilities. The test in (3) was also satisfied on the facts, as disclosure was likely to affect adversely the claimant's attendance and participation in therapy meetings.

As Lord Woolf CJ made clear in *A* v *B (A Company) and Another* [2002] 2 All ER 545, central to any claim for breach of confidence would be the existence of an interest of a private nature. The less evidence there was of any private interest the greater the probability that it would be outweighed by the right to freedom of expression, although he stressed that each case would depend to a large extent on its own facts. He observed:

'A duty of confidence will arise whenever the party subject to the duty is in a situation where he either knows or ought to know that the other person can reasonably expect his privacy to be protected. ...The range of situations in which protection can be provided is therefore extensive. Obviously, the necessary relationship can be expressly created. More often its existence will have to be inferred from the facts. Whether a duty of confidence does exist which courts can protect, if it is right to do so, will depend on all the circumstances of the relationship between the parties at the time of the threatened or actual breach of the alleged duty of confidence.'

It is thus more likely that a duty of confidence will arise in situations if an intrusion relates to a situation where a person can reasonably expect his privacy to be respected. The bugging of someone's home or the use of other surveillance techniques were cited as obvious examples of such intrusions, but his Lordship noted that the fact that information is obtained as a result of unlawful activities does not mean that its publication would necessarily be restrained by an injunction on the grounds of breach of confidence.

Who is bound by the duty of confidentiality?

On the basis of *Campbell* v *MGN Ltd* (above) the court will take an objective view to determine whether or not the recipient of the information in question is 'clothed in conscience with the duty of confidentiality'. Traditionally the courts have been willing to recognise, for example, that details of dealings between a husband and wife were held to be protected by a duty of confidence: see *Argyll* v *Duke of Argyll* [1967] Ch 302. In *A* v *B (A Company) and Another* (above) the court noted that where one party to a sexual relationship outside marriage wishes to divulge details of it there is a conflict between one party's right to privacy and the other party's right of freedom of expression. The more stable the relationship the greater will be the significance attached to it by the courts. Hence the courts will be willing to extend a duty of confidentiality to stable relationships outside marriage, but not fleeting or transient affairs (ie 'one night stands'). See further *Theakston* v *MGN Ltd* [2002] EMLR 22, where the court observed that a transitory engagement in a brothel was at the very limits of what could be protected by the law of confidence, as the relationship between a prostitute in a brothel and the customer was not confidential in nature. The mere fact that sexual activity had taken place did not, of itself, create a relationship of confidentiality. The court was willing, however, to grant an injunction to prevent the publication of photographs taken of the claimant at the brothel without his consent.

What is the link between breach of confidence and article 8?

Where the party seeking to disclose information, whether in visual or aural form, is a private body art 8 cannot be directly invoked, the 1998 Act imposing a duty to abide by the Convention on public, not private, bodies. The response of the courts has been to develop a concept of indirect horizontal effect for Convention rights, as identified in *Douglas* v *Hello! Ltd* [2001] IP & T 391. In such cases the court, as a public body, acts in conformity with the Convention by developing the common law, which does bind private parties, in conformity with Convention rights, such as the right to privacy. Hence the doctrine of breach of confidence has been developed by the courts to provide a common law right to privacy that stops short of applying art 8 between private parties

Keene LJ was willing to accept, in principle, that guests invited to a wedding on the basis that they would not take any unauthorised photographs did come under a duty of confidentiality to the hosts, so that the publication of any unauthorised photographs could be prohibited as a breach of confidence. On the facts, however, he felt that as the claimants had sold the rights to publish exclusive pictures to a mass circulation magazine the intrusion in question became less serious.

This incremental approach to the imposition of a law of privacy on private parties was subsequently endorsed in *Venables* v *News Group Newspapers Ltd* [2001] 1 All ER 908, where the court rejected the contention that the European Convention on Human Rights gave rise to free-standing rights and obligations as between private parties in domestic law (national newspapers not being public bodies for these purposes). Note that in both of these cases the courts were willing to recognise a duty of confidence notwithstanding the absence of any contractual relationship or indeed any relationship at all between the parties.

The balancing act carried out by the courts

As Lord Woolf CJ emphasised in *A* v *B (A Company) and Another* (above), any interference with the freedom of the press to publish has to be justified in the public interest. Whilst a court will have regard to whether or not publication is in the public interest, it does not follow that publication of any given material has to be desirable in order for publication to be in the public interest.

As was observed by Morland J in *Campbell* v *MGN Ltd* (above), even those in public life who openly court publicity are entitled to respect for their private lives provided this restriction can be justified within the terms of art 10(2) of the European Convention on Human Rights. On the facts the defendant newspaper was justified in publishing information that showed the claimant to have misled the public as to her having had problems with drug abuse. It had overstepped the mark, however, in publishing details of the claimant's treatment. The court was bound to give effect to art 8 by extending the protection of confidentiality to such material.

Regarding the position of those in the public eye, Lord Woolf CJ observed (in *A* v *B (A Company) and Another*):

'A public figure is entitled to a private life. The individual, however, should recognise that because of his public position he must expect and accept that his actions will be more closely scrutinised by the media. Even trivial facts relating to a public figure can be of great interest to readers and other observers of the media. Conduct which in the case of a private individual would not be the appropriate subject of comment can be the proper subject of comment in the case of a public figure. The public figure may hold a position where higher standards of conduct can be rightly expected by the public. The public figure may be a role model whose conduct could well be emulated by others. He may set the fashion. The higher the profile of the individual concerned the more likely that this will be the position. Whether you have courted publicity or not you may be a legitimate subject of public attention. If you have courted public attention then you have less ground to object to the intrusion which follows. In many of these situations it would be overstating the position to say that there is a public interest in the information being published. It would be more accurate to say that the public have an understandable and so a legitimate interest in being told the information. If this is the situation then it can be appropriately taken into account by a court when deciding on which side of the line a case falls. The courts must not ignore the fact that if newspapers do not publish information which the public are interested in, there will be fewer newspapers published, which will not be in the public interest. The same is true in relation to other parts of the media. In drawing up a balance sheet between the respective interests of the parties courts should not act as censors or arbiters of taste. ... If there is not a sufficient case for restraining publication the fact that a more lurid approach will be adopted by the publication than the court would regard as acceptable is not relevant. If the contents of the publication are untrue the law of defamation provides prohibition.'

Remedies for breach of confidence

Although damages may in some cases be an adequate form of compensation, in the vast majority of cases the confider will be seeking an injunction to prevent a threatened breach of confidence. Once information has been disclosed there is clearly little that can be done to prevent its wider publication.

In *Venables* v *News Group Newspapers Ltd* (above) the claimants had been convicted of the murder of a two-year-old boy. They were sentenced to be detained at Her Majesty's Pleasure. The Lord Chief Justice made certain directions regarding their release on parole on attaining the age of 18. Such was the notoriety of the claimants' crime that there were fears that, once released into the community, they might be subjected to revenge attacks from members of the victim's family, or the members of the wider public. To prevent this plans were made for the claimants to be given new identities on release from custody. In order to prevent any sections of the media, in particular tabloid newspapers, from releasing details of the claimants' whereabouts once released, or their new identities, the claimants applied for permanent injunctions prohibiting any disclosure of details that might lead to their being identified once released. Several newspapers sought to oppose the application for the injunction on the basis that, if granted, it would be a breach of the right to freedom of expression as provided for by art 10(1) of the European Convention on Human Rights. Granting the injunctions sought the court observed that, whilst art 10 did provide representatives of the media with the right to freedom of expression, that right could be limited by legal restrictions (the common law doctrine of breach of confidence), provided this limitation was for a legitimate purpose (prevention of crime and the protection of the rights of others), and provided the restriction imposed by law was proportionate to the threats faced by the claimants. The court further observed that the extension of the doctrine of breach of confidence in this particular case was justified by the unusual nature of the case and the grave risks faced by the claimants if their new identities and whereabouts became known. This interference with the right to freedom of expression might not have been justified if the only right that the claimants had sought to protect had been the right to privacy. On the facts, however, there was strong evidence to suggest that the claimants' lives might be at risk if details of their whereabouts became known. Hence the threat was to their rights under arts 2 and 3 as well as art 8.

11.5 Press reporting and broadcast media

Under English law the press is free to report facts that can be substantiated, subject to restrictions such as those imposed by the legislation governing contempt of court and official secrets. Thus previous convictions or other salacious facts about the lives of both famous and previously unheard of persons can be 'dredged up' by the press. Justification would be the defence to any action for defamation. An individual whose previous convictions are made public may bring proceedings in defamation if the provisions of the Rehabilitation of Offenders Act 1974 apply. Under the Act a conviction becomes 'spent' if the sentence imposed was less than 30 months imprisonment, and provided it was imposed between five and ten years previously. A defamation action will fail if the person revealing the 'spent' conviction can show that he did not act with malice, and it should be borne in mind that the plaintiff in such a case will not be eligible for legal aid.

For the time being the press has been allowed to retain a large degree of self-regulation under the auspices of the Press Complaints Commission, a body whose origins can be traced back to the establishment of the Press Council in 1953.

Attempts at reform

The issue of introducing legal controls over the press has been bedevilled by the difficulty inherent in balancing the competing interests of free speech and privacy. Indeed the issue of privacy and press freedom has been the subject of four post-war reports: the JUSTICE Report *Privacy and the Law* (1970); the Younger Committee Report (1972) (Cmnd 5012); the Calcutt Committee *Report of the Committee on Privacy and Related Matters* (1990) (Cmnd 1102); and the second Calcutt Report (1993).

The first Calcutt Report came out against the introduction of a new tort of infringement of privacy, chiefly because of the practical difficulties this would involve. As the Report states (para 12.34):

'Any form of legal action in tort suffers from a number of limitations. The individual who has been wronged has the daunting task of mounting and pursuing an action in the courts. Many find the financial risks a deterrent. One of the main shortcomings of a tort of infringement of privacy would be that it would not provide a readily accessible remedy.

Even if legal aid were made available, which we would consider essential, many would still fall outside its scope ... we set ourselves the test of asking whether any proposed remedy would satisfy the criteria of speed, cheapness and readiness of access. We are not persuaded that a tort of infringement of privacy would perform very well against such criteria. We consider this a major weakness.'

The Committee felt that the introduction of a new self-regulatory body, in the form of the Press Complaints Commission (see above) would provide a procedure for complaint which:

'... would undoubtedly be less daunting to many people than having to use a new tort. The people whose privacy we consider most needs protecting should they, for example, become the victim of a crime or a disaster, or suffer from a disfiguring illness, are precisely those who hold no office, play no prominent role in society, have no publicity agent and also probably lack the means to sue. Thus, while we have not based our rejection of a general tort of infringement of privacy on accessibility alone, it is, nevertheless, an important factor in deciding whether the case for a tort has been made out ...' (para 12.36)

The Committee went on to recommend (inter alia) the introduction of a new criminal offence of surreptitious unlawful surveillance by means of a technical device; a tort related to such unlawful surveillance; and a tort of disclosure of unlawfully obtained information.

The second Calcutt Report, published in January 1993, was highly critical of the Press Complaints Commission, claiming that it had been an ineffectual self-regulatory body, dominated by those with the interests of the Press at heart. The second Report contained two significant proposals. First, it recommended new criminal offences outlawing unauthorised entry into private property, photography, placing a surveillance device, or telephone tapping, conducted with the intention of obtaining information. Liability would extend to editors and proprietors of newspapers who instructed reporters to gather information by these means. Defendants would be able to rely on defences that they had acted to prevent crime, protect public safety or to prevent the public from being misled. Individuals who had suffered such intrusions would be able to invoke the civil courts in order to obtain an injunction to prevent disclosure of illegally obtained information.

The second major proposal was the replacement of the Press Complaints Commission with a statutory press tribunal, funded by the Crown, empowered to apply a Code of Practice. The tribunal would have had the power to prevent the publication of material in breach of the Code, investigate complaints, aid conciliation, award compensation and impose fines, enforce publication of retractions, apologies, and adjudications. Under the proposals the tribunal would have been empowered to impose a fine of up to one per cent of a publication's net annual revenue. Individuals would face a maximum fine of £5,000. In March 1993 the National Heritage Select Committee report on privacy and media intrusion recommended a new self-regulatory Press Commission and the appointment of an Ombudsman to investigate complaints. Significantly perhaps, in January 1994, the

PCC responded by appointing Professor Robert Pinker as its Privacy Ombudsman, empowering him to act, without a complaint actually being received, to ensure that the press complied with its own Code of Practice.

In addition, the Lord Chancellor's Department published its own consultation paper on the law relating to privacy in July 1993, which proposed a new cause of action that could be invoked in cases of infringement of privacy causing substantial distress to the plaintiff in circumstances where a person of ordinary sensibilities would have similarly suffered substantial distress. Privacy was there taken to include details concerning an individual's health, communications, family life and relationships. The proposals also envisaged a right to be free from harassment or molestation. A defendant would be permitted to raise defences that he had lawful authority for his actions, had the consent of the plaintiff, that the disclosure was protected by privilege, or that the disclosure was in the public interest. The paper envisaged actions being brought in the county courts, with awards of damages up to £10,000. A major weakness of the proposals, on which no action has been taken to date, was the absence of any provision of legal aid.

Despite these recommendations, the Conservative government reaffirmed its commitment to press self-regulation, claiming that there was insufficient public support for new civil or criminal restraints, and declaring itself wary of any administrative controls that would smack of government censorship of the press. In its paper (*Privacy and Intrusion: The Government Response to the House of Commons National Heritage Select Committee* (1995)), the Conservative government suggested that members of the public whose privacy has been infringed should be able to claim compensation from a fund set up by the newspaper industry, and that the Code of Practice should be strengthened in certain respects. The paper also recommended better lines of communication between editors and the PCC and greater publicity to increase public awareness of the role of the PCC.

The Press Complaints Commission

The task of the PCC is to enforce the Code of Practice, which was framed by the newspaper and periodical industry. The PCC comprises 16 members, a chair appointed by the newspaper and publishing industry, eight members of the public and seven representatives of the press. It meets once a month, and usually adopts an informal procedure.

The preamble to the PCC Code of Practice (published in December 1999) provides that:

> 'All members of the press have a duty to maintain the highest professional and ethical standards. This code sets the benchmark for those standards. It both protects the rights of the individual and upholds the public's right to know. The Code is the cornerstone of the system of self-regulation to which the industry has made a binding commitment. Editors and publishers must ensure that the Code is observed rigorously not only by their staff but also by anyone who contributes to their publications. It is essential to the workings of

an agreed code that it be honoured not only to the letter but in the full spirit. The Code should not be interpreted so narrowly as to compromise its commitment to respect the rights of the individual, nor so broadly that it prevents publication in the public interest.

It is the responsibility of editors to co-operate with the PCC as swiftly as possible in the resolution of complaints. Any publication which is criticised by the PCC under on of the following clauses must print the adjudication which follows in full and with due prominence.'

The Code itself provides that:

'Everyone is entitled to respect for his or her private and family life, home, health and correspondence. A publication will be expected to justify intrusions into any individual's private life without consent. The use of long lens photography to take pictures of people in private places without their consent is unacceptable.'

For these purposes private places are public or private property where there is a reasonable expectation of privacy. The Code goes on to provide that journalists and photographers should not obtain, nor seek to obtain, information or pictures through intimidation, harassment or persistent pursuit, and should not photograph individuals in private places without their consent. Specific provision is made in sections 6 and 7 of the Code for cases involving children. Significantly the use of material obtained by journalists using clandestine listening or recording devices is prohibited, subject to any such publication being in the public interest. For these purposes the public interest includes:

'(i) Detecting or exposing crime or a serious misdemeanour.
(ii) Protecting public health and safety.
(iii) Preventing the public from being misled by some statement or action of an individual or organisation.'

In determining whether the public interest arguments are made out the Commission will have regard to the extent to which material has, or is about to, become available to the public. In cases involving children the Code demands that editors must demonstrate 'an exceptional public interest to override the normally paramount interest of the child'.

The current version of the Code reflects changes made in the wake of the death of the Princess of Wales (ie restrictions on pursuit etc), and those made in light of the incorporation of the European Convention on Human rights into domestic law.

Like its predecessor the Press Council, the PCC has no coercive power and cannot award compensation or fine publishers. It can merely censure errant journalists and editors, and ask for any adverse adjudications to be given appropriate publicity by the publisher found to be at fault. Notwithstanding that it is a non-statutory body, if the PCC refuses to investigate a complaint, or does so but concludes that there has been no breach of the Code, a complainant could, in theory, seek judicial review of its decision: see the principles enunciated in *R* v *Panel on Take Overs and Mergers, ex parte Datafin* [1987] QB 815. A successful challenge would, however, require proof of manifestly unreasonable decision, or one vitiated by a grave departure from the standards of fairness required at common law: see further *R v Press Complaints Commission, ex parte Stewart-Brady* [1997] EMLR 185.

In a sense it could be argued that, with the incorporation of the European Convention on Human Rights, the need to address the issue of further legal protection of privacy has disappeared. In truth much depends upon how the United Kingdom courts interpret their duty under the Human Rights Act 1998. On the one hand the courts might take on the role of developing a jurisprudence relating to privacy that is particularly relevant to the domestic context but, on the other hand, they will be hamstrung by the need to have regard to the right to free speech under art 10, and the suggestion in s12 of the 1998 Act that if in doubt a court should perhaps give precedence to art 10.

Broadcast media

Until the enactment of the Broadcasting Act 1996, complaints alleging unwarranted infringement of privacy in, or in connection with the obtaining of material included in, television and radio programmes were adjudicated upon by the Broadcasting Complaints Commission (BCC), created by the Broadcasting Act 1990. The 1996 Act (by virtue of s106) creates a new body, the Broadcasting Standards Commission (BSC), which effectively represents a merger of the BCC and the Broadcasting Standards Council.

Under the Code of Conduct drawn up by the BSC (see s107 of the 1996 Act) broadcasters must act fairly and should proceed on the premise that the private lives of individuals are of no legitimate interest to others. As the current Code provides (at para 14)

> 'The line to be drawn between the public's right to information and the citizen's right to privacy can sometimes be a fine one. In considering complaints about the unwarranted infringement of privacy, the Commission will therefore address itself to two distinct questions: First, has there been an infringement of privacy? Second, if so, was it warranted? An infringement of privacy has to be justified by an overriding public interest in disclosure of the information. This would include revealing or detecting crime or disreputable behaviour, protecting public health or safety, exposing misleading claims made by individuals or organisations, or disclosing significant incompetence in public office. Moreover, the means of obtaining the information must be proportionate to the matter under investigation.'

The Code also confirms (para 15) that privacy can be infringed during the obtaining of material for a programme, even if none of it is broadcast. This reflects the ruling in *R v Broadcasting Complaints Commission, ex parte Lloyd* [1993] EMLR 419, where the court held that the forerunner of the BSC had been right to uphold an invasion of privacy complaint raised by the proprietor of a dating agency, about whom the BBC had been trying to produce an investigative film item. The complainant had been subjected to persistent attempts to interview and photograph himself and his family by those compiling material for the programme, and claimed that these activities amounted to an invasion of his privacy. The court ruled that the fact that none of the material was eventually used in the programme was irrelevant to the issue of the Commission's jurisdiction, provided there was a nexus between the material broadcast and the matter complained of.

The Code recognises that 'People in the public eye, either through the position they hold or the publicity they attract, are in a special position' (para 17), and can thus expect to have their activities more closely scrutinised by the broadcast media. It goes on to point out, however, that this does nor mean that, in respect of personal matters, those in the public eye or their immediate family or friends forfeit the right to privacy.

Broadcasters should resort to the use of secret recording techniques only where it is 'necessary to the credibility and authenticity of the story': para 18. The Code nevertheless recognises that secret filming and recording may be the only way to obtain evidence to support an investigation into a matter of genuine public interest.

Whilst the Code envisages the use of 'doorstepping' techniques to question persons currently in the news, and that surprise can be 'a legitimate device to elicit the truth especially when dealing with matters where there is an overriding public interest in investigation', it goes on to provide that repeated attempts to take pictures or to obtain interviews when consent has been refused can amount to an infringement of privacy: see paras 25–27.

An invasion of privacy can arise not only where a person's private life is made public, but also where they experience suffering and distress arising out of a tragic event, and that suffering and distress is then made public. Broadcasters have to tread a fine line between reporting the event and intruding into private grief. The Code provides that broadcasters 'should take care not to reveal the identity of a person who has died, or victims of accidents or violent crimes unless and until it is clear that the next of kin have been informed': para 28.

The broadcasting of programmes that revisit tragic events may also involve an invasion of privacy, causing distress to surviving victims or relatives in retelling the story. Paragraph 31 of the Code provides that the victim or their immediate families should be informed of the intended broadcast, but significantly it does not provide that a broadcast against the wishes of those involved will necessarily amount to an unwarranted invasion of privacy. In *R* v *Broadcasting Complaints Commission, ex parte Granada Television* (1994) The Times 16 December the appellants were responsible for the broadcasting of two programmes, both of which contained details of tragic deaths. One concerned a child who had been raped and murdered, the other of a young woman who had died as a result of an allergy. The parents of the deceased did not consent to the broadcasts and suffered distress as a result of having seen them by chance. In both cases the parents complained to the Broadcasting Complaints Commission that the broadcasts amounted to an invasion of privacy, and the Commission upheld the complaints. The appellants contended that there could be no invasion of privacy where the material broadcast was already in the public domain and did not relate to the complainants themselves. Confirming the correctness of the Commission's decision, the Court held that, as the Broadcasting Act 1990 Act did not contain a definition of privacy, it could be inferred that Parliament intended that the question of whether or not an infringement of privacy had occurred should be dealt with as one of fact and degree by the Commission itself. Whilst the Court would be willing to intervene in an extreme case where the Commission's interpretation of privacy could not be substantiated on any grounds, the present case was not regarded as falling within that category. The fact that the details had been in the public domain did not prevent their republication from amounting to an invasion of privacy, and it was unacceptably narrow to argue that the fact had to concern the complainant personally. Once the Commission concluded that an invasion of privacy had occurred it had jurisdiction to determine whether or not that invasion had been warranted. On the facts the Commission's determination could not be impeached.

The particular position of children is reflected in the Code, para 32 of which provides that children:

> '... do not lose their rights to privacy because of the fame or notoriety of their parents or because of events in their schools. Care should be taken that a child's gullibility or trust is not abused. They should not be questioned about private family matters or asked for views on matters likely to be beyond their capacity to answer properly. ... Similarly, children under 16 involved in police enquiries or court proceedings relating to sexual offences should not be identified or identifiable in news or other programmes.'

The protection provided by the 1996 Act enures for the benefit of individuals and not representative organisations: see s111(7), which restates similar provisions from the 1990 Act. The effect of this provision is illustrated by the litigation resulting from BBC's broadcasting, in 1993, of an edition of *Panorama*, which dealt with the rise in the number of lone parent families. The National Council for One-Parent Families, a pressure group, objected to the tone and content of the programme on the grounds that it gave a false picture of the problems of lone parenting and its causes, and lodged a complaint about the programme with the BCC. The BBC sought judicial review of the BCC decision to receive the complaint on the ground that it lacked jurisdiction to do so, as ss144(7) and 150 of the Broadcasting Act 1990 required a complainant to have a direct interest in the subject matter of the programme. Allowing the application and granting a declaration to the effect that the BCC, in concluding that the National Council for One Parent Families was a person with a direct interest in the content of the *Panorama* programme, had misdirected itself in law, the court observed that there was nothing in the 1990 Act to indicate that Parliament had intended that the BCC should have power to entertain complaints from organisations purporting to represent hundreds of thousands of people. In particular, Brooke J doubted whether permitting such a form of challenge would be consistent with the United Kingdom's obligations under the European Convention on Human Rights: see *R* v *Broadcasting Complaints Commission, ex parte British Broadcasting Corporation* (1995) The Times 24 February.

Limited companies, by contrast, can make complaints regarding unfair treatment and invasion of privacy. In *R* v *Broadcasting Standards Commission, ex parte British Broadcasting Corporation* (2000) The Times 12 April the Court of Appeal held that the BSC had been correct in ruling that covert filming of sales transactions in Dixons stores, carried out by the BBC for a consumer affairs programme investigating allegations that refurbished goods were being sold as new, could be the subject of a complaint under ss110 and 111 of the Broadcasting Act 1996. Lord Woolf MR, noting that the 1996 Act might well extend further in protecting privacy in certain situations than art 8 of the European Convention on Human Rights, observed that there was no doubt that a company could be unfairly treated in a television broadcast and there was nothing in the 1996 Act to suggest that companies should not enjoy the same safeguards as individuals. A company could engage in activities of a private nature that needed protection from unwarranted intrusion. If this were not the case it might be difficult under the Act to persuade broadcasters to observe proper standards when reporting items about companies. On the facts the BBC had failed to justify why it had resorted to covert filming. Notwithstanding that the covert filming took place in areas to which the public had access, the fact that customers and employees were being filmed without their consent added to the weight of the company's argument. Again the fact that the film in question was never broadcast did not detract from the strength of the complainant's case.

11.6 Security of communications and data protection

The use of surveillance devices by law enforcement agencies raises obvious issues regarding the extent to which the right to privacy ought to give way to the wider public interest in preventing and detecting criminal activity. The European Convention on Human Rights recognises that the right to privacy is not absolute, but equally any interference with that right must be as prescribed by law, and must be proportionate. The problem with domestic law until comparatively recently was that activities such as telephone tapping were authorised administratively, as opposed to being subject to any regime of clear legal control. In *Malone* v *United Kingdom* (1985) 7 EHRR 14 the European Court of Human Rights ruled unanimously that the then current law relating to interception of communications was insufficiently precise. The Court accepted that such interception might be necessary in order to investigate crime, but again stressed that this should be in accordance with the law and, in the absence of any clear law, the United Kingdom was unable to satisfy this condition.

In the wake of the ruling of the European Court of Human Rights in the *Malone* case the United Kingdom government was obliged to introduce legislation to provide a legal framework for the interception of communications by agents of the state, in particular the tapping of telephone lines. In its White Paper *The Interception of Communications in the United Kingdom* (1985) (Cmnd 9438) the government indicated its desire to introduce legislation that would:

'... provide a clear statutory framework within which the interception of communications on public systems will be authorised and controlled in a manner commanding public confidence.'

The result was the Interception of Communications Act 1985, which created the offence of intercepting a communication in the course of its transmission by post or by a public telecommunication system unless a warrant has been issued by the Secretary of State. Since 1985 there have been significant developments in telecommunications. The human rights climate has changed with the incorporation of the European Convention on Human Rights, and various deficiencies ion the 1985 Act have become apparent, not least the issue of telephone calls made on 'private' systems. For example, in *Halford* v *United Kingdom* (1997) 24 EHRR 523, the European Court of Human Rights ruled that the right to privacy extended to telephone calls made from the workplace if no warning was given by an employer that calls would be monitored. If such calls were intercepted on an internal communications system, there would be a breach of art 8. The interception could not be justified as being in accordance with the law because, given that the 1985 Act did not apply to private telephone systems, there was no relevant law covering such interceptions.

In *Khan* v *United Kingdom* Application No 35394/97 (2001) 31 EHRR 45 art 8 was successfully invoked before the European Court of Human Rights in relation to the use by police officers of a surveillance device attached (without permission) to the exterior of the premises in order to record the conversations of suspected drugs dealers. The respondents accepted that the applicant's privacy had been invaded by the eavesdropping, but contended that it was permissible as being 'in accordance with law and justified in a democratic society'. Rejecting this contention the Court noted that, at the time the surveillance had taken place the only regulation took the form of Home Office guidelines (*Covert Listening Devices and Visual Surveillance (Private Places)* (1984)), under which the chief constable of the relevant force had to be satisfied that, where devices were to be used to record conversations in places where a citizen would normally be entitled to presume privacy, such surveillance was required because the investigation concerned major organised crime, particularly violence. Given the absence of statutory controls, and the fact that the guidelines were not readily available to the public, the Court concluded that it could not be said that the violation of the applicant's privacy had been in 'accordance with the law': see further *PG and JH* v *United Kingdom* (2001) The Times 19 October.

In an attempt to update the law on the interception of communications, and to introduce a regulatory framework for other forms of surveillance, Parliament enacted the Regulation of Investigatory Powers Act 2000.

This major piece of legislation replaces the Interception of Communications Act 1985 and introduces additional safeguards in respect of covert surveillance. In doing so it complements provisions of the Police Act 1997 and the Intelligence Services Act 1994.

Chapter I of Part I deals with the interception of communications. Much of this restates what was in the 1985 Act, but changes have been made to deal with certain anomalies and uncertainties that became apparent under that Act, particularly problems of compliance with the European Convention on Human Rights as regards communications on private telephone systems, and technological advances, in particular the growth in the use mobile phones, the internet and e-mail communication. Hence s1 provides that it is an offence for a person, intentionally and without lawful authority to do so, to intercept, at any place in the United Kingdom, any communication in the course of its transmission by means the public postal service or public telecommunication system. It becomes an offence (subject to certain exceptions) to intentionally and without lawful authority intercept, at any place in the United Kingdom, any communication in the course of its transmission by means of a private telecommunication system. The House of Lords' decision in *DPP* v *Morgan* [2000] 2 All ER 522 confirms that a 'communication' for these purposes need comprise no more than the transmission of electronic impulses, such as might be generated when a number is dialled.

Interception is lawful if the sender and receiver consent to the interception; the sender consents to the interception and interception is authorised under Part II of the 2000 Act (which deals with authorised surveillance operations); the interception is conducted under specific provisions relating to prisons, or international mutual assistance agreements; or the interception is pursuant to a warrant issued under s5.

In granting a warrant s5 provides that the Secretary of State must believe that it is necessary to do so on one of the following grounds: the interests of national security; preventing or detecting serious crime; or of safeguarding the economic well-being of the United Kingdom. In any event the conduct authorised by the warrant must be proportionate to what is sought to be achieved by that conduct. The Act sets out at length, in s6, the office holders, such as chief constables and security service officials who may apply for an intercept warrant. Warrants must be for a specified period and (where appropriate) relate to a specified property. Under s12 the Secretary of State can impose a requirement on communication service providers (eg telecommunications and Internet service providers) to maintain intercept capabilities. This has raised concerns about the 'routine' monitoring of e-mail traffic.

Section 15 sets out various general safeguards relating to the use and disclosure of information obtained following the granting of intercept warrants. Section 17 (in terms similar to s9 under 1985 Act) provides that no evidence shall be adduced and no question in cross-examination shall be asked, in any court proceedings, which (in either case) tends to suggest that an offence has been committed under s1 by any servant of the Crown, or that any warrant has been issued. This rather opaque provision is actually designed to prohibit questioning in court that might expose the sources of information that led the police or other authorities to apply for a warrant. Hence the evidence obtained as a result of a warrant having been granted would not be admissible, as this too might result in the inadvertent disclosure of sources.

Equally evidence obtained through the use of a warrant will not be subject to the disclosure regime that governs evidence in criminal trials (ie it will not be made available to assist the defendant). The grounds for issuing a warrant are to prevent or detect serious crime, not to obtain evidence to be used for a prosecution in a court of law.

Section 17 therefore prohibits the use of evidence obtained by intercepts in all cases, other than those where the communication has been intercepted for the purposes of enforcing an enactment concerned with the provision of postal or public telecommunications services: see further *DPP* v *Morgan* (above) overruling *R* v *Rasool; R* v *Choudhary* [1997] 1 WLR 1092 and *R* v *Owen; R* v *Stephen* [1999] 1 WLR 949. Unauthorised disclosure of material obtained by means of an intercept warrant, or disclosure of the existence of a warrant is an offence under s19 punishable with up to five years' imprisonment.

Chapter II of Part I of the 2000 Act deals with the security of and access to communications data (ie traffic data indicating that telephone calls were made between specific numbers at particular time). Law enforcement agencies may need to obtain traffic data for the same reasons that an intercept warrant might be sought under Chapter I of Part I. Again authorisation will have to be sought beforehand and, if granted, telecommunications providers will be under an obligation to provide the traffic data requested. The information obtained might, for example, provide evidence of the 'clickstream' of an Internet user accessing various sites, or send and receiving e-mails.

Part II of the 2000 Act provides a framework for obtaining authorisations to engage in various forms of surveillance. The three forms of surveillance specified are: (i) directed surveillance; (ii) the use of covert human intelligence sources; and (iii) intrusive surveillance.

Directed surveillance is covert surveillance that is not intrusive – for example the use of devices that can pick up conversations from a distance, without being placed on premises – where the device is used to collect private information. Covert human intelligence sources encompasses the use of undercover agents where a relationship is formed with a source to obtain information. Covert for these purposes means that the person subject to surveillance is not intended to be aware that it is taking place. These two forms of surveillance will be lawful if authorised as required under the Act. The grounds for authorisation in both cases are, broadly, that the surveillance is required in order to investigate matters affecting (inter alia): national security; preventing or detecting crime or of preventing disorder; the economic well-being of the United Kingdom; the interests of public safety; the protection of public health; or the assessing or collecting any tax, duty, levy or other imposition. Authorisation should only be granted if the use of surveillance is proportionate in the circumstances. In addition, where undercover officers are used to 'befriend' a suspect and obtain information, there must be evidence that the operation is being properly managed and supervised by senior officers.

Intrusive surveillance involves covert surveillance using 'bugging' devices.

Authorisation for this form of surveillance can be granted, under s32, by the Secretary of State (or a senior authorising officer acting on his behalf) provided the requirement of proportionality is met, and the surveillance is related to the interests of national security; preventing or detecting serious crime; or the interests of the economic well-being of the United Kingdom.

Significantly, law enforcement and intelligence agencies resorting to these forms of surveillance are not under a legal duty to obtain prior authorisation – the effect of these provisions is that if they do, the surveillance will be lawful. Section 80 of the 2000 Act makes it clear that just because an authorisation framework is provided does not mean that it therefore becomes unlawful to engage in any such conduct, provided it is not otherwise unlawful under the terms of the Act. Failure to obtain authorisation could, however, leave the authorities concerned open to claims under the Human Rights Act 1998 regarding invasion of privacy, as the actions will not have been regulated by law. Sections 33–40 of the Act regulate applications for intrusive surveillance authorisations by the police, the NICS and customs officials. Broadly, these provisions are very similar to Part III of the Police Act 1997, indicating the role played by the Surveillance Commissioner in authorising intrusive surveillance.

Part III of the 2000 Act deals with access to encrypted data by law enforcement agencies. The assumption underpinning these provisions is that criminals and terrorists may be passing information in an encrypted form (ie in a form that can only be made intelligible if the encryption 'key' is provided). At its most simple the encryption key could simply be the password used to protect a text file. Under s53 it becomes criminal offence to refuse to disclose any such encryption key when the disclosure is required by virtue of s49(3). As with other parts of the Act, the basis for this intervention would be national security, the economic well being of the United Kingdom, or preventing and detecting serious crime. These measures have caused considerable controversy as they raise the prospect of a defendant being imprisoned where he has genuinely forgotten or lost the encryption key.

Part IV of the 2000 Act sets out the framework for oversight of the operation of the authorisations machinery and the functions of the intelligence services in this regard. The Interception of Communications Commissioner, a senior judicial figure, replaces the Commissioner appointed under the 1985 Act. He will review the Secretary of State's role regarding the granting of intercept warrants and the operation of the regime for acquiring communications data. The Act also provides for the continued existence of a tribunal to consider complaints arising under the provisions of the 2000 Act. The tribunal is the only forum (short of having resort to Strasbourg) where a human rights claim arising under the Act can be considered. Under s67(8) decisions of the tribunal are protected by an 'ouster clause' to the effect that 'determinations, awards, orders and other decisions of the tribunal (including decisions as to whether they have jurisdiction) shall not be subject to appeal or be liable to be questioned in any court.' Tribunal rules approved by the Secretary of State may also provide for hearing of a complaint in the absence of the complainant (s69(4)(a)); and in secret: s69(4)(b). The Tribunal may also withhold the full reasons for its decisions: see s69(4)(c).

Data protection

In its White Paper of 1984 the government recognised the need for some legislation controlling the use of personal information stored in computers:

'First, because of the threat to privacy posed by the rapid growth in the use of computers, with their ability to process and link at high speed information about individuals. There have been few reported instances in this country of information held on computers being misused so as to threaten the personal privacy of individuals. But the ease and scale of misuse which the versatility of computers makes possible is significantly greater than with manual records. Secondly, without legislation, firms operating in the United Kingdom may be at a disadvantage compared with those based in countries that have data protection legislation.'

The resultant legislation was the Data Protection Act 1985, now superseded by the Data Protection Act 1998, enacted to ensure compliance with both the right to privacy enshrined in art 8 of the European Convention on Human Rights, and the provisions of the EC Data Protection Directive 95/46/EC.

Under the 1998 Act data is defined as information which being processed by computer, or forms part of a relevant filing system or accessible record. The data protection principles provide that the data may not be processed unless a number of conditions are met. Normally the person providing the data should be told of the reason for collecting the data, how it will be processed, and his or her consent should be obtained. Other requirements are that the data will only be used for specified and lawful purposes, and will not be further processed in any manner incompatible with that purpose or those purposes. The personal data held should be only that required for the specified purpose and should be accurate and, where necessary, kept up to date. The data should not be kept for longer than is necessary safeguards should be in place to ensure that data cannot be unlawfully processed or divulged. Additional safeguards apply to sensitive personal data, defined as data relating to a data subject's racial or ethnic origin, political opinions, religious beliefs, trade union membership, physical or mental health or condition, sex life, or criminal record. Note that in *Campbell* v *MGN Ltd* (above), the claimant was awarded compensation under s13 of the Data Protection Act 1998 because the defendant newspaper was found to have been in breach of the Act as regards its processing of data concerning the claimant's physical or mental health.

The provisions of the Act are administered by an Information Commissioner (a change consequent upon the enactment of the Freedom of Information Act 2000), who can reject applications to register as a holder of information, issue enforcement notices for non-compliance, and even inspect premises and records. Appeal from his decision lies to the Information Tribunal (formerly the Data Protection Tribunal). Within the limitations imposed by the Act, individuals can, upon payment of a fee, request details of the information that is held on them. Under s40 of the Freedom of Information Act 2000 personal data held on third parties is exempt from disclosure if such disclosure would contravene the provisions of the Data Protection Act 1998. By virtue of Part VII of the 2000 Act, however, Data Protection Act 1998 rights of subject access and data accuracy are, with certain modifications and exemptions, extended to all personal information – not just that held in automated systems.

Additional safeguards are provided by s4 of the Electronic Communications Act 2000, which makes it a criminal offence (subject to certain exceptions) to disclose information relating to the private affairs of an individual or business if it has been obtained in the process of providing cryptography support services and consent has not been given to that disclosure. The offence is punishable by a two-year term of imprisonment following trial on indictment.

11.7 The right not to divulge information

The law recognises that there are situations where an individual can claim a legal right not to divulge information. In some cases this can be seen as an aspect of privacy, where the information is of a sensitive nature and its disclosure would cause embarrassment and distress to the person concerned, or their close family. In many cases, however, the right to maintain secrecy is invoked by those who seek some tactical advantage in litigation, or who wish to ensure a supply of information from informants who do not wish to be identified.

Legal professional privilege

In litigation, communications between lawyer and client attract legal professional privilege, which effectively prevents the court from ordering disclosure. The rationale for this privilege is clearly that individuals should be able to discuss their cases freely with their legal advisers. In order to determine whether or not the privilege will apply, a 'dominant purpose' test is applied. In *Waugh* v *British Railways Board* [1980] AC 521 the widow of a man who had been killed in a railway accident sought production of a report compiled for the safety inspectorate to assist them in determining the cause of the accident. The report stated that it was to be passed on to British Rail's solicitors to enable them to advise British Rail. The court held that, as the report had been drawn up, principally, to assist in accident prevention, it could order disclosure: see also *Peach* v *Commissioner of the Metropolis* [1986] 2 All ER 129.

In *R* v *Secretary of State for the Home Department, ex parte Daly* [2001] 3 All ER 433 the House of Lords held that a policy of excluding prisoners (regardless of status) from their cells whilst the cells were searched was a breach of art 8 of the European Convention on Human Rights as it went further than was necessary in securing the legitimate aim of ensuring that prisoners were not secreting prohibited articles. A particular aspect of the policy that the House of Lords found unacceptable was the checking of correspondence between prisoner and lawyer to ensure that legal professional privilege was not being abused: see further *R* v *Ashworth Special Hospital Authority and Another, ex parte N* (2001) The Times 26 June (monitoring of inmates' calls permissible but not if corresponding with lawyers on a matter of legal professional privilege).

Information supplied in confidence

Information supplied in confidence may also be protected on the grounds that it is in the public interest to do so: see for example *Rodgers* v *Home Secretary* [1973] AC 388; *D* v *National Society for the Prevention of Cruelty to Children* [1978] AC 171; and *Bookbinder* v *Tebbit* [1992] 1 WLR 217.

A subpoena duces tecum can compel a third party to attend trial with any relevant documents, but generally mere witnesses cannot be compelled to reveal what they have seen, or provide information: see *A Health Authority* v *X and Others* [2001] Lloyd's Rep Med 349 and *H (A Healthcare Worker)* v *Associated Newspapers Ltd* [2002] EMLR 425.

The exceptional situations where the production of documents in the possession of non-parties before the trial can be ordered are:

1. Personal injury litigation/fatal accident claims, eg to obtain hospital records where the health authority is not a party to the litigation. In *Paterson* v *Chadwick* [1974] 2 All ER 772 the plaintiff sued the defendant solicitor for allowing a personal injury action to become statute-barred. Even though the action appeared to be one based on a claim of professional negligence, the court held that the hospital should be required to disclose its records relevant to the injury, since the matter arose out of a personal injuries case.
2. Inspection of banker's books under court order.
3. Where a third party has inadvertently or knowingly assisted in the wrongdoing complained of. In *Norwich Pharmacal Ltd* v *Customs and Excise Commissioners* [1974] AC 133 the Customs and Excise was ordered to disclose information on who was importing fertiliser in breach of the plaintiff's patent. Similarly, in *Ashworth Hospital Authority* v *MGN Ltd* [2002] 4 All ER 193, a newspaper was compelled to reveal the source of information concerning the convicted murderer Ian Brady who was on hunger strike at the hospital. The House of Lords held that the *Norwich Pharmacal* jurisdiction to order the delivery up of material was not contingent upon establishing that the party in possession of the material was a wrongdoer. It was sufficient that the party in possession was involved in some way.

Lord Woolf CJ explained in *Ashworth*:

'Under this jurisdiction, there is no requirement that the person against whom the proceedings have been brought should be an actual wrongdoer who has committed a tort or breached a contract or committed some other civil or criminal wrongful act. In *Norwich Pharmacal Co* v *Comrs of Customs and Excise* ... itself, the Customs and Excise Commissioners were an entirely innocent party. The commissioners had, however, because of their statutory responsibilities become involved or mixed up in the illicit importation of the chemicals manufactured abroad which Norwich Pharmacal alleged infringed their patent. The *Norwich Pharmacal* case clearly establishes that where a person, albeit innocently, and without incurring any personal liability, becomes involved in a wrongful act of another, that person thereby comes under a duty to assist the person injured by those acts by giving him any information which he is able to give by way of discovery that discloses the identity of the wrongdoer. While therefore the exercise of the jurisdiction does require that there should be wrongdoing, the wrongdoing which is required is the wrongdoing of the person whose identity the claimant is seeking to establish and not that of the person against whom the proceedings are brought.'

The court, he felt, should exercise its discretion to determine where and how the line would be drawn to distinguish between parties involved in the wrongdoing and parties that were mere onlookers:

'It is sufficient that the source was a wrongdoer and MGN became involved in the wrongdoing which is incontestably the position. Whether the source's wrongdoing was tortious, or in breach of contract in my judgment matters not. If there was wrongdoing then there is no further requirement that [the] conduct should also be wrongful. It is sufficient ... that there was "involvement or participation". As MGN published the information which was wrongfully obtained, the answer as to whether there was involvement or participation must be an emphatic Yes.

... Although this requirement of involvement or participation on the part of the party from whom discovery is sought is not a stringent requirement, it is still a significant requirement. It distinguishes that party from a mere onlooker or witness. The need for involvement, the reference to participation can be dispensed with because it adds nothing to the requirement of involvement, is a significant requirement because it ensures that the mere onlooker cannot be subjected to the requirement to give disclosure. Such a requirement is an intrusion upon a third party to the wrongdoing and the need for involvement provides justification for this intrusion.'

The protection of journalistic sources

At common law it is a criminal offence to refuse to answer questions, when directed to do so by a trial judge, punishable by imprisonment. In certain circumstances this may result in pressure being placed on a journalist to reveal the source of confidential information that has been passed on to him. In *Attorney-General* v *Mulholland and Foster* [1963] 2 QB 477 the court confirmed that journalists had no common law legal privilege protecting them from proceedings for contempt where they refused to identify the source of information considered material to a proper disposal of an action. See further *British Steel Corporation* v *Granada Television Ltd*

[1981] AC 1096, where the House of Lords ruled that Granada Television should reveal to British Steel the name of the British Steel employee who had provided the television company with details of British Steel's corporate strategy.

The matter has now been placed on a statutory footing with the enactment of s10 of the Contempt of Court Act 1981, which gives journalists a limited defence if they wish to withhold their sources of information. It provides that:

> 'No court may require a person to disclose, nor is any person guilty of contempt of court for refusing to disclose, the source of information contained in a publication for which he is responsible, unless it be established to the satisfaction of the court that disclosure is necessary in the interests of justice or national security or for the prevention of disorder or crime.'

The scope of this provision was examined in *Secretary of State for Defence* v *Guardian Newspapers Ltd* [1984] 3 WLR 986. A document entitled *Deliveries of Cruise Missiles to RAF Greenham Common – Parliamentary and Public Statements* was prepared in the Ministry of Defence on or about 20 October 1983. It was classified as 'secret' and only seven copies left the ministry. The next day a photocopy of one of the copies arrived at the news desk of *The Guardian* newspaper where, apparently, none of the staff knew from whence it had come or who had delivered it. The editor, after inquiries, decided that it was authentic and concluded that the national interest would not be damaged by its publication, which subsequently occurred on 31 October. On 11 November, the Treasury Solicitor wrote to the editor asking him to deliver up the document. On 17 November solicitors acting for *The Guardian* replied, to the effect that certain markings on the document might disclose, or assist in the identification of, the source of the information, and although the editor did not know the source, in accordance with the well-established convention of journalism which had been given statutory force by s10 of the 1981 Act, he was not prepared to take any steps which might lead to the disclosure. The Court of Appeal held that by virtue of s18(1) of the Copyright Act 1956 the Crown had a strong prima facie right to be treated as the owner of the copy document. The interests of justice and those of national security required the immediate return of the document in the defendant's possession and, accordingly, exceptions to the operation of s10 regarding the immunity from disclosure of a source of information had been established. On appeal, the House of Lords was unanimous in its view that the Crown had adduced sufficient evidence to establish that the delivery up of the document was required in the national interest. Note that for these purposes the duty to disclose the source of the information took the form of a duty to reveal the information that might, indirectly, reveal the identity of the informant.

As Lord Bridge later observed in *X Ltd* v *Morgan-Grampian (Publishers) Ltd* [1991] 1 AC 1:

> '... if non-disclosure of a source of information will imperil national security or enable a crime to be committed which might otherwise be prevented, it is difficult to imagine that any judge would hesitate to order disclosure. These two public interests are of such

overriding public importance that once it is shown that disclosure will serve one of those interests, the necessity of disclosure follows almost automatically.'

In determining whether or not disclosure of sources should be ordered 'in the interests of justice' Lord Bridge went on, in *X Ltd* v *Morgan-Grampian (Publishers) Ltd*, to point out that the party seeking disclosure had to go further than simply demonstrating that he needed to identify the source of the information in order to exercise his legal rights, or avert a legal wrong. Other factors might include the effect of disclosure on the litigant's proprietary interest, the manner in which the information was obtained, and the public interest in the material published, as for example where it revealed iniquity. On the facts the House of Lords held that the defendant journalist, William Goodwin, should provide the evidence in his possession that would assist the plaintiffs in identifying who had passed on confidential information relating to their refinancing negotiations. In *Goodwin* v *United Kingdom* (1996) 22 EHRR 123 the European Court of Human Rights was asked to consider the extent to which the house of Lords' decision in *X Ltd* v *Morgan-Grampian (Publishers) Ltd* was consistent with art 10. The Court at Strasbourg, applying the same test as the House of Lords, ruled that the order to disclose had been a violation of Goodwin's right to freedom of expression, contrary to art 10. Given the enactment of the Human Rights Act 1998 the domestic courts will have a firmer grasp of the need to ensure that any disclosure order under s10 of the 1981 Act is consistent with the legitimate aims of any restrictions imposed on the right to free speech provided for by art 10.

Two cases illustrate how the wider public interest can become a dominant factor in whether or not disclosure is ordered. In *Interbrew SA* v *Financial Times Ltd and Others* [2002] EWCA Civ 274 a disclosure order was granted in respect of a financial analyst's report on South African Breweries that had been obtained by a third party (the source) and fraudulently altered by the source with a view to creating a false market in the shares of South African Breweries. The report was then passed on to the defendant newspapers where it was used as the basis for articles that were subsequently published. The publications had a significant impact on share values in certain companies. Critical to the decision to order disclosure was the fact that the source could not have been claiming to act in any wider public interest. On the contrary, all the evidence suggested that the source had acted either with a view to personal gain, or at least out of malevolence towards the applicants. This was not, therefore, a case where it could be said that requiring journalists to disclose their sources would in any way inhibit the flow of information to journalists that it might be in the public interest to have disclosed. As Sedley LJ observed:

'... is the public interest in the doing of justice sufficient in the particular circumstances of this case to make disclosure necessary? ... What in my judgment matters critically, at least in the present situation, is the source's evident purpose. It was on any view a maleficent one, calculated to do harm whether for profit or for spite, and whether to the investing public or Interbrew or both. ... The public interest in protecting the source of such a leak is in my judgment not sufficient to withstand the countervailing public interest in letting Interbrew seek justice in the courts against the source.'

In *Ashworth Hospital Authority* v *MGN Ltd* (above) disclosure was felt to be necessary partly to deter disclosures for purely venal reasons and partly to ensure public confidence in the security of medical records. As Lord Woolf CJ went on to explain:

> 'The fact that journalists' sources can be reasonably confident that their identity will not be disclosed makes a significant contribution to the ability of the press to perform their role in society of making information available to the public ... [the] situation [has to be] exceptional ... if disclosure of sources is to be justified. The care of patients at Ashworth is fraught with difficulty and danger. The disclosure of the patients' records increases that difficulty and danger and to deter the same or similar wrongdoing in the future it was essential that the source should be identified and punished. This was what made the orders to disclose necessary and proportionate and justified. The fact that Ian Brady had himself disclosed his medical history did not detract from the need to prevent staff from revealing medical records of patients. Ian Brady's conduct did not damage the integrity of Ashworth's patients' records. The source's disclosure was wholly inconsistent with the security of the records and the disclosure was made worse because it was purchased by a cash payment.'

What the courts are engaged in, therefore, is essentially a balancing act, with the public interest in a free press with access to sources of information to be weighed against the need to protect the legitimate interest that a party might have in maintaining the confidentiality of information. Hence in *Camelot* v *Centaur Communications plc* [1997] NLJ 1618 the Court of Appeal ruled that the interests of justice were best served by ordering disclosure of a source so that the plaintiffs might identify a disloyal employee, given that the material in question did not disclose any wrongdoing on the part of the plaintiffs, and the fact that there was no public interest in the information concerned being made public earlier than the plaintiffs wished it to. The Court recognised that its decision might be a deterrent to others who might feel it right to pass on confidential material to the press, but Schienmann LJ took the view that, as the law stood, informants would always be required to take a calculated risk as to whether a court would order disclosure of sources or not

By contrast, in *John and Others* v *Express Newspapers and Others* [2000] NLJ 615, the Court of Appeal refused to order disclosure of a journalistic source, notwithstanding that the resultant publication threatened to undermine the doctrine of legal professional privilege. The decision concerned a draft advice produced by a barrister for the claimant's solicitors, which was retrieved from a waste paper bin in chambers. It subsequently found its way into the hands of a journalist writing for a national newspaper. Again the court adverted to the balancing act involved under s10 of the 1981 Act, weighing the competing interests of the free press and public confidence in legal professional privilege. It is significant that it was persuaded to exercise its discretion against disclosure on the grounds that: (i) those acting for the claimant had made no effort to inquire into how the document had been obtained; and (ii) there was no evidence to suggest that if such an inquiry had been conducted the source of the information could have been identified. As Lindsay J observed in *Saunders* v *Punch Ltd* [1998] 1 WLR 986 (at 997): 'To an extent, whether disclosure of a source is "necessary" in the interests of justice can depend on whether the person seeking disclosure has made any attempt other than by applying to the court to find the source for himself.'

11.8 Sexuality, privacy and family life

Issues of privacy that bring art 8 into play can arise in a wide variety of circumstances. Privacy can be violated by direct intentional intrusion. Violations can also arise collaterally, where administrative practices or legal requirements force individuals to reveal information they feel should remain confidential. Sexuality and gender issues have provided considerable litigation on this point.

In *Dudgeon* v *United Kingdom* (1981) 4 EHRR 149 the European Court of Human Rights upheld (by a majority) a claim that the Northern Ireland laws prohibiting buggery between consenting adult males amounted to a violation of the right to privacy under art 8, as the police had relied upon the law to justify questioning the applicant about his sex life. The Homosexual Offences (Northern Ireland) Order 1982 was introduced to meet the requirements of the Court's ruling.

Similarly, in *ADT* v *United Kingdom* (2000) The Times 8 August, the European Court of Human Rights held that s13 of the Sexual Offences Act 1956, as amended by s1(2)(a) of the Sexual Offences Act 1967 (male homosexual acts in private not unlawful provided no more than two persons present), did amount to a violation of art 8, where the applicant had been convicted of gross indecency between men, after the police had seized his video tapes of sexual acts he had performed at his house with up to four other consenting adult males. Whilst the Court was satisfied that the interference with the applicant's private life was in accordance with the law, in that s13 of the 1956 Act and s1(2) of the 1967 Act provided for a clear scheme of prohibitions and sanctions, it could not accept that the domestic law was, on the facts, necessary in a democratic society. The applicant's activities were non-violent, raised no general public health concerns and were restricted to a small number of consenting adults. They were, therefore 'genuinely private', leading the court to adopt a narrow margin of appreciation in reviewing the domestic law. On this basis the interference caused by the domestic law could not be justified.

The Ministry of Defence policy prohibiting individuals with homosexual proclivities from serving in the armed forces was also subjected to the scrutiny of the European Court of Human Rights when viewed in the light of art 8. In *Lustig-Prean and Becket* v *United Kingdom; Smith and Grady* v *United Kingdom* (1999) The Times 11 October the Court held that the policy violated art 8, noting that the investigations into the homosexuality of the applicants had been intrusive and constituted grave interferences with their private lives. The Court was unwilling to accept alleged homophobia amongst members of the armed forces as a justification for the policy. To the extent that such prejudice existed the Court felt that it was incumbent upon the United Kingdom government to take steps to eradicate it, as was the case with racial or gender-based discrimination. The Court was also influenced by the fact that other contracting states appeared to be adopting more liberal policies on the admission of homosexuals to their armed forces.

Transsexuals

Applicants claiming that their right to privacy has been violated because their changed sexual status has not been recorded by variations to their birth certificates have, until recently, met with less success. In *Rees* v *United Kingdom* (1986) 9 EHRR 56 (woman having sex change operation to become a man) and *Cossey* v *United Kingdom* [1991] 2 FLR 492 (man having sex change operation to become a woman) the Court recognised that the margin of appreciation allowed to signatory states permitted them to insist on a system of recording births that identified the sex of a child when born. In *Rees* the Court noted the importance of the fact that the register of births recorded facts of legal significance and the establishment of family ties in connection with succession, legitimate descent and the distribution of property. The European Court of Human Rights rejected the argument advanced in *X, Y, and Z* v *United Kingdom* (1997) 24 EHRR 143 to the effect that it was a breach of art 8 to refuse to register as the father of a child a person who had undergone female to male gender re-assignment surgery, and whose partner had conceived by artificial insemination. Given the margin of appreciation granted to signatory states, they were entitled to adopt the view that only someone who was a 'biological male' could be registered as a child's father.

In *Sheffield and Horsham* v *United Kingdom* [1998] 2 FLR 928 the European Court of Human Rights saw no reason to depart from the above decisions regarding the refusal of signatory states to alter birth certificates, but the Court did stress the need for states to keep the matter under review in the light of emerging medical evidence. Pending such evidence the Court was not persuaded that the frequency of incidents when the applicants would have to produce documents showing their sex at birth was such as to amount to a disproportionate interference with the right to respect for their private lives. The Court also observed that, as regards the right to marry enshrined in art 12, the marriage there referred to meant a traditional marriage between person who were of the opposite biological sex, and that the right was concerned to protect marriage as the basis of family life. To allow the applicants to succeed under art 12 would result in an impairment of the very basis on which art 12 had been included in the Convention.

The illogicality of a signatory state recognising the condition of sexual dysphoria to the extent of providing gender re-assignment surgery through its national health service, yet refusing to permit any such patient to alter official documents to record his or her new gender, was finally recognised in *I* v *United Kingdom; Goodwin* v *United Kingdom* [2002] NLJ 1171. The Court held that to prohibit alteration of birth certificates did amount to a violation of art 8, and went on to hold that, as a consequence, there was no longer any justification in denying a transsexual the right to marry on the basis that his or her intended partner had the same birth sex as the transsexual.

The right to family life

Article 8 could, in theory, be invoked by those who feel that their right to adopt an 'alternative' lifestyle is being hampered by that state, but note that in *Buckley* v *United Kingdom* (1996) 23 EHRR 191 the applicant, a gypsy, unsuccessfully argued that the planning laws that led to her being forbidden to site caravans on land that she had purchased for her own occupation amounted to a violation of art 8. The planning legislation was regarded by the European Court of Human Rights as having 'legitimate aims', and as having been applied in a non-discriminatory fashion. Note that the applicant had also sought to argue that both the Caravan Sites Act 1968 and the Criminal Justice and Public Order Act 1994 were discriminatory in seeking to penalise or incriminate those who led a gypsy lifestyle, but the Court declined to consider these questions given that no specific action had been taken against the applicant under the auspices of either piece of legislation.

In *R* v *Secretary of State for the Home Department, ex parte Mellor* [2000] 3 FCR 148 the applicant was a prisoner serving a life sentence for murder. He requested that a sample of his semen be taken so that his wife, who he had married whilst he was in prison, could be artificially inseminated. The applicant feared that by the time the tariff period of his sentence had been served and he became eligible for release his wife would be too old to have children. The Secretary of State refused the request stating that it was his department's policy to accede to such requests only in the most exceptional circumstances. It was also contended that there was no need for the procedure and that there were doubts as to the stability of the applicant's relationship with his wife. The applicant sought judicial review of the refusal, stressing that prisoners retained all civil rights not expressly or impliedly removed as a result of incarceration. In particular, he contended that his right to found a family had not been given sufficient weight by the Secretary of State.

Dismissing the application, the court accepted that, whilst art 8 of the European Convention on Human Rights did require respect for family life where it existed, it did not necessarily give rise to any right to start a family. Article 12 could not be prayed in aid to create any such right either. Prisoners did not have any right as such of access to facilities for artificial insemination. The Secretary of State therefore had a discretion as to whether or not to allow access to such facilities, and the adoption of a policy to govern the exercise of that discretion was lawful provided, as in the present case, the policy was rational. Further, it was legitimate for the Secretary of State to take into account factors such as the interests of the unborn child, and public concern over the provision of artificial insemination facilities to prisoners serving custodial sentences. Note that although the decision was made prior to the Human Rights Act 1998 coming into effect, it serves as a good example of the court carrying out the balancing act required when considering arguments relating to alleged violation of those rights where the interest of both the individual and society at larger have to be considered.

In *Hatton* v *United Kingdom* (2001) The Times 8 October, art 8(1) was successfully invoked to challenge the government's decision to permit noisier aircraft to take off and land at Heathrow Airport during the night-time. The court acknowledged that interference with the rights guaranteed by art 8(1) could be permitted where this was 'in accordance with the law and necessary in a democratic society in the interests of ... the economic well-being of the country ... or for the protection of the rights and freedoms of others', but concluded that in striking the required balance in the particularly sensitive field of environmental protection mere reference to the economic well-being of the country was not sufficient to outweigh the rights of others. The positive duty upon a signatory state was to minimise, as far as was possible, the interference with art 8(1) rights by trying to find alternative solutions and by generally seeking to achieve its aims in the least onerous way as regards human rights. On the facts the modest steps at improving the night noise climate were not capable of constituting the measures necessary to protect the applicants' position. The United Kingdom had, therefore, failed to strike a fair balance between its aims as regards economic well-being and the applicants' effective enjoyment of their right to respect for their homes and their private and family lives.

12

Freedom of Expression: Article 10 of the European Convention on Human Rights

12.1 The constitutional context

12.2 Criminal law restraints upon freedom of expression

12.3 State control of the media

12.4 Contempt of court

12.5 Defamation

12.1 The constitutional context

The concept of free speech is seen as being one of the basic rights that is key to the proper working of a mature political constitution. As Lord Steyn observed in *R v Secretary of State for the Home Department, ex parte Simms; Same, ex parte O'Brien* [1999] 3 All ER 400 (at p408d–f):

> 'Freedom of expression is, of course, intrinsically important: it is valued for its own sake. But it is well recognised that it is also instrumentally important. It serves a number of broad objectives. First, it promotes the self-fulfilment of individuals in society. Secondly, in the famous words of Mr Justice Holmes (echoing John Stuart Mill), "the best test of truth is the power of the thought to get itself accepted in the competition of the market.": *Abraham* v *United States* 250 US 616, at 630 (1919), per Holmes J (dissent). Thirdly, freedom of speech is the lifeblood of democracy. The free flow of information and ideas informs political debate. It is a safety valve: people are more ready to accept decisions that go against them if they can in principle seek to influence them. It acts as a brake on the abuse of power by public officials. It facilitates the exposure of errors in the governance and administration of justice of the country ...'

Similarly, in *R* v *Shayler* [2002] 2 All ER 477, Lord Bingham observed that:

> 'Modern democratic government means government of the people by the people for the people. But there can be no government by the people if they are ignorant of the issues to be resolved, the arguments for and against different solutions and the facts underlying those arguments. The business of government is not an activity about which only those

professionally engaged are entitled to receive information and express opinions. It is, or should be, a participatory process. But there can be no assurance that government is carried out for the people unless the facts are made known, the issues publicly ventilated. Sometimes, inevitably, those involved in the conduct of government, as in any other walk of life, are guilty of error, incompetence, misbehaviour, dereliction of duty, even dishonesty and malpractice. Those concerned may very strongly wish that the facts relating to such matters are not made public. Publicity may reflect discredit on them or their predecessors. It may embarrass the authorities. It may impede the process of administration. Experience however shows, in this country and elsewhere, that publicity is a powerful disinfectant. Where abuses are exposed, they can be remedied. Even where abuses have already been remedied, the public may be entitled to know that they occurred. The role of the press in exposing abuses and miscarriages of justice has been a potent and honourable one. But the press cannot expose that of which it is denied knowledge.'

Given that the British constitution is largely unwritten, it is not surprising too that, historically, there has been no express legal basis for the right to freedom of expression in English law. As with other aspects of individual liberties, the citizen has been free to do as he or she pleases, subject to the restrictions imposed by the substantive law. As Lord Goff observed in *Attorney-General* v *Guardian Newspapers Ltd (No 2)* [1990] 1 AC 109 at 283–284:

'... we may pride ourselves on the fact that freedom of speech has existed in this country perhaps as long as, if not longer than, it has existed in any other country in the world ... we in this country (where everybody is free to do anything, subject only to the provisions of the law) proceed rather upon an assumption of freedom of speech, and turn to our law to discover the established exceptions to it.'

This is in stark contrast to the approach adopted under the European Convention on Human Rights, art 10 of which provides:

'(1) Everyone has the right to freedom of expression. This right shall include freedom to hold opinions and to receive and impart information and ideas without interference by public authority and regardless of frontiers. This article shall not prevent states from requiring the licensing of broadcasting, television and cinema enterprises.
(2) The exercise of these freedoms, since it carries with it duties and responsibilities, may be subject to such formalities, conditions, restrictions or penalties as are prescribed by law and are necessary in a democratic society, in the interests of national security, territorial integrity or public safety, for the prevention of disorder or crime, for the protection of health or morals, for the protection of the reputation or rights of others, for preventing the disclosure of information received in confidence, or for maintaining the authority and impartiality of the judiciary.'

Whilst the Convention remained simply a treaty to which the United Kingdom was a signatory its provisions were at best persuasive as far as courts deciding cases on the basis of domestic law were concerned. As will have been seen from Chapter 9, the enactment of the Human Rights Act 1998 has effected the incorporation of certain key Convention rights into domestic law, including art 10. In essence it means that the courts now have to interpret domestic legislation so as to ensure compliance with art 10 in so far as this is possible, and it is now unlawful for any public authority to act in a way which is inconsistent with the Convention rights.

In this context it is perhaps significant that Lord Steyn, in *R* v *Secretary of State for the Home Department, ex parte Simms; Same, ex parte O'Brien* (above), was keen to emphasise what he described as a 'principle of legality' whereby it was presumed that, in enacting primary or secondary legislation, Parliament did not seek to undermine or erode long standing principle of constitutional law relating to civil liberties such as freedom of expression, unless there were clear indications that such had been Parliament's intent. Hence the House of Lords held that prohibitions on prisoners talking to journalists were unlawful because of the important role journalists had played in investigating possible miscarriages of justice. To the extent that the Home Office had opted to operate a blanket ban on oral interviews by journalists, it was unlawful as it undermined the fundamental civil liberties of the applicants, not only to freedom of expression but in respect of access to justice.

Within the United Kingdom, the numerous laws restricting freedom of expression can be seen as an attempt to balance competing rights: the right to say and write anything one chooses to, as against the rights of others not to be offended, abused, scandalised or have their privacy invaded by such activities. As a matter of public law, whilst the State has an interest in protecting itself from betrayal or subversion, individual citizens may contend that they have a right to know what is being done by the state on their behalf.

12.2 Criminal law restraints upon freedom of expression

Sedition and disaffection

The state enforces certain key restraints on freedom of expression by means of imposing criminal sanctions to deter transgressions. Many of these offences exist to protect public order or national security. Thus, at common law it is an offence to publish a seditious libel or to utter seditious words. In *R* v *Burns* (1886) 16 Cox CC 355, sedition was defined as:

> 'An intention to bring into hatred or contempt, or to excite disaffection against the person of Her Majesty, or the government and constitution of the United Kingdom as by law established, or either House of Parliament, or the administration of justice, or to excite Her Majesty's subjects to attempt, otherwise than by lawful means, the alteration of any matter in church or state by law established, or to raise discontent or disaffection amongst Her Majesty's subjects, or to promote feelings of ill-will and hostility between different classes of such subjects.'

In *R* v *Caunt* (1948) 64 LQR 203 Birkett J directed the jury that proof of an intention to promote violence was an essential part of the offence. It is assumed, therefore, that a successful prosecution would have to involve proof of an intention to promote violence and disorder over and above the strong criticism of public affairs. In any event, many activities which would previously have been regarded as coming within the scope of sedition are now covered by other, more appropriate, offences, for example under the Public Order Act 1986.

An individual will incur liability under the Incitement to Disaffection Act 1934 if he maliciously and advisedly endeavours to seduce a member of the armed forces from his duty or allegiance to the Crown, or has in his possession or under his control any document of such a nature that the distribution of copies among members of the forces would constitute that offence, and he intends to commit the offence. For example, in *R v Arrowsmith* [1975] QB 678, the appellant was convicted, under the 1934 Act, of possessing, and distributing near army barracks, leaflets which might seduce soldiers from their duty of serving in Northern Ireland.

Similarly s91 of the Police Act 1996 prohibits acts calculated to cause disaffection among police officers or to induce them to withhold their services or commit breaches of discipline.

Racism

Offences related to stirring up racial hatred are contained in ss17–23 of the Public Order Act 1986, s17 defining racial hatred as hatred against a group in Great Britain defined by reference to colour, race, nationality, or ethnic origin. The use of words, or behaviour, or the displaying of written material, in a public place, which is intended to, or is likely to, stir up racial hatred is prohibited by s18. The publication or distribution of such material is prohibited by s19. The possession of racially inflammatory material is prohibited by s23. Sections 20–22 deal with the issues arising from plays and other public performances that may stir up racial hatred.

Blasphemy

As a starting point it should be noted that art 9 of the ECHR provides for a right to freedom of religion in the following terms:

> '(1) Everyone has the right to freedom of thought, conscience and religion; this right includes freedom to change his religion or belief and freedom, either alone or in community with others and in public or private, to manifest his religion or belief, in worship, teaching, practice and observance.
> (2) Freedom to manifest one's religion or beliefs shall be subject only to such limitations as are prescribed by law and are necessary in a democratic society in the interests of public safety, for the protection of public order, health or morals, or for the protection of the rights and freedoms of others.'

Difficulties inevitably arise where those espousing opposing religious beliefs, or even no religious beliefs are seen as undermining or insulting the religious views held by others. Under domestic law, freedom of expression on religious matters is limited in a number of ways, most notably by the offence of blasphemy.

The House of Lords in *R v Lemon* [1979] AC 617 defined blasphemy as involving the vilification of Christ, the Christian religion, the Bible, or any subject sacred to Christians. The existence of the common law offence is a highly symbolic restriction on free speech, largely reflecting the special position of the established church within the state. As Lord Sumner stated in *Bowman* v *Secular Society* [1917] AC 406, blasphemy was criminal because it tended to 'shake the fabric of society generally'.

Notwithstanding the decision in *Lemon*, there have been very few successful prosecutions for blasphemy during the twentieth century. In 1921 a defendant named Gott was sentenced to nine months' imprisonment for publishing *Rib Ticklers or Questions for Parsons*. In the *Lemon* case, which involved the prosecution of the editor of *Gay News* for publishing a poem in which a Roman soldier expressed homosexual love for Christ, it was held that, for a successful prosecution for blasphemy, it was not necessary that a breach of the peace should be a likely or intended result of the publication, nor was it necessary that the accused should intend to blaspheme, the offence being one of strict liability.

In *R* v *Bow Street Magistrates, ex parte Choudbury* [1991] 1 QB 429 the Divisional Court refused an application for judicial review of the magistrates' refusal to issue a summons for blasphemy in respect of the Salman Rushdie book *Satanic Verses*. The court noted that the Law Commission had recommended the abolition of the offence, and accepted that, in the light of this, it might not have been desirable to extend the ambit of the existing offence to other religions.

The Law Commission Working Paper, *Offences Against Religion and Public Worship* (No 79), referred to in *Choudbury*, based its conclusions on the need to promote free speech, the fact that most serious instances of blasphemy could now be prosecuted under other public order offences, the inappropriateness of giving special protection to Christianity in what was now a multi-faith society, and the unfairness that could result from the imposition of strict liability.

The Blasphemy (Abolition) Bill, a measure effectively identical to that appended to the Law Commission's paper, aimed at abolishing the common law offence, was introduced in the House of Lords in March 1995 but failed to gain a second reading.

Perhaps surprisingly, the United Kingdom's blasphemy laws were, indirectly, relied upon by the European Court of Human Rights as justifying the British Board of Film Classification's refusal to grant a certificate to a video entitled *Visions of Ecstasy* which depicted the erotic fantasies of St Teresa of Avila, a sixteenth-century Carmelite nun, on the grounds that it was blasphemous and would give deep offence to Christians. The Court took the view (by seven votes to two) that, whilst there had been an interference with the applicant's right to free expression under art 10 of the European Convention on Human Rights, that interference had been prescribed by law, had been in pursuit of a legitimate aim, and had been necessary in the interests of a democratic society. The Court accepted that, whilst blasphemy was not a concept availing itself of close legal definition, the British Board of Film Classification had acted within its powers under s4(1) of the Video Recordings Act 1984, and hence the restrictions in question were prescribed by law. The fact that

English law only extended the protection afforded by blasphemy to the Christian religion did not alter the fact that the law, per se, pursued a legitimate aim. Although practice varied amongst states that were signatories to the Convention, it was not possible for the Court to conclude that the protection afforded by the law of blasphemy in the United Kingdom was 'unnecessary', particularly given that fact that it sought to protect rights to freedom of thought and religion enshrined in art 9. Whereas the Court might have taken a stricter line had the application involved a restriction on political comment, a wider margin of appreciation would be granted to states where questions related to intimate personal convictions were concerned. Signatory states were better placed than the court to judge the need for such restrictions: see *Wingrove* v *United Kingdom* (1997) 24 EHRR 1.

Balancing free speech and religious tolerance

During the passage of the Human Rights Bill great concern was expressed by religious organisations as to the effect of incorporation on their rights to act in accordance with their religious beliefs, and by sections of the media concerned at the impact of a right to privacy on the common law notion of free speech. Section 11 of the 1998 Act provides that the incorporation of the Convention should not be regarded by a court as necessarily restricting any other rights and freedoms conferred on an individual by common law or statute. Section 12 goes on to deal more specifically with the issue of free speech by providing (in s12(4)) that the courts must have

> '... particular regard to the importance of the Convention right to freedom of expression and, where the proceedings relate to material which the respondent [ie person against whom the application for relief is made] claims, or which appears to the court, to be journalistic, literary or artistic material (or to conduct connected with such material), to –
> (a) the extent to which –
> (i) the material has, or is about to, become available to the public; or
> (ii) it is, or would be, in the public interest for the material to be published;
> (b) any relevant privacy code.'

Where a court is considering whether to grant any relief which, if granted, might affect the exercise of the Convention right to freedom of expression, and the respondent is neither present nor represented, no such relief should be granted unless the court is satisfied: '(a) that the applicant has taken all practicable steps to notify the respondent; or (b) that there are compelling reasons why the respondent should not be notified': s12(2)(a) and (b). Further 'no such relief is to be granted so as to restrain publication before trial unless the court is satisfied that the applicant is likely to establish that publication should not be allowed': see s12(3).

Section 13 provides that a court determining a question arising under the 1998 Act that 'might affect the exercise by a religious organisation (itself or its members collectively) of the Convention right to freedom of thought, conscience and religion' must 'have particular regard to the importance of that right.'

The usefulness of both ss12 and 13 must be questioned. They seek to assist the courts in the interpretation of domestic legislation and Convention rights, but ultimately the United Kingdom courts will be bound by the jurisprudence of the European Court of Human Rights as regards the 'hierarchy' of rights (ie whether freedom of expression outweighs the right to privacy). If domestic courts restrict the scope of Convention rights in a manner that is contrary to the rulings of the European Court of Human Rights, the way lies open to have the matter determined at Strasbourg with the prospect of the United Kingdom being found in breach of its Convention rights, notwithstanding incorporation.

Criminal libel

Criminal libel covers those serious cases of libel where mere damages are not appropriate as a remedy. It is very rare and not encouraged by the courts. Leave of a High Court judge is required before a prosecution can be commenced. A rare example of criminal libel being invoked was provided by the litigation in *Goldsmith* v *Pressdram Ltd* [1976] 3 WLR 191, where Wien J granted an order enabling a private prosecution for criminal libel to be brought by Sir James Goldsmith against *Private Eye* in respect of repeated allegations that Goldsmith was involved in a conspiracy to obstruct the course of justice, concerning the disappearance of Lord Lucan. In justifying the decision, Wien J observed that the press did not have licence to publish scandalous or scurrilous matter that was, in the view of the court, wholly without foundation.

Obscenity: common law offences relating to obscenity

The common law has always provided for some sort of criminal sanction in respect of publications deemed to be obscene: see *Curll's Case* (1727) 17 St Tr 153. Whilst the key prohibitions are now to be found in statute (see below) there are still two key common law offences that continue to play something of a residual role in providing some means of censoring publications and other displays: conspiracy to corrupt public morals, and conspiracy to outrage public decency. In *Shaw* v *Director of Public Prosecutions* [1962] AC 220 the appellant published the *Ladies Directory* which advertised prostitutes and their services. The House of Lords upheld the appellant's conviction for conspiring to corrupt public morals despite assertions that no such offence existed at common law. Justifying the decision of the majority Viscount Simon stated:

> '... there remains in the courts of law a residual power to enforce the supreme and fundamental purpose of the law, to conserve not only the safety and order but also the moral welfare of the state.'

His Lordship further suggested that prosecutions for common law conspiracy could be used where doubt existed as to whether a conviction of obscenity under the

Obscene Publications Acts could be obtained. Similarly, in *Knuller Ltd* v *Director of Public Prosecutions* [1973] AC 435, the appellant was convicted of conspiring to corrupt public morals on the basis of his publishing a magazine containing advertisements by homosexuals seeking to meet other homosexuals. It was held that it was no defence that under the Sexual Offences Act 1967 homosexual acts between consenting males in private had ceased to be an offence.

The offence of conspiring to outrage public decency also serves to fill gaps in the obscenity legislation, although the scope of the offence is far from clear. In *R* v *Gibson and Sylveire* [1991] 1 All ER 439 the appellants were convicted of the offence having displayed earrings made from human foetuses in an art gallery owned by one of the appellants. The court regarded the motive of the appellants in mounting the display as irrelevant if in fact the jury concluded that the display would be or was an outrage to public decency.

Obscenity: statutory offences relating to obscenity

There is a patchwork of statutory measures, stretching back over 170 years, attempting to regulate the production, marketing and even possession of purportedly obscene items. For example, s4 of the Vagrancy Act 1824 made it an offence to expose to view in any public place any obscene print, picture or other indecent exhibition. The first Obscene Publications Act was enacted in 1857, although it lacked any definition of obscenity, whilst s42 of the Customs Consolidation Act 1876 granted officers the power to seize and destroy indecent or obscene books and articles imported into the United Kingdom. More recently, s11 of the Post Office Act 1953 made it an offence to send indecent or obscene articles through the post, and the Children and Young Persons (Harmful Publications) Act 1955 made it an offence to publish horror comics, ie stories told in pictures portraying the commission of crimes, acts of violence or cruelty, or incidents of a repulsive or horrible nature.

The basis of the modern law is to be found in the Obscene Publications Acts of 1959 and 1964. Section 1 of the 1959 Act, in attempting to define the meaning of the word 'obscene', follows the definition laid down in *R* v *Hicklin* (1868) LR 3 QB 360. An obscene article is one whose effect, if taken as a whole, is such as tends to deprave and corrupt persons who are likely, having regard to all relevant circumstances, to read, see or hear the matter contained or embodied in it. The book or article must be taken as a whole so that it is no longer possible to select parts of the publication out of context, as for example was attempted by prosecuting counsel in the case concerning the book *Lady Chatterley's Lover*. A magazine which has many articles in it can, however, be within the definition even if only one article is held to be obscene: *R* v *Anderson* [1972] 1 QB 304. Further, obscenity is not necessarily limited to sexual matters – it may encompass matters such as drug taking: see *John Calder (Publishers)* v *Powell* [1965] 1 QB 509.

The 1959 Act requires that, for the material in question to be regarded as obscene, the prosecution must satisfy the court that it will tend to 'deprave and corrupt' those who are likely to read, see or hear it, as the case may be. Byrne J in the 'Lady Chatterley' case gave this definition of the phrase to the jury:

> '... to deprave means to make morally bad, to pervert, to debase, or corrupt morally. The words "to corrupt" mean to render morally unsound or rotten, to destroy the moral purity or chastity of, to pervert, to ruin a good quality, to debase, to defile ... just as loyalty is one of the things which is essential to the well-being of the nation, so some sense of morality is something that is essential to the well-being of a nation, and to the healthy life of the community ... and accordingly, anyone who by his writing tends to corrupt that fundamental sense of morality is guilty of an obscene libel.'

The difficulty with this definition is that juries have not been able or willing consistently to apply it. Modern-day jurors and magistrates are likely to be much more liberal in their views and are unlikely to be persuaded that anything less than an explicit portrayal or description of sexual activity is obscene in this sense.

Hence, in *R* v *Clayton and Halsey* [1963] 1 QB 163, where a police officer was shown obscene material, the court decided he was unlikely to be depraved and corrupted. However it is no defence that the sort of people likely to obtain particular material are already depraved and corrupted. In *R* v *O'Sullivan* [1995] 1 Cr App R 455 the appellant was observed by police whilst delivering and collecting pornographic material from a garage, and working behind the counter of a sex shop where the items were sold. He was also found to have pornographic video cassettes in his possession. The appellant was convicted of having obscene articles for gain contrary to s2(1) of the Obscene Publications Act 1959, and he appealed on the ground that the material in question was not obscene. In particular he contended that the trial judge should have directed the jury to consider whether the publications would tend to deprave and corrupt those likely to see the material (ie customers of the sex shop) as opposed to those who might possibly see the material. Dismissing the appeal the Court of Appeal held that for a conviction the jury had to:

1. be satisfied beyond all reasonable doubt that the defendant had the relevant articles in his possession with a view to publication for gain;
2. decide what publication the defendant had in contemplation;
3. consider what further publication, for example by giving, lending, or selling, could reasonably be expected to follow from the original contemplated publication; and
4. be satisfied that the effect of any of those contemplated publications would be to deprave and corrupt a more than negligible proportion of those likely to see the relevant matter.

'Publishing' for the purposes of the 1959 Act includes distributing, circulating, selling, hiring, showing pictures or playing records.

Section 2(5) gives a publisher a defence if he can show that he 'had not examined the article ... and had no reasonable cause to suspect' that what was published was obscene. Section 4 gives those charged with the offence of publishing an obscene article a defence if it can be shown that the publication was for the public good, in the interests of science, literature, art or learning, or other objects of general concern. Evidence can be given on the literary, artistic or scholastic merits of a piece of work, but evidence cannot be given of whether the publication is for the public good: that is for the jury to decide. In *R* v *Calder and Boyars Ltd* [1969] 1 QB 15 the Court of Appeal held that the jury had two questions to answer:

1. Was the book obscene?
2. Having assessed the strength of the literary, sociological or ethical merit which they consider the book to possess, has the publication, on balance, been shown to be justified as being for the public good?

Under the 1959 Act, as strengthened by the 1964 Act, the police may obtain warrants to search for and seize obscene material held for publication for gain. The courts also have powers to order the forfeiture and destruction of such material.

The law relating child pornography was strengthened further by the enactment of the Protection of Children Act 1978 which creates offences of taking, permitting to be taken, possessing or publishing indecent photographs of children under the age of 16: see further *R* v *Graham-Kerr* [1988] 1 LR 1098 and *R* v *Owen* [1988] 1 WLR 134. Section 84 of the Criminal Justice and Public Order Act 1994 Act extends the scope of the offences under the 1978 Act to include 'pseudo-photographs' which encompasses data stored on a computer disk or by other electronic means, thereby bringing within the ambit of the law the growing field of computerised child pornography. In *R* v *Fellows; R* v *Arnold* [1997] 2 All ER 548 the Court of Appeal confirmed that liability under these provisions extended to images held in digital form on a computer connected to the Internet, and that they were 'distributed or shown' for the purposes of the legislation by being made accessible to other users of the Internet.

The Indecent Displays (Control) Act 1981 prohibits the public display (ie visible to the public) of any indecent matter, provided that exceptions are made where entry to an exhibition of indecent items is by payment or where warning signs are exhibited at the entrance prohibiting entry by those under the age of 18. Curiously, a photographer could quite legally take an indecent picture of a 17-year-old girl, but she would not be legally entitled to enter premises where the picture was being displayed for the public to view. Exceptions are also made in respect of displays in art galleries and museums.

Obscenity: cinemas and theatres

Obscenity in films to be shown in cinemas may be regulated under statute and administratively. Local authorities, acting under the Cinematograph Act 1952 and the Cinemas Act 1985, are empowered to licence cinemas, and attach conditions to the licences that are granted. These can refer to the type of films shown and the courts have held that the conditions attached can apply to the morality of the films. A usual condition is that no film can be shown unless it has been approved by the British Board of Film Censors, essentially an administrative body performing a non-statutory form of cinema censorship. The Board will pay particular attention to the age of persons to be admitted to view a film when granting it a certificate for public viewing. Although the Board has no power to stop a film being shown or to enforce any cuts or to impose and enforce its classification, it is very influential and local authorities usually follow its recommendations.

The classification powers of the British Board of Film Censors were extended to videos by virtue of the Video Recordings Act 1984. It is an offence under the 1984 Act to supply to the public any video recording that has not been granted a certificate, unless the recording falls within an exempt category: see for example *Wingrove* v *United Kingdom* (above)

Prior to the enactment of the Theatres Act 1968, plays had to be granted a licence by the Lord Chamberlain before they could be performed for the public. The 1968 Act removed this requirement, but there is still a need for premises used for showing plays to be licensed by the local authority, although no conditions as to the content of the performances can be attached. The law relating to obscenity, incitement to racial hatred and breaches of the peace still applies to theatrical performances, but for a prosecution to be commenced the permission of the Attorney-General is required. Under the civil law any defamatory statements made in plays are libellous.

Official Secrets Acts 1911–1989

Section 1(1) of the Official Secrets Act 1911 provides, inter alia, that it is an offence, punishable with 14 years' imprisonment if any person, for any purpose prejudicial to the safety or interest of the state, publishes or communicates to any other person any secret official code word or any sketch, plan, model, article, or note, or other document or information which might be or is intended to be directly or indirectly useful to an enemy. Whether or not the defendant has acted for a purposes that is prejudicial to the state is to be determined by reference to the evidence submitted by the executive: see *Chandler* v *DPP* [1964] AC 763. Section 2 of the 1911 Act was for many years the subject of severe criticism for creating more than 2,000 offences and being in effect a 'catch-all' provision. It was not consistently enforced and a number of well-publicised prosecutions, such as those of Clive Ponting and Sarah Tisdall, both civil servants, lent strength to calls for its reform. Broadly the section made it an offence for a person receiving information in confidence from the government to communicate it to anyone who was not authorised to receive it unless it was in the interests of the state for him to do so. Even information that was not confidential was protected by the section and there were many difficulties of interpretation. Section 2 was eventually repealed and replaced by provisions in the

Official Secrets Act 1989, which came into force in March 1990. The 1989 Act is designed to protect more limited classes of official information. It also clarifies the position of members of the security and intelligence services.

Section 1 of the 1989 Act imposes a stringent duty on members or retired members of the security and intelligence services and those notified that they are subject to the section. It provides that such a person commits an offence if without lawful authority he discloses any information or document he has received in the course of such work or while such notification is in force. Other Crown servants or government contractors working in the security or intelligence fields are only guilty of an offence if they make a damaging disclosure of information or documents. A damaging disclosure is defined as one that causes damage to the work of or any part of the security and intelligence services or would be likely to do so. It is a defence to any of these charges if the defendant had no reasonable cause to believe that the information related to security and intelligence and, in the case of Crown servants or government contractors only, that they did not know the disclosure would be damaging. Note the heavier liability placed on members of the security and intelligence services.

Sections 2 and 3 of the 1989 Act respectively make it an offence for a Crown servant or government contractor without lawful authority to make a damaging disclosure in the field of defence and international relations. The phrase 'damaging disclosure' is precisely defined in the context of defence and international relations by the respective sections. Similar defences to charges under ss2 and 3 are provided as those for s1, noted above.

Section 4 of the 1989 Act makes it an offence for a Crown servant or government contractor or such retired employees to disclose information the disclosure of which results in the commission of an offence, facilitates escape from legal custody or impedes the prevention or detection of offences or the apprehension or prosecution of suspected offenders. Again, defences similar to those noted above are provided.

A person who receives a disclosure that is outlawed by the Act himself commits an offence if he discloses the information without lawful authority where he had reasonable grounds for belief that the information would be protected by the Act. A defence is provided if the defendant did not have reasonable cause to believe the disclosure would be damaging or if it is not in fact damaging.

What is conspicuous by its absence from the 1989 Act is any recognition that a disclosure might be lawful because it is in the public interest that the information concerned be made public. An attempt to challenge this was made in *R* v *Shayler* [2002] 2 All ER 477, where the defendant, who had supplied a newspaper with information for publication claiming that his motivation had been to show that the British people were being put at risk of harm as a result of the inadequacies of the security services, contended that the stricter controls placed on security service members by the 1989 Act were in breach of art 10 of the European Convention on Human Rights, and that, in any event, he should have been allowed to argue the defence of duress of necessity in respect of the disclosures. The House of Lords held that neither serving nor former members of the security services were permitted any public interest defence in respect of disclosures that contravened the Official Secrets Act 1989. Further, s1 of the 1989 Act was compatible with art 10 of the ECHR, therefore the defendant should stand trial on the charges that had been brought against him. There was scope, on the facts, for the application of any defence based on necessity.

Under the 1989 Act members or former members of the intelligence and security services with concerns about the activities of those services have a number of courses of lawful action open to them. These include discussing concerns with a staff counsellor, raising issues about breaches of the criminal law with the Attorney-General, the Director of Public Prosecutions or the Head of the Metropolitan Police, and raising issues about maladministration with the Home Secretary, other relevant ministers, or the Secretariat of the Parliamentary Intelligence and Security Committee. In the light of these possibilities, alerting the press was not seen as justifiable by the House of Lords.

Regarding the existence of any public interest defence for disclosures Lord Bingham observed:

'It is in my opinion plain, giving ss1(1)(a) and 4(1) and (3)(a) their natural and ordinary meaning and reading them in the context of the OSA 1989 as a whole, that a defendant prosecuted under these sections is not entitled to be acquitted if he shows that it was or that he believed that it was in the public or national interest to make the disclosure in question or if the jury conclude that it may have been or that the defendant may have believed it to be in the public or national interest to make the disclosure in question. The sections impose no obligation on the prosecution to prove that the disclosure was not in the public interest and give the defendant no opportunity to show that the disclosure was in the public interest or that he thought it was. The sections leave no room for doubt.'

Regarding the extent to which s1 of the 1989 Act was compatible with art 10 of the ECHR Lord Bingham set out the tests as being: (i) whether or not the restriction was prescribed by law; (ii) if so, whether the restriction sought to achieve one or more of the objectives permitted by art 10(2); (iii) if so, whether or not the restriction was necessary in a democratic society – in relation to which he observed that:

' "Necessary" has been strongly interpreted: it is not synonymous with "indispensable", neither has it the flexibility of such expressions as "admissible", "ordinary", "useful", "reasonable" or "desirable". ... One must consider whether the interference complained of corresponded to a pressing social need, whether it was proportionate to the legitimate aim pursued and whether the reasons given by the national authority to justify it are relevant and sufficient under art 10(2).'

Concluding that there was a pressing social need for the restrictions imposed under the 1989 Act Lord Bingham observed:

'There is much domestic authority pointing to the need for a security or intelligence service to be secure. The commodity in which such a service deals is secret and confidential information. If the service is not secure those working against the interests of the state, whether terrorists, other criminals or foreign agents, will be alerted, and able to take evasive action; its own agents may be unmasked; members of the service will feel unable to rely on each other; those upon whom the service relies as sources of information will feel unable to rely on their identity remaining secret; and foreign countries will decline to entrust their own secrets to an insecure recipient.'

As to whether the scheme provided for under s1 of the 1989 Act, whereby a member of the security services could take up his concerns about security with a senior civil servant, Lord Bingham commented:

'One would, again, hope that requests for authorisation to disclose would be granted where no adequate justification existed for denying it and that authorisation would be refused only where such justification existed. But the possibility would of course exist that authority might be refused where no adequate justification existed for refusal. ... In this situation the former member is entitled to seek judicial review of the decision to refuse, a course which the OSA 1989 does not seek to inhibit. ... For the appellant it was argued that judicial review offered a person in his position no effective protection, since courts were reluctant to intervene in matters concerning national security and the threshold of showing a decision to be irrational was so high as to give the applicant little chance of crossing it. ... There are in my opinion two answers to this submission. First the court's willingness to intervene will very much depend on the nature of the material which it is sought to disclose. If the issue concerns the disclosure of documents bearing a high security classification and there is apparently credible unchallenged evidence that disclosure is liable to lead to the identification of agents or the compromise of informers, the court may very well be unwilling to intervene. If, at the other end of the spectrum, it appears that while disclosure of the material may cause embarrassment or arouse criticism, it will not damage any security or intelligence interest, the court's reaction is likely to be very different. Usually, a proposed disclosure will fall between these two extremes and the court must exercise its judgment, informed by art 10 considerations. The second answer is that in any application for judicial review alleging an alleged violation of a Convention right the court will now conduct a much more rigorous and intrusive review than was once thought to be permissible.'

The Freedom of Information Act 2000

Whilst the reforms introduced by the Official Secrets Act 1989 Act helped to clarify the law to some extent, domestic law was still nevertheless criticised in that it did not provide for a positive 'right to know' in the form of a Freedom of Information Act, such as is found in many other jurisdictions, for example the United States, Canada and Australia.

In April 1994 the Conservative government signalled its willingness to accept some increased openness in government as indicated by the publication of the *Code of Practice on Access to Government Information* (Cmnd 2290). Under the Code useful information (not necessarily in the form of original documents) was, in theory, available from those bodies who came within the jurisdiction of the Parliamentary Commissioner for Administration (the Ombudsman), and other agencies. The weaknesses of the system were, first, that if the Ombudsman concluded that information should be disclosed, the relevant department could still ignore his recommendation without fear of any legal sanctions. Second, it was for the department itself to determine the 'usefulness' of the information sought. In most countries that have freedom of information legislation the 'need to know' concept is judged from the perspective of the person seeking the information.

In the manifesto upon which it fought and won the 1997 general election the Labour Party pledged itself to introducing a Freedom of Information Act once in office. Following the election, in December 1997, the White Paper *Your Right to Know* was published, setting out details of proposals for a Freedom of Information Act. It describes the proposed Act as being designed to:

> '… help open up public authorities and other organisations which carry out public functions. First, it will empower people, giving everyone a right of access to the information that they want to see. Secondly, it will place statutory duties on the bodies covered by the Act to make certain information publicly available as a matter of course.' (para 2.5)

The Act eventually received the Royal Assent in December 2000. It is an extremely complex and detailed piece of legislation and what follows is an overview of the salient points. The Act creates a qualified statutory right to information held by certain specified public bodies, and provides for a supervisory framework to ensure the effective operation of the disclosure scheme, through both administrative supervision and the establishment of an appeals procedure.

Public bodies to whom an application for disclosure can be made

The statutory right of access to information created by s1 of the Act provides that any person making a request for access to information to a public authority is entitled to be informed as to whether or not the information is held and, if it is, to have that information communicated to him. The right to information is heavily qualified by the exemptions provided for in the Act, considered below.

For these purposes a public authority is as defined in ss3–7 and Sch 1 to the Act. This definition brings within the scope of the provisions any government department, the House of Commons, the House of Lords, the Northern Ireland Assembly, the National Assembly for Wales, local government bodies, national health service bodies, educational institutions, police forces, the armed forces (save for certain exceptions), and a range of quangos from the Advisory Board on Restricted Patients to the Zoos Forum. Publicly owned companies are also subject to the Act, ie a company wholly owned by the Crown or wholly owned by any public authority listed in Sch 1 other than a government department.

The rules relating to applications

Section 16 of the Act places public authorities under a general duty to provide advice and assistance, so far it is reasonable to expect them to do so, to persons who propose to make, or have made, requests for information. An application for disclosure must specify the information sought to enable the public authority to identify and locate the information requested – no duty to disclose arises if the request is insufficiently specific: see s1(3). An application must be in writing and may not be anonymous: s8(1). A public authority is entitles to charge a fee for providing the information sought and must normally respond to an application within 20 working days.

Procedural grounds for refusing an application for information

An application can be refused where the relevant public body estimates that the cost of complying with the request would exceed the appropriate cost limit (as specified by the Secretary of State in regulations): see s13. The cost limit will vary depending on the nature of the information sought. Vexatious or repeated requests can also be refused: see s14. A repeated request is taken to be one that is identical or substantially similar to a request already made by the applicant, unless there has been a reasonable interval between requests.

Substantive grounds for refusing disclosure

Section 2 of the Act provides that there is no duty on a public authority to disclose information which, by virtue of the provisions of Part II of the Act, is classified as being subject to an absolute exemption (see below). Where information does not fall within the absolutely exempt categories it can still be withheld if 'in all the circumstances of the case, the public interest in maintaining the exclusion of the duty to confirm or deny outweighs the public interest in disclosing the information': see s2(2)(b).

Material subject to absolute exemption from disclosure

There are a number of categories of material subject to absolute exemption, as specified by s2(3). Information which is reasonably accessible to the applicant by other means is subject to an absolute exemption (see s21 and the exception as regards information contained in a historical record in the Public Record Office, see further s64), as is information supplied by, or relating to, bodies dealing with security matters: see s23. Under s23(2) a minister of the Crown can certify that the information to which the application relates is covered by the exemption, and such certification will be regarded as conclusive evidence of that fact, subject to the appeals procedure considered below: see s60. Court records are protected by the absolute exemption (s32) as is any information required for the purposes of avoiding parliamentary privilege: s34. Certain documents relating to the formulation of government policy held by the House of Commons or the House of Lords are absolutely exempt by virtue of s36 and s2(3), as certain personal information governed by the Data Protection Act 1998: see s40. An absolute exemption is extended to information obtained by a public authority in circumstances where disclosure of the information to the public would constitute an actionable breach of confidence: see s41. The absolute exemption also applies to where the disclosure is prohibited by or under any enactment, is incompatible with any EC obligation, or would constitute or be punishable as a contempt of court: see s44.

Material that may be exempt from disclosure

In some cases arising under Part II of the Act information is declared to be exempt because it falls within a particular class. For example information relating to the inner workings of government is protected by s35 which provides that information relating to the formulation or development of government policy, Ministerial communications, or information relating to the provision of advice by any of the law officers or any request for the provision of such advice, is exempt from the duty to disclose. This has to be read in conjunction with s2 of the Act which, as outlined above, provides that information not subject to an absolute exemption may still be withheld if the public interest in withholding the information outweighs the public interest in disclosure. A similar approach is taken to communications about the granting of honours (s37), information protected by legal professional privilege (s42), commercial interests (s43), and information held by public authorities relating to the investigation of crime: s30.

As regards some categories of information not covered by an absolute exemption under Part II of the Act, the legislation specifies a 'potential harm' test to be applied in determining whether or not disclosure should be made. Hence, under s26 information relating to defence is exempt information if its disclosure under the Act would, or would be likely to, prejudice the national defence or the capability, effectiveness or security of the armed forces. Information relating to international relations is exempt under s27 if disclosure would be likely to, prejudice (inter alia) relations between the United Kingdom and any other state or international organisation or court. Section 28 creates a similar exemption regarding the disclosure of information that would prejudice relations between any two administrations in the United Kingdom. Under s29 information relating to the economy can be withheld if its disclosure would be likely to prejudice the economic interests of the United Kingdom or the financial interests of any administration in the United Kingdom. Under s36 information held by a public authority which is not exempt by virtue of s35 (see above) may still be exempt if the person specified under the Act is of the reasonable opinion that disclosure would, or would be likely to, prejudice the maintenance of the convention of the collective responsibility, or the free and frank provision of advice, or the free and frank exchange of views for the purposes of deliberation, or would otherwise prejudice, or would be likely otherwise to prejudice, the effective conduct of public affairs. Such 'catch-all' provisions have provided much ammunition to critics of the Act who claim that it might even make it more difficult to obtain information held by government departments than was the case before the Act came into effect.

Special provision is made in respect of environmental information by virtue of ss39 and 74, which seek to give effect to the provisions of the Aarhus Convention as regards the provision of access to environmental information.

Where a public authority, in reliance on Part II of the Act, determines that information is exempt from disclosure, it must give the applicant a notice which states that fact, specifies the exemption in question, and states why the exemption applies: see s17.

Under s63 information comprising a historical record cannot be exempt information by virtue of s28 (relations between UK administrations), s30(1) (investigations by public authorities), s32 (court records), s33 (audit functions), s35 (formulation of government policy), s36 (disclosure prejudicial to the conduct of public affairs), s37(1)(a) (communications with the royal family), s42 (legal professional privilege) or s43 (commercial interests). For these purposes information comprises a historical record at the end of the period of 30 years beginning with the year following that in which it was created. Information relating to the granting of honours under s37(1)(b) ceases to be exempt after 60 years. Information protected by s31 (eg the prevention or detection of crime, apprehension or prosecution of offenders, administration of justice) ceases to be exempt after 100 years.

Challenging the decision of a public body regarding disclosure

The Act creates the post of Information Commissioner to whom applicant can complain if they wish to challenge the way in which a public body has discharged its obligations under the Act regarding the disclosure, or non-disclosure, of information.

When a complaint is received the Commissioner is obliged to come to a decision in respect of it provided the complainant has exhausted any complaint procedures provided by the public body, there has been no undue delay in making the complaint, and provided the complaint is not frivolous or vexatious. Where a complaint is upheld by the Commissioner he will serve a decision notice to that effect on the relevant public authority specifying the steps which must be taken by the authority for complying with the Act. Under s52 the Commissioner can serve an enforcement notice on a public authority that fails to comply with its duties under the Act – ultimately failure to comply can be dealt with as a contempt of court: see s54. Where necessary the Commissioner can serve a public authority with an information notice in order to obtain the information needed to deal with a complaint. An important limitation on the Commissioner's powers is provided for by s53, which states that an 'accountable person', in most cases a Cabinet minister, can issue a certificate to the effect that a government department or other public body specified by the Secretary of State need not comply with a decision or enforcement notice. Any such certificate must be laid before the House of Commons.

Following consideration of a complaint the Commissioner may disclose to the Parliamentary Ombudsman, the Health Service Ombudsman or Local Government Ombudsman any information if it appears to the Commissioner that the information relates to a matter which could be the subject of an investigation by an Ombudsman.

Sections 57–61 provide for a right of appeal to the Information Tribunal (exercisable by applicant or public body) in respect of notices issues by the Commissioner. Under s58 an appeal can be allowed if the Tribunal determines that the notice issued by the Commissioner is not in accordance with the law or, to the extent that the notice involved an exercise of discretion by the Commissioner, if it determines that he ought to have exercised his discretion differently. The Tribunal also has the power to substitute such other notice as could have been served by the Commissioner, and can review any finding of fact on which the notice in question was based. A further right of appeal to the courts exists in respect of a point of law arising out of a determination of the Tribunal. Section 60 empowers the Tribunal to determine appeals against ministerial certificates issued under ss23(2) or 24(3) (security issues).

Supervision of the disclosure regime

The supervisory framework created by the Freedom of Information Act 2000 is to be found in Part III. The Secretary of State is required, under s45, to issue a Code of Practice providing guidance to public authorities as to the practice which it would, in his opinion, be desirable for them to follow in connection with the discharge of their functions regarding the handling of requests for information, particularly the provision of advice and assistance to those making such requests, and the provision of complaints procedures. The Lord Chancellor, under s46, is required to issue a Code of Practice providing guidance to public authorities as to the practice which it would, in his opinion, be desirable for them to follow in connection with the keeping, management and destruction of their records. The Information Commissioner, under s47, is required to promote good practice by public authorities as regards the discharge of their duties under the Act and must take steps to inform the public regarding the operation of the Act. The Commissioner is further required, by virtue of s49, to lay annually before each House of Parliament a general report on the exercise of his functions under the Act.

12.3 State control of the media

The press

A free and independent press is generally seen as one of the hallmarks of a healthy, mature and liberal democracy, providing its readership with a range of political criticism and also engaging in investigative journalism that can reveal the improper use of political power. Any attempts by the state to curtail the freedom of the press, in peacetime at least, should therefore be viewed with a degree of circumspection. All governments engage, to varying degrees, in what is known as 'news management', which involves feeding the press such information as the government of the day wants to have reported, but this process clearly relies upon the acquiescence of the press. A more specific method of controlling what is reported is that overseen by the Defence, Press and Broadcasting Committee, a non-statutory body which has as its function the issuing of 'D' Notices. The Committee has no legal status but it is made up of some senior civil servants, and its full-time secretary is paid by the Ministry of Defence. The function of the Committee is to give informal confidential advice to the editors of newspapers on whether or not they should publish any article concerning defence or security matters. Merely disregarding a 'D' Notice is not itself an offence but it can leave a newspaper or publisher open to prosecution under the Official Secrets Act. If, on the other hand, clearance has been given, a publisher should be safe from prosecution, although this is not necessarily the case, as the *Sunday Telegraph* discovered to its cost when publishing an article concerning the war in Biafra. In practical terms the ' D' Notice system depends for its success on goodwill. As James Michael wrote in *The Politics of Secrecy* (1982):

> 'The "D" Notice system is the most explicit example of what is either self-censorship or responsible journalism, depending on who is speaking.'

Broadcast media

The British Broadcasting Corporation (BBC) is a body constituted by royal charter, first granted in 1926 and renewed in May 1996 (see Cmnd 3248). It is empowered to make broadcasts by virtue of an Agreement with the Secretary of State for Culture Media and Sport (replacing the former licence and agreement arrangement): see further Cmnd 3152 (1996). The BBC is controlled by nine governors appointed on advice from the Prime Minister. There is obviously considerable ministerial influence in terms of the renewal of the Agreement, the determination of the licence fee upon which the BBC depends for its income. Under the Agreement the BBC is required to broadcast impartial reports on the proceedings of both Houses of Parliament and to refrain from broadcasting programmes which might offend against good taste and decency or promote violence. The Secretary of State also has powers to prevent the broadcast of other material as detailed in the Agreement.

The Independent Television Commission (ITC) licences and regulates all commercial television broadcasting services, ie broadcasts not provided by the BBC. It derives its powers from the Broadcasting Act 1990, as amended by the Broadcasting Act 1996, and replaces the Independent Broadcasting Authority. Like the BBC, the ITC has a duty to ensure that the independent television companies do not broadcast anything that could offend against good taste or decency or lead to crime or violence, and must provide politically impartial programmes, involving a balanced reporting of current affairs, and an equitable distribution of time for party political broadcasts: see further Chapter 5. Both the BBC and the ITC are required to allow the government the right to broadcast any announcement so long as it is an official statement not a policy statement. The Independent Radio Authority performs a similar function to the ITC in relation to commercial radio.

The duty to ensure political impartiality is complimented by the prohibition on political advertising on commercial television and radio laid down in the 1990 Act, as amended by the 1996 Act, although difficult questions can nevertheless arise as to what constitutes a 'political' advertisement.

In *R* v *Radio Authority, ex parte Bull and Another* [1997] 3 WLR 1095 Amnesty International, applied for judicial review of the Radio Authority's refusal to allow its adverts to be broadcast because Amnesty International's objects were mainly of a political nature, and thus prohibited by s92(2)(a) of the Broadcasting Act 1990. Dismissing the application, the Court of Appeal held that the restriction on free speech imposed by s92 was to be interpreted narrowly so that it should only apply to those bodies whose objects were substantially or primarily political. For these purposes this would be taken to mean that at least 75 per cent of a body's objects were political. The term 'political' in this context was taken to mean that the body had to have as its object the procuration of changes to the law or policies of the United Kingdom or countries overseas. Amnesty's contention that its objects were not political, because what it sought was observance of international law as reflected in art 55 of the United Nations Charter, was rejected because such observance would require a change in the law and policies of many countries. In any event the Court found that the wording of s92(2)(a)(i) gave considerable discretion to the Authority in this matter and the court would respect that in considering any attempt to impugn the quality of the Authority's decision-making. The Court would not intervene unless the authority's decision could be shown to be irrational, which was not the case here. It is perhaps worth noting a point raised by the court at first instance to the effect that there were sound reasons of public policy for restricting access to paid political advertising on broadcast media, not least the intrusive nature of such advertising, and the advantage that would be afforded, if such advertising was permitted, to those political campaigners with the deepest pockets.

This legal and administrative framework for the regulation of broadcasting does give rise to questions relating to control and accountability. As indicated above, the Secretary of State has certain powers to intervene and regulate the content of programmes to be broadcast, even to the extent of prohibiting broadcasts in certain circumstances: eg the ban on the broadcasting of statements made by IRA supporters that was brought into effect in October 1988, upheld in *R* v *Secretary of State for the Home Department, ex parte Brind* [1991] 2 WLR 588.

The extent to which individual citizens can invoke the law to challenge a decision to broadcast a particular programme is less clear. Such challenges have been mounted, usually on the grounds of offending good taste and decency, but have failed on their merits: see *Attorney-General (ex rel McWhirter)* v *IBA* [1973] QB 629 (interim injunction granted but then dismissed) and *R* v *IBA, ex parte Whitehouse* (1985) The Times 4 April. In this context, the decision of the Court of Session – *Houston* v *BBC* 1995 SLT 1305 (see Munro [1995] NLJ 518 and [1996] NLJ 1433) – to uphold the interim interdict granted at the behest of the Labour Party to prevent the BBC from broadcasting an interview with John Major on the eve of the Scottish local elections, on the grounds that it would contravene the BBC's duty of impartiality, is all the more surprising, and indeed worrying.

The Broadcasting Standards Commission, created under s106 of the Broadcasting Act 1996 in place of the Broadcasting Complaints Commission and the Broadcasting Standards Council, will be:

1. under a duty to prepare a code giving guidance to broadcasters regarding practices to be followed in connection with the portrayal of sex and violence (s108);
2. under a duty to monitor programmes to which the Act applies; and is empowered to adjudicate upon any complaints made in relation to such matters: s110.

12.4 Contempt of court

Contempt of court is a significant constitutional issue because it raises the prospect of conflict between two important principles. On the one hand there is a public interest in the media being able to report on court proceedings (where appropriate), in journalists and others being able to comment critically on the nature of court proceedings, and in ensuring that press freedom is not unduly restricted by interim injunctions prohibiting the publication of potentially sensitive or confidential material. On the other hand there is the need to protect the processes of the law, to ensure that trials are fair and not prejudiced by media comment, and to ensure that interim court orders are not undermined by improper publication of material.

The law relating to contempt is somewhat complex and far reaching, based on a combination of common law principles and the provisions of the Contempt of Court Act 1981. A broad distinction that can be made at the outset is between civil contempt on the one hand and criminal contempt on the other. Civil contempt, punishable at common law, normally involves a failure to comply with an order of the court. Typically this will be an injunction, order of mandamus, or order of specific performance. Further, where a trial judge has been given an undertaking by one of the parties that certain action will, or will not, be taken, it is a contempt of court for that undertaking to be ignored. In *Harman* v *Home Secretary* [1984] 2 WLR 338, a solicitor, who had been granted access to Home Office documents on the undertaking that they would only be used by her in the preparation of her client's case against the Home Office, subsequently made them available to a journalist from *The Guardian* newspaper, who in turn wrote an article based on the information provided. The House of Lords held (Lords Simon and Scarman dissenting) that the solicitor was in contempt of court in making the documents available to the press, notwithstanding the fact that they had been read out in court in the course of the proceedings, because the undertaking that they should only be used for the purposes of the trial was still effective: see also *M* v *Home Office* [1992] QB 27. Despite the categorisation of such contempts as 'civil' it should be noted that a judge in a civil court does have the power to order the imprisonment of a contemnor, impose a fine and cause his assets to be sequestrated.

Criminal contempt of court, by contrast, involves publication of material prejudicing a fair civil or criminal trial, interference with the course of justice (ie bribing or threatening jurors and witnesses), publication of material that undermines the administration of justice generally, and contempt in the face of the court.

Publications prejudicing a fair trial: the Contempt of Court Act 1981

The publication of material intended to prejudice a fair trial has always been a criminal contempt at common law. There was concern, however, regarding the scope of the offence, and the extent to which the legitimate right of the media to comment on matters concerning civil and criminal liability was being unduly restricted: see *Phillimore Committee on Contempt of Court* (Cmnd 5794 (1974)). The real impetus for reform came from the ruling of the European Court of Human Rights: see *Attorney-General* v *Times Newspapers* [1974] AC 273 and *Sunday Times* v *United Kingdom* (1979) 2 EHRR 245. The *Sunday Times* had published a series of articles which were severely critical of Distillers Ltd, manufacturers of the drug Thalidomide. The drug was implicated in over 400 cases of women who had given birth to children with physical deformities. After writs had been issued against Distillers Ltd, but prior to the action being set down for trial, the *Sunday Times* sought to publish an article containing details about the tests that had been carried out by Distillers Ltd prior to the drug being marketed. Distillers Ltd applied for an injunction to prevent publication of the article on the grounds that it would prejudice any subsequent trial. The House of Lords ultimately upheld the injunction, noting that it was a contempt to use the power of the press to pressurise a litigant into settling an action by publishing articles in which a litigant was held up to vilification.

The European Court of Human Rights held that the common law position, as expounded by the House of Lords, violated art 10 of the European Convention on Human Rights, because it amounted to a restriction on freedom of expression that was not necessary in a democratic society for maintaining the authority and impartiality of the judiciary. The United Kingdom government had little option but to legislate, the result being the Contempt of Court Act 1981. The Act does not replace the common law on criminal contempt (indeed s6(c) specifically preserves the position at common law regarding conduct intended to impede the administration of justice), but does clarify the position regarding the so-called 'strict liability rule', ie where a publisher did not intend that a publication should interfere with the administration of justice.

Under the 1981 Act, the rule that 'conduct may be treated as a contempt of court as tending to interfere with the course of justice in particular legal proceedings regardless of intent to do so' (s1), applies to publications which create 'a substantial risk that the course of justice in the proceedings in question will be seriously impeded or prejudiced': s2(2). Further, the proceedings in question must be 'active', and the first Schedule of the Act gives some guidance on this issue. Regarding criminal proceedings, the Act is supposed to come into operation when a person is charged or summoned or at the time of his arrest. The issue of a warrant for a person's arrest is also taken as a relevant starting point for the Act. As far as civil proceedings are concerned the Act applies only after the case has been set down for trial. This indicated a significant change in the law as formerly (see the *Sunday Times* case, above) the law of contempt would have restricted comment from the date when proceedings were initiated, ie writs served. A related point deals with the status of the Act regarding appeals. Here the starting point is the granting of leave to appeal by the court. Therefore the media is not subject to the Act once criminal trials are concluded by acquittal or sentence and once other proceedings at first instance and all appeals are concluded by being discontinued, disposed of or withdrawn.

Defences

There are a number of defences that can be raised where the 'strict liability' rule is invoked. Firstly, s3 of the Act gives a publisher a defence of 'innocent publication or distribution' if he does not know or has no reason to suspect that the relevant proceedings are active. The same applies if he has no reason to suspect that the contents of a publication contain a contempt. The crucial test is whether the publisher or distributor could not reasonably have discovered either that proceedings were active or that a book or magazine contained within it a contempt: see *R* v *Griffiths* [1957] 2 QB 192.

The second defence provided in the 1981 Act applies to the contemporaneous reporting of proceedings. The court, however, retains the power to postpone any report if it is deemed necessary for avoiding a substantial risk of prejudice to the administration of justice: s4(1) and (2).

Third, s5 of the 1981 Act provides:

> 'A publication made as or as part of a discussion in good faith of public affairs or other matters of general interest is not to be treated as a contempt of court under the strict liability rule if the risk of impediment or prejudice to particular legal proceedings is merely incidental to the discussion.'

The effect of this section was considered at length by the House of Lords in *Attorney-General* v *English* [1982] 2 WLR 278, where proceedings under the Act were initiated against the editor and publishers of the *Daily Mail* newspaper in respect of an article entitled 'The Vision of Life that Wins My Vote' – an article written in support of a candidate in a parliamentary by-election. The candidate, Ms Carr, had been born without arms and was standing as an independent 'Pro-Life' candidate; the main basis of her election campaign was the stopping of the practice, that she alleged had been developed in some British hospitals, of killing newborn handicapped babies. Public interest in the question of whether severely handicapped babies should be allowed to die had been aroused by a Court of Appeal decision two months earlier ordering a surgeon to carry out a life-prolonging operation on a Down's syndrome baby despite the refusal of the parents to give their consent to the operation. Shortly before the publishing of the article in question, a Sunday newspaper had published an article asserting that the termination of life of unborn, hopelessly handicapped babies was morally justifiable. Ms Carr published her election address three days later and the article in question in the present case was published nine days later on 15 October. Coincidentally, on 13 October, there commenced the trial of Dr Arthur, a consultant paediatrician on a charge of murdering a three-day-old Down's syndrome baby by giving instructions that a drug should be administered that caused the baby to die of starvation. Dr Arthur pleaded not guilty. The article in question made no mention of Dr Arthur's trial. However, apart from passages such as: 'Are human beings to be culled like livestock? No more sick or misshapen bodies, no more disturbed or twisted minds, no more hereditary idiots or mongoloid children. Babies not up to scratch to be destroyed, before or after birth, as would also the old beyond repair', the article also contained the following: 'Today the chances of such a baby surviving would be very small indeed. Someone would surely recommend letting it die of starvation or otherwise disposing of it.'

Clearly the article was a 'publication' within s2(1) of the Contempt of Court Act 1981. Since an intention to prejudice the trial was not alleged, the issues in question were, firstly, whether or not the nature and circumstances of the publications were such as to satisfy s2(2) of the 1981 Act so that the strict liability rule might apply, and, second, whether or not the publication escaped the strict liability rule by virtue of coming within s5. The Divisional Court had held that the article did create a substantial risk of seriously impeding Dr Arthur's fair trial as required by s2(2) for the strict liability rule to apply. It further held that the onus of proving that the conditions of s5 applied lay on the defendants and that they had not discharged this burden since the article contained accusations – that babies were killed or allowed to die – which were 'unnecessary' and not therefore merely incidental to the 'discussion in good faith of public affairs or other matters of general public interest' which alone was protected by s5. 'Discussion' was, in the court's view, limited to 'the airing of views and the propounding and debating of principles and arguments' and did not include the making of 'accusations'. On appeal, the House of Lords held that the nature and circumstances of the publication satisfied s2(2). If a publication put at risk the outcome of a trial or the need to discharge the jury without proceeding to a verdict, that was risking serious prejudice to the legal proceedings. The adjective 'substantially' was meant to exclude risks that were remote only. The publication of the article in question on the third day of Dr Arthur's trial did involve a more than remote risk that the jury verdict might be affected. The House of Lords went on to hold, however, that the onus of proving that the conditions of s5 were satisfied did not necessarily lie on the defendants and in the present case s5 applied. 'Discussion' should not be regarded as limited only to the 'airing of views and the propounding and debating of principles and arguments' but could include also assertions of fact.

Indeed, in the absence of any assertion of fact that 'mercy killing' did take place, the article in question would be no more than a contribution to the discussion of a purely hypothetical problem which would be quite remote from all public affairs and devoid of any general public interest to readers of the *Daily Mail*. The risks to Dr Arthur's fair trial were merely incidental to the bona fide discussion of Ms Carr's election policy and of the wider question of the justifiability of mercy killing. To hold otherwise would have prevented Ms Carr from gaining publicity for her election campaign and prevented all public discussion of the issue of mercy killing between February and November 1981 whilst the proceedings in Dr Arthur's case were active. Section 5 was intended to prevent the 'gagging' of just such bona fide public discussion. Lord Diplock observed:

> 'There is, of course, no question that the article in the Daily Mail of which complaint is made by the Attorney-General was a "publication" within the meaning of s2(1). That being so, it appears to have been accepted in the Divisional Court by both parties that the onus of proving that the article satisfied the conditions stated in s2(2) lay upon the Attorney-General and that, if he satisfied that onus, the onus lay upon the appellants to prove that it satisfied the conditions stated in s5. For my part, I am unable to accept that this represents the effect of the relationship of s5 to s2(2). Section 5 does not take the form of a proviso or an exception to s2(2). It stands on an equal footing with it. It does not set out exculpatory matter. Like s2(2) it states that publications shall not amount to contempt of court despite their tendency to interfere with the course of justice in particular legal proceedings.'

Having agreed that the article fell within s2(2) of the Act he continued:

> 'The article, however, fell also within the category dealt with in s5. It was made, in undisputed good faith, as a discussion in itself of public interest, viz [Ms Carr's] candidature as an independent Pro-Life candidate. It was also part of a wider discussion on a matter of general public interest that had been proceeding intermittently over the last three months, upon the moral justification of mercy killing and in particular of allowing newly born hopelessly handicapped babies to die. So it was for the Attorney-General to show that the risk of prejudice to the fair trial of Dr Arthur, which I agree was created by the publication of the article at the stage the trial had reached when it was published, was not merely incidental to the discussion of the matter with which the article dealt.'

Consider also *Attorney-General* v *Times Newspapers and Others* (1983) The Times 12 February, where the *Daily Mail* published an article about Michael Fagan (who had been discovered trespassing in the Queen's bedroom at Buckingham Palace) suggesting that Fagan was a 'rootless neurotic with no visible means of support'. The court took the view that the article clearly impugned the honesty of Fagan, thus prejudicing any subsequent trial for burglary, but no liability for contempt would ensue as the article came within s5 of the Act, being a discussion of the poor security arrangements made for the Queen.

Proceedings protected by the 1981 Act

Part of the rationale for the law of contempt is the need to protect the legal process from being undermined by prejudicial comment in the media, but this in turn begs the question as to what constitutes legal proceedings for this purpose. For example, at common law, in *Attorney-General* v *BBC* [1981] AC 303, the House of Lords held that the law of contempt did not apply to the activities of a local valuation court because (per Viscount Dilhorne, Lord Fraser and Lord Scarman) it was a court which discharged administrative functions and was not, therefore, a court of law. According to Lord Salmon, while a local valuation court has some of the attributes of the long established 'inferior courts' such as county courts, magistrates' courts, courts martial, coroner's courts and consistory courts, public policy required that in the interests of freedom of speech and freedom of the press, the principles relating to contempt of court should not apply to it or to the host of other modern tribunals which might be regarded as inferior courts. Viscount Dilhorne, in attempting to state a general rule, commented:

> '... I think that a distinction has to be drawn between courts which discharge judicial functions and those which discharge administrative ones; between courts of law which form part of the judicial system of the country on the one hand and courts which are constituted to resolve problems which arise in the course of administration of the government of this country. In my opinion a local valuation court comes within the latter category. It discharges functions formerly performed by assessment committees. It has to resolve disputes as to the valuation of hereditaments. While its decisions will affect an occupier's liability for rates, it does not determine his liability. It is just part of the process of rating.'

In an effort to clarify this point, s19 of the 1981 Act provides that 'court' includes any tribunal or body exercising the judicial power of the State. Hence the courts have been willing to recognise situations where tribunals have attracted the protection of the 1981 Act, for example in *Pickering* v *Liverpool Daily Post and Echo* [1991] 2 WLR 513, where the House of Lords accepted that the 'novel jurisdictions' of the Mental Health Tribunal, and the need for privacy in its proceedings, justified its classification as a 'court' for these purposes: see further *X* v *United Kingdom* (1981) 4 EHRR 188. Similarly, in *Peach Grey & Co (A Firm)* v *Sommers* [1995] 2 All ER 513, a case involving proceedings before an industrial tribunal, the court suggested that factors indicating that the law of contempt would apply were the fact that it: was presided over by a legally qualified person; sat in public; decided cases affecting the rights of parties; could compel the attendance of witnesses; could administer the oath; heard from parties permitted legal representation; had to give reasons for its decisions; and made decisions which could be taken on appeal, on a point of law, to the Employment Appeal Tribunal.

Publications prejudicing a fair trial: contempt at common law and in criminal proceedings

As indicated above, the common law relating to criminal contempt will still be applicable to publications falling outside of the scope of the 1981 Act. This can be of significance where there are publications concerning criminal proceedings that are imminent but have not yet been instigated, and the prosecution alleges that the publication was calculated or likely to interfere with the course of justice and was intended to have such an effect.

In *Attorney-General* v *News Group Newspapers* [1989] QB 110 the Attorney-General applied for the respondents to be fined for contempt in respect of a series of articles alleging that a doctor had raped an eight-year-old girl. The authorities had determined, on the evidence, not to prosecute the doctor, and the respondents, through *The Sun* newspaper, offered to pay for a private prosecution of the doctor. The court was satisfied that, had the articles appeared at a time when proceedings where pending, they would have prejudiced a fair trial, and that the intention of the editor of *The Sun*, that the articles should have had such an effect, could be inferred from his conduct. A key issue before the court, therefore, was whether there could be liability in a criminal case where no formal steps had yet been taken to commence proceedings. Watkins LJ was persuaded that the circumstances in which a criminal contempt at common law could be committed were not limited to those cases where the proceedings were pending. As he observed:

> 'The common law surely does not tolerate conduct which involves the giving of encouragement and practical assistance to a person to bring about a private prosecution accompanied by an intention to interfere with the course of justice by publishing material about the person to be prosecuted which could only serve to and was so intended to prejudice the fair trial of that person. This is especially so where the publisher of them makes plain that he believes the person referred to in the articles is guilty of serious crime.
>
> ... [T]he common law is not a worn out jurisprudence rendered incapable of further development by the ever increasing incursion of parliamentary legislation. It is a lively body of law capable of adaptation and expansion to meet fresh needs calling for the exertion of the discipline of the law ... [T]he need for a free press is axiomatic, but the press cannot be allowed to charge about like a wild unbridled horse. It has, to a necessary degree, in the public interest, to be curbed ... [T]he respondent here had very much in mind particular proceedings which it was determined, as far as it lay within its power and influence, to ensure took place. If it is necessary for the Attorney-General to establish that proceedings were imminent, he has, I think, done so. In my judgment where a prosecution is virtually certain to be commenced and particularly where it is to be commenced in the near future, it is proper to describe such proceedings as imminent. Such was the case here.'

The respondents were fined £75,000 and ordered to pay costs.

Publications prejudicing a fair trial: contempt at common law and breach of court orders

The courts have the power to grant interlocutory injunctions to prevent the disclosure or publication of material where such publication would defeat the purpose of the prospective trial. Breach of an injunction is punishable by way of proceedings for contempt. Most injunctions are granted on an interim basis, but permanent injunctions can also be granted if the circumstances so warrant: see *Venables* v *News Group Newspapers Ltd* [2001] 1 All ER 908.

As the court observed in *Imutran Ltd* v *Uncaged Campaigns Ltd* (2001) The Times 30 January in determining whether or not to grant an interlocutory injunction to prevent publication a court should go beyond the balance of 'convenience test' laid down in *American Cyanamid Co* v *Ethicon Ltd* [1975] AC 396, which suggested that an injunction should be granted if the applicant had a 'real prospect of success' at trial. Following the enactment of s12(3) of the Human Rights Act 1998 the test was now one of likelihood of success – ie a higher standard of probability will now be applied.

The potential for such injunctions to impinge upon the right to freedom of expression is self-evident and the courts will have to weigh these competing factors in mind when considering whether to grant any such injunction and the scope of the injunction granted. This is particularly the case where injunctions are sought to protect sensitive government information.

Although no injunction was granted in *Attorney-General* v *Jonathan Cape Ltd* [1976] QB 752, Lord Widgery CJ re-affirmed the existence of the equitable doctrine that no man should be allowed to profit from his own wrongdoing, namely the unauthorised publication of material received in confidence. In that case the court ruled that there was insufficient evidence that the workings of government would be damaged by the publication of Richard Crossman's diaries, but the court clearly indicated that in an appropriate case it would not hesitate to act. The Attorney-General had won on the point of principle, and the ensuing Radcliffe Committee report (Cmnd 6386 (1976)) led to much stricter guidelines being laid down concerning ministerial disclosures. In this respect note that, under the terms of the Public Record Acts 1958 and 1967, Cabinet papers are not normally made public for at least 30 years.

The ruling in *Attorney-General* v *Jonathan Cape Ltd* in fact served as a prelude to the most celebrated case of a government seeking refuge in the civil remedy of an action for breach of confidence, the so-called 'Spycatcher' litigation.

A former member of MI5, Peter Wright, became disturbed by what he saw as foreign infiltration of the secret services. He approached a House of Commons select committee with his evidence, but his complaints were not taken up. He retired to Australia from where he proposed to publish his memoirs, in the form of the book *Spycatcher* that revealed much about the workings of the security services. Whilst the government sought an injunction to prevent its publication in Australia, several newspapers in the United Kingdom sought to publish extracts from the book. The Attorney-General was granted an injunction to prevent the publication of extracts by *The Observer* newspaper, even though the nature of the revelations in the extracts was becoming well known. The basis for the injunction was not so much that confidentiality had to be maintained, but more that no disclosure had been authorised by the government. Other newspapers moved to publish the extracts from *Spycatcher* on the basis that they were not prevented from doing so by the injunction, as this was directed at *The Observer*. The courts ruled, however, that publication in any other newspaper would amount to a contempt of court, as it would have had the effect of undermining the injunction already granted.

By July 1987 *Spycatcher* had been published in the United States, and *The Observer* returned to court in an attempt to have the interim injunction prohibiting publication of extracts discharged, on the basis that there was nothing left to protect. At first instance the court agreed, noting that British citizens returning from the United States were able to purchase the book at any airport bookstall. This ruling was reversed by the Court of Appeal however, subject to the relaxation on restrictions that would have prevented accurate reporting of the debates on the issue in Parliament. Ultimately the question of whether the interim injunction should be discharged reached the House of Lords: *Attorney-General* v *Guardian Newspapers Ltd and Others* [1987] 3 All ER 316. By a majority of three to two, it was held that, pending a trial of the main issue, the interim injunction would remain. Lord Brandon thought the maintenance of the injunction might serve to deter further disclosures, whilst Lord Ackner, referring to the fact that the Attorney-General had been unable to prevent publication in the United States, felt that to lift the injunction now would be seen as surrendering to the American constitutional right to free speech. Lord Bridge and Lord Oliver, dissenting, expressed grave misgivings as regards the implications of maintaining the injunctions. Lord Oliver, in particular, pointed out that in the absence of a constitutional right to freedom of expression (the case clearly pre-dated the Human Rights act 1998), the liberty of the press was of paramount importance.

By the time the matter came to trial, international publication of *Spycatcher* had become much more widespread, and the High Court and the Court of Appeal recognised that granting a final injunction to prevent publication in the United Kingdom would be futile: [1988] 3 All ER 545. The Attorney-General nevertheless appealed to the House of Lords: *Attorney-General* v *Observer Ltd and Others* [1988] 3 WLR 776. It was held (Lord Griffiths dissenting in part) that no final injunction to restrain a breach of confidence would be granted unless it could be shown to be in the public interest to do so. Where the information had already been published abroad, little further damage would be prevented by an injunction.

It is interesting to note that the Attorney-General had attempted to obtain an injunction to prevent any future publication of confidential material divulged by Peter Wright. The House of Lords refused to grant any such general prohibition, declaring that each incident would have to be dealt with in its own right.

If material enters the public domain, therefore, it is now very unlikely that the courts will be willing to grant it any further protection from re-publication by way of an injunction. In *Attorney-General* v *Times Newspapers Ltd* (2001) The Times 31 January the court confirmed that it would not be appropriate to grant an injunction in terms that required editors to seek clearance from the Attorney-General before deciding whether or not to publish. The decision was one for the editor to take, mindful of the consequences of any misjudgment on his part.

Whether any given publication is deemed to have had the effect of undermining an order of the court very much depends on the facts of each case. In *Attorney-General* v *Newspaper Publishing plc* [1997] 1 WLR 926 *The Independent* newspaper, in its coverage of the Court of Appeal hearing that led to the acquittal of the defendants in the 'Matrix Churchill' case, included details of documents for which the Crown had claimed public interest immunity. The Court of Appeal had ruled that, although the documents were to be disclosed to the defendants and their advisers, they were not to be used for any other purposes. The newspaper had acquired copies from a source independent of the defendants. The Court of Appeal's order was not expressly binding on third parties or the world at large, but the Attorney-General contended, nonetheless, that the publication of the documents amounted to a contempt because it involved an interference with the administration of justice. Dismissing the application, Lord Bingham CJ observed (at p936b–c):

> 'It is not in our view necessary to show that the administration of justice in the relevant proceedings has been wholly frustrated or rendered utterly futile. But it is, we think, necessary to show some significant and adverse effect upon the administration of justice. Recognising that the restraints upon freedom of expression should be no wider than are truly necessary in a democratic society, we do not accept that conduct by a third party which is inconsistent with a court order in only a trivial or technical way should expose a party to conviction for contempt.'

The Court also confirmed that there was insufficient evidence of mens rea on the part of the journalists involved, citing with approval the passage from *Attorney-General* v *Newspaper Publishing plc* [1988] Ch 333 at 374–375 where Sir John Donaldson MR had observed that it had to be established, to the criminal standard of proof, that the alleged contemnor had, by his actions:

> '... intended to impede or prejudice the administration of justice. Such an intent need not be avowed or admitted, but can be inferred from all the circumstances, including the foreseeability of the consequences of the conduct. Nor need it be the sole intention of the contemnor. An intent is to be distinguished from a motive or desire.'

See further on this point *Attorney-General* v *Punch Ltd and Another* (2001) The Times 30 March.

Other forms of contempt

Undermining the judiciary

Proceedings for contempt at common law may be brought where a publication imputes bias on the part of a judge, although such cases are rare. The leading authority is the Privy Council decision in *Ambard* v *Attorney-General for Trinidad and Tobago* [1936] AC 322, where Lord Aitken observed:

> '... whether the authority and position of an individual judge, or the due administration of justice, is concerned, no wrong is committed by any member of the public who exercises the ordinary right of criticising, in good faith, in private or public, the public act done in the seat of justice. The path of criticism is a public way; the wrong-headed are permitted to err therein; provided that members of the public abstain from imputing improper motives to those taking part in the administration of justice, and are genuinely exercising a right of criticism, and not acting in malice or attempting to impair the administration of justice, they are immune. Justice is not a cloistered virtue; she must be allowed to suffer the scrutiny and respectful, even though outspoken, comments of ordinary men.'

See also *R* v *New Statesman (Editor), ex parte DPP* (1928) 44 TLR 301, where an article alleging that birth control pioneer Marie Stopes could not hope to expect a fair trial before Avory J was held to be a contempt of court, notwithstanding that no punishment was imposed.

Again the balance has to be struck between healthy debate on legal and political matters on the one hand, and the need to ensure that the dignity and authority of the judiciary, and public confidence in the judicial process, are not undermined by unjustified criticism.

Outraging the court

Contempt in the face of the court relates to unacceptable behaviour whilst the court is sitting. This may involve insulting or unseemly behaviour, a refusal to comply with the trial judge's directions, or even physical assault on others present. The trial judge has a common law power to regulate such behaviour and can deal with contemners summarily as arbiter of fact and law: see *Balogh* v *St Albans Crown Court* [1975] QB 73 (D attempting to let off a cylinder of nitrous oxide during a trial) and *Morris* v *Crown Office* [1970] 2 QB 114 (demonstration in the body of the court).

12.5 Defamation

Defamation is a tort, in respect of which damages can be obtained, that can take one of two forms: if transitory in nature, such as the spoken word or gestures, it is referred to as slander; if in a more permanent form, such as the printed word, or a broadcast, it is referred to as libel. The essence of the tort is that, as a result of things said, done, or published by the defendant, the plaintiff has suffered the hatred, ridicule, contempt of others such that would tend to lower him in the estimation of right thinking members of society. Slander is only actionable if the plaintiff can show special damage, otherwise actions in defamation are notable for being one of the few surviving cases where a jury might still be used to settle an issue of civil liability, and indeed the issue of quantum. The balance to be struck by the courts is, again, on the one hand to ensure that individuals and publishers are free to express such opinions as they wish (particularly in the form of political criticism, or in exposing corruption), whilst on the other hand ensuring that individuals are not needlessly and unjustifiably vilified, or have their reputations ruined. In this respect it is important to note that the courts have held that local authorities cannot sue for defamation in respect of adverse comments made concerning their political activities: see *Derbyshire County Council* v *Times Newspapers Ltd and Others* [1993] 2 WLR 449. Lord Keith agreed with the view of the majority that it was not in the public interest to permit democratically elected local government bodies to bring actions for defamation, his reasoning being that the threat of a civil action might inhibit legitimate public comment on, or criticism of, the activities of a local authority. He added that although the same conclusion would have been reached by reference to art 10 of the European Convention on Human Rights, such reference was unnecessary as 'the common law of England is consistent with obligations assumed by the Crown under the Treaty in this particular field'.

Similarly, in *Goldsmith* v *Bhoyrul* [1997] 4 All ER 268, the court ruled that the principle that those in public life should be exposed to a degree of criticism should be extended to political parties, the public interest in free speech outweighed any unfairness that might be caused by not permitting such organisations to sue for defamation. As Buckley J observed:

> '... it seems to me that the public interest in free speech and criticism in respect of those bodies putting themselves forward for office or to govern is also sufficiently strong to justify withholding the right to sue. Defamation actions or the threat of them would constitute a fetter on free speech at a time and on a topic when it is clearly in the public interest that there should be none.'

Note that the law of defamation could still be invoked by an individual candidate to protect his own reputation. Hence a criticism of a political party could be libellous if it, of necessity, cast imputations on the character of an identifiable individual member of that party, or one of its candidates.

Defences

At common law, a defendant in a defamation action can plead justification, ie that the impugned statement is essentially true. Where the statement is essentially an expression of opinion the defendant may be able to plead 'fair comment', provided he was expressing his view of a matter of public interest, was not motivated by malice, and that the statement did not contain any significant factual errors.

No action in defamation can be sustained in respect of material to which absolute privilege attaches, in particular statements made during proceedings in Parliament, statements made during judicial proceedings, and reports of the Parliamentary Commissioner for Administration. The protection given to statements made in Parliament is a consequence of the parliamentary privilege that protects any member from impeachment in respect of things said during proceedings in Parliament. Significant amendment to this privilege was effected by s13 of the Defamation Act 1996 which effectively provides that an MP can waive his parliamentary privilege if he wishes to rely on evidence of statements made during parliamentary proceedings in order to pursue an action for defamation: see further Chapter 6, section 6.9. Absolute privilege also extends to fair and accurate reports of proceedings in public before any court in the United Kingdom, the European Court of Justice and the European Court of Human Rights: see further s14 Defamation Act 1996.

Qualified privilege is a defence to defamation in respect of statements made by a defendant in the course of his performing a legal, social or moral duty, where the statements are directed to another person who has a corresponding interest in receiving the material, and where the defendant is not motivated by malice, ie he believes the statement to be accurate.

Significantly, in *Reynolds* v *Times Newspapers Ltd and Others* [1999] 3 WLR 1010, an attempt was made to establish political comment and the reporting of political matters as a new category of publication automatically attracting qualified privilege. The defendant newspaper published an article about the resignation of the plaintiff, Albert Reynolds, formerly the Prime Minister of Ireland. The article was critical of the plaintiff's alleged involvement in the appointment of a former Irish Attorney General to the post of President of the Court. The gist of the criticisms was that the plaintiff had knowingly misled the Irish parliament.

Lord Nicholls acknowledged the important role played by the press in keeping the public informed. It performed, he said, vital functions both as 'bloodhound' and 'watchdog'. He also expressed the view that, in respect of political discussion, the courts should be slow to conclude that the public had no 'right to know'. Any residual doubts regarding whether or not material should be made public should normally be resolved in favour of disclosure. He rejected, however, the contention that there could be a defence of qualified privilege based simply on the fact that the subject matter complained of constituted political information or reporting. A proper balance could be struck between press freedom and the protection of an individual's reputation by granting political reporting qualified privilege provided certain factors were satisfied. A claim to qualified privilege stood or fell on the basis of the 'duty-interest' test. As regards articles containing statements of opinion on matters of public interest, sufficient protection was afforded to an individual's reputation by the fact that the publication would not attract qualified privilege if it was shown to have been actuated by malice. In cases where a publication contained assertions of fact further safeguards were required because those receiving the information were unlikely to be able to check the veracity of the assertions, and because a newspaper could not normally be compelled to reveal its sources, thus making proof of malice virtually impossible. He added, significantly, that the past track record of the press in the United Kingdom indicated that the matter could not be left to self-regulation or the observance of ethical journalistic practices.

His Lordship went on to identify ten factors (although he stressed that his list was not to be regarded as exhaustive) that could have a bearing upon whether or not an assertion of fact, not motivated by malice, attracted the protection of qualified privilege. These were: the seriousness of the allegation; the extent to which the material was in a matter of public interest; the source of the information; the steps taken to verify the information; the status of the information; the urgency of the matter; whether the plaintiff had been invited to comment; whether the article indicated the plaintiff's view of the allegation; the strength of the assertion of fact; and the timing of the publication. The fact that a newspaper was unwilling to disclose its sources should not count against it in weighing these factors. Whether or not, having regard to such factors, a publication attracted qualified privilege would be a matter for the trial judge. Whether or not the publication was actuated by malice would be a question for the jury. On the facts the Court of Appeal had been correct, in this case, in concluding that the defendant's publication should not attract qualified privilege.

Notwithstanding the various ringing declarations in their Lordships' speeches regarding the importance of a free press the decision does little to clarify the position of the editor having to decide whether or not to publish political information of a sensitive nature. What the decision does make clear is that there is no automatic protection at common law in respect of mistakes made by the press in publishing matters as political fact that turn out to be erroneous. The press may be given the benefit of the doubt but whether or not this is the case can only be resolved at the conclusion of lengthy and expensive litigation. In such circumstances obiter statements about the duty of the press to inform the public carry little weight. In theory 'responsible' journalists, ie those that check their sources and behave ethically should benefit from the decision in that they can expect their work to attract qualified privilege, but much will depend on the view of the judge presiding over any consequent libel action.

Subsequent attempts by the Court of Appeal to clarify the circumstances when the 'duty – interest' test would be satisfied have not significantly advanced the matter. In *Loutchansky* v *Times Newspapers Ltd and Others (No 2)* (2001) The Times 7 December Lord Phillips MR expressed the view that in determining whether or not there was a duty to publish, as required by the test for qualified privilege, the courts should be mindful of the interest of the public in a modern democracy in free expression and, more particularly, in the promotion of a free and vigorous press to keep the public informed. Qualified privilege would be made out where it could be shown that it would have been irresponsible not to publish, but it was by no means the case that qualified privilege would not be available simply because non-publication might not be regarded as irresponsible. He added, however, that without evidence of responsible journalism a claim to qualified privilege was bound to fail.

Until the defence of 'offer of amends' contained in the Defamation Act 1996 is implemented (see below) journalists will have to pick their way gingerly through the thicket of conditions laid down by Lord Nicholls.

Note that the defence of qualified privilege is also available to those who publish fair and accurate reports of proceedings in Parliament; for the scope of this defence see now s15 of the Defamation Act 1996.

What was the common law defence of innocent publication has been replaced with a statutory defence created by s1 of the Defamation Act 1996. The 1996 Act provides that in defamation proceedings a person has a defence if he shows that: he was not the author, editor or publisher of the statement complained of; he took reasonable care in relation to its publication; and he did not know, and had no reason to believe, that what he did caused or contributed to the publication of a defamatory statement. The author is the person who is the originator of the statement, but does not include a person who did not intend that his statement be published at all; the editor is the person having editorial or equivalent responsibility for the content of the statement or the decision to publish it; and the publisher is defined as a commercial publisher, that is, a person whose business is issuing material to the public, or a section of the public, who issues material containing the statement in the course of that business. The defence is further extended to printers, distributors, and those who broadcast live programmes.

In determining whether a person took 'reasonable care', or had reason to believe that what he did caused or contributed to the publication of a defamatory statement, regard shall be had to: the extent of his responsibility for the content of the statement or the decision to publish it; the nature or circumstances of the publication; and the previous conduct or character of the author, editor or publisher. Hence, the defence might not be available to the distributor of a publication that had a bad reputation for defaming others.

As indicated above, the 1996 Act also creates a new defence based upon the defendant's offer to make amends. The defence (not yet brought into effect) will replace the defence of unintentional defamation created under s4 of the Defamation Act 1952. The defendant must be prepared to make a suitable correction of the statement complained of and a sufficient apology to the aggrieved party; to publish the correction and apology in a manner that is reasonable and practicable in the circumstances, and; to pay to the aggrieved party such compensation (if any), and such costs, as may be agreed or determined to be payable. An offer to make amends cannot be made if a defence to the action has already been served. Once an offer has been accepted the party accepting the offer may not bring or continue defamation proceedings in respect of the publication concerned against the person making the offer. If an offer to make amends is not accepted by the aggrieved party, the fact that the offer was made is a defence to defamation proceedings, provided the maker of the defamatory statement did not know or believe that it was false and defamatory.

Damages

The prospect of excessive and ruinously large awards of damages in favour of plaintiffs bringing legal actions can act as a significant deterrent to those who seek to publish potentially defamatory material. The extent to which this might amount to a violation of art 10 of the European Convention on Human Rights was considered in *Tolstoy Miloslavsky* v *United Kingdom* Case 8/1994/455/536 (1995) 20 EHRR 442. The applicant, who had been successfully sued for libel in the High Court, the jury having awarded damages against him of £1.5 million, three times the largest sum awarded up to that date, sought to appeal against the decision. The Registrar of the Court of Appeal granted the plaintiff an order to the effect that the applicant would only be permitted to proceed with an appeal if he lodged a sum in excess of £124,000 with the court as a security against costs. The applicant failed to produce the sum and his appeal was dismissed. The European Court of Human Rights held that, given the state of English law at the time the award was made, there had been a violation of art 10. All sides agreed that the prospect of an award of damages for libel could act as a fetter on the right of freedom of expression, hence the role of the court was to determine whether or not it was a restriction that was permitted within the scope of art 10. The first criterion was that any restriction had to be 'prescribed by law'. The Court acknowledged that a degree of flexibility had to be granted to signatory states in this respect, and that the size of an award of damages could not necessarily be forecast with any accuracy, given that such matters were determined by juries, and that reasons were not given for the size of awards. On this basis the first criterion was met. Second, the restriction had to pursue a legitimate aim. The Court was satisfied that the protection of the reputations of others was such a legitimate aim. Third, there was the question of whether the award of damages at such a level was necessary in a democratic society. Given the size of the award there were serious doubts as to whether the substantive domestic law at the time of the trial provided for a requirement of proportionality. Further, as the law then stood, the Court of Appeal was unable to interfere with an award unless it was so unreasonable that it could not have been the decision of sensible people. Hence the Court ruled that art 10 had been violated because the restriction on free speech had not been justified under that article.

The Court further observed that it was in agreement with comments made in *Rantzen* v *Mirror Group Newspapers (1986) Ltd* [1993] 3 WLR 953, to the effect that art 10 was relevant to the issue of awards for libel since, although it did not form part of domestic law, it reflected the rules of the common law in relation to freedom of expression. In the *Rantzen* case the Court of Appeal expressed the view that the right of a jury in a libel action to award unlimited damages was difficult to reconcile with the wording of art 10, in light of the requirement to show that any limitation on freedom of expression, such as the law of defamation, had to be necessary in a democratic society. The Court doubted whether such large awards were so necessary to protect the reputation of plaintiffs. In order to show that the award of damages was a restriction on free speech 'prescribed by law', it was essential that the jury be given guidance on the basis of previous decisions.

Changes introduced in the Courts and Legal Services Act 1990 empowered the Court of Appeal to overturn 'excessive' awards, but the litigation in the *Tolstoy Miloslavsky* libel action predated these reforms: see further *John* v *MGN Ltd* [1997] QB 586.

In this regard it should also be noted that ss8 and 9 of the Defamation Act 1996 introduce a new summary procedure for the disposal of defamation actions where there is either 'no realistic prospect of success' for the plaintiff, or no defence. If the court is satisfied that summary relief will adequately compensate the plaintiff for the wrong he has suffered it can grant: a declaration that the statement was false and defamatory of the plaintiff; an order that the defendant publish or cause to be published a suitable correction and apology; damages not exceeding £10,000 or such other amount as may be prescribed by order of the Lord Chancellor; or an order restraining the defendant from publishing or further publishing the matter complained of. Whilst these changes may be of direct benefit to the impecunious plaintiff who is more interested in clearing his name than in obtaining a huge award in damages, certain issues remain unresolved that have serious implications for the freedom of the press. If a declaration is granted, is it binding on other publishers? If this is the case will a publisher be in contempt of court even if he is unaware of the existence of the declaration? Would anyone other than the defendant publisher have locus standi to challenge the request for the declaration?

13

Freedom of Assembly and Association: Article 11 of the European Convention on Human Rights

13.1 Introduction

Prior to the enactment of the Human Rights Act 1998 English law contained little in the way of positive rights to associate freely with others, to demonstrate or march in support of an issue or organisation. The constitutional arrangement familiar to generations of lawyers was that individuals were free to act as they wished, subject only to the express restrictions provided by the common law and statute. The 1998 Act incorporates the European Convention on Human Rights, art 11 of which provides:

'(1) Everyone has the right to freedom of peaceful assembly and to freedom of association with others, including the right to form and to join trade unions for the protection of his interests.

(2) No restrictions shall be placed on the exercise of these rights other than such as are prescribed by law and are necessary in a democratic society in the interests of national security or public safety, for the prevention of disorder or crime, for the protection of health or morals or for the protection of the rights and freedoms of others. This article

shall not prevent the imposition of lawful restrictions on the exercise of these rights by members of the armed forces, of the police or of the administration of the state.'

The way in which the English courts will have to respond to the incorporation of the Convention is considered in more detail in Chapter 9. It should be noted here, however, that it becomes unlawful, under s6(1) for any public authority to act in a manner that is incompatible with any Convention rights protected by the 1998 Act (such as art 11), and that the courts will have to have regard to those rights in interpreting domestic legislation, whether passed before or after incorporation.

What follows is an examination of the main aspects of the current domestic law, but this should be read mindful of the legislative context now provided by art 11, and with a view to assessing the extent of compliance with its requirements.

13.2 Freedom of association

As indicated above, historically individuals are free to associate with each other under English law subject to a number of significant legal limitations. The Public Order Act 1936 s1 places a general prohibition on the wearing of political uniforms in any public place or at any public meeting except for uniforms worn on ceremonial, anniversary or other special occasions where public disorder is not likely to be provoked. (The Prevention of Terrorism (Temporary Provisions) Act 1989 contains a similar prohibition in respect of proscribed organisations.) Section 2 of the 1936 Act creates an offence of controlling, managing, organising or training an association of persons for the purpose of usurping the functions of the police or the armed forces or for the use or display of physical force in promoting any political object. In 1963, for example, the leaders of Spearhead, a neo-Nazi organisation, were convicted under s2. Similarly, the Unlawful Drilling Act 1819 prohibits assemblies for the purpose of training or drilling in the use of arms or practising military exercises without lawful authority.

The Prevention of Terrorism (Temporary Provisions) Act 1989, as amended by the Criminal Justice Act 1993, contains, in Part I of the Act, a series of offences that may be committed by persons supporting proscribed organisations. Two organisations are proscribed under the Act: the Irish Republican Army and the Irish National Liberation Army. By s1 of the Act, it is an offence to belong or profess to belong to such an organisation, to solicit or invite financial or other support for it, to make or receive contributions to its resources, or to arrange, assist in the arrangement of, or address its meetings. Members of the armed forces, the police and senior civil servants may be prevented by their conditions of service from engaging in political activities and may not therefore join political associations.

13.3 Freedom of assembly

Notwithstanding the rights now provided by art 11, domestic law provides for restrictions that Parliament and the courts have felt it necessary to impose on the freedom to assemble in public, in the interests of maintaining order.

The right to hold meetings on private and public property

There is no legal right to hold a meeting on private premises without the consent of the owner or occupier. Unless permission has been granted a person holding such a meeting becomes a trespasser and the owner or occupier of the premises may use reasonable force in evicting the trespasser. Meetings in public places are subject to a number of limitations. Places such as Hyde Park Corner or Trafalgar Square, which are traditionally used for public meetings, are Crown property and there is no right to hold meetings there. The permission of the Secretary of State for the Environment, Transport and the Regions is needed, and he can impose restrictions on any meeting.

Many local authority premises are also subject to regulations governing meetings. If there are bye-laws that require permission to be obtained for a meeting on local authority property, then holding one without permission will be a criminal offence. Local authorities have a wide discretion to stop meetings being held in their parks or buildings, but their decisions are open to judicial review. A decision to refuse permission for any meeting, or a meeting by a particular organisation, may be unreasonable under the principles laid down in *Associated Provincial Picture Houses Ltd* v *Wednesbury Corporation* [1948] 1 KB 223.

There is, however, a statutory right under the Representation of the People Act 1983 for candidates in general or local elections to have access to local authority premises for the purpose of holding election meetings. It has been argued that this statutory right ought to be extended to all meetings, following decisions by some local authorities to refuse the extreme right-wing political groups permission to hold meetings on their premises.

Police powers of entry to private meetings

Following *Thomas* v *Sawkins* [1935] 2 KB 249 it appears that the police have a power to enter a public meeting even though it is held on private premises and permission to enter has been withheld, if they reasonably apprehend a breach of the peace. In that case a meeting was held against the Incitement to Disaffection Bill. Two police officers entered the meeting and the organiser asked them to leave. One police officer grabbed him and then 30 other officers entered the meeting. Thomas prosecuted the police officer for battery. The magistrate held that the police had a right to enter the meeting, and therefore there was no battery. The view of the Divisional Court was that if the police apprehended both the possibility of seditious speeches and a breach of the peace, they had a power of entry. Section 17(6) of the Police and Criminal Evidence Act 1984 expressly retains the constable's common law power to enter premises to deal with a breach of the peace. The power is not limited to entry of premises open to the public. In *McLeod* v *Commissioner of the Metropolitan Police* [1994] 4 All ER 553 the plaintiff's husband, from whom she was divorced, obtained a court order, concerning the division of chattels that were matrimonial property, under which he was entitled to seize them from the house that plaintiff shared with her mother. The plaintiff's husband arrived to collect the property in several vans, accompanied by a number of police officers. The plaintiff arrived home from work whilst the vans were being loaded and remonstrated with the police officers, who indicated that the operation was to proceed and that the vans would not be unloaded. The plaintiff sought unsuccessfully to recover damages for trespass to goods and property against the police, the court confirming that, at common law, police officers had the power to enter private premises if they reasonably believed that a breach of the peace was likely to occur in the near future. The contention that *Thomas* v *Sawkins* [1935] 2 KB 249 should be limited to entry into private property where a public meeting was being held was expressly rejected. See further *McConnell* v *Chief Constable of Greater Manchester* [1990] 1 WLR 364; *Lamb* v *DPP* [1990] Crim LR 58; and *McQuade* v *Chief Constable of Humberside Police* (2001) The Times 3 September.

Imposing conditions on public assemblies

The Public Order Act 1986, in s14 (as amended by ss70 and 71 of the Criminal Justice and Public Order Act 1994) provides that a senior police officer may impose conditions in relation to public assemblies if, having regard to the time or place at which and the circumstances in which any public assembly is being held or is intended to be held, he reasonably believes that:

1. it may result in serious public disorder, serious damage to property or serious disruption to the life of the community, or
2. the purpose of the persons organising it is the intimidation of others with a view to compelling them not to do an act they have a right to do, or to do an act they have a right not to do.

The section states that he may give directions imposing on the persons organising or taking part in the assembly such conditions as to the place at which the assembly may be (or continue to be) held, its maximum duration, or the maximum number of persons who may constitute it, as appears to him necessary to prevent such disorder, damage, disruption or intimidation.

It should be noted, however, that, on the basis of *DPP* v *Ballie* [1995] Crim LR 426, even if there is prima facie evidence that an individual is organising a gathering, the police will have no power to issue an order under s14 unless there are sufficiently clear details of the likely time and location of the proposed gathering for the police to 'have regard to' as required by that section.

Section 16 defines 'public assembly' as an assembly of 20 or more persons in a public place that is wholly or partly open to the air. Under ss14A, B and C (added by the 1994 Act) a chief officer of police is empowered to apply to the relevant local authority for an order prohibiting trespassory assemblies on land to which the public does not normally have a right of access, provided that there are grounds to reasonably believe that the owner of the land has not granted permission for the assembly and that the trespassory assembly may result in either serious disruption to the life of the community, or significant damage to land or buildings of historical, archeological or scientific importance. It is an offence to organise or participate in any such trespassory assembly in the knowledge that a banning order has been granted. Whether or not an individual was, at a material time, a party to the demonstration and march to which a s14 order applied will be a question of fact for the court. If it concludes that he was then failure to comply with the terms of the order will justify arrest and conviction under s14(5): see further *Broadwith* v *Chief Constable of Thames Valley Police Authority* [2001] Crim LR 924. This raises the question of how a person taking part in a march which is the subject of a s14 order can disassociate himself from the march so that the order ceases to apply to him. Under s14C a police constable has the power to intercept and stop those reasonably believed to be proceeding to a trespassory assembly, and direct them not to proceed to the assembly. Disobedience to an order under this provision is a summary offence in relation to which a constable may exercise a power of arrest without a warrant.

When these amendments were made to s14 it was widely thought that what Parliament had in mind was the type of activities that have taken place in the vicinity of the ancient monument at Stonehenge, particularly around the time of the summer solstice celebrations, and it not entirely surprising, therefore, that the first challenge to the ambit of an order made under s14A should have arisen as a result of arrests made near that site. *DPP* v *Jones* [1999] 2 All ER 257 concerned an order granted on 22 May 1995, pursuant to s14A(2) of the Public Order Act 1986, prohibiting the holding of any trespassory assembly within a four-mile radius of the Stonehenge site. On 1 June 1995 the police found a number of persons congregating in the vicinity of the Stonehenge site, some displaying banners and playing music. On determining the number of persons involved exceeded 20, the police ordered the assembly to disperse, arresting those who refused to do so. A number of the demonstrators were, in due course, convicted of the offence of trespassory assembly under s14B(2) of the Public Order Act 1986 and, following successful appeals to the Crown Court, the prosecutor appealed by way of case stated to the Divisional Court. Two questions were put before the Court: (i) where there was in force an order under s14A(2) and, on the public highway within the area and time covered by the order, there was a peaceful assembly of 20 or more persons which did not obstruct the highway, did such assembly exceed the public's right of access to the highway so as to constitute a trespassory assembly within the terms of s14A; and (ii) in order to prove an offence under s14B of the Public Order Act 1986, was it necessary for the prosecution to prove that each of the 20 or more persons present was exceeding the limits of the public's rights of access or merely that 20 or more persons were present and that some of them were exceeding the limits of the public's right of access?

Allowing the prosecutor's appeal the Court held that even though an assembly was peaceful and did not amount to an obstruction of the highway, if there was a s14A order in force, any assembly of 20 or more persons would amount to a trespassory assembly within the terms of s14A. Further, it was not necessary for the prosecution to prove that each of the 20 persons comprising the assembly was exceeding the limits of the public's right of access. It was sufficient that the person charged had been one of that number and had known that the assembly was prohibited by the order. The Court rejected the view that any assembly on the highway was lawful provided it was peaceful and did not amount to an obstruction. The right to use the highway to pass and repass did include the right to carry out activities that were necessarily incidental thereto, such as passing the time of day with an acquaintance, but this did not extend to holding assemblies of 20 or more persons. The defendants appealed to the House of Lords where it was held, (Lords Slynn and Hope dissenting) that the approach adopted in the Divisional Court had been wrong and that its decision should be reversed.

Lord Irvine criticised the reasoning in the Divisional Court, particularly the view expressed by Collins J to the effect that the use of the highway for peaceful purposes such as assembly automatically exceeded the public's right of reasonable use. As Lord Irvine observed (at pp262j–263a):

> 'The question to which this appeal gives rise is whether the law today should recognise that the public highway is a public place, on which all manner of reasonable activities may go on ... [In my view] ... it should. Provided these activities are reasonable, do not involve the commission of a public or private nuisance, and do not amount to an obstruction of the highway unreasonably impeding the primary right of the general public to pass and repass, they should not constitute a trespass. Subject to these qualifications, therefore, there would be a public right of peaceful assembly on the public highway.'

It had been contended that the owner of the land should be the arbiter of what constituted a reasonable use of the land but Lord Irvine rejected this approach on the ground that it would result in inconsistencies and would be difficult to apply where the use in question had persisted over a long period of time. He concluded (at p265c–g):

> '[The law is that] the public highway is a public place which the public may enjoy for any reasonable purpose, provided the activity in question does not amount to a public or private nuisance and does not obstruct the highway by unreasonably impeding the primary right of the public to pass and repass: within these qualifications there is a public right of peaceful assembly on the highway.
>
> Since the law confers this public right, I deprecate any attempt artificially to restrict its scope. It must be for the magistrates in every case to decide whether the user of the highway under consideration is both reasonable in the sense defined and not inconsistent

with the primary right of the public to pass and repass. In particular, there can be no principled basis for limiting the scope of the right by reference to the subjective intentions of the persons assembling. Once the right to assemble within the limitations I have defined is accepted, it is self-evident that it cannot be excluded by an intention to exercise it. Provided an assembly is reasonable and non-obstructive, taking into account its size, duration and the nature of the highway on which it takes place, it is irrelevant whether it is premeditated or spontaneous: what matters is its objective nature. To draw a distinction on the basis of anterior intention is in substance to reintroduce an incidentality requirement. For the reasons I have given, that requirement, properly applied, would make unlawful commonplace activities which are well accepted. Equally, to stipulate in the abstract any maximum size or duration for a lawful assembly would be an unwarranted restriction on the right defined. These judgments are ever ones of fact and degree for the court of trial.'

Lord Irvine did not feel it necessary to have recourse to art 11 of the European Convention on Human Rights (the right to peaceful assembly) in order to determine the appeal, the common law, in his view, being sufficiently clear and unambiguous. He was willing to accept, however, that if, contrary to his view, the common law was not clear, it was '... uncertain and developing, so that regard should be had to the Convention in resolving the uncertainty and in determining how it should develop ...'. On this basis he would have been prepared to invoke art 11 to support the conclusion that an assembly on the highway would not necessarily be trespassory. He concluded (at p26b–d):

'The effect of the Divisional Court's decision in this case would be that any peaceful assembly on the public highway, no matter how minor or harmless, would involve the commission of the tort of trespass. Its conclusion is that all peaceful assemblies on the highway are tortious, whilst seeking to justify that state of affairs by observing that peaceful assemblies are in practice usually tolerated. In my judgment it is none to the point that restrictions on the exercise of the right of freedom of assembly may under art 11 be justified where necessary for the protection of the rights and freedoms of others. If the Divisional Court were correct, and an assembly on the public highway always trespassory, then there is not even a prima facie right to assemble on the public highway in our law. Unless the common law recognises that assembly on the public highway may be lawful, the right contained in art 11(1) of the Convention is denied. Of course the right may be subject to restrictions (for example, the requirements that users of the highway for purposes of assembly must be reasonable and non-obstructive, and must not contravene the criminal law of wilful obstruction of the highway). But in my judgment our law will not comply with the Convention unless its starting-point is that assembly on the highway will not necessarily be unlawful. I reject an approach which entails that such an assembly will always be tortious and therefore unlawful. The fact that the letter of the law may not in practice always be invoked is irrelevant: mere toleration does not secure a fundamental right.'

The decision is significant in that it arguably represents a shift in emphasis from the notion of negative rights (ie freedom to do as one pleases subject to the limitations imposed by the law) towards a concept of positive rights. Such a change is perhaps not surprising given the impact of the Human Rights Act 1998.

'Raves'

Section 63 of the Criminal Justice and Public Order Act 1994 seeks to address the use of open land for so-called 'raves', defined as a gathering on land in the open air of 100 or more persons at which amplified music is played during the night and is such that by reason of its loudness and duration and the time at which it is played likely to cause serious distress to the inhabitants of the locality. 'Music' is further defined as 'sounds wholly or predominantly characterised by the emission of a succession of repetitive beats'. An officer of at least the rank of superintendent may give directions to those gathering for a rave, or taking part in one, to leave the land in question and remove any property brought onto the land. Failure to comply with any such direction constitutes a summary offence, and any constable who reasonably suspects that such an offence is being committed can arrest without a warrant. Section 64 provides the police with the power to seize sound equipment, and s65 provides a further power to intercept those reasonably believed to be proceeding to a rave and direct them not to proceed.

'Mass trespass'

Criminal liability for involvement in so-called 'mass trespass' upon land, originally introduced by s39 of the Public Order Act 1986, is now provided for by ss61 and 62 of the Criminal Justice and Public Order Act 1994. The provisions, which seem to be specifically targeted at the activities of persons leading a nomadic lifestyle ('new age travellers' etc), state that a police constable is empowered to order the removal of trespassers (ie two or more persons) from land where he reasonably believes that:

1. they are present with the common purpose of residing there for any period; and
2. reasonable steps have been taken by or on behalf of the occupier to ask them to leave; and either
3. any of the persons has caused damage to the land or property on the land or used threatening or abusive or insulting words or behaviour towards the occupier, his family or agents; or
4. the trespassers have between them six or more vehicles (a reduction from 12 under the 1986 Act) on the land.

For these purposes 'land' does not include land forming part of a highway other than footpaths, bridleways, byways or cycle tracks. Subject to certain statutory defences, failure to comply with a constable's direction under this section is an offence in relation to which a person can be arrested without a warrant, and in relation to which a constable has the power to seize vehicles involved. A person removed from land under these provisions is prohibited from returning for the following three months.

Aggravated trespass

Section 68 of the Criminal Justice and Public Order Act 1994, primarily aimed at the activities of groups such as hunt saboteurs, animal rights protesters attempting to prevent the transport of live animals, or demonstrators attempting to disrupt road building programmes, provides the police with the power to deal with those committing aggravated trespass on open land. Aggravated trespass arises where a person is present on land (excluding highways other than footpaths, bridleways, byways or cycle tracks) without the owner's permission, and he commits acts intended to intimidate others present on the land so as to deter them from engaging in any lawful activity, or intended to obstruct or disrupt such activities. Activity for these purposes means human activity, hence trespass in order to destroy crops would fall outside s68: see *Tilly* v *DPP* [2002] Crim LR 128. The actual occupation of land itself can amount to an act intended to intimidate others present on the land but only if it is 'distinct and overt' from the original trespass: see *DPP* v *Barnard* (1999) 96 (42) LSG 40. There should be supporting evidence of what the defendant was actually doing.

In *Winder and Others* v *DPP* (1996) The Times 14 August the court adopted a broad approach to the concept of disruption so as to include acts that it regarded as more than merely preparatory to causing disruption (eg running after a hunt intending to blow a horn). Given the wording of s68, if D enters property he knows to be unoccupied, it may be difficult to show that the actus reus is made out. Similarly, where a demonstration involves blocking a road, it will almost certainly fall outside the scope of the offence, because the demonstrators are not on private land. Peaceful protest may well fall outside of this section, as the defendant will not have the necessary mens rea, ie he will not intend to intimidate others, or obstruct or disrupt their activities. Given that the offence requires a specific intent to intimidate or obstruct others, it would seem that a defendant who was intoxicated would have an absolute defence to any charge under the section. The section creates a summary offence for which a person can be arrested by a constable without a warrant if the constable reasonably suspects that such an offence is being committed. Liability only arises where the defendant enters land to interfere with a lawful activity, hence no offence under the section would be committed where the defendant acts to prevent cruelty to animals that amounts to a criminal offence. A senior police officer may, under s69, direct persons to leave land if he reasonably believes that they have committed or intend to commit the offence of aggravated trespass, or if he reasonably believes that two or more persons are trespassing on land in the open air and are present there with the common purpose of intimidating persons so as to deter them from engaging in a lawful activity or of obstructing or disrupting a lawful activity. Again, failure to comply with such a direction is, subject to certain statutory exceptions, a summary offence in relation to which a constable in uniform may exercise a power of arrest without a warrant.

Local authorities also have powers to direct unauthorised campers to vacate land occupied without the permission of the owner. If such a direction is ignored a local authority can apply for a magistrates' order compelling the occupiers to leave: see s78 of the 1994 Act. In *Shropshire City Council* v *Wynne* (1997) The Times 22 July the Divisional Court confirmed that magistrates do not have a discretion to refuse such an order, for example on the grounds that they believe the local authority to be acting unreasonably. A magistrate can only decline to make a s78 order where there are special grounds, for example where the person who is the subject of the order has given an undertaking that the site will be vacated by a particular date.

Meetings on the highway

At common law, the highway is land dedicated to the public use for the primary purpose of passing and repassing by pedestrians and traffic, and any activities that are reasonably incidental thereto; see *Dovaston* v *Payne* (1795) 2 H Bl 527. The owners of the highway can sue anyone in trespass who uses the highway for an improper (ie unreasonable) purpose. The surface of the highway is usually vested in the local authority, but adjacent landowners have an interest in the subsoil and can also sue in trespass and nuisance. There have been many cases illustrating the concept of reasonable use. In *Hickman* v *Maisey* [1900] 1 QB 752 a racehorse trainer successfully sued in trespass a person who stood on the highway to time the trainer's racehorses. Similarly, in *Harrison* v *Duke of Rutland* [1893] 1 QB 142 a person who objected to the Duke shooting grouse walked up and down a highway across the grouse moor opening and closing his umbrella so as to frighten the birds. He was held to be an unreasonable user of the highway and therefore a trespasser who could not complain when the Duke's gamekeeper used reasonable force to eject him from the moor. In a more recent authority, *Hubbard* v *Pitt* [1976] QB 142, Forbes J gave the following examples of permissible use:

> 'Thus a tired pedestrian may sit down and rest himself. A motorist may attempt to repair a minor breakdown. Because the highway is used also as a means of access to places abutting on the highway, it is permissible to queue for tickets at a theatre or other place of entertainment, or for a bus.'

Lord Clyde, in *DPP* v *Jones* [1999] 2 All ER 257, expressed the concept of reasonable use of the highway in these terms (at p286b–c):

> '... the public's right [to use the highway] is fenced with limitations affecting both the extent and the nature of the user. So far as the extent is concerned the user may not extend beyond the physical limits of the highway. That may often include the verges. It may also include a lay-by. Moreover, the law does not recognise any jus spatiendi which would entitle a member of the public simply to wander about the road, far less beyond its limits, at will. Further, the public have no jus manendi on a highway, so that any stopping and standing must be reasonably limited in time. While the right may extend to a picnic on the verge, it would not extend to camping there.'

He accepted that there was a general common law right of assembly, but did not accept that this necessarily extended to the highway. As he observed (at pp286f–287a):

'In the generality there is no doubt but that there is a public right of assembly. But there are restrictions on the exercise of that right in the public interest. There are limitations at common law and there are express limitations laid down in art 11 of the Convention on Human Rights. I would not be prepared to affirm as a matter of generality that there is a right of assembly on any place on a highway at any time and in any event I am not persuaded that the present case has to be decided by reference to public rights of assembly. If a group of people stand in the street to sing hymns or Christmas carols they are in my view using the street within the legitimate scope of the public right of access to it, provided of course that they do so for a reasonable period and without any unreasonable obstruction to traffic. If there are shops in the street and people gather to stand and view a shop window, or form a queue to enter the shop, that is within the normal and reasonable use which is a matter of public right. A road may properly be used for the purposes of a procession. It would still be a perfectly proper use of the road if the procession was intended to serve some particular purpose, such as commemorating some particular event or achievement. And if an individual may properly stop at a point on the road for any lawful purpose, so too should a group of people be entitled to do so. All such activities seem to me to be subsidiary to the use for passage. So I have no difficulty in holding that in principle a gathering of people at the side of a highway within the limits of the restraints which I have noted may be within the scope of the public's right of access to the highway.'

Under s137(1) Highways Act 1980, it is a criminal offence for any person to wilfully to obstruct the free passage along a highway without lawful authority or reasonable excuse. If the highway is obstructed a constable can arrest those causing the obstruction. Obstruction, in this context, is a very flexible term. In *Gill* v *Carson* [1917] 2 KB 674, it was held that there was no necessity to show that anyone was actually obstructed, whilst in *Homer* v *Cadman* (1866) 55 LJMC 110, it was held that it is no defence to show that there was a way around the obstruction; a street stall erected on a wide pavement, leaving plenty of room for people to pass, will still constitute an obstruction. In *Arrowsmith* v *Jenkins* [1963] 2 QB 561, Lord Parkes rejected the contention that the prosecution had to show that there was an intention to obstruct the highway, stating that if a person does an act according to their free will which results in an obstruction, it will be sufficient for the offence of obstruction. Reasonable use of the highway will constitute a reasonable excuse for these purposes: see *Nagy* v *Weston* [1965] 1 All ER 78. In *Hirst and Agu* v *Chief Constable of West Yorkshire* (1986) 85 Cr App R 143, Glidewell LJ explained that, for the defence of lawful excuse to arise, the activity in question must of itself be inherently lawful. If it is not the question of reasonable excuse does not arise. In that particular case the appellants had been demonstrating their opposition to the fur trade by congregating on the highway outside a shop selling fur garments. The convictions for obstruction were quashed because the Crown Court had not expressly addressed the question of whether or not their campaigning activities were lawful. In *DPP* v *Jones* (above), Lord Irvine, referring to *Hirst and Agu*, noted that there was a 'symmetry in the law between the activities on the public highway which may be trespassory and those which may amount to unlawful obstruction of the highway.'

Lord Hutton in *DPP* v *Jones* (above) was also of the view that the law as to trespass on the highway should conform with the law relating to wilful obstruction of the highway under s137 of the Highways Act 1980 – ie that a peaceful assembly on the highway may be a reasonable use of the highway, noting in particular that the public's right to use the highway should be extended 'in accordance with the enlarged notions of people in a country becoming more populous and highly civilised' provided those rights were not extended in a manner that was inconsistent with the maintenance of 'the paramount idea that the right of the public [in relation to the highway] ... was that of passage.'

Pickets and picketing

Picketing by strikers usually involves a few of them standing at the works gate and informing their fellow workers that a strike is taking place. Mass picketing is simply picketing in large numbers. There are three ways in which pickets can become involved with the law. First, if the picketing is unlawful then the employer can use the civil law to obtain an injunction ordering the pickets to stop. Second, the pickets may be prosecuted for breaches of the criminal law. Finally, anyone can obtain an injunction to stop pickets who are unreasonable users of the highway: *Hubbard* v *Pitt* [1976] 1 QB 142.

Generally there is no 'right' to picket because it will not be a reasonable use of the highway unless for passing and repassing. However, under s220 of the Trade Union and Labour Relations (Consolidation) Act 1992, picketing is lawful if it is in contemplation or furtherance of a trade dispute and at or near the strikers' own workplace for the purpose only of peacefully obtaining or communicating information or peacefully persuading any person to work or to abstain from working. This provision provides pickets with immunity in respect of civil actions for trespass or for inducing breach of contract. It follows from this that picketing someone else's place of work is illegal and the employer can obtain an injunction to stop it. This is so-called secondary picketing. For the picketing to be legal it must fall within each of the following categories:

1. the people picketing must be employees, their trade union officials or those sacked during the dispute;
2. the only places that can be picketed are the entrances to the premises, or if there is more than one place of work or it is impracticable to picket the workplace (for example seamen), then they can picket those offices of their employer from which they receive their instructions or pay packets, or depot or garage from which their vehicles operate;
3. the picketing is only lawful if it is peaceful; and
4. unless the picketing is in furtherance of a trade dispute, it is unlawful.

The 1992 Code of Practice provides that pickets and their organisers should ensure that in general the numbers of pickets does not exceed six at any entrance to a workplace. The Code is not law, and hence is not legally binding, but the courts must take it into account when considering whether to grant an injunction.

In *Hubbard* v *Pitt* [1976] 1 QB 142 it was held that consumers picketing an estate agent could be stopped by an injunction. The practice of stopping vehicles in order to persuade their occupants not to cross a picket line is not specifically allowed by s220 of the 1992 Act. In *Hunt* v *Broome* [1974] AC 587 it was held that if pickets seek to compel a person to refrain from work and seek to prevent him from attending his place of work he may use force if necessary to cross the picket line.

Section 220 of the 1992 Act does not provide protection from the criminal law, hence it provides no protection in respect of charges of obstruction. More than 10,000 criminal charges were brought in England and Wales for offences committed in connection with the miners' dispute in 1984–85. More than 4,000 charges were brought under s5 of the Public Order Act 1936: 1,500 for obstructing the police; 1,000 for criminal damage; 640 for obstructing the highway; and 360 for assaulting a police officer. Other offences committed included murder, riot, unlawful assembly and affray

Processions

Processions along the highway, being mobile, will generally be lawful at common law since the highway is being used for passage. However, if the procession goes beyond reasonable use, then it may constitute a public nuisance. This offence is rare but it was used in the case of *R* v *Clarke (No 2)* [1964] 2 QB 315. Clarke was charged with inviting others to obstruct the highway around Whitehall. The police had blocked the path of the demonstration and Clarke was said to have told the crowd to go around the blockade. It was argued that this amounted to an incitement to commit a public nuisance. The accused was convicted and given a sentence of 18 months' imprisonment. The conviction was quashed on appeal. The Court held that the question that must be asked was whether there had been an unreasonable use of the highway. It was held to be irrelevant that some obstruction had occurred if the use of the highway was reasonable.

Processions and the Public Order Act 1986, ss11, 12 and 13

Under the Public Order Act 1986 advance notice of public processions must be given in certain circumstances. Section 11 provides that proposals to hold a public procession must be notified to the police if it is a procession intended to demonstrate support for, or opposition to, the views or actions of any person or body of persons; or publicise a cause or campaign; or mark or commemorate an event. Written notice must be given to the police not less than six clear days before the date of the procession, or as soon as is practicable. The organisers commit an offence if they fail to satisfy these requirements or, if in general, the conduct of the procession differs from that indicated in the notice. For example, the provisions of s11 were invoked in respect of the activities of animal rights activists blockading ports used for the export of live animals during early 1995, on the basis that notice had not been given as required by the Act.

The Public Order Act 1986, ss12 and 13, replaces the provisions first enacted in s3 of the Public Order Act 1936. The 1936 Act was enacted following disorder caused by Fascist marches in the East End of London. Powers to control the route of processions had long existed, in the Metropolitan Police Act 1839 and the Town Police Clauses Act 1847, but s3 of the 1936 Act introduced for the first time the power to ban processions. These provisions are now contained in ss12 and 13 of the 1986 Act. They are directed to preventing serious public disorder rather than dealing with it when it has occurred. The framework of control has two stages, in order to ensure that banning orders are used only as a measure of last resort. Section 12 provides that:

'(1) If the senior police officer, having regard to the time or place at which and the circumstances in which any public procession is being held or is intended to be held and to its route or proposed route, reasonably believes that –

(a) it may result in serious public disorder, serious damage to property or serious disruption to the life of the community, or

(b) the purpose of the persons organising it is the intimidation of others with a view to compelling them not to do an act they have a right to do, or to do an act they have a right not to do,

he may give directions imposing on the persons organising or taking part in the procession such conditions as appear to him necessary to prevent such disorder, damage, disruption or intimidation, including conditions as to the route of the procession or prohibiting it from entering any public place specified in the directions.'

If, however, it is considered that these powers will not be sufficient to prevent serious disorder, then the second stage of the process is used. Section 13 provides that:

'If at any time the chief officer of police reasonably believes that, because of particular circumstances existing in any district or part of a district, the powers under s12 will not be sufficient to prevent the holding of public processions in that district or part from resulting in serious public disorder, he shall apply to the council of the district for an order prohibiting subject to the consent of the Home Secretary (s13(2)) for such period not exceeding three months as may be specified in the application the holding of all public processions (or of any class of public procession so specified) in the district or part concerned.'

In the City of London or the metropolitan police district, the Commissioner of Police for the City of London or the Commissioner of Police of the Metropolis may make such orders with the consent of the Home Secretary: s13(3) and (4). Prohibitions imposed under these provisions can be challenged by way of an application for judicial review on the ground that they unreasonable or disproportionate to the threat to public order presented by the procession.

Gatherings in the vicinity of Parliament

Under s52 of the Metropolitan Police Act 1839 the Commissioner of Police of the Metropolis may make regulations for preventing obstruction of the streets within the vicinity of Parliament. Any contravention of those regulations is a criminal offence. Although this is a wide power there are some limits to it. In *Papworth* v *Coventry* [1967] 1 WLR 633 the accused was convicted of ignoring a s52 order that the streets around Parliament should be kept clear. He appealed on the grounds that the seven protesters could not have caused an obstruction. The appeal was upheld. The police also have the power to stop potential disorderly processions by bringing the possible demonstrators before the magistrates before the demonstration. They may then be bound over to keep the peace. Should they refuse to be bound over they can be imprisoned for up to six months.

Breach of the peace

Arrest for breach of the peace has, for many years, provided police officers with a useful residual power to prevent and control outbreaks of public disorder. Breach of the peace, as such, is not an offence: see *R* v *County Quarter Sessions Appeals Committee, ex parte MPC* [1948] 1 KB 260, but a threatened or actual breach of the peace provides a police officer, or private citizen, with a summary power of arrest, and an individual who resists the exercise of the power of arrest, where exercised by a constable, runs the risk of being charged with obstructing a police officer in the execution of his duty, contrary to s89(2) of the Police Act 1996. A person arrested for breach of the peace may be brought before a magistrates' court and bound over to keep the peace, a power that can be traced back to the Justices of the Peace Act 1361: see s115 Magistrates' Court Act 1980. Sureties will sometimes be required, in default of which the defendant can be imprisoned for up to six months. The criminal standard of proof has to be satisfied in relation to the alleged breach of the peace: see *Percy* v *DPP* [1995] 3 All ER 124.

   Given that it can be used to prevent individuals meeting in public or making speeches, it is important that the nature of breach of the peace should be clearly defined. The reality is that the concept remains, to some extent, shrouded in uncertainty. In *R* v *Howells* [1982] QB 416 Watkins LJ, giving the judgment of the court, attempted to define breach of the peace in the following terms:

'... we cannot accept that there can be a breach of the peace unless there has been an act done or threatened to be done which either actually harms a person, or in his presence his property, or is likely to cause such harm, or which puts someone in fear of such harm being done ...'

Whilst the above does provide a useful working definition, it has been criticised for suggesting that a threat of violence could amount to a breach of the peace. It would be preferable, perhaps, to say that a police officer has a power to arrest for an anticipated breach of the peace where such threats are made. The extent to which this lack of specificity might amount to a violation of rights protected by the European Convention on Human Rights was considered in *Steel and Others* v *United Kingdom* (1998) 5 BHRC 339. The applicants fell into two categories. In the first group were those who had taken part in demonstrations against blood sports and road building programmes and had engaged in direct confrontation, for example by standing in front of those about to fire rifles at birds, or blocking the way in front of earth moving equipment. In the second category were those applicants whose protests had been more passive, for example holding up banners and distributing leaflets protesting at arms sales. In relation to the first group the European Court of Human Rights concluded that the arrest and detention of the applicants for breach of the peace had not amounted to a violation of the Convention. The Court noted that although (as indicated above) breach of the peace was, technically, not an offence under English law, it amounted to an offence for the purposes of art 5 of the ECHR (a point conceded by the United Kingdom government). The Court looked to the substance rather than the form. The requirement under art 5 was that an offence should be prescribed by law with sufficient clarity so that an accused person would be able to foresee the legal consequences of any given action. The Court was satisfied that, through case law, the concept of breach of the peace had been clarified in English law to the extent that it could be defined as arising when a person caused harm (or appeared likely to do so) to persons or property, or acted in a manner the natural consequence of which was to provoke others to violence. There was also a clear power of arrest in such circumstances. On the facts the Court was satisfied that the behaviour of the applicants in the first category had warranted arrest for breach of the peace as defined. Further, the binding over orders issued in respect of these applicants made it sufficiently clear that they were being asked to refrain from committing similar breaches of the peace within the following 12 months. In respect of the second category of applicants, however, the Court concluded that, as their protest had been entirely peaceful, there had been no basis for their being arrested for breach of the peace, and hence there had been a violation of art 5(1). The Court also held that the detention of applicants in the second category amounted to a violation of the right to freedom of expression under art 10 of the Convention. Given that their protests were peaceful, the interference with their rights under art 10 had been disproportionate to the aim of preventing disorder and protecting the rights of others.

Note that the European Court of Human Rights accepted that a breach of the peace could occur or be apprehended where a person acted in a way that could provoke other persons to violence. This suggests that a police officer can arrest the person behaving in the provocative manner, rather than those likely to be provoked into committing acts of violence. A number of other authorities support this view. In *Nicol and Selvanayagam* v *DPP* [1996] Crim LR 318, the court upheld binding over orders in respect of defendants who had tried to disrupt an angling competition by blowing horns. Similarly in *R* v *Morpeth Ward Justices, ex parte Ward and Others* [1992] Crim LR 497, where the applicants, anti-blood sports demonstrators who had entered a field where a shooting party had gathered, engaged in noisy disruptive behaviour intending to impede the shoot. They were subsequently summonsed for breach of the peace and bound over to keep the peace. Their challenge to the magistrates' order, on the basis that the elements of the offence of breach of the peace had not been made out, and thus the magistrates had not had jurisdiction to make the orders in question, was rejected by the Court on the ground that magistrates could exercise their powers of bindover provided there was evidence that the Queen's peace was threatened by the conduct of the defendant. The Court felt that it was not necessary to show that any other person had been put in bodily fear by the conduct, provided that a natural consequence of the conduct was that it would provoke others to violence.

The concept of 'lawfulness' is, however, linked to the reasonableness of the individual's behaviour in the circumstances: see again *Nicol and Selvanayagam* v *DPP*. For example, in *Beatty* v *Gillbanks* [1882] 9 QBD 308, it was held that Salvation Army marchers were not guilty of a breach of the peace simply because their procession might cause bystanders to react violently. More recently, in *Redmond-Bate* v *DPP* (1999) 163 JP 789, the Divisional Court confirmed that a public preacher, exercising her right to free speech, could not be arrested for breach of the peace simply because her views were unpopular. Sedley LJ observed that a precondition for a police officer exercising his power to arrest for breach of the peace was a reasonable belief, based on his perceptions at the time, that the person he intended to arrest was about to cause a breach of the peace. It was, in his view, important that the court assessed the likelihood of any breach of the peace based on what the officer had known at the time and not with the benefit of hindsight. Where such preventative action was taken by a police officer it should be directed at the person whose actions were likely to cause the disturbance. The Crown Court had been in error in concluding that lawful conduct could, if persisted in, lead to a conviction for wilful obstruction. Only if there was a reasonable apprehension that lawful conduct would provoke violence by interfering with the rights of others was an officer empowered to intervene.

There are a number of difficulties with this approach. First it is difficult to reconcile with *Duncan* v *Jones* [1936] 1 KB 218. In that case Duncan intended to hold a meeting outside a government training centre. At a previous meeting there had been a disturbance. As she was about to start speaking a police officer asked her to move about 150 yards down the road. She refused to move and was arrested and charged with obstructing a police officer in the execution of his duty. The Divisional Court, upholding her conviction, found that she must have realised that a probable consequence of holding the meeting was a disturbance, and further found that the police officer had reasonable grounds for believing that a breach of the peace might ensue and therefore was under a duty to stop the meeting taking place.

Secondly, it perhaps pays insufficient regard to the practicalities of policing a modern society. It is significant that in *Redmond-Bate* v *DPP* the appellant had attracted a crowd of over 100 persons who were listening to her speech on the steps of Wakefield cathedral. Some of those gathered were shouting abuse at her. It was far easier for the police to defuse the potentially violent situation in this case by removing the appellant from the scene, rather than arresting large numbers of those who gathered to listen and shout abuse. In the light of the Divisional Court's ruling what should the police officer have done? Wait for actual violence to break out? In this case the appellant was putting forward views reflecting her religious persuasion. One wonders whether the court's view would have been the same if, for example, the speaker had been espousing a far more disreputable theory, such as the idea that the Nazi holocaust never happened. One can imagine a large crowd becoming quickly enflamed by this. Who would the police remove?

Further support for the position adopted by the arresting officer in *Redmond-Bate v DPP* can be found in Lord Slynn's speech in *R v Chief Constable of Sussex, ex parte International Trader's Ferry Ltd* [1999] 1 All ER 129. Animal rights protestors, demonstrating against the export of livestock from the port of Shoreham, had made it impossible for the applicant company to conduct its business. The chief constable advised that he only had the resources to keep the port open for two days a week. The drivers were, on a number of occasions, informed by the police that they should not proceed to the port to deliver livestock because of the danger that doing so might provoke the demonstrators to commit a breach of the peace. The drivers were also advised that if they persisted in proceeding towards the port they would be arrested for obstruction. Responding to the '*Beatty v Gillbanks*' argument Lord Slynn observed:

> 'The police, in the performance of their duty, here sought to protect people exercising a lawful trade from the acts of violent demonstrators acting unlawfully and threatening a breach of the peace. When, with their finite resources of officers and finance, the police could do this they did so. Only when their resources were insufficient did they not provide the protection and, in order to prevent a breach of the peace, on rare occasions, they told the lorry drivers to turn back. I do not accept that *Beatty v Gillbanks* lays down that the police can never restrain a lawful activity if that is the only way to prevent violence and a breach of the peace. Professor Feldman in "*Civil Liberties and Human Rights in England and Wales*" (1993) at p791 writes: "Furthermore, the police have a duty to prevent reasonably apprehended and imminent breaches of the peace, and failure to obey instructions reasonably directed to that end constitutes the offence of obstructing a constable in the execution of his duty. That being so, the decision in *Beatty v Gillbanks* tells us nothing about how the very wide discretion to act preventively in apprehension of a breach of the peace should be exercised." '

Attempting to reconcile these conflicting approaches the Court of Appeal in *Bibby v Chief Constable of Essex Police* (2000) The Times 24 April held that the common law power to arrest for breach of the peace should only be exercised in relation to D where a sufficiently real and present threat to the peace arose; that threat came from D; D's conduct clearly interfered with the rights of others; D's conduct was unreasonable; and the natural consequence of D's conduct would be 'not wholly unreasonable violence' from a third party.

Where D's actions are unlawful and may cause damage to property, but do not create any threat of violence, a court can, in theory, impose a binding over order prohibiting D from engaging in any activity that could be 'contra bonos mores', or contrary to what the majority of citizens would consider to be proper behaviour. The difficulty with such an order is that it is a very vague restriction on D's behaviour that may prevent him from exercising his civil rights. In *Hashman* v *United Kingdom* (1999) The Times 1 December, the European Court of Human Rights held that anti-blood sport protestors who had been made the subject of such a binding over order after having attempted to disrupt hunt meetings had not had their rights under the Convention adequately protected. In particular the order was seen as a restriction on the right to free speech enshrined in art 10. The concept of behaviour 'contra bonos mores' was regarded by the Court as too vague to be equated with a limitation on the right to free speech that was 'prescribed by law'.

13.4 Offences under the Public Order Act 1986

The Public Order Act 1986 effected the repeal of several common law and statutory offences, such as riot, rout, unlawful assembly and affray, and provided three replacements: riot, violent disorder and affray.

Riot

Section 1(1) redefines the offence of riot. It provides that:

> 'Where 12 or more persons who are present together use or threaten unlawful violence ... and the conduct of them (taken together) is such as would cause a person of reasonable firmness present at the scene to fear for his personal safety, each of the persons using unlawful violence for the common purpose is guilty of riot.'

A person guilty of riot is liable on conviction on indictment to imprisonment for a term not exceeding ten years or a fine or both.

Violent disorder

Section 2(1) creates the offence of violent disorder. It provides that:

> 'Where three or more persons who are present together use or threaten unlawful violence and the conduct of them (taken together) is such as would cause a person of reasonable firmness present at the scene to fear for his personal safety, each of the persons using or threatening unlawful violence is guilty of violent disorder.'

A person guilty of violent disorder is liable on conviction on indictment to imprisonment for a term not exceeding five years or a fine or both, or on summary conviction to imprisonment for a term not exceeding six months or a fine or both. See further *R* v *McGuigan* [1991] Crim LR 719 and *R* v *Worton* [1990] Crim LR 124.

Affray

The offence of affray is now set out in s3 of the Public Order Act 1986, which provides as follows:

'(1) A person is guilty of affray if he uses or threatens unlawful violence towards another and his conduct is such as would cause a person of reasonable firmness present at the scene to fear for his personal safety.

(2) Where two or more persons use or threaten the unlawful violence, it is the conduct of them taken together that must be considered for the purposes of subsection (1).

(3) For the purposes of this section a threat cannot be made by the use of words alone.

(4) No person of reasonable firmness need actually be, or be likely to be, present at the scene.

(5) Affray may be committed in private as well as in public places.'

A threat of unlawful violence may take a very obvious form, such as driving a car at another: see *R* v *Hind* [1999] Crim LR 842. It may also, however, be implied, as in *I* v *DPP* [2001] 2 All ER 583 where it was held that the carrying of dangerous weapons such as petrol bombs by a group of persons could constitute a threat of violence within the meaning of s3(1). Whether it did so in a particular case would be a matter for the court to decide having regard to the facts of the case.

There can be no liability under s3 if the threats of violence are directed at persons not at the scene. As Lord Hutton observed in *I* v *DPP* (a case where youths had been convicted of affray having congregated in the vicinity of a block of flats carrying petrol bombs):

'... the overt carrying of petrol bombs [could not have] constituted a threat of violence to anyone in the vicinity, including the police on arrival at the scene, because the magistrate found that no one other than the police was present at the scene, and he also found by clear implication that the group of youths constituted no threat towards the police as the group dispersed immediately the police carrier came into view. ... In order to constitute an offence under s3 there must be a threat of violence towards another person ... it does not necessarily follow that because a person is present at a location where a gang are carrying petrol bombs there is a threat of violence towards that person. Whether there is a threat of violence towards a person present at the scene constituted by the carrying of a weapon or weapons will depend on the facts of the actual case, but that issue does not arise in the present case because, apart from the police officers towards whom there was no threat, no one was present at the scene.'

Hence the threat has to be towards a person actually present, even though the test of causing 'a person of reasonable firmness present at the scene to fear for his personal safety' is based on the reaction of a notional third party who need not be present: see further *R* v *Sanchez* [1996] Crim LR 572. Although there need not actually be any third person present for the offence to be made out, such a direction is necessary because the offence was enacted for the protection of the innocent bystander, as opposed to the person towards whom the violence was aimed. In assessing whether the threat was 'against another' it was not necessary to show that another person had actually perceived a threat: see *Swanston* v *DPP* (1997) The Times 23 January. The offence of affray could be made out even if the person threatened was unaware of the threat (for example because his back was turned) or where the identity of the person threatened was not known – for example where the occupants of flats overlooking a communal area observed the gathering of armed youths. A further relevant factor might be whether an assault by A upon B took place in circumstances that permitted the innocent bystander to move out of harm's way, thus reducing the fear of any interference with his personal safety.

Subsection 3(3) provides that for the purposes of the offence of affray, a threat cannot be made by the use of words alone. In *R* v *Dixon* [1993] Crim LR 579 the appellant had been involved in a domestic argument with his common law wife. The police were called and the appellant made off, accompanied by his dog. When eventually cornered by the police, the appellant ordered the dog, which was in an agitated state, to attack the officers. Two officers suffered bites in an attack by the dog. The dog returned to the appellant who then ordered it to kill the officers. At this point the officers retreated awaiting reinforcements. The appellant was convicted of affray, and appealed on the grounds that his words alone could not constitute the affray; that there was insufficient evidence to show that the dog had been responding to his commands; and that the trial judge may have given the jury the impression that passivity on the part of the appellant might be sufficient actus reus for the offence. Dismissing his appeal, the Court of Appeal held that, whilst the offence could not comprise the use of words alone, in the instant case the prosecution had relied upon the actions of the appellant in deliberately setting the dog on the officers and the words he had uttered at the time. The prosecutor was not required to prove that the dog had responded to the commands uttered by the appellant. The actus reus of the offence comprised the words spoken to the dog, coupled with the dog being in a highly agitated state. The decision perhaps raises the questions as to whether the mere presence of the dog should have been regarded as sufficient to convert what would otherwise have been words alone into an affray, where the instructions given might cause fear in the reasonable bystander. The requirement of something more than words alone is further confirmed in *R* v *Robinson* [1993] Crim LR 581; and see also *R* v *Davies* [1991] Crim LR 469. A person guilty of affray is liable on conviction on indictment to imprisonment for a term not exceeding three years or a fine or both, or on summary conviction to imprisonment for a term not exceeding six months or a fine or both.

Fear or provocation of violence

Section 4(1) largely replaces s5 of the Public Order Act 1936 with an offence of causing fear or provocation of violence:

> 'A person is guilty of an offence if he –
> (a) uses towards another person threatening, abusive or insulting words or behaviour, or distributes, or

(b) displays to another person any writing, sign or other visible representation which is threatening, abusive or insulting,

with intent to cause that person to believe that immediate unlawful violence will be used against him or another by any person, or to provoke the immediate use of unlawful violence by that person or another, or whereby that person is likely to believe that such violence will be used or it is likely that such violence will be provoked.'

Also, see *Edwards* v *DPP* (1996) (CO/293/96).

Atkin v *DPP* (1989) 89 Cr App R 199 held that the words must be used in the presence of, and earshot of, the person to whom they are directed. No offence is committed under s4 where the behaviour complained of occurs in a dwelling house: *R* v *Va Kun Hua* [1990] Crim LR 518. In *R* v *Horseferry Road Justices, ex parte Siadatan* [1990] Crim LR 598 the Divisional Court refused to allow an application for judicial review of the decision not to prosecute the publishers of Salman Rushdie's *The Satanic Verses* under s4(1). The court felt that as the 1986 Act created criminal liability it was to be construed narrowly, and that in any event the disturbances created by the book's publication did not amount to the provocation of immediate violence. *R* v *Afzal* [1993] Crim LR 791 confirms that, in relation to the charge of threatening behaviour contrary to s4, the trial judge should, where appropriate, direct the jury to consider whether or not the violence might have been lawful, eg where it was threatened by way of self-defence, since actual violence by way of reasonable self-defence would not be unlawful.

The jury should be directed to consider the effect of the threats on the victim, in particular whether the victim apprehended immediate violence (as opposed to being immediately put in fear of some general non-specific threat of violence). Some cases will obviously lie at the margins of liability – for example *DPP* v *Ramos* [2000] Crim LR 768, where D was convicted of a racially aggravated form of the offence under s4(1)(b) in relation to letters sent to an Asian community centre warning of a bombing campaign that he was going to carry out; the conviction was upheld even though the letters did not clearly indicate when the bombing would take place.

Section 154 of the Criminal Justice and Public Order Act 1994 added a further offence, namely causing intentional harassment alarm or distress, by the addition of a s4A to the 1986 Act. Under s4A:

'(1) A person is guilty of the offence if, with intent to cause another harassment, alarm, or distress, he –
(a) uses threatening, abusive or insulting words or behaviour or disorderly behaviour, or
(b) displays any writing, sign or other visible representation which is threatening, abusive or insulting,
thereby causing another person harassment, alarm or distress.'

The offence can be committed in a public or private place, except where both parties are in private dwellings. A constable may arrest without a warrant anyone he reasonably suspects to be guilty of committing the offence. The new offence is effectively an aggravated form of the offence created by s5 of the 1986 Act – ie causing harassment, alarm or distress – and shares many of its features.

Using threatening, abusive or insulting words or behaviour

Under s5(1) (as amended by the Public Order (Amendment) Act 1996):

> 'A person is guilty of an offence if he –
>
> (a) uses threatening, abusive or insulting words or behaviour, or disorderly behaviour, or
>
> (b) displays any writing, sign or other visible representation which is threatening, abusive or insulting,
>
> within the hearing or sight of a person likely to be caused harassment, alarm or distress thereby.'

It is a matter of fact for the court to determine whether or not this has occurred. For the purposes of s5, a police officer may be the person harassed or alarmed by the defendant's words. As Glidewell LJ observed in *DPP* v *Orum* (1989) 88 Cr App R 261:

> 'I find nothing in the context of the 1986 Act to persuade me that a police officer may not be a person who is caused harassment, alarm or distress by the various kinds of words and conduct to which s5(1) applies. I would therefore answer the question in the affirmative, that a police officer can be a person who is likely to be caused harassment and so on. However, that is not to say that the opposite is necessarily the case, namely, it is not to say that every police officer in this situation is to be assumed to be a person who is caused harassment. Very frequently, words and behaviour with which police officers will be wearily familiar will have little emotional impact on them save that of boredom. It may well be that in appropriate circumstances, justices will decide ... as a question of fact that the words and behaviour were not likely in all the circumstances to cause harassment, alarm or distress to either of the police officers. That is a question of fact for the justices to be decided in all the circumstances: the time, the place, the nature of the words used, who the police officers are and so on.'

See further *R* v *Ball* (1990) 90 Cr App R 378. Disorderly conduct is not defined by the 1986 Act but, on the basis of *Chambers and Edwards* v *DPP* [1995] Crim LR 896, is to be given its ordinary and everyday meaning and whether it is made out is a question of fact for the court at first instance. In general terms, the expression does not require proof of threatening, abusive or insulting behaviour as these are matters dealt with elsewhere in the Act. A constable may arrest a person without warrant if he engages in offensive conduct which the constable warns him to stop, and he engages in further offensive conduct immediately or shortly after the warning. The maximum penalty on summary conviction is a fine.

Section 5 provides for three specific defences. First, that the defendant had no reason to believe that there was anyone within hearing or sight of his conduct who was likely to be harassed, alarmed or distressed; second, that he was inside a dwelling and had no reason to believe that the conduct would have been seen or heard by anyone outside; and, third, that his conduct was reasonable. These are all objective tests: see *DPP* v *Clarke and Others* [1992] Crim LR 60 and *DPP* v *Fidler and Morgan* [1992] Crim LR 62. In relation to the issue of reasonableness: see further *Kwasi Poku* v *DPP* [1993] Crim LR 705.

Like all Public Order Act 1986 offences, s5 has to be interpreted in the light of the Human Rights Act 1998. The possibility arises that s5 may be seen as an interference with the right to free expression under art 10 of the European Convention on Human Rights. Hence in *Percy* v *DPP* (2002) The Times 21 January, a conviction under s5 imposed after the defendant, demonstrating outside an American airbase, had defaced the flag of the United States of America in protest at military action by that country, was set aside on the basis that the prosecution was a disproportionate interference with art 10 rights. This is not a decision to the effect that s5 of the Public Order Act is incompatible with art 10 of the European Convention on Human Rights. The restrictions imposed by s5 passed the 'prescribed by law' test despite the vagueness of the terms deployed. If P's expression was reasonable within the terms of s5(3) of the 1986 Act the burden fell upon the prosecution to show that the interference with Convention rights caused by the use of s5 was both legitimate and proportionate.

Racially motivated offences

Sections 17–23 of the 1986 Act deal with various forms of incitement to racial hatred, replacing s5A of the 1936 Act. The 1986 Act creates six offences, all of which require the consent of the Attorney-General if proceedings are to be instituted. All of these offences concern conduct which is threatening, abusive or insulting and which is intended or which is likely, having regard to all the circumstances, to stir up racial hatred. They are: using such words or behaviour or displaying such materials (s18); distributing or directing such materials (s19); presenting or directing a public play which involves such words or behaviour (s20); distributing, showing or playing a recording of such visual images or sounds (s21); certain participation in a broadcast or cable programme service which includes such images or sounds (s22); and possessing such material or recordings with a view to its being displayed, published, distributed, broadcast or included in a cable broadcast service (s23). Section 30 empowers a court by or before which a person is convicted of an offence connected with football to make an exclusion order prohibiting him from entering premises to attend a prescribed football match.

The Crime and Disorder Act 1998 as amended by the Anti-terrorism, Crime and Security Act 2001, adds a number of racially or religiously aggravated versions of public order offences under the 1986 Act, specifically s4 (causing fear or provocation of violence), s4A (intentional harassment, alarm or distress) and s5 (harassment, alarm or distress). For these purposes an offence is racially aggravated if (under s28 of the 1998 Act) if:

'(a) at the time of committing the offence, or immediately before or after doing so, the offender demonstrates towards the victim of the offence hostility based on the victim's membership of, or association with members of, a racial group; or
(b) the offence is motivated (wholly or partly) by hostility towards members of a racial group based on their membership of that group.'

For these purposes a 'racial group' means a group of persons defined by reference to race, colour, nationality (including citizenship) or ethnic or national origins.

Public order measures relating to football matches

Public concern over the violence and disorder that seems to accompany many high profile football matches, especially international games, has prompted successive governments to introduce a legislative framework providing for various types of orders aimed at restricting the freedom of movement of those who might create public disorder at the time matches and tournaments are being held.

The Football (Disorder) Act 2000, prompted by further outbreaks of violence and public disorder involving England football supporters attending the Euro 2000 championship in Belgium and the Netherlands, builds upon previous legislation, such as the Public Order Act 1986, the Football Spectators Act 1989, the Football (Offences) Act 1991 and the Football (Offences and Disorder) Act 1999. The 2000 Act provides the police with extended powers to combat and prevent outbreaks of public disorder prior to or after football matches, and to impose restrictions on those travelling to locations where football matches are to be held. The Act includes preventative measures designed to ensure that those intending to travel to football matches held outside the jurisdiction are prevented from doing so.

Section 1 of the 2000 Act, which amends Part II of, and Schedule 1 to, the Football Spectators Act 1989, makes provision for banning orders which combine the effect of domestic football banning orders and international football banning orders provided for under earlier legislation. A Chief Officer of police may apply for a banning order in respect of a person residing in the area for which he is responsible if it appears to him that the person has at any time caused or contributed to any violence or disorder in the United Kingdom or elsewhere. The court will be able to make the banning order on a complaint (as well as a conviction), where it believes that there are reasonable grounds to believe that such an order would help to prevent violence or disorder at or in connection with particular football matches. A person made subject to a banning order will be required to report to a police station during a specified period (ie whilst a particular football match or tournament is being held).

For the purposes of banning orders 'violence' is defined to include violence against persons or property and includes 'threatening violence and doing anything which endangers the life of any person.' 'Disorder' is very widely construed to include: stirring up hatred against a group of persons defined by reference to colour, race, nationality; using threatening, abusive or insulting words or behaviour or disorderly behaviour; and displaying any writing or other thing which is threatening, abusive or insulting. These activities do not have to have taken place in connection with football.

Enforcing authorities are empowered to require individuals subject to banning orders to surrender their passports to prevent travel to specified football matches played outside the United Kingdom. Police constables are given the power, during control periods (ie normally in the five day period leading up to a particular game) to require individuals to appear before a magistrates' court within 24 hours to answer a complaint for the making of a banning order and, for that purpose, to give certain powers of arrest and detention. The grounds for a police constable exercising this power are that he has reasonable grounds to suspect that the person he is dealing with has at any time caused or contributed to any violence or disorder in the United Kingdom or elsewhere.

Where a banning order is made on complaint a right of appeal to the Crown Court is provided.

13.5 Martial law

The exact meaning of the phrase 'martial law' in the United Kingdom law is unclear. Many writers emphasise its ambiguity. It is sometimes used to denote an extreme form of the situation discussed above in which the military aid the civil authorities to maintain order. Martial law can be defined as the suspension of the ordinary law, and the substitution therefore of discretionary government by the executive exercised by the military. The suspension of the ordinary law in this context means that the ordinary courts of the land are suspended or otherwise unable to sit. Martial law certainly does not mean military law, which is a special branch of the law applying to members of the armed forces. During a period of martial law, military courts may be set up to administer justice while the ordinary courts are unable to function, but this is quite different from the ordinary function of courts martial applying military law subject to appeal in the civil courts. Military administration of occupied enemy territory in time of war is also sometimes called martial law. Where a true state of martial law obtains, the actions of the military are immune from interference by the civil courts.

Whether martial law is recognised by the common law is uncertain. Writers did not usually distinguish between martial law and military law. Martial law is lawful only in time of war, being illegal in time of peace under the Petition of Rights 1628, but war may have a different meaning in this context from the usual one of armed conflict between states. Apparently, it is for the civil courts to decide whether at any particular time insurrection has given rise to a state of war so that, for example, military courts could be set up: see *R* v *Allen* (1921) 2 IR 241. This is in contrast to the conclusiveness of a ministerial certificate declaring that at a certain time the United Kingdom is at war with another state: see *R* v *Bottrill, ex parte Kuechenmeister* [1947] KB 41.

There is no standard procedure whereby authority is handed over by the government to the military to commence a period of martial law. It is not the case that martial law obtains at all times during which the United Kingdom is at war with another state. *DF Marais* v *GOC Lines of Communication, ex parte Marais*

[1902] AC 109 was a decision of the Judicial Committee of the Privy Council on a petition for special leave to apply from a decision of the Supreme Court of the colony of the Cape of Good Hope. Marais had been arrested by the military in an area in which martial law had been declared. It was argued for him that his detention was unlawful because the ordinary courts were still functioning, that if he were guilty of any crime he should be prosecuted in the ordinary way, and that his detention by the military was therefore illegal and he should be forthwith released. The petition was refused. Lord Halsbury LC said:

> '[Their Lordships] are of opinion that where actual war is raging acts done by the military authorities are not justifiable by the ordinary tribunals, and that war in this case was actually raging, even if their Lordships did not take judicial notice of it, is sufficiently evidenced by the facts disclosed by the petitioner's own petition and affidavit. ... The fact that for some purposes some tribunals had been permitted to pursue their ordinary course is not conclusive that war was not raging. ... The truth is that no doubt has ever existed that where war actually prevails the ordinary courts have no jurisdiction over the action of the military authorities.'

The idea that the ordinary courts may be 'allowed' to sit by the military seems very doubtful: see for example Molony CJ in *R (Garde)* v *Strickland* (1921) 2 IR 317 at p326. The better view seems to be that the fact of the ordinary courts continuing to sit is no more than a factor in answering the real question as to whether a state of war exists.

In *R* v *Allen* (1921) 2 IR 241 the court of the King's Bench in Ireland refused writs of prohibition, habeas corpus and certiorari against the decision of a military court which had passed a sentence of death on a person convicted of being found in possession of arms and ammunition. The authority for this trial and the sentence was a proclamation of martial law in certain parts of South Ireland and a proclamation that persons found in possession of arms and ammunition would be liable to suffer death on conviction by such a court. The court accepted the point in *Marais* that the fact of the ordinary courts continuing to sit is not conclusive of the question whether a state of war exists. It also decided, in line with most modern authority, that military courts set up under martial law are not truly courts at all, but only committees set up to carry into execution the discretionary powers assumed by the government: see also Lord Halsbury in *Tilonko* v *Attorney-General of Natal* [1907] AC 93 and Viscount Cave in *Re Clifford and O'Sullivan* [1921] 2 AC 570.

As Molony CJ observed in *R (Garde)* v *Strickland* (above):

> 'The proceedings of a military court derive their sole justification for authority from the existence of actual rebellion, and the duty of doing whatever may be necessary to quell it and to restore peace and order ...'

This does not mean that the court will inquire into the necessity for each act: the rule appears to be that once it recognises the necessity of martial law, it will not claim jurisdiction, at any rate until after the war is over. In *Egan* v *Macready* (1921) 1 IR 265, O'Connor MR decided that habeas corpus should be issued on facts similar to those in *Allen*. He based his decision on the Restoration of Order (Ireland) Act 1920, which he said, governed the existing situation and therefore made recourse to a military court unnecessary and illegal. He said:

> 'The argument based on military necessity was pressed strongly and I fully recognise that in a case not touched by special legislation it is not for the civil court to decide whether a military act was necessary or not. That must be left to the military authority. But I think that it should at least appear that there may have been the necessity. Now, the evidence offered by the military in this case seems to me to negative the bringing the prisoner before a military court rather than a court martial ...'

If, apart from the act, the second last sentence is meant to assert that, for example, if no reasonable man could have found the act necessary, the court intervene, it is contrary to the proposition in *Marais* that the court simply has no jurisdiction during the war.

After the war, it is not clear to what extent there can be redress for action taken under martial law. Usually Parliament passes Acts of Indemnity. It may be that acts that no reasonable man could have found necessary will be punishable, even if only the military commander is alone liable at least where his orders were not patently illegal.

13.6 Emergency powers in time of war

Most of the special powers taken by the government in time of war are nowadays conferred by statute. During the First World War the government acted under the Defence of the Realm Acts 1914–15. Section 1(1) of the 1914 Act provided that:

> 'His Majesty in Council has power during the continuance of the present war to issue regulations for securing the public safety and defence of the realm.'

It also said that such regulations could authorise the trial and punishment of persons committing offences against them. This was a very wide power to pass delegated legislation, though its exercise was limited by the doctrine of ultra vires. See, for example, *Chester v Bateson* [1920] 1 KB 829. In *R v Halliday, ex parte Zadig* [1917] AC 260 a regulation made under the 1914–15 Acts was held not to be ultra vires in purporting to give to the Secretary of State unrestricted powers to detain a person – even a British subject – on security grounds. After the First World War, most acts done in the prosecution of the war were protected from legal action by the Indemnity Act 1920.

Emergency powers were again taken by the government during the Second World War under the Emergency Powers (Defence) Acts 1939 and 1940. Regulations that could be made under the 1939 Act included those that appeared to His Majesty:

> '... to be necessary or expedient for securing the public safety, the defence of the realm,

the maintenance of public order and the efficient prosecution of any war in which His Majesty may be engaged, and for maintaining supplies and services essential to the life of the community.'

Various matters were expressly specified as proper subjects for these regulations, such as dealing with offenders against them, detention of people for security reasons, taking possession of property and entering and searching premises. The imposition of charge was authorised. Provision was made by the Emergency Powers (Defence) (No 2) Act 1940 for the making of regulations for the trial of persons whether or not members of the armed forces in special military courts, should the military situation require it. Such regulations were never in fact made. Some of the regulations were interpreted by the courts in ways very favourable to the executive. The most famous instance, perhaps, is *Liversidge* v *Anderson* [1942] AC 206 in which regulation 18B(1) on the internment of certain persons was taken to be satisfied by honesty and good faith on the part of the Secretary of State, even though it expressly required him to have reasonable cause to believe in the hostile origin or associations of the person to be detained, and in the necessity of detaining him for those reasons. The Acts expired in 1946.

13.7 Peacetime emergencies and terrorism

Emergency Powers Act 1920

The Act of 1920 (as amended by the Emergency Powers Act 1964) permits the proclamation of a state of emergency to last no more than a month (renewable) if at any time it appears to Her Majesty that there have occurred, or are about to occur, events of such a nature as to be calculated, by interfering with the supply and distribution of food, water, fuel or light, or with the means of locomotion, to deprive the community, or any substantial portion of the community, of the essentials of life. Provision is made for the communication of the proclamation to Parliament, even when it is not sitting. During the emergency the Act authorises the making of regulations for securing the essentials of life to the community. As the powers given are very wide, and intended to be used during very disruptive strikes, it is expressly provided that no regulations under the Act shall make it an offence to take part in a strike or peacefully to persuade others to do so. The provisions were last invoked to deal with strikes during the winter of 1973–74.

Anti-terrorist legislation

The origins of the modern anti-terrorist legislation can be traced back to the Prevention of Violence (Temporary Provisions) Act 1939, which conferred powers on the Secretary of State to make expulsion, prohibition and registration orders against persons reasonably suspected of involvement in acts of violence designed to influence public opinion or government policy with respect to Irish affairs, and enabled the police to arrest and detain such persons. Although stated to be temporary these provisions were regularly renewed until 1954 when they were allowed to lapse. The resurgence of terrorist activity by republican para-military organisations, and in particular the perpetration of a mainland bombing campaign in which civilians as well as members of the military were targeted, led the Labour government to introduce what became the Prevention of Terrorism (Temporary Provisions) Act 1974. As the short title to the Act suggests, it was intended to be a temporary measure, and was subject to renewal on an annual basis.

The 1974 Act was replaced, with modifications and additions, by the Prevention of Terrorism (Temporary Provisions) Act 1976 and, following review by the Shackleton Committee in 1978 and by the Jellicoe Committee in 1983, the 1984 Act. The operation of the 1984 Act was, in turn, considered in 1987 by the Colville Committee, resulting in the enactment of the Prevention of Terrorism (Temporary Provisions) Act 1989, as amended and augmented by the Prevention of Terrorism (Additional Powers) Act 1996 and the Criminal Justice (Terrorism and Conspiracy) Act 1998.

The 1974 Act and its successors were effectively replaced by the enactment of the Terrorism Act 2000, which made sweeping changes to the law relating to the criminalisation and policing of terrorist activities. Unlike its predecessors the Terrorism Act 2000 does not require annual renewal, although Parliament receives an annual report on the operation of the Act.

Part I of the 2000 Act sets out the framework for the operation of the powers it provides by defining 'terrorism' to include action that involves any of the following: serious violence against a person; serious damage to property; endangering a person's life; creating a serious risk to the health or safety of the public or a section thereof; or an action designed seriously to interfere with or seriously to disrupt an electronic system.

Terrorism can also include the use or threat of action is designed to influence the government or to intimidate the public or a section of the public and the use or threat is made for the purpose of advancing a political, religious or ideological cause. The 'action' in question can include action outside the United Kingdom. Any action taken on behalf of what the Act goes on to define as a proscribed organisation will also fall within the scope of the statutory definition of terrorism.

Part II of the Act provides for a new regime to designate certain groupings as proscribed organisations. One of the main differences between the new and the old regimes is that under the new Act proscription will apply throughout the United Kingdom, and will not be limited to terrorist organisations connected with Northern Ireland (previously the Irish Republican Army and the Irish National Liberation Army).

The power to proscribe an organisation, on the basis that it commits or participates in acts of terrorism, prepares for terrorism, promotes or encourages terrorism, or is otherwise concerned in terrorism, remains vested in the Secretary of

State and is subject to the affirmative resolution procedure in Parliament. Under the previous regime it was open to a proscribed organisation to challenge the decision to proscribe by way of an application for judicial review (although there were no reported instances of this). Under the 2000 Act an organisation subject to a proscribing order is given the right to challenge the decision. Under s4 it may apply to the Secretary of State for an order of de-proscription. If unsuccessful it can appeal to the Proscribed Organisations Appeal Commission. The Commission is required to allow such an appeal if it 'considers that the decision to refuse was flawed when considered in the light of the principles applicable on an application for judicial review': s5(3). Section 6 provides for a further right of appeal on a point of law to the relevant Court of Appeal.

Sections 11–13 provide for certain offences related to membership and support of a proscribed organisation. These offences carry the possibility of ten years' imprisonment upon conviction. Support for these purposes extends beyond simply providing financial assistance. Part III of the 2000 Act effectively replicates the provisions of earlier anti-terrorist legislation providing for the seizure of property, that is the proceeds of terrorist activity or property provided to support terrorist activity. Fundraising for proscribed organisations remains a criminal offence.

Other specific offences created by the Act include: providing instruction or training in the making or use of weapons (s54); directing the activities of a proscribed organisation (s56); possessing an article in circumstances which give rise to a reasonable suspicion that his possession is for a purpose connected with the commission, preparation or instigation of an act of terrorism (s57); collecting information for a proscribed organisation: s58.

Where a terrorist investigation is being undertaken (defined in s32 as, inter alia, 'an investigation of … the commission, preparation or instigation of acts of terrorism … an act which appears to have been done for the purposes of terrorism, the resources of a proscribed organisation') the police are provided with particular powers relating to cordoning off areas where investigations are taking place, for example the scene of a bomb blast.

Under s41 a police constable may arrest without a warrant any person whom he reasonably suspects to be a terrorist. Section 40 provides that a 'terrorist' for these purposes includes a person who is a member, supporter, fundraiser, money launderer or weapons trainer for a proscribed organisation. It also includes anyone who is or has been concerned in the commission, preparation or instigation of acts of terrorism. Where a person is arrested under s41 the provisions of Sch 8 apply. These provide that an officer of at least the rank of superintendent may authorise a delay of up to 48 hours in permitting access to a solicitor if he has reasonable grounds for believing that not delaying access will result in (inter alia): interference with or harm to evidence of a serious arrestable offence; interference with or physical injury to any person; and alerting of persons who are suspected of having committed a serious arrestable offence but who have not been arrested for it.

Despite the fact that the European Court of Human rights held, in *Brogan* v

United Kingdom (1989) 11 EHRR 117, that detention without charge for more than four days was in breach of art 5(3) of the European Convention on Human Rights, the United Kingdom has successfully argued that it should be permitted to derogate from the requirements of that article because of the exceptional threat posed by the terrorist situation in Northern Ireland: see *Brannigan and McBride* v *United Kingdom* (1994) 17 EHRR 539.

Schedule 8 para 29 of the 2000 Act provides that, where a person has been detained following arrest under s41, a police officer of at least the rank of superintendent may apply for a warrant of further detention in respect of an arrest under s41. The application will be made to a judicial authority. The maximum detention period permitted under these provisions is seven days from the time of arrest under s41.

Where an authorisation has been granted by a senior officer (as might be the case during a time of heightened security) a constable in uniform is provided with powers under ss44–47 to stop and search persons and vehicles for articles of a kind which could be used in connection with terrorism. Failure to comply with the directions given by a police constable exercising his powers of stop and search is an offence contrary to s47.

The Criminal Justice (Terrorism and Conspiracy) Act 1998 created the offence of conspiring in the United Kingdom to commit criminal acts abroad. Section 59 of the 2000 Act complements these provisions by making it an offence to incites another person to commit an act of terrorism wholly or partly outside the United Kingdom, provided the act incited would have constituted one of a number of listed offences had it been carried out in the United Kingdom. The list includes offences such as murder, ss18, 23 and 24 of the Offences Against the Person Act 1861, criminal damages and explosives offences. It is immaterial whether or not the person incited is in the United Kingdom at the time of the incitement.

Whilst still designed to counter the threat of terrorism arising from both sides of the sectarian divide in Northern Ireland, the 2000 Act encompassed a wider range of terrorist activities, including those with religious, ideological, political or economic motivations. The need for a wider definition of terrorism was, to some extent, borne out by terrorist attacks on New York in September 2001 and the consequent international ramifications. By way of response Parliament gave the authorities more far-reaching powers in the Anti-terrorism, Crime and Security Act 2001.

The 2001 Act is a lengthy and complex piece of legislation, running to almost 130 sections, spread across 14 Parts and has 8 Schedules. Parts 1 and 2 provide extended powers to confiscate terrorist property and to make freezing orders in respect of bank accounts and similar assets. Part 3 extends the basis upon which public authorities can disclose information where a criminal investigation is taking place.

It is, however, Part 4 of the 2001 Act that has attracted perhaps most attention. Under s21 the Secretary of State may issue a certificate in respect of a person where he reasonably believes that the person's presence in the United Kingdom is a risk to national security, and suspects that the person is a terrorist. For these purposes 'terrorist' is defined as a person who '(a) is or has been concerned in the commission, preparation or instigation of acts of international terrorism, (b) is a member of or belongs to an international terrorist group, or (c) has links with an international terrorist group': see s21(2).

If a person is certified as a terrorist under s21 he or she can be detained indefinitely without charge. The rationale for these exceptional powers is that there may be cases where there is insufficient evidence to charge a suspected terrorist or the suspect may be subjected to the death penalty if deported to another country.

Legal challenge to certification can only be brought as provided for under the 2001 Act – in effect the normal jurisdiction of the courts has been ousted.

Appeal against certification lies to the Special Immigration Appeals Commission (SIAC). On an appeal the SIAC must cancel the certification if it considers that there are no reasonable grounds for a belief or suspicion of the kind referred to in s21, or it considers that for some other reason the certificate should not have been issued. If the Commission determines not to cancel a certificate it must dismiss the appeal. In any event certification is subject to review under s26, the SIAC being placed under a duty to hold a first review of each certificate issued under s21 as soon as is reasonably practicable after the expiry of the period of six months beginning with the date on which the certificate is issued.

Section 28 of the Act places the Secretary of State under a duty to appoint a person to review the operation of ss21–23 within 14 months of the provisions coming into effect. The certification power, unless renewed, expires at the end of the period of 15 months beginning with the day on which the Act was passed.

Index

Old Bailey Press

The Old Bailey Press integrated student law library is tailor-made to help you at every stage of your studies from the preliminaries of each subject through to the final examination. The series of Textbooks, Revision WorkBooks, 150 Leading Cases and Cracknell's Statutes are interrelated to provide you with a comprehensive set of study materials.

You can buy Old Bailey Press books from your University Bookshop, your local Bookshop, direct using this form, or you can order a free catalogue of our titles from the address shown overleaf.

The following subjects each have a Textbook, 150 Leading Cases/Casebook, Revision WorkBook and Cracknell's Statutes unless otherwise stated.

Administrative Law
Commercial Law
Company Law
Conflict of Laws
Constitutional Law
Conveyancing (Textbook and 150 Leading Cases)
Criminal Law
Criminology (Textbook and Sourcebook)
Employment Law (Textbook and Cracknell's Statutes)
English and European Legal Systems
Equity and Trusts
Evidence
Family Law
Jurisprudence: The Philosophy of Law (Textbook, Sourcebook and
   Revision WorkBook)
Land: The Law of Real Property
Law of International Trade
Law of the European Union
Legal Skills and System
   (Textbook)
Obligations: Contract Law
Obligations: The Law of Tort
Public International Law
Revenue Law (Textbook,
   Revision WorkBook and
   Cracknell's Statutes)
Succession

Mail order prices:	
Textbook	£15.95
150 Leading Cases	£11.95
Revision WorkBook	£9.95
Cracknell's Statutes	£11.95
Suggested Solutions 1999–2000	£6.95
Suggested Solutions 2000–2001	£6.95
Suggested Solutions 2001–2002	£6.95
Law Update 2003	£10.95
Law Update 2004	£10.95

Please note details and prices are subject to alteration.

To complete your order, please fill in the form below:

Module	Books required	Quantity	Price	Cost
		Postage		
		TOTAL		

For Europe, add 15% postage and packing (£20 maximum).
For the rest of the world, add 40% for airmail.

ORDERING

By telephone to Mail Order at 020 8317 6039, with your credit card to hand.

By fax to 020 8317 6004 (giving your credit card details).

Website: www.oldbaileypress.co.uk

By post to: Mail Order, Old Bailey Press at Holborn College, Woolwich Road, Charlton, London, SE7 8LN.

When ordering by post, please enclose full payment by cheque or banker's draft, or complete the credit card details below. You may also order a free catalogue of our complete range of titles from this address.

We aim to despatch your books within 3 working days of receiving your order.

Name

Address

Postcode   Telephone

Total value of order, including postage: £

I enclose a cheque/banker's draft for the above sum, or

charge my   ☐ Access/Mastercard   ☐ Visa   ☐ American Express
Card number

☐☐☐☐ ☐☐☐☐ ☐☐☐☐ ☐☐☐☐

Expiry date   ☐☐☐☐

Signature: ....Date: ....